United States History from 1865

HARPERCOLLINS COLLEGE OUTLINE

United States History from 1865

20th Edition

John A. Krout

Arnold S. Rice, Ph.D.
Kean College of New Jersey

HarperPerennial
A Division of HarperCollins*Publishers*

For Marcia, Noah Bruce, and Myong Ae, who mean everything

UNITED STATES HISTORY FROM 1865. (Twentieth edition). Copyright 1933, 1935, 1937, 1940, 1941, 1946, 1947, 1948, 1949, 1951, 1953, 1955, 1960, 1961, 1965, 1967, 1969, 1971 by Harper & Row Publishers, Inc. Copyright © 1973 by John A. Krout. Copyright © 1977 by John A. Krout and Arnold S. Rice. Copyright © 1991 by HarperCollins Publishers, Inc. All rights reserved. Printed in the United States. No part of this book may be used or reproduced in any manner whatsoever without written permission except in the case of brief quotations embodied in critical articles and reviews. For information address HarperCollins Publishers, Inc., 10 East 53rd Street, New York, N.Y. 10022

An American BookWorks Corporation Production
Project Manager: Jonathon E. Brodman
Editor: Robert A. Weinstein

Library of Congress Cataloging-in-Publication Data

Krout, John Allen, 1896–
  United States history from 1865 / John A. Krout, Arnold S. Rice.
—20th ed.
    p.   cm.
  Includes bibliographical references and index.
  ISBN 0-06-467100-3 (pbk.)
  1. United States—History—1865— —Outlines, syllabi, etc.
I. Rice, Arnold S.   II. Title
E661.K76 1991
973—dc20   90-56013

Contents

OTHER BOOKS IN THE HARPERCOLLINS COLLEGE OUTLINE SERIES

ART
History of Art 0-06-467131-3
Introduction to Art 0-06-467122-4

BUSINESS
Business Calculus 0-06-467136-4
Business Communications 0-06-467155-0
Introduction to Business 0-06-467104-6
Introduction to Management 0-06-467127-5
Introduction to Marketing 0-06-467130-5

CHEMISTRY
College Chemistry 0-06-467120-8
Organic Chemistry 0-06-467126-7

COMPUTERS
Computers and Information Processing 0-06-467176-3
Introduction to Computer Science and Programming
    0-06-467145-3
Understanding Computers 0-06-467163-1

ECONOMICS
Introduction to Economics 0-06-467113-5
Managerial Economics 0-06-467172-0

ENGLISH LANGUAGE AND LITERATURE
English Grammar 0-06-467109-7
English Literature From 1785 0-06-467150-X
English Literature To 1785 0-06-467114-3
Persuasive Writing 0-06-467175-5

FOREIGN LANGUAGE
French Grammar 0-06-467128-3
German Grammar 0-06-467159-3
Spanish Grammar 0-06-467129-1
Wheelock's Latin Grammar 0-06-467177-1
Workbook for Wheelock's Latin Grammar
    0-06-467171-2

HISTORY
Ancient History 0-06-467119-4
British History 0-06-467110-0
Modern European History 0-06-467112-7
Russian History 0-06-467117-8
20th Century United States History 0-06-467132-1
United States History From 1865 0-06-467100-3
United States History to 1877 0-06-467111-9
Western Civilization From 1500 0-06-467102-X

Western Civilization To 1500 0-06-467101-1
World History From 1500 0-06-467138-0
World History to 1648 0-06-467123-2

MATHEMATICS
Advanced Calculus 0-06-467139-9
Advanced Math for Engineers and Scientists
    0-06-467151-8
Applied Complex Variables 0-06-467152-6
Basic Mathematics 0-06-467143-7
Calculus with Analytic Geometry 0-06-467161-5
College Algebra 0-06-467140-2
Elementary Algebra 0-06-467118-6
Finite Mathematics with Calculus 0-06-467164-X
Intermediate Algebra 0-06-467137-2
Introduction to Calculus 0-06-467125-9
Introduction to Statistics 0-06-467134-8
Ordinary Differential Equations 0-06-467133-X
Precalculus Mathematics: Functions & Graphs
    0-06-467165-8
Survey of Mathematics 0-06-467135-6

MUSIC
Harmony and Voice Leading 0-06-467148-8
History of Western Music 0-06-467107-7
Introduction to Music 0-06-467108-9
Music Theory 0-06-467168-2

PHILOSOPHY
Ethics 0-06-467166-6
History of Philosophy 0-06-467142-9
Introduction to Philosophy 0-06-467124-0

POLITICAL SCIENCE
The Constitution of the United States 0-06-467105-4
Introduction to Government 0-06-467156-9

PSYCHOLOGY
Abnormal Psychology 0-06-467121-6
Child Development 0-06-467149-6
Introduction to Psychology 0-06-467103-8
Personality: Theories and Processes 0-06-467115-1
Social Psychology 0-06-467157-7

SOCIOLOGY
Introduction to Sociology 0-06-467106-2
Marriage and the Family 0-06-467147-X

Available at your local bookstore or directly from HarperCollins at 1-800-331-3761.

Preface

The *United States History from 1865* gives considered emphasis to the events of the immediate past. Although I have tried to avoid exaggerating the significance of recent trends, at the same time I have accorded thorough recognition to these developments, many of which could serve as guides to the nation in the twenty-first century. Thus this book treats carefully such topics as the huge federal budget deficit, the entertainment and informational revolution effected by television, the announced end of the Cold War, and the persistent Middle East turmoil.

Since chronology is the underpinning of history, a chronological arrangement determines the pattern of this book. In addition, a topical sequence for a specific subject can be traced through the index.

A bibliography for each chapter includes general works with which every observer of the American past should be acquainted, and it also lists special studies.

I hope students find that this book not only provides a useful digest of material for courses in American history, but also serves as a worthwhile historical framework for courses in American government, society, or culture.

Arnold S. Rice

1

The Reconstruction Period

1863   Lincoln announces his Reconstruction plan
1864   Lincoln pocket-vetoes Wade-Davis bill
1865   Civil War ends
         Lincoln assassinated; Johnson becomes president
         Freedmen's Bureau established
         Joint Committee on Reconstruction created
         Thirteenth Amendment ratified
1865–1866   Black Codes passed
1866   Civil Rights Act
         Ku Klux Klan founded
1867   Tenure of Office Act
1867–1868   Reconstruction Acts
1868   Johnson impeached but acquitted
         Fourteenth Amendment ratified
1870   Fifteenth Amendment ratified
1870–1871   Enforcement Acts
1872   General Amnesty Act
1875   Civil Rights Act
1877   Hayes withdraws remaining troops from South

The Civil War worked a revolution in the life of the American people in many respects more profound than did the American Revolution. During the Reconstruction period, which lasted from the surrender of the Confederate forces in 1865 to the removal of the last Union occupation troops in 1877, the South was the scene of bitter strife, as its status in the federal government and the plans for its rebuilding were debated. From the

Reconstruction period emerged new patterns of government, economy, and society that transformed the southern states.

FRAMING AND IMPLEMENTING A RECONSTRUCTION POLICY

The views among the political leaders who tried to formulate and carry out a program for the rehabilitation of the former Confederate states were so mixed that the American people were badly confused.

The Prostrate South

War always disfigures. And a civil war often scars the face of society so greatly that it is hardly recognizable. This was true of the South during the Reconstruction period. Confederate soldiers, returning home after the surrender of General Robert E. Lee, found destruction, poverty, and hopelessness all about them.

ECONOMIC CHAOS

Throughout the former Confederacy farmhouses, barns, and mills had been burned; bridges and railroad tracks had been destroyed; towns had been looted and their inhabitants driven out. Plantation owners had lost their slaves, and they could not afford the capital for agricultural equipment to replace slave labor. Business was at a standstill, except for speculative enterprises that preyed on people left destitute by war.

SOCIAL CONFUSION

The war had destroyed the whole structure of southern society. Aristocratic planters, shorn of their wealth and power, yielded reluctantly to the growing influence of bankers, merchants, and small farmers. The changing status of blacks, as they made the transition from slaves to wage earners, created serious social tensions between them and whites.

POLITICAL UNCERTAINTY

The collapse of the Confederacy had stalled most political processes in the South. State and local governments had to be organized; the new state governments had to establish normal relations within the Union. In the nation's capital and throughout the North, political leaders differed sharply over what should be done and how it should be done. There were bitter quarrels among the leaders of the dominant Republican party concerning the proper basis for political reconstruction.

Framing a Policy   The approaches of presidents Abraham Lincoln and Andrew Johnson on the one hand and of Congress on the other for the readmission of the former Confederate states to the Union were so opposed that a rift between the executive and legislative branches of the government soon occurred that was unprecedented in the nation's history.

THE "CONQUERED PROVINCES" THEORY

Some members of Congress, including such influential Republican leaders as Senator Benjamin F. Wade of Ohio and Representative Thaddeus Stevens of Pennsylvania, argued that secession was an illegal act and that southerners must pay a heavy penalty for having committed it. By having engaged in this crime, the southern states had placed themselves outside the protection of the Constitution. They must now be treated as "conquered provinces," which Congress had the constitutional power to govern.

LINCOLN'S 10 PERCENT PLAN

President Lincoln brushed aside the "conquered provinces" theory, although he knew it had support from important members of his own party. He believed that the right to secede did not exist. Therefore, despite attempts to sever relations by force of arms, the southern states had never left the Union but had merely been "out of their proper practical relation" to it. (In 1869 the Supreme Court in *Texas* v. *White* upheld the position that the Union was constitutionally indestructible.) Lincoln was convinced that he should help the southern people to quickly resume their former status within the Union. In December 1863, he presented a two-part plan for reconstruction. First, the plan pardoned all southerners (except high Confederate officials and those who had left United States government or military service to aid the Confederacy) who would swear allegiance to the United States and accept "all acts of Congress passed during the existing rebellion with reference to slaves." Second, it authorized the establishment of a new government, with representation in the national government, for any state if one-tenth of its qualified voters (as registered in 1860) would take the required loyalty oath.

THE WADE-DAVIS BILL

Lincoln's moderate plan ran into strong opposition among the congressional leaders of his own party. They feared that the president would "let the South off too easily" and that former Confederate officials would return immediately to political power in their states. In July 1864, Congress passed the stringent Wade-Davis bill. Named after its sponsors, Senator Benjamin F. Wade of Ohio and Representative H. Winter Davis of Maryland, it provided that a majority of white male citizens had to take a loyalty oath before a civil government could be organized in a seceded state. It also excluded from the electorate of such states former Confederate officeholders and military personnel who had "voluntarily borne arms against the United

States." Lincoln defeated the bill with a pocket veto; that is, he failed to sign it into law before the adjournment of Congress. Thereupon Wade and Davis issued a manifesto accusing him of "dictatorial usurpation."

THE JOHNSON PLAN

The assassination of President Lincoln on April 14, 1865, was a particular blow to those who favored a policy of moderation. His unfinished work fell into the hands of his vice-president, Andrew Johnson, a pro-Union Democrat from Tennessee. In the 1864 election Johnson had been placed with Lincoln on the Republican party ticket (temporarily calling itself the Union party) to emphasize unity and attract wide support. The new president attempted to carry forward his predecessor's plan with minor changes, but the tactless Johnson had little skill in handling strong-willed members of Congress. He granted amnesty to all former Confederates (except certain high leaders and large property holders) who were willing to take an oath to uphold the Constitution. By successive proclamations he set up provisional governments (adapted to current conditions and of a temporary nature) in the former Confederate states. He authorized the loyal white citizens to draft and ratify new state constitutions and to elect state legislatures, which were to (1) repeal the ordinances of secession; (2) repudiate the Confederate state debts; and (3) ratify the Thirteenth Amendment to the Constitution, prohibiting slavery.

Implementing a Policy

Members of the Republican party who opposed the Johnson reconstruction plan came to be called Radicals. The Congress that convened in December 1865 soon came to be dominated by this group, which was led by Senator Charles Sumner of Massachusetts and Representative Thaddeus Stevens of Pennsylvania.

MOTIVES OF THE RADICAL REPUBLICANS

In opposing the president's policy, the Radicals exhibited a curious blend of high moral purpose and partisan self-interest, in which the following were important factors: (1) personal animosity toward Johnson on the part of senators and representatives who believed him unworthy of the presidency; (2) fear of executive encroachment upon the authority of Congress; (3) the desire to safeguard the interests of freedmen (blacks freed from slavery as a result of the Civil War); (4) resentment over the speedy return of former Confederates to political power in the South; (5) the determination of the Republican politicians to establish their own party in the South; and (6) the hope, shared by northern businessmen, that the removal of southern influence from Congress would result in a program of government aid to industry.

THE THIRTEENTH AMENDMENT

On one issue there was complete agreement among all northern political leaders: that the slaves must be given their freedom. Thus in February 1865, Congress passed the Thirteenth Amendment, prohibiting slavery within the nation. Ratification of the amendment by the required number of states was obtained by the following December, and it thus became part of the Constitution.

THE BLACK CODES

Beginning in November 1865, and continuing into 1866, southern legislatures that had been elected under Johnson's lenient reconstruction plan passed the so-called Black Codes, a series of laws that regulated the status of the freedmen. Although these laws conferred some rights of citizenship upon the newly freed slaves, they helped to ensure white supremacy by narrowly restricting the political, economic, and social activities of blacks. The Black Codes varied in severity from state to state. Blacks were, for example, denied the right to hold public office, to serve on juries, to bear arms, or to engage in any occupation other than farming without obtaining a license. The immediate effect in the North of the Black Codes was increased support for the Radical Republican position.

THE FREEDMEN'S BUREAU

In March 1865, Congress created the Bureau of Refugees, Freedmen, and Abandoned Lands (popularly called the Freedmen's Bureau). Its role was to provide the newly emancipated blacks with the basic necessities of life and to protect their civil rights, as well as to care for the abandoned lands of the South. In February 1866, the legislators passed a bill extending the life of the bureau indefinitely. Johnson vetoed this bill on the grounds that the states affected by it had not been represented in Congress when it was passed and that its provision for the military trial of civilians violated the Constitution. A later bill, however, enlarging the powers of the Freedmen's Bureau, was passed over Johnson's veto in July 1866.

THE JOINT COMMITTEE ON RECONSTRUCTION

In December 1865, Congress refused to seat the senators and representatives who had been elected by the provisional state governments set up under the Johnson plan. (According to the Constitution, each house of Congress is empowered to judge the election and qualifications of its own members.) Instead, the Republicans in Congress, led by Stevens, immediately created the Joint Committee on Reconstruction, with a total of fifteen senators and representatives. The committee was to examine the entire question of political reconstruction and make new proposals for congressional action.

THE CIVIL RIGHTS ACT

In April 1866, Congress passed over the president's veto the Civil Rights Act, conferring citizenship upon blacks and assuring them equal treatment with whites before the law. Johnson had maintained that the measure invaded states' rights and would revive the spirit of rebellion.

THE FOURTEENTH AMENDMENT

As the quarrel with Johnson grew more violent, the Radical Republican faction insisted upon the political punishment of former Confederates. The basis of their attack first took the form of a proposal to amend the Constitution. The Joint Committee on Reconstruction proposed the Fourteenth Amendment to the Constitution. Congress passed it in June 1866, and promptly referred it to the states for ratification.

By its provisions: (1) citizenship was conferred upon every person born or naturalized in the United States and state laws that abridged the privileges of any citizen or deprived any person of "life, liberty, or property without due process of law" were prohibited; (2) a state that deprived any of its male inhabitants of the ballot (the concern was for blacks) was to suffer a reduction of representation in Congress proportionate to the number denied the right to vote (this provision could have been carried out only with enforcement legislation, which Congress never enacted); (3) former Confederates were barred from holding federal and state offices if they had filled similar posts before the Civil War (this disability could be removed by a two-thirds vote of each house of Congress); and (4) the Confederate debt was repudiated and the United States debt affirmed.

Tennessee quickly ratified the Fourteenth Amendment and was readmitted to the Union. The other Confederate states rejected the amendment upon the advice of Johnson, who considered it unconstitutional. Even so, by July 1868, the Fourteenth Amendment had been ratified by the required number of states and was incorporated into the Constitution.

THE 1866 CONGRESSIONAL ELECTIONS

President Johnson and the Radical Republicans fought for political supremacy in the congressional elections of 1866. The supporters of the administration denounced the Fourteenth Amendment and urged a policy of conciliation toward the defeated South. But in many congressional districts voters found that their only choice on the ballot was between a Radical Republican and a Democrat who had opposed Lincoln's wartime policies. The result was scarcely in doubt, and the Radicals scored an overwhelming victory.

THE RECONSTRUCTION ACTS

In March 1867, some months after the congressional elections, Congress passed—over the president's veto—the Reconstruction Act. It divided the ten states still unreconstructed into five military districts, with a major general in command of each. For each state to be restored to the Union, the following procedure was required: (1) A constitutional convention, elected by blacks and loyal whites, was to frame a state constitution guaranteeing suffrage for all males, including blacks; (2) this constitution would need to be approved by Congress; (3) qualified voters were to elect a state legislature pledged to ratify the Fourteenth Amendment; and (4) with the ratification of the Fourteenth Amendment the state could apply for representation in Congress. Later that year and in the following year Congress passed three supplementary Reconstruction Acts that outlined administrative and legal procedures.

THE IMPEACHMENT OF JOHNSON

The leaders of the Radical faction in Congress were hindered by their inability to control the presidential office. Realizing that Johnson was personally unpopular, they determined to humiliate him and thus remove any constitutional check on their policies.

With the Tenure of Office Act, passed over Johnson's veto in March 1867, Congress forbade the president to remove federal officeholders, including members of his own cabinet, without the consent of the Senate. When Secretary of War Edwin M. Stanton, who was in sympathy with the Radicals, refused to carry out a presidential order, Johnson dismissed him without the Senate's consent. The House of Representatives promptly impeached the president for "high crimes and misdemeanors," among which were eleven charges, including violation of the Tenure of Office Act.

At the trial, which took place during March–May 1868, with Chief Justice Salmon P. Chase presiding, Johnson was ably defended by his lawyers, who argued that the Tenure of Office Act was unconstitutional. In the final vote of the Senate, which was sitting as the jury, the Radicals failed by one vote (35 to 19) to secure the two-thirds majority required by the Constitution for conviction. Seven moderate Republicans voted with the Democrats to acquit the only president ever impeached by the House of Representatives. Johnson's victory helped preserve the authority and independence of the presidential office. (In 1887 Congress repealed the Tenure of Office Act.)

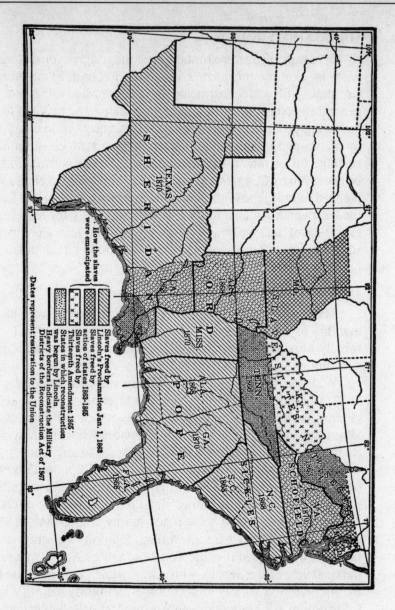

Emancipation and Restoration of Southern States

THE SOUTH IN TRANSITION

The policy of military reconstruction, which was pushed vigorously by the Radicals, hastened changes in the economic and social life of the South and the upper classes, which had been dominant before the Civil War, began to lose their political power.

The Changing Political Scene

After the registration of voters required under the Reconstruction Acts of 1867, there were approximately 700,000 blacks on the lists and about 625,000 whites. In some districts the black vote was marshaled and controlled by ambitious but unprincipled whites.

CARPETBAG GOVERNMENTS

Blacks sat in most of the conventions that drafted the new state constitutions, making up about one-third of the total membership. In the state legislatures there were many inexperienced, yet on the whole able and honest, representatives, both white and black. Making up the group of white legislators were the "carpetbaggers" and "scalawags." The former were northerners who had gone south after the Civil War. Since a number of them carried cheap traveling bags made of carpeting material, they were scornfully called "carpetbaggers." The motives of the carpetbaggers were mixed. Many wanted to help blacks adjust to freedom; others anticipated power and fortune through business and political enterprises.

Those southern whites who cooperated with the carpetbaggers and the freedmen to aid the Radical program were called "scalawags" (a slang term for "rascal"). As with the carpetbaggers, their motives were mixed. Many were eager to help both blacks and lower-class whites achieve security in a rebuilt South. Others were interested in political preferment and lucrative contracts during a period of widespread confusion.

Some legislatures elected in the southern states in 1868–69 indulged in extravagance and fraud, leaving an aftermath of public debts and burdensome taxes. But as supporters of Radical Reconstruction pointed out, the carpetbag governments were no more corrupt than a number of northern municipal administrations and state legislatures or the whole executive branch of the federal government under President Ulysses S. Grant.

REFORMERS

There were in the southern states a number of white and black leaders who were determined to make life better for the average citizen of the region. Each of the state constitutional conventions drafted liberal documents that guaranteed civil liberties and universal male suffrage. In almost every state an attempt was made to base representation in the legislature on electoral districts substantially equal in population. Several legislatures enacted laws providing for an enlarged court system. Although fraud tainted some of the appropriation bills passed by the Reconstruction legislators, many other expenditures were for worthy purposes. Greater state support for hospitals and asylums was authorized. Notable were the efforts to build more schools and to provide better educational opportunities for both whites and blacks.

THE FIFTEENTH AMENDMENT

Virginia, Georgia, Mississippi, and Texas were not able to satisfy congressional requirements for rejoining the Union until 1870. They were readmitted on the condition that their legislatures ratify the Fifteenth Amendment, passed by Congress in February 1869, prohibiting any state from denying suffrage on the grounds of "race, color, or previous condition of servitude." Approval of the amendment by the required number of states had been obtained by March 1870, and it had thus become part of the Constitution.

THE KU KLUX KLAN

By 1868 most southern states had ratified the Fourteenth Amendment and had thus been permitted to rejoin the Union. Southern whites soon turned to nonpolitical methods in their efforts to undo the results of Radical Reconstruction and to restore "white supremacy."

Secret societies—such as the Ku Klux Klan, which was founded in Pulaski, Tennessee, in 1866; the Knights of the White Camellia; and the Boys of '76—became the instruments of a policy of ugly terrorism designed to frighten blacks into renouncing their new political power and economic and social gains. The Klan became the most notorious of these organizations. Taking refuge under white hoods and robes, its members, on gruesome "night-riding" missions, used whips, branding irons, ropes, torches, guns, and knives on blacks and even their white supporters.

Southern whites who disliked the violent tactics of the Klan and other secret societies turned to more subtle forms of coercion. Blacks were denied employment and were kept from the polls not by force but by psychological intimidation.

THE "ENFORCEMENT ACTS"

Southern resistance led to three laws, called the Force Acts, for the enforcement of the congressional program. The Enforcement Act of May 1870 imposed heavy penalties for violations of the Fourteenth and Fifteenth amendments. The Enforcement Act of February 1871 placed congressional elections under the control of federal authorities. The Enforcement Act (also called the Ku Klux Klan Act) of April 1871 gave the president military authority to suppress violence in the southern states. In 1871 President Grant used these powers to subdue the Klan in South Carolina.

**The Return
of the
Conservatives**

Despite the Fourteenth and Fifteenth amendments to the Constitution and the Enforcement Acts, the Radical Republicans lost ground in the South after 1870.

THE GENERAL AMNESTY ACT

In 1872 a combination of Democrats and moderate Republicans, who disliked the severity of military Reconstruction, pushed through Congress the General Amnesty Act. This legislation restored political privileges to thousands of former Confederates and hastened the collapse of governments based on black votes. By 1876 only South Carolina, Florida, and Louisiana were still in the hands of the Radical Republicans.

WITHDRAWAL OF FEDERAL TROOPS

As a result of a compromise among certain elements in the Republican party and some leaders of the southern Democrats—which arose out of the disputed presidential election of 1876—President Rutherford B. Hayes withdrew all federal troops from the South in 1877. The state governments still in Republican hands quickly fell to the southern Democrats.

SUPREME COURT DECISIONS

In 1873 the Supreme Court, deciding cases that arose from the disputed grant of a state legislature to a slaughterhouse company, restricted the application of the Fourteenth Amendment. It held that the amendment was not intended to protect civil rights in general but only United States citizenship rights. In 1875 Congress passed the Civil Rights Act, prohibiting racial discrimination in public places, such as restaurants, hotels, and theaters. The measure was never enforced, and in 1883 the Supreme Court declared it unconstitutional, on the ground that the Fourteenth Amendment prohibited acts of discrimination by the states but did not prohibit acts of discrimination by private persons.

THE LEGACY OF RECONSTRUCTION

It is hard to balance the good and the evil features in the congressional program of reconstruction. It is even difficult to determine whether the policies of the federal government during the Reconstruction period were responsible for all of the political, economic, and social developments of the post–Civil War years in the former states of the Confederacy. Less vigorous northern control might have resulted in similar political, economic, and social changes.

Political Readjustments

The most obvious political consequence of congressional policies in the South was the adherence of the great majority of southern whites to the Democratic party.

THE SOLID SOUTH

In the immediate postwar years most southern whites came to believe that the Republican party as a whole was the party of blacks and corrupt whites who despised the Old South. As a result, many areas in the former slave states knew only a one-party system. Whoever captured a Democratic nomination on the state or local level was virtually certain of winning the ensuing election. In presidential elections between 1876 and 1920 the Republican party carried not a single state from the old Confederacy.

THE BOURBONS

Within the one-party system the leaders of the Democrats came to be known as Bourbons (from the name of a European royal family whose descendants were known for clinging obstinately to ideas adapted to a past order). This extremely conservative faction consisted mainly of the former planter class and many southern whites who had made money during the Reconstruction period.

DISFRANCHISEMENT OF BLACKS

While avoiding violence, the Democratic leaders still managed to steadily reduce the number of blacks who could meet the qualifications for the suffrage. Several devices were used: (1) the literacy test, so constructed that most blacks could not pass; (2) the poll tax (a tax levied on adults, the payment of which was required for voting); (3) property requirements; and (4) the "grandfather clause" of newly revised state constitutions, granting the suffrage only to those whose fathers or grandfathers had voted before 1867. (The last device, of course, barred blacks but made it possible for uneducated whites to vote.)

Economic Rehabilitation

The political confusion of the postwar decade slowed all the southern states in their efforts to promote the economic well-being of their citizens.

DISRUPTION OF THE PLANTATION SYSTEM

The revolutionary changes brought about by the war compelled southern landholders to reduce the size of their plantations. Having insufficient money to hire laborers, some landowners sold off large portions of their acreage. But the majority preferred to try a plan of cultivation using tenant farmers, white or black, who themselves did not possess enough money to pay a cash rental. Known as sharecropping, the system entailed the tenant farmer (the sharecropper) giving to the landowner as rent a portion (usually half) of the crop he raised by his labor.

RISE OF THE MERCHANT

If the landowner did not supply the tools, seed, and draft animals that the sharecropper needed, the latter was frequently forced to pledge another share of his crop to the local merchant in order to secure credit for his working requirements. This was called the crop-lien system. Many small farmers who owned their land were also forced to engage in the crop-lien system, often pledging their entire crop to the merchant in return for sup-. plies. This proved to be an expensive system of credit. The small farmers were compelled to confine their production to crops having a widespread and constant demand, such as cotton or tobacco. They became, in a sense, economically enslaved to the merchant-creditors.

INDUSTRIAL DEVELOPMENT

As the South of the great plantations disappeared, a new industrial order arose. The exploitation of coal, iron, phosphates, and lumber slowly gathered momentum. The less prosperous people in the rural districts drifted into towns to work in factories, usually located where cheap water power was available. The increase in railroad mileage began to keep pace with the output of coal and iron and with the multiplication of cotton mills.

Social Tensions

It is not easy to measure the effect of the Reconstruction years in the process of social readjustment throughout the South.

STATUS OF BLACKS

In many communities the bitterness engendered by imposed government and military occupation under the Radical Republicans brought about conflicts between the native whites and the newly liberated blacks, thus curbing the blacks' development. The breakup of the large plantations into smaller farms often meant the loss of work for blacks. Those who drifted into mill towns or got employment in mines and factories found that their labor was exploited almost as vigorously as it had been during the years of slavery.

CLEAVAGES AMONG NATIVE WHITES

The independent small farmers, heavily in debt, and the sharecroppers grew ever more hostile toward the Bourbon representatives of the former planter aristocracy and the new merchant-creditor group.

"The New South"

In 1886 Henry Grady, editor of the *Atlanta Constitution*, coined the phrase "The New South" to denote primarily economic developments in the region after the Reconstruction period.

LOOKING TO THE FUTURE

Grady asserted that the South, instead of bemoaning the past, should look to the future with hope and confidence. But the phrase, which gained wide acceptance, told only part of the story at the close of the nineteenth century. Although southerners made successful efforts to balance agriculture with new industries, much needed to be accomplished.

REMAINING PROBLEMS

There was a vigorous leadership trying to remake the South economically, but many critical problems remained: (1) the southern economy had not escaped the control of northern financiers; (2) southern political leaders remained far more interested in sectional than national problems; (3) many farmers, both white and black, still lived in poverty; and (4) mindful of heavy personal losses during the Civil War and the Reconstruction period, most southern voters refused to accept tax programs that would have provided funds for the social services needed to rebuild after the war's destruction.

Selected Readings

GENERAL WORKS:

Bowers, Claude G. *The Tragic Era* (1929)

Dunning, William A. *Reconstruction, Political and Economic* (1907)

Foner, Eric. *Reconstruction: America's Unfinished Revolution, 1863–1877* (1988)

Franklin, John Hope. *Reconstruction: After the Civil War* (1961)

McPherson, James. *Ordeal by Fire: The Civil War and Reconstruction* (1982)

Patrick, Rembert W. *The Reconstruction of the Nation* (1967)

Randall, James G., and David Herbert Donald. *The Civil War and Reconstruction* (1961)

Stampp, Kenneth M. *The Era of Reconstruction* (1965)

SPECIAL STUDIES:

Beale, Howard K. *The Critical Year: A Study of Andrew Johnson and Reconstruction* (1930)

Benedict, Michael Les. *The Impeachment and Trial of Andrew Johnson* (1973)

Bentley, George R. *A History of the Freedmen's Bureau* (1955)

Coulter, E. Merton. *The South During Reconstruction* (1947)

Cruden, Robert. *The Negro in Reconstruction* (1969)

Current, Richard N. *Those Terrible Carpetbaggers: A Reinterpretation* (1988)

Du Bois, W. E. Burghardt. *Black Reconstruction* (1935)

Gillette, William. *Retreat from Reconstruction, 1865–1879* (1980)

Kutler, Stanley A. *Judicial Power and Reconstruction Politics* (1968)

Litwack, Leon. *Been in the Storm So Long: The Aftermath of Slavery* (1979)

McKitrick, Eric L. *Andrew Johnson and Reconstruction* (1960)

Perman, Michael. *The Road to Redemption: Southern Politics, 1869–1880* (1984)

Rable, George C. *But There Was No Peace: The Role of Violence in the Politics of Reconstruction* (1984)

Trelease, Allen W. *White Terror: The Ku Klux Klan Conspiracy and Southern Reconstruction* (1971)

2

Government Affairs and Political Pursuits

1868   Grant elected president

1869   "Black Friday" scandal

1871   Tweed Ring destroyed

1872   Grant reelected president

1873   Crédit Mobilier scandal

       "Salary Grab" Act

1874   Sanborn Contracts scandal

1875   Whiskey Ring scandal

1876   Belknap scandal

       Disputed presidential election between Hayes and Tilden

1877   Compromises of 1877: Hayes chosen as president; remaining troops withdrawn from South

1880   Garfield elected president

1881   Garfield assassinated; Arthur becomes president

1883   Pendleton Act

1884   Cleveland elected president

1886   Presidential Succession Act

1887   Electoral Count Act

       Cleveland vetoes Dependent Pension bill

       Tenure of Office Act repealed

1888   Benjamin Harrison elected president

1889   Agriculture Department created

1890   McKinley tariff

1892 Cleveland reelected president

1893 Panic of 1893

1894 Coxey's Army

Wilson-Gorman tariff

In the last third of the nineteenth century each administration—whether Democratic or Republican—was hampered by factional quarrels or a lack of constructive leadership—or both. From the beginning of Ulysses S. Grant's first term of office in 1869 to the end of the second Grover Cleveland term in 1897, the professional politicians were slow to face the new issues that arose out of economic changes. They appeared to be more interested in winning elections and dispensing patronage. Since the most important national problems—the regulation of industry, the control of the railroads, the settlement of management-labor disputes, the support of beneficial tariff schedules, the maintenance of a satisfactory currency system—were apt to cut across party lines and impair party discipline, the political leaders either avoided them or dealt with them only in evasive generalizations. Demands for reform were met with responses slowly and over strong opposition from the politicians.

GRANT AND SCANDALS

The period of Grant's presidency was marked by scandals. Corruption, which many believed resulted from the effects of the Civil War, pervaded the times. The unprecedented growth of big business during the Reconstruction period, with its pursuit of more and more profits, led many to discard the older, absolute moral code in favor of a freer or "looser" personal one. Corruption existed not only at the federal level of government but also at the state and local levels. The corrupt activities of many carpetbag state governments in the South and of the New York City ring of politicians headed by William M. "Boss" Tweed were exposed to the American people. Although Grant was personally honest, his reputation as chief executive suffered from his failure to reestablish a moral tone in government.

Election of 1868

During the 1868 presidential campaign the Radicals within the Republican party emerged not only as the champions of a vigorous reconstruction policy but also as the defenders of northern manufacturing, banking, and railroad interests against the agricultural interests of the West and South.

DEMOCRATS

The delegates to the Democratic national convention adopted a platform that denounced as unconstitutional the congressional program of reconstruction. They pledged support to the Ohio Idea, an inflationary proposal that government bonds, whenever possible, be paid not in gold but in greenbacks (the popular name for the paper money issued during the Civil War). But Democratic support for this Midwest-oriented financial policy was weakened by the nomination for president of Governor Horatio Seymour of New York, who repudiated the greenback idea. Francis P. Blair, Jr., a former representative from Missouri who had contributed greatly to keeping his border slave state loyal to the Union, was chosen to run for vice-president.

REPUBLICANS

The delegates to the Republican national convention adopted a platform that endorsed congressional reconstruction and demanded payment in gold of the public debt. The Radicals, having made certain that General Ulysses S. Grant was one of their number, succeeded in moving the party to nominate him for president and Speaker of the House Schuyler Colfax for vice-president.

THE CAMPAIGN

The Republicans reiterated throughout the campaign that their party had saved the Union. The image of Governor Seymour paled alongside that of General Grant, the symbol of strength and success during the Civil War.

GRANT'S VICTORY

In the electoral college Grant defeated Seymour, 214 to 80. The votes of 650,000 newly enfranchised blacks in the southern states—under the military power of the federal government—helped to give the Republican candidate his 310,000-popular-vote majority.

The Grant Administration

Grant's naïveté and lack of political experience proved severe handicaps to him and the nation.

THE PRESIDENT

Grant was inclined to regard the presidential office as a gift bestowed upon him by the American people in gratitude for his military service to the nation. Neither by temperament nor by training was he qualified to set a high standard of political ethics.

THE CABINET

Grant's cabinet initially included three men of outstanding ability: Secretary of State Hamilton Fish, Secretary of the Interior Jacob D. Cox, and Attorney General Ebenezer R. Hoar. Cox and Hoar soon retired in disgust, however, and the president came under the influence of such shrewd politicians as Senator Roscoe Conkling of New York and Representative Benjamin F. Butler of Massachusetts. Civil service positions were filled with Grant's relatives and friends, as well as with minor party workers and their protégés.

Political Corruption

Businessmen sought and received favors from government officials for a price; politicians shamelessly used public office as a source of private profit.

"BLACK FRIDAY"

Grant's admiration for and association with men of wealth unwittingly involved him in the attempt by financiers James Fisk and Jay Gould in 1869 to get command of a large part of the nation's gold supply in order to dictate their own price for the precious commodity. While spreading the rumor that Grant was against the government selling its own gold, Fisk and Gould bought much of the privately held gold, thus shooting up the price of the dwindling supply on the market. Many businesses that needed gold in their transactions were being ruined. On September 24, 1869 ("Black Friday"), when the price of gold was at its highest, the Grant administration took belated action. Secretary of the Treasury George S. Boutwell sold $4 million in government gold, and the price plummeted, bringing ruin to a number of speculators.

THE CRÉDIT MOBILIER

In 1872 rumors of graft and political corruption in connection with the Crédit Mobilier, a construction company that had built the Union Pacific Railroad in the 1860s, were verified in part. The principal stockholders of the Union Pacific had been the founders of the Crédit Mobilier, in which capacity they took exorbitant profits for building the line. A congressional investigation in 1873 produced evidence that Democratic representative Oakes Ames of Massachusetts, in order to influence legislation benefiting the railroad interests, had distributed shares of Crédit Mobilier stock among congressional leaders, including Vice-President Colfax, who at the time had been serving as Speaker of the House of Representatives.

THE TWEED RING

Symptomatic of business and political corruption were the frauds, totaling perhaps as much as $100 million, committed against the residents of New York City by a group of politicians headed by William M. "Boss" Tweed, the leader of Tammany Hall, the Democratic political machine in Manhattan. The persistent investigative work sponsored by the *New York Times* and the striking cartoons of Thomas Nast in *Harper's Weekly* finally helped to bring about the destruction of the Tweed Ring in 1871.

Election of 1872

Some members of the Republican party, calling themselves Liberal Republicans, were critical of the policies and tactics of the Grant administration and strove to prevent the president's reelection.

LIBERAL REPUBLICANS

The center of the anti-Grant movement in the Republican party was in Missouri, where such Liberal Republican leaders as Senator Carl Schurz and Governor B. Gratz Brown favored a more conciliatory attitude toward former Confederate supporters in the state and resented the dominance of the Radical Republicans in national affairs. These Republicans were especially critical of Grant's policy toward the South. The Liberal Republican national convention included the champions of a variety of political reform movements. Besides the opponents of Radical Reconstruction policies, there were civil service reformers and advocates of lower tariff rates as well as crusaders against the corruption of the Grant administration. The delegates passed over such reformers as the diplomat Charles Francis Adams of Massachusetts and Senator Lyman Trumbull of Illinois to select *New York Tribune* editor Horace Greeley as their standard-bearer. Governor Brown of Missouri was chosen as his running mate.

DEMOCRATS

The delegates to the Democratic national convention followed the lead of the Liberal Republicans in nominating Greeley for president and Governor Brown for vice-president. Although the brilliant but eccentric Greeley had been a vitriolic critic of the Democrats, they accepted him as their candidate because a fusion with the Liberal Republicans seemed the only chance to prevent Grant's reelection.

REPUBLICANS

The Republican national convention nominated Grant for president and Senator Henry Wilson of Massachusetts for vice-president.

THE CAMPAIGN

Rather than forcefully coming to grips with the basic issues of the day, the majority of party spokespersons, although not the two presidential candidates themselves, rapidly fell to mudslinging. Greeley was castigated for, among other things, an attitude toward the South so "soft" that it bordered on treason. Grant was denounced as an obtuse, drunken tyrant.

GRANT'S LANDSLIDE VICTORY

Grant carried all but three border states (Missouri, Kentucky, and Maryland) and three southern states (Georgia, Tennessee, and Texas). Major factors in Grant's overwhelming victory were Greeley's personal unpopularity and the Republicans' control of the South. The Liberal Republican movement, however, was not without results. It threw a sufficient scare into the administration to cause the president to advocate civil service reform, a downward revision of the tariff, and modification of the recent policy toward the South.

Continuance of Political Corruption

Despite the promises he had made during his bid for reelection, Grant was either unwilling or unable to put his political house in order, and his second term was marked by a series of government scandals.

THE "SALARY GRAB"

The nation was incensed in 1873 when Congress voted salary increases to members of all three branches of the federal government, including a 50-percent raise for senators and representatives to be retroactive for the preceding two years. Public protest forced Congress to repeal its own "back-pay steal" the following year, although the increases voted for the president and Supreme Court justices were, for constitutional reasons, not rescinded.

THE SANBORN CONTRACTS

In May 1874, a House of Representatives committee reported that Secretary of the Treasury William A. Richardson had permitted a friend, John D. Sanborn, to retain exorbitant commissions for collecting unpaid internal revenue taxes for the Department of the Treasury. Richardson promptly resigned in order to escape a vote of censure by the House.

THE WHISKEY RING

Through ingenious probing, Benjamin H. Bristow, who had succeeded Richardson as secretary of the treasury, uncovered a conspiracy of revenue officials and distillers—which included Grant's private secretary—to defraud the government of tax revenues on the sale of whiskey.

THE BELKNAP SCANDAL

In March 1876, Secretary of War William W. Belknap abruptly resigned in order to escape impeachment. He had accepted bribes for granting the rights to sell supplies to the Indian tribes.

REPUBLICAN DOMINANCE AND INTRAPARTY STRIFE

Factional rivalries within the dominant Republican party seemed more important to many professional politicians of the party than did the many and serious national issues that needed attention during the period from 1876 to 1884.

Election of 1876

The voting returns in 1876 produced the most disputed election in the nation's history.

DEMOCRATS

The Democratic national convention chose as its standard-bearer Governor Samuel J. Tilden of New York, who had won national fame for his successful prosecution of the Tweed Ring in New York City. Governor Thomas A. Hendricks of Indiana was selected as the candidate for vice-president.

REPUBLICANS

Avoiding several prominent leaders who had been too closely linked to the Grant administration, the Republican party selected as its nominee the honest and conscientious governor of Ohio, Rutherford B. Hayes. Representative William A. Wheeler of New York was chosen as his running mate.

THE CAMPAIGN

Both candidates were straightforward representatives of American business interests. During the campaign Tilden focused on the corruption of the Grant administration, while Hayes asserted that the Republican party had saved the nation during the Civil War and the era of Reconstruction.

COMPROMISE OF 1877

Tilden won 4,300,000 popular votes to Hayes's 4,036,000. Tilden carried states with a total of 184 votes in the electoral college, one short of the necessary majority. Hayes received 165 votes. In dispute were twenty electoral votes, which both candidates claimed. In Oregon the Democratic governor declared one of the Republicans named to the electoral college technically ineligible to cast his ballot. In South Carolina, Florida, and Louisiana there were charges of fraud involving nineteen electoral votes. (Those southern states were just passing from the control of carpetbaggers, scalawags, and freedmen into the control of the Bourbons.)

To avert any possibility of serious disturbances, Congress created a fifteen-member electoral commission to pass judgment on the disputed votes. Five members of the Senate (three Republicans and two Democrats), five members of the House of Representatives (three Democrats and two Republicans), and five justices of the Supreme Court (three Republicans and two Democrats) were named to the commission. (It had been expected that Justice David Davis, an independent, would be selected by his colleagues on the Supreme Court as the fifteenth member of the commission, but, having just been chosen to the Senate from Illinois, he was ineligible.) The decision was eight to seven—along straight party lines—on every disputed point in favor of the Republican, Hayes. The nation acquiesced in the decision after southern Democratic leaders had received informal assurances from Republican politicians that federal troops would be withdrawn from the South.

The Hayes Administration

Hayes's term of office was far from tranquil. Relations with the Democrats in Congress were difficult. The Republican party was troubled by factionalism. The reform wing constantly demanded that the Republican party be cleansed of its unscrupulous members.

THE PRESIDENT

Although Hayes was no crusading reformer, he worked hard to give the nation honest and efficient leadership. In economic matters he represented the views of American business.

THE CABINET

The members of Hayes's official family were unusually able. Reformers were particularly pleased by the selection of noted lawyer and former attorney general William M. Evarts of New York as secretary of state, Senator John Sherman of Ohio as secretary of the treasury, and former senator Carl Schurz of Missouri as secretary of the interior. The president's appointment of David Key, a Democratic senator from Tennessee, as postmaster general demonstrated his conciliatory attitude toward the South.

Political Quarreling

During Hayes's term of office hostility was rife between two elements within the Republican party and between the president and the Democratic-dominated Congress.

STALWARTS AND HALF-BREEDS

Within the Republican ranks there were bitter quarrels between the Stalwarts and the Half-Breeds. The former were staunch supporters of the recent Grant regime and looked to Senator Roscoe Conkling of New York for leadership. The latter (so called because of their "half-breed" Republicanism) were of a more liberal bent, favoring Hayes's southern policy and civil service reform, and they rallied around the authority of Senator James G. Blaine of Maine. Important members of the Stalwart faction were Representative Benjamin F. Butler of Massachusetts, former senator Zachariah Chandler of Michigan, and Senator John A. Logan of Illinois. Prominent Half-Breeds included Representative James A. Garfield of Ohio and Representative George F. Hoar of Massachusetts. This intraparty rivalry gave the reform element an occasional chance to determine party action. Factional strife, however, had more to do with power than with policy.

AN OPPOSITION CONGRESS

The president's relations with Congress were far from peaceful, for the Democrats controlled the House of Representatives during his entire term and the Senate for the latter two years. In the lower house the Democratic majority set up a committee to investigate the disputed election of 1876 in order to embarrass Hayes. The president in turn vetoed congressional appropriation bills when the Democrats, in attempting to repeal the Enforcement Acts that compelled the observance of the reconstruction program, attached what he considered to be one or another objectionable rider (a clause appended to a bill to secure a goal entirely distinct from that of the bill itself). This partisan quarreling prevented the passage of a sound program of legislation.

Election of 1880

Hayes's refusal to seek reelection seemed to remove the chief obstacle in the path of the Stalwarts, who were making a vigorous attempt to control the Republican organization and force former president Grant on the party and the nation for another term.

DEMOCRATS

The Democratic national convention nominated for president a distinguished Civil War general, Winfield S. Hancock of Pennsylvania. Former representative William H. English of Indiana was chosen as Hancock's running mate.

REPUBLICANS

At the Republican national convention a deadlock developed between the Stalwart supporters of Grant and the Half-Breed supporters of Blaine. On the thirty-sixth ballot Grant's opponents concentrated their strength and led a stampede of delegates to a compromise candidate, Representative James A. Garfield of Ohio. Since Garfield was a member of the Half-Breed faction of the party, the anti-Grant delegates attempted to pacify the Stalwarts by nominating for vice-president one of Senator Conkling's most trusted lieutenants, Chester A. Arthur of New York, who two years earlier had been removed from a New York Custom House post in a reform maneuver by Hayes.

THE CAMPAIGN

The Republicans discovered early in the campaign that the animosities aroused during their convention were not easily forgotten. But Grant and

Conkling finally agreed to speak for Garfield and thus present a united front against the Democrats. At a time when the voters could have profited from some guidance in deciding important economic and social issues, they received little help from the two presidential candidates.

In ability and achievement there was little difference between Garfield and Hancock, and both men were essentially conservative in their views on national questions. Partisan strife and personal rivalries still held the center of the political stage.

GARFIELD'S NARROW VICTORY

Garfield was elected with 9,000 more popular votes than Hancock. In the electoral college, however, Garfield achieved a more substantial success: He received 369 votes to Hancock's 155.

The Short-Lived Garfield Administration

Garfield was unable to prove himself as president, as he was assassinated a few months after assuming the office.

THE INFLUENCE OF BLAINE

Immediately following Garfield's election, he indicated that Senator Blaine, whom he appointed secretary of state, would exercise a commanding influence in the new administration. The result was an unseemly quarrel between Senator Conkling and the president. When Garfield used the control of political appointments in New York in such a way as to build a Garfield-Blaine machine, Conkling defied the administration. The controversy became ever more acute.

ASSASSINATION

On July 2, 1881, Garfield was shot in the Washington, D.C., railroad station by a crazed and disappointed office seeker, Charles T. Guiteau, who was heard to shout "I am a Stalwart and Arthur is president now." The president died two months later.

The Arthur Administration

The death of Garfield elevated to the presidency Chester A. Arthur. As president, Arthur quickly surprised those who believed that, as a machine-oriented politician, he would not be equal to the tasks of the office.

THE PRESIDENT

Arthur refused to use the presidency to reward his former political cronies, and he expended much energy in attempting to end the factional strife within the Republican party.

THE CABINET

The new president gradually changed the membership of his cabinet so that the influence of Blaine and his intimates declined. Senator Frederick T. Frelinghuysen of New Jersey replaced Blaine as secretary of state, while jurist Charles J. Folger of New York became secretary of the treasury. Robert T. Lincoln, the son of President Lincoln, was retained as secretary of war.

A Surplus of Government Funds

As the government's income from various taxes piled up a surplus, members of Congress yielded to the temptation to support one another's proposed legislation for expensive public works in their districts.

PORK-BARREL APPROPRIATIONS

During the 1870s there was a marked increase in pork-barrel appropriations (expenditures for projects, such as building roads and bridges, deepening rivers and harbors, and establishing military installations—which are allocated more for local political patronage than for needed improvements). Arthur forthrightly criticized what he considered to be wasteful expenditures of government funds, even when it was argued that the money was readily available.

AN OVERRIDDEN VETO

When an appropriations bill authorizing the use of $18 million for river and harbor improvements of dubious need was sent to President Arthur for his signature, he vetoed it. Although his veto was overridden, he won the esteem of a large part of the nation for his sober action.

Reform of the Civil Service

The assassination of President Garfield seemed to be a consequence of factional quarrels over political appointments. It shocked the nation into a realization of the evils of the spoils system (the practice of regarding public offices and their financial rewards as plunder to be distributed to members of the victorious party in an election).

PLANNING THE MERIT SYSTEM

After the Civil War the merit system of appointing and promoting civil service employees slowly made headway. In 1865 Republican Representative Thomas A. Jenckes of Rhode Island, who had conducted a systematic study of the British civil service, introduced a bill in Congress to set up competitive examinations for specific federal government offices. In 1871 President Grant appointed a commission that experimented—unsuccessfully—with examinations for some positions. President Hayes cast his lot with the enemies of the spoils system. He issued an executive order forbidding the extraction of political contributions from federal officeholders; he gave Secretary of the Interior Carl Schurz a free hand to institute the merit system in his department; he renamed Thomas L. James, a champion of civil service reform, to the postmastership of New York City; he removed two of Conkling's leading supporters from New York Custom House posts for violating a regulation against political campaigning by government employees. The National Civil Service Reform League, founded in 1881 by

George William Curtis, the editor of *Harper's Weekly*, served to unite the efforts of those in favor of the merit system.

THE PENDLETON ACT

Indignation became widespread as revelations of political corruption marked the trial of President Garfield's assassin. In his first message to Congress, President Arthur indicated his willingness to cooperate with the legislative branch in ending the practice of granting civil service positions as political rewards. The result was the Pendleton Act. Named after its sponsor, Democratic senator George H. Pendleton of Ohio, the measure was passed in January 1883, by a Republican-controlled Congress that was motivated, in part, by the expectation that the measure would safeguard Republican officeholders in the event of Democratic successes in the 1884 congressional elections.

The Pendleton Act provided for the president to appoint a three-member bipartisan commission to draft and administer competitive examinations to determine on a merit basis the fitness of applicants for office. The act also prohibited the collection of funds from federal officeholders for party campaign purposes. A list of federal positions obtainable through the merit system (approximately 10 percent of the total) was established, and the president was authorized to expand the number as he saw fit. By substituting merit for political influence in federal appointments, the Pendleton Act established the basis for the present-day federal civil service system.

Tariff Legislation

A tariff is a system—called a schedule—of taxes (specifically, duties) placed by the federal government on imported goods. In the post–Civil War period the Republican party, when in control of Congress, redeemed its campaign pledges by passing legislation to increase tariff rates.

TRADITIONAL PARTY POSITIONS

The tariff used to play a significant role in American politics. The Republican party traditionally advocated a higher tariff, one that "protected" domestic manufacturers from foreign competition by imposing high rates on foreign goods so as to discourage their importation. The Democratic party traditionally supported a revenue tariff, one that provided income for the federal government and therefore had low rates, so as not to discourage imports. But Republicans endorsed the tariff not only for protective purposes but also as a favored means of raising revenue for the government. And some Democrats even subscribed to free trade, the international exchange of goods unimpeded by any restrictions.

TINKERING WITH THE SCHEDULES

Protection, initially justified as a help for "infant" industries that were being developed in the face of established foreign competition and subsequently justified as compensation to industry for increased internal revenue taxes, was generally accepted as an important factor in the growth of American industry. The modification of rates in 1870, 1872, and 1875 was designed to respond to the protests of the nonindustrial West and South without abandoning the protective principle.

THE TARIFF OF 1883

During the presidential campaign of 1880 there was much discussion about revising the tariff schedules to meet the needs of domestic manufacturers on a scientific basis. Two years later a congressionally sponsored fact-finding commission, after conducting a thorough investigation of the tariff question, surprised the nation by recommending a substantial reduction of duties. Congress, however, ignored the advice of the experts and in 1883 passed an act that was a caricature of genuine reform. The rate reductions averaged scarcely 2 percent.

THE RETURN OF THE DEMOCRATS TO POWER

The balloting in the election of 1884 brought a political upheaval that enabled the Democrats to secure the presidential office for the first time in twenty-eight years.

Election of 1884 Since the scandals of the Grant administration the Republicans had been on the defensive. They could win the election only if they carried the independent voters who since the Civil War had tended to support their ticket. But in 1884 the Republicans suffered defeat, and contributing to it were defections from their own ranks.

DEMOCRATS

The Democratic national convention chose as its presidential nominee Governor Grover Cleveland of New York, who was widely known as a competent and courageous administrator. For vice-president the delegates named Thomas A. Hendricks, Tilden's running mate in the disputed election of 1876.

REPUBLICANS

The Republican national convention refused to give the nomination to the incumbent Arthur, although he desired it and, it was widely held, deserved it on the basis of his creditable accomplishments as president.

Disregarding the small but vigorous reform element, the delegates instead yielded to the magnetism of Blaine and on the fourth ballot selected him in a frenzy of rejoicing. Senator John A. Logan of the former Stalwart faction was chosen as his running mate.

THE CAMPAIGN

Many reformers within the Republican ranks announced that they would bolt their party if the Democrats chose a nominee whom they could support. Cleveland was such a candidate. The regular Republicans sneeringly nicknamed the bolters mugwumps (from the Indian for "great chief").

CLEVELAND'S NARROW VICTORY

The election was close, with Cleveland receiving only 60,000 more popular votes than did Blaine. In addition to the active support of Cleveland by the mugwumps, reasons for the Democratic victory included (1) the unenthusiastic campaigning for Blaine on the part of former Stalwarts; (2) the belief that Blaine had used his political position to further his own financial interests (in 1876 the "Mulligan Letters" had pointed to his acceptance of money for securing a land grant for an Arkansas railroad); and (3) the resentment of Catholic voters, particularly in the pivotal state of New York, over the Reverend Samuel D. Burchard's campaign remark that the Democrats were the party of "rum, Romanism, and rebellion."

The Cleveland Administration

Although Cleveland soon made it known that he regarded public office as a public trust, he had difficulty in persuading others that his administration would conduct itself accordingly.

THE PRESIDENT

Cleveland is generally considered the ablest chief executive since Abraham Lincoln. He was honest, efficient, imbued with common sense, and above all not subject to control by others. Cleveland was stronger than his party, for he embodied the hopes of most political reformers, regardless of party affiliation.

THE CABINET

In choosing his official family, Cleveland sought men of ability, even if they lacked experience in government office. Outstanding appointees were former senator Thomas F. Bayard of Delaware as secretary of state, New York City financier William C. Whitney as secretary of the navy, and Senator L. Q. C. Lamar of Mississippi as secretary of the interior.

Cleveland's Independent Actions

As a person of great integrity, Cleveland was frequently embarrassed by partisan pressure when dealing with legislative matters and patronage (the control of political appointments). Many of his recommendations to Congress, such as those to revise the tariff rates and to conserve the diminishing acreage of public lands, were either ignored by the legislators or blocked by the Republican leaders.

EXTENDING THE CIVIL SERVICE LIST

With their first national victory in twenty-eight years, Democratic leaders insisted that 100,000 federal jobs be given to faithful party workers, and Cleveland reluctantly permitted the removal of some Republican officeholders for this purpose. He showed his interest in reform, however, by adding almost 12,000 positions to the list of offices obtainable on a merit basis.

REPEAL OF THE TENURE OF OFFICE ACT

When Cleveland dismissed a federal district attorney in Alabama, the Senate, invoking the Tenure of Office Act passed during the Andrew Johnson administration, demanded that Cleveland submit the papers relating to the removal. This Cleveland refused to do, insisting that the removal of federal officers was an executive prerogative. Thereupon the Senate censured the president. But in 1887 Congress repealed the Tenure of Office Act. By his action Cleveland had helped to strengthen the independence of the presidency.

THE PENSION CONTROVERSY

The mounting surplus in the Treasury Department prompted Congress to be generous in granting pensions to Union veterans of the Civil War. The original modest appropriations for pensions to disabled veterans increased greatly with the passage in 1879 of the Arrears of Pension Act, which granted back payments for service-connected disabilities. Soon pension agents were touring the nation, persuading veterans to file claims. By 1885 the pension roll contained almost 350,000 names. Claimants whose cases were not approved by the Bureau of Pensions turned to Congress, where willing legislators sponsored private pension bills, many of which were frauds. Cleveland attempted to investigate each of those bills, and his research led him to veto more than two hundred, although he approved more private pension bills than had any of his predecessors. Congress abandoned the test of service-connected disability in the Dependent Pension Bill of 1887, which provided that any veteran who had served for three months and was incapable of earning a livelihood could receive a pension. But Cleveland vetoed the bill on the grounds that it would tend to "pauperize" the former servicemen and that it was too soon after the war for so comprehensive a pension policy.

Government Reorganization and Reform

The Cleveland administration saw the need to improve the workings of government. Measures were enacted in a spirit of nonpartisanship unusual for the period.

THE PRESIDENTIAL SUCCESSION ACT

In November 1885, the death of Thomas A. Hendricks, the fifth vice-president to die in office, prompted the legislators to take action. In 1886 Congress passed the Presidential Succession Act, providing that in case of the removal, death, resignation, or inability to serve of both the president and the vice-president, the members of the cabinet, in order of the creation of their offices, should succeed to the duties of the presidency.

THE ELECTORAL COUNT ACT

Intended to prevent a disputed presidential election (such as that of 1876), the Electoral Count Act, passed by Congress in 1887, authorized each state to decide contests over the appointment of its electors and the reporting of its electoral returns. If opposing sets of returns were submitted, the Senate and House of Representatives, voting separately, were empowered to decide which result to approve. If the two houses of Congress disagreed, the returns certified by the state's governor were to be accepted.

DEPARTMENT OF AGRICULTURE

In 1889 Congress enlarged the Department of Agriculture and made its head a member of the cabinet. The new department was established to gather and distribute information on farming matters and to administer laws dealing with all aspects of agriculture.

The Tariff in Fiscal Policy

The Cleveland administration regarded the tariff as one facet of the government's overall fiscal policy, which had resulted in the accumulation of a surplus of funds through an extensive program of taxation.

SURPLUS OF FUNDS

During the 1880s the excess of federal government income over expenditures averaged $100 million annually. The surplus was embarrassing, because it indicated to the taxpayers that they were bearing an unnecessary burden; it reduced the amount of currency in circulation and thus available for normal business needs; and it encouraged Congress to make pork-barrel appropriations.

CLEVELAND'S TARIFF MESSAGE

President Cleveland was opposed to using the surplus funds for large-scale government expenditures; he believed that a reduction of taxes would lower the surplus sufficiently. In his view, the tariff remained the chief obstacle in the way of tax reform. In his third State of the Union message to Congress, in December 1887, the president not only denounced the existing tariff duties as a "vicious, inequitable, and illogical source of unnecessary taxation" but also maintained that the protective principle was responsible for the growth of large business combinations that eventually increased prices by stifling competition. The only solution, he emphasized, was the downward revision of tariff rates. Presidential pressure persuaded the Democratic-controlled House of Representatives to pass the Mills bill in 1888, providing for a drastic reduction of tariff rates, but the Republican-controlled Senate soon replied with the Aldrich bill, which called for a high protective tariff. There was a stalemate.

A REPUBLICAN REVIVAL

In the election of 1888 both major parties tried to make enough concessions to the discontented farmers and laborers to solidify their ranks against a protest vote. The Republicans were more successful than the Democrats in convincing the nation that their party was the protector equally of all three elements of economic society—businessmen, factory workers, and farmers.

Election of 1888

The major campaign issue had been largely determined by Cleveland's demands for a general lowering of tariff rates.

DEMOCRATS

The Democratic national convention enthusiastically renominated Cleveland. For vice-president the delegates selected former senator Allen G. Thurman of Ohio.

REPUBLICANS

After Blaine had declined to become a candidate, the Republican national convention selected as its nominee Benjamin Harrison of Indiana, a corporation lawyer and grandson of President William Henry Harrison. Levi P. Morton of New York, a banker who had served as minister to France, was chosen as his running mate.

THE CAMPAIGN

To a remarkable degree the tariff issue overshadowed all others. Party lines held relatively firm, with the Democrats proposing a lowering of tariff duties and the Republicans advocating the maintenance of high protective rates. The Democrats were placed on the defensive by the aggressive and well-financed Republican drive. Cleveland was accused, without justification, of subscribing to a policy of removing all restrictions on trade, including tariffs, and thus benefiting British manufacturers at the expense of American manufacturers. The Republicans also made a strong appeal to Union veterans, whom Cleveland had antagonized by his views on pensions and by his order for the return to the southern states of Confederate battle flags captured during the Civil War. Neither Cleveland nor Harrison addressed himself to the needs of laborers and farmers.

HARRISON'S VICTORY

Although Cleveland received a plurality of more than 100,000 popular votes, he lost such pivotal states as New York, Pennsylvania, and Ohio, with their large number of electoral votes. In these states the Republicans had effectively mobilized the strength of businessmen behind their ticket. Harrison achieved victory with 233 votes in the electoral college to Cleveland's 168.

The Harrison Administration

The executive branch under Harrison reflected the views and had the enthusiastic support of the nation's business interests.

THE PRESIDENT

Harrison was dignified in demeanor and conservative in opinion: He was an able lawyer but an inept politician.

THE CABINET

Rather than relying upon the advice of his cabinet members, most of whom were fairly competent, the new president depended heavily on the counsel of three prominent Republicans (one of whom did serve in the cabinet): James G. Blaine, once again secretary of state; Thomas B. Reed of Maine, Speaker of the House of Representatives; and William McKinley of Ohio, chairman of the House Committee on Ways and Means (the committee concerned with methods and resources for raising the necessary revenue to meet national expenses).

High Protection

The deadlock on the tariff between the Democratic-controlled House of Representatives and the Republican-controlled Senate that had developed during the last year of the Cleveland administration was broken during the Harrison administration.

THE McKINLEY TARIFF

The tariff matter was resolved when the Republicans gained control of the House of Representatives and retained their majority in the Senate in the 1888 election. The result was the McKinley tariff of 1890, named after William McKinley, who guided the legislation through the House of Representatives. On the theory that prosperity flowed directly from protection, McKinley and his colleagues raised the level of duties to a new peak, attaining an average rate of approximately 50 percent. Rates on woolen goods, cotton goods, and steel products were increased, while the protective principle was extended to some farm products, including wheat, potatoes, butter, and eggs. To soothe consumers, raw (unprocessed) sugar was put on the free list (the American Sugar Refining Company was a beneficiary of this move), and, as a unique concession to the domestic producers of raw sugar, they were granted a bounty of two cents a pound on their product. This strategy reduced revenues and thus decreased the federal surplus. The act also included innovative reciprocity provisions. The president was empowered to impose duties on commodities on the free list, such as sugar, molasses, coffee, tea, and hides, if the nations exporting these items discriminated against the products of the United States.

OPPOSITION TO PROTECTION

As soon as the McKinley bill was signed into law, in October 1890, prices on protected commodities were raised by producers in anticipation of the effect of the protective schedules. The Democrats used an "increase in the cost of living" argument as an effective weapon against the Republicans in the congressional elections of 1890. The Democratic landslide was partly a result of the voters' repudiation of the Republicans because of the apparent effects of the protective tariff.

Developments in Congress

The attention of the American people at the time was naturally turned not toward the lackluster president but toward the aggressive legislative branch of the federal government.

THE REED RULES

Through the use of parliamentary tactics permissible under the rules of the House of Representatives, the Democratic minority attempted to obstruct the president's recommendations for legislation. Speaker of the House Reed changed the rules to speed up legislative processes, an action considered arbitrary by the Democrats. After a sharp controversy between the two parties in the lower house, the new rules that Reed had unilaterally imposed were adopted as standard procedure. They provided that the Speaker should entertain no dilatory motions and that physical attendance should be sufficient basis for determination of a quorum. (Under the old rules, when the Democrats had wanted to delay action on a matter, they had refused to answer the roll call even though physically present, thus preventing a quorum; that is, the minimum number required to conduct business.) The new rules increased the efficiency of conducting House business, but in so doing they greatly enlarged the power of the Speaker. As the initiator and vigorous wielder of the new rules, Reed soon gained the title "Czar."

THE "BILLION-DOLLAR CONGRESS"

Despite Harrison's plea that the "problem" of a surplus of federal funds be solved by reducing taxes, the Republican-controlled Congress actually dissipated the surplus through increased expenditures. Between 1889 and 1891, Congress appropriated a total of $1 billion, the largest sum yet spent by a peacetime session. Among the appropriations were those for the return to the northern states of the direct tax collected during the Civil War; an extensive program of river and harbor improvements; the construction of additional steel ships as part of a naval modernization program begun during the Arthur administration; and implementation of the Dependent Pension Act of 1890, which was similar to the bill vetoed by Cleveland three years earlier. The Fifty-first Congress thus became known as the "Billion-Dollar Congress."

A DEMOCRATIC REAPPEARANCE

As a result of the 1892 election, Grover Cleveland returned to the presidency. During his second term the hostility of the agrarian West and South toward the industrial East became more intense as the result of a severe economic depression and the financial policies of the government.

Election of 1892

The dramatic feature of the election was the emergence of the Populists as a strong minor party of protest. Nevertheless, the overwhelming number of voters remained loyal to the major parties.

DEMOCRATS

Having Cleveland's permission to promote his candidacy, a group of eastern bankers and businessmen marshaled a number of state delegations pledged to the former president. In an unusual manifestation of party unity, he received on the first ballot the two-thirds vote required by the convention rules for nomination. As a concession to midwesterners, former representative Adlai E. Stevenson of Illinois was nominated for vice-president.

REPUBLICANS

Blaine, whose record as secretary of state had commanded general admiration, permitted his name to be presented for the presidential nomination. But Harrison, although unpopular among the Republican party workers, who considered him too reserved and unsympathetic, controlled enough delegates to win the nomination on the first ballot. Chosen as his running mate was Whitelaw Reid, editor of the *New York Tribune*.

POPULISTS

Composed of western and southern farmers and eastern laborers, the new third party nominated agrarian-oriented politician James B. Weaver of Iowa for president and agrarian reformer James G. Field of Virginia for vice-president. The Populist platform advocated a variety of reforms to help the farmers and laborers.

THE CAMPAIGN

Although the two major parties differed on the tariff issue, with the Democrats advocating a general lowering of rates and the Republicans supporting the continuance of high protective duties, there were only slight differences in their platforms and in the candidates' statements on any other matter. The Republicans, however, were considerably weakened by a number of factors: (1) the hostility of reformers to Harrison's neglect of the merit system; (2) widespread resentment over higher prices following the McKinley tariff of 1890; (3) anger in the South over the Republican attempt to force federal control of elections on the southern states (a federal election bill had passed the House of Representatives but had not come to a vote in the Senate); and (4) disgust with the Republican-controlled Congress for having used up the federal surplus at a time when it was feared that an economic depression was beginning.

CLEVELAND'S VICTORY

In popular votes, Cleveland received 5,556,000 and Harrison 5,176,000. The Democrats won a complete victory, capturing the presidency and control of both the Senate and House of Representatives for the first time in thirty-six years. The Populists received 1,041,000 popular votes, thus making their party a force to be reckoned with.

The Second Cleveland Administration

When Cleveland took the oath of office for the second time he became the first and so far the only chief executive to serve two nonconsecutive terms.

THE PRESIDENT

After leaving the White House four years earlier, Cleveland had engaged quite successfully in the practice of law. He returned to office a much more conservative man.

THE CABINET

The membership of Cleveland's official family was strikingly conservative. Walter Q. Gresham of Indiana, a Republican leader who had criticized some of his party's positions, was secretary of state; John G. Carlisle of

Kentucky, who had served with distinction in both houses of Congress, was secretary of the treasury; Richard Olney of Massachusetts, a highly successful corporation lawyer, was attorney general.

The Panic of 1893

Cleveland had scarcely been inaugurated, when the nation found itself in the grip of a panic that led to a severe depression that lasted four years. Certain factors had foreshadowed economic trouble: (1) the enormous increase in government expenditures, while income remained stationary, until the federal surplus was changed to a deficit; (2) the hoarding of gold as investors in Europe, already experiencing a depression, began to sell their American stocks and bonds in order to secure the precious metal; and (3) the acute uneasiness of the business community when in April 1893 the gold reserve in the Treasury Department fell for the first time below the $100 million mark.

BUSINESS FAILURES

The depression was precipitated in May 1893 by the failure of the National Cordage Company, a rope-manufacturing concern. Within six months thousands of business firms became insolvent, hundreds of banks closed, and scores of railroads went into bankruptcy. By the spring of 1894 close to 20 percent of the work force was unemployed.

COXEY'S ARMY

Bands of jobless men, loosely organized into "armies," roamed the countryside. Some sought relief measures from state and local governments. Coxey's Army, some several hundred men led by "General" Jacob S. Coxey, an Ohio businessman, marched on Washington, D.C. in April 1894 and presented to Congress a petition for inflation of the currency and a federal program of public works. But after Coxey and two aides were arrested for walking on the Capitol lawn, their followers quickly disbanded.

Tariff Legislation

Once more the tariff issue came to the fore.

THE WILSON-GORMAN TARIFF

Early in 1894 the House of Representatives passed the Wilson bill, which provided for (1) the inclusion of raw materials such as coal, iron ore, lumber, wool, and unprocessed sugar on the free list; (2) the reduction of the rates on such finished products as iron and steel wares, cotton and woolen goods, and silk and linen articles; (3) the repeal of the bounty granted under the McKinley tariff to the domestic producers of unprocessed sugar; and (4) the imposition of a tax of 2 percent on incomes of $4,000 and over, in order to make up for the loss of revenue from the reduced duties. The Senate added to the Wilson bill 634 amendments, removing some raw materials from the free list and raising the protective rates to an average of approximately 40 percent. The resulting Wilson-Gorman bill bore a marked resemblance to the McKinley tariff. After acrimonious debate the House accepted the amendments. Although Cleveland did not veto the bill, he refused to sign it, allowing it to become law in 1894 without his signature.

UNCONSTITUTIONALITY OF THE INCOME TAX

In 1895 the Supreme Court, in *Pollock v. Farmers' Loan and Trust Co.*, declared the income-tax provision of the Wilson-Gorman tariff unconstitutional on the grounds that it was a direct tax and therefore subject to the requirement that such a tax must be apportioned among the states according to population.

Selected Readings

GENERAL WORKS

Josephson, Matthew. *The Politicos, 1865–1896* (1938)
Morgan, Wayne H. *From Hayes to McKinley: National Party Politics, 1877–1896* (1969)
White, Leonard D. *The Republican Era, 1869–1901* (1958)

SPECIAL STUDIES:

Davison, Kenneth. *The Presidency of Rutherford B. Hayes* (1972)
Dobson, John. *Politics in the Gilded Age* (1978)
Hoogenboom, Ari. *Outlawing the Spoils: A History of the Civil Service Reform Movement, 1865–1883* (1961)
Mandelbaum, Seymour. *Boss Tweed's New York* (1965)
Marcus, Robert D. *Grand Old Party: Political Structure in the Gilded Age, 1880–1896* (1971)
Nevins, Allan. *Grover Cleveland: A Study in Courage* (1932)
———. *Hamilton Fish: The Inner History of the Grant Administration* (2 vols., 1936)
Peskin, Allan. *Garfield* (1978)
Reeves, Thomas. *Gentleman Boss: The Life of Chester Alan Arthur* (1975)
Sproat, John G. *"The Best Men": Liberal Reformers in the Gilded Age* (1968)
Woodward, C. Vann. *Reunion and Reaction* (1951)

3

The Rise of Industrialism

In the quarter century after 1865, the nation witnessed the rise of big business. The tremendous expansion of business enterprise was significantly accelerated by the influence of the period's dominant economic theory, which favored the free play of individual initiative. However, the monopolistic practices of the large industrial firms and the abuses of the railroads—both of which the states were constitutionally prohibited from controlling because of their interstate nature—eventually forced the federal government to take action in the public interest.

By the 1870s the American worker had learned that so far as he or she was concerned, the most important effect of industrialization was the transformation of the skilled artisan into a factory worker. The consequences of this change for the individual included the loss of any bargaining power usually enjoyed by skilled workers; the impersonality of employer-employee relations in the new corporations; and increased competition for jobs resulting from an expanded labor force that now included former slaves, women, children, and immigrants. For unskilled laborers weekly wages of ten dollars or less and a workday of ten hours or more were common. In addition, working conditions in factories were unhealthy and often dangerous.

THE SHAPE OF INDUSTRY

Industrial enterprise is a pursuit that has for its end the production and supply of commodities. It is a form of business activity that is distinguished by such a large scale that major problems of capital and labor are often involved. Following the Civil War the development of American industry was so extensive that the entire population was affected.

Manufacturing

A handful of significant characteristics marked manufacturing in the post–Civil War years. Readily observable was the evolution of the small shop into the large factory.

A NATIONAL MARKET

The opening of the West converted the entire territory of the United States into a domestic market. The development of a far-flung transportation system put all sections of the market within reach of the eastern manufacturing centers. Congressional enactment of tariff barriers protected many goods from foreign competition.

ABUNDANT RESOURCES

The discovery and utilization of the nation's natural resources also aided the growth of manufacturing. The mining frontier contributed gold, silver, and copper. Large deposits of iron ore were found in Pennsylvania and in the Great Lakes region, where the Mesabi range of Minnesota was especially accessible. Oil was discovered in Pennsylvania and in the Southwest. The great northwestern forests were added as the source of lumber. Coal, which became vitally important as a source of energy, could be mined in a number of regions, especially in the central Appalachian Mountains.

AN ADEQUATE LABOR SUPPLY

Following the Civil War the supply of labor was augmented by veterans seeking jobs and by persons, including many women and children (whose employment was not at the time restricted), attracted from farms to the new manufacturing centers. The largest source of factory labor, however, came from the millions of immigrants—mostly from eastern and southern Europe—who arrived in the United States during the last quarter of the nineteenth century. Political unrest and religious persecution abroad, inducements offered by American manufacturing firms, and generally non-restrictive immigration policies were factors that caused foreigners to flock to the United States. Lacking skills or bargaining power, most of those immigrants had to work long hours for low wages.

TRANSPORTATION

Advances in transportation in the latter part of the nineteenth century were crucial to manufacturing. The railroads carried raw materials to the manufacturing centers and carried finished goods to the domestic markets and to ports for shipment overseas. And such refinements as the air brake, various signal devices, and the refrigerator car increased the value of railroads to manufacturing.

TECHNICAL IMPROVEMENTS AND INVENTIONS

The records of the Patent Office tell an impressive story of how old businesses were revolutionized and new ones created by the invention and improvement of machinery and industrial processes. The process for making steel by blowing air through cast iron in its molten state was discovered in the 1850s by the Englishman Henry Bessemer and the American William Kelly. Thomas A. Edison and his laboratory associates were responsible for such significant inventions as the dynamo, the incandescent lamp, and the alkaline storage battery. Charles Goodyear's process for the vulcanization of rubber to make it stronger and resistant to heat and cold and Eli Whitney's system of interchangeable parts (although both inventors had accomplished their work earlier) came into widespread use after the Civil War. All of these devices enabled manufacturers to produce goods more cheaply and in ever-increasing quantities.

Of clear importance to manufacturing were developments in communications. The amount of telegraph wire in use throughout the nation tripled within six years after the close of the Civil War. As the telegraph helped unite remote sections of the nation, the transatlantic cable, successfully laid in 1866 by Cyrus W. Field, brought other countries of the world into closer business contacts with the United States. Within a few years of its invention in 1876, Alexander Graham Bell's telephone, in addition to becoming a familiar convenience in thousands of American homes, revolutionized business methods throughout the nation.

CORPORATE ORGANIZATION

The form of business organization changed rapidly after 1850. The individual proprietorship and the partnership gave way to the corporation chartered under state law. During the 1850s and 1860s the obvious advantages of this organization—relative permanence, limited liability of the stockholders, and the opportunity for promoters to acquire large amounts of capital—induced manufacturers to seek corporate charters for their enterprises. Upon these foundations were later erected the elaborate structures designed to insure monopolistic control by particular business firms.

TERRITORIAL EXTENSION

Although the northeastern states, which had been the first to feel the impulse of industrialization, still retained their primacy in the production of commodities, manufacturing rapidly expanded into other sections of the nation. New population shifts in the 1870s, for example, made Chicago the center of the meat-packing industry, carried flour-milling from northern New York to Minneapolis, and brought several of Pennsylvania's great iron and steel mills into Ohio and Illinois. In the 1880s manufacturing also began to occupy an important place in the economic life of the South, where the textile, tobacco, and lumber industries benefited from the cheap labor and accessibility to raw materials.

The Business Cycle

In every part of the world where the process of industrialization was relatively rapid, speculative enterprises intensified the fluctuations in the business cycle—a recurring succession of prosperity, crisis, liquidation, depression, and recovery. Thus prosperous years were swallowed up in crisis, quickly followed by depression. The United States had experienced depressions in 1819, 1837, and 1857, but the collapse that followed the flourishing post–Civil War years was more severe than usual, for it was on a wider front and in a more industrialized economy.

THE PANIC OF 1873

The collapse of business prosperity in the United States was but a phase of the world depression resulting mainly from the following conditions: (1) a series of international conflicts, culminating in the Franco-Prussian War of 1870–71; (2) the too-rapid expansion of railroads in central and eastern Europe; and (3) the inflation of national currencies, which adversely affected international exchange rates. In the United States the panic brought to an end a period of increased production of farm commodities, raw materials, and manufactured goods; excessive construction of railroads and public works;

and inflated currency and rising prices, which had persuaded investors to put their savings into speculative enterprises. The sudden insolvency in September 1873 of the Philadelphia banking and brokerage firm controlled by Jay Cooke, who had gained fame and huge profits by helping the Union government sell its bonds during the Civil War, precipitated the panic. Cooke and his associates had formed a syndicate to finance the Northern Pacific Railroad. Their operations brought more capital into railroad construction than the receipts from passenger and freight traffic warranted. The attempts of creditors to collect on their loans threw some 5,000 firms into bankruptcy within a year of the Jay Cooke failure. In September 1873, the New York Stock Exchange was forced to close for ten days. Prices plummeted. During the following year 3 million men were thrown into the ranks of the unemployed. Farmers were forced to sell their grain and livestock at substantial losses.

PROPOSALS FOR INFLATION

Price levels remained low for several years after the crisis. As a result, numerous proposals were offered to secure an inflation of the currency in order to raise prices artificially and thus stimulate trade. Many wanted the government to issue paper money, backed not by a set amount of precious metal such as gold or silver but by "the faith and resources of the nation." Others demanded that the total amount of coins in circulation be increased by laws that would compel the government to mint coins of silver (then being mined in large quantities) as freely as it minted gold coins. Both groups maintained that prosperity could be induced by greatly increasing the amount of paper money in circulation, which would devalue the dollar and thus increase the value of the businessmen's commodities, the farmers' crops, and the workers' labor. Farm groups as well as labor organizations supported inflation as the solution to the business cycle.

THE DEVICES OF INDUSTRY

It was generally believed that freedom of competition in industry would compel efficient methods on the part of the producer and insure fair prices for the consumer. But as industrial competition became more intense, businessmen, fearing its effect on profits, sought to limit competition by combinations that would concentrate control in ever-larger corporations.

Laissez Faire

This was the motto of eighteenth-century French economists who protested excessive government regulation of industry.

APPLICATION OF THE ECONOMIC DOCTRINE

Laissez faire means "to let [people] do [as they choose]." The doctrine emphasized that government, although responsible for the maintenance of peace and the protection of property rights, must not interfere with private enterprise, neither hindering through regulation nor helping through subsidy. In other words, government should pursue a hands-off policy. In the United States laissez faire as an economic theory was popularly summarized: "The government of business is no part of the business of government."

GOVERNMENT GENEROSITY

As a matter of fact, the American government pursued a hands-off policy that soon turned into a hands-outstretched one. During the quarter century following the Civil War, politicians—whether Democratic or Republican— seldom opposed the generosity of the government in its support of businessmen. This help took various forms: (1) government grants of land and loans to the railroad owners; (2) high tariff rates maintained to protect American industrialists against foreign competition; and (3) banking and financial policies that benefited investors at the expense of other elements in the nation. Thus individual initiative often realized its objectives only with government support.

LEADERS OF BUSINESS

Many Americans during the late nineteenth century seemed to believe that individual businessmen, by being permitted to pursue their own self-interest without external restrictions, were responsible for the great industrial progress of the nation. They were inclined to admire the more prominent leaders of business—John D. Rockefeller and Stephen V. Harkness in oil, Andrew Carnegie and Elbert H. Gary in steel, Cornelius Vanderbilt and James J. Hill in railroads, and John P. Morgan and Jay Cooke in banking— and to excuse the sharp practices in which such men often engaged.

Social Darwinism

This was a theory that attempted to justify the activities of American businessmen of the period.

THE DARWINIAN THEORY

In the nineteenth century British naturalist Charles Darwin proposed the theory that in nature there is among living creatures a struggle for survival and that only the fittest survive.

APPLICATION TO INDUSTRY

William Graham Sumner, a professor of sociology at Yale University, applied the Darwinian theory to American economic and social life. In his writings, which received widespread attention, he asserted that in the struggle for economic survival, wealthy businessmen obviously proved themselves to be the fittest. As an extension of this basic premise, American economic and social reformers were acting counter to natural selection by attempting to save the unfit, who were unable to sustain themselves in the struggle for survival.

The Trend Toward Monopoly

Various devices were used by the large corporations as they strove to secure dominant positions in their particular fields of enterprise. Businessmen argued that unrestrained competition had become so intense that they had been compelled to correct the "evils of competition" by mergers and consolidations.

THE POOL

Early used by the railroads, the pool took the form of an agreement by which several supposedly competing companies established prices, regulated output, and divided markets among themselves. Since such agreements were not recognized by law they could be easily broken and thus proved largely unsatisfactory.

THE TRUST

This form of combination was first tested when John D. Rockefeller, the founder of the Standard Oil Company, organized the Standard Oil Trust in 1879. Rockefeller's ingenious attorneys worked out a plan whereby a group of corporations that engaged in the refining and transportation of petroleum entrusted their stocks to a small board of trustees, which was authorized to control the new combination. The original stockholders of the various corporations received in return for their stock "trust certificates," which entitled them to dividends from the earnings of the trust. As revised in 1882, the Standard Oil Trust included seventy-seven companies, whose total stock was held in trust by a nine-member board. These companies represented 90 percent of the nation's oil refineries and pipelines. The trust was later used in modified form to create steel, sugar, beef, and other monopolies.

THE HOLDING COMPANY

When some states prosecuted trusts on the grounds that they were unlawfully restraining trade, industry leaders began to experiment with the holding company. This was a corporation that, while neither manufacturing a product nor delivering a service, held a sufficient share of stock to control one or more subsidiary companies that did produce goods or perform services. The holding company became important in the 1890s, after such states as New Jersey, Delaware, and West Virginia modified their corporation laws to permit the chartering of this kind of combination.

THE REGULATION OF INDUSTRY

An increasing number of voters during the 1880s and 1890s came to doubt the prevailing theory that government should abstain from meddling in business affairs. They vigorously questioned the assumption that the individual left to his own discretion would always adopt plans and procedures in the public interest. They insisted that there was a public interest that had to be protected against the private interest. Many Americans were suspicious of all big corporations. They idealized earlier generations, when production was on a small scale and most business firms were individual proprietorships or partnerships. To them big corporations meant trusts, and trusts meant the threat of monopolistic control.

Criticism of Laissez Faire

Although Americans generally appreciated the cheaper prices made possible by large-scale production, they feared that most business managers were more interested in controlling prices than in quality production under conditions of maximum efficiency.

MOLDERS OF PUBLIC OPINION

During the 1880s and 1890s the popular magazines and sensational newspapers reported on the unfair practices of monopolistic corporations. Economists and journalists, such as Henry George, Edward Bellamy, and Henry D. Lloyd, were among the leading proponents of government regulation of industry, usually for the purpose of maintaining freedom of competition.

SMALL PRODUCERS

Farmers complained that the power of the large corporations to determine prices resulted in high transportation costs for the produce they shipped and excessive charges for the manufactured goods they purchased. Small businessmen accused their more powerful competitors of using unfair methods to force them out of business.

CONSUMERS

Impressed by congressional investigations into the monopolistic methods of the great railroad systems, many consumers demanded equally searching examinations of the way in which large corporations used their control of the market to charge exorbitant prices. They called upon government to restore that freedom of trade that would permit the law of supply and demand to determine prices.

Antitrust Legislation

Since corporations received their charters from the states, the early response to demands for action by small producers and consumers came from the state legislatures. Later the federal government took steps.

STATE ACTION

The states did little more than apply the rules of common law forbidding agreements, written or unwritten, in restraint of trade. By 1890 fifteen states had passed laws defining in somewhat specific terms various practices of corporations that would be punished as actions in restraint of trade. Those laws were of little effect, however, since corporations chartered in states that had no restrictive legislation could trade across state lines. Also, since the plea of former senator Roscoe Conkling before the Supreme Court in *San Mateo County v. The Southern Pacific Railroad* (1882), the federal courts had tended to interpret the Fourteenth Amendment so as to protect corporations against any state legislation that might deprive them of "life, liberty, or property without due process of law." (Corporations were considered "persons" under the law.)

THE SHERMAN ANTITRUST ACT

So widespread was the popular sentiment against the trusts that in 1889 Republican president Benjamin Harrison recommended action by Congress, and in 1890 the legislature followed his suggestion by passing the Sherman Antitrust Act. Named after its sponsor, Republican senator John Sherman of Ohio, the act used a principle of English common law to declare illegal "every contract, combination in the form of trust or otherwise, or conspiracy, in restraint of trade or commerce among the several states, or with foreign nations." It authorized prosecutions by federal district attorneys and suits for damages by any individual or firm injured by a company in violation of the act's provisions. During the first decade of the act's existence, the federal government was not aggressive in seeking criminal indictments. This inactivity can be blamed neither on the conspicuously loose phrasing of the statute nor on the attitude of the judiciary. Although the Supreme Court held in *United States v. E. C. Knight Company* in 1895 that the control by the sugar trust of 95 percent of the refining of sugar was not an illegal restraint of interstate trade, in subsequent decisions handed down by the Court the majority opinion prepared the way for successful prosecution. But the Harrison, Cleveland, and McKinley administrations did not want to undertake a vigorous campaign against the trusts.

THE RAILROAD SYSTEMS

Of paramount importance in the process of industrialization were the railroads, which united all sections of the nation, bringing raw materials and foods to the industrial centers and carrying finished products to the domestic markets and to ports of shipment for foreign trade. Eastern manufacturing firms, western mining companies, and the growing communities on the Pacific coast enthusiastically sponsored plans to bind together distant parts of the nation with miles of steel rails.

Railroads East of the Mississippi

In the eastern states, railroad construction, which had proceeded rapidly in the 1850s, was checked by the Civil War. But even before the cessation of hostilities building was resumed.

NEW LINES AND INVENTIONS

Between 1865 and the financial panic of 1873, more than 30,000 miles of track were laid; by 1880, despite the depression years, mileage in operation had reached 93,000. During the same period the railroad companies began to substitute steel for iron, adopted a standard gauge for their tracks, improved their engines, introduced the air brake perfected by George Westinghouse in 1868, and used Pullman cars, invented by George Pullman (his sleeping car was introduced in 1859, his dining car in 1868, and his parlor car in 1875).

DOMINANT LINES

During the 1860s and 1870s the trend toward consolidation of the shorter rail lines established many of the nation's great rail systems: (1) the New York Central, organized by Cornelius Vanderbilt, which ran from New York City to Chicago; (2) the Erie, which expanded its service across New York State until its director, Daniel Drew, together with financiers Jay Gould and James Fisk, engaged in stock manipulations that threw the line into bankruptcy; (3) the Pennsylvania, which reached Cleveland, Chicago, and St. Louis; (4) the New York, New Haven, and Hartford, which came to dominate New England; (5) the Baltimore and Ohio, which pushed steadily beyond the Ohio River to Chicago; (6) the Illinois Central, managed by Edward H. Harriman, which traversed the Mississippi Valley from Chicago to New Orleans; and (7) the Atlantic Coast Line, formed from over a hundred small independents.

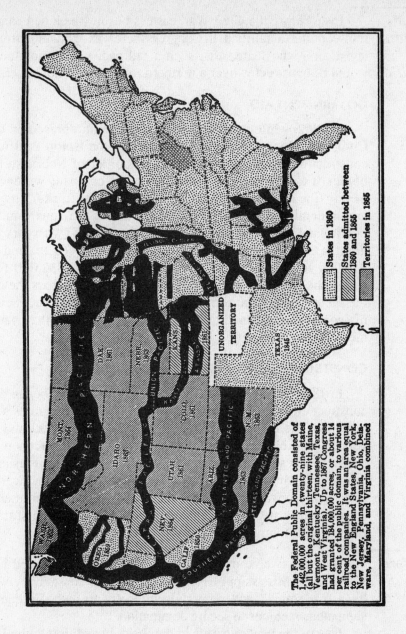

Political Organization of the West and Land Grants to Railroads

The Transcontinental Union Pacific and Central Pacific

Even before the Civil War, eastern businessmen had campaigned for a transcontinental railroad. In Congress there was opposition from the southern legislators, who feared that such a railroad, which most people assumed would be constructed over a northern route, would not benefit the South.

GOVERNMENT AID

In 1862, while the southern states were unrepresented because of the Civil War, Congress granted a charter to the Union Pacific Company to construct a railroad from the eastern border of Nebraska to the eastern border of California. The promoters of the company were to receive right of way (the land occupied by the railroad for its tracks), free use of timber and minerals on public land, and a grant of ten-square-mile sections of public land for every mile of track they laid. (Two years later the land grant was doubled.) In addition, Congress agreed to lend the company $16,000 for every mile built across the plains, $32,000 for every mile across the plateaus, and $48,000 for every mile across the mountains. At the same time similar terms were accorded the Central Pacific, a California corporation formed to build a line from within that state eastward to meet the Union Pacific.

CONSTRUCTION METHODS

In 1867 the building of the transcontinental line began in earnest. The construction gangs (including thousands of Irish immigrants who worked for the Union Pacific and thousands of Chinese immigrants hired by the Central Pacific) labored feverishly to overcome the difficulties inherent in spanning a region of desert wastes, wooded plateaus, and precipitous mountains. The promoters, whose ingenuity was tested in meeting engineering problems, were richly rewarded for their efforts. The Union Pacific and the Central Pacific met near Ogden, Utah, in May 1869, and the first transcontinental railroad was completed.

Other Western Railroads

By 1890 twelve important rail systems had expanded into the region between the Mississippi River and the Pacific coast. They were organized by a few shrewd and powerful entrepreneurs, who frequently used unscrupulous methods to secure domination.

Five of the new railroads in the West, in addition to the Union Pacific–Central Pacific combination, were transcontinental lines: (1) the Great Northern, under James J. Hill; (2) the Northern Pacific, organized by Jay Cooke and then taken over by Henry Villard; (3) the Southern Pacific, organized by the controllers of the Central Pacific, Collis P. Huntington and Leland Stanford, and then taken over by Jay Gould; (4) the Atchison, Topeka, and Santa Fe, under Cyrus K. Holliday; and (5) the Chicago, Milwaukee, St. Paul, and Pacific, under Alexander Mitchell.

PATTERNS OF FINANCING

The financial arrangements that made possible the building of the Union Pacific set the pattern for many other early western railroads. Capital for new construction came from the sale by the railroads of much of the land granted them by the federal and state governments, loans from federal and state governments, loans from county and municipal governments eager for rail facilities, and private investments by Americans and Europeans.

GOVERNMENT STIMULUS

Land grants from the federal and state governments greatly supplemented the monetary loans to the western railroads. More than 130 million acres owned by the federal government and approximately 55 million acres owned by the various state governments were granted to railroad corporations. For every three dollars invested by private individuals, the government advanced two dollars in the form of loans. Later on, government on the various levels decided to refrain from exacting repayment of the balance (in many cases a considerable amount) on the loans.

Effects of the Transcontinental Rail System

The completion of the transcontinental railroads had important and varied effects on many aspects of American society.

INFLUENCE ON MANUFACTURING AND TRADE

The transcontinental lines created a national market within which farm commodities, raw materials, and manufactured goods could be freely exchanged. Frontier farms and western mining communities could supply urban centers of the East. Manufacturers were encouraged by the expanding market and easy access to raw materials to seek higher profits in mass production at lower cost per unit. Foreign trade also expanded rapidly. Within three years of the completion of the Union Pacific, exports to and imports from China and Japan had risen more than 100 percent.

INFLUENCE ON POPULATION

The high cost of construction caused many transcontinental railroad promoters to dispose of great portions of their land grants as rapidly as possible. Aggressively making known the availability of property at reasonable prices and along newly built rail lines, they sold off to enterprising cattle ranchers, sheepherders, and farmers land that the federal and state governments had given them, thus stimulating migration into the trans-Mississippi West. Through advertising and by sending agents abroad, railroad companies actively sought immigrants as railroad construction workers and to purchase land. Large numbers of Europeans and Asians were thereby brought to the American West.

INFLUENCE ON POLITICS

As many Americans moved farther westward, new territories were organized to become states. In the federal government the influence of the new states was felt especially in the Senate (where each state, regardless of population, has two votes). A political revolt of the West against eastern business interests soon developed, which climaxed in the 1890s.

ABUSES OF THE RAILROADS

Those responsible for the management of the great rail systems were charged with committing a number of abuses in the promotion, construction, and operation of the lines.

Speculative and Political Abuses

The accusations against many railroad owners and managers cited speculative trickery and political pressure, the latter frequently of an exceedingly immoral kind.

SPECULATIVE PROMOTION

Even the imaginative skill of a railroad operator such as James J. Hill of the Great Northern or the efficiency of one such as Edward H. Harriman of the Illinois Central could not obscure the fact that too many American railroads were constructed by speculators who knew little about the needs of the nation and paid scant attention to legal requirements. They were guilty of (1) promoting lines in regions where the absence of competition enabled them to charge exorbitant rates; (2) selling large quantities of securities (stocks and bonds) of unsuccessful lines to the residents of the localities that the lines pretended to serve; and (3) imposing excessive expenses on railroads undertaking new projects by paying huge profits to themselves as directors of the construction companies that were commissioned to lay the tracks.

POLITICAL CORRUPTION

There was a growing concern during the 1870s and 1880s over the interference in state legislation by powerful railroad lobbyists (persons who solicit members of a legislative body in the lobby or elsewhere in an effort to influence them to pursue a certain course of action). Pressure was exerted in various ways to secure legislation favorable to the railroads or to block legislation that restricted them. By resorting to extensive distribution of free passes among officeholders, generous contributions to party campaign funds, and outright bribery of legislators, the railroads gained "protection" but also incurred ill will.

Financial Abuses   The practices of some owners and managers embraced a wide range of financial dishonesty.

FRAUDULENT SALE OF SECURITIES

European investors were successfully approached to put their money into American lines that had sold more stock than the law permitted. In a few instances powerful directors sold bonds and pocketed the proceeds, thus increasing the corporation's liabilities without adding to its assets.

MARKET MANIPULATION

Daniel Drew, Jay Gould, and James Fisk, who controlled the Erie, were typical of those owners who used valuable railroad properties to build up private fortunes through the unscrupulous manipulation of securities on the stock exchange. They knew little, and cared less, about managing a transportation system.

"STOCK-WATERING"

Investors complained that there were railroad directors who engaged in the practice of overcapitalization, or "stock-watering" (the phrase originally referred to the practice of feeding salt to livestock to make them thirsty, then having them fill themselves with water before being weighed for market). By selling more stock than was represented by the actual physical value of the railroad, those directors had given investors stock containing "water"; that is, the par (nominal) value of each share of stock was higher than what it should have been to indicate the true asssets of the line.

Unfair Rate-Making   In the view of the shippers, the greatest sins of the common carriers (public transportation systems) were their rate-making policies.

POOLING AGREEMENTS

In order to prevent cutthroat competition, which would take the form of rate wars, many of the railroads entered into pooling agreements, which provided either for a division of territory among the members of the pool or for a proportionate division of the profits at the end of the business year. Thus genuine competition among the lines was eliminated and the rates remained as high as the traffic would bear.

DISCRIMINATION BETWEEN PLACES

The "long haul–short haul evil" grew out of a tendency of the railroads to favor shippers who operated from important terminal points (stations central to considerable areas), where there was competition among lines. As a result, the shipper using two terminal points paid low rates, while the shipper using way stations (intermediate stations between principal stations), where there was no competition between carriers, paid a proportionately higher rate for the same service. For example, the same shipment could be sent from New York City to Chicago at a lower rate than was charged for the shorter distance between Rochester, New York, and Toledo, Ohio.

REBATES

The small shipper bitterly complained that his larger competitor was the recipient of favors from the railroads in the form of secret rebates (parts of payments returned after open fee transactions), which brought freight costs far below the rates advertised by the railroads in their published schedules. The carriers maintained that as a result of the growth of big business, this practice was forced upon them by the powerful industrial entrepreneurs in their war on the independent producers.

CONTROL OF THE RAILROADS

Despite the obvious benefits resulting from the rapid extension of lines into all parts of the nation, protests against the methods of the railroad owners increased, resulting eventually in a variety of regulatory measures.

State Regulations

Mounting protests finally brought attempts by several state legislatures to control the practices of the common carriers.

RAILROAD COMMISSIONS

In 1869 Massachusetts created the first commission with supervisory powers. Its record of correcting abuses through investigation and conference caused other eastern states, notably New York and New Hampshire, to set up similar bodies to hear complaints and report discriminatory practices.

FIXING MAXIMUM RATES

Primarily because of the lobbying of an association of farmers called the Patrons of Husbandry—or, more popularly, the Grange—western states began passing laws to fix maximum rates for the transportation of passengers and freight. Illinois set up a commission that was given power to prepare rate schedules; Wisconsin, Minnesota, and Iowa established carrying charges by direct legislative action; several other states adopted constitutional amendments empowering the legislature to deal with railroad abuses, including excessively high rates.

Judicial Review of State Legislation

The railroads appealed to the courts to protect them against state regulation, but the trend of early decisions was against the carriers. During the 1870s, in the so-called Granger cases, the Supreme Court held that when property became "clothed with a public interest" its owner must "submit to be controlled by the public for the common good."

MUNN V. ILLINOIS

In 1877 the Supreme Court decided that an Illinois law fixing the maximum rates for the storage of grain in elevators did not deprive the warehouse owners of property rights without due process of law.

PEIK V. CHICAGO AND NORTHWESTERN RAILROAD

In 1877 the Supreme Court, distinguishing between intrastate (within the boundaries of a state) commerce and interstate (between two or among many states) commerce, maintained the right of Wisconsin to regulate railroad rates within the state, even though such regulation might incidentally affect persons outside the state. A majority of the justices believed that the states should be permitted to handle their railroad problems without judicial interference "until such time as Congress should legislate on this matter."

THE WABASH RATE CASE

The principles established in the Granger cases were apparently reversed by the Supreme Court in 1886 when it handed down the decision in *Wabash, St. Louis, and Pacific Railway Company v. Illinois*, known as the Wabash Rate Case. An Illinois statute that attempted to prevent rate discrimination by railroads that passed through its territory was held unconstitutional on the grounds that the control of interstate commerce was exclusive to Congress. The effect of the decision was to limit each state's jurisdiction to intrastate commerce and to render ineffective most of the rate-making legislation of the previous fifteen years.

Congressional Action

For a number of years before the decision in the Wabash Rate Case crippled the power of the states over interstate commerce, Congress had been considering proposals for federal control of the railroads. Every presidential campaign after 1868 was marked by the demand of the minor parties that Congress regulate railroad rates. The Labor Reform party in 1872, the Prohibition party in 1876, the Greenback party in 1880, and the Greenback-Labor party in 1884 cited the outstanding railroad abuses and called upon the federal government to take action. Within the two major parties there was considerable sentiment favoring congressional legislation. The Windom report to the Senate in 1874, the McCrary bill passed by the House of Representatives in 1874 but defeated in the Senate, and the Reagen bill, which was passed by the House of Representatives in 1878 but which the Senate refused to consider, all kept the issue alive.

THE CULLOM COMMITTEE INVESTIGATION

In 1885 the Senate appointed a special committee of five, headed by Republican senator Shelby M. Cullom of Illinois, to investigate the subject of federal control of interstate commerce. The committee, after protracted hearings in every section of the nation, filed a 2,000-page report, which concluded that "upon no public question is public opinion so nearly unanimous as upon the proposition that Congress should undertake in some way the regulation of interstate commerce."

THE INTERSTATE COMMERCE ACT

The congressional debates over the Cullom report resulted in the Interstate Commerce Act—the first attempt of the federal government to control private business enterprise in the public interest. The act, passed by Congress in 1887, forbade the railroads (1) to form pooling agreements; (2) to charge more for a short haul than for a long haul under the same conditions of traffic; and (3) to grant secret rebates. It also required them to post their rates and to give a ten-day public notice of any rate change. A bipartisan commission of five, called the Interstate Commerce Commission, was created to supervise the accounting systems, rate schedules, and business methods of the roads; to hear complaints from shippers; and to assist the attorney general in prosecuting offenses. Even an able and conscientious commission, however, found its efforts ineffective for several reasons: (1) its inability to compel witnesses to testify; (2) the numerous appeals to the courts from commission rulings; (3) the success of the attorneys representing the railroads in winning appeals from the commission's orders; and (4) the Supreme Court's tendency to interpret the Interstate Commerce Act in such a way as to restrict the commission's control over the long haul–short haul system and secret rebates. For years the nation waited for Congress to remedy the situation by futher regulatory legislation, but that did not come until the first decade of the twentieth century.

AIMS AND TACTICS
OF MANAGEMENT AND LABOR

Management and labor shared a common desire for national prosperity. But they had divergent sets of aims and tactics to get their own pieces of the economic "pie." This condition made for an adversarial relationship.

Management

Most employers of the late nineteenth century distrusted labor's attempts to organize and took active measures to hinder the efforts.

AIMS

Operators of business firms sought to achieve the greatest profits possible by increasing production through the most efficient use of materials and labor.

TACTICS

The tactics of management against labor included (1) the "yellow-dog" contract (a worker's agreement not to join a union during the period of his or her employment); (2) the blacklist (a list circulated among employers of workers reputed to hold opinions or engage in actions contrary to the employers' interests); (3) the injunction (a court order whereby one is required to do or refrain from doing a specified act) to restrain unions from actions harmful to employers; (4) the open shop (an establishment in which employment is not determined by union membership or nonmembership); (5) company police and company spies; and (6) use of strikebreakers (called "scabs" by workers) to fill the jobs of strikers.

Labor

American workers strove to adjust themselves to the new industrial order of the latter part of the nineteenth century and to organize effectively to improve their status.

AIMS

During the half century following the Civil War the labor movement had three principal aims: higher wages, shorter hours (the common demand was for an eight-hour workday), and safe and sanitary working conditions. But the labor movement was concerned with more than these goals. Among its secondary aims were (1) the establishment of federal and various state bureaus of labor; (2) the abolition of child labor; (3) the abolition of contract labor (laborers imported by an employer from a foreign nation); (4) recognition of the principle of collective bargaining (negotiation of contract terms between an employer or group of employers on one side and a union or number of unions on the other); (5) institution of compulsory arbitration of management-labor disputes; and (6) laws providing for worker compensation (insurance for pay that a worker may recover from an employer in the case of a job-related accident).

TACTICS

Among the tactics of organized labor were (1) the strike; (2) picketing; (3) the boycott (engaging in a concerted refusal to have anything to do with the products or services of an employer—and attempting to convince consumers to do the same—in order to force acceptance of certain conditions desired by a union); and (4) the closed shop (an establishment in which the employer by agreement hires and retains in employment only union members in good standing). Because their task was a more difficult one, the leaders of labor were often less successful than the leaders of industry in mobilizing their forces. In their attempts to weld the workers of the nation into a united and class-conscious group, the labor leaders had to cope with (1) the entrance of blacks, both skilled and unskilled, into the ranks of paid labor; (2) the presence of many poorly paid women in certain crafts; (3) an increase in the number of foreign-born workers, divided by language, religion, and national tradition; and (4) the activities of radicals holding to abstract theories for the reorganization of the social order, without sufficient regard for practical difficulties.

INFLUENTIAL LABOR UNIONS

As industrialists formed ever-larger business units, the factory workers tried to create organizations large and strong enough to bargain on equal terms with employers. Eventually small local craft unions (also called horizontal unions), the membership in which was limited to workers in the same craft, gave way to large national industrial unions (also called vertical unions), which admitted to membership workers in an entire industry irrespective of their occupation or craft.

The National Labor Union

The earliest instance of bringing various craft unions into a single national organization was the establishment in 1866 of the National Labor Union, mainly through the efforts of William H. Sylvis, head of the iron molders' union. But since many of Sylvis's associates were allied with skilled craftsmen, they often failed to win the confidence of the factory workers.

OBJECTIVES

In its program the National Labor Union demanded the elimination of monopoly in industry, the establishment of a federal department of labor, the abolition of contract labor, the arbitration of labor conflicts, and the enactment of laws providing for the eight-hour workday in factories.

GROWTH AND DECLINE

The leaders of the union turned to politics to further their organization's objectives, entering the political field as sponsors of the National Labor Reform party. In the presidential election of 1872 the party made a notably poor showing, however, contributing significantly to the rapid dissolution of the National Labor Union.

The Knights of Labor

For more than a decade after the collapse of the National Labor Union, the forces of labor were represented mainly by the Noble Order of the Knights of Labor, founded in 1869 under the leadership of Uriah S. Stephens, a tailor who had helped organize the garment cutters of Philadelphia.

OBJECTIVES AND METHODS

The Knights of Labor stressed (1) industrial unionism; (2) the inclusion of all workers—skilled and unskilled, regardless of the craft or industry—in a single great organization; (3) the formation of local assemblies of workers on the basis of their residence rather than their occupational affiliation; and (4) highly centralized control of the local assemblies by the national body. In furthering industrial solidarity, members pledged themselves "to secure for the workers the full enjoyment of the wealth they create, and sufficient leisure in which to develop their intellectual, moral, and social faculties."

Their programs included such specific objectives as (1) the eight-hour workday; (2) equal pay for equal work for men and women; (3) the abolition of labor of children under fourteen; (4) the prohibition of contract foreign labor; (5) the arbitration of labor disputes; (6) the establishment of bureaus of labor statistics on both the federal and state levels; (7) safety and sanitary codes for industry; (8) laws compelling employers to pay laborers on a weekly basis; (9) the creation of cooperatives (associations for buying or selling goods to the better advantage of its members by eliminating the middlemen's profits); (10) the imposition of an income tax; and (11) government ownership of railroad and telegraph lines.

Although the Knights of Labor held as one of their main tenets that disputes should be arbitrated, they relied increasingly upon strikes and boycotts to achieve their objectives. In the political arena the organization fought aggressively for its program, but not until its influence began to wane did it view favorably the idea of a labor party.

GROWTH AND DECLINE

The Knights of Labor expanded rapidly under the leadership of Terence V. Powderly, a former machinist, reaching its greatest strength in 1886, when 5,892 local chapters reported over 700,000 members. However, a series of unsuccessful strikes in 1886 marked the beginning of the union's decline. Its complete collapse was hastened by (1) the growing public belief that many members favored the use of violence in industrial disputes; (2) the hostility of skilled workers toward an organization that minimized the interests of the craft union; (3) the failure of most of the producers' cooperatives in which the Knights of Labor had invested funds; (4) a confusion among the leaders, the majority of whom were largely concerned with the direct goals of higher wages, shorter hours, and good conditions of employment, while others focused on idealistic social reform measures; (5) the revolt by many of the local assemblies against centralized control by the national body; and (6) the organization's ineffective handling of the large numbers of unskilled workers, many of whom were transient.

The American Federation of Labor

The increasing dissatisfaction of skilled craftsmen with the objectives and methods of the Knights of Labor resulted in the formation in 1881 of the Federation of Organized Trades and Labor Unions of America and Canada, reorganized in 1886 as the American Federation of Labor (AFL).

OBJECTIVES AND METHODS

Samuel Gompers and Adolph Strasser, who together had revived the Cigarmakers' Union, were influential in organizing the American Federation of Labor and formulating its philosophy. The AFL was a league of separate and quite autonomous craft unions, each of which retained strong local powers, with the authority of the central body strictly limited. The specific objectives of the AFL were quite similar to those of the Knights of Labor, and for a time the two organizations cooperated. Gradually, however, the AFL concentrated its efforts upon a campaign for the "bread and butter" issues—higher wages, shorter hours, and safer and more sanitary conditions of employment within the various crafts. The organization also vigorously advocated the restriction of immigrants, who competed with native-born Americans for jobs.

The weapons of the AFL came to be the strike, the boycott, and collective bargaining. Refusing to sponsor an American labor party or to ally itself with any one political party, it used its political power to secure immediate objectives rather than to champion a comprehensive program for the reorganization of society.

GROWTH AND ACHIEVEMENT

Elected first president of the AFL, Gompers held that position except for one term until his death almost forty years later. Despite the pressure of a small socialist minority among its members, the AFL remained conservative, defending the capitalist system while criticizing its imperfections. Membership increased from 190,000 in 1890 to 550,000 in 1900 to more than 2 million in 1915. However, since the vast majority of the nation's industrial workers did not belong to the AFL, its victories had little direct effect on American labor in general. AFL achievements included (1) the development within the national organization of strong craft unions with effective programs, aided by large funds, for sickness and unemployment benefits; (2) the establishment of the eight-hour workday in several trades; (3) the recognition by an increasing number of employers of labor's right to bargain collectively; and (4) the slow but steady growth of labor's influence upon the federal and state legislatures.

The Industrial Workers of the World

In 1905 leaders of the radical wing of unionism together with militant socialists founded the Industrial Workers of the World (IWW) to oppose conservative policies in the labor movement. William D. "Big Bill" Haywood, who had been an officer in the Western Federation of Miners, was its most prominent head.

OBJECTIVES AND METHODS

The IWW sought to bring all the workers of the nation into a single industrial union. It strove to overthrow the capitalist system and establish in its place a socialist one. Spurning the middle-class reformers and moderate socialists alike, the IWW championed direct action—the mass strike and sabotage.

GROWTH AND DECLINE

The IWW appealed chiefly to migratory laborers in the lumber camps, mines, and harvest fields of the far West. Various states took action against the organization because of its radical views and actions, and in 1918 the federal government imprisoned its most influential leaders for their opposition to American entry into World War I. By the mid-1920s the membership, which at its height numbered 60,000, had disintegrated.

MANAGEMENT-LABOR CONFLICTS

In the unequal struggle between the employers, powerful and always well organized, and the unions, weak and often without experienced leaders, workers resorted to strikes, picketing, and boycotts as their only effective weapons.

Confrontation

Between 1880 and 1900 there were close to 25,000 strikes, involving more than 6 million workers. Almost half ended in failure, while another 15 percent ended in compromise.

RAILROAD STRIKES

Symptomatic of the extensive management-labor unrest in the 1870s were the railroad strikes of 1877, which started when employees of the Baltimore and Ohio Railroad walked off their jobs because of a reduction in wages. Soon most of the roads east of the Mississippi, and eventually some western lines, were involved. Rioting, resulting in bloodshed and destruction of railroad property, was more than the local authorities could handle, and state militia companies were called into action. Finally President Hayes sent federal troops to restore order and to protect nonstriking workers who crossed the picket lines.

THE HAYMARKET INCIDENT

Despite the failure of the railroad strikes, industrial warfare grew more intense. On May 4, 1886, a mass meeting organized by anarchists was held in Chicago's Haymarket Square to protest police tactics against strikers at the local McCormick Harvester Company plant. When the police tried to disperse the crowd, someone threw a bomb at them. Seven policemen were killed and a number were injured. Both sides then opened fire, resulting in the deaths of two civilians and injuries to both policemen and civilians. Although the person who hurled the bomb was never identified, eight anarchists were convicted of inciting a crowd to riot and four were hanged. The Haymarket Square incident injured the labor movement throughout the nation, for public opinion unwarrantedly accused the Knights of Labor of affiliating with anarchists, condoning violence, and being responsible for the so-called Haymarket Riot.

THE HOMESTEAD STRIKE

The wave of antilabor hysteria that followed the Haymarket affair had scarcely subsided when in June 1892 violence again flared, this time at the Homestead, Pennsylvania, plant of the Carnegie Steel Company, where members of the Amalgamated Association of Iron, Steel, and Tin Workers, a relatively strong and conservative union, struck to protest a reduction in wages. In an attempt to destroy the union, the company employed some 300 Pinkerton detectives to protect strikebreakers. (In the late nineteenth century the Pinkerton National Detective Agency was actively engaged in supplying armed men to employers in management-labor disputes.) In desperation the strikers fired on and killed several Pinkerton detectives. After the state militia had restored order, the strike was called off, and the Amalgamated Association of Iron, Steel, and Tin Workers, its spirit and funds exhausted after a five-month strike, collapsed.

THE PULLMAN STRIKE

In the depression year of 1893 the Pullman Palace Car Company, near Chicago, sought to prevent the loss of dividends to its stockholders by reducing the wages of its employees and dismissing many workers. As a result, in June 1894 the employees went on strike. The members of the American Railway Union tried to help the strikers by refusing, at first in the Chicago area, to handle any trains carrying Pullman cars. As the boycott spread over the middle and far West, the Railroad Managers' Association fought back vigorously. Attorneys for the Railroad Managers' Association secured a federal court injunction, under the Sherman Antitrust Act, to prevent the strikers from interfering with the carrying of the United States mail and with interstate commerce "as a conspiracy in restraint of trade." When the strikers ignored the court order, the government made two moves. First, President Grover Cleveland sent federal troops into the Chicago area, ostensibly to assure delivery of the mail but actually to maintain order, a presidential action that Governor John P. Altgeld of Illinois protested as unnecessary; second, Attorney General Richard Olney instructed government attorneys to press charges against officers of the American Railway Union on the grounds that they were in contempt of court. Eugene V. Debs, president of the union, was sentenced to a six-month prison term for refusing to obey the injunction. The strike disintegrated. (While in prison Debs spent much time reading about socialist theory. He emerged an ardent opponent of capitalism and some years later became the head of the Socialist Party of America.)

Debs sought a writ of *habeas corpus* (an inquiry into the lawfulness of the restraint of a person who is imprisoned) in the Supreme Court, which the justices denied in 1895. They based their decision not on the Sherman Antitrust Act but on the grounds that the jurisdiction of the federal government over interstate commerce and the carrying of the mail authorized use of the injunction to prevent obstruction of those activities. This marked the first effective use of the injunction against a union.

Effects of Confrontation

More significant than the failure of any one set of actions by workers was the evidence that public opinion was opposed to such union tactics as strikes, picket lines, and boycotts. Organized wage earners were fully aware of the fact that the force of government on both the federal and state levels usually entered management-labor disputes in support of the employers.

PUBLIC OPINION TOWARD LABOR

Most Americans were unhesitatingly responsive to the individual laborer's grievances concerning long hours, low wages, and unsafe and unsanitary working conditions. However, they were suspicious of unions that conducted a strong offensive against the employer class as a whole. Many people believed, in accordance with the basic tenets of laissez faire, that collective bargaining could not determine wages, which were set by economic competition. Many were slow to admit that labor could win shorter hours, higher wages, and satisfactory working conditions without defying the operation of "natural" economic laws, or that it could organize without resorting to violence. Not until the 1920s did the labor movement enjoy a favorable climate of public opinion.

JUDICIAL RESTRICTIONS ON LABOR

If labor leaders had long found it hard to defend a union's right to bargain collectively, their task became much more difficult after the passage of the Sherman Antitrust Act of 1890. The law, designed to prevent corporations from engaging in monopolistic practices, was eventually turned against unions, which were seen as "combinations in restraint of trade." The federal courts repeatedly held that the Sherman Antitrust Act was applicable to unions, and attorneys for employers used the act to secure injunctions against strikes and boycotts.

LABOR LEGISLATION

Despite the obstacles encountered by the labor movement, some of its objectives were enacted into law. The eight-hour workday was instituted in 1868 for federal employees engaged in public works projects and established in 1892 for all federal employees. The immigration of Chinese laborers, who had been competing for jobs with native-born workers in the far West, was suspended in 1882. The Erdman Act, passed by Congress in 1898, provided for the mediation of disputes involving railroads engaged in interstate commerce and their employees, and it prohibited the use of the yellow-dog contract by interstate railroads. (Ten years later the Supreme Court declared the latter provision unconstitutional on the grounds that it violated the freedom of contract and property rights of the railroads.) Although the Supreme Court generally maintained that state laws regulating employment were unconstitutional, it upheld certain of those laws as valid exercises of the states' police power. Thus in 1898 the Court sustained in *Holden v. Hardy* a Utah law establishing maximum working hours for miners and in 1908 in *Muller v. Oregon* an Oregon law setting maximum working hours for women. In 1907 Congress passed the Hours of Service Act, limiting, in the interest of public safety, the number of consecutive hours that railroad employees could work.

Selected Readings

GENERAL WORKS:

Cochran, Thomas C., and William Miller. *The Age of Enterprise* (1942)
Garraty, John A. *The New Commonwealth, 1877–1890* (1968)
Hacker, Louis M. *The Triumph of American Capitalism* (1940)
Kirkland, Edward C. *Industry Comes of Age: Business, Labor, and Public Policy, 1860–1897* (1961)
Rayback, Joseph G. *A History of American Labor* (1959)
Taft, Philip. *Organized Labor in America* (1964)
Tarbell, Ida M. *The Nationalizing of Business, 1878–1898* (1936)
Ware, Norman J. *The Labor Movement in the United States, 1860–1895* (1929)

SPECIAL STUDIES:

Benson, Lee. *Merchants, Farmers, and Railroads* (1955)

Cochran, Thomas C. *Railroad Leaders* (1953)

Dick, William M. *Labor and Socialism in America: The Gompers Era* (1972)

Dubofsky, Melvyn. *Industrialism and the American Worker, 1865–1920* (1975)

————. *We Shall Be All: A History of the Industrial Workers of the World* (1969)

Fine, Sidney. *Laissez Faire and the General Welfare State: A Study of Conflict in American Thought, 1865–1901* (1956)

Fink, Leon. *Workingmen's Discovery: The Knights of Labor and American Politics* (1983)

Fogel, Robert W. *Railroads and American Economic Growth* (1964)

Foner, Philip. *Women and the American Labor Movement* (2 vols., 1979)

Grob, Gerald N. *Workers and Utopia: A Study of Ideological Conflict in the American Labor Movement, 1865–1900* (1961)

Gutman, Herbert. *Work, Culture, and Society in Industrializing America* (1976)

Harris, William H. *The Harder We Run: Black Workers Since the Civil War* (1982)

Josephson, Matthew. *The Robber Barons* (1934)

Kaufman, Stewart. *Samuel Gompers and the Origins of the American Federation of Labor* (1973)

Kolko, Gabriel. *Railroads and Regulation, 1877–1916* (1965)

Lindsey, Almont. *The Pullman Strike* (1942)

Livesay, Harold C. *Andrew Carnegie and the Rise of Big Business* (1975)

Mink, Gwendolyn. *Old Labor and New Immigrants in American Political Development: Union, Party, and State, 1875–1920* (1986)

Nevins, Allan. *Study in Power: John D. Rockefeller* (2 vols., 1953)

Porter, Glenn. *The Rise of Big Business* (1973)

Rosenblum, Gerald. *Immigrant Workers: The Impact on American Labor Radicalism* (1973)

Salvatore, Nick. *Eugene V. Debs: Citizen and Socialist* (1982)

Temin, Peter. *Iron and Steel in Nineteenth-Century America* (1964)

Trachtenberg, Alan. *The Incorporation of America* (1982)

4

The Settlement and the Revolt of the West

1849   California gold rush

1859   Comstock Lode discovered

1862   Homestead Act
       Morrill Act

1867   Grange founded

1873   Coinage Act
       Timer Culture Act

1875   Resumption Act
       National Greenback party founded

1876   Custer and his troops killed in battle at the Little Bighorn

1877   Desert Land Act
       Greenback-Labor party founded

1878   Bland-Allison Act

1881   Jackson, *A Century of Dishonor*

1887   Dawes Act

1890   Census Bureau announces end of frontier
       Sherman Silver Purchase Act

1892   Populist party founded

1893   Sherman Silver Purchase Act repealed

1896   McKinley elected president

1906   Burke Act

*W*hile the South was being humbled during the Civil War and the Reconstruction years, the foundations of a new economic order were being established in the West. Several factors contributed to the settlement of the West. Among them were the courage and perseverance of the pioneers; the skill of business interests possessed of abundant capital and an adequate labor supply; and a government policy of support and encouragement. The domain of prairie, plateau, mountain, and desert beyond the Mississippi River possessed remarkable resources. Before they could be utilized, however, the West had to be made accessible to settlement. The building of transcontinental railroads made it possible to transport people and goods to and from the region. In topography and climate the West offered a wide range of opportunities for mining, ranching, and large-scale farming. There were three waves of migration: First came the miners, then the cattlemen, and finally the farmers.

Growing dissatisfaction with the failure of both major parties to come to grips with the serious economic issues affecting their welfare caused the farmers to engage in a political revolt in the 1890s. The political power of the business interests was seriously threatened during that decade, as the farmers of the West and South, joined by many wage earners of the East, launched proposals for radical reform measures against the bulwark of big business. Although the conservative forces won the important election of 1896, the demands of the farmers and laborers had to be reckoned with thereafter, and many were eventually adopted by both the Democratic and Republican parties.

THE INDIANS

The arrival of the whites in the West quickly changed Indian life. War, the introduction of diseases such as measles and tuberculosis, extensive killing of the bison, being forced onto reservations—all these created almost unendurable hardships for the Indians of the western plains.

Overcoming the Indians

Complete utilization of the vast natural resources of the western regions was impossible so long as the nomadic Indian tribes, which relied for subsistence on the bison (commonly called buffalo) herds of the Great Plains, retained their hunting grounds. These Plains Indians, probably numbering more than 225,000 at the end of the Civil War, were skilled fighters and often resisted the encroachments of the white settlers with violence.

FRONTIER HOSTILITIES

While some tribes, such as the Crow and northern Arapaho, were generally friendly to the whites, the more militant southern Arapaho, Cheyenne, Comanche, and Kiowa were determined to halt the advance of settlers into the Great Plains and the intermountain areas farther west. During the decade after the Civil War, hundreds of skirmishes took place between United States military forces and the Indian tribes. At times as many as 30,000 troops were in the field to protect the emigrants moving along the Missouri River and farther westward.

COLLAPSE OF THE SIOUX

The Sioux nation in the northern Great Plains constituted one of the most difficult challenges for the army commanders, as it was large, powerful, and ably led. Skirmish after skirmish occurred. In 1876 General George A. Custer and the two hundred men under his immediate command were killed in battle at the Little Bighorn River in Montana. However, the Sioux's courageous campaign against United States troops was slowly contained, and by 1880 the northern frontier was relatively quiet. But the price had been high in lives and in money, shocking the government into a reconsideration of its Indian policy.

EXTERMINATING THE BUFFALO

The Plains Indians depended upon the flesh of buffalo for food, upon their hides for clothing, and upon many other parts for additional articles of daily use. An important factor in the decline of militant resistance on the part of the Indians was the slaughter by professional hunters and sportsmen of the buffalo herds. Buffalo robes were in great demand during the quarter century after the Civil War. Scout and showman William F. "Buffalo Bill" Cody claimed that he had shot 4,280 in the northern herds within less than two years. By 1885 only a few straggling herds remained of the more than 15 million animals that had roamed the plains twenty years earlier. Although the species survived under government protection, the main economic support of the nomadic Indians was gone.

Formulating a National Policy for the Indians

A more enlightened policy of dealing with the Indian tribes slowly took shape. But it was framed only after the record had been filled with needless wars and massacres, fraudulent seizures of Indian lands, and the work of dishonest traders. For many years the Department of War, which advocated "extermination," worked at cross purposes with the Bureau of Indian Affairs within the Department of the Interior, which at times supplied the Indians with hunting rifles, usable of course in combat.

THE RESERVATION SYSTEM

As actual warfare between United States troops and Indian warriors diminished, the government forced tribes onto reservations, where they were almost completely dependent on the taxpayers' bounty, which was never adequate for their needs. The aim of the reservation policy was to assimilate the Indians into an agricultural economy. By 1885 there were 171 reservations in more than a score of states and territories.

But the administration of the reservation system was notoriously corrupt. Government agents made fortunes by supplying Indians under their jurisdiction with shoddy goods, selling them prohibited liquor, and cheating them out of their rightful lands through fraudulent real-estate deals. Meanwhile traders, miners, cattlemen, and railroad builders prodded the government to encroach upon Indian reservations.

THE REFORM MOVEMENT

Humanitarians, stirred in part by Helen Hunt Jackson's *A Century of Dishonor* (1881), a report on the degradation of reservation Indians —tried to modify or supplant the system. Among the reformers there was a sharp division between those who wanted to preserve old tribal customs and those who desired to hasten the assimilation of the Indians.

THE DAWES ACT

Government action was initially confined to a program of increased appropriations for schools to train young Indians in arts and crafts, farming, and animal husbandry. Congress at least partially accepted the idea that Indians should be more adequately prepared for a place in American society when it passed the Dawes Act in 1887. This measure modified the reservation system by granting 160 acres of land and United States citizenship to the heads of Indian families who would agree to abandon their tribal allegiance. The right to sell the land was withheld for twenty-five years. The motive behind this legislation was twofold: first, to encourage Indians to become assimilated into the nation; and second, to satisfy the land hunger of white settlers. Land on the Indian reservations not needed for allotment to former members of the tribes was opened to settlement.

THE BURKE ACT

Cattlemen and farmers, seeking new homesteads in the trans-Mississippi West, profited more from the Dawes Act than did the Indians. After some thirty years even the reformers admitted that title to private property and the rights of citizenship had not improved the status of many Indians. The Burke Act, designed to correct the defects of the Dawes Act, was passed in 1906. It provided new incentives for those making the transition from tribal membership to individual citizenship. Citizenship was generally not granted to Indians receiving land allotments until they had completed the twenty-five-year probationary period specified in the Dawes Act, but those who proved competent in managing the land could become citizens in a shorter time. (In 1924 legislation was passed conferring citizenship on all Indians.)

THE MINING FRONTIER

One of the magnets pulling settlers westward through the Indian barriers, and drawing squatters (those who occupied land without possessing a legal title) into the regions where nomadic tribes had long roamed, was the discovery by venturesome prospectors of the rich mineral deposits beyond the Mississippi River.

The Boom

During the third quarter of the nineteenth century many of the mineral resources of the West were rapidly discovered and almost as rapidly exploited.

STRIKES

The discovery of a rich mineral deposit was called a strike. Gold was found not far from present-day Sacramento, California, in 1848, leading to the rush there the following year by prospectors not only from all over the United States but also from overseas. More gold deposits were discovered in 1858 in the Pikes Peak district of what is now Colorado. The Comstock Lode (a lode is an ore deposit that fills a fissure in rock), discovered in 1859 on the site of present-day Virginia City, Nevada, produced large amounts of both gold and silver. In 1874 gold was discovered in the Black Hills section of what is now South Dakota. Copper was found in 1881 near present-day Butte, Montana. A number of abundantly rich silver deposits were unearthed during the 1880s in the Coeur d'Alene Mountains district of what is now Idaho.

MINING CAMPS

In his writings, Bret Harte, among others, captured the mood and manner of the settlers who put together the hastily built wooden towns that provided shelter and recreation for enthusiastic seekers of wealth. Saloons, dance halls, hotels, and gambling houses were apt to be established earlier than schools or churches. Indeed, some of the so-called boom towns had enjoyed a brief prosperity and been largely abandoned before law and order could be established.

After the Boom Despite the usual pattern of discovery and boom (in many a case it was discovery and bust), mining soon became the chief industry of the mountainous regions of the West. The economic structure of many communities rested on mining.

GETTING OUT THE WEALTH

Some mining booms, such as the one at Pikes Peak, ended quickly. The resources of gold, silver, lead, copper, and other minerals were abundant in the West, but it required more than enthusiasm and the techniques of placer mining, (extracting mineral particles from surface deposits), such as panning, at a stream, to get out the ore. In Montana and Idaho, as in Colorado and Nevada, the greatest wealth came after placer mining had been replaced by more elaborate processes, requiring heavy machinery and a considerable outlay of money. As a result, profits went more often to absentee capitalists than to resident prospectors.

THE IMPACT OF THE MINING FRONTIER

Before the frontier days had ended, the mining industry had produced enduring influences by (1) stimulating settlements that brought new states into the Union (Nevada in 1864, Colorado in 1876, Montana in 1889, Idaho and Wyoming in 1890); (2) providing gold and silver in such quantities that the volume of currency kept pace for a time with the increasing needs of business enterprise; (3) offering new opportunities for the investment of capital in speculative, but often highly profitable, mining ventures; (4) emphasizing the need for the reorganization of the structure of American business so that larger amounts of capital could be used under the corporate form of investment; (5) giving many settlers in new communities a chance to work out procedures of self-government necessary to combat violence and social anarchy; and (6) inducing an increased demand for better transportation, which was met by stage coaches and railroads.

THE CATTLE COUNTRY

The westward thrust of rail facilities brought boom times to the Great Plains once the threat of Indian attack was removed. Cattlemen discovered that the treeless grasslands were ideal for grazing livestock and rapidly exploited their lush growth. After the Civil War, cattle were driven northward from Texas to rail centers for shipment to the East.

The Life of the Cowboy

The difficult and lonely work of the cowboy (also known variously as a cowhand, cowpoke, or cowpuncher) has become one of the most colorful facets of American folklore.

UTILITARIAN GARB

Living in the saddle, the cowboy wore utilitarian garb, consisting of such items as a broad-brimmed sombrero, neckerchief, spurred boots, and sturdy workpants, the latter probably made by Levi Strauss. Often equipped with a revolver, he carried a length of rope to catch cattle.

DUTIES

The cowboy's main job was to protect the cattle as they grazed on the range and as they were driven to market. The cowboy had many duties to perform on the ranch and on the roundup (gathering cattle together on the range by riding around them and driving them inward, which was done when calves needed branding or older animals were to be selected for shipment to market). The most strenuous work of all, perhaps, was on the long drive—moving hundreds and sometimes thousands of cattle hundreds of miles from the range to the "cow towns."

The Long Drive

Ever larger herds were driven from Texas to rail centers in Wyoming, Kansas, and Missouri for shipment to stockyards in the East.

TRAILS AND "COW TOWNS"

The cattlemen of Texas soon discovered the advantages of fattening their stock, called Texas longhorns, on the free, open range of the plains, which were still part of the public domain. There were four main trails to the cow-town rail centers northward: (1) the Goodnight-Loving Trail (named after Charles Goodnight and Oliver Loving, the two cattlemen who laid it out), ending at Cheyenne, Wyoming; (2) the Western Trail, ending at Dodge City, Kansas; (3) the Chisholm Trail (named after Jesse Chisholm, a trader who had previously established the route for trading purposes), ending at Ellsworth, Abilene, or Wichita, all in Kansas; and (4) the Sedalia Trail, ending at Sedalia or Kansas City, both in Missouri.

PEAK AND DECLINE OF THE ENTERPRISE

The period from 1875 to 1885 was the heyday of the long drive, cowboys, the open range, and the cattle barons. During this time almost 300,000 cattle annually were fattened on the free pasture land and shipped to eastern stockyards. At the peak, profits rose as high as 40 percent.

Good times, however, did not survive the following factors: (1) the advance of the farmers' frontier, which meant fencing off of the grazing lands; (2) legislation in some states providing for the close inspection of Texas longhorns or prohibiting driving the animals across their boundaries; (3) competition from the livestock raisers on the farms of the Midwest; (4)

the ability of the cattle buyers in the cow towns to determine prices and the railroad owners to set freight rates; and (5) overexpansion of the cattle industry on a speculative basis. With the disappearance of the open range, western cattle raising lost its most picturesque feature.

THE FARMERS' FRONTIER

The farmers, who had followed the miners and the cattlemen, formed the last group to settle the West. Government benefits, new inventions, and rail facilities opened the West to an agricultural population.

Land Policies

In the disposal of its public lands the United States had always been generous, and that generosity reached its zenith during the period following the Civil War.

THE HOMESTEAD ACT

This act, passed in 1862, provided that any head of a family who was a citizen, or declared his intention of becoming a citizen, could acquire 160 acres of surveyed land by paying a small registration fee and residing on the land for five years. So rapid was the response to this invitation that by 1880 almost 20 million acres had been occupied by people alleging to be homesteaders. Despite a number of fraudulent claims, most of this land was soon under cultivation by bona fide settlers.

ADDITIONAL LEGISLATION

The Homestead Act was chiefly beneficial in bringing farmers into the forested and humid areas of the national domain. Its emphasis on the small-acreage farm proved a handicap to those who desired to cultivate the treeless and semi-arid region of the Great Plains. Congress yielded to pressure from the exploiters of the trans-Mississippi West and passed the Timber Culture Act in 1873 and the Desert Land Act in 1877 to encourage the staking out of larger holdings by prospective homesteaders. The Timber Culture Act provided additional land allotments to persons who used a portion of their original allotments for treeplanting. The Desert Land Act authorized as additional land allotments semi-arid land to be sold at $1.25 an acre to persons who agreed to irrigate it. However, neither act contributed greatly to the westward advance of the farmers' frontier.

OTHER OPPORTUNITIES TO SECURE LAND

Many settlers could not qualify under the Homestead Act or found the land allotment by such legislation insufficient for large-scale agriculture on the Great Plains. But they had other opportunities to secure land. The state governments, which under the Morrill Act of 1862 had received generous allotments of land for the endowment of agricultural and mechanical colleges, sold their acreage on satisfactory terms, and the transcontinental railroads that had received grants of land offered much of theirs at reasonable rates. All too often, however, prospective settlers seeking to buy land were victimized by speculative interests.

The Life of the Farmer

Rather than the miners or the cattlemen, the farmers gradually became the dominant force in the taming of the "Wild West."

NEW METHODS AND TOOLS

To move homesteaders into the vast areas of the Great Plains required more than the legislative assistance of the federal government. The open ranges of the cattle country had to be enclosed, and neither deep furrows nor high hedges proved satisfactory substitutes for wooden fences, the timber for which the region lacked. Cheap barbed wire, patented in 1874, finally provided the necessary fencing. At the same time, plows and mowers suitable to the plains appeared on the market. But agriculture was not practicable in the semi-arid sections until the twentieth century, when sophisticated irrigation techniques came into use.

CATTLEMEN VERSUS FARMERS

The ranchers viewed the farmers, whom they called nesters, as their natural enemies. The fences, so necessary for an agricultural economy, broke up the open ranges of the West, and the farmers' search for water took from the grazing cattle easy access to customary water holes. The rivalry in some districts turned into open warfare in the 1880s. But the nesters had found their decisive weapon in the barbed wire, which could be used to set off their homesteads from the open range.

AGRARIAN IMMIGRANTS

The bulk of the settlers in the prairie states of the Mississippi Valley and in the Great Plains came from the older states. They were attracted to the West by cheap land, improved rail transportation, and the opportunity to harvest the large crops that agricultural machinery made possible. Thousands of foreign immigrants, principally Germans and Scandinavians, also helped swell the populations of Wisconsin, Minnesota, Iowa, Nebraska, Kansas, North Dakota, and South Dakota.

CLOSING OF THE FRONTIER

Between 1870 and 1880 an area equal to that of Great Britain was brought under cultivation, and the agrarian frontier claimed most of the nation's arable land. In 1890, although much western land still remained to be settled, the Bureau of the Census announced the end of a frontier line. (By definition, a frontier region was a large inhabitable area having fewer than two people per square mile.) The frontier was held by some historians, notably Frederick Jackson Turner, to be the greatest force in the shaping of American democracy. The existence of free, open territory with abundant natural resources was perhaps most important in forming American tendencies to individualism, inventiveness, and expansionism. However, Turner's idea that the frontier served as a safety valve during periods of economic distress in the cities of the East was disputed by his critics. They argued that the frontier was of limited value to most urban laborers, who lacked the means to move to the West. After 1890 the West became a place for consolidation and conservation. Expansion was then sought overseas.

THE FARMERS' GRIEVANCES

Fundamental to the discontent of the farmers was their belief that they were not receiving a share of the national income commensurate with their contributions to American life.

Farm Environment

During the last third of the nineteenth century most farmers in the United States lived either along the frontier of settlement or in comparative isolation on small farmsteads in more populous areas.

DIFFICULTIES IN LIFE-STYLE

From planting time to harvest, the average farmer was a hard worker in the fields, and leisure was usually as monotonous as toil. Though independent, farmers were too often isolated and thus denied many advantages and conveniences that their fellow Americans in towns and cities took for granted.

RELIANCE ON RAINFALL

Farmers had always been the recipients of nature's bounty but also the victims of its uncertainties. In a particular way this was the fate of the western farmer in the post–Civil War period. Many ambitious tillers of the soil had pushed into areas where the average annual rainfall was insufficient for farming without irrigation. In the early 1880s rainfall on the western plains was abnormally heavy, but from the mid-1880s to the mid-1890s an extended drought ruined thousands who had gambled that the rains would continue.

Economic Conditions

During the last third of the nineteenth century farmers complained bitterly about the low prices for their products and the high prices for manufactured goods, including agricultural equipment, that they had to buy.

FINANCIAL COSTS

Constantly in need of money between harvests, for the purchase or repair of farm machinery and tools, fertilizer, and other supplies, farmers grew more and more indignant at the high interest rates for the bank loans that they were compelled to seek. Because of a higher rate of taxation on landed property (which was always visible to the tax assessor) than on personal property, the farmers' taxes were higher in proportion to their ability to pay than were the taxes of the financiers and the factory workers. Farmers were charged excessive railroad freight rates compared with those required of industrial shippers. They also objected to economic discrimination created by tariffs; they bought protected products and sold unprotected ones.

INCREASED PRODUCTION

The growing number of new farms, cultivated more efficiently with better machines, such as the gang plow, disk harrow, thresher, and grain binder, made for tremendously increased production. This large supply was responsible for declining crop prices because of the operation of the supply-and-demand principle in an unprotected market. Furthermore, there was increasing competition from Canadian, Russian, and Argentine wheat growers.

FARM OWNERSHIP

As a result of the farmers' unfavorable economic situation during the last third of the nineteenth century, mortgage foreclosures increased greatly. The number of persons working farms as tenants rather than owners also increased, as farms became larger, more specialized, and more dependent on ready cash. Prevalent in the South was sharecropping, in which the landlord furnished tenants with land, equipment, and shelter in return for a share of the harvest proceeds, and the crop-lien system, in which the farmers pledged a portion or all of their crops to a merchant for supplies.

THE AGRARIAN REACTION

The declining prices of agricultural products in the post–Civil War period brought into sharp focus the protest of the farmers. They insisted that new machines, more cultivated acres, and larger markets were not enabling the farm population to keep its proportionate share of the national income. To help themselves they began to join a number of organizations and to support different movements.

The Grange

Popularly known as the Grange (the name given to the local chapter), the Patrons of Husbandry was a ritualistic society formed in 1867 through the efforts of Oliver H. Kelley, a Post Office Department clerk, to promote rural social activity as an antidote to the loneliness and monotony of farm life. It was not long before the Grangers began engaging in a program that had economic and political objectives as well as social aims. Within a few years the Grange had approximately 700,000 members, most of whom were from the midwestern grain-growing states.

THE COOPERATIVE MOVEMENT

The Grangers organized cooperatives to reduce the cost of the commodities that they purchased and to increase the price of the crops that they produced. In the 1870s the Grangers were operating plow and harvester factories, elevators for the storage of grain, meat-packing plants, loan companies, and retail stores. However, most of those cooperatives were wrecked by inexperienced and inefficient management, internal dissension, and the aggressive hostility of private competitors.

POLITICAL ACTION

By supporting sympathetic candidates, most of whom were affiliated with minor party movements, the Grangers fought for influence in many state legislatures—and won a number of notable triumphs. Illinois passed a law fixing the maximum rates of railroads and the maximum charges of grain-storage companies. Wisconsin and Iowa, whose legislatures were under tight Granger control, enacted laws regulating railroad freight rates. Minnesota established a commission to supervise all public utilities, including the railroads. The political power of the Grangers in some of the prairie states enabled them to send to Congress senators and representatives who acted as their spokesmen. In the so-called Granger cases of the 1870s the Supreme Court upheld a state's right to establish maximum fees to be charged by railroads and public utilities, but in the 1880s the Court reversed itself regarding the competence of a state to regulate railroad traffic. By that time, however, the farmers had turned to organizations and movements other than the Grange.

The Greenback Movement

Farmers were debtors. To help themselves in their plight they supported the Greenback movement, which espoused a policy of inflation.

ADVOCACY OF INFLATION

During the quite extended periods between harvests, when profits were realized, farmers found themselves borrowing money to repair and buy machinery, to make mortgage payments, and to pay for family articles. Because of that and to halt the trend of decreasing prices for agricultural products, the farmers advocated inflation. The debtor class generally—and the farmers particularly—strongly supported the Greenback movement, which would have the government issue paper money to bring about inflation of the currency—a cheapening of the value of money. This would not only increase prices but also ease the payment of debt. (If wheat sold at $1 a bushel, a farmer would need to sell 1,000 bushels to settle a $1,000 loan—disregarding, of course, the interest. If, however, wheat sold at an inflated $2 a bushel, a farmer would need to sell only 500 bushels to repay a $1,000 loan.) Although the farmers would have to pay more for manufactured products, they would still be at an advantage because, while they received higher prices for their crops, their debts would remain the same. Attaining inflation by increasing the amount of currency in circulation could be done in two ways: by issuing more paper money not backed by gold or silver, or by issuing silver coins.

DEMAND FOR THE REDEMPTION OF GREENBACKS

During the Civil War the federal government issued approximately $430 million in paper money to help pay for its military operations. These paper notes were called greenbacks, from the color of the ink used to print them. The greenbacks were not supported by gold or silver as security but were buttressed solely by the confidence of the people in the government. After the Civil War the creditor class generally, and eastern business interests particularly, demanded a government policy of sound money, by which they meant removing from circulation most of the paper money and making redeemable in gold that which remained. On the other hand, western farmers became ever more active in the movement for cheaper money.

THE RESUMPTION ACT

Disregarding the sharp protests from the agricultural West, Congress passed the Resumption Act in January 1875, providing that, of the total amount of greenbacks, $300 million worth should remain in circulation and that after January 1, 1879, they should be redeemable at face value in gold. A reserve of $100 million in gold was set up by the government for this purpose. By bringing greenbacks up to the value of gold-backed money, the Resumption Act produced deflation and a consequent lowering of prices. But in 1878 lobbyists for the inflation-minded farmers succeeded in having Congress modify the measure by halting the redemption of greenbacks into gold when the value of paper money in circulation reached $346,681,016— an amount that was allowed to remain in the currency.

THE GREENBACK PARTY

The extreme inflationists answered the federal deflationary policy by organizing the National Greenback party in 1875. The following year the Greenbackers nominated Peter Cooper, a New York City iron manufacturer and philanthropist who believed in an inflationary policy, for president. In 1878 the Greenback party merged with the National Labor Reform party, and the new Greenback-Labor party received approximately 1,000,000 votes in the congressional elections and sent fourteen representatives to the lower house. In 1880, 1884, and 1888 the Greenback-Labor party offered presidential candidates to the American people, but its standard-bearers made poor showings and the strength of the third party quickly declined.

The Silver Movement

The advocates of cheap money eventually came to the conclusion that the free and unlimited coinage of silver would provide a more satisfactory currency than would a further issuance of greenbacks.

The Democratic and Republican parties were both divided over the silver issue, with westerners apt to be more sympathetic than easterners toward inflationary proposals. Regardless of party affiliation, the debt-ridden farmers argued for cheapening the value of the dollar by having the government mint silver coins as freely as it minted gold ones.

THE "CRIME OF '73"

In 1873 Congress passed the Coinage Act, ending the minting of silver dollars. This demonetization (abandoning the use of a precious metal as money) abolished bimetallism (the use of two metals, ordinarily silver and gold, for coinage) and placed the nation on the gold standard (having gold as the currency's only base). Some years later the silver advocates blamed declining prices on the scarcity of hard (metallic) money and traced this lack to the Coinage Act, calling it the "Crime of '73."

THE BLAND-ALLISON ACT

Farmers in the West and South and western silver-mine owners allied themselves in lobbying for congressional action to resume the coinage of silver. The farmers' case was well known to the nation. The tillers of the soil now had effective allies. Silver-mine owners and those interested in the development of regions in which silver was produced loudly demanded that "something be done for silver." They pointed out that the price of commercial silver had been sharply declining, since new deposits in Nevada and Colorado made large quantities available on the market, while exports of the metal had fallen off because of its decreased use in European and Latin American coinage systems.

A combination of western Republican and southern Democratic voters carried through Congress the Bland-Allison bill, authorizing the Treasury Department to purchase between $2 million and $4 million worth of silver bullion (metal in the mass, as opposed to being in a coined state) each month at the prevailing market price and to coin silver dollars. President Hayes vetoed the bill on the grounds that it allowed dollars of cheaper value to be used in the payment of pre-existing debts, but the measure was passed over his veto in 1878. The Bland-Allison Act, however, did not provide the inflation hoped for by the farmers. A succession of conservative "sound money" secretaries of the treasury, using the discretionary power granted them under the terms of the act, authorized monthly purchases of silver bullion only at the $2 million minimum amount.

THE SHERMAN SILVER PURCHASE ACT

Farmers and western silver-mine owners continued to press their demands. In 1890 Congress acquiesced with the Sherman Silver Purchase Act, authorizing the Treasury Department to purchase 4.5 million ounces of silver bullion each month at the prevailing market price and paying for it in newly issued treasury notes called silver certificates, which would be redeemable at face value in either gold or silver.

REPEAL OF THE SHERMAN SILVER PURCHASE ACT

Vast numbers of silver certificates were redeemed in gold, draining the gold reserve, which by June 1893 had fallen below the generally accepted "safe" mark of $100 million. In August President Cleveland, a longtime foe of inflationary policies, informed a special session of Congress that the developing financial panic was directly related to the fear that the nation was going to substitute silver for gold as its monetary base. Cleveland called for the prompt repeal of the Sherman Silver Purchase Act. With the aid of the eastern Republicans in Congress the president won his case, but he incurred the bitter animosity of the western and southern wings of his own Democratic party.

Populists

The political climax of agrarian discontent in the 1870s and 1880s was the organization of the Populist party, which enrolled Grangers, Greenbackers, and Laborites, plus many who had been active in the inflationist ranks of the two major parties.

FORMING THE PARTY

During the 1880s the western and southern states saw a phenomenal increase in the number of agrarian organizations. These groups were soon consolidated into two powerful associations: the Northwestern Alliance and the Southern Alliance. Such colorful leaders emerged as Jerry "Sockless Jerry" Simpson and Mary Ellen Lease, both of Kansas, James B. Weaver of Iowa, Ignatius Donnelly of Minnesota, Benjamin R. "Pitchfork Ben" Tillman of South Carolina, and Thomas E. Watson of Georgia. These organizations and leaders finally united to compete with the two major political parties. In February 1892, at St. Louis, Missouri, delegates formally organized the People's Party of the U.S.A., known as the Populist party. It held its first national nominating convention the following July at Omaha, Nebraska, to choose its presidential and vice-presidential candidates.

THE PLATFORM

The new third party adopted a platform expressing the grievances of decades. The planks dealing with economic reform called for (1) free and unlimited coinage of silver and gold at the ratio of sixteen to one (in minting coins the government had considered sixteen ounces of silver to be equal in value to one ounce of gold); (2) an increase in the amount of currency in circulation (then approximately twenty dollars per person) to fifty dollars per person; (3) the enactment of an income tax that was graduated (rate increases in proportion to increased earnings); (4) the reduction of various kinds of federal and state taxes; (5) the government ownership and operation of railroads and telegraph and telephone lines; (6) the appropriation by the government of all land held by corporations in excess of their actual needs; (7) the prohibition of alien ownership of land; (8) the establishment by the government of a postal savings system; and (9) the use of government funds to facilitate the marketing of farm products and to extend short-term rural loans. As an invitation to the industrial wage earners of the East, other planks favored (1) the restriction of "undesirable" immigration (to lessen competition for jobs); (2) the establishment of the eight-hour workday for government employees; and (3) the abolition of the Pinkerton detective system, which was used, often violently, against labor unions. The planks that were politically based advocated (1) a single term for the president and vice-president; (2) direct election of United States senators (then appointed by state legislatures); (3) use of the secret ballot; and (4) adoption by the states of the initiative (permitting voters to propose laws) and the referendum (permitting voters to accept or reject laws already passed).

THE FIRST CAMPAIGN

The Populists presented their first ticket to the nation in the election of 1892, nominating former Greenback representative James B. Weaver of Iowa for president and agrarian reformer James G. Field of Virginia for vice-president. Weaver's popular vote totaled 1,041,000. He received the entire electoral vote of Kansas, Colorado, Idaho, and Nevada and one vote each from North Dakota and Oregon, making a total of twenty-two. In accordance with third-party strategy, in the Midwest the Populists allied themselves with the Democrats against the dominant Republicans, while in the South they cooperated with the Republicans in an effort to defeat the dominant Democrats.

Election of 1896

The battle for the presidency in 1896 was the most momentous since the 1860 election, on the eve of the Civil War. The farmers of the West and South and the laborers of the East made a strong bid against the business interests.

DEMOCRATS

Bitterness and confusion were rife at the Democratic national convention. The delegates from the West and South, particularly those from rural areas, were in open revolt against the Cleveland administration, then drawing to a close. From the outset the convention was dominated by the supporters of silver coinage. In the Nebraska delegation was a young former representative who had become well known as a gifted crusader for inflation—William Jennings Bryan. At one point in the proceedings Bryan, a masterful orator, made an impassioned plea for silver coinage, the last words of which achieved fame: "You shall not press down upon the brow of labor this crown of thorns, you shall not crucify mankind upon a cross of gold." So deeply stirred were the delegates that on the fifth ballot Bryan was nominated for president. As a conciliatory gesture to the East, Arthur Sewall, a Maine banker, was nominated for vice-president.

The platform repudiated the Cleveland administration. Adopted after spirited debate, it demanded the free and unlimited coinage of silver and gold at the present legal ratio of sixteen to one. The other planks included (1) a demand that tariff schedules be imposed solely to provide federal revenue; (2) criticism of the Supreme Court for declaring unconstitutional the income-tax provision of the 1894 Wilson-Gorman tariff; (3) denunciation of the government's use of the injunction in management-labor disputes; and (4) a demand for the enlargement of the powers of the Interstate Commerce Commission in dealing with the railroads.

REPUBLICANS

The most influential leader at the Republican national convention was Mark Hanna, a Cleveland businessman with large coal and iron interests, whose career in Ohio politics had demonstrated his conviction that there should be an intimate affiliation between the business community and the Republican party. He was determined that the presidential nominee should be his close friend William McKinley, who after having been a seven-term representative from Ohio had served as governor of that state. So effectively had Hanna lined up the Republican delegates that the convention required only one ballot to nominate McKinley for president. Named for second place on the ticket was Garret A. Hobart of New Jersey, a businessman, lawyer, and state legislative leader.

Hanna was determined that the platform should pledge the maintenance of the gold standard. He adroitly handled a threatened revolt of the western silver advocates. In the end a plank supporting gold was adopted, and only thirty-four delegates, led by Senator Henry M. Teller of Colorado, bolted the convention. In addition the platform contained planks favoring a protective tariff, generous pensions for Union veterans of the Civil War, enlargement of the navy, and federal arbitration of management-labor disputes involving interstate commerce.

POPULISTS

The adoption of the Democratic party platform was an open invitation to the Populists, who held their national convention two weeks after Bryan was nominated, to join the Democratic ranks. Such a fusion was opposed by some of the most devoted Populist leaders, but the general membership, eager for victory, nominated the Democrat Bryan for president and former Populist representative Thomas E. Watson of Georgia for vice-president. In twenty-six of the forty-five states the Populist and Democratic tickets were combined.

THE CAMPAIGN

The Republican campaign, astutely controlled by Mark Hanna, appealed to the propertied classes and emphasized the "dangerous radicalism" of the Democrats. McKinley, gracious and dignified, received delegations of voters at his home in Canton, Ohio. In contrast to the Republican candidate's front-porch campaign, Bryan traveled approximately 15,000 miles, making more than 600 speeches in twenty-nine states, addressing masses of debt-ridden farmers, poorly paid industrial workers, and small shopkeepers.

McKINLEY'S VICTORY

McKinley won 7,111,000 popular votes to Bryan's 6,509,000 (227,000 of which were Populist). In the electoral college, McKinley captured 271 votes to Bryan's 176; he took every state east of the Mississippi River and north of the Ohio River, as well as West Virginia, Kentucky, Minnesota, Iowa, North Dakota, Oregon, and California. Most of the West and South went to Bryan. It was believed by many contemporary political analysts that the fact that the season was an especially good one for farmers caused Bryan to lose many votes.

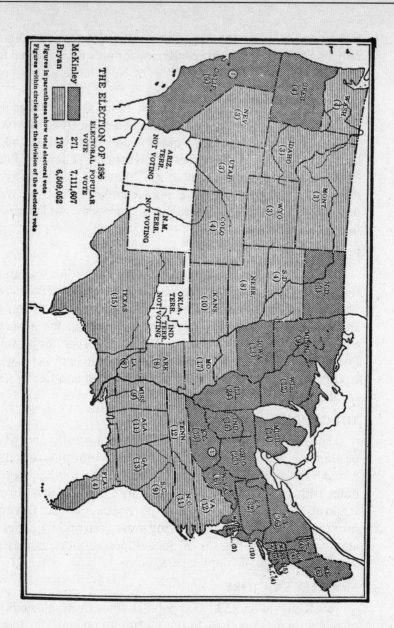

The Election of 1896

All told, the decisive Republican victory meant the defeat of the farmers and laborers in their greatest struggle against the industrialists, the continuing dominance of business interests in government affairs, and the triumph of eastern conservative financiers in the realm of monetary policy. The agrarian crusade had been transformed for a time into a battle over the currency. Although the farmers and laborers were defeated in their fight with the businessmen, within fifteen years their demands would be sponsored by both the Democratic and Republican parties.

The McKinley Administration

The manufacturing and trading interests of the nation looked to the executive branch of the government, with McKinley at its head, for assistance and encouragement. They were clearly not disappointed with the support they received.

THE PRESIDENT

William McKinley was unfailingly dedicated to his church, his invalid wife, and his party. As chief executive he made good use of his long-standing habit of compromise and conciliation to achieve his political objectives.

THE CABINET

The McKinley cabinet was, not surprisingly, a model of conservatism. The elderly—and increasingly forgetful— Republican senator John Sherman of Ohio became secretary of state. (Mark Hanna was appointed to Sherman's vacated Senate seat.) Heading the Department of the Treasury was Chicago banker Lyman J. Gage, a staunch defender of the gold standard. McKinley later made changes in his cabinet, appointing the widely experienced diplomat John Hay as secretary of state and the highly successful New York City corporation lawyer Elihu Root as secretary of war.

Selected Readings

GENERAL WORKS:

Billington, Ray Allen. *Westward Expansionism* (1967)
Buck, Solon J. *The Agrarian Crusade* (1920)
Destler, Chester M. *American Radicalism, 1865–1901* (1946)
Durden, Robert F. *The Climax of Populism* (1966)
Hicks, John D. *The Populist Revolt* (1931)
Hine, Robert. *The American West* (1984)
Pollock, Norman. *The Populist Response to Industrial America* (1962)
Webb, Walter P. *The Great Plains* (1931)

SPECIAL STUDIES:

Ambrose, Stephen E. *Crazy Horse and Custer: The Parallel Lives of Two American Warriors* (1975)
Atherton, Lewis. *The Cattle Kings* (1951)
Brown, Dee. *Bury My Heart at Wounded Knee: An Indian History of the American West* (1971)

Coletta, Paolo E. *William Jennings Bryan: Political Evangelist, 1860–1908* (1964)

Dary, David. *Cowboy Culture* (1981)

————. *Entrepreneurs of the Old West* (1986)

Durham, Philip, and Everett L. Jones. *The Negro Cowboys* (1965)

Dykstra, Robert R. *The Cattle Towns* (1968)

Fite, Gilbert C. *The Farmer's Frontier* (1966)

Glad, Paul W. *The Trumpet Soundeth: William Jennings Bryan and His Democracy, 1896–1912* (1960)

Hagan, William T. *American Indians* (1961)

Hoffmann, Charles. *The Depression of the Nineties: An Economic History* (1970)

Jackson, Donald. *Gold Dust* (1980)

Jones, Stanley L. *The Presidential Election of 1896* (1964)

Knoles, George H. *The Presidential Campaign and Election of 1892* (1942)

Koenig, Louis. *Bryan* (1971)

Merrill, Horace S. *Bourbon Democracy of the Middle West, 1865–1896* (1953)

Myres, Sandra. *Westering Women and the Frontier Experience, 1800–1915* (1982)

Nugent, Walter T.K. *Money and American Society, 1865–1880* (1967)

Paul, Rodman W. *Mining Frontiers of the Far West, 1848–1880* (1963)

Roe, Frank G. *The Indian and the Horse* (1955)

Shannon, Fred A. *The Farmer's Last Frontier* (1945)

Unger, Irwin. *The Greenback Era* (1964)

Woodward, Vann C. *Tom Watson, Agrarian Rebel* (1938)

Young, Otis E., Jr. *Western Mining* (1970)

5

The United States as a World Power

1867	United States purchases Alaska
	Napoleon III withdraws troops from Mexico
	United States occupies Midway Islands
1872	Tribunal adjudicates *Alabama* claims dispute
1878	United States establishes naval base in Samoa
1889	Pan-American Union founded
1894	Republic of Hawaii established
1898	*Maine* sunk
	United States goes to war with Spain
	Teller Amendment
	United States annexes Hawaii
1899	Treaty of Paris ratified, ceding Puerto Rico, Guam, and the Philippines to the United States
	Hay announces open-door policy in China
1900	United States acquires American Samoa
	McKinley reelected president
	Foraker Act
	Boxer Rebellion
1901	Platt Amendment
1901–1903	Supreme Court rules on Insular Cases
1902	Organic Act
1916	Jones Act on the Philippines

1917 Jones Act on Puerto Rico

For some time after the Civil War the United States attempted to pursue its professed intention of isolationism. But Americans gradually turned their attention from internal events to international affairs and overseas expansion. Toward the end of the nineteenth century the United States developed a desire for overseas expansion, which led to the Spanish-American War in 1898. This war, won by the United States with few casualties and little cost in money and time, brought about a revision of American foreign policy. The resulting acquisition of island territories in the Caribbean Sea and the Pacific Ocean presented a new challenge: to establish principles and procedures for governing overseas possessions. The United States thus emerged from semi-isolation to become a world power—with all the benefits and hazards accruing to that status.

POLITICAL DIPLOMACY IN ACTION

During the three decades following the Civil War the United States had no purposeful foreign policy. Relations with other nations were determined either by events in domestic politics or by accident.

Isolation— Reality or Myth?

Although isolation was only a state of mind in the United States from 1865 to 1898, to the inhabitants of the nation it was nothing less than stark reality. Americans were aware of the importance of foreign markets for the products of their factories and farms, but they were little concerned with the stakes of international diplomacy.

THE POLITICIAN AS SECRETARY OF STATE

A remoteness from the main currents of world affairs was evidenced in the activities of the secretaries of state who served between 1865 and 1898. With the possible exceptions of William H. Seward in the Johnson administration and Hamilton Fish in the Grant administration, all were politicians much more concerned with events at home than with developments abroad. Unimaginative they may have been, and perhaps aggressive in some controversies, but they practiced a diplomacy that was straightforward and peaceful in its objectives.

THE FOREIGN SERVICE

American ambassadors and ministers (diplomatic representatives ranking below ambassadors and usually accredited to nations of lesser importance) were too often chosen because they enjoyed enough wealth to lavishly entertain foreign dignitaries or had rendered conspicuous service to the party in power. They were occasionally men of ability. So inconsequential were the stakes of diplomacy, however, that few of them had a chance to distinguish themselves. The changing administrations in Washington were more concerned with the work of consular officials charged with the care of the commercial interests of American citizens.

Traditional Policies in Foreign Relations

From the pre–Civil War period two traditional policies persisted in American foreign relations: the adherence to the principles of the Monroe Doctrine and the expansion of American commercial interests in the Pacific.

ENFORCING THE MONROE DOCTRINE IN MEXICO

The statement of foreign policy issued by President James Monroe in 1823 and since known as the Monroe Doctrine declared in essence that the Western Hemisphere was no longer open to colonization by European nations; that the United States would not interfere in purely European affairs; and that European nations were not to interfere in the affairs of existing Western Hemisphere republics. In 1864 Emperor Napoleon III of France, in flagrant violation of the Monroe Doctrine, placed Archduke Maximilian of Austria upon an unstable Mexican throne. Secretary of State Seward protested, though in vain since the United States was then involved in the Civil War and could not enforce the Monroe Doctrine.

With the conclusion of hostilities the American government ordered troops to take up positions along the Mexican border. War seemed imminent. But Seward was able to achieve a diplomatic victory when Napoleon III's troubles in Europe caused him to withdraw his military forces from Mexico in 1867. Without French support Maximilian lost the throne and was executed by his former subjects. Thus the attempt of a European power to intervene in the affairs of an independent Western Hemisphere republic was thwarted.

DEFINING A POLICY FOR THE PACIFIC

Secretary Seward stated clearly the traditional basis of his nation's commercial interests in the Pacific. In 1867, finding Russia eager to divest itself of its outpost on the North American continent, he persuaded Congress to purchase Alaska for $7.2 million. With its rich natural resources, Seward hoped that the area would start the United States on an expansionist policy. In 1867 he also arranged for the United States to formally occupy the Midway Islands. At the same time he urged eventual acquisition of the Hawaiian Islands.

RELATIONS WITH GREAT BRITAIN

There was extensive American ill will toward Great Britain during the decades following the Civil War. The anti-British feelings stemmed from the belief, growing out of the Revolutionary War and the War of 1812, and perpetuated by many American historians and publicists, that Great Britain was the traditional enemy of the United States; the fact that the governing classes in Great Britain had apparently desired the permanent dissolution of the United States to result from the Civil War; the view of many politicians that the best way to cultivate the Irish-American vote was to "twist the British lion's tail"; and a resentment of the patronizing attitude of many British commentators on things American.

Legacy of British Policy During Civil War

The policy of Great Britain toward the United States government during the Civil War left a legacy of bitterness between the two nations that was finally settled diplomatically.

THE "ALABAMA" CLAIMS

Great Britain's failure during the Civil War to strictly enforce its neutrality laws made possible the construction in British shipyards of vessels that were to fly the Confederate flag. The claims pressed by the United States against Great Britain for damages inflicted upon northern shipping by these cruisers, the most famous of which was the *Alabama*, came to be known as the *Alabama* claims. Secretary Seward was ignored by the British government when he called for a diplomatic settlement. Great Britain, however, changed its attitude when it watched the United States deal effectively with the Fenian Brotherhood, a secret organization of Irish-Americans intent upon achieving the independence of Ireland. In 1865 the Fenians began using the United States as a base for sporadic raids into Canada. The Department of State was so vigilant in suppressing these violations of Canada's frontiers that British leaders finally responded by settling all outstanding differences between Great Britain and the United States.

THE TREATY OF WASHINGTON

Negotiations extended over several years. In 1869 Reverdy Johnson, the American ambassador to Great Britain, and Lord George Clarendon, the British foreign secretary, reached an agreement, known as the Johnson-Clarendon Convention, providing for the settlement of demands outstanding on both sides since 1853. The Senate refused to ratify the agreement, but Secretary of State Hamilton Fish successfully reopened negotiations. The Treaty of Washington, ratified by the Senate in 1871, authorized (1) the submission of the *Alabama* claims to an international tribunal; (2) the making of a new arrangement to protect the rights of American fishermen operating off the shores of Canada; and (3) the settlement by arbitration of the disputed water boundary between British Columbia and the state of Washington.

Meeting at Geneva, Switzerland, in 1872, the tribunal that had been created under the terms of the Treaty of Washington to adjudicate the *Alabama* dispute refused to accept United States claims for indirect damages by the British-built Confederate vessels but awarded $15.5 million for direct damages, which Great Britain promptly paid.

Other Disputes

Relations between the United States and Great Britain continued to be unfriendly during the last third of the nineteenth century.

THE NEWFOUNDLAND FISHERIES DISPUTE

For decades fishermen from Maine and Massachusetts had operated off the shores of the Canadian Province of Newfoundland, basing the right to fish on a treaty between the United States and Great Britain dating from the early nineteenth century. Resenting the American fishermen, the Newfoundland legislature passed irksome restrictions upon their activities. Quarrels over fishing rights were halted by the Treaty of Washington, but in 1885, when the fisheries clauses of the treaty were terminated, Canada began seizing American fishing vessels in Canadian waters. In response, an angry Congress authorized President Cleveland to close American ports to Canadian ships and goods. The State Department finally worked out an informal agreement with the British government that remained in effect until 1912.

THE BERING SEA CONTROVERSY

During Cleveland's first term the United States, in an attempt to protect the herds of seals in the Bering Sea, west of Alaska, arbitrarily seized Canadian sealing vessels, contending that the Bering Sea was under American dominion. During the Harrison administration, after Secretary of State Blaine and British foreign secretary Lord Robert Salisbury had exchanged acrimonious diplomatic notes, Blaine finally agreed to submit the dispute to arbitration. In 1893 an international tribunal decided against the United States on every point of law, although it provided some rules for protection of the seal herds.

THE VENEZUELAN BOUNDARY ADJUSTMENT

Of all the disputes between the United States and Great Britain in the post–Civil War decades, the one that brought the two nations closest to war was the controversy over the Venezuelan boundary. The long-contested line of demarcation between the republic of Venezuela and the British colony of Guiana became an especially sensitive issue when gold was discovered in the disputed region in the 1880s. Three times (in 1886, 1890, and 1894) the

United States volunteered to act as mediator, but the offers were rejected by both Great Britain and Venezuela. Finally, in 1895, when it appeared that Great Britain was attempting to use the boundary controversy as a means to acquire substantial mineral-rich territory, Secretary of State Richard Olney sent several sharp notes to the British government, in which he asserted (1) that the United States was bound under the Monroe Doctrine to protect the territorial integrity of Venezuela; (2) that the United States was "practically sovereign" on the South American continent and its decrees were "law upon the subjects to which it confines its interposition"; and (3) that arbitration was the only way to settle the boundary line.

When Foreign Secretary Lord Salisbury denied the applicability of the Monroe Doctrine and refused to submit the disputed boundary to arbitration, President Cleveland sent a message to Congress in December 1895 requesting approval of the appointment of a commission to draw the boundary line, which the United States would be bound to defend against any British aggression. This stirring presidential message roused the nation, although Lord Salisbury was correct in branding the Olney dispatches as a completely novel interpretation of the Monroe Doctrine. But the war spirit subsided when it became evident that responsible leaders in the American Congress and in the British Parliament desired peace. Through the efforts of the United States, representatives of Great Britain and Venezuela signed a treaty in 1897 providing for the boundary dispute to be submitted to an international board of arbitration. The decision, rendered in 1899, was in basic accord with the claims of Great Britain, making Venezuela regret its reliance on American support.

RELATIONS WITH LATIN AMERICA

A serious defect in United States foreign policy during the last third of the nineteenth century was the failure to establish enduring friendships with the independent republics of Latin America.

Application of the Monroe Doctrine

The interest of the United States in its neighbors to the south was based upon one of the Monroe Doctrine's principles—that European nations were not to interfere in the affairs of the republics of the Western Hemisphere.

THE UNITED STATES AS MEDIATOR

Since peace was often threatened by quarrels over international boundaries, the United States frequently offered its services as a mediator (its "good offices"). In 1876 the United States arbitrated a boundary dispute between Argentina and Paraguay. In 1880 its good offices were accepted by Colombia and Chile in all controversies that they could not settle through direct negotiation. In 1881 it helped Mexico and Guatemala, as well as Argentina and Chile, settle boundary disputes. The same year it intervened in the quarrel between Peru and Chile over the provinces of Tacna-Arica and earned the ill will of Chile by its efforts to achieve a compromise. It tried hard to bring to an end the War of the Pacific (1879 to 1884), which pitted Chile against Bolivia and Peru.

ATTITUDE OF LATIN AMERICAN NATIONS

In the hands of United States diplomats the Monroe Doctrine could be a two-edged sword. The gratitude of Latin American nations for the protection the Doctrine provided against European interference was often overshadowed by their resentment over the position of superiority assumed by the United States.

Blaine's Pan-American Policy

No secretary of state since Henry Clay (who served in the 1820s) had worked harder than James G. Blaine to promote the interests of the United States in Latin America.

ORIGINS OF THE PAN-AMERICAN UNION

Much of Blaine's effort, however, was nullified by his aggressive insistence that commercial contracts be worked out along the lines laid down by the State Department. During his brief tenure as secretary of state under President Garfield, Blaine arranged for a conference of Western Hemisphere nations in Washington, D.C., but his immediate successor, Frederick T. Frelinghuyssen, abandoned the project. The first International Conference of American States did eventually meet during 1889–90 in Washington, D.C., and Blaine, who had resumed the office of secretary of state under President Harrison, presided over deliberations. He gained little satisfaction from it, however, as the delegates refused to approve his proposals for a customs union (an association of nations that have abolished restrictions on trade among themselves and have adopted a common trade policy toward other nations). The sole tangible result of the conference was the establishment of the International Bureau of American Republics (later called the Pan-American Union) to help the exchange of commercial information.

AGGRESSIVELY MAINTAINING ORDER

Under Blaine's direction the State Department was eager to maintain order in Latin America. When the American minister in Chile, Patrick Egan, assumed a truculent attitude toward a government that in 1891 had taken control by force, Blaine supported him. Later that year Blaine used a mob's attack on American sailors on shore leave in Valparaiso, Chile, as a pretext for a belligerent tone that brought the United States to the verge of war with the Latin American republic. Although Blaine secured an official apology from Chile, his attitude created among Latin Americans an impression of unrestrained aggressiveness on the part of the United States.

THE LURE OF THE PACIFIC

Into the early 1890s most Americans showed little interest in their government's relations with foreign nations. However, a change in sentiment was already becoming evident, particularly noticeable in the favorable reaction throughout the nation to American expansion in the Pacific.

Emergence of the New Imperialism

The growing desire of the United States to acquire territory beyond its continental borders was the result of several factors.

MARINERS AND MISSIONARIES

Although many Americans failed to realize it, there was much in the new wish for overseas possessions that was old. In the Pacific the expansion was largely the result of attitudes developed during the era of clipper ships and whaling vessels. The zeal of Christian missionaries who had for decades longed to reform the people of Asia to the ways of their gospel was also a major factor. Mariners and missionaries were the American pioneers in Samoa and Hawaii.

THE SETTLEMENT OF THE WEST

The westward advance of the continental United States ended with the close of the frontier in the early 1890s. Pioneering habits were then transferred overseas. Those who had settled in the far West maintained a great economic interest in the Pacific region, if only because of geographic proximity.

THE SEARCH FOR MARKETS

The growing industrialization of the United States spurred expansion into the Pacific. Every decade after 1870 brought an increase in United States exports and, more significantly, an accompanying rise in the proportion of manufactured goods to agricultural products. As the industrial system grew, the need for new markets for manufactured articles gave added impetus to the demand that American political control over the Pacific be strengthened.

IMPORTANCE OF SEA POWER

Although the United States had never maintained a large standing army, its people had long cherished the tradition of the American navy. But naval strength declined after the Civil War. In the 1880s work was begun to improve the navy by adding newly constructed steel vessels. This marked the government's acceptance of the concept that the navy should be capable of successfully meeting any potential foe in the Atlantic or the Pacific. This new policy was popularized by the writings of Alfred Thayer Mahan, a career naval officer who was one of the world's leading authorities on the subject of the importance of sea power, particularly in relation to a nation's commercial expansion.

Samoa

An early example of the changed attitude of many Americans toward overseas imperialism was the peaceful penetration of the Samoan Islands. Contacts with the islanders, first stimulated by the pre–Civil War trade with China, passed through several stages.

TRADING CONCESSIONS

Casual relations established by American traders led in 1872 to the negotiation of a treaty, which the Senate failed to ratify, granting the United States a coaling station. In 1878, however, the Senate approved a treaty that gave the United States certain trading rights and permitted it to establish a naval base at the harbor of Pago Pago.

POLITICAL CONTROL

During this time Germany and Great Britain were also granted trading rights in Samoa, and they and the United States entered into an often fierce competition for favored treatment by the Samoans. This rivalry aroused a nationalistic spirit that was only partially satisfied when, in 1889, the three nations established over Samoa a joint protectorate (a relationship in which a nation, without having legal possession, exercises governmental powers over a smaller and weaker territorial unit, especially in the areas of defense and foreign relations).

In 1899 Great Britain relinquished its claims in Samoa in return for concessions elsewhere. Germany took over two of the islands. The United States retained the rest, including Tutuila, with its fine harbor of Pago Pago, which provided an important naval base in the Pacific. The following year the Senate ratified the treaty.

Hawaii

Acquisition of the Hawaiian Islands was the result of forces similar to those that brought the United States colonial responsibilities in Samoa.

EARLY CONTACTS

As early as the 1820s, New England missionaries had established themselves on several of the Hawaiian Islands. Their descendants were joined by traders and sailors on the clipper ships and whaling vessels. All these groups steadily augmented the American population in the islands.

SUGAR PLANTERS

Within a generation, the production of sugar became the chief interest of Americans in Hawaii. Those sugar planters who were Americans—and a majority were—worked tirelessly for closer relations with the United States. In 1875 they secured a tariff agreement between the United States and the islands, which greatly stimulated the sugar trade. The McKinley tariff of 1890, however, while removing the duty on raw sugar imported into the United States, also provided to the domestic producers of raw sugar a bounty of two cents per pound on their product. Thus the Hawaiian sugar planters lost their favored position and began to seek annexation as their best prospect.

OVERTHROW OF THE MONARCHY

The government of Queen Liliuokalani, who ascended to the Hawaiian throne in 1891, was determined in its opposition to foreigners. The American minority in the islands became alarmed when the queen proclaimed that Hawaii was for the Hawaiians. In 1893 the foreign elements staged a revolution. When the American minister to Hawaii, John L. Stevens, gave his support to the temporary revolutionary government, American marines landed to "preserve order."

CLEVELAND'S REJECTION OF ANNEXATION

President Benjamin Harrison, who favored annexation, left office before a treaty could be acted upon. The incoming president, Grover Cleveland, withdrew the proposed annexation treaty from the Senate and appointed James H. Blount, a former representative from Georgia who was known as an anti-imperialist, as special commissioner to investigate the situation. After receiving Blount's report, which criticized American involvement in the recent uprising, Cleveland attempted to restore the government of Queen Liliuokalani on the condition that she pardon all the revolutionists. The queen refused, and the revolutionary government continued in power. On July 4, 1894, this government proclaimed the Republic of Hawaii, and in the following month it was formally recognized by the United States.

VICTORY OF THE ANNEXATIONISTS

When William McKinley became president in 1897, sentiment in favor of annexation was strong. Acquiring the Republic of Hawaii, said the expansionists, was highly desirable because (1) it might otherwise fall under the control of a foreign power; (2) it would provide a badly needed naval base in the Pacific; and (3) it would offer opportunities for American commercial investment. These arguments were reinforced in the minds of many citizens by the belief that the United States was destined to control the Pacific and that the nation had a duty to take both the Christian gospel and American democratic institutions to the people of that area. A formal protest against annexation by Japan also spurred the move, and the war with Spain in 1898 gave added impetus. All these considerations brought about the annexation of Hawaii by a joint resolution of Congress, which President McKinley signed on July 7, 1898.

The Far East

Upon acquiring island possessions in the Pacific, the United States was compelled to become much more actively interested in the course of events in the Far East.

THE OPEN-DOOR POLICY

Among the champions of overseas expansion was John Hay, who became secretary of state in 1898. Hay particularly wanted to maintain the stable relationship already established among the foreign powers in the Far East for the benefit of American trade. He was alarmed by the activities of a half-dozen foreign powers in a China that was weakened and dispirited after having been defeated in a recent war with Japan. Each of the powers assumed in China a sphere of influence (a geographic area more or less under the control of a nation considered to have paramount political or economic interests in the region). Hay asked Great Britain, Germany, Russia, France, Italy, and Japan to agree to an open-door policy—that no nation within its sphere of influence would interfere with the normal commercial and transportation activities of other nations. The foreign powers reluctantly agreed to Hay's doctrine, thus ensuring to American traders equal treatment with the citizens of those nations that had previously received economic concessions from China.

THE BOXER REBELLION

Foreign activity in China was threatened by a society of ultrapatriotic Chinese known in English as Boxers. Early in 1900 the Boxers, fully committed to acts of terrorism, demanded that the "foreign devils" be driven from China. In June 1900, the Boxers attacked members of the foreign community in the capital, Peking (later spelled Beijing). The United States assumed the lead in organizing an international relief force, which arrived in Peking in time to rescue the majority of besieged foreigners. When some of the foreign powers used the Boxer Rebellion as a pretext for discarding the open-door policy and partitioning China, Hay successfully argued for the preservation of China as a "territorial and administrative entity," with, however, certain restrictions on the nation's sovereignty.

WAR WITH SPAIN

The Spanish-American War caused the people of the United States to move rapidly along the path of empire already clearly defined by the nation's more enthusiastic expansionists.

The Situation in Cuba

Throughout the nineteenth century the United States frequently showed its concern over the fate of its close neighbor Cuba, which was Spain's chief possession in the Caribbean.

THE AMERICAN POLICY

Early in the nineteenth century the American government expressed fear lest Spanish control of Cuba be replaced by that of a more formidable European power. In the 1850s Americans debated the possibility of acquiring Cuba, by either purchase or seizure. In the last quarter of the century, as American commercial contacts and financial investments in Cuba increased, the government was inclined to support a policy that promised to maintain stable political and economic conditions on the island.

THE CUBAN INSURRECTION

A rebellion of the Cubans against Spanish authority, lasting from 1868 to 1878, not only brought devastation to large areas of the island but also led to Spanish charges that Americans were aiding the rebels in violation of international law. The Spanish mistreated American citizens in Cuba and in 1873 summarily executed Americans (along with other nationals) who were crew members of the arms-running ship *Virginius*, which illegally flew the American flag. But since the United States at this time had no desire for war, it acted with moderation. The period following the insurrection left the Cuban leaders resentful over the Spanish government's unfulfilled reform promises. Many of them went to the United States, where they disseminated propaganda for Cuban independence.

THE CUBAN WAR OF INDEPENDENCE

Continuing Cuban discontent with Spanish rule flared into open revolt in 1895, when prices for Cuban sugar and tobacco sharply declined, as a result of two factors that affected the American market: the financial panic of 1893 and the Wilson-Gorman tariff of 1894, with its high import duties. The island experienced widespread economic depression. Nevertheless, the wealthier classes in Cuba and most Americans with investments there were opposed to the revolutionists' demands for independence. The revolutionists therefore embarked on a campaign of widespread destruction of such property as sugar plantations, in which Americans had extensive investments, hoping by this action to induce United States intervention. The Spanish government sent General Valeriano Weyler to suppress the uprising. Deciding that the revolutionists would never be defeated unless they were deprived of arms and other supplies from the population, Weyler began confining civilians in camps closely supervised by Spanish troops. Although Weyler's policy was misrepresented in sensational accounts in several American newspapers, there was some justification for his nickname, Butcher, because of the brutal effects of his concentration camps. Many noncombatants, including women and children, lacking proper food and sanitation, became victims of starvation and disease. Equally brutal, however, were the guerrilla tactics of the revolutionary forces.

American Demands for Military Intervention

The United States government endeavored to maintain a policy of strict neutrality regarding the situation on the Caribbean island, but an increasing number of citizens voiced their sympathy for the Cuban revolutionists.

CLEVELAND'S ATTITUDE

During the last months of his second term, President Cleveland strove both to maintain genuine neutrality and to persuade the Spanish leaders that a measure of Cuban self-government was the surest way to establish political stability and economic order. Cleveland feared, however, that the growing demand in the United States for intervention would compel his successor, McKinley, to act accordingly.

THE WAR FACTION

American intervention in Cuba was not desired by those holding the largest financial interests on the island, since they believed that Spain would eventually restore stability. The groups most enthusiastic for a war to secure Cuban independence were (1) humanitarians who believed that Spanish policy, as exemplified by the actions of Weyler, was both arbitrary and cruel; (2) "jingoes" (those who favor a belligerent foreign policy), who felt that Spain should be chastised; (3) certain Republican politicians who hoped that a successful struggle with Spain would increase support for the McKinley administration; (4) a few public officials, such as Assistant Secretary of the

Navy Theodore Roosevelt and Republican senator Henry Cabot Lodge of Massachusetts, who were nationalistic in spirit and eager to have the United States become a world power; and (5) some newspaper publishers, notably William Randolph Hearst of the *New York Journal* and Joseph Pulitzer of the *New York World*, who printed exaggerated accounts of Spanish atrocities, while deemphasizing the atrocities of Cuban revolutionists, to increase their papers' circulation. It has been argued by many that the single most important factor in pushing the United States into war with Spain was the activity of the "yellow press," journalism that holds reader interest by dealing with sensational items or ordinary news sensationally distorted (so named after the "Yellow Kid," the first comic strip printed in color, which appeared in the *New York Journal* and the *New York World*).

THE DE LÔME LETTER

The position of the war faction was strengthened when, on February 9, 1898, Hearst's *New York Journal* printed a letter that the Spanish minister to the United States, Enrique Dupuy de Lôme, had written to a friend in Cuba. This private communication had been stolen from the mails in Havana by Cuban revolutionists, who made it available to the Hearst organization. The letter contained slurs against President McKinley, calling him "weak" and "a bidder for the admiration of the crowd." To spare his government embarrassment, de Lôme promptly resigned. But the anger of the American people over the letter remained undiminished.

THE SINKING OF THE *MAINE*

On February 15, 1898, the United States battleship *Maine*, which had been ordered to Havana Harbor to protect American life and property, blew up and sank, with the loss of 260 of its crew. An American naval court of inquiry was unable to determine whether the explosion had been the work of hostile Spanish loyalists or of Cuban revolutionists who hoped that the destruction of the warship would induce American intervention, or had been entirely accidental. Although the Spanish authorities, anxious to prevent American military involvement in Cuba, had good cause for not committing such an act, those in the United States who were eager for war attributed the explosion to them. The war faction made "Remember the *Maine*" a popular slogan, which rapidly aroused sentiment throughout the nation for American intervention to liberate Cuba from Spain.

McKINLEY'S WAR MESSAGE

Although he personally wanted to avert war, President McKinley realized that a policy of "peace at any price" might split his party and wreck his administration. On April 11, 1898, therefore, he sent a message to Congress, charging that, as the Spanish government was unable to suppress the Cuban rebellion, American military intervention was necessary to establish peace on the island. Between the time McKinley wrote his message and the time he transmitted it to Congress, Spain had already capitulated to the United States demands that it (1) proclaim an armistice; (2) close the concentration camps; and (3) enter into negotiations with the revolutionists. But the pressure for war was so great, not only in Congress but throughout the nation, that McKinley could resist it no longer. On April 19, Congress adopted a joint resolution for military intervention, which McKinley signed the next day. Attached to the document as its final clause was the Teller Amendment (sometimes called the Teller Resolution), sponsored by Republican senator Henry M. Teller of Colorado, which disclaimed any intention by the United States to exercise control over Cuba, pledging that the government of the island would be left to its inhabitants as soon as peace had been restored.

Preparation for Hostilities

During the three decades following the Civil War the United States had neglected to maintain an up-to-date and efficient military organization, primarily because no powerful foe posed a threat to the nation. In the war with Spain the American people paid the price for this unpreparedness.

THE ARMY

For years Congress had been miserly in its appropriations for the Department of War. Furthermore, many high-ranking officials in the department had been appointed for political reasons rather than for administrative or technical skills. When the war with Spain began, department routine foundered. The necessary tasks of doubling the size of the regular army of 30,000 men and training 200,000 volunteers were not accomplished with the speed and efficiency that the war demanded. The performance of the War Department was distressing to the American people, who began to learn that inferior equipment, spoiled food, improper clothing for a tropical climate, poor sanitation facilities, and inadequate medical services could cause more deaths than did actual fighting on the battlefield.

THE NAVY

Because of the nature of the war, the brunt of the fighting fell upon the navy of 26,000 men, which was far better prepared than the army. This was the first test for the new steel ships, which had been under construction since 1883. In addition to the North Atlantic Squadron under Rear Admiral William T. Sampson, the Flying Squadron under Commodore Winfield S. Schley, and the Asiatic Squadron under Commodore George Dewey, the Department of the Navy put into service more than a hundred auxiliary ships. The number of naval personnel had already been doubled, and contracts had been placed for munitions and other supplies—all with speed and efficiency.

War on Two Fronts

With the outbreak of war, Spain became vulnerable not only in its Caribbean colonies but also in its Pacific possessions. Despite serious blunders by both civil and military authorities, the United States won the war with a weak Spain with relative ease.

THE PHILIPPINE CAMPAIGN

The first United States blow for Cuban independence was struck not in the Caribbean but in the far-distant Philippine Islands. Commodore Dewey's Asiatic Squadron had been on the alert for two months, as a result of secret orders sent by Assistant Secretary of the Navy Theodore Roosevelt to immediately engage the Spanish fleet in the Philippines should war break out. Dewey's fleet steamed from its base near Hong Kong to Manila Bay. There on May 1, 1898, it destroyed the Spanish fleet, which was ill-equipped and had poorly trained crews. Dewey then imposed a blockade until the arrival of army forces, which captured the city of Manila on August 13.

THE CARIBBEAN CAMPAIGN

Rear Admiral Sampson and Commodore Schley, responsible for blockading Cuban ports, were not able to prevent the most important Spanish fleet, under the command of Admiral Pascual Cervera, from entering the harbor of Santiago, on Cuba's southeastern shore. There Cervera's ships took a position well protected by land batteries. American naval forces then blockaded the harbor and waited for the arrival of the army from the United States to begin a coordinated operation in the Santiago area. On June 22, 1898, 17,000 troops under the command of General William R. Shafter landed to the east of Santiago. The joint operation against the city was brief and decisive. It consisted of two phases: the action of the land troops to the north and east of the city and the action of the naval forces blockading the harbor.

In the battles of El Caney and San Juan Hill, both occurring on July 1, the American army gained control of the heights to the north and east of Santiago and began preparations for the bombardment of the Spanish fleet below. In a victorious charge led by Theodore Roosevelt during the battle of San Juan Hill, the First United States Volunteer Cavalry Regiment, nicknamed the Rough Riders, achieved a large measure of fame. (The Rough Riders had been organized by Roosevelt, who had resigned as assistant secretary of the navy and become second in command of the volunteer regiment.)

Cervera made a desperate effort to break through the blockade. In the ensuing battle his entire fleet was destroyed. On July 17 Santiago surrendered. After the termination of the Santiago operation, American troops were dispatched to capture the nearby Spanish colony of Puerto Rico, which they did after meeting but feeble military resistance.

AMERICAN WAR COSTS

Of the approximately 275,000 men who served, 5,462 died and 1,604 were wounded in combat. Only 385 of the deaths were battle casualties, most of the remainder being caused by disease, attributed to improper food, poor sanitation, and inadequate medical attention. As for financial costs, the United States spent approximately $250 million in the conflict.

The Treaty of Paris

The terms of the peace settlement with Spain immediately impressed upon the American people how far and how fast they had traveled along the road of expansionism.

NEGOTIATIONS

Through the good offices of the French government, on August 12, 1898, representatives of the United States and Spain signed a protocol (a preliminary memorandum that serves as a basis for a final diplomatic action) calling for a peace conference in Paris in October. President McKinley appointed Secretary of State William R. Day, publisher Whitelaw Reid of the *New York Tribune*, Republican senators Cushman K. Davis of Minnesota and William P. Frye of Maine, and Democratic senator George Gray of Delaware to the peace delegation. Gray was the sole anti-expansionist of the group. The future status of the Philippines—whether all of the islands, some, or none should be retained by the United States—caused the most disagreement among the members of the American commission.

PROVISIONS

McKinley settled the issue of the Philippines with his conviction that the nation favored retaining all of the islands and that humanitarianism (the desire, in the president's words, to "uplift and civilize" the Filipinos), as well as economic and strategic considerations, justified doing so. The main provisions of the treaty, which was signed on December 10, 1898, were the following: (1) Cuba was granted independence, and Spain agreed to assume the Cuban debt; (2) Puerto Rico, Guam, and the Philippines were ceded to the United States; and (3) the United States paid Spain $20 million for the Philippines.

RATIFICATION

The final realization of American expansion, which was implemented by the Treaty of Paris, was the result of varied motives: (1) to increase the prestige of the nation by having it play a larger role in world affairs; (2) to tap the expanding trade with the Far East; (3) to frustrate the naval and commercial designs of rivals Germany and Japan in the Pacific; and (4) to "uplift and civilize" the peoples of the Caribbean and the Pacific. Nevertheless, the president encountered great difficulty in persuading the Senate to ratify the treaty. A determined anti-expansionist force was rapidly developing in the nation. Even before the treaty was signed, the influential Anti-Imperialist League had been organized. Its members—led by historian Charles Francis Adams, economist and sociologist William Graham Sumner, and liberal Republican leader Carl Schurz—denounced the acquisition of colonial possessions as a policy that would have Americans control millions of people hostile to their rule and, in so doing, impose heavy burdens upon the national treasury. In the Senate some Republicans, under the leadership of George F. Hoar of Massachusetts, condemned any attempt to govern distant overseas possessions. The Democratic party sought to derive political gains out of the debate over ratification. Although he was opposed to overseas expansion, William Jennings Bryan, as the titular head of the party, persuaded some Democratic senators to vote for ratification, hoping to make the new imperialism an issue on which the Democrats might achieve victory in the election of 1900. Thus the McKinley administration got the treaty ratified with the aid of Democratic votes on February 6, 1899.

A COLONIAL EMPIRE

The administration of its new overseas possessions and relations with an independent Cuba presented the United States with constitutional, political, and economic problems that it had never before experienced.

Election of 1900

Imperialism was the paramount issue in the 1900 contest for the presidency.

DEMOCRATS

William Jennings Bryan was made the presidential nominee by acclamation. Adlai E. Stevenson, who had been vice-president during Cleveland's second term, was selected as his running mate. A strong anti-imperialist policy for the nation was recommended by the platform.

REPUBLICANS

The delegates to the Republican national convention renominated William McKinley for president with great enthusiasm. Theodore Roosevelt, who after returning from the Spanish-American War a dashing hero had been elected governor of New York, was chosen for second place on the ticket. The Republican platform praised the McKinley administration for its conduct of a "righteous war" against Spain and its assumption of a "moral duty" in the Philippines after the conflict.

THE CAMPAIGN

Bryan endeavored to spread the gospel of anti-imperialism. Denunciation of the trusts, condemnation of the protective tariff, and support of the unlimited coinage of silver received less attention from the Democratic candidate than did his demand that the nation repudiate the course of empire upon which the Republicans had embarked. Republican leaders assailed Bryan throughout the campaign as an impractical radical.

McKINLEY'S VICTORY

McKinley received 292 electoral votes to Bryan's 155. Only four states outside the quarter-century-old solid South were carried by the Democratic candidate. From the outset Bryan's cause had been hopeless. The nation was enjoying widespread prosperity at home and heightened prestige abroad. The voters were ready to assume the burdens of empire and to reward the party that had brought a revival of manufacturing and commercial activity.

The Insular Cases

A fundamental question regarding the status of the overseas dependencies was this: Does the Constitution follow the flag?

OPPOSING POSITIONS

Imperialistically inclined Americans asserted that the newly acquired territories did not become routinely incorporated into the United States and that the inhabitants of those possessions did not hold the same rights granted to the citizens of the United States by the Constitution. Anti-expansionist Americans, on the other hand, maintained that the very fact of acquisition made each new possession a fully integrated part of the United States, thus giving its inhabitants all the constitutional benefits enjoyed by other citizens of the United States.

DISTINCTIVE PROCEDURE IN ADMINISTERING EACH POSSESSION

In a set of rulings known as the Insular Cases (1901–03) the Supreme Court settled the status of the island possessions by laying down the principle that not all provisions of the Constitution need apply to those who lived under the American flag but outside the continental boundaries of the United States. Thus the Constitution did not follow the flag. In effect, Congress was virtually free to administer each particular island possession as it saw fit.

Puerto Rico

In the decades following the war with Spain the United States endeavored to lead the people of Puerto Rico toward self-government and stable economic conditions.

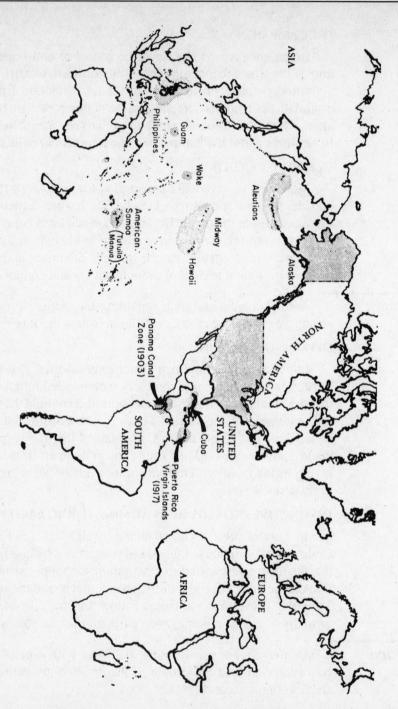

The United States as a Colonial Power, 1900

MOVEMENT TOWARD SELF-GOVERNMENT

In 1900 Congress passed the Foraker Act, making Puerto Rico an unincorporated territory—a status midway between that of a colony and a territory, with no provision for eventual statehood. The president of the United States was empowered to appoint the governor-general, who headed the executive branch of the island's government, and to name the members of the upper house of the two-house legislature, while Puerto Rican voters elected representatives to the lower house.

The Jones Act, passed in 1917, conferred American citizenship upon all Puerto Ricans and made the upper house of the legislature elective. In 1947 Congress passed a law granting Puerto Ricans the right to elect their own governor. The following year journalist and legislative leader Luis Muñoz Marín became the first elected governor. Muñoz Marín served four consecutive four-year terms and became very popular for his promotion of economic and social reforms.

In 1952 President Harry Truman signed a joint resolution of Congress that approved a new constitution drafted by the islanders themselves. Under it Puerto Rico became voluntarily associated with the United States as a commonwealth (a colony that achieves a self-governing, autonomous status but remains associated in a loose political federation with its former ruling power). In a number of referendums beginning in the 1960s, the people of Puerto Rico expressed their preference regarding the political status of the island: about 60 percent of those polled favored retaining the commonwealth; about 35 percent, statehood; about 5 percent, independence.

ECONOMIC CONDITIONS

As Puerto Ricans moved toward self-government, they made efforts to improve their standard of living. Almost entirely devoted to the production of sugar in order to meet the tremendous demand from the United States, the island was unable to produce sufficient foodstuffs or other commodities for its fast-growing population. During the 1950s the Puerto Rican government made a determined effort, with assistance from the United States, to develop the production of agricultural commodities other than sugar and to stimulate industrial enterprise.

The Philippines

The most severe challenge to American colonial policy was the development of procedures for governing the Philippine Islands.

THE AGUINALDO INSURRECTION

When the Spanish-American War began, Emilio Aguinaldo, a municipal official who had recently led an unsuccessful revolt against Spanish control of his homeland, formed a native army to aid the American forces. He hoped that after the anticipated American victory was achieved he would be installed as president of a new Philippine republic. When he realized that the

United States would keep the islands, he organized an insurrection, which was finally suppressed by American troops in 1902.

ESTABLISHMENT OF CIVIL GOVERNMENT

While the American army was still fighting Aguinaldo's insurrectionists, President William McKinley appointed two commissions to report on political conditions in the islands. The first Philippine Commission, which was investigative in nature, affirmed that the ultimate goal for the islands should be independence. The second Philippine Commission, led by William Howard Taft, who was then a federal judge, set up civil government on the islands. In 1901 Taft was appointed head of the executive branch, eventually receiving the title of governor-general. In 1902 Congress passed the Organic Act, which outlined the conditions under which the Filipinos could participate in their own government. The act provided for a two-house legislature, the upper house consisting of the members of the second Philippine Commission and the lower house consisting of representatives elected by Filipino voters.

THE JONES ACT OF 1916

Passed by a Democratic-controlled Congress and signed into law by Democratic president Woodrow Wilson in 1916, the Jones Act was in harmony with the basic Democratic party platforms since 1900, favoring a steady progression toward ultimate independence for the Philippines. Under the act, although the head of the executive branch of the government was still to be an American governor-general, five of the executive departments were to be led by Filipinos. The upper house of the legislature was made elective, as the lower house had been for fourteen years.

REPUBLICAN POLICY

The governor-general through the eight years of the Wilson administration, Francis B. Harrison, pursued a notably liberal course, which gave impetus to the demand both in the islands and in the United States for immediate Philippine independence. But beginning in 1921 each of the three Republican presidents of the next dozen years—Harding, Coolidge, and Hoover—exhibited his party's reluctance to grant early independence.

THE TYDINGS-McDUFFIE ACT

The overwhelming Democratic victory in the election of 1932 was a stimulus to the Philippine independence movement. In January 1933, toward the end of the Hoover administration, the outgoing Congress passed over the president's veto the Hawes-Cutting Act, providing for the independence of the Philippines after a ten-year transition period. The Philippine legislature refused to ratify the act, however, because of certain provisions on immigration and imports. In 1934 the Democratic-controlled Congress passed and the Philippine legislature unanimously ratified the Tydings-McDuffie Act. This measure established the Philippines temporarily as a commonwealth, with the provision that complete independence would be granted in 1946. Manuel Quezon, who had held a number of government positions, became president of the Philippines Commonwealth and prepared the way for independence.

Despite a five-year occupation of the islands by Japan during World War II, there was no delay in bestowing independence, as promised, in 1946. Manuel Roxas, who had served the American-sponsored government on the islands in various capacities, was elected the first president of the Republic of the Philippines.

Relations with Cuba

Although the United States withdrew its military forces from Cuba as soon as order had been restored, it imposed upon the newly established island republic certain conditions that kept it under American control.

THE PLATT AMENDMENT

The United States established in Cuba a military government headed by Major General Leonard Wood. In 1901, with American support, a convention of Cuban delegates drafted a constitution for the new nation. As a condition for the withdrawal of American forces, the delegates were compelled to accept provisions that had been passed by Congress as a rider to an army appropriations bill. These provisions, known collectively as the Platt Amendment after their sponsor, Republican senator Orville H. Platt of Connecticut, stipulated that (1) Cuba would sign no treaty impairing its sovereignty without the consent of the United States; (2) Cuba would not incur a debt unless the interest could be met out of current revenues; (3) the United States could intervene to preserve the independence or the political and social stability of Cuba; and (4) Cuba would grant to the United States land for the establishment of naval bases. (Under the terms of the last clause the United States built at Guantanamo Bay in the eastern part of the island a naval station, which it continues to operate.)

In 1902 American troops sailed for home. The following year the Platt Amendment was incorporated into a treaty between the United States and Cuba. In 1934 the Platt Amendment was repealed as part of Franklin D. Roosevelt's policy to improve relations between the United States and Latin America.

MILITARY INTERVENTION

While the Platt Amendment was in effect, diplomatic pressure was usually sufficient to bring compliance with American wishes. However, military forces were dispatched to the island on three occasions: in 1906 to quell disorderly protests by a political party that had suffered defeat in a recent election; in 1912 to restore order when blacks engaged in an insurrection against white control in one of the provinces; and in 1917 to put down a political revolt against the government.

ECONOMIC PENETRATION

After the Spanish-American War commercial contacts between Cuba and the United States increased rapidly. By the early 1920s nearly three-fourths of Cuba's imports consisted of American goods, while more than four-fifths of its exports went to the United States. Americans soon came to control a wide range of economic enterprises in the island republic, including sugar production and railroading. Thus Cuba, while in the strict sense politically independent, became in a full sense economically dependent upon its powerful neighbor to the north.

Selected Readings

GENERAL WORKS:

Battistini, Lawrence H. *The Rise of American Influence in Asia and the Pacific* (1960)

Beisner, Robert. *From the Old Diplomacy to the New, 1865–1900* (1975)

Campbell, Charles. *The Transformation of American Foreign Relations, 1865–1900* (1976)

Dobson, John. *America's Ascent: The United States Becomes a Great Power, 1880–1914* (1978)

Healy, David F. *U.S. Expansionism: The Imperialist Urge in the 1890s* (1970)

LaFeber, Walter. *The New Empire* (1963)

May Ernest R. *Imperial Democracy: The Emergence of America as a Great Power* (1961)

Weinberg, Albert K. *Manifest Destiny* (1935)

SPECIAL STUDIES:

Anderson, David. *Imperialism and Idealism: American Diplomacy in China, 1861–1898* (1985)

Beisner, Robert L. *Twelve Against Empire: The Anti-Imperialists, 1898–1900* (1968)

Campbell, Charles S., Jr. *Special Business Interests and the Open Door Policy* (1951)

Challener, Richard D. *Admirals, Generals, and American Foreign Policy, 1898–1914* (1973)

Dennett, Tyler. *John Hay* (1933)

Foner, Philip S. *The Spanish-Cuban-American War and the Birth of American Imperialism* (2 vols., 1972)

Freidel, Frank. *The Splendid Little War* (1958)

Healy, David F. *The United States in Cuba, 1898–1902* (1963)

Hunt, Michael. *The Making of a Special Relationship: The United States and China to 1914* (1983)

Iriye, Akira. *Pacific Estrangement: Japanese and American Expansion, 1897–1911* (1972)

Karnow, Stanley. *In Our Image: America's Empire in the Philippines* (1989)

LaFeber, Walter. *Inevitable Revolutions: The United States in Central America* (1984)

Langley, Lester. *The United States and the Caribbean, 1900–1970* (1980)

Millis, Walter. *The Martial Spirit* (1931)

Morgan, H. Wayne. *America's Road to Empire: The War with Spain and Overseas Expansion* (1965)

Paolino, Ernest. *The Foundations of American Empire* (1973)

Perez, Louis, Jr. *Cuba under the Platt Amendment, 1902–1934* (1986)

Perkins, Dexter. *The Monroe Doctrine, 1867–1907* (1937)

Pletcher, David M. *The Awkward Years: American Foreign Relations Under Garfield and Arthur* (1961)

Pratt, Julius W. *The Expansionists of 1898* (1936)

Stanley, Peter. *A Nation in the Making: The Philippines and the United States, 1899–1921* (1974)

Thomson, James, Peter Stanley, and John Perry. *Sentimental Imperialists: The American Experiences in East Asia* (1981)

Young, Marilyn B. *Rhetoric of Empire: American China Policy, 1895–1901* (1968)

6

The Progressive Era

1895   Hearst becomes owner of *New York Journal*
Crane, *The Red Badge of Courage*
1897   Dingley tariff
1901   McKinley assassinated; Theodore Roosevelt becomes president
Hay-Pauncefote Treaty
Socialist party of America founded
1902   Newlands Act
1903   Hay-Herran Treaty
Commerce and Labor Department established
Elkins Act
Hay-Bunau-Varilla Treaty
Wright Brothers make first airplane flight
Porter, *The Great Train Robbery*
1904   Roosevelt elected president
Roosevelt Corollary stated
Tarbell, *History of the Standard Oil Company*
Steffins, *Shame of the Cities*
1905   Roosevelt mediates Russo-Japanese War
Ochs becomes owner of *New York Times*
1906   Hepburn Act
Meat Inspection Act
Pure Food and Drug Act
De Forest makes first broadcast of human voice
Sinclair, *The Jungle*

1907 Ziegfeld begins his annual Ziegfeld Follies

1907–1908 "Gentlemen's Agreement"

1908 Taft elected president

Ford produces the Model T

1909 Payne-Aldrich tariff

National Association for the Advancement of Colored People (NAACP) founded

1909–1910 Ballinger-Pinchot controversy

1910 Mann-Elkins Act

1911 Supreme Court orders dissolution of Standard Oil Company

1912 Progressive ("Bull Moose") party founded

American troops occupy Nicaragua

Wilson elected president

1913 Underwood tariff

Federal Reserve Act

Sixteenth Amendment ratified

Seventeenth Amendment ratified

Armory Show on modern art held

1914 American troops occupy Veracruz, Mexico

Panama Canal opens

Federal Trade Commission Act

Clayton Antitrust Act

1915 American troops occupy Haiti

Griffith, *The Birth of a Nation*

1916 Federal Farm Loan Act

Keating-Owen Act

Adamson Act

La Follette Seamen's Act

American troops occupy Dominican Republic

1916–1917 American troops pursue Pancho Villa into Mexico

1917 United States purchases Virgin Islands

1920 Nineteenth Amendment ratified

*P*rogressivism developed as a doctrine for dealing with the far-reaching impact of the enormous industrialization after the Civil War. The United States had to contend with, among other things, the monopolistic practices of the large manufacturing firms; the abuses of the rapidly extending railroad systems; the changing status of the labor force, which was being transformed from skilled artisans into factory workers; the plight of farmers as they cultivated more efficiently with better machines and thus increased production, with consequent declining prices for their crops; and the demanding problems brought about by the vast growth of cities. The adherents of the progressive movement (called progressives whether their party affiliation was Democratic or Republican) endeavored to make government organization and processes on the federal, state, and local levels more democratic and to foster legislation that would directly benefit the people economically and socially.

The period made memorable by Theodore Roosevelt began in 1901 and lasted for the almost twelve years during which he and William H. Taft were in the White House. The era was one of vigorous effort to remodel the structure of government, to further democratize its processes, and to make it an arbiter of social justice. For close to eight years the exuberant style of Roosevelt gave a new meaning to the presidency. His hand-picked successor, Taft, although possessing none of the Roosevelt style, did achieve many of the widely demanded reforms of the period.

In 1913, after sixteen years of Republican rule, Democrat Woodrow Wilson was in the White House. Wilson had a strong sense of right and wrong, which he applied to the handling of domestic matters and international relations. In his first term he brought the progressive movement to its climax. In domestic matters he supported a number of reforms relating to the tariff, banking and currency, trusts, labor, and agriculture.

In foreign affairs, the period of territorial acquisitions resulting from the Spanish-American War was quickly followed by military intervention and commercial penetration, something deeper than the considerable trade activity that had previously taken place. The United States was also forced to deal extensively not only with nations in Latin America and the Far East but also with the European powers that had established themselves in those regions. In foreign policy the era of Theodore Roosevelt was marked by the aggressive actions of the United States to expand its role as a world power. Woodrow Wilson, in his conduct of foreign policy, attempted to diminish American imperialism and to promote the development of democracy in the smaller nations.

ELEMENTS OF
THE PROGRESSIVE MOVEMENT

Progressivism was a widely accepted reform movement that held sway from about the time Theodore Roosevelt assumed the presidency in 1901 until the United States entered World War I in 1917.

Political Progressives

At all three levels of government—federal, state, and local—efforts by a number of committed and vigorous political leaders propelled the progressive movement forward.

THE FEDERAL LEVEL

All three presidents of the period of progressivism—Theodore Roosevelt, William H. Taft to a lesser degree, and Woodrow Wilson—supported many of the goals of the progressive movement.

THE STATE LEVEL

Republican governor Robert M. La Follette of Wisconsin was the first progressive chief executive at the state level. His program of reform, called the Wisconsin Idea, was, among other things, leveled against the corruption of political bosses and the abuses of business interests, particularly the railroads. Other governors who drew nationwide attention as progressives were Republicans Hiram Johnson of California and Charles Evans Hughes of New York. Democrat Woodrow Wilson distinguished himself as a progressive governor of New Jersey before he was elected to the presidency.

THE LOCAL LEVEL

The most notable of the many progressive mayors across the nation were Democrat Tom L. Johnson of Cleveland and Republican Samuel M. "Golden Rule" Jones of Toledo. Johnson worked ceaselessly to eliminate the political, economic, and social faults and abuses that existed in his city. He was widely considered the most competent person up to his time to serve as head of a municipality. Among the many reforms Jones implemented in Toledo were both an eight-hour workday and minimum wages for municipal employees.

The Muckrakers

The term muckrakers was applied to a group of writers who stirred public opinion to the point of action by exposing abuses in business and corruption in politics.

ORIGIN OF THE TERM

The term originated with President Roosevelt, who, although concurring with the basic accusations of the crusading writers, criticized them for their focus on sensationalism. The president compared them with a character in

John Bunyan's seventeenth-century allegory *Pilgrim's Progress* who was so intent on piling up the filth with his muckrake that the only direction in which he looked was downward.

INFLUENTIAL PRACTITIONERS

Some of the best-known muckrakers were Frank Norris, whose novels *The Octopus* (1901) and *The Pit* (1903) attacked the Southern Pacific Railroad and the Chicago grain market, respectively; Ida M. Tarbell, whose *History of the Standard Oil Company* (1904) condemned the practices of that monopolistic corporation; Lincoln Steffens, whose *Shame of the Cities* (1904) exposed corruption in various municipal governments across the nation; and Upton Sinclair, whose novel *The Jungle* (1906) decried conditions in the Chicago meat-packing plants. Several popular magazines of the period, including *Collier's*, *Cosmopolitan*, *Everybody's*, and *McClure's*, provided the muckrakers with a forum for some of their most sensational disclosures.

IMPORTANCE OF THE GROUP

Although President Roosevelt was not always willing to recognize his indebtedness to the muckrakers, his own crusade for social justice was significantly aided by the work of such writers. Such results as legislation for the protection of consumers and federal suits against various trusts can be traced to the muckrakers.

Direct Government

The charge by critics that American legislative bodies were dominated by privileged interests and therefore did not truly represent the people as a whole led to a demand that the will of the people be translated more directly into governmental action.

THE INITIATIVE

First adopted by South Dakota in 1898, the initiative permits a certain portion of the voters (usually about 10 percent) to initiate by petition a law, which is then submitted to either the state legislature or the people for approval. Twenty-two states have at various times tested the initiative.

THE REFERENDUM

Like the initiative, the referendum was first used by South Dakota in 1898. It permits a certain portion of the voters (usually about 10 percent), by signing a petition, to have submitted to the voters for their acceptance or rejection a law that has passed the legislature. In some states the referendum procedure allows the state legislature to submit to the voters a proposed bill for their acceptance or rejection. If accepted, the bill becomes a law.

THE RECALL

This plan to make public officials more responsive to the people's will was first used in Los Angeles in 1903. The recall permits a certain portion of the voters (usually about 25 percent), by petition; to start proceedings to remove an officeholder before the expiration of the term for which he has been elected or appointed. Its use in connection with the recall of judges, as provided in the constitution of Arizona, aroused bitter controversy, but there have been few examples of summary removal of officeholders in any of the three branches of government.

THE DIRECT PRIMARY

Introduced in Wisconsin in 1903 during La Follette's governorship, the direct primary is a preliminary election in which the voters directly nominate candidates of their own party to run in a general election. By 1933 some form of the direct primary was used in all but six of the states. But the hopes of the reformers that the device would break the power of the bosses at party nominating conventions proved overoptimistic.

THE SEVENTEENTH AMENDMENT

The champions of direct government were particularly insistent in their demand for the popular election of United States senators. They charged that selection by the state legislatures resulted in a Senate brought into being by an alliance between wealthy businessmen and unscrupulous politicians. They persuaded state after state to permit the voters to express a senatorial preference that the legislature was bound to accept. At the same time, the progressives worked hard to secure a constitutional amendment to implement their objectives. Passed by Congress in 1911 and ratified in 1913, the Seventeenth Amendment to the Constitution provided for the direct election of senators.

Municipal Reform

The progressives' vigorous attack upon the structure and administration of municipal government led to reforms that broke the power of city political machines in various parts of the nation.

THE COMMISSION PLAN

In 1900 Galveston, Texas, following a destructive hurricane, experimented with a new form of government—the commission plan. The system spread quickly. Under this plan all municipal functions are vested in a small group of elected persons, usually five, each of whom is responsible for the management of an administrative department. The commission, all of whose members theoretically hold equal power, determines policy as a body. One of the commissioners serves as ceremonial head of the municipal government. By 1914 more than 400 of the nation's smaller cities had tried the plan, some with such indifferent results that they abandoned it.

THE CITY-MANAGER PLAN

In 1914 Dayton, Ohio, adopted the city-manager type of municipal organization, a plan patterned after a system introduced six years earlier by Staunton, Virginia. The Dayton approach was widely imitated. Under the city-manager plan a commission of elected persons, acting in the capacity of a board of directors, appoints a nonpolitical city manager to administer the government as if it were a business concern. As in the case of the commission plan, the results did not prove uniformly satisfactory.

Women's Suffrage

The progressive era was marked by a notable extension of suffrage, as state after state gave women the right to vote.

STATE ACTION

The egalitarian philosophy of the far western frontier, the entrance of women into certain trades and professions, the opening of institutions of higher education to women—these all gave impetus to the campaign for women's suffrage after the Civil War. Wyoming was the first state to grant the ballot to women, having been admitted to the Union in 1890 with the provision already established by law. By the end of the Taft administration, in 1913, eight states—Kansas, Colorado, Idaho, Utah, Arizona, Washington, Oregon, and California—had given women the right to vote.

THE NINETEENTH AMENDMENT

Many advocates of women's rights believed that a constitutional amendment was the ultimate solution to the issue of equal political rights for men and women. Susan B. Anthony, a social reformer and leader in the women's suffrage movement, proposed such an amendment in 1869; nine years later it was introduced in Congress. There it languished for more than forty years. In 1919 Congress passed the Nineteenth Amendment to the Constitution, granting nationwide women's suffrage—a testimonial to the effective work of such feminists as Anthony, Elizabeth Cady Stanton, and Carrie Chapman Catt. Ratification in August 1920 permitted women to vote in the presidential election that year.

State and Municipal Welfare Action

The progressives were responsible for a good deal of state and municipal welfare legislation passed during the Roosevelt and Taft administrations.

THE STATE LEVEL

A number of states enacted laws that regulated hours and wages of workers; restricted the type and amount of labor performed by women and children; provided for workers' compensation; granted public aid to widowed or deserted mothers with dependent children and to the aged; and set health and safety standards for industry.

THE MUNICIPAL LEVEL

Progressive reforms in the cities included the establishment of settlement houses to supply various educational, leisure, medical, and other services to congested urban communities; slum clearance; and the setting up of recreational facilities.

The Socialist Challenge

Although the socialist movement in the United States had its start immediately after the Civil War, socialists attracted little attention until they formed the Socialist party of America in order to offer alternative programs to those of the progressives.

GOAL

The Socialist Labor party, established in 1876, and the Social Democratic party, founded in 1897, united in 1901 to form the Socialist party of America, headed by Eugene V. Debs. The party set for its ultimate goal the establishment of public ownership and operation of the means of production and distribution, according to the principles of the German social philosopher Karl Marx. The Socialist party of America advocated the following preliminary steps for achieving its goal: (1) reduction of workday hours; (2) enactment of unemployment insurance; (3) government ownership of railroad lines, telegraph companies, telephone firms, and other public utilities; (4) nationwide adoption of the initiative, referendum, and recall; and (5) implementation of proportional representation (an electoral system designed to represent in a legislative body each political group or party in optimum proportion to its actual voting strength in a community). The socialists denounced the programs of the progressives as the futile "tinkering" of the bourgeoisie (the middle class, engrossed in material interests).

ELECTORAL PERFORMANCE

The first substantial vote received by a socialist candidate in a presidential election was in 1912, when Debs polled 897,000 votes. In the election of 1920, with women voting for the first time, Debs secured 919,000 votes. From the election of 1928 on, although the party's candidate was repeatedly its able head, Norman Thomas, the electoral strength of the organization declined.

THEODORE ROOSEVELT AND THE SQUARE DEAL

The assassination of President William McKinley by a crazed anarchist on September 6, 1901, threw the conservative Republican leaders into a panic. They feared that the young and dynamic vice-president, now elevated to the presidency, might put into effect too many of his progressive ideas. With his constant exuberance Roosevelt gave a new dimension to the office. He manifested a lively concern that his administration should afford what he referred to as a square deal for all Americans: businessmen, laborers, farmers, and consumers. Roosevelt's impact lay in his unusual ability to arouse the people to an awareness of their civic duties, rather than in any notable progress toward social justice under his leadership.

The Roosevelt Administration

Implicit in everything that Roosevelt did as president was his theory that the one who held that office should be the leader in the formulation of all governmental policies.

THE PRESIDENT

Roosevelt exuded a zest for living that few, if any, of his predecessors in the White House had ever matched. He was a person of varied talents—outdoorsman, writer, politician. His fellow Americans affectionately called the colorful Roosevelt "Teddy."

FIRST STATE OF THE UNION MESSAGE

The new president's first State of the Union message was transmitted to Congress in December 1901, less than three months after he was thrust into office. Calculated to calm the fears of his party associates, the message was nevertheless a blueprint for far-reaching reforms. Roosevelt called for (1) greater control of corporations by the federal government; (2) more authority for the Interstate Commerce Commission; (3) conservation of natural resources; (4) extension of the merit system in the civil service; (5) construction of an isthmian canal; and (6) a vigorous foreign policy.

THE CABINET

Wanting to suggest continuance of the previous administration's policies, Roosevelt retained the McKinley cabinet intact. Thus the distinguished John Hay and Elihu Root remained as heads of the departments of state and war, respectively. Eventually, however, he made changes in all of the posts except one. The members of the official family were, on the whole, men of ability, but the strong-willed Roosevelt dominated them all.

The Coal Strike

Roosevelt's concern for a square deal for all Americans prompted his actions in a strike that took place in the anthracite coal fields.

THE MINERS' GRIEVANCES

For many years miners in the anthracite coal districts of eastern Pennsylvania, unable to effect a satisfactory organization to protect their interests, had been exploited by the mine operators. They had grievances regarding (1) long hours; (2) low wages; (3) being compelled to live in company houses and to trade at company stores; and (4) the refusal of the operators to recognize the union and collective bargaining. When the mine owners refused to arbitrate these grievances, the miners went on strike in May 1902.

THE WHITE HOUSE CONFERENCE

In October 1902, with the strike dragging on, Roosevelt invited the mine owners and John Mitchell, president of the United Mine Workers, to confer with him in the White House. But the president's attempt to mediate failed completely, as the mine owners still refused to make any concessions.

SETTLEMENT

Soon after the conference at the White House, Roosevelt quietly began exerting pressure in financial circles to resolve the conflict. He also threatened to use federal troops to run the mines. The operators were finally persuaded to agree, as the miners had already done, to Roosevelt's plan for a board of arbitration to review the issues in the dispute. In March 1903, the board decided to grant a 10-percent wage increase and a nine-hour workday, but it failed to recognize the union. The decision became the basis of peace between management and labor in the anthracite coal districts for the next fifteen years.

Election of 1904

Having served three and a half years of McKinley's term, Roosevelt was eager to become president in his own right.

DEMOCRATS

The delegates to the Democratic national convention, turning aside from the "radicalism" of William Jennings Bryan and ignoring the claims of *New York Journal* publisher William Randolph Hearst for the presidential nomination, selected a conservative New York jurist, Alton B. Parker. Henry G. Davis of West Virginia, a merchant and former senator, was chosen as the vice-presidential nominee.

REPUBLICANS

For a time Roosevelt had feared that the ultraconservative wing of his party would oppose him for the presidential nomination and support Mark Hanna. But Hanna's death early in 1904 removed all likelihood of opposition, and Roosevelt was nominated by acclamation at the Republican national convention. Senator Charles W. Fairbanks of Indiana was selected his running mate.

THE CAMPAIGN

At issue in the campaign was whether the people were in favor of a continuation of the policies and style of Theodore Roosevelt.

ROOSEVELT'S VICTORY

Roosevelt was elected by an electoral vote of 336 to 140 for Parker. He carried every state outside the solid South. In popular votes, Roosevelt received 7,628,000 to Parker's 5,084,000.

Handling the Trusts

Roosevelt was opposed to any program to destroy the trusts, but he advocated close governmental regulation of industry under the terms of the Sherman Antitrust Act of 1890, which so far had not been vigorously enforced.

THE NORTHERN SECURITIES CASE

The first assault in the battle against business combinations in restraint of trade occurred in 1902. Attorney General Philander C. Knox filed suit against the Northern Securities Company, a holding company that had a controlling share of stock in the Northern Pacific, the Great Northern, and the Chicago, Burlington, and Quincy railroads. The president, who had declared that the most powerful corporation, like the humblest citizen, should be compelled to obey the law, was pleased that the government won its case in the lower federal courts and that the Supreme Court, in 1904, upheld the decision.

FEDERAL LEGISLATION

Congress failed to undertake a comprehensive modification of the Sherman Antitrust Act, which Roosevelt had urged. It did pass several measures designed to help enforce the act, however. The Expedition Act of 1903 gave precedence on federal court calendars to cases arising from alleged nonobservance of the Sherman Antitrust Act or the Interstate Commerce Act. Within the Department of Commerce and Labor, established in 1903, was the Bureau of Corporations, which was authorized to investigate possible violations of antitrust prohibitions. Congress appropriated a special fund of $500,000 for bringing suit against illegal business combinations.

FEDERAL PROSECUTIONS

During the almost eight years of the Roosevelt presidency, the Justice Department obtained twenty-four indictments against the trusts. The most significant of the judicial decisions, some rendered during the succeeding Taft administration, were (1) the injunction, in 1905, forbidding the member firms of the beef trust to engage in certain practices designed to restrain competition; (2) the suit, in 1911, that resulted in the dissolution of the Standard Oil Company of New Jersey, a holding company with a monopoly in the oil-refining business; and (3) the order, in 1911, requiring the reorganization of the American Tobacco Company, found to be an illegal combination. In the course of deliberating alleged violations of the Sherman Antitrust Act, the Supreme Court formulated what became known as the "rule of reason"—only "unreasonable" combinations in restraint of trade should be prohibited.

Regulating the Railroads

Roosevelt constantly recommended a more comprehensive regulation of the railroads by extending the power of the Interstate Commerce Commission, which had been crippled by judicial limitation.

THE ELKINS ACT

This measure, passed in 1903, struck at the practice of secret rebates, which had been declared illegal by the Interstate Commerce Act of 1887. According to the Elkins Act, the recipient, as well as the grantor of the rebate, was made liable to prosecution. Further, the agent or official of the railroad was held legally responsible for any deviation from regular published rates.

THE HEPBURN ACT

By increasing the power of the Interstate Commerce Commission, the Hepburn Act, passed in 1906, made a great advance toward government regulation of the railroads. The act (1) raised the membership of the commission from five to seven; (2) the commission authority over express companies, ferries, and pipelines; (3) granted the commission power to reduce unreasonably high and discriminatory rates, subject to judicial review; (4) placed the burden of proof in all legal disputes upon the carrier rather than the commission; (5) forbade the railroads to transport commodities in the production of which they were themselves interested; and (6) established a uniform system of accounting to be used by the carriers. Although the Hepburn Act fell short of conferring upon the Interstate Commerce Commission the absolute power to fix rates, it made the commission an effective agency for the first time since its creation twenty years earlier.

SUPPORTIVE JUDICIAL DECISIONS

After the passage of the Hepburn Act the federal courts showed an increasing disposition to lend support to the decisions of the commission. In 1910 the Supreme Court laid down the principle that the railroads could expect protection from the federal courts only if they proved "beyond any reasonable doubt" that their property was being confiscated. At the same time, however, the judiciary as a whole refused to sanction extreme penalties imposed upon railroads or shippers found guilty of violating the law. In 1907 the higher courts set aside the decision of Judge Kenesaw M. Landis of the Second District Court imposing a fine of over $29 million on the Standard Oil Company of Indiana for accepting secret rebates from the railroads.

Conservation

No part of Roosevelt's program was carried forward more energetically or more successfully than his campaign for the conservation of natural resources.

EXPOSING NATIONAL WASTE

Roosevelt's outstanding achievement in the conservation movement was his arousal of widespread public interest in halting the squandering of natural resources. The generosity of the federal government in transferring portions of the public domain (land owned or controlled by the government) to private ownership had resulted in wasteful exploitation of the nation's lumber, coal, petroleum, natural gas, and metals. Aided by such associates as Gifford Pinchot, chief of the Forest Service of the Agriculture Department, and James R. Garfield, secretary of the interior, Roosevelt undertook to educate the American people to support conservation and to secure legislative action for this purpose.

THE NEWLANDS ACT

Recommended by Roosevelt, the Newlands Act, passed in 1902, provided for the appropriation of most of the money received from the sale of public lands in the West and Southwest to finance the construction of irrigation projects. Within five years twenty-eight projects in fourteen states were underway.

NATIONAL PARKS AND FORESTS

Roosevelt was not the originator of the campaign for the establishment of national parks, but he gave vigorous support to those who were trying to preserve regions of great natural beauty. In addition, to prevent the forests from being virtually depleted, he set aside 148 million acres as timber reserves.

INTERNAL WATERWAYS

Conservation also included the use of the system of inland bodies of water to facilitate transportation, to promote irrigation projects, and to develop water-power sites. To supervise such activities, Roosevelt appointed the Internal Waterways Commission.

NATIONAL CONSERVATION COMMISSION

In 1908 Roosevelt held a governors' conference at the White House to discuss the fundamental issues relating to conservation. The result of the conference was Roosevelt's appointment of the National Conservation

Commission, with Gifford Pinchot as chairman, and the creation of thirty-six state boards to cooperate with the national body.

Consumer Protection Laws

The scandal arising from supplying spoiled canned meat to servicemen during the Spanish-American War and the writings of muckrakers such as Upton Sinclair on the meat-packing industry resulted in legislation for the protection of consumers.

THE PURE FOOD AND DRUG ACT

Passed in 1906, the Pure Food and Drug Act forbade the adulteration or fraudulent labeling of foods and drugs sold in interstate commerce.

THE MEAT INSPECTION ACT

Also passed in 1908, the Meat Inspection Act provided for the supervision of conditions of sanitation in meat-packing firms engaged in interstate commerce and for federal inspection of the meat they sold.

TAFT AND REFORM

Although Taft was much more conservative in temperament than Roosevelt, he nevertheless sympathized with the political reformers of his time and approved of many of their objectives. In listing the achievements of his four years in office, his admirers included the vigorous prosecution of illegal combinations in restraint of trade, the extension of the merit system to new branches of the civil service, the adoption of the eight-hour workday for employees on government contracts, and the passage of legislation reserving additional public lands from private enterprise. But Taft frequently took issue with the methods of the political reformers and criticized the haste with which they attempted to put their progressive ideas into effect.

Election of 1908

At the end of his second term Roosevelt could have been nominated again for president, but he declined to be a candidate, basing his decision largely on a desire to observe the two-term tradition established by George Washington. Without the zestful Teddy in the running, the election was dull from start to finish.

DEMOCRATS

Once more dominant in Democratic circles, William Jennings Bryan was chosen by the national convention of the party to be its standard-bearer for the third time. Indiana lawyer and progressive state legislator John W. Kern was nominated for vice-president.

REPUBLICANS

The Republican national convention was a Roosevelt-dominated affair. The delegates were wild admirers of the president. At his behest they nominated Taft to be their standard-bearer and adopted a platform that had been drafted in the White House. Representative James S. Sherman of New York was chosen as Taft's running mate.

THE CAMPAIGN

The vigorous orator Bryan was unable to make any headway in the campaign against the easygoing Taft. Indeed, there was much in the Republican position on the various issues that met with Bryan's approval.

TAFT'S VICTORY

Taft won 321 electoral votes to Bryan's 162. The Democratic candidate had thus regained for his party some of the ground lost by presidential candidate Alton B. Parker four years earlier.

The Taft Administration

Taft set himself a twofold task: to carry forward in his own right the policies that his predecessor had so effectively dramatized and to reconcile the progressives and the conservatives within the Republican party.

THE PRESIDENT

Taft was a hearty and placid 350-pound man whose judicial temperament made it impossible for him to assume the dynamic role that Roosevelt had played so successfully in the progressive movement. As a result, Taft seemed inclined to restrain the zealous liberals rather than to win over the conservatives to the cause of reform.

THE CABINET

Most of the members of Taft's official family were lawyers who emphasized the legal limitations on presidential prerogative and the difficulties of implementing the progressive program. Two influential cabinet members were Secretary of State Philander C. Knox of Pennsylvania, a former attorney general and United States senator, and Secretary of War Henry L. Stimson, a former United States attorney.

Tariff Revision

The first significant test of Taft's leadership both as president of the United States and as leader of the Republican party arose out of attempts to revise the tariff.

PROTESTS AGAINST PROTECTION

In 1897 the Republican-controlled Congress passed, and President McKinley signed into law, the protective Dingley tariff, with an average rate of 57 percent. The high tariff, which had then seemed reasonable to the Republican party, became the object of vigorous attacks as the prices of protected American manufactured goods increased more rapidly than did workers' wages. In 1907 Roosevelt declared that the tariff needed revision. In the 1908 campaign Taft pledged that he would interpret the plank on tariff revision in the Republican platform to mean a reduction in rates.

THE PAYNE-ALDRICH TARIFF

The House of Representatives passed the Payne bill, which provided for a modest general lowering of rates and the placing of coal, iron ore, and hides on the free list. Through the sponsorship of protectionist Republican Nelson W. Aldrich of Rhode Island, the Senate added 847 amendments to the Payne bill, almost all of which provided for increased rates. The amended bill was fought by a group of midwestern progressive Republican senators, ably led by Robert M. La Follette of Wisconsin. After a lowering of some duties in response to strong requests from Taft, Congress in 1909 passed the Payne-Aldrich bill, which removed coal and iron ore from the free list and established rates that came to an average of approximately 40 percent. Thus the tariff remained decidedly protectionist.

Eager to persuade the progressive Republicans that the new tariff should be accepted in the interest of party harmony, Taft signed the Payne-Aldrich bill into law, subsequently asserting that as a tariff it was "the best bill that the Republican party ever passed." This statement put the progressives immediately on their guard against the recently installed president.

The Ballinger-Pinchot Controversy

Conservationists were apprehensive over the plans of Richard A. Ballinger, whom Taft had promoted from superintendent of the General Land Office to secretary of the interior.

BALLINGER'S ACTIONS

Ballinger concluded that Roosevelt had exceeded his legal powers in reserving certain public lands, and he soon opened them once more to private leasing. He also restored to private operation water-power sites in Wyoming and Montana and he approved the claims of private interests to valuable coal lands in Alaska. For those acts he was severely criticized in published articles by Louis R. Glavis, a special agent of the Field Division of the Interior Department, and Gifford Pinchot, head of the Forest Service.

PINCHOT'S DISMISSAL

Taft, distressed by the publicity attending the quarrel in the administration, removed Glavis in September 1909, and dismissed Pinchot in January 1910, after the latter had carried his charges to Congress. Pinchot was quick to rally Roosevelt's supporters and persuade them that Taft was a traitor to the former president's conception of conservation. The accusation was unjust to Taft, but he had to bear the brunt of public antagonism toward Ballinger, who was permitted to resign in 1911.

Reform in the House of Representatives

Although Taft was not directly involved in the battle between conservatives and progressives in the House of Representatives, the revolt of the progressive Republicans, popularly called "insurgents," against Speaker Joseph G. Cannon's rule clearly indicated the president's inability to control his party.

CANNONISM

Republican Joseph G. "Uncle Joe" Cannon of Illinois, as Speaker of the House of Representatives, exercised enormous power in connection with the legislative process. He served on and appointed the other members to the significant Committee on Rules, which determined the routine procedures of the House. He chose the membership and designated the chairmen of all other standing (permanent) committees. Cannon wielded his considerable influence in such a way as to aid the conservatives and hinder the progressives.

THE REVOLT OF 1910

Republican insurgents rose in revolt against Cannon's dictatorial tactics in March 1910. Through a coalition with the Democratic minority, they succeeded in having the House adopt an amendment to its rules of procedure (proposed by Republican George W. Norris of Nebraska), depriving the Speaker of the power to appoint members to the Rules Committee and barring him from serving on it. The Rules Committee was made elective. Further, the following year the Democrats, then in the majority, through the adoption of a resolution by the House, denied the Speaker even the right to appoint standing committees. The success of the Republican insurgents was a defeat for Taft, who had given indirect support to Speaker Cannon in the struggle.

Further Regulation of the Railroads

The desire to strengthen and refine government regulation of the railroads was widespread. The Taft administration gave support to that end.

THE MANN-ELKINS ACT

Through the efforts of congressional progressives of both major parties, legislation was passed during the Taft administration that corrected certain defects in the Hepburn Act. In 1910 President Taft signed into law the Mann-Elkins Act. It (1) gave the Interstate Commerce Commission's authority to supervise telephone, telegraph, cable, and wireless companies; (2) empowered the commission on its own to institute proceedings against carriers for violations of the law; (3) authorized the commission to suspend all new rates until it was satisfied of their reasonableness; and (4) created a new Commerce Court (which was in existence for three years) to expedite the handling of rate cases.

THE PHYSICAL VALUATION ACT

Through the efforts of the progressive Republicans, under the leadership of Senator Robert M. La Follette of Wisconsin, Congress passed in 1913 (three days before the Taft administration came to a close) the Physical Valuation Act. It empowered the Interstate Commerce Commission to make a study with the objective of determining the value of the property held by the various railroads. The purpose of the study, which took the commission eight years to complete, was to provide a basis for setting rates that would represent a reasonable profit to the lines on their investment.

Government Reorganization and Reform

The record of the Taft administration for progressive measures compared favorably with that of the Roosevelt administration. This could be readily seen in the area of government reorganization and reform.

THE POSTAL SAVINGS BANK ACT

Upon the recommendation of Taft, Congress in 1910 established the postal savings bank system, whereby certain post offices were authorized to receive deposited funds and pay interest on them.

THE SIXTEENTH AMENDMENT

Passed by Congress in 1909 and ratified in 1913, just as the Taft administration was coming to an end, the Sixteenth Amendment to the Constitution permitted the imposition of a graduated income tax without regard to apportionment among the states according to population.

DEPARTMENTS OF COMMERCE AND LABOR

From the Department of Commerce and Labor, Congress created in 1913, on Taft's last day in office, two separate departments: the Department of Commerce and the Department of Labor, whose heads would both be cabinet members. The Department of Commerce was authorized to help supervise and advance the nation's commerce, domestic and foreign. The Department of Labor was set up to improve the status of wage earners in all aspects of their working conditions.

WILSON AND THE NEW FREEDOM

In his campaign for the presidency in 1912 the Democratic candidate Woodrow Wilson expressed a body of ideas for a program he called the New Freedom. In essence, it sought to curb any business that enjoyed a monopoly and to restore an earlier condition of competition. Wilson was victorious at the polls and entered the White House as the first Democrat after sixteen years of Republican rule. More significant than a switch of party control, however, is the fact that in his first term he brought the progressive movement to its zenith. In pursuing his domestic policy, Wilson totally rejected the concept that the American system should be scrapped. He desired to preserve that system, but also to strengthen it through reform. He had a strong sense of right and wrong, which he applied to the handling of domestic matters, supporting a number of reforms relating to the tariff, banking and currency, trusts, labor, and agriculture. When the United States entered World War I the attention and efforts of those imbued with progressive zeal switched from domestic reform to worldwide hostilities and their concomitant miseries. Progressive activity virtually ceased.

Election of 1912

A deep split in the Republican party had brought into being the new rival Progressive party and thus made certain the victory of the Democratic candidate for president.

DEMOCRATS

The Democratic national convention witnessed a spirited contest between the conservative and liberal forces within the party. Speaker of the House Champ Clark of Missouri was the front-runner, with both conservative and liberal delegates in his following. The extreme conservatives supported Governor Judson Harmon of Ohio and Representative Oscar W. Underwood of Alabama. The liberals rallied behind Governor Woodrow Wilson of New Jersey, who described himself as a "progressive with the brakes on."

It appeared that Clark was going to win the nomination. However, William Jennings Bryan dramatically denounced the "sinister influences" of the financial sector endorsing Clark. On the fourteenth ballot he switched from Clark to Wilson, carrying many of his followers with him. Wilson was finally nominated on the forty-sixth ballot. The delegates chose Governor Thomas R. Marshall of Indiana for second place on the ticket. The party platform invited the support of those who were willing to enlist in the war against political and economic privilege.

REPUBLICANS

The Republican national convention was a scene of turmoil. After weeks of indecision, former president Theodore Roosevelt agreed to become a candidate for the nomination. Then came an unseemly scramble for delegates between the incumbent Taft and Roosevelt. Wherever the delegates were chosen by state conventions or hand-picked by the bosses, Taft had the advantage. In states that permitted the voters to express their individual preferences, Roosevelt was clearly the choice. The convention was controlled by the Taft forces. It proceeded, amid great confusion and wrangling, to grant the occupant of the White House another nomination. Vice-President James S. Sherman was also renominated.

PROGRESSIVES

More than a year before the election, liberal insurgent Republicans tried to mobilize the progressive sentiment of the country. In January 1911, several Republican senators formed an organization called the Progressive Republican League, which announced the following political aims: (1) direct election of senators; (2) direct primaries; (3) direct election of delegates to national nominating conventions; and (4) state adoption of the initiative, referendum, and recall.

Initially the league merely advocated progressive principles. In October 1911, it endorsed Senator Robert M. La Follette of Wisconsin for the Republican nomination against President Taft. La Follette, who had won national fame for his successful battle against the power of large corporations in his own state, promptly started a vigorous drive to rouse the voters from their lethargy. Although former president Roosevelt had been supporting the liberal insurgent Republicans ever since the summer of 1910, he refused to join the league or to support La Follette.

Roosevelt charged that the Republican nomination had been "stolen" from him by irregular tactics. With evangelical fervor his followers undertook the task of helping to form a new party, called the Progressive party. In August 1912, the Progressive party held its first convention in Chicago, where two months earlier its hero, La Follette, had been rejected by the Republicans at their convention. La Follette was the logical leader of liberal insurgent Republicans openly at war with the party leadership. The revolt against Taft no longer appeared hopeless. However, many of La Follette's supporters seized on a pretext to switch to Roosevelt at the convention, and La Follette was shunted aside. Roosevelt was nominated for president by acclamation, while Republican governor Hiram Johnson of California was nominated for vice-president. The schism in the Republican ranks was complete. The Progressive party was nicknamed the "Bull Moose" party, from Roosevelt's frequent use of the term to describe someone full of strength and vigor.

THE CAMPAIGN

During the campaign the positions of all three presidential candidates were very much alike on a host of political, economic, and social reforms. Where the three men differed was on the issues of the tariff and the handling of trusts. In keeping with the traditional Republican position, both Taft and Roosevelt called for a protective tariff, although one with lower rates than the existing Payne-Aldrich tariff. Representing the traditional position of his party on the tariff, Wilson advocated the passage of a new tariff for revenue purposes only.

As for government handling of trusts, Roosevelt presented views known collectively as the New Nationalism, which looked to even stricter federal regulation of trusts than had previously been exercised—but not an elimination of them. Although Taft used a different phraseology, he supported a policy of stricter trust regulation that was virtually indistinguishable from the one advocated by Roosevelt. Wilson, however, sought the elimination of business monopoly as an inherent evil.

WILSON'S VICTORY

Wilson captured forty states, with a total of 435 electoral votes; Taft secured only Vermont and Utah, with their 8 electoral votes; Roosevelt carried six states, with 88 electoral votes. The House of Representatives and the Senate went Democratic by wide margins. The overwhelming nature of the Democratic victory was plainly due to the split in the Republican party.

The Wilson Administration

Wilson viewed the presidency as a means of securing the legislation needed to make government responsive to the will of the people.

THE PRESIDENT

Wilson was a model of independence, firmness, and energy. He wrote and spoke with a rare eloquence. During his first term he used executive power creatively, notably in dealing with Congress.

INAUGURAL ADDRESS

After taking the oath of office, Wilson delivered a stirring inaugural address, summoning "all honest men, all patriotic, all forward-looking men" to join him in service to the nation. In his presentation he itemized "things that ought to be altered," including the tariff, banking and currency, and industry.

THE CABINET

Wilson felt compelled to select William Jennings Bryan to head the cabinet as secretary of state, in recognition of Bryan's considerable influence within the Democratic fold and also his significant support at the party's 1912 convention. Testimony to the power of the southern wing of the Democratic party was the fact that more than half of those chosen for the remaining cabinet posts had been born and raised in the South. The following cabinet members were to become well known for particular competence: Georgia-born New York City businessman William G. McAdoo as secretary of the treasury; North Carolina newspaper editor Josephus Daniels as secretary of the navy; and former Texas Democratic representative Albert S. Burleson as postmaster general.

UNOFFICIAL ADVISOR

Edward M. House, known as "Colonel" House, who had been active in the politics of his state of Texas, became the president's most trusted advisor. Wilson admired him for his combination of idealism and common sense. He turned to him often for counsel, particularly in foreign affairs.

Revision of the Tariff

The Democratic party's traditional opposition to the principle of the protective tariff was firmly supported by the new administration, alerting the nation to expect an early and strong attempt at tariff reduction.

WILSON'S ROLE

After Congress decided to deal with the tariff issue, Wilson went to the Capitol a number of times to consult with leaders of his party on the strategy that would most effectively achieve a lowering of tariff duties. When it seemed that lobbyists representing special interest groups would be able to block some of the proposed reductions in rates, he took a variety of effective approaches, including a direct appeal to the American people for their moral support.

THE UNDERWOOD TARIFF

Passed in 1913, the Underwood tariff provided for the first substantial lowering of duties in over half a century. Its distinctive features included (1) a reduction of rates on close to 1,000 commodities considered no longer in need of protection against foreign competition; (2) an increase of rates on almost 100 articles deemed luxury in nature; (3) an expansion of the free-items list to include such important products to American consumers as iron, steel, and wool; and (4) the imposition of a graduated income tax as permitted by the recently ratified Sixteenth Amendment to the Constitution (to compensate for anticipated loss of revenue from the new schedule of duties). Before the effect of the measure upon either foreign trade or governmental finances could be determined, the beginning of World War I brought about a period of abnormal economic activity.

Reorganization of Banking and Currency

Wilson argued forcefully for the creation of a banking system capable of supplying currency that would expand and contract in amount according to the needs of business.

BACKGROUND TO ACTION

By the end of the nineteenth century the United States had experienced half a dozen financial panics. In 1907 another occurred. The brief but sharp Panic of 1907 demonstrated the inelasticity of the monetary system and the inflexibility of the credit structure in the United States. In 1912 the House Committee on Banking and Currency, through a subcommittee chaired by the Democratic Arsène Pujo of Louisiana, began investigating the extent of the concentration of financial power in a small group of banking firms. The report of the Pujo Committee, published early in 1913, declared that there existed a "money trust," consisting of a few Wall Street banking houses whose control of money and credit had serious ramifications throughout the manufacturing, trade, and transportation establishments of the nation. The effects of the Panic of 1907 and the findings of the Pujo Committee were used by Wilson as evidence in the case he made for banking and currency reform.

THE FEDERAL RESERVE ACT

From his White House office Wilson played an effective role in both the framing of the Federal Reserve Act and in the parliamentary maneuvering that secured its passage in 1913. In short, the act created a flexible credit structure so that funds could be transferred promptly from one section of the nation to another as the need arose and instituted an elastic currency system so that the supply of money could be expanded and contracted according to business requirements.

The act established the Federal Reserve System, which operated as follows: (1) The nation was divided into twelve districts, based upon economic and geographic considerations, with a federal reserve bank in each; (2) each federal reserve bank dealt not directly with the public but with the banks in its district that joined the system as member banks, serving those banks primarily by depositing their cash reserves and extending them loans; (3) the Federal Reserve Board, composed of a bipartisan group of financial experts, supervised the system; (4) the Federal Reserve Board could regulate the supply of credit available in every section of the nation by raising or lowering the interest rate that each federal reserve bank would charge member banks seeking loans from it, which action would in turn raise or lower the interest rate member banks charged private individuals for loans, thereby giving flexibility to the national credit structure; and (5) each federal reserve bank could issue into the money supply in circulation federal reserve notes, the amount of which could be expanded or contracted depending on the needs of business, thus providing an elastic currency system.

Regulation of Industry

Having expounded the proposition that "private monopoly is indefensible and intolerable," Wilson urged legislation to supersede the Sherman Antitrust Act, which, in large part due to the imprecision of its language, had never been adequately enforced. Somewhat reluctantly, Congress presented two measures to the president for his signature.

THE FEDERAL TRADE COMMISSION ACT

This act, passed in 1914, established a five-member bipartisan commission to prevent interstate businesses from using unfair methods of competition. Under the provisions of the measure, the Federal Trade Commission was authorized to (1) require annual and special reports from corporations; (2) conduct investigations of corporations reported to be engaged in unfair practices in interstate commerce; and (3) issue orders to corporations to "cease and desist" from using those practices considered in violation of the law. Some unfair trade practices the commissioners were particularly alert to were deceptive advertising, mislabeling of containers, and adulteration of products.

THE CLAYTON ANTITRUST ACT

Designed to regulate the nation's monopolies, the Clayton Antitrust Act, passed in 1914, declared illegal the following business practices: (1) price discriminations in interstate trade to the extent that they were destructive of competition; (2) excessive acquisition of one corporation's stock by another; and (3) interlocking directorates in large-scale business enterprises engaged in interstate commerce. The act stipulated that agricultural associations and labor unions were exempt from its terms. The section on labor prohibited the use of injunctions in labor disputes, except in certain cases, and provided that strikes, peaceful picketing, and boycotts were not to be considered practices in restraint of trade and thus were not violations of federal law.

Aid to Labor

Labor leaders exercised an influence on the Wilson administration that was reflected not only in the labor provisions of the Clayton Antitrust Act but also in several separate pieces of legislation.

THE LA FOLLETTE SEAMEN'S ACT

In addition to requiring high standards of safety and sanitation for the crews of American commercial ships, this act, passed in 1915, also regulated the hours, food, and payment of wages to sailors.

THE KEATING-OWEN ACT

This act, passed in 1916, banned from interstate trade articles produced in factories employing children under fourteen years of age. In 1918, however, in *Hammer* v. *Dagenhart*, the Supreme Court declared the act unconstitutional on the grounds that it had the effect of regulating conditions of labor within the state and thus infringed upon powers reserved to the states by the Constitution.

THE ADAMSON ACT

This law, passed in 1916, established the eight-hour workday and the granting of time-and-a-half pay for overtime work for employees of railroads engaged in interstate commerce.

Aid to Agriculture

The Wilson administration lent its support to proposed legislation that would benefit farmers.

THE SMITH-LEVER ACT

This law, passed in 1914, provided for home instruction in farming methods under the joint supervision of the Department of Agriculture and the various state agricultural colleges.

THE FEDERAL FARM LOAN ACT

This measure, passed in 1916, established a farm-loan bank in each of twelve districts of the nation. Cooperative farm-loan associations holding membership in a farm-loan bank were authorized to make available to farmers long-term loans for mortgages at a lower rate of interest than could be obtained at the commercial banks.

AN AGGRESSIVE FOREIGN POLICY

Theodore Roosevelt personally handled the nation's foreign affairs to a degree that none of his predecessors had even approached. His always dynamic and sometimes flagrantly aggressive manner of doing so ensured that other nations would regard with care the role of the United States in world affairs. His style came to be called "big stick diplomacy," a phrase originating from a remark he made before becoming president: "I have always been fond of the West African proverb: 'Speak softly and carry a big stick; you will go far.' "

When Taft succeeded Roosevelt as chief executive, he fully embraced the goal of directing a foreign policy that would increase American participation and influence abroad. To attain that goal he relied on business and financial pursuits, a method called "dollar diplomacy."

The Democrat Wilson determined that the expansionist objectives and techniques pursued by his two Republican predecessors be promptly discarded. He began his administration resolved that its diplomatic basis would be anti-imperialism. He rejected both military intervention in the affairs of weak countries and the use of diplomatic relations to foster American economic enterprise overseas. The new conduct of dealing with the nations of the world would rest on morality. However, despite his declared idealistic approach to diplomacy, realities both at home and abroad were such that Wilson eventually found himself directing a foreign policy that was virtually indistinguishable from that of Roosevelt and Taft.

The Panama Canal

Acquiring island possessions in both the Atlantic and the Pacific dramatically emphasized to Americans the desirability of an isthmian canal between the two oceans under the control of the United States.

THE HAY-PAUNCEFOTE TREATY

In 1850 the United States and Great Britain signed the Clayton-Bulwer Treaty, by which each nation agreed never to exercise exclusive control over nor to fortify an isthmian canal, nor to colonize any part of Central America. But after adhering to the terms of the treaty for half a century, the United States was able to secure cancellation of the agreement in the Hay-Pauncefote Treaty. Signed in 1901, the new agreement permitted the United States exclusively to build and control a canal but stipulated that the use of the waterway should be accorded to all nations on equal terms. Although it was not written into the treaty, in a written communication during negotiations the British conceded the right of the United States to fortify the canal.

THE HAY-HERRAN TREATY

As soon as the Hay-Pauncefote Treaty was concluded, Congress began considering where the waterway should be constructed—in the republic of Nicaragua or in the isthmus of Panama, a province of the republic of Colombia. The proposed route through Panama was chosen, and Congress paid $40 million for the rights to the New Panama Canal Company (a French firm that had tried to build a canal in the 1880s and still held the franchise for the project). The next step was to negotiate with Colombia for a transfer of sovereignty over the strip of Panamanian territory containing the proposed canal route.

In 1903 the Hay-Herran Treaty was signed with Colombia, by which the South American nation granted the United States a ninety-nine-year lease over a canal zone six miles wide, in return for $10 million and an annual payment of $250,000 beginning nine years after the treaty was ratified by both nations. Much to the disgust of President Roosevelt and many other Americans, the Colombian senate rejected the treaty, hoping that an eager United States would then offer better financial terms.

THE PANAMANIAN REVOLUTION

Colombia's refusal to ratify the Hay-Herran Treaty angered large numbers of Panamanians. They foresaw a loss of prestige and income if the waterway were not located in their province. Panama had long felt that it was being misruled by Colombia. During the second half of the nineteenth century inhabitants of the province had engaged in more than fifty uprisings against the national government.

It was no surprise, therefore, when on November 3, 1903, Panama revolted against Colombia and declared itself a republic. The revolutionists were successful because of United States action. Roosevelt ordered a warship to Panama, ostensibly to maintain the free and uninterrupted right of way across the isthmus guaranteed to the United States by a treaty with Colombia 1846. What the vessel accomplished, in fact, was to prevent Colombia from landing troops in the province to suppress the uprising.

THE HAY-BUNAU-VARILLA TREATY

Two weeks after the revolution the United States promptly negotiated with Panama, which Roosevelt had already formally recognized, the Hay-Bunau-Varilla Treaty. The agreement granted the United States the perpetual control of a canal zone in Panama ten miles wide. The new Latin American republic would receive from the United States $10 million and an annual payment of $250,000 beginning nine years after the treaty was ratified by both nations. Ratification was easily achieved on both sides. In 1921, after Roosevelt's death and in a move to bring the United States and Colombia closer together after all that had transpired between them, the Senate approved a treaty that—without providing any reason—called for a payment of $25 million to Colombia.

CONSTRUCTION OF THE CANAL

Excavation for the canal was begun in 1904, but it was hampered by tropical diseases, particularly malaria and yellow fever, among workmen. Colonel William C. Gorgas, a physician in the Army Medical Department, was put in charge of a comprehensive sanitation program. He soon rid the canal zone of malaria and yellow fever. In 1907 Lieutenant Colonel George W. Goethals of the Army Corps of Engineers was appointed to direct the construction job as chief engineer. In 1914 the first ship passed through the Panama Canal.

THE PANAMA CANAL TOLLS ACT

The moral tone Wilson attempted to inject into American diplomacy was evidenced in his solution to the spirited dispute between the United States and Great Britain concerning the use of the isthmian waterway. The Panama Canal Tolls Act, passed in 1912, during the Taft administration, imposed a schedule of tolls upon vessels using the soon-to-be-completed canal but provided that ships of the United States engaged in the coastwise trade were to be accorded free passage through the waterway. Great Britain protested, claiming that the Hay-Pauncefote Treaty stipulated that use of the canal be made available to all nations on equal terms. Americans who defended the act asserted that the phrase "all nations" in the treaty should exclude the United States as the proprietor of the canal—that "all nations" signified, in effect, all *other* nations. Wilson strongly urged that Congress repeal the act on the grounds that the British interpretation of the Hay-Pauncefote Treaty was correct. The legislators complied in June 1914, shortly before the Panama Canal was opened. The administration's success in settling the tolls controversy had the practical effect of winning Great Britain's support for Wilson's dealings with a politically unsettled Mexico.

Relations in the Caribbean

The growing interests of the United States in the Caribbean, tremendously stimulated by the acquisition of the Panama Canal Zone, caused the Roosevelt administration to develop a theory of responsibility for the preservation of order in that area. Under Roosevelt's direction, the Monroe Doctrine was reinterpreted to justify the intervention of the United States in the domestic and foreign affairs of the Latin American nations. Wilson's attitude toward the nations of the Caribbean was less than idealistic, since the opening of the Panama Canal, with the attendant necessity of establishing an appropriate defense of the interoceanic waterway, dictated an American presence in the Caribbean. But Wilson was motivated more by a desire to promote the political and economic stability of the nations close to the canal than to carry out a program of economic imperialism.

THE VENEZUELAN DEBT DISPUTE

In 1902 Great Britain, Germany, and Italy, in an effort to force settlement of the debts owed their citizens by the government of Venezuela, dispatched warships to the South American nation and imposed a blockade of its ports. Roosevelt feared that the debt controversy might lead to a violation of the Monroe Doctrine by the foreign powers involved. By exercising diplomatic pressure behind the scenes, particularly against Germany, Roosevelt helped convince the European nations to decide to grant Venezuela's plea that the issue of the debts be submitted to arbitration. According to the final decision, rendered in 1904, the claims of the European nations were reduced collectively to one-fifth of what they had been, and Venezuela agreed to apply 30 percent of its customs receipts to pay the determined sums.

THE DRAGO DOCTRINE

The Venezuelan incident caused the Argentine minister of foreign affairs Luis M. Drago to formulate a doctrine that a European power must not resort to military intervention to achieve the payment of debts owed its citizens by a Western Hemisphere nation. At the Second International Peace Conference, held in the Hague in 1907, the United States delegation secured the adoption of a resolution supporting a modified version of the original Drago Doctrine: that a nation must not resort to force to collect debts owed its citizens by another nation unless the nation in default refused to submit the matter to arbitration, or, having done so, failed to abide by the decision rendered.

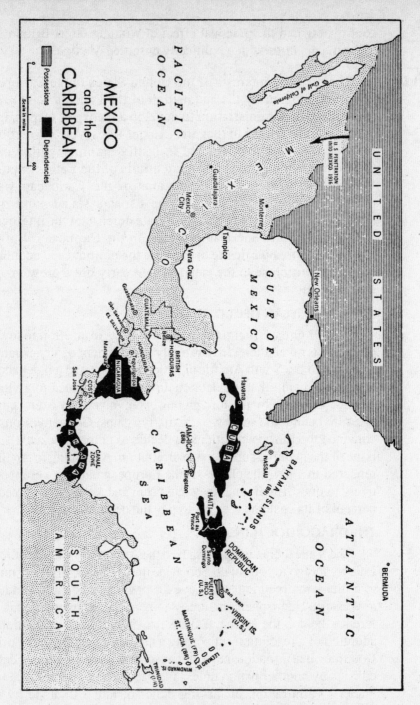

Mexico and the Caribbean

THE ROOSEVELT COROLLARY

As had been the case with Venezuela, the Dominican Republic was heavily in debt to citizens of various European nations. In 1901 France, Italy, and Belgium threatened to use force to collect payment. To prevent such an action, Roosevelt in his fourth state of the union message to Congress, delivered in December 1901, announced: "Chronic wrongdoing, or an impotence which results in a general loosening of the ties of civilized society, may in America" compel the United States "to the exercise of an international police power." This amplification of the Monroe Doctrine came to be known as the Roosevelt Corollary. A new direction in American foreign policy was begun. The Roosevelt Corollary was to lead to intervention by its formulator or one of his successors in the Dominican Republic, Haiti, and Nicaragua.

THE DOMINICAN REPUBLIC

The first application of the Roosevelt Corollary was in the Dominican Republic only weeks after its promulgation. In 1905 the Roosevelt administration negotiated with the Dominican Republic a treaty by which the United States would manage the Caribbean nation's custom houses and oversee the payment of its foreign debts. When the Senate refused to ratify the treaty, Roosevelt carried out the terms of the agreement by executive order. This manifestation of "international police power" was widely criticized in the United States and aroused grave apprehension throughout Latin America.

In 1907 the United States and the Dominican Republic signed a treaty formalizing existing American control of Dominican finances. In 1916 a revolution in the Dominican Republic threatened the treaty arrangements, and military intervention was necessary to maintain the peace. For a number of years a provisional government, supported by American troops, gave the Dominican people orderly rule, despite their protests against the occupation. In 1924 a new treaty on Dominican finances, superseding that of 1907, was signed and American military forces left the nation.

HAITI

After Haiti's creditors in Europe had pronounced the republic bankrupt and threatened to take drastic measures, the Wilson Administration imposed in 1915 a military occupation and forced the Haitian government to sign a treaty that established American control of finances, public works, sanitation facilities, and the police force. The resistance of many Haitians to the occupation caused frequent disorders, but American officials went forward with instituting financial reforms, constructing buildings and highways for public use, and improving sanitation. Not until 1934 were the last of the American civilian administrators and military personnel withdrawn from the republic.

NICARAGUA

In 1912, toward the close of the Taft administration, American marines were landed in Nicaragua to put an end to political disorder there. In the second year of the occupation the Wilson administration negotiated the Bryan-Chamorro Treaty with the Central American republic. Ratified by the Senate in 1916, the treaty granted the United States the exclusive right to construct a canal through Nicaragua, a renewable ninety-nine-year lease to the Great Corn and the Little Corn Islands, and permission to establish a naval base on the Gulf of Fonseca. The marines left in 1925 but returned in 1926 to quell civil disturbances and then stayed until 1933.

PURCHASE OF THE VIRGIN ISLANDS

In 1917 the Wilson administration purchased the Danish West Indies for $25 million, which the United States had been endeavoring to acquire from Denmark for more than a decade. The primary motive behind the acquisition was the desire to use the islands as a naval defense station for the Panama Canal. The United States renamed the territory the Virgin Islands of the United States and instituted a program of limited self-government. In 1927 the inhabitants were made citizens of the United States.

Relations with Mexico

Since the Jefferson administration the United States had given *de facto* recognition (acceptance of a government as the controlling power in reality, although not yet permanently established) to any foreign government that came into being, whatever the circumstances that led it to power. Determined to replace this policy with one that used moral criteria for recognizing foreign governments, Wilson was given an opportunity to do so in dealing with revolution-torn Mexico.

THE REVOLUTION AGAINST DIAZ

In 1910 the long rule of Mexico's despotic president Porfirio Diaz was brought to a close by a revolution led by Francisco I. Madero. The liberal government established under Madero attempted to implement a program of reforms, a notable component of which was the breaking up of large estates and the parceling out of sections to the landless peasants. In 1913 Madero was assassinated in a counterrevolution on behalf of the landholders, led by General Victoriano Huerta, who set up a reactionary regime with himself as provisional president.

THE QUARREL WITH HUERTA

Although more than twenty nations promptly gave *de facto* recognition to the Huerta government, the Wilson administration refused to do so. It charged that the Huerta government did not represent the will of the people and that it was responsible for the murder of Madero. A revolution against Huerta began, led by Madero's former ally, Venustiano Carranza. Wilson announced he would pursue a policy of "watchful waiting." Months later he decided to abandon that policy. He permitted American arms to be shipped to the Carranza faction and set up a blockade of Veracruz to prevent European munitions from reaching Huerta. The Huerta regime retaliated with acts of reprisal against United States citizens in Mexico, culminating in the arrest of a group of American sailors at Tampico in April 1914. Informed that a ship was approaching Veracruz with munitions for Huerta, American troops occupied the city. War between the United States and Mexico seemed imminent.

MEDIATION BY THE ABC POWERS

To avert war, Argentina, Brazil, and Chile (the ABC Powers) volunteered to mediate the dispute, and their offer was accepted. The mediators proposed that Huerta relinquish his office and a government be established that would implement political and economic reforms. Although Huerta formally rejected the proposal, he resigned within a month. In 1915 the United States and a number of Latin American nations, including the ABC Powers, gave *de facto* recognition to a government formed in Mexico with Carranza as president.

THE PURSUIT OF VILLA

Carranza was unable to restrain his former associate Francisco "Pancho" Villa, whose band began to attack resident foreigners and finally, in March 1916, crossed the border and raided Columbus, New Mexico. With Carranza's reluctant consent, Wilson sent General John J. Pershing with 15,000 troops into Mexico to apprehend Villa. This expeditionary force failed to capture Villa, and it was withdrawn in January 1917, as the likelihood of American entry into World War I increased.

Relations with Japan

Japan's easy victories in wars with China and Russia, making it the dominant power in the Far East at the beginning of the twentieth century, convinced many Americans that the Japanese were a threat to the interests of the United States in the area.

ROOSEVELT AND THE RUSSO-JAPANESE WAR

Commercial and territorial rivalry between Russia and Japan in neighboring China and Korea resulted in a war between the two powers in 1904. President Roosevelt realized that an overwhelming defeat of either belligerent would upset the balance of power in the Far East, and he was sure that such unrivaled strength on the part of one nation would adversely affect American interests in the region. He thus intervened to bring the war to an end by inviting the two nations to engage in discussions at which he would serve as mediator.

Representatives from Russia and Japan conducted their negotiations at the navy yard in Portsmouth, New Hampshire, and in September 1905 signed a treaty terminating hostilities. Due largely to Roosevelt's opposition, Japan received neither the financial reparations nor the full territorial gains it had pressed for. In fact, the treaty negotiations began to undermine the friendship that had existed between the United States and Japan since the 1880s, after Japan had been "opened" to the Western world by American commodore Matthew C. Perry. In 1906 Roosevelt was awarded the Nobel Prize for peace for his efforts as mediator.

THE TAFT-KATSURA MEMORANDUM

During the summer of 1905, while the president of the United States was bringing Russia and Japan together at Portsmouth, a secretly drafted document, the Taft-Katsura Memorandum, was signed by the United States and Japan. Under the terms of the memorandum, Japan acknowledged American sovereignty over the Philippines and the United States acknowledged Japanese control of Korea. Further, the two nations pledged to cooperate with each other to maintain peace in the Far East.

WORLD CRUISE OF THE UNITED STATES NAVY

Roosevelt was eager to prevent Japan from interpreting his role in the treaty negotiations ending the Russo-Japanese War as indicating fear of Japanese power. Accordingly, in December 1907, he sent a major part of the United States fleet on a fourteen-month world cruise as a demonstration of American naval strength.

THE ROOT-TAKAHIRA AGREEMENT

The effect of the American naval cruise upon relations between the United States and Japan was immediately realized. While the ships were still under way, Japanese leaders suggested that the United States and Japan attempt to achieve accord on the varied issues relating to the Far East. The result was the Root-Takahira Agreement of 1908, by which the two nations agreed (1) to maintain the *status quo* (the existing state of affairs at the time in question) in the Pacific; (2) to respect each other's territorial possessions in the Pacific; (3) to uphold the open-door policy in China; and (4) to preserve the political independence and territorial integrity of China.

Relations with Europe

Realizing that any upset in the balance of power in Europe could weaken American security, Roosevelt decided to play a role in the diplomatic affairs of the continent. This course of action meant a departure from the established American policy of noninvolvement in purely European concerns.

THE ALGECIRAS CONFERENCE

In 1905 French efforts to establish a protectorate over the North African nation of Morocco clashed with German commercial activity in the region.

Fearing that the conflict over Morocco might start the war in Europe that many had been expecting for years, President Roosevelt arranged for an international conference to settle Morocco's future status. In 1905 the United States and eight European nations, including France, Germany, Great Britain, and Russia, met in Algeciras, Spain. The outcome of the conference revealed the powerful influence of the United States. The formula the delegates accepted for the international regulation of trade, banking, and internal peacekeeping in Morocco did not differ substantially from the American proposals.

THE SECOND HAGUE CONFERENCE

In 1899 twenty-six nations, including the United States, had participated in the International Peace Conference in the Hague, the Netherlands. Known as the First Hague Conference, it had established the Permanent Court of Arbitration for the adjudication of international disputes, which came to be called the Hague Court. The Second International Peace Conference, which was suggested by Roosevelt, took place in the Hague in 1907, with forty-four nations in attendance. The accomplishments of the Second Hague Conference were disappointing. As in the first conference, the limitation of armaments was placed on the agenda with no settlement being reached in the matter. The American delegation pressed for the adoption of a court of international justice, which would be much more comprehensive in scope than the Hague Court. However, this proposal did not succeed. The Second Hague Conference ended with a recommendation for a third conference, but preparations for it were halted when World War I broke out.

Dollar Diplomacy

Unlike his predecessor, Roosevelt, who had used conspicuously aggressive approaches in conducting foreign affairs, Taft was inclined to employ economic means to reach diplomatic objectives. Both supporters and critics of the Taft administration called this policy dollar diplomacy.

THE CHINESE CONSORTIUM

In 1909 Taft's secretary of state, Philander C. Knox, persuaded American financiers to join with their British, French, and German counterparts in a consortium to construct a railroad in China (a consortium is an international business combination created for the financial assistance of another nation or for the control of a particular industry in another nation). Three years later Taft gave his approval to a more ambitious undertaking—a government loan to the newly proclaimed republic of China in which American bankers were invited to participate.

THE EFFECTS OF ECONOMIC EXPANSIONISM

The investment of American money abroad, which so many called dollar diplomacy, was described by Taft as merely an effort "directed to the increase of American trade." He sincerely hoped that American dollars would help American diplomats maintain the balance of power in the Far East, thus perpetuating such foreign-policy interests of the United States as the open-door principle in China and the preservation of the political independence and territorial integrity of that nation. During the first decade of the twentieth century the growth of American foreign investments seemed to follow the pattern of European economic imperialism. However, the American interest in overseas trade rarely led to the attempt to impose political control over foreign lands.

A CONFIDENT SOCIETY

The period 1900–20 was a social era that had a flavor all its own—an all-pervading confidence in the future of the nation that came with the new century. The era's social conditions grew out of two sets of historical circumstances. First, the tremendous industrial expansion in the three decades after the Civil War produced a mass society with new needs and values. Second, a late-nineteenth-century direction in foreign policy resulted in the emergence of the United States as an empire-rich global power. This imperialism added to the characteristics of mass society a chauvinistic awareness of the nation's power and potential.

A result of late-nineteenth-century industrialization and imperialism was the end of the old American society—insulated, detached, restrictive, prim—and the birth of a new. The period 1900–1920 brought the realization to Americans that they were part of a "modern" mass society, to which each individual had a charge to adapt. (Of course there were some who, unwilling or unable to come to terms with this society, tried to salvage the customs and traditions of the old order.) A "modern" America meant, among other things, the following: the struggle of blacks for equality, the employment of women, the tremendous growth of the cities, the arrival and assimilation of a large number of immigrants from eastern and southern Europe, a new philosophy of and methodology for education, a testing of the old religious beliefs, and the extraordinary influence of new advances in technology and medicine.

The Population   Between 1900 and 1920 the population of the United States rose from about 76 million to about 105 million—an increase of approximately 40 percent.

RACIAL AND ETHNIC BACKGROUND

Of the total population in 1900, 66.1 million (87 percent) were whites; 8.8 million (11.4 percent) were blacks; 250,000 were American Indians; and 120,000 were Asians, mostly Chinese and Japanese. By 1920 whites numbered 93.3 million; blacks, 10.5 million; American Indians, 400,000; and Asians, 140,000. Of the white population in 1900, approximately 13.4 percent had been born abroad, while another 20.5 percent had at least one foreign-born parent. As a result of the large immigration (mainly from eastern and southern Europe) during the next two decades, the number of foreign-born increased to 14 million. In 1920, about 85 percent of the black population lived in the South and more than 80 percent of the foreign-born population lived in the North.

EMPLOYMENT

The tremendous extent of American economic growth early in the twentieth century is reflected in national income statistics. In 1900 the total was $36.5 billion; by 1920 it had soared to $60.4 billion. During this period virtually everyone who sought work was able to find it. In 1920 close to 42.5 million persons (including approximately 8.5 million women) were employed. There was a steady percentage decline in those who worked on farms. In 1900 fewer than 40 percent of those employed engaged in farm work; twenty years later fewer than 25 percent did so.

Blacks

In 1900, thirty-five years after emancipation, the vast majority of blacks still lived in the South, where all aspects of life—political, economic, and social—were hard.

CONDITIONS IN THE SOUTH

By the turn of the century southern whites had undone virtually all black advancement of the Reconstruction period and had restored "white supremacy." The number of blacks who could meet suffrage qualifications was steadily reduced, so that by 1900 very few blacks voted. After the Civil War southern plantation owners lost their slaves and had insufficient money to hire laborers. Most turned to sharecropping, a plan that continued well into the twentieth century.

Socially, blacks were kept separated from whites by so-called Jim Crow laws. (The name is believed to be derived from a character in a popular minstrel song.) Beginning in the 1880s statutes that legalized racial segregation were enacted by southern states and municipalities. The Supreme Court in *Plessy v. Ferguson* (1896) decided that a Louisiana law requiring "separate but equal" facilities for whites and blacks on railroad cars was constitutional. This doctrine was soon extended in the South to other public facilities, including educational institutions. The schools for whites were almost without exception superior to those for blacks.

LEADERS

There was disagreement among black leaders on which strategy to employ in the battle for equal treatment in a predominantly white society. The most prominent black leader was Booker T. Washington, who founded Tuskegee Institute in Alabama as a technical school for blacks. Washington advocated that blacks refrain from agitating for political rights and social advancement but instead strive for economic equality with whites through vocational training. He maintained that once blacks had demonstrated diligence and competence in the nation's work force and played a positive role in the nation's economy, substantial gains along political and social lines would surely follow. Many black leaders opposed Washington's position. Among these was the militant and highly intellectual W. E. B. Du Bois, a professor at Atlanta University. Du Bois asserted that while vocational education was good for the majority of blacks, the "talented tenth" should study academic subjects in order to prepare for professional careers that would both satisfy them and enable them to guide their race. Meanwhile, blacks should agitate unflaggingly for complete equality—political, economic, and social.

ORGANIZATIONS

In 1909 a group of whites and blacks founded the National Association for the Advancement of Colored People (NAACP) to combat racial discrimination. The NAACP employed a variety of methods but concentrated on legal action. Much of the organization's efforts was devoted to combating lynchings, of which there were more than 1,300 between 1900 and 1920. In 1910 the National Urban League was organized by a biracial group to help blacks who migrated from the rural South adjust to city life.

The Employment of Women

The most notable change for American women was their increased participation in the job market.

THE VIEWS OF MEN

In 1900 the vast majority of men disapproved of employment for women, who, they asserted, were both mentally and physically unequal to most jobs. They believed that for married women to neglect home responsibilities for outside work was deplorable. Almost all men in labor unions vigorously opposed the unionization of women because they feared competition for jobs.

THE NUMBER AT WORK

The number of employed women soared with rapidly increasing demand for labor caused by tremendous industrial expansion. In 1900 approximately 1.3 million women worked; by 1920 about 8.5 million did so. Virtually all continued to attend to the housekeeping chores after work.

WAGES

Ordinarily, when a woman performed the same job that a man did, she would receive wages about half of his. For women factory workers in 1900, weekly wages of ten dollars or less and a workday of ten hours or more (six days a week) were common.

OPPORTUNITIES FOR THE EDUCATED

There were other job opportunities for women who had the required education. Women (in most places only if they remained unmarried) could pursue careers in teaching, nursing, or secretarial service. Women teachers not only usually received about half of what their male colleagues got for the same duties but were also closely restricted in their social conduct, being expected to maintain a decorous image. Women could become shop clerks, but they had little chance of rising to supervisory positions.

DISCRIMINATION AGAINST BLACK WOMEN

Discriminated against for most types of jobs, black women usually became domestics, earning less than half the pay of white female factory employees and working almost twice the number of hours.

"New Immigrants"

Before the 1880s most immigrants to the United States came from northern and western Europe. Attracted to the West by cheap land, thousands of the "old immigrants" swelled the population of the prairie states of the Mississippi Valley and the Great Plains. Like native-born white Americans in social practices, they adapted well to American society. In the late nineteenth century industrial development created increasing opportunities for workers in the urban centers. Beginning in the 1880s the "new immigrants," from eastern and southern Europe, predominated.

CHARACTERISTICS

Between 1880 and 1920 close to 24 million persons entered the United States. Most of them settled in the cities. Practically all had fled from poverty, but many had fled also from political and religious persecution. The new immigrants, because of language and education barriers and their tendency to cluster in cities, had difficulty assimilating into the dominant American culture.

CONTRIBUTIONS

The new immigrants filled the factories and the shops. Several national groups soon took the lead in particular economic enterprises. Italians built bridges, laid railroad tracks, and dug sewers; Jews from eastern Europe manufactured clothing; Poles, Czechs, and Hungarians mined coal and worked in the steel plants; Greeks operated restaurants. The new immigrants also gave to the older American culture an awareness of Europe's treasures in art, literature, and music. In addition they enriched the language with expressive words and phrases and embellished the diet with ethnic foods that soon became staples of American cuisine.

Asians

During the late nineteenth century the American government suspended immigration from China. Early in the twentieth century it virtually prohibited immigration from Japan.

CHINESE

After the mid–nineteenth century, Chinese laborers were welcomed on the West Coast so long as they were needed for such work as railroad construction. In the 1870s, as it became apparent that, especially in California, the Chinese were competing for jobs with native-born Americans, a movement developed to restrict their immigration. It was maintained that the Chinese were socially unassimilable and that their lower economic life-style endangered the American standard of living. Consequently, in 1882 President Chester A. Arthur signed the Chinese Exclusion Act, which suspended immigration from China for ten years. The exclusion principle was renewed periodically thereafter until 1965.

JAPANESE

Early in the twentieth century California discriminated against the large number of Japanese laborers who had come to the state seeking better job opportunities. Resentment flared in Japan over this situation. What rankled in particular was the action of the San Francisco School Board in ordering all Asian students to attend a separate school. Anticipating a rupture in American-Japanese relations, President Theodore Roosevelt decided to intervene. What followed was a series of diplomatic notes during 1907–1908 between the United States and Japan, embodying the "Gentlemen's Agreement." Japan promised to deny passports to Japanese laborers seeking to emigrate to the United States, while the United States agreed not to prohibit Japanese immigration completely. Although Japan scrupulously observed the agreement, in 1924 the entire body of American immigration regulations was overhauled, and immigration from Japan was totally prohibited.

Growth of Cities

One of the most significant social changes resulting from American industrial expansion was urban growth. As the cities began to offer more and better opportunities for employment, people left the rural areas for urban centers. The growth of cities had a tremendous influence on national thought and action.

RATE OF EXPANSION

At the turn of the century the United States was still predominantly rural. But over the next two decades the urban growth rate was 650 percent greater than the rural growth. In 1900 approximately 33 percent of the population lived in places with more than 8,000 inhabitants; by 1920 the percentage had increased to 44. As for cities, in 1900 only thirty-seven had more than 100,000 residents; twenty years later the number of such cities was sixty-seven.

THE URBAN MIDDLE CLASS

Some of the foreign-born joined the native-born to swell the ranks of the middle class, composed principally of business and professional people, bureaucrats, and some skilled artisans. A segment of this class acquired wealth through the ingenious manipulation of investments in factories, banks, railroads, and mines. Their business methods were generally admired and widely imitated by those who had not attained great financial success. Their power was recognized in all parts of the nation, even if their standards of social conduct and canons of cultural taste were viewed with disfavor by the more sophisticated.

REFORMERS

While most business leaders were involved in adding to their fortunes, a small group of other Americans grappled with the difficult problems presented by the disorderly growth of cities. They strove to provide satisfactory housing, transportation, fire protection, and police service. A few individuals persisted in attacking the poverty, disease, alcoholism, and crime that thrived in the congested byways of the cities. Among the reformers in journalism were Joseph Pulitzer, publisher of the *New York World*; Jacob Riis, reporter for the *New York Evening Sun*; and Lincoln Steffens, writer for *McClure's* magazine. Other reformers included Jane Addams, founder of the Hull House neighborhood center for the poor in Chicago; Lillian D. Wald, who organized a visiting-nurse program in New York City; Carry Nation, a hatchet-wielding smasher of saloon property first in Kansas and subsequently in several other states; and Louis H. Sullivan, a Chicago-based practitioner of a modern architectural style.

Education

Americans were beginning to realize that the home and organized religion were becoming less influential in educating the young. They thus made an ever-increasing commitment to public education to prepare their children for the challenges of a vibrant society.

ELEMENTARY EDUCATION

Elementary education underwent an extraordinary change both in curriculum and in teaching methods. Administrators and teachers began to doubt the traditional belief that the value of education lies in developing mental discipline through arduous abstract learning. Most influential in establishing a new direction for elementary schools was John Dewey, a professor at Columbia University. Dewey maintained that, rather than preparing a child for life, a classroom should be life itself. The teacher should be a knowledgeable and sympathetic guide to classroom activities. Hundreds of professors who had become dedicated followers of Dewey's philosophy prepared elementary schoolteachers to implement his philosophy in the classroom.

SECONDARY EDUCATION

Between 1900 and 1920 enrollment in the nation's secondary schools increased remarkably, from approximately 500,000 to about 2 million. The only goal of secondary education before the turn of the twentieth century was to prepare students for study at a college or university. After 1900, secondary schools assumed other purposes. First, they attempted to develop both intellectual and social skills to meet the challenges of a complex and rapidly changing nation. Second, they added to the college preparatory course other programs, such as commercial studies, industrial technology, and home economics.

Further significant developments were the extension of the high school downward through the establishment of the junior high school and upward through the creation of the junior college.

HIGHER EDUCATION

In 1890 there were approximately 240,000 students in American colleges and universities; by 1920 the number had increased to more than 530,000. The major trend in higher education was the replacement of the fixed curriculum by elective study programs. The trend accepted the idea that individuals at that educational level ought to know what their own needs and interests were and recognized that certain traditional subjects were not in keeping with modern social and scientific developments. Enrollment in graduate schools increased from approximately 500 in 1900 to more than 2,500 by 1920.

Religion

Within the two wings of Christianity—Protestantism and Roman Catholicism—and also within Judaism, there was a split between the conservatives, or traditionalists, who clung to the old doctrines and rituals of their faith, and the liberals, or modernists, who were inclined to test old religious beliefs by the standards of recent social and scientific advances.

PROTESTANTISM

Modernists within Protestantism were drawn to the social gospel movement, whose influential leaders were two ministers, Congregationalist George Washington Gladden and Baptist Walter Rauschenbusch. Through the application of biblical teachings to the social problems resulting from industrialization, the movement attempted to heal economic and social ills—indeed, ultimately to reform industrial society itself. In 1908 the Federal Council of the Churches of Christ in America was organized by more than thirty Protestant denominations and adopted the social creed, which espoused the abolition of child labor, the implementation of safer and more sanitary working conditions for women, the institution of a shorter workday, and the establishment of pensions for retired workers.

Conservatives among Protestant clergy and laymen were apprehensive. They held tenaciously to a fundamentalist (literal) acceptance of every biblical idea and a denial of scientific discoveries that seemed contrary to traditional religious beliefs. Conservative Protestants, strong in rural areas, welcomed traveling evangelist preachers. Among revivalists who proclaimed "old-time" religion, none had more drawing power than the colorful Reverend William A. (Billy) Sunday.

ROMAN CATHOLICISM

In striking contrast to the segmentation within Protestantism, Roman Catholicism enjoyed a notable unity brought about by the Church's highly refined structure and close control of its affairs. In 1907 the Church repudiated modernism insofar as it would weaken traditional religious beliefs. However, it did accept the role of trying to ameliorate harsh economic and social conditions resulting from industrialization. The most striking development within Catholicism in the United States was its increase in adherents, from approximately 9 million in 1890 to more than 18 million in 1920. Much of this increase was due to immigration from the largely Catholic regions of eastern and southern Europe.

JUDAISM

During the first three-quarters of the nineteenth century most Jewish immigrants came from Germany. As a group they quickly became Americanized and soon achieved a good measure of economic and social status. Under the leadership of Rabbi Isaac Mayer Wise, they had developed by 1900 a branch within their faith called Reform Judaism. Although the moral principles of the religion were retained, many rituals and traditions were abandoned. Between 1880 and 1920 approximately 2 million Jews entered the United States, the majority from Russia and Russian-controlled Poland. Fleeing persecution, they tended to cling to Orthodox Judaism, with its emphasis on strict observance of ancient religious laws, rituals, and traditions. During the early twentieth century an ever-larger group, believing that Reform Judaism had gone to extremes and that Orthodox Judaism was not adjusting to the realities of twentieth-century culture, brought forth a program of Conservative Judaism—a position between the other two branches. This period also found the Jews rapidly supplanting Roman Catholics as the main object of whatever religious discrimination there was in the nation.

Technology

As the twentieth century began, Americans were confident, even exhilarated, that technology would soon solve all problems, bringing about "the good life." By 1900 Americans were quite used to such everyday objects as electric lighting, the telephone, and the phonograph, all of which had been invented during the previous quarter of a century. The railroad system, developed during the latter half of the nineteenth century, continued to be instrumental in maintaining a thriving economy. Other inventions—the automobile, the airplane, and the radio—became major influences.

THE AUTOMOBILE

The first practical automobiles were built in the 1890s and were primarily steam-driven vehicles. The best known was the Stanley Steamer. The electric car also enjoyed some popularity. Meanwhile, American automakers experimented with vehicles containing an internal combustion engine that used gasoline. In 1901 Ransom E. Olds, who gave his name to the Oldsmobile, established the assembly-line system of manufacturing cars. A few years later Henry M. Leland, who produced the Cadillac, pioneered the use of expertly engineered interchangeable parts. Both these techniques were fully exploited by automaker Henry Ford.

In 1908 Ford produced the first Model T. Within five years he was producing over five hundred such cars a day, which were popularly referred to as Flivvers and Tin Lizzies. Production mounted rapidly to keep up with the demand. In 1914 Ford introduced the moving assembly line, in which the car's frame moved on a main conveyor belt while other belts brought parts to be used by workmen in assembling the vehicle. By such efficient production methods, Ford managed to decrease the price of his cars almost every year. By 1916 they were selling for less than $400. The American people enjoyed a mobility that they had never before experienced. The automobile industry by 1920 was already the third largest in the nation. In that year close to 2 million automobiles were sold in the United States. The producers of such automobile components as steel, glass, and rubber enjoyed similar expansion, as did the petroleum industry. The need for a comprehensive national network of paved streets and highways was also realized.

THE AIRPLANE

Inventors in the United States and Europe attempted to build a machine that would carry human beings into the air. The American Samuel P. Langley made some notable progress. On December 17, 1903, at Kitty Hawk, North Carolina, the brothers Wilbur and Orville Wright made the first human flight in a power-driven, heavier-than-air machine. Orville piloted the gasoline-powered airplane, staying in the air for twelve seconds and traveling 120 feet. But the development of aviation was slow until its military possibilities were perceived.

THE RADIO

In 1901 the Italian Guglielmo Marconi built a sending station in England and a receiving station in Newfoundland and then picked up the first overseas wireless signals. In 1906 the American Lee De Forest broadcast the human voice for the first time. The following year De Forest made possible long-distance radio communication. In 1910 the first musical broadcast took place in New York City from the Metropolitan Opera House. Woodrow Wilson became the first president to speak over the radio when he addressed American troops returning from Europe after World War I. But the radio did not realize its full potential until the 1920s, when commercial broadcasting began.

Medicine

Medicine enjoyed such progress that Americans became unquestionably healthier.

REFORM OF MEDICAL SCHOOLS

A major indication of progress was the reform of medical schools. As a result of a comprehensive study in 1910, approximately half the nation's medical schools were forced to close, while those that remained greatly improved their courses of study and methods of instruction.

COMBATING DISEASE

Between 1900 and 1920 the national death rate declined from 17.7 to 13.1 per 1,000. These statistics reflect the near eradication of malaria, diphtheria, and smallpox. There was much more effective control (assisted by state and municipal boards of health through improved sanitation programs) of typhoid fever and typhus. Physicians achieved success against syphilis with a European-developed chemical preparation and against tuberculosis with an ever-refined sanatorium treatment. In 1909 the industrialist John D. Rockefeller donated $1 million for the elimination of hookworm disease, from which more than half the children of the South suffered.

A MASS CULTURE

Early in the twentieth century many of the nation's leaders in art, literature, and music made a determined effort to produce works that would appeal to the masses of Americans. At the same time they strove to retain the quality of their output. There were two significant movements in art and literature: realism and naturalism. As for orchestral and operatic music, the nation had not yet come into its own in terms of native-born composers and performers. The musical theater was still greatly influenced not only by American vaudeville but also by European operetta. By 1920 motion pictures were well on their way to becoming the most influential art form—the true art of a mass culture. As art, literature, music, and motion pictures reflected the values of mass culture, so too did the developing popular team sports.

Art

In painting there were important stirrings of a movement called realism, whose roots lay in nineteenth-century European art. American painters in this genre portrayed, without romanticizing, scenes of ordinary life. They were quickly followed by the naturalists, who delineated on their canvases what could be called the ugliness of life. American architecture struck out in excitingly significant changes.

PAINTING

The most influential painters of the late nineteenth century subscribed to the doctrine of art for art's sake: that what the artist painted did not matter; what mattered was how it was painted. This doctrine was popularized by the writings and lectures of James A. McNeill Whistler. His most famous painting is a portrait titled *Arrangement in Gray and Black, No. 1* (1871) but popularly known as *Whistler's Mother*. John Singer Sargent achieved a reputation as a brilliant portraitist. John La Farge is considered the founder of mural painting in the United States.

Two of the greatest realists of the period were Thomas Eakins and Winslow Homer. Younger American painters extended the realism of Eakins and Homer to naturalism. A movement arose called the Eight, or the Ashcan School, which included Robert Henri and John Sloan. Members of the movement dealt with seamy urban scenes. Greatly influenced by the Ashcan School was the painter George Bellows.

In 1913 a group of forward-looking American artists, including Henri and Bellows, organized the International Exhibition of Modern Art in New York City. Popularly called the Armory Show, the exhibition was an introduction of modern art to the American people.

SCULPTURE

The last art in the United States to develop a contemporary mode was sculpture. Although the works of Daniel Chester French varied greatly in both subject matter and style, French excelled in rendering the human figure along realistic lines. His most notable achievement is the stupendous figure of Abraham Lincoln (1922) in the Lincoln Memorial in Washington, D.C. The preeminent sculptor of the period was Augustus Saint-Gaudens, whose figures are distinguished by an energetic, lifelike expression.

ARCHITECTURE

Dominating American architecture from the latter nineteenth century through the early twentieth century was the revival of the Renaissance style and, to a somewhat lesser degree, the classic Greek and Roman styles from which it was derived. These styles were popularized by the architectural firm of McKim, Mead & White. Two of its greatest achievements were the Boston Public Library (1895) and the no longer existing Pennsylvania Railway Station (1910) in New York City.

Louis H. Sullivan propounded the theory that "form follows function"; that is, a building's architecture should be organically related to its use. Sullivan created a style that was both functional and distinctly American. This was readily observable in the early skyscrapers that he designed. The first skyscraper was built in 1884 in Chicago. The design of the sixty-story Woolworth Building (1913) in New York City, produced by the architect Cass Gilbert, greatly influenced the construction of skyscrapers for a number of years.

Literature

The major development in literature during the early twentieth century was the quest for realism and naturalism. Realism in literature is the attempt to portray life objectively. The writers make every effort to observe society without subjectivity, every effort to refrain from idealizing or romanticizing their material. Following close on realism was naturalism, which extended realism as far as possible, portraying life in all its harshness.

THE NOVEL

During the late nineteenth century William Dean Howells was a pioneer of realism. He enormously influenced younger writers and introduced new trends to the American public. His best-known work is *The Rise of Silas Lapham* (1885). Professionally influenced by Howells was his close friend Henry James, who was to become the most skilled writer of realism. Two of his most praised works are *The Ambassadors* (1903) and *The Golden Bowl* (1904). A friend of James's was Edith Wharton. In such novels as *The House of Mirth* (1905) and *The Age of Innocence* (1920) Wharton deals with the emptiness of rigid social convention among wealthy New Yorkers in the early twentieth century.

A notable regionalist author was Willa Cather. Her novels *O Pioneers* (1913) and *My Antonia* (1918) exalt the strength of spirit of immigrant families on the Great Plains. Booth Tarkington established himself as an amiable delineator of the genteel life in the small towns of the Midwest.

Credited with introducing naturalism into American literature is Stephen Crane, who died in 1900 at the age of twenty-nine. His novel *Maggie: A Girl of the Streets* (1893) deals with a young woman who ultimately commits suicide after realizing the hopelessness of life in a slum; his novel *The Red*

Badge of Courage (1895) portrays a young Civil War soldier who gradually rises above cowardice as he sheds his illusions about war and encounters its realities. An influential practitioner of naturalistic writing was Frank Norris. His *McTeague* (1899) is a grim study of San Francisco slum life. *The Octopus* (1901), which treats the struggle between wheat growers and railroad owners, and *The Pit* (1903), which deals with speculation on the Chicago grain market, were significant contributions to the early twentieth-century muckraking movement. Another muckraker was Upton Sinclair, whose novel *The Jungle* (1906) graphically exposes unsanitary conditions in the Chicago meat-packing plants. Jack London also contributed to the development of the naturalistic tradition. His most famous novel is *The Call of the Wild* (1903).

POETRY

The best-known poets of the early twentieth century were William Vaughn Moody, Edwin Markham, Vachel Lindsay, and (Alfred) Joyce Kilmer. Kilmer, who was killed in World War I, achieved fame for "Trees" (1914), containing the well-known lines "Poems are made by fools like me, / But only God can make a tree."

DRAMA

The plays produced in the United States were overwhelmingly those by Europeans. The works of the realists, the Norwegian Henrik Ibsen and the Swede August Strindberg, and the naturalist German Gerhart Hauptmann were exceedingly popular with sophisticated American playgoers. Meanwhile, American dramatists were attempting to establish a distinctly native drama. Clyde Fitch was the period's most successful playwright. Playgoers would have to wait until the 1920s for the advent of a new and vibrant, unmistakably American drama.

Some of the most competent and appreciated actors of the period were John Drew, Ethel Barrymore, and Maude Adams, who in 1905 played for the first time the title role in James M. Barrie's *Peter Pan*.

NEWSPAPERS

A new trend in American journalism began in 1895 when William Randolph Hearst purchased the *New York Journal* and sought to surpass the circulation of Joseph Pulitzer's *New York World*, a well-written newspaper of high standards. Hearst introduced a style that held reader attention by treating the news sensationally, often to the point of distortion. To retain its own readers and capture others, the *New York World* felt compelled to do the same. After 1898 Pulitzer withdrew from the race with Hearst and returned the *New York World* to its more responsible traditions.

During the heyday of the sensationalist press a half-century-old news-paper with a lagging circulation was purchased by Adolph S. Ochs and developed into one of the world's most distinguished newspapers: the *New York Times*.

A development in American journalism that had widespread effects was the emergence of newspaper chains. Edward Scripps started the first chain, which eventually included more than thirty newspapers. However, the most prominent newspaper chain was Hearst's. With an empire that eventually included forty large-circulation newspapers, Hearst exercised a tremendous influence on American society and culture.

Music

During the early twentieth century a number of American symphony orchestras and the Metropolitan Opera House ranked with the world's best musical organizations. But few of the musicians, singers, and conductors and even fewer of the composers were Americans. The musical theater in the United States was greatly influenced by a European source, the operetta, but also by American vaudeville, which had a particular impact on the shows of George M. Cohan and Florenz Ziegfeld.

ORCHESTRAL COMPOSERS AND COMPANIES

The most important American composers were the romanticist Edward MacDowell and the avant-gardist Charles Ives. MacDowell is best known for his piano pieces, but he also wrote numerous orchestral works, including the esteemed *Indian Suite* (1892), which uses American Indian melodies. Ives was a daring innovator in twentieth-century music, employing dissonance and unusual rhythms. His works frequently incorporate elements of American folk music.

The New York Philharmonic Symphony Orchestra, which began in 1842 and is the oldest symphony orchestra in the world, attracted two outstanding conductors: the German-born Walter Damrosch and the Austrian Gustav Mahler, who was also a world-renowned composer. In 1900 the Boston Symphony Orchestra, which was founded in 1881, occupied its new headquarters, Symphony Hall, whose brilliant acoustics immediately placed it in the ranks of the world's greatest concert halls. That same year the Philadelphia Orchestra was founded. Beginning in 1912, under the dynamic and flamboyant leadership of the London-born Leopold Stokowski, it quickly assumed its place as one of the world's finest orchestras.

OPERA

The Metropolitan Opera House in New York City, which was established in 1883, quickly became the foremost operatic company in the United States. The Italian tenor Enrico Caruso made his debut at the Metropolitan in 1903 and was the preeminent star of the house until shortly before his death in 1921. Other outstanding singers of the company were soprano Geraldine Farrar, soprano Emma Eames, and the Italian baritone Giuseppe de Luca.

MUSICAL THEATER

Performances of orchestral music and opera were attended by a small segment of the population, but millions of Americans took delight in the lighter tunes of musical theater.

American operettas had by and large a frankly sentimental plot and contained many highly pleasant, sweeping melodies. The most successful composer of operettas was the Irish-born Victor Herbert. Some of his most popular works were *Babes in Toyland* (1903), *The Red Mill* (1906), and *Naughty Marietta* (1910).

Former vaudevillian George M. Cohan became the jack-of-all-trades in the early twentieth-century American musical theater: He frequently starred in shows that he produced, directed, and wrote the book, music, and lyrics for. Among the most successful of his typically exuberant shows were *Little Johnny Jones* (1904) and *Forty-five Minutes from Broadway* (1906). He composed a host of highly esteemed songs, including "The Yankee Doodle Boy" (1904), "Give My Regards to Broadway" (1904), "You're a Grand Old Flag" (1906), and the most popular American song of World War I, "Over There" (1917).

As a theatrical producer, Florenz Ziegfeld brilliantly fathomed what an audience wanted and gave it to them: elaborate sets, beautiful women in lavish costumes, and top-flight comedians. In 1907 he introduced the first of his annual Ziegfeld Follies, revues that remained popular for almost twenty-five years. Among his stars were the mugging Fanny Brice; the eye-rolling Eddie Cantor; Al Jolson, who in blackface introduced many popular songs, among them "Mammy" and "Swanee"; Will Rogers, who made homely but shrewd comments on current political and social topics; the bulbous-nosed W.C. Fields; and the black woebegone Bert Williams.

MODERN DANCE

Starting early in the twentieth century, and emanating in large part from the creative ideas of American performers, modern dance was in its ascendancy during the late 1930s. The new form's exponents rejected completely the artificial formality with which dance, particularly ballet, had become encumbered. The first and the most influential leader of the movement was Isadora Duncan, who gave performances conveying the ultimate in flowing simplicity and naturalness. Ruth St. Denis, a contemporary of Duncan's, choreographed dances based mainly upon Asian and American Indian themes. In 1915 St. Denis and her husband, the innovative and stylistically virile dancer Ted Shawn, founded the Denishawn dance company, which until its closing in the early 1930s was both a performing troupe and a school. The former helped to gain public acceptance for modern dance; the latter trained performers, choreographers, and teachers.

BANDS

An important facet of American musical activity consisted of band concerts. Many communities organized their own bands, made up of unpaid local citizens, which gave weekly open-air performances throughout the summer season. But paramount in this genre were the professional bands that, during national tours and resort engagements, provided the American people with their best opportunity to listen to a large ensemble of highly skilled instrumentalists led by able directors. The repertory of these bands consisted mostly of marches (attesting to the band's military origins), but they also performed selections from orchestral music, opera, and the musical theater. By far the most famous bandmaster was John Philip Sousa. He also became the nation's best-known composer of band music. His approximately hundred marches include what is almost the official American patriotic march, "The Stars and Stripes Forever" (1897).

After World War I the popularity of concert bands diminished rapidly as the American people's taste in lighter music shifted from the simple sounds of these bands to the sophisticated rhythms of dance bands.

Motion Pictures

In 1900 few imagined that the embryonic motion picture would become the most influential art form (as well as a far-reaching method of communication) of the first half of the twentieth century.

BEGINNINGS

In the United States motion pictures were first projected on a screen in a New York City theater by Thomas A. Edison in 1896. Included in the short program were a dance sequence and part of a boxing match. The first film to relate a sustained story was *The Great Train Robbery* (1903), directed by Edwin S. Porter. In 1905 McKeesport, Pennsylvania, opened the first nickelodeon, a name given to a theater (often a converted storeroom) that showed a motion-picture program, usually with piano accompaniment, for five cents. Within two years approximately 5,000 nickelodeons had begun operation. Soon companies were formed to meet the increasing desire for motion-picture entertainment. Company heads such as Louis B. Mayer, Jesse Lasky, and Samuel Goldwyn became the pioneers of American film production. Hollywood quickly became the nation's movie center, as early film directors went to California because of its good weather with plentiful sunshine, necessary since filming had to be done outdoors.

DIRECTORS

Two famous film directors were D. W. (David Wark) Griffith and Mack Sennett. Griffith introduced such techniques as the flashback, the fade-out, the close-up, panning, and montage. Griffith's masterpiece is *The Birth of a Nation* (1915), a work on the Civil War and Reconstruction whose high technical and artistic merit is unfortunately marred by antiblack bias. Sennett specialized in slapstick comedies. Hallmarks of his films are the wild chasing after wrongdoers by the Keystone Kops and the prancing about of bathing beauties at the seaside.

STARS

By 1920 a number of motion-picture actors and actresses had become "stars." One of the very biggest stars was the incomparable comedian Charlie Chaplin. Mary Pickford ("America's Sweetheart") portrayed endearing, innocent girls. Lillian Gish was invariably a shy victim of life's painful happenings. Theda Bara was the "vamp" (a slang term for a sultry woman who uses her wiles on men). The handsome and muscular Francis X. Bushman was the first "lover" to adorn the screen. Pearl White earned a wide popular following as the heroine in breathtaking serials, such as *The Perils of Pauline* (1914). William S. Hart played the grim-faced, strong-willed cowboy in more than twenty-five westerns.

Sports

From the beginning of the twentieth century the developing popular team sports, exhibiting as they did the worth of group cooperation on the one hand and group competition on the other, both reflected and influenced mass culture, affecting participants and spectators.

BASEBALL

If any sport can be said to be the national game of the United States it is baseball, an outgrowth of the English game of cricket. The first professional baseball team, organized in 1869 in Cincinnati, Ohio, was soon joined by a host of teams in other cities. In 1876 the National League was established; in 1900 the American League was organized. The major leagues began to achieve much success as a number of first-rate players drew fans to baseball parks. Among these were Honus Wagner, Christopher (Christy) Mathewson, and Tyrus (Ty) Cobb.

BOXING

During the post–Civil War period boxing was a less than popular American sport; indeed, it was illegal in most states. In the 1880s it came into its own, largely through the efforts of John L. Sullivan. The world heavyweight boxing champions during the 1890s were Sullivan, James J. Corbett, and Robert P. (Bob) Fitzsimmons. The first heavyweight champion of the new century was James J. Jeffries. John Arthur (Jack) Johnson won the heavyweight championship in 1908, becoming the first black to hold the title. In 1915 he lost the crown to Jess Willard.

FOOTBALL

American football developed from the English game of rugby. In 1869 Princeton and Rutgers played the first intercollegiate game. Walter C. Camp, football coach and later athletic director at Yale University, is often called the father of American football. In 1889 he originated the practice of selecting an annual All-American college football team. More significantly, he devised many of the rules and patterns of play associated with the modern game.

BASKETBALL

In 1891 James A. Naismith, a Young Men's Christian Association physical-education instructor, invented basketball. Seeking a game that could be played indoors in cold weather, he gave his students, divided into two teams, a soccer ball to play with and hung a peach basket at each end of the gymnasium. Most of the rules he devised have remained unchanged. In 1896 the first intercollegiate game was played between Yale and Wesleyan. At the beginning of the twentieth century the game rapidly became popular among both young men and young women in high schools and colleges throughout the nation.

Selected Readings

GENERAL WORKS:

Allen, Frederick Lewis. *The Big Change: America Transforms Itself, 1900–1950* (1952)

Beale, Howard K. *Theodore Roosevelt and the Rise of America to World Power* (1956)

Chambers, John, II. *The Tyranny of Change: America in the Progressive Era, 1900–1917* (1980)

Croly, Herbert. *The Promise of American Life* (1909)

Ekirch, Arthur. *Progressivism in America* (1974)

Faulkner, Harold U. *The Quest for Social Justice, 1898–1914* (1931)

Link, Arthur S. *Woodrow Wilson and the Progressive Era, 1910–1917* (1954)

Link, Arthur S., and Richard L. McCormick. *Progressivism* (1983)

May, Henry F. *The End of American Innocence: A Study of the First Years of Our Own Time, 1912–1917* (1959)

Mowry, George E. *The Era of Theodore Roosevelt, 1900–1912* (1958)

Noble, David. *The Progressive Mind, 1890–1917* (1981)

O'Neill, William. *The Progressive Years* (1975)

SPECIAL STUDIES:

Anderson, Donald F. *William Howard Taft: A Conservative's Conception of the Presidency* (1973)

Beston, Beverly. *Women Vote in the West: The Woman Suffrage Movement, 1869–1896* (1986)

Blum, John M. *The Republican Roosevelt* (1954)

––––––. *Woodrow Wilson and the Politics of Morality* (1964)

Brownlow, Kevin. *Hollywood: The Pioneers* (1979)

Burton, David. *Theodore Roosevelt: Confident Imperialist* (1968)

Chalmers, David M. *The Social and Political Ideas of the Muckrakers* (1964)

Collin, Richard H. *Theodore Roosevelt, Culture, Diplomacy, and Expansion* (1985)

Cooper, John Milton, Jr. *The Warrior and the Priest: Woodrow Wilson and Theodore Roosevelt* (1983)

Cruden, Robert. *Ministers of Reform: The Progressives' Achievements in American Civilization, 1889–1920* (1982)

Franklin, John Hope. *From Slavery to Freedom: A History of Negro Americans* (1974)

Gardner, Lloyd. *Wilson and Revolutions, 1913–1921* (1976)

Handlin, Oscar. *The Uprooted* (1973)

Hoffman, Frederick J. *The Modern Novel in America, 1900–1950* (1951)

Hudson, Winthrop S. *Religion in America* (1973)

Hunter, Sam, and John Jacobus. *American Art of the 20th Century* (1974)

Kelsey, Carl. *The American Intervention in Haiti and the Dominican Republic* (1922)

Knight, Edgar W. *Fifty Years of American Education* (1951)

Kolodin, Irving. *The Story of the Metropolitan Opera, 1883–1966: A Candid History* (1966)

LaFeber, Walter. *Inevitable Revolutions: The United States in Central America* (1983)

———. *The Panama Canal* (1978)

Link, Arthur S. *Wilson* (5 vols., 1947–1965)

Woodrow Wilson: Revolution, War, and Peace (1979)

Marks, Frederick, III. *Velvet on Iron: The Diplomacy of Theodore Roosevelt* (1979)

McCullough, David. *The Path Between the Seas: The Creation of the Panama Canal, 1870–1914* (1977)

Minger, Ralph E. *William Howard Taft and United States Foreign Policy* (1975)

Morris, Edmund. *The Rise of Theodore Roosevelt* (1979)

Mowry, George E. *Theodore Roosevelt and the Progressive Movement* (1946)

Mueller, John H. *The American Symphony Orchestra: A Social History of Musical Taste* (1951)

Munro, Dana G. *Intervention and Dollar Diplomacy in the Caribbean, 1900–1921* (1964)

Nerr, Charles. *An Uncertain Friendship: Theodore Roosevelt and Japan, 1906–1909* (1967)

Oliver, John W. *History of American Technology* (1956)

Penick, James. *Progressive Politics and Conservation: The Ballinger-Pinchot Affair* (1968)

Pringle, Henry F. *The Life and Times of William Howard Taft* (2 vols., 1939)

Rae, John B. *The Road and the Car in American Life* (1971)

Rose, Barbara. *American Art Since 1900: A Critical History* (1967)

Schmitt, Karl. *Mexico and the United States, 1871–1973* (1974)

Thorp, Willard. *American Writing in the Twentieth Century* (1960)

Vazquez, Josefina, and Lorenzo Meyer. *The United States and Mexico* (1985)

Warner, Sam Bass, Jr. *The Urban Wilderness: A History of the American City* (1972)

Wiebe, Robert. *Businessmen and Reform: A Study of the Progressive Movement* (1962)

7

World War I

In the summer of 1914 World War I broke out in Europe between the Allies—headed by Great Britain, France, and Russia—and the Central Powers, led by Germany and Austria-Hungary. President Wilson immediately issued a proclamation of neutrality, warning his people not to be thrown off balance by a "war with which we have nothing to do." However, public sympathy with the Allies and opposition to the activity of the Central Powers eventually brought the United States into the war on the side of the Allies. American military and economic powers were swiftly mobilized to support the war effort and contributed greatly to the defeat of the Central Powers.

In the ensuing treaty negotiations, Wilson's desire for a "peace without victory" was thwarted by the nationalistic demands of the leading Allies and by the failure of the United States Senate to agree on terms for participation in the League of Nations, the new organization created to maintain world security.

A NEUTRAL IN DIFFICULTY

Inspired by the hope that the United States might eventually be able to mediate in the European conflict, Wilson tried to maintain American neutrality—but in vain. An affinity existed between the United States and the principal Allies, based on ethnic, cultural, and, to a degree, diplomatic factors. Bolstering this relationship were the sophisticated Allied propaganda and the ever-tightening financial and commercial links between the American people and the Allied governments. At the same time, an intense aversion to Germany, the leading force of the Central Powers, was rampant in the United States. To many Americans the nation was the epitome of militarism and arrogance. But it was the activity of the Central Powers—chiefly Germany's pursuit of its submarine policy—that prompted the United States to relinquish its neutrality in favor of a declaration of war.

British Maritime Policy

The first difficulties of the United States as a neutral were with Great Britain, whose powerful navy attempted to prevent foreign supplies from reaching the Central Powers.

THE AMERICAN PROTEST

The State Department insisted on the following principles: (1) that a long-range blockade of Germany by Great Britain, the enforcement of which required the British fleet to engage in a wide range of restrictive activity, was not recognized by international law; (2) that the British extension of the internationally accepted list of contraband (goods directly used in maintaining a nation's military force) included commodities such as foodstuffs that had been considered noncontraband (goods useful to the civilian economy of a belligerent nation but not essential to its military activity) in the 1909 Declaration of London, which had codified the rights of belligerents and neutrals during war; and (3) that the British navy had no right to intercept American vessels and seizing goods on board bound for neutral nations such as Sweden, Denmark, and the Netherlands.

THE BRITISH REPLY

Great Britain argued (1) that its definition of contraband should not be restricted by the Declaration of London, since the document had never been ratified by the leading naval powers, including Great Britain; (2) that the doctrine of continuous voyage (the right of a belligerent vessel to stop a neutral ship bound for another neutral nation and seize contraband on board if the *ultimate* destination of the goods were to opposing belligerent territory), which had been upheld in American courts during the Civil War, was being applied to stop shipments from the United States to neutral nations only when it was clear that the ultimate destination was Germany; and (3) that the British government would compensate citizens of the United States for their noncontraband goods seized during a search.

German Maritime Policy

The dispute of the United States with Great Britain over maritime policy was quickly overshadowed by the aggressiveness of Germany's submarine policy, which threatened not only the property but also the lives of American citizens.

SUBMARINE ACTIVITY

In February 1915, Germany declared that the waters surrounding Great Britain and Ireland constituted a war zone in which German submarines would destroy all enemy vessels. To avoid "unfortunate mistakes," the German government warned neutral ships to remain outside the zone and advised citizens of neutral nations to refrain from traveling on Allied ships. The United States protested vigorously against the use of submarines without observing the rule of visit and search (according to international law, a belligerent ship was allowed to stop a neutral ship so that personnel of the former could visit and search for contraband; if none was found, the neutral ship was permitted to continue on its way). Germany complained that the United States was allowing Great Britain to violate its rights as a neutral with impunity. It urged the United States to compel Great Britain to abide by the Declaration of London (which presented the Central Powers with a firm legal basis for extensive trade with neutral nations) and suggested that unrestricted submarine warfare would be abandoned if the United States would cease furnishing the Allies with munitions and other supplies.

THE SINKING OF THE *LUSITANIA*

The potential threat of submarines became real when the British liner *Lusitania* was torpedoed off the Irish coast in May 1915, with the loss of 1,198 lives, of which 128 were American. The ship was carrying contraband but was unarmed. Avoiding the clamor for war by many Americans, President Wilson strove through diplomatic pressure to persuade Germany to abandon its attacks on commercial ships. Between May and July, Wilson sent three notes to the German government regarding the *Lusitania* sinking, insisting on the maintenance of neutral rights and demanding that Germany suspend its policy of unrestricted submarine warfare. Fearing that these notes might lead the United States into war, Secretary of State William Jennings Bryan resigned in protest. He was replaced by the well-known international lawyer Robert Lansing, who supported Wilson's policy. In September 1915, Count Johann von Bernstorff, the German ambassador to the United States, informed the State Department that passenger liners would not be sunk by his nation's submarines without protection of the lives of noncombatants.

THE *SUSSEX* AFFAIR

Despite the assurances from von Bernstorff, miscellaneous reports of submarine tactics caused a sense of distrust in the United States. In March 1916, the French passenger steamer *Sussex* was torpedoed in the English Channel, injuring some on board, including two Americans. Wilson sent an ultimatum to Germany that unless it ended its present methods of submarine warfare, the United States would sever diplomatic relations. The official reply to the United States ("the *Sussex* Pledge") gave assurances that Germany would not sink merchant vessels "without warning and without saving human lives." For the next nine months there was little cause for complaint regarding submarine activities.

The Preparedness Campaign

The struggle to defend American neutral rights was paralleled by a campaign to prepare the nation effectively for the possibility of war.

FOR MILITARY INCREASES

Such figures as former president Theodore Roosevelt, Republican senator Henry Cabot Lodge of Massachusetts, former secretary of war Henry L. Stimson, and General Leonard Wood campaigned vigorously for a comprehensive program of military preparedness. Their pleas were reinforced in molding public opinion by the activities of organizations such as the National Security League, the American Defense Society, and the American Rights Committee.

AGAINST MILITARY INCREASES

To counteract the pressure for increased armaments and military forces, peace organizations such as the American Union Against Militarism, the American League to Limit Armaments, the American Neutrality League, and the Women's Peace Party labored valiantly. President Wilson was initially sympathetic to the aspirations of the antimilitarist groups. As German submarine warfare developed, making the likelihood of war for the United States more apparent, the preparedness movement gained strength. In the spring of 1916 Wilson abandoned his earlier position and appealed to the American people to support an increase in the nation's land and sea forces.

DEFENSE LEGISLATION

The drive for preparedness brought tangible results in 1916 in the form of congressional legislation. The National Defense Act provided for the expansion of the regular army to 223,000 men and the national guard to 450,000. The Army Appropriation Act established the Council of National Defense to formulate plans for the efficient use of the nation's resources in the event of war. The Shipping Act created the Shipping Board to build or buy vessels that in wartime might be operated by the government.

Election of 1916

In a relatively spiritless contest the voters endorsed the policy of neutrality and progressive domestic legislation that Wilson had sponsored. In winning votes, the president proved stronger than his party in almost every congressional district.

DEMOCRATS

The delegates to the Democratic national convention renominated Wilson by acclamation. Their choice for vice-president was the incumbent, Thomas R. Marshall.

REPUBLICANS

In an attempt to reunite their party after the recent Taft-Roosevelt imbroglio, the Republicans gave the presidential nomination to Charles Evans Hughes, an associate justice of the Supreme Court and formerly a liberal governor of New York; Hughes had taken no part in the party disputes of 1912. Roosevelt's vice-president, Charles W. Fairbanks, was chosen for second place on the ticket. When the national convention of the Progressive party nominated Roosevelt for president, as it had four years earlier, he declined, recommending that the party disband and urging his followers to vote for Hughes—all in his determination to defeat Wilson.

THE CAMPAIGN

It soon became apparent that in his effort to please every faction of his party, Hughes was unwilling to take a firm stand on the direction of American foreign policy during this critical period. (He was portrayed by political cartoonists as the "Sphinx.") The most forceful argument of the Democrats was their repeated assertion that Wilson, through his efforts on behalf of neutrality and preparedness, had prevented the nation from becoming involved in Europe's quarrel. Their slogan was "He kept us out of war." The Democrats insisted that a vote for Hughes would mean American intervention in the war raging across the Atlantic.

WILSON'S VICTORY

Wilson carried the solid South and the trans-Mississippi West, except South Dakota and Oregon, for a total of thirty states, while Hughes won all but two of the northeastern states. It was the region from which William Jennings Bryan had drawn his strength in three presidential elections that gave Wilson a margin of 277 votes to 254 in the electoral college.

UNITED STATES ENTRY INTO WAR

By 1917 Germany was encouraged by its army's successes on the Eastern Front as well as by domestic unrest in Russia, which would lead to the eventual collapse of Russian military action. German submarines had inflicted vast losses on Allied shipping. Germany's civilian and military leaders began to believe that unrestricted submarine activity was worth the risks it involved. Even if the United States were drawn into the war, it was concluded, German armed forces would be able to achieve total victory in Europe before American troops could significantly contribute to the Allied war effort.

Efforts at Mediation

Still hoping for a negotiated peace settlement in Europe rather than one imposed by the victors upon the vanquished, Wilson increased his efforts to become the mediator.

THE HOUSE MISSION

During January–February 1916, Colonel House was in Europe on behalf of President Wilson to approach British, French, and German leaders regarding a negotiated peace. At that time, however, both the Allies and the Central Powers were confident that they could achieve military victory and were not receptive to the American efforts.

"PEACE WITHOUT VICTORY"

In December 1916, Wilson strongly urged both belligerent groups to state their war aims. The Allies presented their objectives in terms that meant, in essence, the complete defeat of the Central Powers. Germany, speaking for the Central Powers, merely indicated a willingness to discuss conditions for peace at some future time. Soon thereafter, in January 1917, Wilson, in an address before the Senate, made an eloquent appeal to worldwide opinion for "peace without victory." The proposal found no favor among the belligerents.

German Provocations

The American people became increasingly convinced that war was being thrust upon them by the provocative acts of the German government.

RESUMPTION OF SUBMARINE ACTIVITY

With a blatant disregard for its "Sussex Pledge," Germany announced on January 31, 1917, that it would resume unrestricted submarine warfare. In February the United States replied to the submarine threat by severing diplomatic relations with Germany and arming American merchant ships. Wilson, however, refused to give up his hopes for continued neutrality until he was certain that the Germans would carry out their intention. In March German submarines torpedoed five American merchant ships, killing, in all, thirty-six crewmen.

THE ZIMMERMANN NOTE

A few weeks after the German announcement of resumed submarine warfare, British intelligence agents intercepted and made available to Wilson a note written by German secretary for foreign affairs Arthur Zimmermann to his government's minister in Mexico. Zimmermann suggested that, in the event of war between the United States and Germany, a Mexican-German alliance might be arranged that would enable Mexico to recover Arizona, New Mexico, and Texas—territory it had lost as a result of the 1840s war with the United States. Further, Mexico was to urge Japan to disassociate itself from the Allies and to side with the Central Powers. Wilson had the note released to the newspapers. The nation was outraged.

WILSON'S WAR MESSAGE

The president called for a special session of Congress, which convened on April 2, 1917. In his address to the legislators, after characterizing the German submarine campaign as "warfare against mankind," he asked for a declaration of war against Germany to make the world "safe for democracy." On April 4 the Senate responded by passing a resolution that a state of war existed between the United States and Germany; two days later the House of Representatives concurred.

"OVER THERE"

When the United States declared war, the size of its armed forces was extremely small. In answer to requests from the civil and military leaders of the Allies for extensive troop reinforcements, the American government expended tremendous energy, and after some months the first contingent of soldiers sailed—in the phrase of the most popular American wartime song— "over there."

Military Mobilization

The difficult task of creating a large and effective fighting force was accomplished with notable success. There were approximately 200,000 men in the army when the United States entered the war. Embodying the principle of universal conscription, the Selective Service Act of 1917 required all men between the ages of twenty-one and thirty to register with locally established draft boards. Subsequent legislation lowered the minimum age to eighteen and raised the maximum to forty-five. More than 24.2 million men were registered for the draft, of whom some 2.8 million were inducted into the army. As for enlistments, some 2 million men voluntarily entered the regular army, national guard, navy, and marine corps.

THE ARMY

Army draftees as well as regular army and national guard enlistees were trained at thirty-two camps that were speedily constructed throughout the nation, mostly in the South, where the climate was favorable for military maneuvers. General John J. Pershing, who had recently gained fame as the leader of a punitive expedition into Mexico, was placed in command of the troops sent to Europe—called the American Expeditionary Force (AEF). By the end of the war more than 2 million men had gone overseas, of whom some 1.4 million had engaged in active fighting.

THE NAVY

By the end of the war the navy consisted of more than 500,000 men and approximately 2,000 ships. Admiral William S. Sims was in charge of all naval forces abroad. The navy was responsible for aiding the British fleet in enforcing its blockade of Germany and attacking German submarines on the high seas. Probably the greatest service the American navy rendered was its participation in the convoy system (a group of vessels sailing under the protection of an armed escort). Navy craft accompanied scores of convoys of both troop and freight ships across the Atlantic Ocean to protect them from German submarine attacks. In this way more than 2 million men and more than 5 million tons of supplies reached Europe.

THE "AIR FORCE"

The United States did not possess an air force as a separate military unit. By the end of the war approximately 1,000 airplanes had been produced, but only about 200 actually reached Europe, so that American aviators were forced to rely heavily on British and French aircraft. Invented little more than a decade earlier, the airplane (in World War I it was canvas-covered, relatively slow-moving, and capable of holding only one or two fliers) was used mostly for observation of enemy movements and for light bombing raids. Squadrons of fighter pilots from each of the leading nations contended for supremacy of the air. The United States had more than twenty "aces" (pilots who brought down five or more enemy aircraft), including Captain Edward V. (Eddie) Rickenbacker, who got the record among the American fliers by shooting down at least twenty-five German airplanes.

WOMEN IN THE ARMED FORCES

During World War I, for the first time in the nation's history, women were permitted to become members of the armed forces in fields other than nursing. The army employed several thousand women in civilian capacities only, but the navy officially recruited more than 10,000 women as "yeomanettes" and the marine corps some 300 as "marinettes."

Land Campaigns

When the Germans launched massive offensives on the Western Front in the spring of 1918, American troops engaged in a series of campaigns to push the German army back.

CHÂTEAU-THIERRY

In May 1918, the Germans reached Château-Thierry, forty miles from Paris. American forces, aided by French colonial troops, stopped the Germans at this point.

THE SECOND BATTLE OF THE MARNE

The turning point of the war occurred in July–August 1918, with the Second Battle of the Marne, in which the last great German offensive was repulsed decisively by the Allied armies. Approximately 85,000 American troops participated prominently in this fighting, which took place in the valley of the Marne River.

THE ST. MIHIEL SALIENT

Since the first year of the war the Germans had held the town of St. Mihiel and its surrounding region, called the St. Mihiel salient, because the Germans controlled a deep projection into the Allied side of the trench system. In September 1918, about 500,000 American troops, in their first basically independent action, engaged in four days of bloody fighting that flattened the bulge.

THE MEUSE-ARGONNE OFFENSIVE AND THE ARMISTICE

In September 1918, American forces totaling about 1.2 million men began a major offensive in the Argonne forest along the Meuse River, breaking the German lines. The Meuse-Argonne offensive was an important component of an overall advance launched by Marshal Ferdinand Foch of France, supreme commander of the Allied forces. It started the Germans on their last retreat. As it became evident that the Allies were headed for German territory, resistance collapsed and representatives of a newly established republican government in Germany signed an armistice on November 11, 1918, at Foch's headquarters at Compiègne.

AMERICAN WAR COSTS

World War I was up to that time the nation's second most costly war in lives (the number of deaths in the Civil War was exceedingly high) and its most costly in money. About 54,000 Americans were killed in battle and about 63,000 died of disease. Some 200,000 men were wounded in combat. The United States spent an estimated $24.5 billion, approximately three times the amount disbursed for all of its previous wars combined.

THE HOME FRONT

During the war all Americans at home were asked to cooperate in numerous ways to insure victory. Congress rose above the limitations of partisanship, conferring upon the president the almost unlimited powers that he requested. Representatives of both business and organized labor served on the various governmental units that were created in order to transform the economic activity of the nation into one great war machine. The Wilson administration successfully accomplished the difficult task of mobilizing matériel, labor, transportation, and money and dealt in the sensitive area of molding public opinion in support of the armed conflict.

Mobilizing National Resources

To effectively mobilize the national resources for the prosecution of the war, Wilson fashioned the Council of National Defense. This body oversaw the function of several units, each of which managed a particular aspect of wartime effort.

THE WAR INDUSTRIES BOARD

With New York City financier Bernard M. Baruch as chairma[n]
Industries Board coordinated the activities of all of the nation's i[n]
engaged in the war effort. The agency had as its primary objectiv[e]
increase of production and the elimination of waste. Its functions inclu[d]
the conversion of many existing plants from peacetime to wartime operations, the purchasing of equipment, and the allocation of raw materials.

THE WAR LABOR BOARD

This body was established to arbitrate management-labor disputes in
order to prevent work stoppages, which would impede war production. Since
the War Labor Board was created not by a congressional act but by presidential proclamation, its decisions were not enforceable by law. Nevertheless,
the cooperation of both employers and employees was generally easy to get
because of the pervasive desire on the part of both groups to win the war.

THE FOOD ADMINISTRATION

Headed by Herbert C. Hoover, who had recently organized a successful
relief program for war-ravaged Belgium, the Food Administration controlled
production and distribution, reduced waste, and fixed prices of food, and
promoted the observance of wheatless and meatless days.

THE FUEL ADMINISTRATION

This agency was authorized to stimulate the production, regulate the distribution, and restrict the prices of various coal and petroleum products. The Fuel
Administration encouraged civilians to practice voluntary conservation.

THE RAILROAD ADMINISTRATION

By proclamation Wilson placed the railroads under government control.
The Railroad Administration, with Secretary of the Treasury William G.
McAdoo as director general, operated the lines as a unified system. Coordination of rail transportation during the wartime period resulted in marked
savings of time and energy.

THE EMERGENCY FLEET CORPORATION

Created by the Shipping Board, which had been established in 1916
during the preparedness campaign, the Emergency Fleet Corporation had as
its goal the increase of merchant-vessel tonnage for the war effort. Soon the
United States was building two ships for each Allied vessel sunk by German
submarines.

Financing the War

To raise the large amounts of money needed to conduct the war, the
government used the traditional methods of taxation and borrowing.

...nal income-tax rates were revised upward; an excess-profits tax ...sed on corporations; sales taxes were levied on numerous luxury ...rough expanded taxation the government raised more than $11

...MENT BONDS

...lk of the war expenses, however, was met by borrowing from the ...ugh the sale of government bonds. There were four Liberty Loan drives and a final Victory Loan drive, which brought a total of approximately $20.5 billion into the government coffers.

Mobilizing Public Opinion

The government showed considerable concern about solidifying public opinion in support of the war and suppressing criticism against the war.

THE COMMITTEE ON PUBLIC INFORMATION

Directed by George Creel, a Denver journalist, the Committee on Public Information presented the United States government position on the various aspects of the armed conflict to the people at home and abroad through news releases to the press, as well as through pamphlets, posters, films, and speakers.

MEASURES AGAINST DISSENT

Under the terms of the Espionage Act of 1917 and the Sedition Act of 1918 the government was authorized to suppress any form of dissent that it deemed a hindrance to the war effort. The Espionage Act imposed heavy penalties for spying, sabotage, obstructing military conscription, or encouraging insubordination in the armed forces. The measure also provided for the exclusion from the mails of materials considered by government authorities to be "treasonable." The Sedition Act imposed heavy penalties for speaking or writing about the American form of government or the American armed services in what the authorities considered a "disloyal" manner or for advocating the curtailment of war production.

Approximately 1,500 pacifists and antiwar socialists were imprisoned under these laws, which were criticized by civil libertarians as violations of the First Amendment to the Constitution, which prohibits Congress from interfering with freedom of speech, press, and assembly. However, the Supreme Court upheld the laws on the grounds that the government had authority to prevent a "clear and present danger" to the nation and that free speech, press, and assembly had always been subject to some restraint, especially in time of war. The Court, however, reversed some convictions on the grounds that the defendants' acts had not been proved a "clear and present danger." The Department of Justice acted aggressively in ferreting out persons considered obstructionist, while the postal authorities exercised rigorous censorship over material sent through the mails.

THE LOST PEACE

During the war each Allied government prepared its own list of financial and territorial demands to be imposed upon the Central Powers after the anticipated victory was achieved. (The United States was never officially a member of the Allies, insisting that it be identified as the "Associated Power" of the body of belligerents formally known as the "Allied and Associated Powers.") As personified by President Wilson, the United States sought a nonpunitive settlement. The misfortune of the peace negotiations that took place in Paris was that the collective position of the Allied leaders and the position of the American president were never wholly reconciled. Subsequently, the Senate of the United States refused to ratify the settlement that had been reached, the punitive Treaty of Versailles. In so doing it failed to adopt the document's section containing the idealistic covenant of the League of Nations. Thus the United States withheld its support from the world organization that had been conceived as the means of ensuring that the peace would not be lost.

The Background to a Peace Settlement

After United States entry into the war, President Wilson became by general consent the spokesperson for the Allied cause. While his pleas for a war to make the world "safe for democracy" and for a "peace founded upon honor and justice" stirred people everywhere, he did not succeed in eradicating the spirit of selfish nationalism.

NATIONALISTIC AMBITIONS

Many Allied leaders who had been pleased during the fighting with Wilson's idealistic case against the Central Powers found it difficult when the time came for a peace settlement to reconcile their nationalistic objectives with his altruistic pronouncements. Prime Minister David Lloyd George of Great Britain asserted that Kaiser Wilhelm II of Germany should be hanged and that the Germans should be compelled to pay the Allies for all damages sustained as a result of the war. Premier Georges Clemenceau of France demanded not only financial reparations but also territorial concessions. French security could be accomplished, he insisted, only by keeping Germany stripped of military strength so that it could never again wage war. During the war several Allied nations entered into secret treaties under which they would divide among themselves territory taken from the Central Powers. These agreements contained specific pledges regarding precise territorial gains to be realized by Great Britain, France, and Russia and by such other nations as Italy, Japan, and Romania as an inducement to entering the war on the side of the Allies.

THE FOURTEEN POINTS

On January 8, 1918, Wilson presented in an address to Congress a set of fourteen proposals as the "only possible program" for maintaining peace following the war. These were immediately dubbed the Fourteen Points. The first five points, covering a broad range of international relations, proposed, in essence, (1) the abolition of secret diplomacy; (2) freedom of the seas in peace and in war; (3) the removal of international economic barriers and the establishment of equality of trade; (4) a reduction of armaments; and (5) impartial adjustments of colonial claims. The next eight points pertained to specific cases of political or territorial readjustments concerning Russia, Belgium, Alsace-Lorraine, Italy, Austria-Hungary, the Balkan states, the Turkish empire, and Poland. The fourteenth point was the crowning proposal: A "general association of nations" must be formed to afford "mutual guarantees of political independence and territorial integrity to great and small states alike." The Allied leaders appreciated the Fourteen Points as an aspect of propaganda. However, the ambitious postwar plans those leaders had for their nations kept them from formally adopting the proposals as a basis for peace.

The Peace Conference

Between January and June 1919, the victorious nations met in Paris and sometimes in nearby Versailles to draw up a peace settlement that would be dictated to the defeated nations.

ORGANIZATION

More than sixty delegates from twenty-seven Allied and Associated powers participated in the negotiations. Russia was not represented, for it had withdrawn from the war after the communist revolution and had signed a separate peace treaty with the Central Powers. Germany and the other defeated nations were denied participation in the conference. Major matters were submitted for consideration to the Council of Ten, consisting of two representatives from each of the leading powers in attendance: the United States, Great Britain, France, Italy, and Japan. Most issues were ultimately settled by four men, who were soon known as the Big Four: Wilson, Lloyd George, Clemenceau, and Premier Vittorio Orlando of Italy. Wilson's expansive idealism came into immediate conflict with the narrow nationalism of the other three leaders.

WILSON'S DIFFICULTIES

In Paris Wilson faced the enormous task of making the Fourteen Points the foundation of the peace negotiations. The people of Europe relied upon him to satisfy their nationalistic aspirations and to meet their deep economic and social needs. Wilson was handicapped from the very beginning of the conference. The American people had repudiated the Wilson administration by sending a Republican majority to both the Senate and the House of Representatives in the congressional elections held but a month before the president's departure for Paris.

Wilson's choice of associates for the American delegation—Secretary of State Lansing, Colonel House, former army chief of staff General Tasker Bliss, and retired career diplomat Henry White—shocked and angered Republicans, for Wilson had failed to select an influential member of their party to go to Paris. (White was merely a recognized Republican.) Furthermore, Wilson had engendered ill will in the Senate, which under the Constitution must ratify any treaty to which the nation is to become a party. Not only had he failed to choose one of their number to serve on the delegation, but he had not even consulted the Senate on the appointments he did make. Nor did Wilson cultivate the support of the press, leading to bad relations between the president and reporters when he most needed favorable news coverage. Finally, Wilson failed to reach a preconference agreement with the other leaders regarding the disposition of the secret treaties.

The Treaty of Versailles

The Treaty of Versailles, which was a punitive instrument of peace imposed by the victors, pertained solely to Germany. To complete the settlement officially ending the war, a separate treaty was framed for each of the nations that along with Germany had constituted the Central Powers.

PROVISIONS

The treaty compelled Germany to assume the responsibility of having caused the war. By its provisions Germany was committed to (1) surrender Alsace-Lorraine to France and several border areas to three other surrounding nations; (2) transfer all of its colonies to a mandate system, under which they would be administered by various Allied powers, subject to the general supervision of the newly established League of Nations; (3) reduce its army to 100,000 men; (4) relinquish all warships of a substantial size, all military airplanes, and all heavy guns; and (5) make reparations for the entire cost of the war, which was subsequently fixed at approximately $56.5 billion.

GERMANY'S REACTION

Germany insisted that the burden of the terms imposed upon it was crushing. Furious protests by its leaders over the treaty provisions brought no modification. In June 1919, representatives of Germany, in a sullen mood, signed the document.

The League of Nations

It was anticipated that the newly created association of nations would compensate for the deficiencies of the Treaty of Versailles to secure a long-term peace. All countries except the Central Powers and communist-controlled Russia were asked to affiliate with the world organization.

DRAFTING THE COVENANT

At the conference Wilson achieved his supreme goal of having the covenant of the League of Nations written into the Treaty of Versailles. To gain support for this objective, he had to compromise with the British, French, Italian, and Japanese delegates, who vigorously pressed their particular nationalistic claims. Although Wilson was the chief designer of the League of Nations, he received valuable contributions from a number of people, notably David Hunter Miller of the United States, a lawyer and writer on foreign affairs; Lord Robert Cecil of Great Britain, a holder of a succession of cabinet posts; Leon Bourgeois of France, a former premier and a social philosopher; and Jan Christian Smuts of South Africa, a general and a minister of defense. Wilson also incorporated into the covenant several suggestions made by leading Republicans William H. Taft, Charles Evans Hughes, and Elihu Root.

AIMS

Member nations of the League agreed upon the following aims: (1) to respect and preserve the political independence and territorial integrity of one another; (2) to employ military and economic sanctions against nations resorting to aggression; (3) to present to the League for inquiry all controversies that threatened war; (4) to reduce armaments; and (5) to establish a permanent court of international justice (soon known as the World Court), which would arbitrate disputes submitted to it by contending nations.

STRUCTURE

The final form of the covenant provided for the following structure: (1) an Assembly, composed of delegates from all the member nations, each of which had one vote; (2) a Council, composed of representatives from the five leading powers—the United States, Great Britain, France, Italy, and Japan—and representatives from four other nations elected periodically by the Assembly; and (3) a secretary-general to manage the routine affairs of the League. The League headquarters would be in Geneva, Switzerland.

Senate Rejection of the Treaty

After winning his fight at the peace conference in Paris to have the covenant of the League of Nations incorporated into the Treaty of Versailles, Wilson was to lose his struggle with the Senate of the United States over ratification of the treaty.

WILSON'S APPEAL TO THE NATION

Failing to persuade the Senate Committee on Foreign Relations, which Republican Henry Cabot Lodge of Massachusetts chaired, to recommend ratification of the treaty, President Wilson decided to carry his case in person to the American people. In September 1919, he undertook a speaking tour of the middle and far West. But his trip was cut short when his health broke down and he was compelled to return to Washington. There he suffered a stroke that paralyzed the left side of his face and body. While the president was incapacitated for almost two months, his wife, Edith, and the cabinet as unobtrusively as possible attended to much of his work load. Although Wilson had gained larger and more enthusiastic audiences as his speaking tour proceeded, there was no indication that his appeal had aroused the public to demand ratification.

THE LODGE RESERVATIONS

There was criticism of many sections of the treaty, such as those that dismembered the Austro-Hungarian empire, allotted most of the German colonies under the mandate system to Great Britain and its dominions, and granted to Japan rights in the Shantung province of China. But the hostility to the document was primarily toward the covenant of the League of Nations. In September 1919, a few days after Wilson had begun his speaking tour, the Senate Committee on Foreign Relations proposed more than forty amendments and four reservations to the League covenant. After weeks of debate the treaty came to the actual voting stage, with fourteen reservations (called the Lodge Reservations after the committee chairman) having already been passed and added to it. The Lodge Reservations included, among other things, the following: (1) the United States reserved the right to withdraw at any time from the League of Nations; (2) American military forces could not be used to carry out Article X of the covenant of the League (in which member nations pledged to defend the political independence and territorial integrity of one another against aggression) except by an act of Congress; (3) purely domestic questions were to be excluded from consideration by the Assembly and the Council of the League; (4) a mandate could be accepted by the United States only by congressional consent; and (5) the Monroe Doctrine was wholly outside the jurisdiction of the League. President Wilson asserted that the Lodge Reservations had the effect of nullifying the treaty and urged his supporters in the Senate to vote against the treaty if it were coupled with the reservations.

SENATE DIVISIONS

Members of the Senate were divided on the League issue into four groups: (1) the Democratic supporters of Wilson, who favored the ratification of the treaty without changes, led by Senate minority leader Gilbert M. Hitchcock of Nebraska; (2) the mild reservationists, who were willing to accept the treaty with minor changes; (3) the strong reservationists, who favored the ratification of the treaty but only with the Lodge Reservations, to ensure the protection of American interests, led by Henry Cabot Lodge and (4) the "irreconcilables," a faction of fifteen ultra-isolationists who advocated full rejection of the treaty, led by Republicans William Borah of Idaho, Hiram Johnson of California, and Robert M. La Follette of Wisconsin.

THE FINAL VOTE

On November 19, 1919, the Senate voted on the Treaty of Versailles, rejecting ratification either with or without the Lodge Reservations. A combination of Wilson supporters and irreconcilables had defeated the treaty with its reservations. In the spring of 1920 the Senate returned to a consideration of the treaty and the Lodge Reservations. (At this time a fifteenth reservation was adopted, expressing sympathy for self-government for Ireland.) The final test came on March 19. Some Democrats disregarded Wilson's instructions to vote against the treaty with the Lodge Reservations. Even so, the treaty with reservations received fifty-seven ayes and thirty-nine nays, less than the two-thirds vote necessary under the Constitution for ratification.

AFTERMATH

In May 1920, Congress passed a joint resolution declaring the war with Germany at an end, but Wilson vetoed it. On July 2, 1921, Wilson's successor, Warren G. Harding, signed a similar resolution. Subsequently, treaties that did not provide for a League were negotiated with Germany, Austria, and Hungary (the latter two nations had been newly created from the former Austro-Hungarian empire) and were promptly ratified by the Senate. After his inauguration, Harding said bluntly: "The Administration which came into power in March 1921 definitely and decisively put aside all thoughts of entering the League of Nations. It doesn't propose to enter now, by the side door, back door, or cellar door."

Selected Readings

GENERAL WORKS:

May, Ernest R. *The World War and American Isolation, 1914–1917* (1959)
Millis, Walter. *Road to War: America, 1914–1917* (1935)
Paxson, Frederic L. *American Democracy and the World War* (3 vols., 1936–48)
Tansill, Charles C. *America Goes to War* (1938)

SPECIAL STUDIES:

Bailey, Thomas A. *Woodrow Wilson and the Great Betrayal* (1945)
———. *Woodrow Wilson and the Lost Peace* (1944)
Churchill, Allen. *Over Here* (1968)
Coffman, Edward M. *The War to End All Wars: The American Military Experience in World War I* (1968)
Devlin, Patrick. *Too Proud to Fight: Woodrow Wilson's Neutrality* (1974)

Gelfand, Lawrence E. *The Inquiry: American Preparations for Peace, 1917–1919* (1963)

Gregory, Ross. *The Origins of American Intervention in the First World War* (1977)

Kennedy, David. *Over Here: The First World War and American Society* (1980)

Mee, Charles, Jr. *The End of Order: Versailles, 1919* (1980)

Peterson, Horace C., and Gilbert C. Fite. *Opponents of War, 1917–1918* (1957)

Rudin, Harry R. *Armistice, 1918* (1944)

Safford, Jeffrey. *Wilsonian Maritime Diplomacy* (1977)

Seymour, Charles. *American Diplomacy During the World War* (1934)

Stallings, Lawrence. *The Doughboys: The Story of the AEF, 1917–1918* (1963)

Steinson, Barbara. *American Women's Activism in World War I* (1982)

Stone, Ralph. *The Irreconcilables: The Fight Against the League of Nations* (1970)

8

The 1920s: Peacetime Pursuits

1914	Universal Negro Improvement Association (UNIA) founded
1915	Modern Ku Klux Klan founded
1919	Eighteenth Amendment ratified
	Volstead Act
1919–1920	Palmer raids on communists
1920	Nineteenth Amendment ratified
	Harding elected president
	Lewis, *Main Street*
	Fitzgerald, *This Side of Paradise*
	KDKA is first commercial radio station
1921	Emergency Quota Act
	Budget and Accounting Act
	Sacco and Vanzetti trial
1921–1922	Washington Conference
1922	Fordney-McCumber tariff
	Eliot, "The Wasteland"
1923	Harding dies; Coolidge becomes president
	Time magazine begins publication
	Gershwin, *Rhapsody in Blue*
1924	Quota Act
	Senate committee investigates Teapot Dome scandal
	Coolidge elected president

1925   Scopes trial

       Dreiser, *An American Tragedy*

1926   Hemingway, *The Sun Also Rises*

1927   Coolidge vetoes McNary-Haugen bill

       Sacco and Vanzetti executed

       Lindbergh makes transatlantic flight

       Kern, *Show Boat*

       Armstrong forms his jazz band

       The Jazz Singer with Jolson

1928   Kellogg-Briand Pact

       Hoover elected president

       Clark Memorandum

       O'Neill, *Strange Interlude*

1929   Wickersham Commission appointed

       Agricultural Marketing Act

       National Origins Plan becomes operative

       Stock-market crash

1930   Smoot-Hawley tariff

       Hopper, *Early Sunday Morning*

1931   Hoover Moratorium

1932   Stimson Doctrine

1933   Twenty-first Amendment ratified

In the decade following World War I the Republican party and its newfound conservatism held the loyalty of most Americans. The people of the United States desired to return to the quest of peacetime pursuits. However, nagging economic problems pertaining to taxation, agriculture, and tariffs had to be solved. Tired of war and disillusioned by the treaty-making that followed, the people attempted to withdraw from international commitments. Even so, the three Republican administrations did not withdraw the United States into full isolationism. The unprecedented prosperity that characterized the 1920s proved insecurely founded. The decade ended with the stock-market crash— the prelude to the worst depression in the history of the nation.

RETURN TO "NORMALCY"

Politics in the 1920s saw the old issues disappear. Progressive reform, imperialism, war, treaty-making—all were forgotten. The vast majority of voters, desiring to escape from the challenge of Wilsonian idealism and the responsibilities of world leadership, believed that they were returning to "normalcy" (a campaign term used to good effect by the Republican presidential candidate in 1920) by putting the Republican party back in power.

Election of 1920

The issue addressed most extensively in the 1920 campaign was American entry into the League of Nations. The essence of the election, however, was an expression of disapproval of the Wilson administration, arising out of the animosities of the war years and the disappointments of the postwar period.

DEMOCRATS

At the Democratic national convention there were three front-runners for the presidential nomination: Secretary of the Treasury William G. McAdoo; Attorney General A. Mitchell Palmer; and Governor James M. Cox of Ohio. On the forty-fourth ballot the delegates chose Cox to be the party's stand-ard-bearer. The young Franklin D. Roosevelt of New York, who had achieved distinction during World War I as assistant secretary of the navy, was selected as his running mate. The platform advocated the ratification of the Treaty of Versailles, thus providing for American entry into the League of Nations.

REPUBLICANS

In order to prevent a deadlock between the two leading aspirants to the presidential nomination, General Leonard Wood, who had served in the Caribbean and Philippines, and conservative governor Frank O. Lowden of Illinois, the convention settled upon a little-known party regular, Senator Warren G. Harding of Ohio. For vice-president the delegates named Gover-nor Calvin Coolidge of Massachusetts, who had recently gained fame by breaking a police strike in Boston. The platform straddled the League of Nations issue.

THE CAMPAIGN

President Wilson had stated that if the Treaty of Versailles were rejected by the Senate, the issue would be submitted to the people at the next national election in a "great and solemn referendum." Cox made it clear that, if elected, his first duty would be to press for the ratification of the treaty. As the campaign progressed, Harding vacillated on the League issue even more than his party's platform did.

HARDING'S LANDSLIDE VICTORY

Harding received 16,152,000 popular votes to Cox's 9,147,000. He captured every state outside the Democratic solid South; he even cracked that by taking Tennessee. As one prominent Democrat remarked: "It was not a landslide, it was an earthquake." Harding's great victory signified the people's disapproval of the Wilson administration and their desire to have power transferred to the Republican party.

The Harding Administration

Believing that the Constitution meant to keep presidential power within certain prescribed bounds and fully aware of his own limited ability, Harding allowed the Congress and his cabinet to give the nation the leadership it needed.

THE PRESIDENT

Warren Gamaliel Harding was a handsome man of amiable disposition. He hugely enjoyed the ceremonial functions of the presidency, but he found making decisions on the myriad of matters that demanded his attention to be torture.

THE CABINET

While campaigning for the presidency, Harding announced that if elected he would turn to the "best minds" in the Republican party. Considered by contemporaries to be the most distinguished appointees to the cabinet were Secretary of State Charles Evans Hughes, who was a former governor of New York, a former associate justice of the Supreme Court, and the Republican candidate for president in 1916; Secretary of the Treasury Andrew Mellon, the Pittsburgh industrialist and financier; and Secretary of Commerce Herbert C. Hoover, a mining engineer who had successfully directed a program for the relief of Belgium during World War I. In contrast, Albert B. Fall of New Mexico was made secretary of the interior and Harry M. Daugherty of Ohio was made attorney general; both were friends of the president and both were to bring disgrace to the administration.

The Scandals

Harding placed great confidence in his personal friends and political associates. Some of them betrayed that trust.

THE VETERANS BUREAU

In 1925 Charles R. Forbes, the recently resigned director of the Veterans Bureau, received a two-year prison sentence and a $10,000 fine for bribery and conspiracy. He and his associates had made millions by granting government contracts connected with the care of disabled veterans to private interests.

THE ALIEN PROPERTY CUSTODIAN

Thomas W. Miller, the alien property custodian, accepted a $50,000 bribe in a transaction involving the sale for much less than its value of German property confiscated during World War I. In 1927 Miller was sent to prison for eighteen months and fined $5,000 for conspiracy to defraud the government.

TEAPOT DOME

The major disgrace associated with the Harding administration was known as the Teapot Dome scandal. In 1921 Secretary of the Interior Albert B. Fall, after gaining the support of Secretary of the Navy Edwin Denby, convinced President Harding to transfer from the Navy Department to the Interior Department control of naval oil-reserve land at Teapot Dome in Wyoming and Elk Hills in California. Secretly and without asking for bids, Fall then granted drilling rights to private companies operated by oil producers Edward L. Doheny and Harry F. Sinclair, but not until he had received a "loan" of $100,000 from Doheny and three times that much in cash and World War I bonds as a "gift" from Sinclair.

An investigation was begun in 1923 by a Senate committee headed by Democrat Thomas J. Walsh of Montana. Fall resigned from the cabinet and was soon "lent" $25,000 by Sinclair. The Senate investigation led to an indictment of Fall, Doheny, and Sinclair. Their cases dragged on for a number of years. Meanwhile the government canceled the leases to the oil-reserve land. Finally, in 1929, Fall was convicted of bribery, sentenced to one year in prison, and fined $100,000. He became the first cabinet member in the nation's history to go to jail for dishonoring his office. Both Doheny and Sinclair were acquitted of bribery, although the latter received a prison sentence and fine for contempt of court.

CHARGES AGAINST DAUGHERTY

Evidence was produced disclosing that Attorney General Harry M. Daugherty had received sums of money from liquor dealers who were evading the prohibition statutes. It was also discovered that he had not taken the proper course of action to prosecute Forbes and others in the Veterans Bureau for graft. Further, he was implicated in the matter involving alien property custodian Miller. In 1924 Daugherty was forced by President Coolidge to resign. Two years later he was tried in connection with the Miller case for conspiracy to defraud the government but acquitted.

A New Chief Executive

Vice-President Calvin Coolidge was thrust into the presidency by Harding's unexpected death.

HARDING'S DEATH

On August 2, 1923, President Harding died suddenly of a stroke in San Francisco, as he was returning from an official visit to Alaska. The last months of his life had been darkened by his awareness that some of his close advisors had betrayed him and their public trust. Shortly before his death he realized that evidence of gross political corruption would soon be revealed.

COOLIDGE'S SUCCESSION

By insisting that his associates should help in the investigation of corrupt political acts committed during his predecessor's administration, Coolidge quickly won the confidence of the American people, who admired his courage and personal integrity.

Election of 1924

Coolidge sought the presidency in his own right. With prosperity at its height and the Democrats choosing a compromise candidate as conservative as Coolidge, a Republican victory seemed assured.

DEMOCRATS

Trouble developed in the Democratic ranks over a proposed plank in the platform denouncing by name the Ku Klux Klan, an organization designed to maintain the political supremacy of native-born white Protestants. After prolonged and acrimonious debate, the convention rejected by one vote the inclusion of an anti-Klan plank. The platform that was adopted lashed out at the corruption in the Harding administration and proposed a referendum to decide the issue of United States membership in the League of Nations.

When it came to choosing a presidential nominee, the convention was once again split by the Klan issue. The candidate of the anti-Klan delegates was Governor Alfred E. Smith of New York; the candidate of the pro-Klan delegates (although he repeatedly denied any Klan affiliation) was William G. McAdoo of California, who had been Wilson's secretary of the treasury. After the longest deadlock in the history of national political conventions, the delegates chose on the 103rd ballot John W. Davis, originally from West Virginia, who had become a prominent New York City corporation lawyer. For vice-president the liberal governor Charles W. Bryan of Nebraska, brother of William Jennings Bryan, was nominated.

REPUBLICANS

So successful had Coolidge been in removing the stigma of corruption from his party that he was the virtually unanimous choice of the delegates to the Republican national convention. Chosen as his running mate was Charles G. Dawes, a Chicago banker who had served as first director of the budget. The platform was an appeal to the nation's conservative business interests, already feeling the stimulating influence of more prosperous times.

PROGRESSIVES

The dissatisfaction of the eastern laborers and the western farmers with the two major parties resulted in the formation of a new Progressive party. The third party nominated for president the reform-minded Republican senator Robert M. La Follette of Wisconsin. Selected for second place on the ticket was Democratic senator Burton K. Wheeler of Montana. The platform, drafted by La Follette himself, was largely an expression of labor unrest and agrarian discontent.

THE CAMPAIGN

Davis criticized the Republican party for allowing the recently exposed graft in the Harding administration. In Coolidge's few speeches he did not choose to reply to the Davis indictment. La Follette, whose candidacy was endorsed by the American Federation of Labor and the Socialist party, provided what spirit there was in a rather listless campaign. The strategy of each of the major parties was to frighten the voters with the charge that La Follette was a dangerous radical and to proclaim that the best way to defeat him was to vote for its candidate.

COOLIDGE'S LANDSLIDE VICTORY

In popular votes, Coolidge received 15,725,000; Davis, 8,386,000; La Follette, 4,822,000. Coolidge captured the electoral vote of every state in the East, Midwest (except for Wisconsin), and far West, while Davis secured only the solid South and Oklahoma and La Follette won the electoral vote of his home state alone. The big advantage to the Republicans was that the times were so prosperous that most people were not interested in Davis's attacks on the party in power nor in La Follette's recommendations for reform.

The Coolidge Administration

The executive branch under Coolidge achieved a reputation for rectitude as under Harding it had earned a reputation for wrongdoing. But in terms of policy the Coolidge administration accommodated itself as much as had the Harding administration to the needs of American industry and commerce.

THE PRESIDENT

Coolidge was unpretentious and laconic. While not a creative person, he did possess a respectable amount of common sense.

THE CABINET

Wanting to suggest that there would be a smooth transition from the previous administration to his, Coolidge had retained the Harding cabinet intact. Two members who proved a discomfort because of their involvement in Harding administration scandals were Secretary of the Navy Denby and Attorney General Daugherty; both were let go before the 1924 election.

Election of 1928

The Republican candidate represented the Protestant middle class, while the Democratic nominee was an antiprohibitionist Catholic from the city. With continued prosperity a help, the Republican standard-bearer achieved an easy victory.

DEMOCRATS

The Democratic national convention was quite different from the fractious one four years earlier. The delegates, with merely token opposition, nominated Governor Smith of New York on the first ballot. For his running mate they selected Joseph T. Robinson of Arkansas, the Senate minority leader, who as a southerner, Protestant, and prohibitionist balanced the ticket. The Democratic platform pledged the party to international cooperation (American membership in the League of Nations was not mentioned) and an "honest" attempt to enforce the Eighteenth (Prohibition) Amendment.

REPUBLICANS

A year before the Republican national convention, Coolidge issued a short public statement: "I do not choose to run for president in 1928." This made inevitable the nomination of the highly efficient secretary of commerce Herbert C. Hoover. The Republicans chose Hoover on the first ballot and selected for his running mate Charles Curtis of Kansas, the Senate majority leader. The platform, adopted amid much accord, declared against American entry into the League of Nations and demanded full enforcement of the Eighteenth Amendment.

THE CAMPAIGN

In a number of speeches throughout the nation, Smith urged revision of the prohibition laws and accused the Republican party of giving undue attention to the interests of the business community. Compared with the energetic campaign waged by Smith, Hoover's was rather easygoing.

HOOVER'S LANDSLIDE VICTORY

Hoover received 21,392,000 popular votes to Smith's 15,016,000. Hoover won the electoral vote of forty states, including his opponent's home state of New York and five states—Virginia, Tennessee, North Carolina, Florida, and Texas—from the half-century-old solid South. Smith's race for the presidency seemed doomed from the outset. He was handicapped in the South and Midwest by his antiprohibition views, his Catholic faith, and his connection with Tammany Hall (the Manhattan Democratic political machine). But, more important, the American people were experiencing great prosperity and were in no mood to break the spell that appeared to have been induced by Republican rule.

The Hoover Administration

Upon his inauguration Hoover was hailed as a person who could run the complicated machinery of government with skill and efficiency. Four years later he was rejected by a nation consumed by economic despair.

THE PRESIDENT

Hoover was among the most conscientious of the men who have ever occupied the White House. A man of scrupulously correct behavior, he became stiff in dealing with others during the difficult days of his presidency.

THE CABINET

The Hoover cabinet thoroughly reflected the conservative philosophy of the man who selected it. Members of the official family implemented policies that won the appreciation of the business community. More than half the men in the cabinet were millionaires, including Secretary of the Treasury Andrew Mellon.

DOMESTIC ISSUES

In the post–World War I decade there were persistent economic problems that Americans were reluctant to face. Among them were those relating to taxation, agriculture, and tariffs.

The Mellon Fiscal Policy

Andrew Mellon headed the Treasury Department from 1921 to 1932, holding that position longer than any other person in the nation's history. Hailed by his conservative Republican supporters as the "greatest secretary of the treasury since Alexander Hamilton," Mellon was given more and more freedom to set the fiscal policies of the three Republican administrations of the 1920s, until the depression hit at the end of the decade.

BUDGETARY REFORM

In order to reduce government expenditures, Secretary Mellon advocated a reform of the national budget system. The Budget and Accounting Act, passed in 1921, established the Bureau of the Budget, with a director appointed by the president. It required the president to submit to each session of Congress an estimate of federal income and expenditures. Chicago banker Charles G. Dawes was named the first director of the budget; he became the supervisor of the government's economy campaign.

TAX REDUCTIONS

Mellon and the three presidents under whom he served won the acclaim of businessmen for their efforts to decrease tax rates both on corporations and on individuals in the higher personal income brackets. Although taxes were decreased, the increasing prosperity throughout the 1920s enabled the government to collect more than enough revenue to meet current expenses and to apply the surplus to the steady reduction of the national debt.

CONGRESSIONAL REACTION

Mellon's tax program did not meet with full success in Congress. There a combination of Democrats and rebellious Republicans compelled the Harding administration and the early Coolidge administration to accept higher rates on large personal incomes than the Treasury Department had proposed. This political dissent centered in the farm bloc, representing constituencies of the midwestern "corn belt," which insisted that agriculture receive governmental favors equivalent to those conferred upon industry. However, as prosperity reached unprecedented heights from 1924 until the onset of the depression five years later, the people, through their choice of federal legislators, permitted Mellon to pursue his policy as he saw fit.

Aid to Agriculture

The perennial problem of the relation of agriculture to the industrial order became acute immediately after World War I. Because farmers did not share with businessmen and laborers the great prosperity of the 1920s, the government decided to take steps to help them.

WARTIME PROSPERITY

The demands for food during World War I brought unprecedented good times to American farmers. They were tempted by the phenomenal rise in crop prices to increase the productivity of acreage already under cultivation and to buy more acres for new cultivation. The mechanization of agriculture, which progressed rapidly in response to the needs of the warring nations, brought increasing returns to farmers who chose to use the new methods.

PEACETIME REVERSAL

The farmers' prosperous years were few. Peace brought a quick descent to prewar price levels. From 1919 to 1921 the value of farm products was cut in half. The farmers' plight, to which foreclosed mortgages bore mute witness, was the result of (1) the expanding use of land for agricultural purposes, much of it submarginal; (2) the increased productivity per acre due to improved machines and methods; and (3) the decline of agricultural prices in the world market, where the farm surplus of the United States competed with that of other nations.

THE FARM BLOC

Like the Grangers and the Populists of earlier periods, the farmers, through various new organizations, turned to Congress for relief from economic hardships. The pressure exerted by agrarian groups such as the American Farm Bureau Federation and the Farmers' National Council caused the formation in Congress of a bipartisan farm bloc that worked for legislation providing agrarian relief. As a result, Congress passed the Grain Futures Trading Act in 1921 to prevent manipulation of the grain market; the Cooperative Marketing Act in 1922 to exempt agricultural cooperatives from the antitrust laws; and the Intermediate Credit Act in 1923 to extend agricultural loans on easier terms.

THE McNARY-HAUGEN BILL

The basic problem of agricultural surpluses was addressed by the McNary-Haugen bill, which passed Congress in 1927 only to be vetoed by President Coolidge. Its sponsors, Republican senator Charles L. McNary of Oregon and Republican representative Gilbert N. Haugen of Iowa, modified some of the bill's provisions and secured passage of the revised bill the following year, but again Coolidge vetoed it. The central feature of the plan was that the federal government would purchase at relatively high prices farm surplus staples, such as wheat, corn, and cotton, and sell them in the world market, with whatever losses the government might incur to be made up by an equalization fee (the difference between the fixed domestic price and the unfixed world price) imposed upon producers. It was asserted that the fee plan would operate automatically to curb excessive production of any staple. In vetoing the bill Coolidge reasoned that it sanctioned unwarranted price fixing and was, in fact, an incentive to agricultural overproduction.

THE AGRICULTURAL MARKETING ACT

Upon the recommendation of President Hoover, Congress passed the Agricultural Marketing Act in 1929. It attempted, through the storage of surplus crops, to prevent the already low farm prices from falling to ruinous levels. The act created a Federal Farm Board authorized to extend low-interest loans to agricultural cooperatives. Such loans enabled them to purchase and store surplus farm commodities and then to sell those surplus crops at a time when the market supply was low. The act was criticized by many for not providing incentives to farmers to limit their production. Within four years the not-very-successful Federal Farm Board was disbanded.

The Tariff Issue

Despite the growing realization of the interdependence of manufacturing, agriculture, and trade among the nations of the world, there was a significant increase in tariff barriers after World War I.

THE FORDNEY-McCUMBER TARIFF

This measure represented a decisive return by the United States government to protectionist principles, in keeping with the traditional position of the Republican party. The Fordney-McCumber tariff, enacted in 1922, was an elaboration of the emergency tariff of 1921, which had reversed the notably low rates of the Wilson administration's Underwood tariff. It (1) reduced the number of commodities on the free list; (2) increased the rates on agricultural products; (3) charged the Tariff Commission, established six years earlier, with investigating for purposes of comparison production costs at home and abroad; and (4) empowered the president to revise rates up to 50 percent in either direction whenever it seemed advisable on the basis of the commission's report. In general, the act restored the duty levels of the Taft administration's Payne-Aldrich tariff.

THE SMOOT-HAWLEY TARIFF

This tariff provided for the highest rates in the nation's history. The average duty was approximately 60 percent. In May 1930, Hoover had received a petition signed by more than a thousand prominent economists opposing the passage of the Smoot-Hawley bill and urging a presidential veto if Congress approved the measure. The petition argued that the rates would sharply reduce American trade, a situation particularly harmful during the recently begun depression. Hoover signed the bill in June 1930. Within three years, thirty-three foreign countries had retaliated against the high rates by increasing their rates on American products.

The Speculative Mania

Between 1919 and 1929 the people of the United States experienced a rise in their standard of living more remarkable than any change that had taken place in any previous decade. The vast expansion of business enterprise concealed from many economists the highly speculative nature of this period of unprecedented prosperity, which ended in 1929 with the collapse of the stock market.

THE BUSINESS SCENE

The prosperity of the nation was marked by significant changes in the production, distribution, and sale of goods. Business statistics during the 1920s showed the following conditions: (1) a decline in manufacturing costs resulting from the use of standardized methods of operation and the production of uniform goods; (2) a greatly increased number of stockholders; (3) a proliferation of chain stores; (4) an extension of credit to customers through the use of the installment buying plan; and (5) a significant increase of wages in most industries.

SIGNS OF DANGER

Several disquieting features of those boom years were becoming alarming at the beginning of the Hoover administration: (1) Agricultural profits were lagging far behind industrial profits; (2) wages of factory workers were increasing, but not nearly so rapidly as the prices of manufactured goods; (3) the nation's factories and farms were producing more than American and foreign consumers were able to buy, while the high tariff was curtailing the overseas market; (4) consumers were buying an ever-increasing amount of goods on installment, thereby raising the total of outstanding private debts; and (5) an extremely large proportion of the annual national income was being invested in highly speculative manufacturing, mining, and transportation enterprises.

THE STOCK-MARKET CRASH

Hundreds of thousands of Americans were buying securities (stocks and bonds) on the stock exchange for the first time; and many were acquiring their shares on credit. In late October 1929, a panic developed in the New York stock market. Prices of securities dropped with startling speed to low levels. Over 13 million shares were traded on October 24, soon to be known as Black Thursday. Five days later more than 16 million shares were sold, making October 29, soon to be called Black Tuesday, the worst day in the history of the New York stock market. By November 14 approximately $30 billion in the market value of listed stocks had been wiped out. At no previous period had so many Americans been directly involved with corporate securities. The collapse of the New York Stock Exchange, therefore, was the prelude to economic disaster.

A BASIC ISOLATIONISM

The United States in the 1920s found it difficult to cooperate with other nations in any form of collective action to promote peace, for the feeling among Americans of political isolationism and economic nationalism was exceedingly strong. Nevertheless, the United States did engage in some worthwhile international projects.

Dealings with the League of Nations

During the 1920s the United States gradually abandoned its earlier decision to have no dealings with the League of Nations and increasingly cooperated in the nonpolitical aspects of the League's activities.

PARTICIPATION IN INTERNATIONAL CONFERENCES

American delegates participated in such League-sponsored conferences as those on opium-traffic control in 1924 and on tariff reform in 1927. By the beginning of the 1930s the United States had participated in more than thirty-five League conferences and was retaining a permanent corps of "unofficial observers" at League headquarters in Geneva, Switzerland.

THE WORLD COURT

The Harding, Coolidge, and Hoover administrations all favored having the United States join the World Court, which had been established by the League to arbitrate disputes submitted to it by contending members. In 1926, at the prompting of President Coolidge, the Senate approved the protocol of membership with five reservations, but not all these reservations were acceptable to the Court's member nations. In 1929 former secretary of state Elihu Root sponsored the formulation of a revised protocol that seemed more satisfactory, but the Senate refused to ratify the Root formula.

Although the United States never became a member of the World Court, during the 1920s the League of Nations Assembly appointed as judges to the Court two Americans, Columbia University professor John Bassett Moore and former secretary of state Charles Evans Hughes, both of whom served with distinction. After World War II the functions of the World Court were assumed by the International Court of Justice established under the United Nations. American membership in this court was promptly ratified by the Senate.

War Debts and Reparations

Relations with European nations during the 1920s were seriously affected by efforts to collect the sums that the United States had lent to the Allied governments during and immediately after World War I.

THE FOREIGN DEBT COMMISSION

Many Americans believed that the United States should cancel the war debts, since the Allies had used most of the money to buy war matériel from American firms in order to achieve victory not only for themselves but also for the United States. Congress, however, in 1922 created the Foreign Debt Commission, which negotiated agreements with the various nations on the basis of each debtor's ability to pay. The total indebtedness of seventeen nations was set at approximately $10.3 billion. Payments on the loans and accrued interest were spread over a period of sixty-two years.

THE DAWES PLAN

In 1921 the Allied Reparations Commission, set up under the Treaty of Versailles, had fixed Germany's obligation at approximately $33 billion. Although the United States refused to admit that payment of war debts was contingent upon collection of reparations from Germany to the Allies, this was in fact the case. After Germany defaulted on reparations payments, the United States in 1924 proposed, and the European governments accepted, the Dawes Plan. Named after Chicago banker Charles G. Dawes, it substantially reduced the German obligation, set up a new schedule of reparations payments, and advanced a loan to Germany.

THE YOUNG PLAN

As a result of eventual German objections to the operation of the Dawes Plan, revision of the reparations agreement became necessary. In 1929 a commission of experts headed by American lawyer and businessman Owen D. Young arranged new terms partially contingent upon the American policy concerning the reduction of Allied war debts. Called the Young Plan, it reduced the German obligation to $8 billion, payable over a period of fifty-eight and a half years. Further, it established a bank for international settlements to facilitate reparations payments and other processes of international finance.

THE HOOVER MORATORIUM

So alarming was the financial weakness of Germany in the worldwide depression that in 1931 President Herbert Hoover proposed a one-year postponement on all war debts and reparations. This moratorium was not extended in 1932, but several Allied nations failed to make payments on their debts to the United States, and after two more years all but one nation, Finland, defaulted. As for reparations, after 1931 Germany repudiated the remainder of the amount due. Ultimately the United States collected approximately $2.3 billion in war debts and the Allies received about $4.5 billion in reparations from Germany.

The Antiwar Movement

After World War I there was a spirited crusade against war among many nations. Despite its isolationist attitude, the United States participated in several conferences designed to limit armaments and one conference called to outlaw war.

THE WASHINGTON CONFERENCE

At President Harding's invitation, representatives from Great Britain, France, Italy, Japan, China, Belgium, the Netherlands, and Portugal met in Washington D.C., from November 1921 to February 1922 to discuss a reduction of naval armaments and issues relating to the Pacific. The conference drafted nine treaties, three of which were particularly significant. A five-power treaty was signed by the United States, Great Britain, Japan, France, and Italy, the world's leading naval powers, whereby they agreed to observe a ten-year "naval holiday" in the construction of capital ships (those over 10,000 tons) and to fix the tonnage of their capital ships at a ratio of 5 to 5 to 3 to 1.67 to 1.67, respectively. In order to conform to this ratio some ships already built or in construction by the signatories had to be scrapped. A four-power treaty bound the United States, Great Britain, France, and Japan to respect one another's possessions in the Pacific and to confer in the event that any issue threatened to disrupt harmonious relations in the area. A nine-power treaty, signed by all participants at the conference, guaranteed the political independence and territorial integrity of China and reaffirmed support of the open-door policy in that nation.

THE GENEVA NAVAL CONFERENCE

President Coolidge suggested that the signatories to the five-power treaty of the Washington Conference meet in Geneva, Switzerland, to consider limiting the construction of cruisers, destroyers, and submarines. France and Italy, however, declined to participate. In 1927 delegates from the United States, Great Britain, and Japan deliberated for six weeks without coming to agreement on restricting these smaller vessels.

THE KELLOGG-BRIAND PACT

Developing from a suggestion by French foreign minister Aristide Briand that was supported by American secretary of state Frank B. Kellogg, the pact was signed by fifteen nations in Paris in 1928. Ultimately forty-seven other nations became signatories. The pact declared that the subscribers renounced war as an instrument of national policy and agreed to settle all disputes among themselves by peaceful means. Since no machinery was provided for its enforcement, the Kellogg-Briand Pact proved ineffective.

THE LONDON NAVAL CONFERENCE

The danger of a new naval race caused Great Britain to invite the United States, Japan, France, and Italy to participate in a naval disarmament conference in London in 1930. France and Italy soon withdrew from the proceedings, dissatisfied. The United States, Great Britain, and Japan signed a treaty fixing ratios among themselves for cruisers, destroyers, and submarines and extending to 1936 the naval holiday set by the Washington Conference.

THE GENERAL DISARMAMENT CONFERENCE

Representatives of thirty-one nations, including the United States, began meeting in Geneva early in 1932 to discuss general disarmament. An American proposal for the abolition of all offensive armaments failed to be adopted. After prolonged negotiations interspersed by two long adjournments, the conference came to an end in 1934, having achieved no success.

The Manchurian Crisis

Defying the covenant of the League of Nations, treaties concluded at the Washington Conference, and the Kellogg-Briand Pact, Japan engaged in a military operation to secure control of Manchuria. The United States denounced the Japanese move but was unwilling to apply force to halt it.

JAPANESE AGGRESSION

In September 1931, Japanese troops marched into and then occupied the Chinese province of Manchuria, using as a reason an explosion on the South Manchurian Railroad. Within a year Japan had established a puppet state called Manchukuo.

THE STIMSON DOCTRINE

In January 1932, Hoover's secretary of state, Henry L. Stimson, in identical notes to Japan and China, declared that the United States would not recognize any agreement that impaired the political independence or territorial integrity of China or that adversely affected the open-door policy. This declaration of nonrecognition soon came to be known as the Stimson Doctrine.

THE LYTTON REPORT

Hoover announced that he would cooperate with the League of Nations in the Manchurian crisis, although he was opposed to the use of economic sanctions against Japan then being considered. In December 1931, the League appointed the British Earl of Lytton chairman of a commission, which included an American representative, to investigate the whole matter. The commission's report condemned Japan but also proposed that Manchuria become an autonomous state under Chinese sovereignty but Japanese control. In February 1933, the League adopted the Lytton Report, and the following month Japan gave notice of its withdrawal from the organization.

Relations with Latin America

Presidents Coolidge and Hoover tried to promote a better understanding among the republics of Latin America and the United States.

MEXICO

In the early 1920s first the Alvaro Obregon and then the Plutarco E. Calles administrations in Mexico made efforts to enforce a provision of the 1917 constitution that all mineral resources belonged to the people. American firms operating oil fields and mines in Mexico became alarmed. President Calles's decision in 1925 to dispossess all foreign oil and mining companies brought a warning from Secretary of State Frank B. Kellogg that "the government of Mexico is now on trial before the world."

As tensions mounted, President Coolidge named his close friend, New York City banker Dwight W. Morrow, ambassador to Mexico. Morrow served from 1927 to 1930. His sympathetic and skillful handling of a sensitive situation won him acclaim in both the United States and Mexico, and he succeeded in securing satisfactory modifications of the Mexican Petroleum Law, which restricted foreign corporations. In addition, Morrow mediated a dispute between the Roman Catholic hierarchy in Mexico and the government arising out of legislation nationalizing church property.

PAN-AMERICAN CONFERENCES

At various conferences of the American republics the United States engaged in conciliatory diplomacy toward its neighbors to the south. In 1923 a pan-American conference in Santiago, Chile, adopted a resolution that any dispute between republics of the Western Hemisphere should be settled by peaceful means, a principle the United States formally endorsed. In 1928 President Coolidge, in an opening address to a pan-American conference in Havana, Cuba, stated: "All nations here represented stand on an equal footing." The participating countries signed a treaty providing for the arbitration of virtually all types of disputes in the Western Hemisphere.

THE CLARK MEMORANDUM

In 1928 Undersecretary of State J. Reuben Clark drafted a memorandum that clarified the current American interpretation of the Monroe Doctrine. Approved by both the Coolidge and Hoover administrations, the Clark Memorandum declared that the United States would not again claim the right to intervene in the internal affairs of a Latin American country through "the exercise of an international police power." It thus repudiated the Roosevelt Corollary to the Monroe Doctrine. The Clark Memorandum, which was published by the Hoover administration in 1930, was greeted with much satisfaction throughout Latin America.

RECOGNIZING NEW GOVERNMENTS

In 1931 Secretary of State Stimson declared that the United States would no longer use the criterion of moral basis, first employed by President Wilson, as a test for the diplomatic recognition of a new Latin American government.

THE ROARING TWENTIES

The decade after World War I—the Roaring Twenties—was marked by an almost frenzied acceleration in the tempo of American life and by a desire for personal pleasure. The social ambiance of the 1920s was largely determined by the effects of World War I. During the war there was a suspension of the old-fashioned absolute moral code and the subsequent substitution of a more free and individual morality. This meant, among other things, the weakening of religious influence and parental authority, which permitted such activities as drinking illicit liquor, dancing the Charleston, engaging in uninhibited discussions of sexual matters, and amorous caressing in public.

As a result of their wartime opportunities, blacks showed a newfound dignity. Women also enjoyed increased independence; they had engaged in many new types of jobs as part of the war effort and quickly began to demand greater freedoms as their right. The strict conservation policies of the government during the war included confining the use of grains almost exclusively to food, thus greatly limiting their use for liquor production. This gave impetus to the ultimate success of the long drive for prohibition, which could not be effectively enforced and gave rise to a large-scale traffic in illicit liquor. During the war Americans had also allowed the government to suppress criticism, mobilize labor and other resources, and raise money through bond drives and increased taxation. But the war was over too quickly for the United States to fully expend its ultrapatriotic psychological feelings. Thus after the war the nation permitted itself to deport aliens, to mistrust and mistreat political radicals, and also to accept the idea of "one-hundred-percent Americanism."

Fads

The 1920s were conspicuously abundant in fads.

NEW AMUSEMENTS

People used their leisure time to experience new amusements, including: marathon dancing, flagpole sitting, goldfish swallowing, solving crossword puzzles, and playing mah-jongg (an ancient Chinese game).

ATTIRE

Young men affected low-crowned, flat-topped porkpie hats with a turned-up brim, bell-bottomed trousers, and long raccoon coats; young women took to straight, long-waisted dresses so short that they exposed the knees (sometimes rouged), below which were rolled-down stockings.

POPULAR EXPRESSIONS

The period was notably prolific in the coining of imaginative words and phrases. Some popular expressions were "the bee's knees" and "the cat's meow" for an impressive person or thing, "flapper" for a young woman who rejected constraint and convention in conduct and apparel, and "speakeasy" for a place where illicit liquor was sold.

Blacks

The association of black servicemen with whites during World War I and the high wages earned by large numbers of blacks employed in war industries located in the North gave the nation's blacks a feeling of dignity that they had never before experienced. White racist organizations exploited the resulting feelings of those whites who resented the developing black pride.

MIGRATION TO THE NORTH

During World War I approximately 350,000 blacks moved from the South to the North to work in war plants. After the war blacks continued to go north. During the 1920s burgeoning business enterprises hired black workers, as the white labor supply was curtailed by federal restriction of immigration.

DISCRIMINATION

Although blacks in the North enjoyed political rights, such as voting and running for office, they did encounter economic and social discrimination. The blacks who moved to the North crowded into cities. Black sections containing large numbers of dwellers and limited housing quickly deteriorated physically. Because of their separation from whites through neighborhood housing patterns, black children attended schools that were segregated, not by law but in reality. And the schools for blacks were often inferior to those for whites.

RACIAL PRIDE

The most significant movement among the black masses was racial nationalism. Its most ardent proponent was Jamaican-born Marcus Garvey. In 1914 he founded the Universal Negro Improvement Association (UNIA), which espoused worldwide black unity and emphasized the worth and glory of African civilization. The UNIA dismissed as futile any efforts to achieve integration. Garvey advocated a back-to-Africa program. The UNIA quickly disintegrated after Garvey was convicted of mail fraud related to his activities. But his persuasive appeal to racial pride gave blacks an enhanced self-esteem that had a lasting effect.

The Independence of Women

During the decade American women achieved an increased independence—political, economic, and social.

THE SUFFRAGE

Women voted in large numbers in the presidential election of 1920, the first one open to them. But in general they did not soon "take" to politics. Very few of them ran for public office. Even so, the granting of the vote to women was an important psychological advance in the movement to attain full equality between the sexes.

NEW OPPORTUNITIES IN EMPLOYMENT

There were opportunities for women previously denied them in the business sector. (Careers in teaching and nursing were still the most commonly pursued.) In years past women had been relegated to secretarial service, but they could now aspire to being, for example, writers for advertising concerns, editors for publishing houses, agents for realty firms, or buyers for department stores.

RELIEF IN HOUSEKEEPING

Perhaps the most significant independence that women achieved was that of being relieved of many tedious and time-consuming housekeeping chores. The introduction and developing general use of electrical housekeeping appliances had a revolutionary impact upon women's lives. Although the first refrigerators and washing machines had appeared early in the twentieth century, they were not widely manufactured and sold until the 1920s. In addition to those appliances, a few others, including the vacuum cleaner, were available. Furthermore, new processing methods increased the amount and variety of foods in cans, jars, and boxes. The rapid increase in commercial bakeries eliminated the necessity for housewives to make their own breads, cakes, and pies.

Restriction of Immigration

As a direct consequence of World War I, the United States reversed its traditional immigration policy during the 1920s.

THE DEMAND FOR LIMITATION

Before 1914 the United States permitted virtually unrestricted immigration from Europe, barring only those aliens considered likely to adversely affect public health, safety, or morals. The United States, representing in the minds of many the epitome of the New World, was proud to be an asylum for the oppressed of the Old World. In addition, the nation needed cheap labor to exploit its abundant mineral wealth, to build its railroads, and to operate the machinery in its factories. Yet there was a growing demand for a selective immigration policy.

THE LITERACY TEST ACT

Bills providing for a literacy test for immigrants had been vetoed by Grover Cleveland in 1896, William H. Taft in 1913, and Woodrow Wilson in 1915. Finally, in 1917 Congress succeeded in passing over Wilson's veto an act requiring immigrants to be able to read and write a language, whether English or another.

THE EMERGENCY QUOTA ACT OF 1921

When it appeared to many at the close of World War I that "the world was preparing to move to the United States," Congress rather hastily adopted a policy of restriction. The Emergency Quota Act of 1921 limited immigration from Europe in any one year to 3 percent of the number of each nationality resident in the United States according to the census of 1910. The total number of immigrants who would be permitted to enter the United States was set at approximately 357,000 annually.

THE QUOTA ACT OF 1924

This measure further restricted the number of people permitted to settle in the United States. It limited immigration from Europe in any one year to 2 percent of the number of each nationality resident in the United States according to the census of 1890, with the total number of immigrants set at approximately 164,000 annually. Changing the census base from 1910 to 1890 drastically reduced the quotas of immigrants coming from eastern and southern Europe. It increased the proportion of immigrants from northern and western Europe. As for non-European nations, the act exempted the Western Hemisphere from its terms but totally prohibited immigration from Asia.

THE NATIONAL ORIGINS PLAN

The Quota Act of 1924 called for a set of permanent regulations to take effect three years later, but the calculations for establishing new quotas proved so difficult that the regulations did not become operative until 1929. According to the National Origins Plan, the total number of immigrants from outside the Western Hemisphere was restricted to approximately 150,000 annually. Each country was given a quota based on the proportion that the number of persons of that "national origin" residing in the United States bore to the total American population in 1920. But each European country was permitted to send at least 100 people a year. All immigration from Asia was still prohibited. Although the quota system did not apply to Canada or the independent nations of Latin America, so wide was the latitude for administrative discretion that State and Labor Department officials were able to restrict selectively even nonquota groups by requiring certain qualifications, such as the holding of property. Mexican immigration, for example, was greatly reduced as a result of this administrative action. The National Origins Plan remained in effect until 1965, when the entire body of American immigration regulations was overhauled.

The Labor Movement

With the higher standard of living that the prosperous 1920s made possible, the core of organized labor lost much of its militancy.

MODERATE UNIONISM

Before 1920 organized labor had grown steadily. But in the post–World War I decade it declined both in activity and prestige. The conservative American Federation of Labor reported more than 4 million members in 1920 but fewer than 3 million in 1930. Several circumstances explain the decline in moderate unionism: (1) It clung to its commitment to the craft-type labor organization in an evermore industrialized society; (2) it failed to come to grips with the problem of technological unemployment; (3) it was still disinclined to enroll blacks, who in larger numbers were entering into important trades; (4) it developed nothing to offer unskilled laborers; and (5) it had difficulty making union benefits attractive in the face of increasing company programs of health protection, unemployment insurance, recreational facilities, and profit sharing.

RADICAL UNIONISM

The activities of the radical wing of American labor were curbed by the anticommunist campaign of the federal and various state governments during the post–World War I period. The leftist Industrial Workers of the World never recovered from this onslaught, and by 1925 it had virtually disappeared. In labor circles, workers who were communists at first strove to capture moderate unions by a policy of boring from within, but by the end of the decade they had begun a concentrated drive to form new industrial unions committed to the intensification of the class struggle. In 1928 radical workers were responsible for the establishment in the United States of the Communist party, which, however, was never able to poll more than 60,000 votes for its presidential candidate.

Prohibition

Probably no public issue was so widely discussed during the 1920s as the prohibition of the manufacture and sale of intoxicating beverages.

BACKGROUND

National prohibition was the culmination of a long campaign. From its inception in the early nineteenth century, the movement rested upon the conviction that intoxicants (1) had an injurious effect upon the mind and body; (2) led users into vice and crime, thus constituting a menace to the life and property of others; (3) sent many to asylums and prisons, the maintenance of which required heavy taxes; and (4) reduced workers' efficiency, thus increasing management problems. The organizations particularly effective in the prohibition movement were (1) the Prohibition party, formed in 1869, which in its platform placed destruction of the liquor traffic above every other issue; (2) the Woman's Christian Temperance Union, established in 1874, which undertook a spirited educational campaign; and (3) the Anti-Saloon League, organized in 1893, which mobilized the sentiment of evangelical Protestantism so that it wielded great political influence.

THE EIGHTEENTH AMENDMENT

So successful were the tactics of the Anti-Saloon League that by the fall of 1917 the legislatures of more than half the states had banned the liquor traffic and fully two-thirds of the people of the nation were living in areas that were "dry" by either state or local legislation. In December 1917, Congress passed the Eighteenth Amendment to the Constitution, prohibiting the manufacture, sale, or transportation of intoxicating liquors. Ratification by the required number of states was achieved with ease by January 1919.

THE VOLSTEAD ACT

This act, passed over President Wilson's veto in October 1919, provided the machinery for implementing the Eighteenth Amendment. It defined as intoxicating any beverage containing one-half of 1 percent alcohol. Administration of the act was assigned to the Bureau of Internal Revenue, a division of the Treasury Department. There were major obstacles to successful enforcement of the Volstead Act, including (1) the opposition to national prohibition of some communities, especially larger cities; (2) the lack of cooperation between federal and local authorities; (3) the corruption of some enforcement agents, who accepted bribes from illicit-liquor traffickers; and (4) the failure of the Treasury and Justice departments to centralize control of enforcement services.

Disrespect for law continually increased. The consumption of illicit liquor became widespread, as did bootlegging (the illegal production or distribution of intoxicating beverages). There was extensive smuggling of liquor from other nations. Rival bootlegging gangs like those of Alphonse (Al) Capone and Dion O'Banion battled each other to retain or expand their areas of operation in Chicago. The difficulties of making the Volstead Act effective caused opponents of prohibition to denounce the Eighteenth Amendment as a failure.

THE WICKERSHAM COMMISSION

In 1929 President Hoover appointed the National Commission on Law Observance and Enforcement. Known as the Wickersham Commission after its chairman, former attorney general George W. Wickersham, the body was charged with conducting an investigation of prohibition and related problems of law enforcement. In 1931 the commission submitted its report, which declared that prohibition was not being effectively enforced but recommended further trial of the Eighteenth Amendment and the Volstead Act.

THE TWENTY-FIRST AMENDMENT

In February 1933, Congress passed—and by December 1933 the required number of states had ratified—the Twenty-first Amendment, which repealed the Eighteenth Amendment. Thereupon control of the liquor traffic reverted to the states. All but eight promptly permitted the manufacture and sale of intoxicating liquors under various types of regulation.

Antiradicalism

During the 1920s fear pervaded the nation that radicalism might destroy American traditions. Even the moderate reforms of the recent progressive era came under suspicion. As a result, some who had been reformers in their younger years now gained prominence as defenders of the existing economic and social order.

THE "RED SCARE"

The success of the 1917 communist revolution in Russia convinced many Americans that the communists ("Reds") and their sympathizers were using the postwar turmoil to secure political power elsewhere in the world, including the United States. Law-enforcement agencies, both federal and state, were put on their guard against radical uprisings. In the fall of 1919 Attorney General A. Mitchell Palmer authorized raids on both acknowledged and alleged communists, resulting in the arrest of more than 4,000 persons, many of whom were apprehended and held in violation of their constitutional rights. At the end of 1919 almost 250 aliens whose views were regarded as dangerously radical were deported to the Soviet Union.

In the spring of 1920 the raids were ended, but that fall a bomb exploded on Wall Street, killing thirty-eight people, sending a wave of fear across the nation, and contributing greatly to the antiradical fervor. Palmer asserted that the Reds were ready to "destroy the government at one fell swoop." By the beginning of 1921, however, the Red scare had abated.

THE BOSTON POLICE STRIKE

A dispute in Boston between the police commissioner and members of the police force over the policemen's right to affiliate with the American Federation of Labor led to a strike in the fall of 1919 involving about three-fourths of the force. To prevent the collapse of law enforcement, Calvin Coolidge, then governor of Massachusetts, dispatched the state militia to the city. Although Coolidge had taken action after Boston was already under control, he won widespread approval by his statement "There is no right to strike against the public safety by anybody, anywhere, anytime."

THE SACCO-VANZETTI CASE

Fear of radicalism was evident in the handling of the case against two acknowledged anarchists, Nicola Sacco and Bartolomeo Vanzetti. In 1921, despite inconclusive evidence, the men were found guilty of murdering a paymaster and a guard in the course of a robbery at a shoe factory in South Braintree, Massachusetts. They received the death sentence, which was stayed for a number of years by appeals from many people both in the United States and abroad who felt that the two men had been convicted because of their anarchist beliefs rather than the evidence presented. They were finally executed in 1927. The Sacco-Vanzetti case forced large numbers of Americans to reappraise their fears of radical views and those who held them.

THE KU KLUX KLAN

The most notorious manifestation of organized hatred was the Ku Klux Klan. Founded in 1915 in Atlanta, Georgia, by a former itinerant preacher, William Joseph Simmons, the organization took firm root in the Deep South, then spread rapidly throughout the nation after 1920, achieving extraordinary success in the Midwest. The Klan drew its membership primarily from the villages and small towns that had been left rather undisturbed by the immigration, industrialization, and liberal thought of modern America. The post–Civil War Klan had attacked mainly blacks, but the Klan of the 1920s added anti-Catholic, anti-Semitic, and antiforeigner sentiments to its creed. So many members, especially in the South, belonged to the evangelical sects that the public came to think that religious fundamentalism was a Klan article of faith. The secret order was preoccupied with the question of morals. Some Klansmen took vigilante action, including "night riding," that might culminate in tarring and feathering, whipping, branding, emasculation, hanging, or burning at the stake.

Although the Klan publicly denied playing a role in politics, it did control the political affairs of many local communities, did elect a number of state officials and some members of Congress, and was a force in the presidential races of 1924 and 1928. In the latter year, when the Democratic party's standard-bearer was the Catholic Alfred E. Smith, the spirit of the Klan was indeed a major factor in the desertion of almost half the states of the solid South to the Republican candidate. At the height of its activity in the mid-1920s the Klan had an estimated 4 million members. But as a result of the nation's increasing wrath toward the organization, by the beginning of the 1930s the membership had withered away to scarcely 50,000.

Religion

Conservative alarm over radicalism had a counterpart in the area of religion, as many were apprehensive that the changing mood of the nation would weaken traditional religious beliefs.

LIBERALS VERSUS CONSERVATIVES

The liberals among Protestant clergy and laymen feared that a fundamentalist (literal) acceptance of every biblical idea and a denial of the discoveries of science would separate the Christian churches from any interaction with modern culture. At times the liberals were inclined to test traditional religious beliefs by the standards of the twentieth century. The conservatives, or fundamentalists, feared that the liberal interpretation of the Scriptures would destroy the power of Protestantism to maintain its evangelical influence in human affairs.

THE SCOPES TRIAL

Among conservative Protestant laypeople none defended their position more forcefully than William Jennings Bryan, who urged state legislatures to prohibit teaching the theory of evolution in the public schools. When John T. Scopes, a young teacher in Dayton, Tennessee, was indicted in a test case for presenting the evolutionary theory to his high-school biology class, Bryan himself served on the prosecution staff. Scopes's defense attorney was Clarence Darrow, the most famous trial lawyer of the period. The arguments of the two distinguished counselors focused the attention of the world on the 1925 trial. Scopes was found guilty of violating the state law and fined $100. The weaknesses of fundamentalist beliefs in opposition to modern science were exposed, however, and thereafter the fundamentalist cause steadily declined.

Technology

The widespread use of automobiles brought about vast changes in the way Americans lived. Many people realized that before long airplane travel would have a similar effect.

THE AUTOMOBILE

Car sales in the United States climbed from approximately 2 million in 1920 to about 4.5 million in 1929. Over half the cars purchased during the early 1920s were manufactured by the Ford Motor Company. In 1929 three firms—the General Motors Corporation, Ford, and the Chrysler Corporation—dominated American automobile manufacturing. By the end of the decade over 21 million cars were on the roads. The automobile in the 1920s revolutionized American society. It gave the people true mobility, freeing regions of the nation from isolation and thus standardizing customs and manners. It brought rural and urban areas closer together. It created the new industry of tourism. It stimulated the growth of the steel and rubber industries, both of which were important suppliers to car manufacturing. It also promoted construction of paved roads.

THE AIRPLANE

The cancellation of government contracts for military aircraft at the end of World War I was a severe setback to the aviation industry. The Post Office Department helped a bit by opening an airmail route between New York City and Washington, D.C., in 1918, but it was eight years before Congress granted subsidies to commercial airlines for carrying the mails.

In 1919 a New York hotel owner offered a $25,000 award to the aviator making the first nonstop flight from New York to Paris. Airmail pilot Charles A. Lindbergh won the award. On May 20, 1927, he took off from Roosevelt Field, in Garden City, Long Island, and made a thirty-three-and-a-half-hour solo flight across the Atlantic Ocean in his airplane *The Spirit of St. Louis.* He landed at Le Bourget Field near Paris amid pressing crowds. This thrilling flight impelled Americans to focus on the vast possibilities of aviation. Some months before Lindbergh executed his feat the Department of Commerce, under the provisions of the Air Commerce Act of 1926, began (1) to establish and regulate a nationwide system of airways (routes designated for regular travel by commercial aircraft carrying passengers, goods, and mail); (2) to aid in the construction of municipal airports; and (3) to set up intermediate landing fields. By 1929 there were forty-eight airways with a combined length of 20,000 miles, serving thirty-five cities that possessed airports. The United States was well on its way into the air age.

Medicine

Perhaps the outstanding stride in American medicine during the 1920s had to do with the treatment not of physical but of mental dysfunction.

PSYCHOANALYSIS

Toward the end of the nineteenth century the Viennese physician Sigmund Freud developed psychoanalysis as a means for treating mental disorders. After World War I Freudian theories gained wide acceptance among American professionals. Freud maintained that mental illness originates in the repression of sexuality and that, in order to cure such illness, the subconscious memories of the sexual repression have to be drawn into consciousness. To accomplish this Freud developed the two main techniques of psychoanalysis: the interpretation of the patient's dreams, which he believed are clues to the subconscious, and free association, in which the patient relates to the psychoanalyst his thoughts without any effort to control them.

INFLUENCE OF THE FREUDIAN THEORY

The influence of Freudianism in the United States (as in the rest of the Western world) on the treatment of the ills of the mind was, of course, enormous, but so too was its impact upon society and culture. Sex became a respectable topic for consideration in the fields of education and religion. Soon the popularizers seized upon psychoanalysis and in a myriad of books, magazines, and newspapers (often less than precise) familiarized the people with the subject's essence and terminology. The idea of investigating the unconscious mind was extensively used in art, particularly painting, and in literature in the stream-of-consciousness device (presenting a character's manifold thoughts and feelings as a flowing process, without reference to logical discourse or a connected sequence).

A VIBRANT CULTURE

Virtually all aspects of American art moved in courses that had been set during the period from the late nineteenth century to World War I. In literature, the novel was still bound by the realism and naturalism of the two preceding decades, but poetry and drama took new approaches both in subject matter and style. To the field of light music the United States made two important contributions: musical comedy and jazz. A revolution oc-curred in the motion-picture industry with the invention of sound film. In sports, professional athletics became big business.

Art

Although painting, sculpture, and architecture continued in the same decades-old trends, there was one notable new development: the emergence of photography as an art form.

PAINTING

American painters were still influenced by the movements developed before World War I. Edward Hopper carried on the tenets of the Ashcan School. *Early Sunday Morning* (1930), evoking a feeling of stark emptiness, is a typical work. One of the many painters who held to abstractionism or semi-abstractionism was John Marin. He worked in vivid watercolors, with scenes of New York City and the Maine seacoast as his most frequent subjects. Each object is represented in semi-abstract form by a few brush-strokes.

SCULPTURE

Lorado Taft, who both worked in and taught sculpture in the Midwest, exerted great influence on that art. He was prolific, specializing in large-scale memorials and fountains. The best-known early sculptures of Gutzon Borglum include two studies of Abraham Lincoln. His masterpiece is the Mount Rushmore National Memorial in the Black Hills of South Dakota.

PHOTOGRAPHY

Perhaps the most significant development in American art during the 1920s was the transition of photography, an approximately seventy-five-year-old science that produced a pictorial record, into an art form. The commanding figure in this movement was Alfred Stieglitz. Immediately preceding and during the first half of the 1920s he produced his most critically acclaimed works, including portraits of his wife (the artist Georgia O'Keeffe), views of Manhattan, and studies of clouds.

Literature

American novelists were still influenced by the realism and naturalism of the early 1900s, continually refining the techniques of these genres. The poets, however, rejected the older forms of their craft and sought innovative approaches. The playwrights produced truly American drama liberated from European influence.

THE NOVEL

With the works of novelists such as Sinclair Lewis, F. Scott Fitzgerald, and Ernest Hemingway, realism became so securely established that a return to idealizing or romanticizing material appeared almost impossible. Sinclair Lewis won fame for his works decrying the values and activities of middle-class life in such novels as *Main Street* (1920) and *Babbit* (1922). F. Scott Fitzgerald is regarded as the principal literary interpreter of the Roaring Twenties with his novels *This Side of Paradise* (1920), *The Beautiful and the Damned* (1921), and *The Great Gatsby* (1925). Ernest Hemingway established himself as one of the most highly praised writers of the 1920s with the publication of two novels, *The Sun Also Rises* (1926) and *A Farewell to Arms* (1929), both of which throw doubt upon the generally accepted values of American and European society. Hemingway's literary style, pointedly and elegantly concise, was greatly admired and much imitated by many contemporary writers.

Carrying on in the naturalistic tradition was Theodore Dreiser, who was to become the period's commanding novelist. His most acclaimed novel, *An American Tragedy* (1925), is the story of a poor and weak-principled young man's ruinous quest for wealth and social position. Sherwood Anderson was a significant writer who rejected both realism and naturalism and focused on a psychological analysis of his characters. His most impressive novel is *Winesburg, Ohio* (1919).

Important for her influence on Fitzgerald, Hemingway, and Anderson is the American author Gertrude Stein, who had a salon in Paris frequented by many European and American artistic and literary figures. Stein originated the term "lost generation" to characterize the disillusioned American intellectual expatriates of the post–World War I period. Stein's own writing is experimental; sound frequently takes precedence over meaning, as in her most famous line, "Rose is a rose is a rose is a rose."

POETRY

Most of the great poets of the 1920s produced works that were so different in form from what had appeared before that Americans of even the preceding generation would not have identified them as poetry. The new poets repudiated the traditional verse form of systematized rhyme and measured rhythm in favor of what came to be called "free verse," and they explored different approaches to accepted syntax and punctuation.

Still holding to the traditional verse form but employing a natural vernacular mode of expression rather than a formal literary one were two New Englanders, Edwin Arlington Robinson and Robert Frost. Frost, possibly the most widely read twentieth-century American poet, wrote verse linked to the people and land of New England. Expressing the ambiance of the Midwest were Carl Sandburg and Edgar Lee Masters. Many of Sandburg's poems are about the common people of farms and industrially developing cities; he treats with a loving sensitivity their economic and social distress and their yearning for a better future. Masters's most important work is *Spoon River Anthology* (1915), a group of epitaphs in free verse uttered by men and women buried in a cemetery. Singular in its pessimism is the poetry of Robinson Jeffers.

Of the decade's great poets, Ezra Pound and T. S. (Thomas Stearns) Eliot were the most original and also the most influential. Their works marked a decisive break with the content and form of nineteenth-century poetry, and their styles became standards for other poets. The poems of both are characterized by profound scholarship. Pound's most significant work is a group of over a hundred poems called the *Cantos*, the first of which was published in 1925 and the last thirty-five years later. The work is an effort to reveal the long and varied story of all the divisions of humankind. Like Pound, the St. Louis–born Eliot spent most of his life in Europe. His poems are extremely complex, using language intricately and containing abstruse references to a diversity of literatures, myths, and religions. His masterpiece "The Wasteland" (1922) caused a stir in the literary world when it appeared.

DRAMA

The 1920s marked the "golden age" of American drama. In their successful attempt to free American theater from European influence and create a native drama, many playwrights, led by the towering Eugene O'Neill, engaged in bold experimentation.

O'Neill is considered the greatest playwright the United States has ever produced. He almost singlehandedly brought about a fundamental change in American drama. The realism and the naturalism in his plays gave their stamp to American drama from the early 1920s on. O'Neill discarded the well-known content and form of past drama and offered to American playgoers strikingly original works. His continued experimentation in subject matter and style encouraged other dramatists to follow suit. His more than a dozen plays of the 1920s exhibit, as do his later ones, an extraordinarily wide range of subject matter and form and include *The Emperor Jones* (1920), *Anna Christie* (1921), and *The Hairy Ape* (1922). *Strange Interlude* (1928) is a detailed psychological study of a woman and her relationships with the three men in her life: her husband, her lover, and her longtime friend. In this play O'Neill uses the spoken "asides" of the Elizabethan drama to let the characters reveal their thoughts.

Two other major dramatists of the period, Sidney Howard and Elmer Rice, were also involved with experimentation. Howard is best known for *They Knew What They Wanted* (1924). Rice's most famous work is the naturalistic *Street Scene* (1929).

Among the most celebrated dramatic performances of the decade were the playing of the title roles by John Barrymore in 1922 in Shakespeare's *Hamlet* and by Walter Hampden in 1923 in Edmond Rostand's *Cyrano de Bergerac*.

THE HARLEM RENAISSANCE

The 1920s saw a flourishing of culture, especially in literature, among black Americans. This surge of creativity is commonly referred to as the Harlem Renaissance, since it was centered in the predominantly black section of New York City. Three outstanding writers of the Harlem Renaissance were James Weldon Johnson, Countee Cullen, and Langston Hughes.

NEWSPAPERS AND MAGAZINES

The most significant development in American journalism was the growing popularity of tabloids. The first one was the *New York Daily News*, founded in 1919. Within half a dozen years it had the largest circulation of any of the nation's newspapers. In 1924 two more tabloids entered the field, the *New York Daily Mirror* and the *New York Daily Graphic*. Competing for reader interest, the tabloids gave extensive coverage to events dealing with crime, particularly murder, and sex.

In periodical publishing the most notable advance was the appearance of a large number of general-interest magazines in addition to the established ones that catered to a special-interest readership. Many of these new publications made a striking impact by using photographs and illustrations. Within a few years the general-interest magazines enjoyed large circulations. Among the most popular was *Reader's Digest*, a pocket-size monthly begun in 1922 that condensed articles from other periodicals. Another notable triumph in periodical publishing was *Time*, a weekly news magazine founded in 1923 by Henry R. Luce and Briton Hadden. *Time's* success motivated the founding of two other influential weekly news magazines, *Newsweek* and *U.S. News and World Report*, both of which began publication in 1933. Magazines that were influential among sophisticated Americans were *The Saturday Review of Literature*, which appeared in 1924, and *The New Yorker*, which was founded in 1925.

Music

During the 1920s the nation's premier bodies engaged in the field of orchestral music and opera continued to perform at a high artistic level. The decade also saw the rapid development of the musical comedy.

ORCHESTRAL COMPANIES AND CONDUCTORS

During the 1920s three of the world's foremost conductors—the Dutchman Willem Mengelberg, the German Wilhelm Furtwängler, and the Italian Arturo Toscanini—held successive posts with the New York Philharmonic Symphony Orchestra. The Boston Symphony Orchestra appointed two distinguished conductors, the Frenchman Pierre Monteux and the Russian Serge Koussevitzky.

OPERA

Throughout the 1920s Giulio Gatti-Casazza, as general manager, maintained the high artistic standards of the Metropolitan Opera House. Among the company's celebrated singers were soprano Rosa Ponselle, the Italian tenor Giovanni Martinelli, and the Russian bass Feodor Chaliapin.

MUSICAL THEATER

The traditional style of American operettas was carried on by composers Rudolf Friml and Sigmund Romberg. Two of the Bohemian-born Friml's most successful operettas were *Rose Marie* (1924) and *The Vagabond King* (1925). The Hungarian-born Romberg composed more than seventy-five operettas, of which the best known were *Maytime* (1917), *Blossom Time* (1921), *The Student Prince* (1924), *The Desert Song* (1926), and *The New Moon* (1928). Among the most popular of his songs are "Sweetheart" from *Maytime*; "Deep in My Heart" from *The Student Prince*; and "Lover Come Back to Me" and "Stout-Hearted Men," both from *The New Moon*.

After World War I American operettas gradually yielded their hold on the public to musical comedies, in which dancing, both solo and chorus, assumed an importance equal to that of the singing. The musical-comedy form that quickly developed was to become one of the most important contributions to theater by the United States. Vincent Youmans wrote the scores for a number of successful musicals, among them *No, No, Nanette* (1925) and *Hit the Deck* (1927).

Toward the end of the 1920s composers such as Jerome Kern and George Gershwin tended to select more realistic stories and to write more sophisticated songs, often with lyrics that conveyed a serious message. Kern wrote numerous successful musicals, including *Sally* (1920), *Show Boat* (1927), and *Roberta* (1933). His outstanding work was *Show Boat*, adapted from the novel of the same name by Edna Ferber, which features the song "Ol' Man River." Gershwin composed several critically acclaimed musicals, most of them in collaboration with his brother, lyricist Ira Gershwin. Among them were *Lady, Be Good!* (1924), which includes the song "Fascinating Rhythm"; *Oh, Kay!* (1926), with "Someone to Watch over Me"; *Funny Face* (1927), with "'S Wonderful"; and *Of Thee I Sing* (1931), with "Who Cares?" Gershwin's most ambitious and widely admired theater piece was *Porgy and Bess* (1935), a folk opera depicting southern black life and from which come the much-esteemed songs "Summertime," "I Got Plenty o' Nuttin'," and "It Ain't Necessarily So." Gershwin also turned his considerable talent to composing orchestral works, such as *Rhapsody in Blue* (1923) and *An American in Paris* (1928), both of which blend the elements of jazz with the classical musical forms.

JAZZ

Perhaps the only truly American art form in the history of world culture is jazz. This music is characterized by syncopated rhythm and contrapuntal ensemble playing, the interspersing of vocal renditions with instrumental performance, and most of all by improvisation of the players. Throughout the 1920s black composers and performers dominated jazz. In the early years of its popularity, jazz was also called ragtime. Among the best-known ragtime pianists was Scott Joplin. By 1910 another form of jazz, the slow melancholy blues, overtook ragtime in popularity. W. C. (William Christopher) Handy composed by far the most popular songs of this type, including "Memphis Blues" (1912) and "St. Louis Blues" (1914).

By the 1920s large numbers of southern black musicians had gone north, most to New York City and Chicago. Among them was Joseph "King" Oliver, who led the much-acclaimed Creole Jazz Band, which included such musicians as trumpeter Louis "Satchmo" Armstrong and cornetist Leon Bismarck "Bix" Beiderbecke, one of the period's few white jazzmen. Armstrong became the preeminent figure in the history of jazz, achieving international renown and influencing virtually every jazz performer. Among the jazz vocalists, Bessie Smith is considered the greatest interpreter of the blues.

Motion Pictures

Early in the 1920s Hollywood developed from the movie center of the United States into the movie center of the world. Motion-picture stars came to be regarded as national heroes and heroines. The introduction of talkies revolutionized the film industry.

DIRECTORS

Two great directors of the era were Cecil B. De Mille and Erich von Stroheim. De Mille specialized in the epic style, winning particular success with the biblical epics *The Ten Commandments* (1923) and *King of Kings* (1927). The Austrian-born von Stroheim's films are characterized by their imaginative subtlety. He achieved wide fame with *Greed* (1923), which was based on Frank Norris's naturalistic novel *McTeague*.

STARS

Rudolph Valentino was the archetypal "Latin lover" of such movies as *The Sheik* (1921) and *Blood and Sand* (1922). Douglas Fairbanks thrilled audiences as a swashbuckling hero in "costume" adventure films, including *The Mark of Zorro* (1921) and *The Thief of Bagdad* (1924).

As for female stars, "America's Sweetheart" Mary Pickford was joined by Clara Bow and Gloria Swanson. Clara Bow personified the Roaring Twenties flapper in the film *It* (1927). Gloria Swanson often portrayed the sophisticated, glamorous "woman of the world."

Lon Chaney was the "Man of a Thousand Faces." A master of makeup, he won acclaim for horror films such as *The Hunchback of Notre Dame* (1923) and *The Phantom of the Opera* (1925), in which he portrayed characters hideous of face and distorted of body.

Charlie Chaplin was still popular as the nation's most beloved comedian. Joining him in the 1920s to form a triumvirate of superb funnymen were the deadpan Buster Keaton and the bumbling Harold Lloyd. *The Navigator* (1924) and *The General* (1926) showed Keaton at his best; *Safety Last* (1923) and *The Freshman* (1925) highlighted Lloyd's talent.

TALKIES

Soon after inventors had succeeded in projecting motion pictures they began to attempt to combine sound with films. The real breakthrough took place in 1927, when Warner Brothers presented *The Jazz Singer* with Al Jolson. Through the use of records, Jolson sang three songs and engaged in a bit of conversation. By the following year the public would fill any theater presenting a sound motion picture—no matter how poor the quality—in preference to viewing a silent film—no matter how artistic the creation. Soon the use of records yielded to the use of the so-called sound strip to one side of the actual film itself. The revolution in the motion-picture industry had begun.

Radio

During the 1920s a combination of electronic skill and financial support from business firms advertising their products and services made possible the rapid development of radio for broadcasting news, public events, music, sports, drama, and comedy.

DEVELOPMENTS

The first American commercial station was KDKA in Pittsburgh, which began broadcasting in 1920. KDKA's coverage of the presidential election returns in 1920 was the first major public event to be broadcast. In 1926 the National Broadcasting Company, a coast-to-coast chain of radio stations, was established to increase the amount of programming and improve its quality; the following year a competing chain, the Columbia Broadcasting System, was inaugurated. In 1927 the government established the Federal Radio Commission to regulate the more than seven hundred stations then in operation. Seven years later this agency was replaced by the Federal Communications Commission, which was given authority to regulate all communication facilities: telegraph, telephone, cable, and radio. Although some influential leaders advocated the use of radio broadcasting as an instrument of mass education, most programs were designed to provide entertainment and to advertise products. Achieving nationwide popularity were such radio personalities as a news and sports reporter, Graham McNamee; a comedy team, the Happiness Boys; and a dance band, the Clicquot Club Eskimos.

INFLUENCE

With tens of millions of listeners tuned in to the same programs, the phenomenon of a nationwide appeal became a reality. More and more the American people listened to the same news reports, thrilled to the same dramatic sketches, laughed at the same comedy routines, and were persuaded through clever advertising to use the same brands of products. All this resulted in a greater uniformity in customs and manners than had ever before existed.

Sports

In the 1920s professional athletics became big business. Promoters found huge profits in baseball, boxing, football, tennis, and golf—all of which catered to the spectators' desire for excitement. Great crowds flocked to see professional athletes, who for the first time in the nation's history achieved the status of heroes.

BASEBALL

In 1920 the reputation of baseball was soiled by scandal. Eight members of the Chicago White Sox were accused of accepting money from gamblers to lose to the Cincinnati Reds in the 1919 World Series. Federal Judge Kenesaw M. Landis was then made commissioner of baseball by the club owners and was given wide authority to regulate the game. With the start of Landis's tenure, which was to last for almost a quarter century, baseball entered its "golden age." Among the decade's most famous players were George Herman "Babe" Ruth, Louis (Lou) Gehrig, and Rogers Hornsby. The incomparable slugger Ruth is widely regarded as America's greatest baseball player.

BOXING

Like baseball, boxing enjoyed a "golden age" in the 1920s. William Harrison "Jack" Dempsey became one of the most celebrated heavyweight boxing champions. Dempsey won the title in 1919 from Jess Willard and lost it in 1926 to James J. "Gene" Tunney.

FOOTBALL

In the decade after World War I college football achieved great popularity. The greatest coach of the period was Knute Rockne, head football coach at Notre Dame University from 1918 until his death in an airplane crash in 1931.

Professional football also grew in popularity. At the beginning of the 1920s the American Professional Football Association was established; its name was changed in 1922 to the National Football League. Turning to professional football and playing with the New York Yankees and the Chicago Bears was Harold "Red" Grange, who had won fame as a halfback at the University of Illinois. By the time James Francis (Jim) Thorpe started to play professional football in the 1920s, he had already achieved an international reputation as perhaps the best all-around athlete in the history of American sports.

TENNIS

Perhaps the greatest player in the history of tennis was William Tatem (Bill) Tilden, Jr. From 1920 to 1930 he won the United States men's singles championship seven times and the British three times. Helen Wills is considered the best woman tennis player of her time. During the 1920s and 1930s she won seven United States and eight British women's singles championships.

GOLF

In the decade after World War I golf grew rapidly and prospered strikingly. During that period Robert Tyre (Bobby) Jones Jr. dominated the sport. The increasing popularity of golf transformed the once highly exclusive country club into a relatively common institution. In virtually every urban community the middle and upper classes strove to establish and maintain a private country club, and hundreds of thousands of business and professional men and women learned to play golf as an important part of the club's social programs.

Selected Readings

GENERAL WORKS:

Allen, Frederick Lewis. *Only Yesterday: An Informal History of the 1920s* (1931)
Faulkner, Harold U. *From Versailles to the New Deal* (1950)
Hicks, John D. *The Republican Ascendancy, 1921–1933* (1960)
Leuchtenburg, William E. *The Perils of Prosperity, 1914–1932* (1958)
Nevins, Allan. *The United States in a Chaotic World, 1919–1933* (1950)
Perrett, Geoffrey. *America in the Twenties* (1982)
Slosson, Preston W. *The Great Crusade and After, 1914–1928* (1930)

SPECIAL STUDIES:

Bagby, Wesley M. *The Road to Normalcy: The Presidential Campaign and Election of 1920* (1962)
Barrett, Marvin. *The Jazz Age* (1959)
Bernstein, Irving. *The Lean Years: A History of the American Worker, 1920–1933* (1960)
Blesh, Rudi. *Shining Trumpets: A History of Jazz* (1975)
Bogan, Louise. *Achievement in American Poetry, 1900–1950* (1951)
Burner, David. *The Politics of Provincialism: The Democratic Party in Transition, 1918–1932* (1968)
Cohen, Warren. *Empire Without Tears: American Foreign Relations, 1921–1933* (1988)
Costigliola, Frank. *Awkward Dominion: American Political, Economic, and Cultural Relations with Europe, 1919–1933* (1985)
Downer, Alan S. *Fifty Years of American Drama, 1900–1950* (1951)

Durso, Joseph. *The All-American Dollar: The Big Business of Sport* (1971)

Edler, Paula. *Governor Alfred E. Smith: The Politician as Reformer* (1983)

Ellis, L. Ethan. *Republican Foreign Policy, 1921–1933* (1968)

Ewen, David. *Composers for the American Musical Theater* (1968)

Fass, Paula. *The Damned and Beautiful: American Youth in the 1920s* (1977)

Fausold, Martin. *The Presidency of Herbert C. Hoover* (1985)

Ferrell, Robert H. *American Diplomacy in the Great Depression: Hoover-Stimson Foreign Policy, 1929–1933* (1957)

Franklin, John Hope. *From Slavery to Freedom: A History of Negro Americans* (1974)

Furniss, Norman. *The Fundamentalist Controversy, 1918–1931* (1954)

Galbraith, John Kenneth. *The Great Crash, 1929* (1955)

Gottfried, Martin. *Broadway Musicals* (1979)

Hoffman, Fredrick J. *The Modern Novel in America, 1900–1950* (1951)

Huggins, Nathan Irvin. *The Harlem Renaissance* (1971)

Iriye, Akira. *After Imperialism: The Search for a New Order in the Far East, 1921–1931* (1965)

McCoy, Donald. *Calvin Coolidge* (1967)

Michener, James A. *Sports in America* (1976)

Moore, Edmund A. *A Catholic Runs for President: The Campaign of 1928* (1956)

Murray, Robert K. *The Harding Era: Warren G. Harding and His Administration* (1969)

————. *Red Scare* (1950)

Nash, George. *The Life of Herbert Hoover* (1983)

Peterson, Theodore. *Magazines in the Twentieth Century* (1964)

Rae, John B. *The Road and the Car in American Life* (1971)

Rice, Arnold S. *The Ku Klux Klan in American Politics* (1962)

Russell, Francis. *The Shadow of Blooming Grove: Warren G. Harding in His Time* (1968)

Sann, Paul. *The Lawless Decade* (1957)

Schickel, Richard. *Movies: The History of an Art and an Institution* (1965)

Schriftgiesser, Karl. *This Was Normalcy: An Account of Party Politics During Twelve Republican Years: 1920–1932* (1940)

Sinclair, Andrew. *Era of Excess: A Social History of the Prohibition Movement* (1962)

Sklar, Robert. *Movie-Made America: A Cultural History of American Movies* (1975)

Soule, George. *Prosperity Decade* (1947)

Taylor, John W. R., and Kenneth Munson. *History of Aviation* (1972)

Thomas, Gordon, and Max Morgan-Witts. *The Day the Bubble Burst: The Social History of the Wall Street Crash of 1929* (1979)

Trani, Eugene, and David Wilson. *The Presidency of Warren G. Harding* (1977)

Wandersee, Winifred. *Women's Work and Family Values, 1920–1940* (1981)

White, Llewellyn. *American Radio* (1947)

White, William Allen. *A Puritan in Babylon: The Story of Calvin Coolidge* (1930)

9

Franklin D. Roosevelt and the New Deal

1932 Reconstruction Finance Corporation (RFC) created

Bonus Army converges on Washington

Roosevelt elected president

1933 Twentieth Amendment ratified

Emergency Banking Act

Civilian Conservation Corps (CCC) created

Federal Emergency Relief Act creates Federal Emergency Relief Administration (FERA)

Agricultural Adjustment Act creates Agricultural Adjustment Administration (AAA)

Tennessee Valley Authority (TVA) created

Home Owners Loan Corporation (HOLC) created

National Industrial Recovery Act (NIRA) creates National Recovery Administration (NRA)

Public Works Administration (PWA) created

Glass-Steagall Banking Act

Civil Works Administration (CWA) created

Roosevelt announces his Good Neighbor policy

Forty-Second Street with Berkeley as choreographer

1934 Securities Exchange Act creates Securities and Exchange Commission (SEC)

National Housing Act creates Federal Housing Administration (FHA)

1935 Supreme Court declares NIRA unconstitutional

Emergency Relief Appropriation Act creates Works Progress Administration (WPA)

Emergency Relief Appropriation Act creates Resettlement Administration (RA)

Emergency Relief Appropriation Act creates National Youth Administration (NYA)

National Labor Relations Act (Wagner-Connery Act)

Social Security Act

Banking Act

Odets, *Waiting for Lefty*

Becky Sharp is first feature-length film in improved Technicolor

1936   Supreme Court declares Agricultural Adjustment Act unconstitutional

Soil Conservation and Domestic Allotment Act

Roosevelt reelected president

Life magazine begins publication

1937   "Court Packing" bill rejected

NBC Symphony with Toscanini as conductor founded

Louis becomes heavyweight boxing champion

1938   Agricultural Adjustment Act of 1938

Food, Drug, and Cosmetic Act

Fair Labor Standards Act

Congress of Industrial Organizations (CIO) founded

Nylon introduced

Wilder, *Our Town*

Berlin, "God Bless America"

Disney, *Snow White and the Seven Dwarfs*

1939   Steinbeck, *The Grapes of Wrath*

Selznick, *Gone With the Wind*

1939–1940   New York World's Fair

The economic expansion of the 1920s with its increased production of goods and high profits culminated in an orgy of speculation that collapsed with disastrous results in 1929. It gradually became apparent that strong measures would be necessary to combat the depression that resulted. In accepting the presidential nomination of the Democratic party in 1932, Franklin D. Roosevelt pledged that if elected he would give the nation what he called a New Deal. Roosevelt assumed the presidency, and the New Deal attempted to cope with the emergency situation by engaging in experimental programs of relief and recovery. The New Deal also enacted long-range reform programs to promote the economic security and social welfare of the American people. In many ways the New Deal represented a continuation of the reform movement begun toward the end of the nineteenth century. But in one sense it did constitute a new direction in government policy. During the 1930s the government turned from a primarily restrictive and coercive philosophy to one of bold activism on behalf of the people.

In the realm of foreign affairs the Roosevelt administration immediately indicated that it was eager to adopt a new policy toward Latin America—that of the "good neighbor."

THE GREAT DEPRESSION

The stock-market crash in late October 1929 marked the beginning of the worst depression in the nation's history. It is commonly referred to as the Great Depression.

Hoover's Response

It was President Hoover's misfortune that his years in the White House coincided with the most difficult phase of the depression. The president took the traditional American view that the surest and quickest way out of a depression was to rely mainly on individual initiative. He clung to the hope that self-help and private charity, with a minimum of governmental intervention, would restore more prosperous times. The federal government was not, however, entirely inactive. The Hoover administration tried several limited remedies that it believed would help businessmen, workers, and farmers.

THE RECONSTRUCTION FINANCE CORPORATION

Hoover finally accepted a plan to "pump" government funds into private business enterprise. In February 1932, he signed the bill passed by Congress establishing the Reconstruction Finance Corporation (RFC) to provide government loans to banks, railroads, insurance companies, building and loan associations, and agricultural credit organizations. Former vice-president Charles G. Dawes was appointed chairman of the RFC, which lent $1.2 billion during its initial six months of operation.

THE RELIEF AND CONSTRUCTION ACT

Hoover and Congress yielded to the pressure for legislating funds for emergency relief. The Relief and Construction Act, signed into law in July 1932, enlarged the range of activity of the RFC by authorizing it to grant approximately $2 billion to states and municipalities for construction of public buildings, aid to agriculture, and emergency relief.

THE FEDERAL HOME LOAN BANK ACT

This measure, passed by Congress in July 1932, provided for the creation of eight to twelve home-loan banks established in different sections of the nation to make loans to mortgage-lending institutions. This in turn permitted these institutions to encourage the purchase of private dwellings, thus stimulating construction and increasing employment.

The Effects of the Depression

The reversal in 1929 of the economic trend was at first regarded as merely temporary, but the nation slowly realized that it would be many years before the damage caused by excessive speculation could be repaired. All Americans—rich and poor, rural inhabitants and urban dwellers, white and black, men and women—were subjected to the ravages of the depression. Businesses by the thousands failed. Workers by the millions were unemployed.

GROSS NATIONAL PRODUCT

The scope of America's suffering could be strikingly seen in the statistics of the gross national product (the total value of the goods and services produced in a nation during a specific period, plus the total of expenditures by both private and public sources and the total of investments by private sources): In 1929 it was about $150 billion and in 1932 it was about $108 billion (a drop of almost 30 percent).

NATIONAL INCOME

From 1929 to 1932 the total national income fell steadily from $81 billion to $41 billion.

BUSINESS FAILURES

Between 1929 and 1932 approximately 85,000 businesses, with assets totaling about $4.5 billion, failed. During that period industrial production declined by almost 45 percent. Thousands of factories stood idle, their doors locked and their machines rusting.

UNEMPLOYMENT

By the end of 1930 over 5 million workers (almost 15 percent of the nonfarm labor force) were unemployed; by the end of 1931 close to 9 million (more than 25 percent of the force) were out of work; by the end of 1932 more than 12 million (almost 40 percent) were looking for jobs. And during that period savings in 9 million bank accounts were wiped out to meet current expenses by families coping with unemployment.

As might be expected, the group that was most severely affected was composed of nonunion unskilled laborers. Organized skilled workers were able to survive better, often by agreeing to a reduction in the length of the workweek, with, of course, a consequent cutback in wages. White-collar employees, such as office workers and shop clerks, were laid off and joined the ranks of those seeking jobs with a lesser social status. Government employees enjoyed a measure of security, those on the federal level more so than those on the state or local. On the latter two levels dismissals as an economy measure were by no means rare. Salaries, such as for public-school teachers, were time and again reduced, and salary payments were frequently postponed until a defaulted payroll could be met through such devices as an advanced collection of taxes and a loan from a private business organization. The professional class, including physicians and lawyers, sustained a drastic reduction in income, since its services were less frequently sought.

Black and women workers faced especially grim circumstances. By the end of 1932 more than half the nation's blacks were unemployed. Women—no matter how needy—who sought work had to contend with job discrimination and were reproached for taking employment away from men with families to support. Black women workers, whose plight had undoubtedly always been the worst of all working groups, found their position deteriorated even further with the onset of the depression.

THE BONUS ARMY

In late May 1932, approximately a thousand unemployed ex-servicemen of World War I converged on Washington, declaring that they would remain there until Congress authorized the immediate cash payment of the twenty-year bonus voted in 1924 for World War I veterans. Other veterans arrived in the city, bringing the total number to more than 15,000 by mid-June. By mid-July most of them had departed, but some 2,000 refused to disband. Believing that the Bonus Army might eventually resort to some kind of violence, President Hoover ordered the use of infantry, cavalry, and tanks to drive it from the capital.

THE NADIR OF NATIONAL MORALE

Perhaps the most serious injury sustained by the American people was spiritual rather than material. In the descent from riches to rags many of them lost self-confidence and felt that their old values had been destroyed. Throughout the nation homeless men built shacks for themselves of flattened tin cans, cardboard, tar paper, and waste lumber, or they lived in abandoned factories or idle freight cars. In New York City homeless men slept in subway stations. A few in the nation died from starvation, but in every community voluntary charitable agencies tried to care for the hungry by setting up soup kitchens and bread lines. Churches and synagogues, community centers, welfare societies, the Red Cross, and the Salvation Army all attempted to help people. An apple-shippers' association devised a plan to market their surplus fruit and at the same time to help the jobless. Soon thousands of apple vendors took charge of the organization's stands on the sidewalks of large cities. The operation brought a pittance to a few, but it chiefly became a symbol of the will of the people to survive on their own and of their reluctance to turn to the government for direct relief.

Election of 1932

With the Republican party handicapped by the generally accepted view that it was responsible for the depression, the Democratic candidate for president appeared a certain victor.

DEMOCRATS

The powerful drive by Governor Franklin D. Roosevelt of New York to become the Democratic presidential nominee had made such an impact that the only question in the minds of the delegates to the national convention was whether a combination could be effected to prevent him from securing the two-thirds vote required by the party's rules for the nomination. When the "stop Roosevelt" movement, led by former Democratic presidential candidate Alfred E. Smith, collapsed, the New York governor was chosen on the fourth ballot. For second place on the ticket the delegates named Speaker of the House John N. Garner of Texas. The platform, which was an unusually brief and specific one, committed the party to the repeal of the Eighteenth (Prohibition) Amendment and to the principle of "continuous responsibility of government for human welfare."

REPUBLICANS

President Hoover controlled the proceedings of the Republican national convention. His nomination on the first ballot was quickly made unanimous. In accordance with his wishes, Vice-President Charles Curtis was also renominated. The platform, drafted by Hoover and his aides, was adopted after a spirited battle over the prohibition plank. As finally approved, it called for a referendum on the issue.

THE CAMPAIGN

Both Hoover and Roosevelt carried out extensive programs of speech-making. Hoover defended his party's policies on the tariff, agricultural relief, and general economic recovery, and he denounced the proposals of the opposition as demagogic appeals. Roosevelt stressed a "new deal" for the "forgotten man" without clearly indicating the specific measures of his program. He accused the Republicans of seeking prosperity by conferring favors on special interests and emphasized that the Democrats believed it the responsibility of government to promote the well-being of the great masses of the people.

ROOSEVELT'S LANDSLIDE VICTORY

The result at the polls was an unprecedented majority for the Democrats. In popular votes, Roosevelt won 22,830,000 to Hoover's 15,761,000. Roosevelt captured forty-two states with 472 electoral votes, while Hoover carried four of the New England states, Pennsylvania, and Delaware, with a total of 59 electoral votes. The victory represented not so much a vote of confidence in the Democratic party and its leaders as a measure of resentment, engendered by the depression, against the Hoover administration.

THE FIRST NEW DEAL

On March 9, 1933, Congress met in a special session called by President Roosevelt to deal with what seemed to be the impending collapse of the American banking system. After Congress passed an emergency act on banking it remained in special session, upon Roosevelt's request, to treat a variety of economic ills, including unemployment among laborers and falling prices for farmers. This session came to a close on June 16, 1933, after enacting a host of measures deemed essential by the Roosevelt administration. The special session of Congress, called the Hundred Days, was a remarkable period of cooperation between the executive and legislative branches of government. The Hundred Days launched the First New Deal, which had as its objective the relief and recovery, and then the reform, of the various economic sectors of the nation.

The Roosevelt Administration   Roosevelt was an unabashed activist in the office of the presidency. He deeply believed in the government's responsibility to ensure to the utmost the economic and social well-being of the people of the United States.

THE PRESIDENT

Roosevelt was an extraordinarily adroit politician. Over the radio on many an evening he spoke in a relaxed style to the American people in "fireside chats." As an orator he had few equals. He was not the first president to agree to press conferences, but he held them more often. Through his masterful give-and-take with reporters, he used them more skillfully than had any of his predecessors to present his views to the American people. Although confined to a wheelchair since 1921 as a result of polio (wearing heavy leg braces, he was able to take a few steps and stand to deliver an address), he exhibited striking self-assurance and unlimited mental and physical energy.

INAUGURAL ADDRESS

Between Roosevelt's election in November 1932 and his inauguration in March 1933, economic conditions had steadily worsened. His inaugural address, however, sounded a high note of confidence. He declared in ringing tones that "the only thing we have to fear is fear itself" and pledged strong executive leadership to resolve the grave economic conditions.

THE CABINET

Roosevelt chose the members of his cabinet with considerable care and skill. Democratic senator Cordell Hull of Tennessee, a powerful legislative leader, became secretary of state. Henry Morgenthau Jr. of New York, a specialist in agriculture and a close friend of the president's, soon joined the cabinet as head of the Department of the Treasury. Harold L. Ickes of Illinois, a former liberal Republican who had become a Democrat, was appointed secretary of the interior and immediately brought reforming zeal to his department. Frances Perkins, who had been an advisor to Roosevelt on social legislation when he was governor of New York, was named secretary of labor. She became the first woman to hold a cabinet post.

THE BRAIN TRUST

During his early years in office Roosevelt consulted a group of unofficial advisors on matters of economic and social reform. Newspaper reporters dubbed it the Brain Trust because its members were academics. Particularly influential in the Brain Trust were Columbia University professors Raymond Moley, Adolph A. Berle Jr., and Rexford Tugwell.

The New Deal Philosophy

Roosevelt's approach to the difficult problems of the depression was to experiment with a host of proposed solutions, whatever their origins. He discarded those that proved to be unworkable and retained those that worked.

A PLANNED ECONOMY

The experiments Roosevelt tried convinced him that the best course for the nation was away from traditional principles of economic individualism and toward a planned economy. Roosevelt and his associates in the administration maintained that by such planning it was possible to establish an enduring balance in the economic system among conflicting sectors of the nation.

KEYNESIAN ECONOMICS

An integral part of the New Deal concept of a planned economy was the theory of British economist John Maynard Keynes. Advocating that depression-ridden governments should "spend their way back to prosperity," Keynes counseled that by implementing comprehensive programs of public works governments would increase employment. Thus the Roosevelt administration was convinced to adopt extensive spending programs.

RELIEF, RECOVERY, REFORM

The watchwords of the New Deal were *relief*, *recovery*, *reform*. The mission of the New Deal lay in, first, relief to persons in need by providing them with money, loans to make mortgage payments, or jobs; second, recovery to the nation as a whole by passing legislation to assist business, labor, and agriculture to reestablish their strength; third, reform of institutions, such as banking, to make for economic and social stability.

Relief for the Unemployed

Any attempt to remedy the fundamental economic and social weaknesses within the nation had to wait until emergency measures could meet the immediate needs of a discouraged people, many of whom were destitute.

CIVILIAN CONSERVATION CORPS (CCC)

A dramatic relief measure was the Unemployment Relief Act, passed in March 1933, which created the Civilian Conservation Corps to provide work for men between the ages of eighteen and twenty-five. They were employed in such projects as reforestation, soil conservation, flood control, and road construction throughout the nation. By the end of 1941 more than 2 million young men had been employed by the CCC.

FEDERAL EMERGENCY RELIEF ADMINISTRATION (FERA)

This agency was established by the Federal Emergency Relief Act in May 1933, to assist states and cities in caring for the unemployed. Under the direction of Harry L. Hopkins, an advisor and close friend of Roosevelt, the FERA matched the funds expended by state and municipal governments in administering their relief projects for the jobless.

CIVIL WORKS ADMINISTRATION (CWA)

Created in November 1933, the Civil Works Administration, headed by Hopkins, provided jobs for approximately 4 million men in such undertakings as road repair and park improvement. The CWA was disbanded the following year and its functions were assumed by the Federal Emergency Relief Administration.

Recovery in Business

The Roosevelt administration made strong legislative moves to help business.

THE NATIONAL INDUSTRIAL RECOVERY ACT (NIRA)

Passed in June 1933, the National Industrial Recovery Act (NIRA) was intended to help business revival by means of self-regulation and in so doing decrease unemployment. The act created the National Recovery Administration (NRA), which supervised the preparation of codes of fair competition by employers, employees, and consumers in each industry. After the codes received the approval of the president, they became binding upon every segment of the industry in question and were to be enforced by law. The codes accomplished such objectives as the abolition of child labor, the limiting of production, the control of prices, and the establishment of minimum wages and maximum hours for workers.

Hundreds of these codes were administered by the NRA under the control of the iron-willed retired brigadier general Hugh Johnson, but few proved effective. Participating firms within each industry displayed the Blue Eagle (symbol of the NRA) and used the motto of the agency, "We do our part." Organized labor achieved a long-standing goal through the NIRA, for Section 7a of the act guaranteed workers the right to bargain collectively. Approximately 500 industries had adopted fair-competition codes and were operating under them when, in 1935, the Supreme Court declared the NIRA unconstitutional on the grounds that it granted the president too much power and that it dealt in commercial activities that were intrastate in nature.

PUBLIC WORKS ADMINISTRATION (PWA)

The NIRA established the Public Works Administration (PWA) for the construction of roads, school buildings, hospitals, dams, bridges, and a variety of other projects to stimulate the economy. The agency cooperated with state and local governments in the granting of contracts to private firms. Under the direction of Secretary of the Interior Ickes, between 1933 and 1939 the PWA spent approximately $5 billion on close to 35,000 construction projects, employing more than 500,000 people.

Recovery in Agriculture

Legislation was sponsored by the Roosevelt administration to strengthen the status of agriculture and to prevent the loss of farms by debt-ridden owners.

THE AGRICULTURAL ADJUSTMENT ACT

This measure, passed in May 1933, was designed to help farmers gain increased profits by encouraging them to reduce their production, which would in turn decrease their surpluses and thus raise the prices of their goods. It was hoped that through this action the farmers' purchasing power would be restored to parity with that of the prosperous and relatively stable five-year period before the outbreak of World War I.

The act created the Agricultural Adjustment Administration (AAA). The AAA was authorized (1) to control production of such commodities as wheat, cotton, corn, rice, tobacco, and hogs by paying cash subsidies to farmers who voluntarily restricted acreage planted in such crops or reduced the numbers of such livestock; (2) to impose taxes upon the processors of agricultural commodities—such as flour millers and meat packers—in order to secure funds to pay the subsidies; and (3) to pay farmers to plant grasses on untilled land that would provide cover for topsoil and prevent dust storms. The act remained in operation until 1936, when it was declared unconstitutional by the Supreme Court.

THE FARM CREDIT ACT

This act, passed in June 1933, set up the Farm Credit Administration (FCA) to provide loans to farmers for production and marketing. The object was to enable farmers to refinance farm mortgages that were in jeopardy of being lost through foreclosures. Within the first two years of its existence the agency helped refinance approximately 20 percent of the farm mortgages in the nation.

THE FRAZIER-LEMKE FARM BANKRUPTCY ACT

This measure, passed in June 1934, provided for a five-year postponement on the foreclosure of farm mortgages. During the five years, a farmer in default of his payments could repurchase his property at a reappraised price. When the Supreme Court invalidated the act the following year, Congress passed, in August 1935, the second Frazier-Lemke Act. This second act allowed for only a three-year moratorium on farm mortgage foreclosures and for a more precise guarantee of the rights of the lending institutions.

Recovery in Housing

The Roosevelt administration sponsored legislation to prevent the loss of homes by financially distressed owners, to encourage the building of new homes and the improvement of existing ones, and to establish a stable procedure for home financing.

HOME OWNERS LOAN CORPORATION (HOLC)

This agency, created in June 1933, was provided with more than $2 billion to refinance the mortgages of nonfarm homeowners who were threatened with losing their properties through foreclosures. The HOLC was in existence for three years, during which time it aided approximately 1 million homeowners.

FEDERAL HOUSING ADMINISTRATION (FHA)

This agency was established by the National Housing Act in June 1934, to insure mortgages made by private lending institutions for the building of new homes and the improvement of existing homes. By 1941 the government had insured $3.5 billion in mortgages.

Reform in Banking

While Congress was enacting the various measures that constituted a program of relief for the unemployed and of recovery in business, agriculture, and housing, it was also considering legislation to bring about long-range reforms in banking.

THE EMERGENCY BANKING ACT

Numerous demands upon banks for the payment of money had forced thousands to suspend operations by the time Roosevelt assumed office. Roosevelt feared that the banking system was on the verge of collapse. On March 5, 1933, he declared an immediate four-day bank holiday, which closed all national banks and the financial institutions affiliated with them. On the single day of March 9, 1933, the Emergency Banking Act was introduced, passed, and signed into law. The act empowered the president to reorganize insolvent national banks. Under its terms a majority of the banks soon reopened.

THE GLASS-STEAGALL BANKING ACT

Passed in June 1933, this significant reform law, among other things, (1) separated commercial banking from investment banking (a specialization primarily in the buying and selling of large blocks of securities); (2) increased the authority of the Federal Reserve Board to prevent member banks of the Federal Reserve System from engaging in excessive speculation; and (3) created the Federal Deposit Insurance Corporation (FDIC) to guarantee bank deposits up to $5,000 (subsequent legislation increased the sum) in the event of the institution's failure.

THE SECURITIES EXCHANGE ACT

This measure, passed in June 1934, provided for the regulation of securities exchanges in order to protect the purchasers of stocks and bonds against fraudulent practices. The Securities Exchange Act set up the five-member Securities and Exchange Commission (SEC) to register and supervise the sale of new issues of stocks and bonds. It also authorized the Federal Reserve Board to control the buying of stocks and bonds on margin (making partial payment of the purchase price).

THE BANKING ACT

This measure, passed in August 1935, strengthened government control of the nation's banking system through a revision of the Federal Reserve Act of 1913. The new law, among other things, (1) changed the title of the Federal

Reserve Board to the Board of Governors of the Federal Reserve System, increased its bipartisan membership of financial experts from six to seven, and enlarged its power over the twelve federal reserve banks; (2) required that all state banks with deposits of $1 million or more join the Federal Reserve System within seven years in order to have their deposits guaranteed by the Federal Deposit Insurance Corporation; and (3) permitted the federal reserve banks to purchase government bonds only in open-market transactions.

The Government as Regional Developer

An earlier demand for a relatively simple plan of government production of electric power led eventually to a rather complex program of government participation in regional development.

BACKGROUND

In the 1920s the advocates of government ownership and operation of electric-power facilities concentrated their efforts upon Muscle Shoals. This gigantic project on the Tennessee River had been built by the government during World War I to produce hydroelectric power and extract nitrate for the manufacture of explosives. In 1928 liberal Republican senator George W. Norris of Nebraska guided a bill through Congress that provided for the creation of a government-owned corporation to work the nitrate plants for the production of fertilizer and to sell the surplus power generated at the hydroelectric station. President Coolidge vetoed the bill on the grounds that the government operation would compete with private enterprise. In 1931 a virtually identical bill passed Congress, only to be vetoed by President Hoover on the same grounds.

THE TENNESSEE VALLEY AUTHORITY ACT

In May 1933, President Roosevelt enthusiastically signed into law the Tennessee Valley Authority Act. The act marked the triumph of Senator Norris's attempt to place the power resources of the Tennessee River at the disposal of the people. It established the Tennessee Valley Authority (TVA), an independent public corporation created not only to work the Muscle Shoals power project but also, more important, to fully develop a region embracing parts of seven states for the economic and social well-being of the people. These states were Tennessee, Virginia, Kentucky, North Carolina, Georgia, Alabama, and Mississippi.

Through the construction of dams, power plants, and transmission lines, many villages and farms in the Tennessee River Valley were supplied with electric current at low rates. TVA electric rates served as a yardstick to measure the reasonableness of rates charged by utility companies. Some other important projects of the TVA were the implementation of a program of flood control, the improvement of navigation on the Tennessee River and its tributaries, and the production of nitrate fertilizer. The standard of living of the approximately 3 million inhabitants of the Tennessee River Valley was quickly raised. During World War II the TVA generated hydroelectric power for the production of the atomic bomb at the government installation in Oak Ridge, Tennessee. Since the establishment of the TVA representatives of big business and conservative politicians have unsuccessfully called for the disbanding of the agency on the grounds that it competes with private enterprise.

The Tariff Issue

As American exports increased rapidly, exceeding imports, nations already in debt to the United States found it difficult to make payments for goods recently bought on credit.

TARIFF WARS

When the Smoot-Hawley tariff, with an average duty of approximately 60 percent, was signed by President Hoover, there were protests from all parts of the world. More than thirty nations struck back at the excessively high rates by increasing their rates on goods from the United States. Many nations passed acts placing all sorts of restrictions on the passage of American-made goods through their customhouses.

THE TRADE AGREEMENTS ACT

Secretary of State Cordell Hull feared not only the economic but also the political effects of tariff wars. He therefore proposed the adoption of reciprocal trade agreements with those nations that traded most extensively with the United States. In 1934 Congress passed the Trade Agreements Act. This act empowered the president, with the advice of economic experts, to negotiate agreements with other nations that revised tariff rates by as much as 50 percent in either direction without the consent of Congress. By 1950 agreements had been reached with some fifty nations in Europe, Asia, and Latin America. By the time the United States next engaged in extensive tariff legislation, in 1962, the average duty was approximately 10 percent.

THE SECOND NEW DEAL

Shortly after the Roosevelt administration received a tremendous vote of confidence from the American people in the congressional elections of 1934, it indicated that it was intent upon sponsoring a group of new projects to help the underprivileged throughout the nation. In his State of the Union message to Congress delivered in January 1935, President Roosevelt declared that his administration was ready to implement a comprehensive program of social reform, having as its basic objective to provide security against unemployment, illness, the cares of old age, and the uncertainty of dependency upon family or friends. This plan of action soon became known as the Second New Deal.

New Directions

Whereas the First New Deal had instituted projects to help businessmen, laborers, and farmers, the Second New Deal gave assistance almost exclusively to laborers and farmers.

CRITICISM OF THE NEW DEAL

That many businessmen by mid-1934 began to resist what they considered the "radical" policies of the New Deal was an indication that the economy was beginning to head in the direction of normalcy. Complaints increased that the Roosevelt administration was undermining the capitalist system with its bold experimentation. Conservatives charged that the government was destroying private enterprise through interference in every phase of business activity.

POLITICAL ENDORSEMENT OF THE NEW DEAL

Whatever the effects of New Deal acts, they were approved by the labor and farm vote in the congressional elections of 1934. In the new Seventy-fourth Congress the Roosevelt administration increased a dominant strength it already enjoyed in the legislative branch. In the Senate the Democratic majority went from 59 to 69 out of 96 members, while in the House of Representatives the number of Democrats rose from 313 to 323 out of 435 members. Although the administration sometimes experienced difficulty in maintaining unity of action among the Democrats, it met with no serious reversals in guiding its legislative program through the new session of Congress.

THE TWENTIETH AMENDMENT

The Seventy-fourth Congress was the first to meet under the terms of the Twentieth Amendment to the Constitution, passed by Congress in 1932 and ratified in 1933. The amendment stipulated that Congress convene each year on January 3, thus abolishing the previous short session of Congress, in which lame-duck legislators (those defeated for reelection and those choosing to retire) would remain in Congress for the special session that began in December and lasted until the following March 4. The amendment also specified that the president and vice-president take office on January 20 following their election rather than on March 4, as had previously been the practice.

Election of 1936

In a campaign marked by a vigorous defense and a bitter denunciation of the New Deal, Roosevelt won a strong reelection victory.

DEMOCRATS

There were no surprises at the Democratic national convention. President Roosevelt and Vice-President Garner were renominated without opposition.

REPUBLICANS

The delegates to the Republican national convention began their proceedings with little confidence that their candidate for president, whoever he might be, could beat Roosevelt in the coming election. The convention chose for its standard-bearer the rather liberal Republican governor Alfred M. Landon of Kansas. Chicago newspaper publisher Frank Knox was named Landon's running mate.

THE CAMPAIGN

The candidates avoided such deep basic issues separating their parties as the philosophy underlying direct federal benefits, the centralization of power in the national government, the delegation of unusual authority to the president, and the relation of a heavily unbalanced budget to the economy of the nation. The Democrats were content to defend their record. The Republicans denounced the Roosevelt administration for reckless experimentation, extravagant spending, unbridled use of patronage, and failure to suppress communism. The conduct of the campaign by the Republicans was hesitant and inept, sharply contrasting with the assurance and proficiency of the politicians who managed the Democratic campaign. Roosevelt skillfully carried the brunt of the battle for his party, while Landon proved a dull campaigner both in his personal appearances and in his radio speeches.

ROOSEVELT'S LANDSLIDE VICTORY

The vote for the president cut across party lines. He was reelected with 27,757,000 popular votes to Landon's 16,684,000. Roosevelt carried every state except Maine and Vermont, thus capturing 523 out of 531 electoral votes.

Relief for the Unemployed

On the basis of the experience secured from the Civil Works Administration of 1933–34, the Roosevelt administration put a more comprehensive plan into operation early in 1935 to overcome persistent unemployment.

WORKS PROGRESS ADMINISTRATION (WPA)

In April 1935, Congress passed the Emergency Relief Appropriation Act, which signified the federal government's turn from direct relief to work relief alone. The act established the Works Progress Administration (WPA), a name that was changed to the Works Projects Administration in 1939. Harold L. Ickes of the Public Works Administration and Harry L. Hopkins of the Federal Emergency Relief Administration each wanted to administer the new agency. Roosevelt chose Hopkins, in large part because he was more inclined to spend large sums and was less heedful of stringent rules.

Within six months of its creation the WPA was employing approximately 2.5 million manual laborers on such projects as the construction or improvement of roads, school buildings, hospitals, power plants, bridges, and parks. The WPA also provided work for the skilled and educated—artists, writers, theater people, musicians, and teachers—by creating the Federal Art Project, the Federal Writers' Project, and the Federal Theater Project. By the time the WPA was terminated in 1943, it had spent approximately $11 billion on close to 1.5 million projects and in so doing had given temporary jobs to about 8.5 million persons. In spite of its achievements, the WPA was criticized by many conservative Americans as being wasteful and inefficient.

NATIONAL YOUTH ADMINISTRATION (NYA)

Established by executive order in June 1935, under the provisions of the Emergency Relief Appropriation Act, the National Youth Administration (NYA) gave part-time employment to needy persons between the ages of sixteen and twenty-five in high schools, colleges, and universities so that they could continue their education. More than 4 million young people had been helped by the time the NYA was disbanded in 1943.

Recovery in Labor

The Roosevelt administration was extremely supportive of organized labor's aspirations for a higher status in American society. The New Deal gained some of its most substantial victories in the field of labor legislation. Changes within the labor movement itself had great influence on the principles written into that legislation.

THE CONGRESS OF INDUSTRIAL ORGANIZATIONS

The activity of labor organizers in the early 1930s raised anew the issue of bringing into organized labor unskilled industrial workers. Within the American Federation of Labor certain unions sponsored industrial unionism as opposed to craft unionism. The most notable of those unions were the United Mine Workers under John L. Lewis, the Amalgamated Clothing Workers of America under Sidney Hillman, the International Ladies' Garment Workers Union under David Dubinsky, and the International Typographical Union under Charles Howard.

At the 1935 national convention of the AFL the organization's president, William Green, and his associates blocked Lewis's attempt to commit the AFL to industrial unionism. A majority of the delegates favored the traditional structure based upon representation of the skilled crafts. However, eight unions that were affiliated with the AFL formed the Committee for Industrial Organization (CIO). Under the leadership of Lewis and his mine workers, the CIO defied the executive committee of the AFL and proceeded to organize along industrial union lines the automotive and steel industries. The CIO soon secured partial recognition from the General Motors Corporation and several subsidiaries of the United States Steel Corporation. In 1937 the AFL expelled the ten unions that were by then within the CIO, which was reorganized the following year as the Congress of Industrial Organizations.

Although most of the craft unions within the AFL continued their long-standing policy of excluding blacks from membership, the CIO from the outset organized workers without regard to race. By 1939 approximately 200,000 black unskilled workers had been enrolled in the CIO, where they experienced a new sense of kinship with white workers. Many women workers responded eagerly to the CIO's organizing drive, becoming union members for the first time in their lives. The International Ladies' Garment Workers Union, for example, in 1939 reported a membership of over 730,000, the vast majority of whom were women who had recently joined the organization and now made up approximately 75 percent of the rolls.

MANAGEMENT-LABOR STRIFE

The vigorous efforts of the CIO to organize workers in the automobile and steel industries brought strikes marked by violence. In the automobile industry dissatisfied workers used a new weapon: the sit-down strike. While ceasing work, they refused to leave plants against which their unions had called a work stoppage. This tactic spread rapidly to workers in many other industries. When employers began to use force to evict sit-down strikers, the labor organizers condoned meeting force with force. When the police fired upon union demonstrators in front of a steel plant in Chicago in 1937, a pitched battle ensued between the two groups in which ten men were killed. In 1939 the Supreme Court declared the sit-down strike illegal.

SECTION 7a OF THE NATIONAL INDUSTRIAL RECOVERY ACT

Despite outbursts of violence, organized labor made great gains in winning public support and in the recognition of its rights by employers. According to Section 7a of the National Industrial Recovery Act of 1933, labor was guaranteed the right "to organize and bargain collectively through representatives of their own choosing." This provision stimulated the growth of unions, greatly increasing their membership.

THE NATIONAL LABOR RELATIONS ACT

After the NIRA was declared unconstitutional by the Supreme Court in 1935, Senator Robert F. Wagner of New York initiated legislation to guarantee labor's right to bargain collectively. The result was the National Labor Relations Act (also called the Wagner-Connery Act), passed by Congress in July 1935. The act created the three-member National Labor Relations Board (NLRB) and authorized it to determine suitable units for collective bargaining, to conduct elections for the choice of labor's representatives, and to prevent interference with such elections. The NLRB was empowered to investigate complaints of unfair labor practices, to issue orders that such practices be stopped, and to petition federal courts to enforce its restraining orders. The NLRB's work was made difficult by the hostility of employers, who felt that the National Labor Relations Act unfairly benefited the working class over the business class, and by the quarrel within the ranks of labor between the AFL and the CIO.

THE FAIR LABOR STANDARDS ACT

This act, passed by Congress in June 1938, was designed as a substitute for the codes of the disbanded NRA as they concerned fair labor standards. For each industry engaged in interstate commerce, a committee composed of employers and employees was to recommend a minimum wage—not less than twenty-five cents an hour, to be raised to forty cents by 1945—compatible with economic conditions in that industry and to establish over a period of time a forty-hour workweek. The act required payment for work over forty hours in a week at the rate of time and a half, prohibited the labor of children under sixteen years of age, and restricted the labor of those under eighteen to nonhazardous jobs.

Recovery in Agriculture

The problems of farmers trying to make a living on inferior land was a constant concern of the Roosevelt administration.

RESETTLEMENT ADMINISTRATION (RA)

Established in May 1935, under the provisions of the Emergency Relief Appropriation Act, the Resettlement Administration (RA) helped farm families move from submarginal to fertile land. It also extended loans at low interest rates to enable particularly needy farm families to purchase new land and equipment. Within four years almost 800,000 families had received rehabilitation aid. Under the auspices of the RA a few suburban communities were also built for low-income city families.

THE SOIL CONSERVATION AND DOMESTIC ALLOTMENT ACT

This act was passed in February 1936, soon after the Agricultural Adjustment Act of 1933 was declared unconstitutional. It attempted to curtail agricultural production, not through a program of crop control (as under the Agricultural Adjustment Act) but through soil conservation. The act authorized the payment of cash subsidies to farmers for planting crops such as alfalfa and clover that would conserve the soil. The intent was to curtail production of staple crops, such as wheat, cotton, corn, and tobacco, which deplete the soil, and to ultimately raise agricultural prices.

THE BANKHEAD-JONES FARM TENANT ACT

The work of the Resettlement Administration was assumed by the Farm Security Administration (FSA), established by the Bankhead-Jones Farm Tenant Act, passed in July 1937. The FSA granted low-interest-rate loans to tenant farmers, sharecroppers, and farm laborers so that they could purchase their own land. In addition, the FSA aided migrant workers and experimented with the resettlement of rural groups in cooperative communities.

THE AGRICULTURAL ADJUSTMENT ACT

With the Agricultural Adjustment Act of 1933 declared unconstitutional by the Supreme Court and with the Soil Conservation and Domestic Allotment Act proving ineffectual, Congress passed a second Agricultural Adjustment Act, in February 1938, in another attempt to decrease agricultural surpluses and thus increase agricultural prices. The secretary of agriculture was authorized (1) to set acreage quotas for staple crops and pay farmers cash subsidies for planting soil-conserving crops; and (2) to set marketing quotas for export crops that were in surplus to such a degree that the prices for them might be adversely affected.

The act also implemented the "ever-normal granary" plan, sponsored by Secretary of Agriculture Henry A. Wallace, which operated as follows: A Community Credit Corporation would store crops that were in surplus to prevent a decline in prices. At the same time it would grant loans to farmers on the stored crops as a substitute for the profits that would have been realized by selling them. The loans were to be repaid when the price of the crops rose and the farmers removed them from storage, selling them at a satisfactory profit. The financing of the various aspects of the program was to come from the federal treasury, rather than from taxes imposed upon the processors of farm commodities as in the act of 1933.

Security for the Needy

In what was to be one of its most far-reaching enterprises, the Roosevelt administration launched the government into assuming a duty (for all time to come) to ensure the security of the needy people of the nation.

EXTREMIST PROPOSALS

One of the reasons for Roosevelt's strong support of attempts to give the people greater security was the appeal of several extremist proposals by groups that were hostile toward the Roosevelt administration. The Share-Our-Wealth movement, led by Democratic senator Huey P. Long of Louisiana, advocated that the federal government guarantee to every family of the nation a homestead worth $5,000 and a minimum annual income of $2,000. The Old Age Revolving Pension plan, originated by Dr. Francis E. Townsend, a California physician, recommended that the federal government pay $200 a month to persons sixty years of age and over, who would be obligated to spend the entire sum within the month. The National Union for Social Justice, headed by the Reverend Charles E. Coughlin, a Michigan Roman Catholic priest who made effective use of the radio to spread his views, urged that the currency be extensively inflated through the use of silver.

THE SOCIAL SECURITY ACT

This act, passed by Congress in August 1935, upon the recommendation of President Roosevelt, provided for (1) a federal program of benefits to retired workers beginning at the age of sixty-five and of benefits to the dependent survivors of deceased workers, based on the employees' earnings before the age of sixty-five, to be paid out of funds derived from a tax on employees and their employers; (2) a program of unemployment compensation administered by the state with grants from the federal government and financed by a similar payroll tax; and (3) federal aid to the states for various projects, such as maternity and infant-care services and assistance to crippled children and the blind.

Other Reform Measures

Among the wide range of acts passed during the New Deal were some measures that were designed to benefit consumers and reform the workings of government.

THE FOOD, DRUG, AND COSMETIC ACT

This measure, passed in 1938, extended the provisions of the Pure Food and Drug Act. It forbade manufacturers of foods, drugs, and cosmetics (1) to mislabel products; (2) to sell products without listing their ingredients on the containers' labels; and (3) to engage in false advertising.

THE CIVIL AERONAUTICS ACT

This act, passed in 1938, created the Civil Aeronautics Authority, which two years later was renamed the Civil Aeronautics Board (CAB), composed of five members appointed by the president with the approval of the Senate. The CAB was authorized (1) to regulate the economic aspects of American aviation service, including the charging of fares; (2) to advise the State Department in its negotiations with foreign countries for the establishment of international standards of aviation activities; and (3) to investigate aviation accidents.

THE ADMINISTRATIVE REORGANIZATION ACT

This measure, passed in 1939, was designed to regroup the many independent units of the federal government in order to improve the efficiency of the executive branch. An executive order established the Federal Security Agency, the Federal Works Agency, and the Federal Loan Agency, the three of which, along with the executive office of the president, assumed control of most of the independent units of the government.

THE HATCH ACT

This act, passed in 1939, forbade federal officeholders who were not on the policymaking level to participate in political campaigns or solicit contributions from people on work relief.

Roosevelt and the Supreme Court

The executive and legislative branches of the government seemed to be in substantial agreement regarding the need for the laws that comprised the recovery and reform programs of the New Deal. It remained for the Supreme Court to decide the constitutionality of the legislation sponsored by the Roosevelt administration.

INVALIDATION OF NEW DEAL LAWS

Decisions of the Supreme Court starting from the last third of the nineteenth century indicated that most justices were opposed to the government's increased role in economic affairs. They were reluctant to sanction government-fostered social improvements that restricted individual initiative. The Court soon showed its hostility toward much of the New Deal reform legislation. In 1935 in *Schechter v. United States* (the "Sick Chicken Case") the Court declared the National Industrial Recovery Act of 1933 unconstitutional on the grounds that it delegated too much power to the president and that it dealt in intrastate commerce. The Court held that a Brooklyn poultry dealer could not be prosecuted for violating National Recovery Administration codes governing the quality of chickens he sold and the level of wages he paid. The justices agreed unanimously that since the retail poultry business was not interstate commerce, Congress had no jurisdiction over it. Roosevelt angrily retorted that this was a "horse-and-buggy" definition of interstate commerce.

In 1936 in *United States v. Butler* the Court, by a 6 to 3 vote, declared the Agricultural Adjustment Act of 1933 unconstitutional on the grounds that Congress possessed no authority to tax for the benefit of a particular segment of society and that the regulation of agriculture was within the jurisdiction of the state governments. In addition, the Court invalidated two other pieces of legislation: the Frazier-Lemke Farm Bankruptcy Act of 1934 and the Guffey-Snyder Bituminous Coal Stabilization Act of 1935, which dealt with the recovery of the bituminous coal–mining industry.

THE COURT-PACKING PLAN

Despite his anger and his fear that the judicial branch would invalidate much New Deal legislation, Roosevelt postponed action until after the 1936 election. He then chose to interpret his overwhelming victory, which cut across party lines, as a blanket endorsement of his policies and quickly made plans to circumvent the Supreme Court. Because six of the nine justices were over seventy, the president struck at them as too old to remain on the bench. He also charged that the Court was violating the Constitution by acting as a "policymaking body." But he avoided a careful analysis of the basis of its decisions.

In February 1937, Roosevelt submitted to Congress a bill called the Reorganization Plan, which was quickly labeled by its foes as the court-packing bill. It proposed the appointment of additional judges in the various federal courts where there were incumbent judges of recommended retirement age who did not choose to resign. In the case of the Supreme Court the recommended retirement age was to be seventy years. The president was to appoint not more than six additional members to supplement nonretiring justices. The storm over the Reorganization Plan so agitated the Senate that the administration could not persuade conservative Democrats to support the measure in that body. This marked the first clear division between the conservative and liberal wings of the party since Roosevelt took office. After the sudden death of Democratic senator Joseph T. Robinson of Arkansas, who had been directing parliamentary tactics on the Reorganization Plan, Roosevelt reluctantly abandoned the contest.

REVERSAL OF THE COURT

In the end the president won the fight with the Supreme Court. In the spring of 1937 the Court sustained several major New Deal laws, among them the Social Security Act of 1935 and the National Labor Relations Act of 1935. Also in 1937 the Court overruled earlier decisions by upholding a state minimum-wage law. Between 1937 and 1939 retirements from and deaths on the Court enabled Roosevelt to appoint four well-known supporters of the New Deal, bringing about such a change in the Court's membership that a reversal occurred in its interpretation of congressional powers over economic and social matters. By 1941 Roosevelt had named seven of the nine justices. With the retirement that year of the moderate chief justice Charles Evans Hughes, the president elevated the liberal associate justice Harlan F. Stone to the position. Among the legislation sustained by the Court with its new members were the Fair Labor Standards Act of 1938 and the Agricultural Adjustment Act of 1938.

EVALUATION OF THE NEW DEAL

The years of the New Deal constituted one of the most controversial periods in the nation's history.

Critics and Defenders

Critics of the New Deal believed that it was destroying the traditional American way of life, while its ardent defenders thought it could do no wrong.

THE FINANCIAL COST

The New Deal's elaborate spending programs to bring about relief and its extensive loans to private enterprise to promote recovery placed an extraordinary financial burden upon the federal government. The Roosevelt administration tried to increase the annual tax revenues. Congress reluctantly yielded to presidential insistence and passed the Revenue Act of 1935, which increased the rates of taxation on individual incomes over $50,000 on gifts, on estates, on corporate earnings, and on excess profits. But taxation did not provide sufficient revenue to pay for the experiments of the New Deal. In 1933 the debt of the United States had stood at approximately $22.5 billion. Six years later it had increased to almost $40.5 billion. Thus deficit financing (the financing of government expenditures by taking loans rather than by levying taxes) had almost doubled the national debt in six years.

COMPARATIVELY SLIGHT INCREASE IN THE NATIONAL DEBT

Later supporters of the New Deal, however, pointed out that this rapid increase of the national debt was slight in comparison to the crushing burden of debt piled up during World War II.

Opposing Historical Views

Historians subsequently expressed antipodal views of the New Deal. Some maintained that it was the culmination of a half-century-long reform movement, while others insisted that it was a new direction in government policy.

A CONTINUATION OF REFORM

In many ways Roosevelt's program was a continuation of the reform movement that had been interrupted by the outbreak of World War I. There were precedents from both Democratic and Republican administrations. The New Deal regulation of business extended some of the principles laid down in the Interstate Commerce Act of 1887, signed into law by a Democratic president, and the Sherman Antitrust Act of 1890, signed by a Republican president. Much of the New Deal farm relief program was foreshadowed by proposals to aid agriculture during the Wilson administration. There were borrowings from the Populists of the latter part of the nineteenth century and the progressives of the early twentieth century. Roosevelt's attacks on the leaders of industry as economic royalists were reminiscent of those conducted against the "money power" by the Populists and the progressives, and a number of New Deal reforms had first been demanded by those groups.

A NEW DIRECTION IN GOVERNMENT POLICY

To most citizens the New Deal revealed the federal government in an entirely new role. Government policy was not merely a restrictive and coercive force but an instrument to enable a democracy to solve its problems with speed and decision. Many believed that the New Deal was primarily a vital agency in providing economic security for all the people.

THE INTERRUPTION OF REFORM

Roosevelt was still urging further reforms to strengthen the nation when the Nazi dictatorship thrust war upon Europe in 1939. Whether the voluminous legislation of the New Deal would have solved the economic and social problems exposed by the Great Depression was never determined, for recovery and reform programs were interrupted by World War II.

TOWARD SOLIDARITY WITH LATIN AMERICA

The Roosevelt administration used its influence in Latin America to promote greater understanding among all the American republics. It did so with a realization that the defense of the United States against increasing German, Italian, and Japanese aggression was linked with that of the rest of the Western Hemisphere.

The Good Neighbor Policy

In his first inaugural address Roosevelt indicated that his administration was eager to adopt a new policy toward Latin America. The president said: "In the field of world policy I would dedicate this nation to the policy of the good neighbor—the neighbor who resolutely respects himself and, because he does so, respects the rights of others." In 1933 Secretary of State Cordell Hull, with the full support of Roosevelt, declared that "no state has the right to intervene in the internal or external affairs of another."

NICARAGUA

In 1933 the American marines, who had occupied Nicaragua since 1912 except for a brief period during 1925–26, were finally withdrawn.

HAITI

In 1934 the American military occupation of Haiti that had been in effect since 1915 was ended. Three years later, in order to forestall overtures by German financial interests, the United States agreed to purchase almost the entire $5 million worth of bonds issued by Haiti for a public-works program.

CUBA

In 1934 the State Department announced the cancellation of the Platt Amendment as far as the provisions regarding the intervention of the United States in Cuban affairs were concerned.

MEXICO

The experiments in socialism undertaken by the Mexican government beginning in 1934 disturbed the United States, but the State Department refrained from interference. When in 1938 Mexico expropriated foreign-owned property, Secretary Hull admitted the right of a sovereign nation to do so and then reminded the Mexican government that it must compensate the dispossessed owners at "fair, assured, and effective values." Mexico rejected Hull's suggestion that the matter be arbitrated and insisted that it would reimburse the owners in its own way and at its own convenience. In 1941 a settlement was reached that proved satisfactory to American investors.

PANAMA

In 1939 the Senate ratified a treaty with Panama that modified the Hay-Bunau-Varilla Treaty of 1903, granting the United States control of a canal zone in Panama. The new treaty settled some of the long-standing grievances of Panama that had stemmed from the former treaty.

THE DOMINICAN REPUBLIC

In 1940 Roosevelt terminated the management of the Dominican Republic's customhouses that the United States had exercised since 1905.

Hemispheric Defense

A series of conferences among the nations of Latin America and the United States led to a system of common defense, through which the Roosevelt administration hoped to deal with any possible threat to the Western Hemisphere from aggressive Germany, Italy, and Japan.

THE BUENOS AIRES CONFERENCE

In 1936 the American nations, including the United States, adopted the Declaration of Buenos Aires, pledging to consult with one another whenever the peace of the Western Hemisphere was threatened by the action of a non-American nation.

THE LIMA CONFERENCE

In 1938 the twenty-one American republics approved the Declaration of Lima. In the declaration they announced their solidarity and affirmed that any threat to peace in the Western Hemisphere from a foreign nation would lead to immediate consultation among all the signatories to the pact.

THE PANAMA CONFERENCE

With the outbreak of war in Europe in September 1939, the American nations undertook to define their neutral position. The following month at a conference in Panama City, in keeping with the desire of the Roosevelt administration to prevent the war from reaching the Western Hemisphere, the American nations approved the Declaration of Panama. The declaration proclaimed the establishment of a safety zone extending for 300 miles around the Western Hemisphere south of Canada and warned belligerent nations to refrain from military action within the designated zone.

THE HAVANA CONFERENCE

In 1940 representatives of the twenty-one American republics adopted the Act of Havana, declaring that an act of aggression by a foreign nation against any one of them would be considered an attack on all of them. The act also provided, in the interest of hemispheric defense, for the American republics to take over a European possession in the Western Hemisphere that was in danger of aggression.

A DEPRESSION-STRICKEN SOCIETY

During the 1930s the striking influence upon American society was the Great Depression. Since the beginning of the twentieth century there had been three recessions, but each was relatively short and mild. However, the economic reversal that began in 1929 and continued for a decade was such that all significant aspects of society, such as education and medicine, were adversely affected.

Education

The shortage of public funds and the high rate of unemployment had an impact upon education throughout the nation.

ELEMENTARY EDUCATION

Elementary schools were seriously affected when boards of education felt the need to reduce their budgets to such an extent that in addition to removing the so-called frills from their programs they also eliminated essential services. With husbands out of work, married couples delayed having children, and elementary-school enrollment between 1930 and 1940 declined from about 23.6 million to about 21 million.

SECONDARY EDUCATION

As was the case with elementary schools, secondary schools also suffered from significant budget reductions. High-school enrollment, however, rose from about 4.7 million to about 7 million, as many teenagers, with little opportunity for employment, continued to attend school longer than they ordinarily would have.

HIGHER EDUCATION

College and university enrollment, approximately 1.1 million in 1930, began to dip for the first half of the decade but then grew to about 1.5 million by 1940. Like elementary and secondary schools, institutions of higher education, as a result of severe budgetary cuts, experienced diminished effectiveness in fulfilling their obligations to students. With college and university graduates scrambling for the few jobs available in a depressed economy, career-preparation programs became increasingly popular, to the detriment of the traditional liberal-arts goal of producing "well-rounded" individuals.

Technology

In 1939–40 the New York World's Fair was held. Based on the theme "The World of Tomorrow" and symbolized by the dual structures of a trylon (a three-sided tapering pillar that rose to 700 feet) and perisphere (a globe 200 feet in diameter), the fair helped advance and popularize the technology of the period.

AIR CONDITIONING

Although the first scientific air-conditioning system was designed at the beginning of the twentieth century, the use of air conditioning did not become widespread until the 1930s, when much-refined central systems and room units were developed.

NYLON

In 1938 the Du Pont company introduced nylon, the product of a decade of research by a team of the firm's chemists.

Medicine

The inability during the depression to buy sufficient and nourishing food and to pay for medical care resulted in a loss of health for millions of Americans. And throughout the decade medical research suffered from a shortage of funds.

HIGH QUALITY OF MEDICINE AND SANITATION

The increase in life expectancy that had been the trend since the beginning of the twentieth century did continue nevertheless, rising from 59.7 years in 1930 to 62.9 years in 1940. This fact attested to the high level of medicine and sanitation in the United States even when hampered by depression shortages.

SULFA DRUGS

The treatment of disease was significantly advanced by the use of a group of chemicals called sulfa drugs, which function by curtailing the growth of bacteria in the body. The diseases against which the sulfa drugs were used effectively included pneumonia, meningitis, and dysentery.

A DEPRESSION-IMPACTED CULTURE

The impact of the depression on American culture was pervasive. Painters and writers in large numbers were propelled into dealing with social problems emerging from an economically distressed nation. The WPA was established by Congress primarily to give employment to manual laborers on construction projects. But the WPA also provided work for artists, writers, theater people, and musicians by creating the Federal Art Project, the Federal Writers' Project, and the Federal Theater Project. For example, under the auspices of the Federal Art Project murals were painted in public buildings, and under the auspices of the Federal Writers' Project state and local histories were written. In operatic music many native-born singers were engaged, in modern dance the height of public appreciation was reached, and in light music swing became the rage. Motion pictures continued to be the most influential art form. Radio reached its zenith, providing in the main a diversion from the depression's ugly reality. With the alleviation during the second half of the 1930s of the economic impairment, professional sports regained the spectator attendance they had enjoyed in the prosperous 1920s.

Art

In painting, the nation's social ills as well as its regional variations were important themes; in sculpture, mere refinement of a long-standing style prevailed. It was in architecture that there occurred the most impressive development: a surge toward unabashed modernity.

PAINTING

Two movements—social criticism and regionalism—were paramount in American painting.

In response to the depression many painters devoted themselves to themes of social significance. Influential in this group were Reginald Marsh, Ben Shahn, and Jack Levine. Of the three, Levine was by far the most "severe" in conveying his compassion for victims of social injustice.

Among some American painters the desire to capture the nation's numerous regional distinctions was dominant. Regionalist Thomas Hart Benton was the decade's leading muralist, executing works for numerous buildings of the federal and various state governments and of colleges and universities. John Steuart Curry painted views of simple agrarian life in his native Kansas. Grant Wood was a regionalist whose best-known painting, *American Gothic* (1930), satirically portrays a somber, overall-clad, pitch-fork-wielding Iowa farmer and his equally somber, full-aproned daughter at his side.

Outside the movements of both social criticism and regionalism was Georgia O'Keeffe, who won acclaim for representing her two most distinctive subjects, greatly enlarged flowers and bleached animal bones.

ARCHITECTURE

By the end of the 1930s a few architects had developed an unequivocally contemporary style that for many years was to have a determinative influence upon American buildings. Leaders in the movement to modernity were Frank Lloyd Wright, Walter Gropius, and Ludwig Mies van der Rohe.

Frank Lloyd Wright is a titan among American architects. He strove against what was traditional and ordinary in architecture with an almost poetic inventiveness. His guiding principle was that a building must be so compatible with its natural setting that it appears to stem from it. Among his many revolutionary techniques was the selective elimination of walls in order to attain both an aesthetic and a practical free-flowing interior space. Wright's style became the essence of residential design in the United States. Beginning in the 1930s an ever-growing respect for his conception of architectural aesthetics and practicality resulted in numerous commissions for nonresidential structures. For his office buildings he developed new techniques, such as using precast concrete blocks and glass walls. Wright's many notable nonresidential structures include the Solomon R. Guggenheim Museum (1959) in New York City.

The 1930s might well have become notable for the design and construction of skyscrapers, but the depression precluded that development. Nevertheless, the decade saw the creation of two splendors of skyscraper architecture in New York City. During 1930–31 the Empire State Building was constructed, and between 1931 and 1939 most of the buildings that constitute the complex of skyscrapers known as Rockefeller Center were erected. The decoration in the buildings of Rockefeller Center were magnificent examples of the period's popular style of design called art deco (a sleekly streamlined form of ornamentation that represents an expression of modern technology).

A new form of architecture, originating in Europe during the 1920s and named the International Style, accentuated stark functional design. This style used inorganic materials, particularly steel and glass. It featured repetitive geometric shapes in a basic asymmetrical plan. The two most influential practitioners of the International Style were Walter Gropius and Ludwig Mies van der Rohe, both of whom were German-born and had settled in the United States. Mies's maxim that "less is more" is reflected in the uncluttered look of his steel-and-glass structures.

Literature

The aloofness from and cynicism toward the smugly prosperous 1920s on the part of novelists, poets, and playwrights yielded in the 1930s to concern for the problems of a depression-torn society.

THE NOVEL

No writer showed greater commitment to portraying the distress of the American people during the depression than did John Steinbeck. His novel *The Grapes of Wrath* (1939) depicts the migration during the 1930s of dispossessed farm families of the drought-ridden midwestern regions to California, where they seek jobs but find themselves cruelly exploited as itinerant agricultural workers. Another novelist who arrestingly conveyed social consciousness was John Dos Passos, whose most famous work is the trilogy *U. S. A.* (1930–36). Naturalist James T. Farrell attained wide recognition with his trilogy *Studs Lonigan* (1932–35). Black author Richard Wright, in his most influential novel, *Native Son* (1940), delineates urban black lower-class life.

Two great novelists whose writings were not part of the social-consciousness trend were Thomas Wolfe and William Faulkner. Wolfe produced four huge intensely autobiographical novels, including *Look Homeward, Angel* (1929). Faulkner, a Mississippian, wrote mostly about the perplexities that beset the South. He paid particular attention to the antagonism between the declining old aristocratic families and the rising new entrepreneurial ones, and how both groups subjected the blacks. Among his novels are *The Sound and the Fury* (1929), *As I Lay Dying* (1930), *Sanctuary* (1931), and *Absalom, Absalom!* (1936). Faulkner handled with finesse such literary techniques as telling the same story through the perceptions of different characters and stream of consciousness.

POETRY

The absorption with innovative verse forms and language usage that was characteristic of poets of the 1920s gave way in the 1930s to a rekindled regard for content. Stephen Vincent Benét gained fame for his early narrative poem "John Brown's Body" (1928), which patriotically recounts the events of the Civil War. Archibald MacLeish's poetry made a case for political and economic liberalism to such a degree that it was sometimes condemned as propaganda.

DRAMA

As the depression worsened, dramatists showed an increasing propensity for social criticism. Clifford Odets's works epitomized this form of protest. In his play about a New York City taxi drivers' strike, *Waiting for Lefty* (1935), he sought sympathy for working-class aspirations.

Three successful dramatists of the period who examined problems more from the individual than the group point of view were Robert Sherwood, Lillian Hellman, and Thornton Wilder. Sherwood's major theme, expressed in such plays as *The Petrified Forest* (1935) and *Idiot's Delight* (1936), was that a person must act in ways that are free and intuitive rather than be limited by society's artificial conventions. Hellman's *The Little Foxes* (1939) portrays members of an avaricious wealthy southern family in the post–Civil War period. Wilder's masterpiece is *Our Town* (1938). In it he suggests that underlying every activity of ordinary daily living is the sacredness of all human experiences from birth to death. Wilder used a number of innovative nonrealistic stage devices.

A highly successful playwrighting team specializing in comedy was that of George S. Kaufman and Moss Hart. The biggest of their many hits was *You Can't Take It with You* (1936).

Among the most accomplished and popular actors of the 1930s were Katharine Cornell, Helen Hayes, and the husband-and-wife team of Alfred Lunt and Lynn Fontanne.

MAGAZINES

A development in periodical publishing was the launch of several magazines that presented news events, many of a human-interest nature, through photographs. The most successful of these pictorial news magazines was the weekly *Life*, founded in 1936 by Henry R. Luce; almost as popular was the biweekly *Look*, which appeared the following year.

Music

Both orchestral music organizations and opera companies were able to maintain high standards of performance despite the public's lessening of financial support. Modern dance, which had developed early in the twentieth century, was gaining in popularity. In the field of light music the glittering swing bands reigned.

ORCHESTRAL COMPOSERS AND CONDUCTORS

Two of the most gifted American composers of orchestral music were Roy Harris and Virgil Thomson. Harris often employed the musical forms of the seventeenth century, but with such imaginative technique that the result appears thoroughly twentieth-century American. Thomson used a direct and simple style; many of his works were based on American folk music. He is best known for writing the scores for three documentary motion pictures.

In recognition of the opportunities to associate radio with classical music, the National Broadcasting Company in 1937 prevailed upon Arturo Toscanini to assume the musical directorship of the NBC Symphony Orchestra, which was being organized with carefully selected virtuoso players. For seventeen years Toscanini led highly acclaimed concerts that were aired from coast to coast.

OPERA

The Metropolitan Opera House engaged many American singers, such as soprano Grace Moore, mezzo-soprano Gladys Swarthout, and baritone Lawrence Tibbett. Highly acclaimed European-born performers in the company were the French soprano Lily Pons and two who were among the foremost twentieth-century Wagnerian singers: the Norwegian soprano Kirsten Flagstad and the Danish tenor Lauritz Melchior.

MUSICAL THEATER

The leading composers of musicals were Irving Berlin and Cole Porter, each of whom wrote the words to nearly all of his own songs, and Richard Rodgers, who collaborated with lyricist Lorenz Hart. Among Berlin's most successful musicals were *As Thousands Cheer* (1933), which contains the song "Easter Parade," and his later, outstanding work *Annie Get Your Gun* (1946), starring Ethel Merman and introducing what became the virtual theme song of the entertainment field, "There's No Business Like Show Business." More than a composer of musicals, Berlin established himself as the premier American songwriter, with approximately a thousand songs, dozens of which achieved a classic status. His output exhibits an astounding versatility of style. Some of his great creations were "Alexander's Ragtime Band" (1911), "God Bless America" (1918), which was introduced in 1938 and became almost a second national anthem; and "White Christmas" (1942). Among Cole Porter's most popular musicals were *Gay Divorce* (1932), which contains the song "Night and Day"; *Anything Goes* (1934), with the song "You're the Top"; and his later, greatest work, *Kiss Me, Kate* (1948), with "So in Love." The Porter hallmarks are the arresting quality of his melodies and the wit and debonair elegance of his lyrics, with their ingenious rhymes. Richard Rodgers and Lorenz Hart collaborated on close to thirty musicals, including such popular works as *On Your Toes* (1936), with "There's a Small Hotel"; *The Boys from Syracuse* (1938), with "Falling in Love with Love"; and *Pal Joey* (1940), with "Bewitched, Bothered and Bewildered." Rodgers brilliantly tailored his melodic style to Hart's always sophisticated, often breezy, and sometimes bitingly cynical lyrics.

MODERN DANCE

During the 1930s a few highly talented performers who had trained at the Denishawn dance company took modern dance in a new direction, advocating, first, an even greater outpouring of feeling simply displayed, and second, in order to highlight the dance itself, the use of severely simple and somber costuming and staging and minimal musical accompaniment. The most influential of this post–St. Denis group was performer, choreographer, and teacher Martha Graham. She founded her own troupe and then her own school. Soon, in large measure because of the efforts of Graham and her company, modern dance reached the zenith of its popularity throughout the nation.

Some years later a new group of modern dance choreographers stripped dance down to its barest essentials of pure movement, to a point perhaps never before thought desirable. The works they produced were not intended to present a theme. Achieving the greatest influence among these new choreographers was Merce Cunningham, who had trained and danced with Graham.

SWING

Jazz of the 1920s led to swing of the 1930s. Swing was characterized by a lively, insistent beat, the frequent submerging of a basic melody through improvisation of the players, and a collective use of syncopated rhythm. The most striking aspect of the music was a "big" sound, produced by an extensive brass section. Swing was usually arranged for a large commercial dance band. Outstanding bandleaders included clarinetist Benjamin (Benny) Goodman; trombonist Alton "Glenn" Miller; trombonist Francis "Tommy" Dorsey; and Edward "Duke" Ellington and William "Count" Basie, each of whom composed for and played piano with his band. Ellington's "Mood Indigo" (1930) and "Caravan" (1937) were favorite pieces. Basie's most popular composition was "One O'Clock Jump" (1938). A majority of the swing bands featured vocalists. By far the most popular singer was the emaciated-looking Francis Albert (Frank) Sinatra, who became an idol of teenage girls who squealed with delight and even swooned while he performed.

Motion Pictures

In the 1930s motion pictures experienced a golden age that extended throughout the 1940s and into the early 1950s. For a very small sum millions of people each week would flock to motion-picture theaters to escape, if only for a few hours, from the throes of the depression.

WIDE APPEAL

In coming to terms with the protracted economic reversal, motion-picture studios were forced to operate within exceedingly low budgets that in many ways cramped the creativity of producers and directors. This led to the issuance of standardized fare—an unbroken succession of motion pictures based on a few popular genres, each type with its own distinctive style, form, and purpose. Nevertheless, many notable films came out of 1930s Hollywood. Throughout the nation hundreds of motion-picture "palaces" were built, scores of them in imitation of exotic Moorish architecture. Quickly gaining wide public acceptance were drive-in movie theaters, the first of which opened in 1933 in Camden, New Jersey. To encourage attendance the movie houses offered double features and periodically presented the audience with gifts, such as dishes, glassware, and cutlery. The effect of all this could be seen at the box office. By the last years of the decade approximately 65 percent of the American people were going to the movies every week.

MUSICALS

One of Hollywood's most widely appreciated contributions was the musical, which featured dancing as well as singing. In films such as *Forty-Second Street* (1933) and *Footlight Parade* (1933), choreographer Busby Berkeley devised and directed resplendent dance sequences. Fred Astaire brought an unmatched debonair quality to both his singing and dancing. Among his best-remembered films are *The Gay Divorcee* (1934) and *Top Hat* (1935), in both of which his partner was Ginger Rogers. Shirley Temple sang and danced her way to stardom in many films, such as *Little Miss Marker* (1934), becoming perhaps the most celebrated child performer in history. Judy Garland had the innocence of a girl and the powerful voice of a great musical-theater singer, both of which she used in a number of films, including *Babes in Arms* (1939), in which her costar was Mickey Rooney, and the incomparable *The Wizard of Oz* (1939).

COMEDIES

The invention of sound motion pictures instantaneously changed the nature of screen comedy. Now spoken jokes became as important as sight gags. A new breed of comedians succeeded the funnymen of a few years earlier. None of the new comedians was better received than the hard-drinking W. C. Fields, the team of the dim-witted Stan Laurel and the pompous Oliver Hardy, and the zany Marx Brothers (the wisecracking

Groucho, the mute Harpo, and the foreign-accented Chico), who appeared in a number of highly popular movies, including *Duck Soup* (1933) and *A Night at the Opera* (1935). A type of screen comedy called screwball emerged, which depicted daily living as a wonderfully enjoyable madcap experience. Director Frank Capra brought out a number of them, including the most celebrated ever made, *It Happened One Night* (1934), with Clark Gable and Claudette Colbert.

DISNEY PRODUCTIONS

In 1928 Walter Elias (Walt) Disney drew what came to be the most famous cartoon character ever created, Mickey Mouse, introduced in a black-and-white short film, *Steamboat Willie*, which was also Disney's first venture into sound. In 1932 he produced the first Technicolor cartoon. In 1938 Disney released the first feature-length animated cartoon, *Snow White and the Seven Dwarfs*. This was followed by other popular full-length cartoons, such as *Pinocchio* (1940) and *Fantasia* (1940), a work comprising a series of animated cartoons, which were visual interpretations of classical music, performed by the Philadelphia Orchestra under the direction of Leopold Stokowski.

GANGSTER FILMS

The violent operations of gangs during national prohibition formed the basis of the early 1930s gangster films. Gaining quick fame by portraying gangsters were Edward G. Robinson, James Cagney, and Humphrey Bogart. Perhaps the most memorable performance of this kind was by Robinson in *Little Caesar* (1931).

HORROR FILMS

Dracula (1931), with Bela Lugosi as the blood-sucking vampire, and *Frankenstein* (1931), with Boris Karloff as the synthetic monster, launched the horror film as a profitable Hollywood staple.

WESTERNS

The sound-film era witnessed the refinement of the western. Gary Cooper and John Wayne starred in a number of them. Wayne appeared in director John Ford's *Stagecoach* (1939), which grippingly captured the western locale's nuances. For the weekly pleasure of youngsters a host of westerns in the "B" (low-budget) picture category were made in a production-line manner, with such cinematic singing cowboys as Gene Autry and Roy Rogers.

ADVENTURE FILMS

In addition to dispensing the escapism so common to many of the genres during the 1930s, adventure films offered to the audience a glimpse (mostly distorted) of the culture of other times and other places. Errol Flynn was the swashbuckling hero in numerous "costume" adventure films, such as *The Adventures of Robin Hood* (1938). Loinclothed Johnny Weissmuller played the title role in the popular series of Tarzan films.

"MESSAGE" FILMS

An important body of films incorporated pleas for rationality, compassion, and courage in dealing with threatening national issues. *Mr. Smith Goes to Washington* (1939) probed corruption in politics; *Dead End* (1937) examined the breeding of crime in slums; and *Confessions of a Nazi Spy* (1939) explored the challenge to American democracy from a foreign dictatorship.

"PRESTIGE" FILMS

Biographies and adaptations of literary classics formed the core of "prestige" films, which garnered the studio usually modest financial reward but much dignity. The best screen biographies starred either George Arliss or Paul Muni. With deftness Muni portrayed Louis Pasteur and Émile Zola. Among the most successful achievements in adapting novels to the screen were the following: *All Quiet on the Western Front* (1930); *Grand Hotel* (1932), with John Barrymore and Greta Garbo; *Wuthering Heights* (1939), with Laurence Olivier and Merle Oberon; and, bringing the decade to a spectacular close, what is regarded as the quintessential Hollywood product, *Gone With the Wind* (1939), adapted from Margaret Mitchell's bestseller, tastefully produced by David O. Selznick, vibrantly directed mainly by Victor Fleming, with an unforgettable musical score by Max Steiner, and starring what has come to be considered a "perfect" foursome: Clark Gable, Vivien Leigh, Leslie Howard, and Olivia de Havilland.

TECHNICOLOR

The most impressive technical advance in filmmaking during the period was the use of color. The breakthrough took place in 1932 with a recently improved form of a process called Technicolor, which had been invented fifteen years earlier by chemical engineer Herbert T. Kalmus. In 1935 *Becky Sharp*, based on the Thackeray novel *Vanity Fair*, was presented as the first feature-length production filmed entirely in improved Technicolor.

Radio

Like motion pictures, radio experienced a "golden age" in the 1930s; it lasted well into the following decade. During the difficult years of the depression the entire family could be entertained continually with the purchase of an inexpensive set.

WIDE APPEAL

The number of radios in use increased from approximately 12.5 million in 1930 to about 44 million in 1940, by which time almost 90 percent of the nation's families owned sets and listened to them an average of a bit over four hours a day. A vast amount of the programming consisted of exceedingly escapist entertainment.

SOAP OPERAS

Much of the morning and early afternoon broadcasting schedule was devoted to serials, dubbed soap operas because many of them were sponsored by soap-product companies. Intended for housewives, the daily fifteen-minute segments focused on the anguishing vicissitudes of the human condition. Some of the most successful of this genre were *Ma Perkins*, *The Goldbergs*, *Our Gal Sunday*, and *The Romance of Helen Trent*.

ADVENTURE SERIALS

Late afternoon and early evening broadcasting contained a host of serials for youngsters. Delighting listeners for years were serials based on well-known comic-strip characters, among the most popular being *Buck Rogers in the Twenty-fifth Century*, *Dick Tracy*, *Little Orphan Annie*, and *Superman*. *Jack Armstrong, the All-American Boy* was about a high-school student who exhibited sterling behavior. In *The Lone Ranger* a daring masked rider on a fiery steed named Silver, aided by his faithful Indian companion Tonto, brought law and order to the western plains.

EVENING FARE

Programming in the evening was directed at the family as a whole. There were situation comedies. The best-known situation comedy of all—indeed, the first big hit of the medium—was *Amos 'n' Andy*. It was about two blacks (played by white actors Freeman Gosden and Charles Correll) who owned a taxi service and were much involved in their social fraternal order. Few white listeners then found the broad delineation of the characters offensive in its basic attitude toward blacks. Another enduring favorite was *Fibber McGee and Molly*. There were comedians. Especially popular were the stingy Jack Benny, the team of the long-suffering George Burns and the scatterbrained Gracie Allen, and the caustic-witted Fred Allen. There were singers. A stellar triumvirate consisted of the warbling baritone Bing Crosby, the crystalline mezzo-soprano Kate Smith, and the nasal tenor Rudy Vallee.

FM

Radio acquired the capacity to carry the full range of sound reproduction by Edwin Howard Armstrong's invention in 1933 of FM (frequency modulation). A method of broadcasting wholly different from the existing AM (amplitude modification), FM transmitted static-free signals of high fidelity that in time became a boon to avid listeners of classical music.

Sports

Not until the easing of the depression during the second half of the 1930s were professional athletics able to attract the great crowds that they had enjoyed in the prosperous 1920s.

BASEBALL

Still retaining its position as by far the most popular spectator sport was baseball. The best-known player was Joseph Paul (Joe) DiMaggio, who won fame for his batting prowess. Improved technology in lighting made possible night baseball; the first major-league night game was played in 1935.

BOXING

On the whole, professional sports followed a policy of excluding blacks (who established their own teams and leagues). The exception was boxing, which made a black, Joe Louis, the preeminent athlete of the period. Louis won the heavyweight championship in 1937; successfully defended his crown a record twenty-five times, scoring twenty-one knockouts; and retired undefeated in 1949, after holding the title longer than anyone else before or since. He was known and respected as the Brown Bomber.

TENNIS

During the 1930s tennis was dominated by John Donald (Don) Budge, the first player to make the sport's grand slam by winning the United States, British, French, and Australian men's singles championships in 1938.

Selected Readings

GENERAL WORKS:

Brogan, Denis W. *The Era of Franklin D. Roosevelt* (1950)

Leuchtenburg, William E. *Franklin D. Roosevelt and the New Deal, 1932–1940* (1963)

Rauch, Basil. *The History of the New Deal, 1933–1938* (1944)

Schlesinger, Arthur M., Jr. *The Age of Roosevelt* (3 vols. to date, 1957–   )

Wecter, Dixon. *The Age of the Great Depression, 1929–1941* (1948)

SPECIAL STUDIES:

Baker, Leonard. *Back to Back: The Duel Between FDR and the Supreme Court* (1967)

Bennett, David H. *Demagogues in the Depression: American Radicals and the Union Party, 1932–1936* (1969)

Bernstein, Irving. *Turbulent Years: A History of the American Worker, 1933–1941* (1969)

Brinkley, Alan. *Voices of Protest: Huey Long, Father Coughlin and the Great Depression* (1982)

Bunche, Ralph. *The Political Status of the Negro in the Age of FDR* (1973)

Burchard, John, and Albert Bush-Brown. *The Architecture of America: A Social and Cultural History* (1966)

Burns, James MacGregor. *Roosevelt: The Lion and the Fox* (1956)

Cronon, Edmund D. *Labor and the New Deal* (1963)

Dallek, Robert. *Franklin D. Roosevelt and American Foreign Policy, 1932–1945* (1979)

Ekirch, Arthur A., Jr. *Ideologies and Utopias: The Impact of the New Deal on American Thought* (1969)

Ewen, David. *Composers for the American Musical Theater* (1968)

Ferrell, Robert H. *American Diplomacy in the Great Depression* (1970)

Freidel, Frank. *Franklin D. Roosevelt* (4 vols. to date, 1952–)

Gellman, Irwin. *Good Neighbor Diplomacy* (1979)

Gottfried, Martin. *Broadway Musicals* (1979)

Graham, Otis L. *An Encore for Reform: The Old Progressives and the New Deal* (1967)

Gunther, John. *Roosevelt in Retrospect* (1950)

Hoffman, Frederick J. *The Modern Novel in America, 1900–1950* (1951)

Kirby, John. *Black Americans in the Roosevelt Era: Liberalism and Race* (1980)

Lash, Joseph. *Dealers and Dreamers: A New Look at the New Deal* (1988)

McCraw, Thomas K. *TVA and the Power Fight, 1933–1939* (1971)

McElvaine, Robert. *The Great Depression: America, 1929–1941* (1984)

McJimsey, George. *Harry Hopkins: Ally of the Poor and Defender of Democracy* (1987)

McKinley, Charles, and Robert W. Frase. *Launching Social Security* (1970)

Milton, David. *The Politics of U.S. Labor: From the Great Depression to the New Deal* (1980)

Morgan, Ted. *FDR: A Biography* (1985)

Patterson, James T. *Congressional Conservatism and the New Deal* (1967)

Pell, Roy V., and Thomas C. Donnelly. *The 1932 Campaign* (1935)

Rayback, Joseph G. *A History of American Labor* (1966)

Romasco, Albert. *The Politics of Recovery: Roosevelt's New Deal* (1983)

Roosevelt, Eleanor. *This I Remember* (1949)

Roosevelt, Elliot, and James Brough. *An Untold Story: The Roosevelts of Hyde Park* (1973)

Scharf, Lois. *Eleanor Roosevelt: First Lady of American Liberalism* (1987)

Schickel, Richard. *Movies: The History of an Art and an Institution* (1965)

Sherwood, Robert E. *Roosevelt and Hopkins* (1948)

Sklar, Robert. *Movie-Made America: A Cultural History of American Movies* (1975)

Taft, Philip. *Organized Labor in American History* (1964)

Terkel, Studs. *Hard Times: An Oral History of the Great Depression* (1970)

Walters, Raymond. *Negroes and the Great Depression* (1970)

Ware, Susan. *Holding Their Own: American Women in the 1930s* (1982)

Weiss, Nancy. *Farewell to the Path of Lincoln: Black Politics in the Age of FDR* (1983)

White, Llewellyn. *American Radio* (1947)

Wood, Bryce. *The Making of the Good Neighbor Policy* (1961)

10

World War II

1935	Italy invades Ethiopia
1935–1939	Neutrality Acts
1938	Germany annexes Austria
1939	Germany annexes Czechoslovakia
	Germany invades Poland
	Great Britain and France declare war on Germany
1940	Germany invades Scandinavia, Low Countries, and France
	Selective Training and Service Act
	Roosevelt reelected president
1941	Lend-Lease Act
	Germany invades Soviet Union
	Roosevelt and Churchill issue Atlantic Charter
	Japan attacks Pearl Harbor
	United States declares war on Japan
	Germany and Italy declare war on United States
1942	Japan invades Philippines
	Battle of Midway
	Allies invade occupied North Africa
1943	Allies invade Italy
1944	Allies invade occupied Western Europe
	Roosevelt reelected president
1945	Yalta Conference
	Germany surrenders
	United Nations founded

Potsdam Conference

United States drops atomic bombs on Hiroshima and Nagasaki

Japan surrenders

In the 1930s the military aggression of the Axis nations—Germany, Italy, and Japan—brought war to Europe and Asia, turning the American people away from a policy of neutrality. In late 1941 the United States was brought into World War II as a result of a Japanese attack on Pearl Harbor. American manufacturing, agriculture, labor, and transportation were mobilized to support the armed forces sent to war against the Axis powers. By early 1942 representatives from twenty-six Allied nations, including the United States, had signed a declaration pledging joint military action until total victory over the Axis was achieved. The strategy of the Allied nations was to defeat Nazi Germany first and then turn to destruction of the Japanese empire.

Administering the defeated Axis partners of the war, Germany and Japan, and helping both to establish themselves within the world community of nations were formidable tasks for the victorious powers. The postwar reconstruction of Germany and Japan was impeded by an ever-worsening disintegration in relations between the Western Allies on one side and the Soviet Union on the other.

During the war the Allied leaders attended a number of conferences to discuss, in addition to war strategy, their design for international cooperation after the anticipated peace was attained. The latter discussions resulted in the formation of the United Nations.

THE APPROACH OF WAR

Despite elaborate neutrality legislation, the Roosevelt administration moved steadily, although at times hesitantly, to prepare the nation for what might become a world war.

Unrest in Europe

Some Americans believed that the Treaty of Versailles had been too severe in the penalties imposed upon Germany. But observing the dictatorship established in 1933 by Adolf Hitler of the National Socialist (Nazi) party, most Americans came to regard the regime as uncompromisingly despotic in its domestic policies and unjustifiably aggressive in its foreign relations. Italy, since 1922 under the dictatorship of Benito Mussolini of the Fascist party, was also a threat to world peace.

ITALIAN AGGRESSION

In 1935 Italy, defying the opposition of the League of Nations, successfully invaded Ethiopia. The following year it joined Germany, which had withdrawn from the League of Nations in 1933, to form an alliance called the Rome-Berlin Axis.

GERMAN AGGRESSION

Germany violated the Treaty of Versailles in 1936 by sending troops into its demilitarized Rhineland area to the west. In March 1938, Germany forcibly annexed Austria. That September, at the Munich Conference, Great Britain and France, in the hope of averting a general war, agreed to German annexation of the western part of Czechoslovakia called the Sudetenland, a region inhabited by German-speaking people. (The Munich Conference soon came to symbolize appeasement.) The following March Germany took over the rest of Czechoslovakia, except for one region that was annexed by neighboring Hungary. In August, 1939, Germany and the Soviet Union announced the conclusion of a nonaggression pact.

The conditions were now set for World War II. It began on September 1, 1939, when Germany invaded Poland, the independence of which the British and the French had guaranteed. Two days later Great Britain and France declared war on Germany.

Attempt at Neutrality and Isolationism

With Germany and Italy acting ever more aggressively, the United States Congress tried to minimize the possibility of the nation becoming involved again in a European war.

THE JOHNSON ACT

Sponsored by Republican senator Hiram Johnson of California, this act, passed in 1934, forbade the sale in the United States of bonds issued by any government that had defaulted in the payment of its obligations to the United States. Since every European nation that had incurred a World War I debt except Finland belonged in this category as a result of failure to repay its debt, the law was regarded as an effective device to prevent American financial involvement in the plans of a European nation seeking to acquire loans for the conduct of war.

THE NYE COMMITTEE

Between 1934 and 1936 a Senate investigating committee, headed by Republican Gerald P. Nye of North Dakota, revealed that enormous profits had been made during World War I by American financiers and munitions makers and suggested that pressure from those groups had forced the nation into the war. Congress was prompted by the findings of the Nye committee into passing a series of neutrality acts.

NEUTRALITY LEGISLATION

In an effort to prevent American involvement in war should it occur anywhere in the world, Congress passed neutrality acts in 1935, 1936, and 1937. The acts varied mainly in the provisions affecting the discretionary powers of the president. Each succeeding act indicated a growing inclination on the part of Congress to keep for itself the control of foreign policy. The Neutrality Act of 1935 authorized the president, after proclaiming the existence of a state of war, to prohibit the export of implements of war to belligerents and to forbid American citizens to travel on belligerent vessels except at their own risk. The Neutrality Act of 1936, which extended the Neutrality Act of 1935 until mid-1937, added a clause prohibiting loans to belligerents. The Neutrality Act of 1937, which was designed to be permanent, compelled the president to take certain actions, and permitted him to take other actions, whenever he determined the existence of a state of war. Among the compulsory prohibitions were (1) the export of implements of war to belligerents; (2) travel by Americans on belligerent ships; and (3) the extension of loans to belligerents. In addition, the president could prohibit (1) the transport of any type of commodity on American vessels to belligerents; and (2) the use of American ports as supply bases for belligerent warships. With these acts the United States relinquished its claims to a neutral's rights at sea during war, which it had so vigorously defended at the start of World War I.

When war broke out with the German invasion of Poland in September 1939, the Roosevelt administration urged Congress to reconsider certain of the mandatory provisions of the 1937 Neutrality Act. The point at issue was the compulsory embargo on implements of war to belligerents. After a spirited debate Congress passed the Neutrality Act of 1939, which amended the act of 1937 to permit the export of arms and munitions to belligerents on a "cash and carry" basis. To satisfy the strongly isolationist congressional bloc, the act contained a provision authorizing the president to designate war zones from which American merchant ships would be barred.

ROOSEVELT'S POLICY

In opposition to the isolationist basis of the neutrality legislation, in October 1937 President Roosevelt delivered an address in which he suggested that the United States take the lead in persuading all peace-loving nations that in the event of international strife they should "quarantine" the aggressor through economic boycott. Finding little support for this policy in Congress, Roosevelt undertook to persuade Germany and Italy that any just demands could be satisfied around the conference table rather than on the battlefield. When his pleas to the dictators for peaceful negotiations brought no results, he advised Congress that there were a variety of means "short of war" to curb the spread of totalitarian power.

ISOLATIONISTS VERSUS INTERVENTIONISTS

The policy advocated by Roosevelt was severely criticized by isolationists, who recommended that the nation refrain from words as well as deeds that might involve it in a struggle for power overseas. By the spring of 1941 the isolationists were exerting an enormous amount of effort to keep the United States out of World War II. Their spokespersons in Congress were Republican senators Gerald P. Nye of North Dakota, Arthur H. Vandenberg of Michigan, and Robert A. Taft of Ohio; Democratic senator Burton K. Wheeler of Montana; and Republican representative Hamilton Fish Jr. of New York. The most effective pressure group working on behalf of an isolationist policy was the America First Committee, headed by Chicago businessman Robert E. Wood. The famous aviator Charles A. Lindbergh, who was an active member of the committee, won a considerable following by urging a negotiated peace between Great Britain and the Axis powers.

On the other hand, those known as interventionists were convinced that the best security for the United States lay in assisting the Allies, through all measures "short of war," to ensure German defeat. The most influential organization espousing interventionist sentiment was the Committee to Defend America by Aiding the Allies, led by Kansas newspaper editor William Allen White.

Preparedness and Defense

With the German attack upon Scandinavia in April 1940 and its invasion of the Low Countries the following month, Americans were shocked into a realization of the implications for them of total war. Their earnest endeavor to take steps to ensure full preparedness and defense began at that time.

ARMAMENTS APPROPRIATIONS

During 1940 Congress appropriated approximately $1.8 billion for armaments. The sum was used for the creation of a two-ocean navy superior to the combined naval power of nations unfriendly to the United States and for the purchase of munitions and other supplies for an army that was being rapidly increased in size to 1.2 million men. These two branches of the service were to be supported by a fleet of 35,000 aircraft.

THE SELECTIVE TRAINING AND SERVICE ACT

In September 1940, Congress authorized the first peacetime conscription in the nation's history. Under the terms of the Selective Training and Service Act, all men between the ages of twenty-one and thirty-five were required to register for possible military service. From the 16.4 million registrants 800,000 were selected by lot for one year of military training. Also, national guard enlistees were given intensive instruction in modern warfare.

WESTERN HEMISPHERE STRATEGY

German conquests in Europe raised questions in the United States concerning the fate of Dutch, French, and possibly British possessions in the Western Hemisphere. Acting upon a statement he made in 1938 that the United States would not permit a foreign power's domination of Canada (a self-governing autonomous state within the British commonwealth of nations), President Roosevelt joined Canadian prime minister William. L. Mackenzie King in creating in 1940 the Permanent Joint Board on Defense to study the defense needs of the Atlantic and Pacific coasts of both nations. Further, Congress passed a joint resolution in 1940 declaring that the United States would not recognize the transfer of title of any territory of the Western Hemisphere from one non-American nation to another.

Election of 1940

The close advisors of President Roosevelt asserted throughout the campaign that his reluctance to run for a third term had been overcome by his conviction that it would be detrimental to the nation to change administrations in the midst of worldwide war.

DEMOCRATS

The delegates to the Democratic national convention, in a rather sullen mood over the possible adverse effects of the third-term issue upon their party's success in the election, permitted the administration leaders to persuade them that the ticket should consist of Roosevelt and his secretary of agriculture, Henry A. Wallace. The platform defended the New Deal record of social legislation and the party's recent achievements in the area of defense.

REPUBLICANS

The national convention of the Republican party passed over such well-known aspirants to the presidency as Senator Robert A. Taft of Ohio and racket-busting district attorney Thomas E. Dewey of New York. The delegates nominated a newcomer to politics, Wendell L. Willkie, who had recently transferred from the Democratic to the Republican party. As head of the Commonwealth and Southern Corporation, a utility holding company, Willkie had been a cogent critic of New Deal policies. His big-business connections were balanced by the nomination for vice-president of Senator Charles L. McNary of Oregon, a noted advocate of farm legislation. As for the platform, it supported many New Deal reform measures but attacked New Deal methods as wasteful, bureaucratic, and dictatorial.

THE CAMPAIGN

There had been forecasts that the campaign would revolve around foreign policy, but the two candidates offered the voters strikingly similar positions. Each favored a strong national defense, all aid to Great Britain short of war, and protection of the Western Hemisphere against aggression. Both promised to keep the United States out of the European conflict. The Democratic candidate virtually repudiated conservative support and promised to extend social legislation, while the Republican candidate accused the Roosevelt supporters of stirring class antagonism for political advantage.

ROOSEVELT'S THIRD VICTORY

The balloting resulted in a third victory for Roosevelt; his success, however, was not so widespread as that of four years earlier. The popular vote was 27,313,000 for Roosevelt and 22,348,000 for Willkie. Roosevelt captured thirty-eight states with 449 electoral votes. Although Willkie secured almost 45 percent of the popular vote, he received only 82 votes in the electoral college, representing ten states chiefly in the farm belt of the Midwest. The Democrats carried both houses of Congress. After the election Willkie promptly called for national unity despite differences of opinion on domestic issues. He was especially insistent that political partisanship play no part in modifying the nation's decision to aid Great Britain and to resist to the utmost totalitarian aggression.

Aid to the Allies

Although a large majority of Americans were anxious to avoid any involvement in World War II, they were eager for Great Britain and France to win. In 1941 the issue of giving aid to the Allies precipitated a bitter debate between the isolationists and interventionists that was finally won by the latter.

TRANSFER OF DESTROYERS

The British were sorely in need of additional destroyers to fight the German submarines that were attacking their merchant ships in the Atlantic. In September 1940, President Roosevelt by executive agreement transferred fifty "over-age" destroyers to Great Britain in exchange for ninety-nine-year leases on eight naval and air bases on British possessions in the Western Hemisphere, ranging from Newfoundland to British Guiana. Amid a furor from the isolationists over the destroyer deal, President Roosevelt defended his action on the sole grounds of Western Hemisphere defense.

THE LEND-LEASE ACT

In March 1941, Congress, over the protests of the isolationist leaders, passed the Lend-Lease Act, authorizing the president to sell, lend, lease, transfer, or exchange arms and other supplies to or with any nation whose defense he considered vital to the defense of the United States. The amount of aid that could be given was limited, but the president was allowed considerable discretion in placing a value upon such goods and in arranging the terms of the delivery.

In June 1941, in violation of their 1939 pact, Germany invaded the Soviet Union. American lend-lease aid was promptly extended to the Soviet Union. By 1942 thirty-five countries, in addition to the British commonwealth nations, had received assistance under the terms of the act. The total in lend-lease aid during the course of World War II amounted to more than $50 billion.

OCCUPATION OF GREENLAND AND ICELAND

In an extensive agreement signed in April 1941 with the Danish minister to Washington, the United States promised to defend the Danish possession of Greenland against invasion in exchange for the right to establish a base there. By agreement with Iceland, which had proclaimed its independence from Denmark after the German occupation of that nation, in July 1941 the United States established a military base in Iceland to prevent its invasion by Germany. By taking such actions the United States made certain that the control of the Atlantic would not pass to any hostile nation.

THE ATLANTIC CHARTER

In August 1941, President Roosevelt and British prime minister Winston Churchill set forth in a joint statement the postwar objectives of their nations, a step that caused the Axis powers to insist that the United States and Great Britain were already in alliance.

Known as the Atlantic Charter, this statement was the result of conversations between Roosevelt and Churchill at secret meetings aboard their respective warships off the coast of Newfoundland. The document stated that both nations (1) renounced territorial aggrandizement; (2) opposed territorial changes contrary to the wishes of the people concerned; (3) respected the right of all people to choose their own form of government; (4) would assist in arranging for all nations equal access to the trade and raw materials of the world; (5) favored cooperation among the nations to improve the economic status and social security of all people; (6) hoped that the peace settlement would enable people throughout the world to "live out their lives in freedom from fear and want"; (7) supported freedom of the seas; and (8) advocated disarmament of aggressor nations.

COMBAT IN THE ATLANTIC

The delivery of lend-lease goods from the United States depended upon the ability of Great Britain to get its merchant vessels back and forth across the Atlantic safely. Those vessels were convoyed by British warships and other warships that had escaped from the ports of nations occupied by German forces. The American navy itself increasingly participated in protecting lend-lease shipments in the Atlantic through the convoy system.

Germany tried to prevent the United States from continuing its lend-lease aid by submarine attacks on ships moving across the Atlantic. In September 1941, President Roosevelt ordered all American naval commanders to "shoot on sight" any Axis submarine entering Western Hemisphere defensive waters, including the waters surrounding Greenland and Iceland. In October 1941, a German submarine attacked and sank the American destroyer *Reuben James* on convoy duty in Icelandic waters, with the loss of seventy-six of its crew. The following month Congress passed an act that authorized the arming of American merchant ships and permitted them to carry goods directly to the ports of belligerent nations.

UNITED STATES ENTRY INTO WAR

The attack on Pearl Harbor quickly ended the debate between isolationists and interventionists over foreign policy and united the American people in a solemn determination to successfully meet one of the greatest crises in the nation's history.

Strained Relations with Japan

In the 1930s Japan attempted through military aggression to secure control of the Far East. The government of the United States denounced the Japanese actions but was unwilling to apply force to prevent them.

INVASION OF CHINA

In July 1937, Japan invaded China and soon controlled the nation's coastal areas. Although the American people became strongly anti-Japanese, their leaders were too much concerned over the threatening situation in Europe to take punitive action in the Far East. A crisis occurred between the United States and Japan when Japanese airplanes in China bombed the American gunboat *Panay* on the Yangtze River, killing two and wounding thirty. But the matter was resolved when the Japanese government issued a formal apology. In late 1938 Japan felt confident enough to warn the world that there would be a "new order" in Asia and it would not include adherence to the decades-old open-door trading principle in China. The American State Department refused to accept any such unilateral abrogation of Japan's previous agreements on the open-door policy.

By 1939 the United States and Japan were carrying on a war of words. Japanese purchases in the United States of materials with military uses, such as aviation gasoline and scrap iron, continued, but the control over their sale became increasingly vigorous. Resentment against Japan quickened

American sympathy for China. Contributions to the relief of Chinese war victims were but one evidence of that sympathy. By 1940 the American government had lent almost $70 million to the Chinese government for the purchase of badly needed supplies. To make such aid possible President Roosevelt refrained from invoking the provisions of the Neutrality Act of 1937 forbidding the extension of loans to belligerents, basing his position on the grounds that there had been no declaration of war.

INCREASED JAPANESE TRUCULENCE

In late 1940 Japan became a member of the Axis powers when it signed a ten-year pact with Germany and Italy pledging to assist one another in case war should occur with a nation not then a belligerent. Beginning in 1941 Japan became ever more truculent toward its neighbors in Asia. The war against China was pressed ruthlessly. Japanese forces occupied Indochina, the southeast Asian possession of France, now that the latter country had been defeated by Germany. Unprepared and unwilling to fight Japan in the Pacific while the fate of Europe was still undecided, the United States continued a policy of appeasement until the summer of 1941, when it finally forbade the export to Japan of aviation gasoline, scrap iron, and other war matériel.

THE KURUSU MISSION

Japan maintained that it desired to reach a peaceful settlement of all outstanding differences with the United States. When the leader of the prowar party, General Hideki Tojo, became prime minister in October 1941, Saburo Kurusu was sent to the United States as a special envoy to join the Japanese ambassador to Washington, Kichisaburo Nomura, in proposing a settlement of the two nations' disagreements in the Pacific. Nomura and Kurusu demanded, among other things, that the United States abandon its support of China, resume trade with Japan in all commodities, and halt its naval expansion program in the Pacific. Secretary of State Cordell Hull made counterproposals for the United States, including the signing of a multilateral nonaggression pact for the Far East and the withdrawal of Japanese forces from China and Indochina.

Japan Strikes the United States

While Nomura and Kurusu were engaged in discussing with Hull the possibilities for a peaceful settlement of differences in the Pacific, Japan struck the United States.

THE ATTACK ON PEARL HARBOR

On December 7, 1941, Japanese airplanes made a surprise attack on the American naval base at Pearl Harbor in Hawaii that began at 7:55 A.M. (local time) and continued for almost two hours. Of the eight battleships stationed at Pearl Harbor, three were sunk, one was grounded, and four were damaged. A small number of lesser warships were disabled, and approximately 175 airplanes were destroyed. In the attack 2,335 American soldiers and sailors were killed and 1,178 were wounded. On the same day Japanese forces assaulted the Philippines, Guam, the British crown colony of Hong Kong, and the British-controlled Malay Peninsula, including its port city of Singapore.

ROOSEVELT'S WAR MESSAGE

The day after the attack on Pearl Harbor President Roosevelt addressed a joint session of Congress. Asserting that December 7, 1941 was "a date which will live in infamy," he asked for a declaration of war against Japan. Within hours Congress passed a resolution to that effect, with but one dissenting vote in the lower house. On December 11 Germany and Italy declared war on the United States, which in turn adopted war resolutions against them.

The Armed Forces

As in World War I, the difficult task of providing people to serve in the armed forces was accomplished with gratifying success. For the second time in less than a quarter-century, young men of the United States were compelled to perform military duty. Popularly called GIs (from an unofficial abbreviation for "government issue"), they did not fail their nation.

CONSCRIPTION AND ENLISTMENT

In December 1941, Congress amended the 1940 Selective Training and Service Act by lowering the minimum draft-registration age to twenty and raising the maximum to forty-four. More than 31 million men were registered, of whom some 9.8 million were conscripted into the various branches of the armed forces. Approximately 5 million men enlisted voluntarily for military service. By the end of the war there were over 11.2 million in the army (including its air force, numbering about 3 million), close to 4.2 million in the navy, approximately 675,000 in the marine corps, and about 250,000 in the coast guard. Almost 260,000 women enlisted for noncombatant duty in all branches of the armed forces. In the army they were popularly known as WACs (for Women's Army Corps) and in the navy WAVEs (for Women Appointed for Voluntary Emergency Service).

TRAINING AND TRANSPORT OF TROOPS

The draftees and enlistees were quite speedily and rather effectively trained at scores of bases, of which some were expanded and others newly built, throughout the nation. By the end of the war approximately 12 million men had gone overseas, of whom about 4.7 million had engaged in combat duty.

AMERICAN WAR COSTS

For the United States, World War II exceeded World War I in loss of life. It was by far its most costly war in financial expenditures. Approximately 293,000 men were killed in battle, while some 116,000 died of other causes (disease or accident). About 670,000 men were wounded in combat. Financial expenditures of the United States amounted to an estimated $315 billion, about ten times the amount spent on all of its previous wars combined.

THE HOME FRONT

Modern warfare requires the total participation of a nation. Those who go to meet the enemy must be buttressed materially as well as spiritually by those they leave at home. When the United States entered the war against the Axis powers, it needed to quickly mobilize national resources: manufacturing facilities, food, labor, and transportation. To raise the huge sums necessary to pay for the war, the old methods of collecting revenue—taxation and borrowing—had to be refined.

Mobilizing Production

By the middle of 1943 the American people had converted their peacetime industrial establishment into the mightiest wartime arsenal that the world had ever seen.

THE WAR PRODUCTION BOARD

The nine-member War Production Board, headed by Donald Nelson, supervised the staggering tasks of constructing many new plants for the manufacture of war commodities and switching many existing plants from peacetime to wartime production. Within a year after the Pearl Harbor attack the nation had produced under the War Production Board more than $47 billion worth of war matériel, including 32,000 tanks, 49,000 airplanes, and merchant ships totaling 8 million tons. By the end of the war the nation had produced 85,000 tanks, 295,000 airplanes, and 70,000 warships and 5,500 merchant ships. Although the manufacture of many peacetime commodities was either curtailed or prohibited in order to facilitate the manufacture of war items, the total industrial production of the nation almost doubled during the war.

THE FOOD ADMINISTRATION

Despite the bumper crops during World War II, it was difficult to meet the extraordinary demand for foodstuffs. The entire problem of the production and distribution of food was placed directly under the supervision of the Food Administration, whose members were appointed by the president. To continue the program of helping the Allies and supplying the American armed services required careful planning, especially since farmers were handicapped by a dwindling work force and shortages of new agricultural machinery and parts to repair old machinery. The armed forces were allocated approximately 30 percent of the American meat supply. Within fifteen months of the United States entry into the war, it had shipped to Great Britain, the Soviet Union, and China more than 7 billion pounds of food.

THE OFFICE OF PRICE ADMINISTRATION (OPA)

Domestic consumption of such foods as sugar, coffee, meat, and butter was partially controlled through the rationing imposed by the Office of Price Administration (OPA). The OPA also fixed prices and rationed other scarce commodities, such as tires and gasoline. The agency's complicated tasks were generally well handled.

Mobilizing Labor

Although the activities of workers were more strictly supervised by the government than at any other time in the nation's history, American laborers escaped the kind of regimentation experienced by workers of most other countries then at war.

ACHIEVEMENT OF WORKERS

Organized labor generally refrained from strikes and other forms of job action during the first years of the war. American workers were spurred to great efforts. Their record of output from 1942 to 1945 surpassed by far any previous record for a comparable period. At the same time, average weekly earnings rose from approximately twenty-five dollars to about forty-five dollars, while the length of the workweek increased from approximately thirty-eight to about forty-five hours.

THE EMPLOYMENT OF WOMEN

The critical need for labor resulting from the nation's wartime production efforts led to the hiring of women in such numbers that their participation in the job market skyrocketed. During the war the employment of women increased from about 12 million to more than 18 million; by its end women made up approximately 35 percent of the labor force. It is significant that women performed exceedingly well in such jobs as truck driving and riveting that had hitherto been denied them as being beyond their physical strength.

THE WAR MANPOWER COMMISSION

The utilization of labor resources was placed under the nine-member War Manpower Commission, with Paul V. McNutt as chairman. The commission handled the task of apportioning the work of approximately 50 million men and about 20 million women in the labor force.

THE NATIONAL WAR LABOR BOARD

Within a month after the United States entered the armed conflict the twelve-member National War Labor Board was established to settle management-labor disputes through mediation and arbitration. When strife flared up in 1943, Congress passed over Roosevelt's veto the War Labor Disputes Act (also called the Smith-Connally Anti-Strike Act), which, among other things, authorized the president to seize plants in which labor disturbances threatened to impede war production. An unsuccessful attempt was made to stabilize wages through the rulings of the National War Labor Board.

Mobilizing Transportation

If the United States had any "secret weapon" during the early years of the war, it was the marvelous efficiency of its transportation facilities.

THE OFFICE OF DEFENSE TRANSPORTATION

During World War I it had been necessary for the government to assume control of the railroads. During World War II, however, railroad operators and employees, working with the temporarily established Office of Defense Transportation, carried unprecedented numbers of troops and amounts of arms and equipment. In 1942 the railroads transported 40 percent more passengers and 30 percent more freight than they had the previous year. This was done with 20,000 fewer locomotives and 600,000 fewer freight cars than they had possessed during World War I.

THE WAR SHIPPING BOARD

The Allies had two countermeasures to the threat of German submarines: first, improved methods for seeking out and destroying underwater vessels; second, the tremendous output of American shipyards. Under the supervision of the War Shipping Board, prefabricated vessels were built within the amazing time of two and a half months or less. This speed made it possible for the American fleet to maintain a supply line from the United States to the Allies in Europe that, after the first few months of the war, was more than adequate.

AIRWAYS

The commercial airlines, although subordinating their activities to war needs, managed to keep many of their normal schedules. Virtually all airplane construction by private firms was for military purposes. Within a year after the Pearl Harbor attack the nation had produced about 49,000 airplanes. In 1943 the output was over 5,500 airplanes a month, compared with approximately 200 a month in 1939.

Financing the War

Between January 1940 and January 1943, the appropriations first for national defense and then for war itself amounted to approximately $220 billion—slightly more than the cost of government from the inauguration of George Washington in 1789 to 1940. During World War II the national debt rose from approximately $47 billion to about $247 billion.

TAXES

By the second year of the war it was estimated that the daily cost of the conflict to the American people was $1.15 for every man, woman, and child, while revenue to the government from taxes was scarcely forty cents per person. Successive tax bills were designed and passed to increase the proportion of the cost of the war to be met through taxation as opposed to borrowing. This was accomplished by (1) adding millions of taxpayers to the rolls through lowering the minimum tax-exempt income; (2) revising upward the personal income-tax rates; and (3) imposing on corporations a virtual confiscation of income that represented excess profits from the war. In 1943 Congress accepted a plan to place collection of personal income taxes on a withholding ("pay-as-you-go") basis.

WAR BONDS

Despite increased revenue from taxes, the federal government relied upon borrowing through the sale of war bonds and small-denomination war stamps to meet the bulk of the war costs. By July 1945, the government had conducted seven highly successful war-bond drives, which had raised approximately $61 billion in all.

Election of 1944

Not since 1864 had the American people been forced to turn aside from the various pursuits involved in conducting a war to engage in the procedure of choosing a president.

DEMOCRATS

When the Democratic national convention began its proceedings, the delegates knew that President Roosevelt desired a fourth term. He was nominated on the first ballot, although the opponents of a fourth term, most of whom were in southern delegations, cast some ninety votes for Senator Harry F. Byrd of Virginia. The drama of the convention came in the struggle of ultraliberal vice-president Wallace for renomination. Although Wallace led on the first ballot, he was finally defeated by an alliance between certain conservative leaders from the South and the leaders of several powerful political machines in northern cities. As a result of a decision to choose a compromise vice-presidential candidate, and thus avoid a rupture between the liberal and conservative wings of the party, Senator Harry S. Truman of Missouri became Roosevelt's running mate.

REPUBLICANS

During the preconvention primaries Wendell L. Willkie, who had been defeated by Roosevelt in 1940, came to the conclusion that he could not again secure the Republican nomination for president. His position among Republicans was still strong, however, and he used his influence to counteract the power of the isolationist wing of the party. Those who were reluctant to make commitments concerning an active United States role in the postwar period probably would have preferred Senator Robert A. Taft or Governor John Bricker, both isolationists from Ohio, as the presidential nominee. But the delegates to the Republican national convention yielded to the apparent popularity of the mildly liberal and internationalist governor Thomas E. Dewey of New York and nominated him with only one dissenting vote. To balance the ticket, Bricker was then chosen for the second slot.

THE CAMPAIGN

As soon as the campaign got under way, it became clear that it would not revolve around the issues: Roosevelt and Dewey held quite similar views on the domestic programs the government should pursue to bring economic security to the American people and on the foreign policy that it should conduct after the war. Week after week Dewey reiterated that, after a dozen years of the New Deal, it was time for the voters to retire the "tired old men" from the executive branch. Only as the campaign entered its latter stage did Roosevelt become actively involved by giving some "tough" speeches in his familiar dynamic style.

ROOSEVELT'S FOURTH VICTORY

Out of 47,969,000 popular votes cast, Roosevelt received a plurality of 2,357,000. In the electoral college he carried thirty-six states with 432 votes, to twelve states with 99 votes for Dewey. Roosevelt's popularity had remained strong.

THE WAR IN EUROPE

The German conquests in Western Europe were swift and devastating. Then the German attack upon the Soviet Union brought stunning initial success. But soon the Soviets responded with a fierce counteroffensive.

Meanwhile the Allied invasions of North Africa and Italy prepared the way for the 1944 landings in France that led to the defeat of Germany. Although the Germans fought stubbornly, their resistance was crushed within a year by the might of the Allied military forces.

German Conquests

During the winter of 1939–40 there was little military action in Western Europe. The Soviet Union took advantage of the situation to conquer the Baltic states: Estonia, Latvia, Lithuania (each of which in 1918 had achieved independence from the newly established Soviet Union), and Finland. But once the German offensives began, first in Western Europe and then against the Soviet Union, they were overpowering.

SCANDINAVIA AND THE LOW COUNTRIES

In April 1940, German seaborne troops invaded Denmark and Norway. Denmark fell quickly, while Norway, aided by British and French forces, resisted for two months. Early in May the highly mechanized German army overran Belgium, Luxembourg, and the Netherlands. In the face of over-whelming German military power, Luxembourg fell in one day, the Netherlands in five, and Belgium in nineteen. The ruthless German invasion of the neutral Scandinavian nations and Low Countries aroused the Americans.

THE FALL OF FRANCE AND THE RESISTANCE OF GREAT BRITAIN

Early in June 1940, Italy entered the war on the side of Germany. France surrendered less than two weeks later, after having been exposed to a punishing new offensive by German forces. The British expeditionary army was then forced to evacuate the continent. Great Britain fought on alone despite extensive and severe bombings by the Luftwaffe (the German air fleet). The American people were quick to applaud British heroism.

INVASION OF THE SOVIET UNION

In June 1941, Germany suddenly invaded the Soviet Union. For six months approximately 3 million German troops drove deep into Soviet territory. By December they were nearing Moscow. But with the bitter winter of 1941–42 the German advance came to a halt, and the Soviets began a powerful counteroffensive.

German Setbacks

By the fall of 1942 the Germans controlled an empire that was at its height, extending from Norway to North Africa and from France to the western reaches of the Soviet Union. In less than two years it collapsed.

THE NORTH AFRICAN CAMPAIGN

In August 1940, Italian troops attacked British territory in North Africa. Six months later German forces were sent to the area to assist in the Italian military operation. For almost two years British troops fought Germans and Italians back and forth across North Africa. In November 1942, an armada

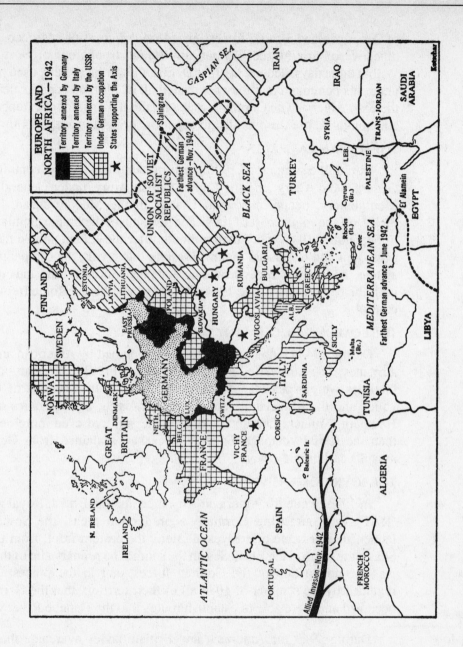

Map of Europe and North Africa - 1942

of American and British forces landed on the coast of Morocco, with the objective of driving the German and Italian troops out of North Africa. Within three days General Dwight D. Eisenhower had so disposed the forces under his command that they controlled all of Morocco and its neighbor to the east, Algeria. The Germans, aided by the Italians, fought stubbornly for six months before they yielded to superior strength in May 1943.

THE ITALIAN CAMPAIGN

During the summer of 1943 the Fifth American Army, commanded by General Mark Clark, and the Eighth British Army, under General Bernard Montgomery, occupied several islands in the Mediterranean, including Sicily, off the south coast of Italy. The invasion of the Italian mainland began in September 1943, more than a month after the Italian people had ousted Mussolini and his fascist regime. Despite this revolt, the campaign in Italy against the German forces sent to defend the nation was long and costly. Not until the beginning of June 1944 did the Allies liberate Rome from German control.

THE BOMBING OF GERMANY

During 1943 Germany was massively bombed by American and British airplanes. The Luftwaffe was knocked out of the sky. German production facilities were repeatedly demolished; the industrial centers of the Ruhr valley and the Rhineland were all but paralyzed; and the cities of Berlin, Hamburg, Munich, Dresden, and Cologne suffered even more destruction than the terrible damage English cities had sustained from German air assaults earlier in the war.

THE SOVIET OFFENSIVE

In 1943, while the American Air Force and the British Royal Air Force (RAF) were attacking Germany's production areas, the Soviet forces launched large-scale offensives all along the eastern front, from the Baltic Sea on the north to the Black Sea on the south. The primary aim of the Soviets was the destruction of the German forces, and in the process they had regained by the summer of 1944 all of their territory that the Germans had occupied and were able to establish routes into the Danube River valley.

Coming to a Close

During 1943 the American and British navies overcame the German submarine menace and opened the sea lanes to the transport of troops and supplies. By June 1944, more than 2 million American troops were in Great Britain, awaiting the invasion of German-occupied France.

THE BATTLE OF FRANCE

In the early hours of June 6, 1944, Allied troops, on orders from Supreme Commander Eisenhower, left their bases in Great Britain and crossed the English Channel to storm the French beaches in the vicinity of Cherbourg.

Preceded by paratroopers and protected by an awesome bombardment from a huge naval fleet, they soon established beachheads and, with the aid of the air force, connected their individual landing zones into one battle front. Within three months of these landings, the Allied armies had conquered Normandy to the northeast, overrun Brittany to the west, chased the Germans north of the Seine River, and assisted the Free French forces of resistance in liberating Paris. In August 1944, new landings were made, with slight losses, on the Mediterranean coast of France near Marseilles. On August 26 General Eisenhower announced the destruction of the German Seventh Army. The Battle of France had been won.

UNCONDITIONAL SURRENDER

German counterattacks just west of the Rhine River proved to be surprisingly determined but were overcome by Allied military power. In December 1944, the Germans mounted an offensive that created a huge bulge in the Allied lines, from which came the name Battle of the Bulge. After yielding some valuable ground, the American and British troops stood firm. One young American officer, Brigadier General Anthony McAuliffe, when the Germans pressed him to surrender, gave the simple but memorable reply: "Nuts!" While incessant bombing pounded much of the western reaches of Germany into rubble, the American First Army reached the Rhine River. In March 1945, the first troops crossed the river southeast of Cologne and moved into the interior of Germany. For the next two months the Allied armies in the west advanced steadily, while the Soviet forces cut through Austria and closed in on Berlin. Hitler, aware that the end was near, took his own life, while other high Nazi officials either committed suicide or went into hiding. On May 7, 1945 at Reims, France, a representative of the German general staff, which had taken over after Hitler's death, accepted the terms of unconditional surrender. May 8 was proclaimed to an expectant world as V-E (Victory in Europe) Day.

THE WAR IN THE PACIFIC

Like the Germans, the Japanese enjoyed a number of early conquests. But a few months after the surrender of Germany in May 1945, there followed the defeat of Japan—hastened by the use of the atomic bomb.

Japanese Conquests

The first half of 1942 was marked by a series of major victories for Japan in the Pacific.

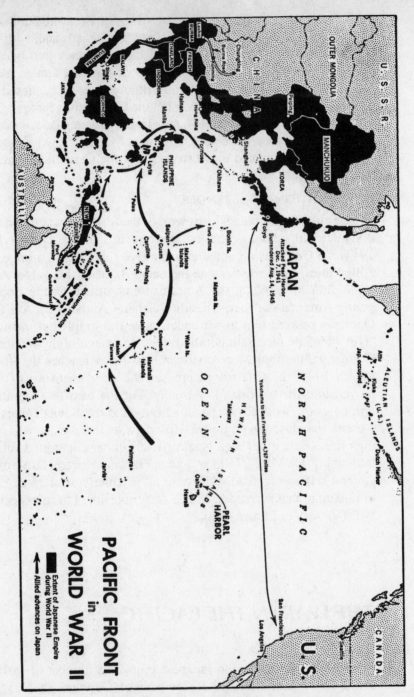

Pacific Front in World War II

BRITISH AND DUTCH POSSESSIONS

The world was astonished by the speed of the Japanese military advance after the attack on Pearl Harbor in December 1941. Within two months Japan had secured the entire British-controlled Malay Peninsula, with its great naval base at Singapore. Three weeks later the Japanese overran the Netherlands East Indies. Early in May 1942, Great Britain retreated from its Burma possession into India. Japanese bases that had been established to the north on Dutch-owned New Guinea and to the east in the Bismarck and Solomon islands, which had been under an Australian mandate, were growing in strength.

FALL OF THE PHILIPPINES

Under the command of General Douglas MacArthur, American and Filipino troops heroically defended the Bataan peninsula and the fortress on the island of Corregidor until resistance was no longer possible. At the order of President Roosevelt, MacArthur transferred his headquarters to Australia in February 1942, but his troops, under General Jonathan Wainwright, held Corregidor until the following May.

THE ALEUTIAN ISLANDS

Soon after Japan had secured the Philippines, its forces to the north moved into the American-owned Aleutians, a chain of islands that extends westward from the tip of the Alaska peninsula. Japanese troops occupied the islands of Attu, Agattu, and Kiska for more than a year before American forces ousted them in the spring of 1943.

Japanese Setbacks

By the late summer of 1942 the Japanese had occupied a million square miles in their triumphant advance, but there it ended. Their retreat was humiliating and costly in both life and material resources.

THE BATTLES OF THE CORAL SEA AND MIDWAY

In April 1942, American airplanes commanded by General James Doolittle dropped tons of bombs on Tokyo, Yokohama, and Kobe. This was the first attack on the Japanese home islands. A few weeks later, American naval and air forces in the Coral Sea stopped an invading force aimed at Australia to the west. The first real defeat for Japan took place in June 1942, with the rout of a strong Japanese naval force proceeding toward the American-owned Midway Islands, to the northwest of Hawaii.

FROM ISLAND TO ISLAND

In August 1942, the Allies launched their counteroffensive in earnest, as American marines, buttressed by air and naval forces, landed on Guadalcanal in the Solomon Islands. For the next two years the Japanese suffered costly defeats in the western Pacific as island after island fell to American forces under General MacArthur and admirals Chester W. Nimitz and William F.

Halsey, ably supported by their allies. From the Solomons the Allies moved into the Marshalls (which had been held by Japan under a League of Nations mandate), the British-owned Gilberts, and the Carolines and Marianas (both also held by Japan under a League mandate). They took Guam and then prepared for the reconquest of the Philippine Islands.

THE BOMBING OF JAPAN

In the spring of 1944, American aircraft factories began to produce special bombers called Superfortresses, which were designed for long flights with heavy bomb loads. Based on airfields in China, which Chinese labor had built almost without tools, these airplanes effectively destroyed the industrial centers of Japan.

CHINA

While the Allied forces moved northward and westward across the islands of the Pacific, ever closer to Japan, the Chinese kept up a heroic resistance to the Japanese occupation of their homeland. They were heartened by increasing support from American air forces in China commanded by General Claire Chennault and by the campaign of Chinese and American troops to reopen the Burma Road, a highway first used in 1938 to carry war supplies to Chinese troops and captured by Japanese forces during the war. At the same time forces of various countries within the British commonwealth of nations were gradually clearing the Japanese out of Burma.

Coming to a Close

With the defeat of Germany in May 1945, the United States strove to speed up the war against Japan.

PREPARING FOR THE ASSAULT ON JAPAN

During the spring of 1945, troops commanded by General MacArthur continued to eliminate pockets of Japanese resistance in the Philippines and cooperated with the Australians in the attack on the partly British- and partly Dutch-owned Borneo to the southwest. To the north of the Philippines the combined operations of the army (along with its air force), navy, and marine corps won Iwo Jima and Okinawa, two islands close to Japan proper. Bases on those islands were prepared by the early summer of 1945 for the final assault on the Japanese home islands.

THE ATOMIC BOMB

Through the cooperative efforts of scientists from many Allied nations as well as a number who had fled from Nazi-controlled nations, the atomic bomb was perfected. The American physicist J. Robert Oppenheimer directed the Los Alamos laboratory in New Mexico, where the bomb was designed and constructed. Making particularly significant contributions were three physicists who were refugees from Nazi-dominated Europe: the

German Albert Einstein, the Italian Enrico Fermi, and the Dane Niels Bohr. The atomic bomb that was developed was the most devastating weapon that the world had ever seen. On August 6, 1945, American airmen dropped the first such bomb on Hiroshima. Approximately 180,000 people were killed or wounded. Three days later a second bomb was dropped, this time on Nagasaki. There were 80,000 immediate casualties. Both cities were virtually obliterated.

UNCONDITIONAL SURRENDER

During a conference of American, British, and Soviet leaders, which assembled in mid-July 1945 in the German city of Potsdam, near Berlin, the United States and Great Britain sent Japan an ultimatum demanding unconditional surrender. At the same time, Soviet premier Joseph Stalin informed President Harry S. Truman that the Soviet Union would soon enter the war against Japan. Two days after the atomic bomb was first used, the Soviet Union moved against the Japanese in Manchuria. The official Tokyo radio station promptly broadcasted an appeal for peace.

After an exchange of notes between the United States and Japan, President Truman announced on August 14 that hostilities had ceased. It was agreed that General MacArthur, appointed the supreme commander for the Allied powers, would rule Japan through Emperor Hirohito until militarism was eliminated and democratic reforms were implemented. On September 2, aboard the battleship *Missouri* in Tokyo Bay, members of a Japanese delegation signed the surrender documents before the representatives of nine of the Allied nations. President Truman proclaimed that September 2 was to be celebrated as V-J (Victory over Japan) Day.

THE DEFEATED NATIONS

In dealing with Germany and Japan the victorious powers concerned themselves with three major tasks: occupying the conquered territories; conducting trials of war criminals; and drafting peace treaties.

Germany

The job of occupying defeated Germany proved long and difficult. On one point the wartime Allied powers could agree: the punishment of German war criminals. As tensions increased between the Western allies and the Soviet Union, it became impossible to frame a peace treaty with Germany.

THE OCCUPATION

A month after Germany surrendered, the nation was divided into four zones of occupation, with the military forces of the United States, Great Britain, France, and the Soviet Union each in charge of a specific zone. The United States commanded the southern sector, Great Britain the northwestern, France the southwestern, and the Soviet Union the eastern. Berlin, which lay within the Soviet sector, was itself divided by the Allies into four occupation zones. General Lucius D. Clay served as military governor of the American zone of occupation. The United States, Great Britain, and France pursued a policy of allowing German officials to assume increasing authority. In 1949 the three western zones were combined to form the Federal Republic of Germany, with Bonn as the capital; the Soviet zone was transformed into the German Democratic Republic, with the Soviet sector of Berlin as its capital. Military occupation then ended in the western zones but continued in the three western sectors of Berlin, since no peace treaty uniting all of Germany had been concluded.

WAR CRIMES TRIALS

Six months after the Germans surrendered, an international military tribunal convened in Nuremberg, Germany, to bring civil and military leaders of the Nazi regime to trial as war criminals. Judges and attorneys from the four nations occupying Germany participated in the first of a series of trials. Associate Justice Robert H. Jackson of the United States Supreme Court served as one of the chief prosecutors. Among the twenty-two defendants taken into custody were reich marshal and Luftwaffe commander Hermann Goering, Hitler's deputy Rudolf Hess, and foreign minister Joachim von Ribbentrop. The crimes the defendants were variously charged with included planning a war of aggression, using slave labor, and exterminating Jews. Twelve of the accused were sentenced to death, seven received prison terms, and three were acquitted. Trials of lesser figures were conducted in each of the four occupation zones. In the American zone approximately 500,000 former Nazis were convicted of war crimes.

THE PEACE TREATY

The drafting of a peace treaty with Germany was impeded by the increasingly deteriorating relations between the Western allies and the Soviet Union. Finally, in 1955, the Western allies signed a treaty with the six-year-old Federal Republic of Germany, by then known as West Germany. According to the treaty provisions, West Germany was granted complete independence, was authorized to develop its own military force, and was required to accept the stationing of Western allied troops. That same year the Soviet Union declared the German Democratic Republic, by then called East Germany, to be fully independent. Thus a general peace treaty with Germany was never concluded. The result was the establishment of two Germanys.

Japan

As was the case with Germany, the victorious powers had to deal with the difficult problems of occupying territory, conducting war-crimes trials, and framing a peace treaty.

THE OCCUPATION

A commission based in Washington, D.C., and consisting of representatives from thirteen Allied nations, including the United States, Great Britain, France, and the Soviet Union, was to direct the occupation of Japan. The commission's activities, however, were hampered by increasing animosity between the Western nations and the Soviet Union. As supreme commander for the Allied powers, General MacArthur ruled Japan. With the exception of a small number of military forces from the British commonwealth of nations, the troops were American. The primary goals of the occupation were to demilitarize and democratize Japan. The occupation ended in 1952. While it lasted, most Japanese were cooperative with MacArthur and his associates.

WAR CRIMES TRIALS

Early in 1946 the International Military Tribunal for the Far East, consisting of representatives from eleven Allied nations, convened in Tokyo to try twenty-five Japanese civil and military leaders for planning an aggressive war and committing crimes against humanity. Seven of the defendants, including former prime minister Hideki Tojo, were hanged; the others received prison sentences. In addition, numerous Japanese army and navy officers were brought to trial for violating the rules of war. Of those accused, approximately 6,000 were found guilty.

THE PEACE TREATY

In 1951 in San Francisco a peace treaty with Japan, which had been drafted under the direction of John Foster Dulles, a New York lawyer and foreign-affairs advisor to the Truman administration, was signed by forty-nine nations. The Soviet Union, which objected to various provisions of the document, refused to become a signatory. The treaty ended the military occupation and recognized the full sovereignty of Japan. The nation was permitted to maintain armed forces for purposes of self-defense only. Japan also agreed to divest itself of its overseas holdings. At the San Francisco conference the United States and Japan concluded a defense treaty providing for the stationing of American armed forces in Japan. Finally, in 1956, Japan signed a separate peace treaty with the Soviet Union.

Italy, Austria, and the Axis Satellites

Hostilities were formally ended with Italy and the Axis satellites—Hungary, Bulgaria, Romania, and Finland—before relations between the Western powers and the Soviet Union began to worsen. The postwar status of Austria, however, was affected by Western-Soviet tensions.

THE OCCUPATION

Italy and the minor Axis nations were occupied by Allied troops. The occupations did not last long, however, since peace treaties signed soon after the war provided for the prompt withdrawal of military forces from these nations. As for Austria, after its liberation from Germany it was divided for a number of years into four occupation zones, with the military forces of the United States, Great Britain, France, and the Soviet Union each in command of a particular zone.

THE PEACE TREATIES

In 1947 the Allied nations signed peace treaties with Italy and the Axis satellites. The United States did not participate in the treaty with Finland, since the two nations had not been at war. The treaties were quite similar in requiring Italy and each of the Axis satellites to surrender territory, to demilitarize, and to make reparations. In 1955 the United States, Great Britain, France, and the Soviet Union signed a treaty with Austria, restoring that nation to full sovereignty and prohibiting a political union with Germany such as had occurred before World War II.

THE UNITED NATIONS

During World War II the leaders of the principal nations that were fighting the Axis powers attended a number of conferences. They discussed not only pressing military affairs but also the nature of the peace they desired and how it could be achieved. Many viewed those wartime meetings as steps toward reaching the goal of a permanent postwar international cooperation for peace. And many hoped that goal had been attained when in 1945 representatives of fifty-one nations signed the charter of the United Nations organization. In 1952 the permanent headquarters of the world body were finally established in New York City.

International Planning for a Peaceful World

The leaders of five Allied nations—the United States, Great Britain, the Soviet Union, France, and China—met in formal conferences over a period of three years to discuss plans for international cooperation after the war.

THE CASABLANCA CONFERENCE

In January 1943, President Roosevelt and Prime Minister Churchill met at Casablanca, in French Morocco, where, after agreeing on a number of military matters, they declared that the war would continue until the "unconditional surrender" of the Axis nations.

THE MOSCOW CONFERENCE

Secretary of State Cordell Hull, Foreign Secretary Anthony Eden of Great Britain, and Foreign Minister Vyacheslav M. Molotov of the Soviet Union conferred in Moscow in October 1943. The three men issued a statement, which came to be known as the Moscow Declaration, that a world organization for the maintenance of peace would be established after the war.

THE CAIRO CONFERENCE

In November 1943, Roosevelt and Churchill met in Cairo with Generalissimo Chiang Kai-shek, the political and military leader of China. There they formally promised to deprive Japan of all territory it had acquired since the latter part of the nineteenth century, with the areas taken from China restored to that country.

THE TEHERAN CONFERENCE

In Teheran, Iran, in November 1943, two days after the Cairo conference was concluded, Roosevelt, Churchill, and Stalin met for the first time. In a joint declaration issued at the close of the conference, the three leaders pledged that their nations would work together to win not only the war but also the peace. The concluding sentence of their declaration was: "We leave here, friends in fact, in spirit, and in purpose."

THE YALTA CONFERENCE

The most fateful of all the wartime conferences took place in February 1945 at the Soviet port of Yalta, in the Crimea. There Roosevelt, Churchill, and Stalin met for the second and final time. They were accompanied by their most important diplomatic and military advisors. It was decided to call a special conference of all the Allies the following April in San Francisco to draft a charter for an association of nations to maintain peace. Further, Roosevelt, Churchill, and Stalin publicly agreed: (1) to divide postwar Germany into American, British, Soviet, and French occupation zones; (2) to readjust the boundaries of Poland, with that nation relinquishing a portion of its eastern area to the Soviet Union and receiving German territory to the north and west as compensation; (3) to guarantee free elections in Poland; and (4) to ensure the establishment of a democratic form of government for all liberated European nations.

A number of agreements made at Yalta were not immediately made public. One secret clause granted the Ukraine and Byelorussia (two of the fifteen historically and ethnically cohesive republics constituting the Soviet Union) membership in the projected postwar association of nations equal to that of independent countries. Other secret provisions pertained to the Far East. The Soviet Union promised to enter the war against Japan after Germany's anticipated surrender. In return for this pledge, the Soviet Union, according to additional secret clauses, would regain the sphere of influence it had enjoyed in Manchuria before the Russo-Japanese War of 1904–05 and receive an occupation zone in Korea. The United States and Great Britain also secretly agreed to self-government for Outer Mongolia, which had been Chinese territory but under Soviet influence.

In the years after the Yalta conference, the American delegation was attacked for having conceded too much to the Soviet Union. Critics argued, for example, that although the Soviet Union did enter the war against Japan, the use of the atomic bomb precluded the need for Soviet military aid in achieving Allied victory in the Far East. Counterarguments were offered in support of the American delegation. Defenders pointed out, for example, that it was widely believed that Soviet aid in the war in the Far East would save the lives of many American servicemen in the final offensive against Japan, especially since those few American leaders who knew of the atomic bomb were unsure about its potential.

THE POTSDAM CONFERENCE

The last meeting during World War II of the leaders of the three principal Allied nations took place during July–August of 1945 at Potsdam, Germany. In attendance were Harry S. Truman, who a few months earlier had become president; Churchill, who was replaced while the conference was in progress by his successor as prime minister, Clement R. Attlee; and Stalin. Germany, but not Japan, had surrendered before the conference began. A declaration was issued at the Potsdam conference calling upon Japan to surrender unconditionally. The conferees agreed on a policy for the occupation of Germany and Japan, which included plans for both the decentralization and democratization of the two Axis nations. At Potsdam the American delegation began to perceive elements of noncooperation by representatives of the Soviet Union that had not been in evidence at the previous wartime conferences.

Drafting the
United Nations
Organization
Charter

In 1944 and 1945, countries fighting the Axis engaged in drawing up a charter for a postwar association of nations to preserve world peace.

THE DUMBARTON OAKS CONFERENCE

Upon Secretary of State Cordell Hull's invitation, representatives of Great Britain, the Soviet Union, and China met with delegates from the United States during August–October 1944 at Dumbarton Oaks, outside Washington, D. C., for a series of discussions concerning an international association after the war. Proposals were drafted that were to serve as the basis for the charter of the hoped-for world organization.

THE SAN FRANCISCO CONFERENCE

During April–June 1945, approximately 300 representatives from fifty-one countries met in San Francisco to draw up the charter of the international association. The American delegation was headed by Secretary of State Edward R. Stettinius Jr. At some of the sessions there were bitter exchanges between the American and Soviet representatives. After weeks of deliberation, the delegates adopted the charter of the United Nations.

Structure of the United Nations

The charter of the United Nations established six major bodies and provided for the setting up of such specialized agencies as might be deemed useful.

GENERAL ASSEMBLY

This body was composed of all member nations, each of which had one vote. The General Assembly had the power to discuss any issue that came under the charter and to recommend a course of action. In addition, it was granted power to supervise the specialized agencies.

SECURITY COUNCIL

This body was composed of five permanent members—the United States, Great Britain, the Soviet Union, France, China—and six (later increased to ten) members elected for overlapping two-year terms by the General Assembly. The Security Council was entrusted with the maintenance of international peace and security, being empowered to take military action for this purpose. Each permanent member was granted the right to veto a decision of the Security Council.

SECRETARIAT

This body was composed of a secretary general and a large staff to manage the routine affairs of the United Nations. As chief administrator of the organization, the secretary general was charged with implementing decisions reached by the General Assembly and the Security Council.

ECONOMIC AND SOCIAL COUNCIL

This body consisted of eighteen (later increased to twenty-seven) member nations that were elected by the General Assembly for overlapping three-year terms. The Economic and Social Council was to investigate all economic, social, cultural, educational, and health problems and then to recommend solutions.

INTERNATIONAL COURT OF JUSTICE

This body consisted of fifteen jurists elected for nine-year terms by the General Assembly and the Security Council. The Court had its headquarters at the Hague, the Netherlands. (It replaced the Permanent Court of International Justice, known as the World Court, of the League of Nations.) The Court was to be the principal judicial organ of the United Nations.

TRUSTEESHIP COUNCIL

This body consisted equally of member nations administering and member nations not administering trust territories. The trust territories were colonial areas unprepared for independence that the United Nations assigned to certain member nations for administration. They included lands previously held under the mandate of the League of Nations and colonies taken from the Axis powers at the end of World War II.

SPECIALIZED AGENCIES

Subsidiary bodies, eventually totaling more than a dozen, were set up to deal with a broad range of economic and social problems. These specialized agencies included the United Nations Education, Scientific, and Cultural Organization (UNESCO), the Food and Agricultural Organization (FAO), the International Labor Organization (ILO), and the World Health Organization (WHO).

Selected Readings

GENERAL WORKS:

Buchanan, A. Russell. *The United States and World War II* (2 vols., 1964)
Davis, Kenneth S. *Experience of War: The United States in World War II* (1965)
Fuller, John F. C. *The Second World War, 1939–1945* (1948)
Keegan, John. *The Second World War* (1990)
Pratt, Fletcher. *War for the World* (1950)
Snyder, Louis L. *The War: A Concise History, 1939–1945* (1960)

SPECIAL STUDIES:

Ambrose, Stephen E. *The Supreme Commander: The War Years of General Dwight D. Eisenhower* (1970)
Anderson, Karen T. *Wartime Women: Sex Roles, Family Relations, and the Status of American Women During World War II* (1981)
Beard, Charles A. *President Roosevelt and the Coming of the War, 1941* (1948)
Borg, Dorothy. *The United States and the Far Eastern Crisis of 1933–1938* (1964)
Buchanan, A. Russell. *Black Americans in World War II* (1977)
Buhite, Russell. *Decision at Yalta* (1986)
Eisenhower, Dwight D. *Crusade in Europe* (1948)
Feis, Herbert. *Churchill, Roosevelt, Stalin* (1957)
———. *The Decision to Drop the Bomb* (1966)

Hartmann, Susan. *The Home Front and Beyond: American Women in the 1940s* (1982)

Headen, Patrick. *Roosevelt Confronts Hitler: America's Entry into World War II* (1987)

Iriye, Akira. *Power and Culture: The Japanese-American War, 1941–1945* (1981)

Jonas, Manfred. *Isolationism in America, 1935–1941* (1966)

Kimball, Warren F. *The Most Unsordid Act: Lend Lease, 1939–1941* (1969)

Langer, Walter L., and Sarell E. Gleason. *The Challenge to Isolation, 1937–1940* (1952)

Larabee, Eric. *Commander in Chief: Franklin Delano Roosevelt, His Lieutenants, and Their War* (1987)

Lingeman, Richard R. *Don't You Know There's a War On? The American Home Front, 1941–1945* (1970)

Morison, Samuel Eliot. *The Two-Ocean War* (1963)

Nalty, Bernard C. *Strength for the Fight: A History of Black Americans in the Military* (1986)

Nevins, Allan. *The New Deal and World Affairs* (1950)

Prange, Gordon. *At Dawn We Slept* (1981)

Rauch, Basil. *Roosevelt: From Munich to Pearl Harbor* (1950)

Rhodes, Richard. *The Making of the Atomic Bomb* (1986)

Sherry, Michael. *The Rise of American Air Power* (1987)

Smith, Gaddis. *American Diplomacy During the Second World War, 1941–1945* (1965)

Spector, Ronald. *The Eagle Against the Sun: The American War with Japan* (1985)

Stainsbury, Keith. *Roosevelt, Stalin, Churchill, and Chiang Kai-shek, 1943: The Moscow, Cairo, and Teheran Conferences* (1985)

Tansill, Charles C. *Back Door to War* (1952)

Utley, Jonathan. *Going to War with Japan, 1937–1941* (1985)

Vatter, Harold. *The American Economy in World War II* (1985)

Walton, Francis. *Miracle of World War II: How American Industry Made Victory Possible* (1956)

Wohlstetter, Roberta. *Pearl Harbor, Warning and Decision* (1962)

Wyman, David. *The Abandonment of the Jews: America and the Holocaust, 1941–1945* (1984)

11

The Quest for Stability at Home and Peace Abroad

1939 Paperback books appear

1941 Welles, *Citizen Kane*

1943 Rodgers and Hammerstein, *Oklahoma!*

1944 Acken develops digital computer

Copland, *Appalachian Spring*

1945 Roosevelt dies; Truman becomes president

1946 O'Neill, *The Iceman Cometh*

1947 Truman Doctrine

Executive order investigates government employees' loyalty

Marshall Plan proposed

Taft-Hartley Act

Defense Department created

CIA created

Williams, *A Streetcar Named Desire*

1948 Marshall Plan implemented

Israel established

Executive order desegregates government departments and armed services

Hiss case

Truman elected president

Long-playing (LP) disks introduced

1948–1949 Berlin Airlift

1949 Point Four Program

Communist party leaders tried and found guilty of subversion

West Germany established

East Germany established

Nationalist Chinese government established on Taiwan

People's Republic of China established

Miller, *Death of a Salesman*

1950 McCarthy begins anticommunist crusade

McCarran Act

North Atlantic Treaty Organization (NATO) formed

Pollock, *Autumn Rhythm*

1950–1953 Korean War

1951 Twenty-second Amendment ratified

Rosenberg case

ANZUS Pact formed

Salinger, *Catcher in the Rye*

"I Love Lucy" with Lucille Ball premieres

1952 Eisenhower elected president

1953 Health, Education, and Welfare Department created

Playboy magazine begins publication

1954 Army-McCarthy hearings

Brown v. Board of Education of Topeka

Southeast Asia Treaty Organization (SEATO) formed

On the Waterfront with Brando

1955 First summit conference, in Geneva

AFL-CIO founded

Salk develops polio vaccine

1955–1956 Montgomery bus boycott

1956 Hungarian revolt

Suez Canal crisis

Eisenhower reelected president

1957 Eisenhower Doctrine announced

Civil Rights Act

Soviet Union launches *Sputnik*

1957–1958 Little Rock high-school desegregation crisis

1958   United States sends troops to Lebanon

National Defense Education Act

Bernstein becomes New York Philharmonic music director

1959   Alaska becomes a state

Hawaii becomes a state

U-2 incident

1960   Civil Rights Act

1962   Carson, *Silent Spring*

On April 12, 1945, Franklin D. Roosevelt died of a massive cerebral hemorrhage. For Harry S. Truman and then Dwight D. Eisenhower to assume the presidency following Roosevelt, who had performed brilliantly in the office for a dozen years, was exceptionally difficult. Although foreign affairs unquestionably dominated the Truman and Eisenhower administrations, many important domestic issues presented themselves. These included government reorganization and reform, the advance of civil rights, the implementation of social legislation, the regulation of labor, and the question of internal security. The conferences among Allied leaders during World War II, followed by the establishment of the United Nations, inspired hope for a lasting peace based on worldwide cooperation. In the postwar period, however, tensions increased between the Western allies, led by the United States, and the communist bloc of nations, led by the Soviet Union. Armed conflict between the two sides finally broke out in Korea.

TRUMAN AND THE DOMESTIC SCENE

The Truman administration faced many important issues—some of them bitterly controversial. Upon congressional acceptance of portions of his comprehensive program of social legislation, known as the Fair Deal, Truman witnessed some improvements in the general condition of the American people. The domestic issue that made for the greatest controversy was that of internal security. The extent of communist infiltration into every sector of society was examined and argued.

The Truman Administration

Truman was fully aware of his strengths and weaknesses. As president, he capitalized on the former and refused to be troubled by the latter.

THE PRESIDENT

Truman projected the image of the common man. But he was truly uncommon in his ability to bear up under long and hard work, to grasp the various aspects of a problem, and to engage in courageous decision making, as well as in his determination to help those in need.

THE CABINET

In office during a period of deep political strife, Truman kept changing cabinet members in order to find skillful administrators who could also be politically helpful. Concerned over the grave international situation, the president paid particular attention to finding a secretary of state. James F. Byrnes, a Democrat who had long represented South Carolina in Congress, was appointed to the post. When Byrnes resigned for reasons of health, he was succeeded by General George C. Marshall, who had been army chief of staff during World War II. Marshall was also forced to resign because of failing health, and he was replaced by Dean Acheson, who had been serving in the State Department for a number of years. Of all the cabinet members, Truman's closest advisors, in addition to Byrnes, were Fred M. Vinson and John W. Snyder, each of whom served as secretary of the treasury.

Government Reorganization and Reform

In order to cope with the tremendous expansion of the federal bureaucracy that developed out of the New Deal and World War II and to treat the difficult domestic and foreign issues in the postwar period, reorganization and reform measures were deemed necessary.

THE HOOVER COMMISSION

In 1947 Congress authorized the establishment of the Commission on Organization of the Executive Branch of Government. Known as the Hoover Commission after its chairman, former president Herbert Hoover, the body was charged with recommending ways to streamline the structure of the executive branch and to economize on its operations. Acting upon the commission's findings, Truman submitted to Congress thirty-six proposals leading to reorganization of the executive branch. All were adopted by Congress, except a plan for the creation of a department of welfare to consolidate government programs in health, education, and welfare.

DEPARTMENT OF DEFENSE

Rivalry among the various armed forces during World War II produced an appreciation of the need for a unified system of defense. In 1947 Congress created the Department of Defense by merging the Department of War and the Department of the Navy. A secretary of defense holding cabinet rank was to have three assistants: secretaries for the army, navy, and air force. James

V. Forrestal, who had previously served as secretary of the navy, was appointed as the nation's first secretary of defense. The act of Congress creating the Department of Defense also established the Central Intelligence Agency, whose responsibility was to gather and evaluate information concerning national security.

THE PRESIDENTIAL SUCCESSION ACT

This measure revised the line of succession to the presidency that had been provided by an 1886 act of Congress. The new act, passed in 1947, placed after the vice-president in line of succession to the office of chief executive the Speaker of the House of Representatives and then the president pro tempore of the Senate (the senator selected to preside over that body in the absence of the vice-president of the United States, who is designated by the Constitution to preside). They would be followed by the members of the cabinet, according to rank.

THE TWENTY-SECOND AMENDMENT

Passed by Congress in 1947 and ratified in 1951, the new amendment to the Constitution prohibited election to the presidency for more than two full terms or the election for more than one term of a president who had served more than two years of an unfinished term. The amendment stemmed from the view that presidential power had so greatly increased during the Franklin D. Roosevelt administration that there should no longer be the possibility of having a multitermed chief executive. Many considered the new addition to the Constitution to have been instituted by a Republican-controlled Congress merely as a reproach to Truman's immediate predecessor.

Labor

When the United States entered World War II it needed to mobilize quickly all national resources, including labor. Most women hired during the war remained in the work force during the postwar period. After the war an epidemic of strikes brought about widespread antilabor feeling, which culminated with the conservative, Republican-controlled Congress attempting to curb "unfair" labor practices. To strengthen its position, the two largest factions of a long-split organized labor movement reunited. But labor still faced many difficulties.

THE EMPLOYMENT OF WOMEN

Of the women hired during World War II, about 65 percent remained at work after the conflict was over. The vast majority of married women who worked during the post–World War II period did so not out of a desire to pursue a career but to help their husbands pay for the increasing number of appealing consumer goods available in an affluent society. By 1960 more than 40 percent of women were employed, totaling approximately 22 million—about 33 percent of the nation's labor force. Compared with men, women were poorly paid; the idea of equal pay for equal work was not prevalent.

MANAGEMENT-LABOR UNREST

In the immediate post-war period relations between management and labor were troubled. As is usually the case, war had caused inflation. When wages lagged behind spiraling prices, workers made demands for wage increases and turned to the strike to compel employers to meet their demands. In 1946 close to 1.75 million persons went on strike. Both United States Steel and General Motors were struck by the unions for months. A strike by maritime workers closed the nation's ports for two weeks. Railroad workers went on strike but cut short their job action when Truman threatened to have the government seize and operate the railroads.

When the United Mine Workers went on strike against the bituminous coal–mining companies, Truman seized the mines. The government retained control of the mines after some operators rejected a contract that had been negotiated between the union and government representatives. John L. Lewis, president of the United Mine Workers, then called on his followers to strike again, this time against government operation of the mines. Lewis soon ordered the miners to resume work while the Supreme Court wrestled with the legal issues. Their decision was in favor of the government, and Lewis agreed to a compromise contract with the mine owners.

THE TAFT-HARTLEY ACT

In an attempt to reduce the number of management-labor disputes and to curb what the conservative Congress believed were "unfair" labor practices, the legislative branch passed the Labor-Management Relations Act in 1947 over President Truman's veto. Commonly referred to as the Taft-Hartley Act after its two Republican sponsors, Senator Robert A. Taft of Ohio and Representative Fred A. Hartley Jr. of New Jersey, the measure amended and superseded the National Labor Relations Act of 1935. It removed some restrictions upon management and added a number of restrictions upon organized labor. Specifically, the Taft-Hartley Act (1) prohibited the closed shop; (2) permitted employers to sue unions for breaking contracts and for damages incurred as a result of a strike; (3) required employers and unions to give sixty days' notice of a decision to modify or terminate a contract; (4) authorized the federal government to take legal action to delay for eighty days a strike that threatened public health or safety; (5) required unions to divulge their financial statements; (6) forbade unions to make contributions to political campaigns; (7) prohibited the paying of union dues by the check-off system (a method whereby the employer collects dues for the union from the workers' pay); (8) compelled union leaders to sign oaths that they were not members of the Communist party; and (9) declared illegal the secondary boycott (a boycott of an employer in order to induce him to bring pressure upon another employer to come to terms with his workers) and the jurisdictional dispute (a dispute involving two or more unions over which one has the right to exclusive control over certain work).

Unions assailed the Taft-Hartley Act as a "slave labor" measure. However, by making organized labor feel a vulnerability it had not recently experienced, the act had the effect of unifying labor. In the following years President Truman repeatedly urged Congress to repeal—or at least modify—the Taft-Hartley Act, but without success.

THE FORMATION OF THE AFL-CIO

As one reaction to the widespread hostility toward it, organized labor assumed a united stand by bringing to an end the two decades of rivalry between the AFL and the CIO. In 1955, after years of discussion, the two groups merged under the name of the American Federation of Labor and the Congress of Industrial Organizations (AFL-CIO) and became a powerful, approximately 15-million-member body. Assuming the presidency of the AFL-CIO was George Meany, who had been the head of the AFL; Walter Reuther, who had been the leader of the CIO, became vice-president, in control of organizing, where appropriate, workers along industrial lines.

The new organization still faced quite serious difficulties within the labor movement. The long-standing and bitter controversy over the value of craft unionism as opposed to industrial unionism still rankled among many members of the organization's two components. Furthermore, approximately 2 million organized laborers, including the railroad workers and the miners, were still not affiliated with the AFL-CIO, preferring to belong to their totally independent unions. In addition, about 50 million workers throughout the nation (more than 75 percent of the total labor force) were not in unions at all. The AFL-CIO undertook to organize unaffiliated workers, a massive task not only because of the sheer numbers to be contacted but also because of the increasing prosperity of the late 1950s, which gave workers a notably higher standard of living and thus made the benefits of union membership seem less substantial.

Election of 1948

The Republican party entered the campaign certain of victory; the Democratic party, with perhaps the sole exception of its nominee, began the campaign prepared for defeat. The election resulted in the most surprising political upset in the nation's history.

DEMOCRATS

The national convention of the Democratic party was a factious affair, beginning with a movement to deny Truman the nomination in favor of someone less controversial. Many party leaders turned to General Dwight D. Eisenhower, then president of Columbia University, while others turned to William O. Douglas, associate justice of the Supreme Court. After both men had made it clear that they were not available, the delegates somewhat reluctantly selected Truman as their candidate. Senator Alben W. Barkley of Kentucky was chosen as his running mate. The platform, which praised the Truman administration for its commitment to increased social legislation and its foreign policy, was most notable for the strong civil rights plank, adopted amid a bitter struggle.

REPUBLICANS

By the time the Republican national convention began its proceedings, there were three leading aspirants to the presidential nomination: Governor Thomas E. Dewey of New York, who, though he had been the party's unsuccessful standard-bearer in 1944, was the acknowledged favorite; Senator Robert A. Taft of Ohio; and former governor Harold E. Stassen of Minnesota. The convention chose Dewey on the third ballot. Governor Earl Warren of California was nominated for the vice-presidential slot. In addition to recommending such measures as civil rights protection, aid to housing, and tax reform, the platform advocated a bipartisan foreign policy.

DIXIECRATS

Following the Democratic convention a rupture occurred in the party. Some conservative southern Democrats formed the States Rights Democratic ("Dixiecrat") party, nominating Governor J. Strom Thurmond of South Carolina for president and Governor Fielding L. Wright of Mississippi for vice-president. The platform they adopted focused on condemning the Democratic party's civil rights program.

PROGRESSIVES

Some members of the ultraliberal wing of the Democratic party also held a separate convention, in which they organized the Progressive party and selected former vice-president Henry A. Wallace for first place on the ticket and Democratic senator Glen Taylor of Idaho as his running mate. The platform advocated a host of economic and social reforms and called for redirection of American foreign policy toward a friendship with the Soviet Union.

THE CAMPAIGN

The divisions within the Democratic party made the Republicans confident of victory. Happy with the predictions of the pollsters that he was certain to win, Dewey conducted an easygoing campaign. In an effort to avoid offending any particular group of voters, he refrained from being specific on the issues confronting the nation. Truman, on the other hand, was an energetic campaigner. Exuding plucky optimism, he traveled to all sections of the country, giving informal speeches in simple, direct language. He dwelled on the Republican-controlled "do-nothing" Eightieth Congress, assailing it for not being interested in the welfare of the people.

TRUMAN'S UPSET VICTORY

In a political upset that confounded the commentators, Truman carried twenty-eight states with 304 electoral votes; Dewey, sixteen states with 189 votes; and Thurmond, four states with 38 votes. Wallace did not win a single state. In popular votes, Truman received 24,179,000; Dewey, 21,991,000; Thurmond, 1,176,000; and Wallace, 1,157,000. The surprising outcome of the election was due to a number of factors—in addition to Truman's courageously masterful campaigning. The overconfident Republican party had conducted its campaign in too sluggish a fashion. Farmers in normally Republican states of the Midwest voted the Democratic ticket because the Democrats—but not the Republicans—were committed to fuller price-support aid to recently declining farm prices. In several northern states attractive Democratic candidates for gubernatorial and congressional offices ran ahead of Truman and helped him carry those states. The anticipated siphoning off of millions of votes from the Democratic party by Wallace never materialized, as many people abandoned the Progressive party because of its increasing domination by radical political elements.

The Fair Deal

Truman recommended to Congress a comprehensive program of social legislation that he regarded as an extension of Franklin D. Roosevelt's New Deal. To emphasize the relationship between the two, Truman referred to his own program as the Fair Deal. Congress passed bills on housing, minimum wages, and the extension of Social Security, which the president signed into law.

THE HOUSING ACT OF 1949

This law provided approximately $2.8 billion for slum clearance and low-rent housing projects.

THE MINIMUM WAGE ACT OF 1949

This measure, by amending the Fair Labor Standards Act of 1938, increased the minimum wage from forty to seventy-five cents an hour.

SOCIAL SECURITY AMENDMENTS OF 1950

The Social Security Act of 1935 was amended to extend coverage to new groups of wage earners, to provide pensions for some who were self-employed, and to increase benefits to retired workers.

Truman's Unachieved Goals

Ahead of his time in believing that the federal government must commit itself to policies that would advance health and education, Truman pushed for enabling legislation. But a coalition of conservatives in Congress, comprised of many Republicans and most southern Democrats, prevented the passage of these progressive and controversial portions of the Fair Deal.

CIVIL RIGHTS

Truman experienced the most disappointing failure in the area of civil rights. In 1946 the president appointed a civil rights committee, which recommended the establishment of a permanent commission to enforce fair employment practices; the denial of federal subsidies to health, education, and housing facilities that practiced racial discrimination; the prohibition of segregation in interstate transportation facilities; and the designation of lynching as a federal crime. In 1948 Truman urgently requested Congress to pass legislation embodying these proposals. When Congress failed to do so, Truman issued an executive order against racial segregation in all government departments and another abolishing it in the armed services.

After his upset victory in the presidential election of 1948, Truman appealed to Congress to enact measures based on the civil rights planks of the platform he had campaigned on. But the conservative southern wing of his own party blocked these proposals. Disappointed and discouraged, Truman resorted to the only course open to him to achieve some limited gains: executive action. For example, in 1951 he appointed the first black judge in the federal court system. Also in 1951 he appointed a committee to oversee the awarding of federal defense contracts, with a charge to bar contracts to companies that practiced racial discrimination in their employment policies.

NATIONAL HEALTH INSURANCE

Congress rejected Truman's proposal for a compulsory health program, in which people would receive medical and dental care through a system of payroll deductions and matching government funds.

FEDERAL AID TO EDUCATION

There was strong bipartisan congressional support for Truman's plan for federal aid to the states to increase and equalize educational opportunity. However, the proposal foundered on the issue of whether assistance should go to parochial schools as well as to public schools.

Internal Security

As in the post–World War I era, the United States was convulsed by fear of widespread communist infiltration in the years following World War II. In the latter period, however, there was greater justification for believing in the existence of communist subversion, prompting the American people themselves to be more receptive to taking drastic measures to prevent it.

TRUMAN'S EXECUTIVE ORDER

As postwar relations between the United States and the Soviet Union rapidly deteriorated, the American people became increasingly suspicious that there were employees within the government who were betraying the nation to the Soviet Union. In 1947, in an effort to ferret out communists, Truman issued an executive order inaugurating a comprehensive investigation of the loyalty of all federal employees. By the end of the probe, which lasted four years, over 3 million government employees had been cleared, approximately 2,000 had resigned, and 212 had been dismissed on the basis of a reasonable doubt as to their loyalty. Further, in what were described as "sensitive" areas of government, Truman consented to the dismissal of persons who were deemed to be not disloyal but—for one reason or another—security risks. The execution of Truman's loyalty probe was severe and thorough. However, this did not prevent the Republican party from exploiting the issue of communists in government through allegations that the Truman administration was too "soft" on communist infiltrators.

THE HISS CASE

In 1948 Whittaker Chambers, an editor of *Time* magazine, while giving evidence regarding a communist organization to which he had belonged in the 1930s, named as a fellow member Alger Hiss, a former official in the Department of State. Chambers admitted to having been a messenger for the Soviet espionage system, asserting that Hiss had passed on to him classified documents. Hiss denied this charge under oath before a federal grand jury. After Chambers produced evidence to corroborate his charge, Hiss was found guilty of perjury and sentenced to five years in prison.

THE ROSENBERG CASE

With the public already alarmed by the Hiss case, another episode took place that lent some credence to the wildest charges of communist infiltration. In 1950 Klaus Fuchs, a naturalized British physicist engaged in atomic research during World War II, confessed that he had supplied the Soviet Union with data on the making of the atomic bomb. Fuchs provided information that led to the arrest of his accomplices in the United States. Julius Rosenberg, a civilian employee in the United States Army Signal Corps during World War II, and his wife, Ethel, were arrested and tried for espionage. The Rosenbergs were found guilty and in 1953 executed in the electric chair. Three other Americans were convicted of being members of this atomic spy ring and received long prison terms.

THE TRIAL OF COMMUNIST LEADERS

The Alien Registration Act of 1940, called the Smith Act after its congressional sponsor, declared it illegal to advocate the overthrow of the United States government by force or to belong to a group dedicated to that end. Put aside during World War II when the United States and the Soviet Union were allied against a common enemy, the act was revived during the postwar period of American-Soviet tensions. In 1949 a dozen leaders of the American Communist party, including national chairman William Foster and national secretary Eugene Dennis, were indicted for violating the Smith Act provisions on subversive activities. Because of ill health Foster did not go on trial, but before the year was over the eleven others were tried, found guilty, and sent to prison.

THE McCARRAN ACT

Determined to strike at communism even harder, Congress in 1950 overrode Truman's veto to pass the Internal Security Act. Known as the McCarran Act after its sponsor, Democratic senator Pat McCarran of Nevada, it required the registration of communist and communist-front organizations, compelled the internment of communists during declared national emergencies, and prohibited the employment of communists in defense work. The McCarran Act also contained a provision forbidding immigration to the United States of anyone who had been a member of a totalitarian organization. This was amended in 1951 to permit exceptions for those who had been forced to belong to such groups.

THE McCARRAN-WALTER ACT

In 1952 Congress passed over Truman's veto an act sponsored by Senator McCarran and Republican representative Frances E. Walter of Pennsylvania that revised existing statutes on immigration and naturalization. The McCarran-Walter Act retained from the Quota Act of 1924 those provisions favoring immigration from northern and western European countries but repealed that portion of the Quota Act that prohibited the immigration and naturalization of people from Asia. The new act gave preferential treatment to would-be immigrants who were relatives of American citizens or who possessed occupational skills deemed useful to American society or the economy. It barred entry into the United States of anyone who had been a member of a communist or communist-front organization. It also provided for the deportation of any immigrant or naturalized citizen who, once in the United States, participated in a communist or communist-front organization.

EISENHOWER AND MODERATE REPUBLICANISM

In 1953, after twenty years of Democratic presidency, the nation installed a Republican chief executive. However, the new president, Dwight D. Eisenhower, disappointed those conservative members of his party who wanted a frontal attack on the laws passed during Roosevelt's New Deal and Truman's Fair Deal. The moderates of both major parties at the time of the Eisenhower administration accepted the principle that the federal government was responsible for the welfare of its citizens.

Election of 1952

"Time for a change" proved to be an effective slogan for the Republican party, which, without alienating its liberal and internationalist wing, succeeded in winning the votes of the conservative and isolationist-oriented Americans in the middle and far West.

DEMOCRATS

The Democratic national convention was wide open because Truman refused to become a candidate. The leading aspirants among the host of contenders for the presidential nomination were Vice-President Alben W. Barkley; Governor Adlai E. Stevenson of Illinois; foreign-affairs specialist and former secretary of commerce W. Averell Harriman; and senators Estes Kefauver of Tennessee, Richard B. Russell of Georgia, and Robert S. Kerr of Oklahoma. On the third ballot the nomination went to Stevenson, who insisted that he was being drafted. For second place on the ticket the convention named Senator John J. Sparkman of Alabama, hoping to thus overcome the disaffection of some southern Democratic leaders.

REPUBLICANS

At the Republican national convention there were two front-runners for the presidential nomination: General Dwight D. Eisenhower (who had just relinquished his position as supreme commander of NATO) and Senator Robert A. Taft of Ohio. The former was supported by the party's liberal and internationalist wing; the latter was the candidate of the more conservative and isolationist "Old Guard" Republicans. After a spirited revolt of many delegates against the Taft supporters, who seemed to have control of the convention committees, the convention gave a first-ballot nomination to Eisenhower. Senator Richard M. Nixon of California, who was presented as a fighter against communist infiltration in the civil service, was selected to be his running mate.

THE CAMPAIGN

Governor Stevenson, with his rare philosophical and literary skill, tried to convince the voters that the nation was threatened by poverty at home and tyranny and war abroad—and that the struggles against those menaces were costly but necessary. But Stevenson could not overcome the personal popularity of General Eisenhower. Perhaps the most effective piece of oratory of the campaign was Eisenhower's simple promise regarding the war that for two and a half years had been going on in Asia between United Nations and communist forces: "I will go to Korea." The American people hoped he could thus end the armed conflict.

EISENHOWER'S VICTORY

Eisenhower received 33,936,000 popular and 442 electoral votes to Stevenson's 27,314,000 popular and 89 electoral votes. The size of this victory, however, did not carry over to the congressional vote. The Republicans won control of the House of Representatives, but by a slim margin. The Republican margin in the Senate was dependent upon liberal senator Wayne Morse of Oregon, who had supported Stevenson in the election as an "independent Republican." To have his legislative program passed by Congress, Eisenhower would thus be compelled to solicit support from conservative Democrats as well as Republicans.

The Eisenhower Administration

Eisenhower did not believe in exercising strong presidential leadership, expressing concern that such a practice did damage to the important—and delicate—balance among the executive, legislative, and judicial branches of government. As president he delegated much authority to his subordinates and relied heavily upon the recommendations of his advisors.

THE PRESIDENT

Eisenhower was a sincere, unpretentious, and kind man. His winning smile topped off an affable manner. He did not possess the gift of eloquence. Finding partisan conflict distasteful, he made a conscious effort to shun it, thus appearing to be "above" politics. Fond of leisure activities, he devoted much time to playing golf, painting, and reading stories about the old West.

THE CABINET

It was clear from the beginning that the Eisenhower cabinet was industrially and commercially oriented. More than half the appointees were businessmen; all except one were millionaires. John Foster Dulles, a New York lawyer who had been a consultant on foreign affairs to the Truman administration, was chosen secretary of state. George M. Humphrey, head of an Ohio-based firm with extensive interests in shipping and steel, became secretary of the treasury. Charles E. Wilson, president of General Motors Corporation, was named secretary of defense. These three became the most powerful figures in the cabinet. In the conduct of American foreign affairs Eisenhower permitted Dulles more control than had been exercised by any previous secretary of state.

ASSISTANT TO THE PRESIDENT

Sherman Adams, a former governor of New Hampshire, was appointed assistant to the president. As head of Eisenhower's personal staff, the extraordinarily hard-working and efficient Adams wielded enormous power in executing the many and varied duties assigned to him. In 1958 he felt compelled to resign after being widely criticized for accepting gifts from a businessman whose operations were being investigated by the government.

Government Reorganization and Reform

The Eisenhower administration made a commitment to continue the work of government reorganization and reform that had been successfully started by the preceding administration.

THE SECOND HOOVER COMMISSION

In 1953 Congress authorized the establishment of the Commission on Organization of the Executive Branch of the Government. Known as the Second Hoover Commission after its chairman, former president Herbert Hoover, it was charged with proposing methods to streamline the structure of the executive branch, a task similar to that of the 1947 Hoover Commission. Most of the commission's recommendations were approved by Congress.

DEPARTMENT OF HEALTH, EDUCATION, AND WELFARE

In 1947 President Truman's proposal for the establishment of a department of welfare to coordinate government-sponsored social programs was defeated by a coalition of congressional conservatives. A few years later the legislative branch took positive action. In 1953 Congress created the Department of Health, Education, and Welfare, the head of which would be a cabinet member. The new department was established to consolidate and supervise the various government agencies that dealt with the health, education, and social and economic welfare of the American people. Eisenhower appointed Oveta Culp Hobby, who had commanded the Women's Army Corps during World War II, as the first secretary of the new department.

Social Legislation During Eisenhower's First Term

Although Eisenhower was elected comfortably to the presidency in 1952, his party had only a narrow margin in the House of Representatives and, with the support of independent Wayne Morse, tied the Democrats in the Senate. The president thus needed and actively sought bipartisan support to enact his legislative proposals into law.

SOCIAL SECURITY AMENDMENTS OF 1954

Congress amended the Social Security Act to provide coverage to new occupational groups, including farmers and state and local government employees, and to increase the amount of pensions to retirees.

THE MINIMUM WAGE ACT OF 1955

This measure increased the minimum hourly wage from seventy-five cents to one dollar.

McCarthyism

There were many politicians who exploited the deep anticommunist feeling in the nation, but no one did so with such vehemence and initial success as Republican senator Joseph R. McCarthy of Wisconsin. Because of his activities his name entered the English language: "McCarthyism" soon came to denote the making of indiscriminate and unsubstantiated charges of subversive activities.

THE SENATOR AND HIS TACTICS

McCarthy first achieved national prominence when, in a speech delivered in West Virginia in February 1950, he charged that he had in his possession a list of "card-carrying" communists in the State Department. But he was never able to prove his case. Over the next few years he alleged that a number of government agencies were infiltrated by communists, communist sympathizers, and "security risks." Anyone who took issue with him was characterized as disloyal or obtuse. He charged with treasonable conduct such persons as General George C. Marshall and Secretary of State Dean Acheson.

THE ARMY-McCARTHY DISPUTE

In 1954 the army accused McCarthy of attempting to obtain preferential treatment for an assistant who had been drafted. McCarthy, who chaired both the Senate Committee on Government Operations and its permanent Subcommittee on Investigations, countered that the army was trying to embarrass him for his investigations of spying at Army Signal Corps facilities at Fort Monmouth, New Jersey. During April–June 1954, televised hearings were held on the two sets of charges. In many confrontations with army counsel Joseph B. Welch, McCarthy's bullying methods were revealed to an estimated 20 million American viewers, with the result that the senator's reputation among his supporters was severely damaged.

CONDEMNATION BY THE SENATE

The public exposure during the hearings of McCarthy's long-standing methods convinced the Senate to take action. In December 1954, by a vote of 67 to 22, it decided to "condemn" his conduct as "unbecoming a member of the United States Senate." His influence was immediately destroyed.

Election of 1956

The result of the 1956 election was a triumphant victory for Eisenhower, who sought a second term, but it was not a success for his party as a whole.

DEMOCRATS

On the first ballot the delegates to the Democratic national convention nominated for president their 1952 standard-bearer, Adlai E. Stevenson. Senator Estes Kefauver of Tennessee was selected for second place on the ticket.

REPUBLICANS

The national convention of the Republican party was a harmonious affair. Neither a heart attack in the summer of 1955 nor an operation for an intestinal ailment in the summer of 1956 could deter Eisenhower from seeking a second term, and he was nominated by acclamation on the first ballot. Vice-President Nixon was chosen as his running mate.

THE CAMPAIGN

With Eisenhower and Stevenson again competing for the presidency, the campaign was in many ways a recapitulation of the one conducted four years earlier. Stevenson, however, shied away from the profundity of thought and eloquence of wit that he had exhibited in 1952, having been convinced by some of his advisors that it had all been too "heavy" for most of the voters.

EISENHOWER'S VICTORY

Eisenhower polled 35,580,000 popular votes to Stevenson's 26,031,000 and received 457 electoral votes to Stevenson's 73. Eisenhower took seven of the states in the solid South, one more than the number he had carried in the region four years earlier. The voters' overwhelming endorsement of the president did not, however, apply to his party. The Democrats captured both houses of Congress.

Social Legislation During Eisenhower's Second Term

After his reelection, Eisenhower began to exert pressure on Congress for his legislative program. Since both houses of that body were controlled by the Democrats, the president sought—as he had been forced to do during his first term—bipartisan support to enact those measures into law. He was, to a degree, successful.

SOCIAL SECURITY AMENDMENTS OF 1956

The Social Security Act was extended to cover new vocational groups, such as physicians and those in the armed services. Also, the eligibility age for receiving pensions was lowered for women to sixty-two and the eligibility age for receiving benefits was lowered for disabled workers to fifty.

SOCIAL SECURITY AMENDMENTS OF 1958

Further amendments to the Social Security Act provided for a substantial increase in benefits to those receiving old-age, survivor's, and disability assistance.

THE NATIONAL DEFENSE EDUCATION ACT

Alarmed by Soviet advancements in space exploration, the American people heaped blame on their educational system. Demands were made for strengthening the entire range of American education, especially the mathematics and science curriculums. In 1958 Congress passed the National Defense Education Act. It authorized the expenditure of $887 million over a four-year period for the following: (1) long-term, low-interest loans to undergraduate college students, with half the loan to be canceled for those who, after receiving their degrees, taught in elementary or secondary schools for at least five years; (2) fellowships for graduate students who agreed to enter college or university teaching; and (3) matching grants with state governments to public schools for the purchase of textbooks and laboratory equipment to improve the teaching of mathematics, science, and modern languages. Later congressional action extended the measure for two more years at a cost of $500 million.

Civil Rights

The issue of extending equality of public treatment to black Americans divided the nation along sectional rather than party lines. As the Truman administration had been supported by many Republicans, in its attempts to broaden the application of civil rights, the Eisenhower administration was supported by many northern Democrats in its efforts to do so. Encouraged by a basic government sympathy, blacks became increasingly active in attempting to improve their status.

BROWN V. BOARD OF EDUCATION OF TOPEKA

By the middle of the twentieth century most public schools in the South were racially segregated by state or local laws, whereas in the North a number of public schools were segregated because of custom or the separation of the white and black races through neighborhood housing patterns. The Supreme Court in the *Plessy v. Ferguson* case of 1896 had decided that a Louisiana law requiring "separate but equal" facilities for whites and blacks on railroad cars was constitutional. The "separate but equal" doctrine for segregation was soon extended in the South to other kinds of public accommodations, including educational institutions. But schools for whites were almost without exception superior to those for blacks.

On May 17, 1954, the Supreme Court, presided over by Chief Justice Earl Warren, handed down a momentous decision on the issue of segregation in the public schools that reversed the Court's earlier position. *Brown v. Board of Education of Topeka* involved a Kansas law requiring segregated classrooms in the state's public elementary and secondary schools. In this case the Court unanimously held that segregation in the public schools was unconstitutional. The justices declared that maintenance of "separate but equal" school facilities for blacks (which was the practice in seventeen states) was a denial of the Fourteenth Amendment's guarantee equal protection of the laws. Writing the opinion for the Court, Chief Justice Warren stated that separating black children from others solely because of their race "generates a feeling of inferiority as to their status in a community that may affect their hearts and minds in a way unlikely ever to be undone" and concluded that "separate educational facilities are inherently unequal." In 1955 the Supreme Court ordered that the desegregation of public schools should begin "with all deliberate speed."

THE MONTGOMERY BUS BOYCOTT

In December 1955, Rosa Parks, a Montgomery, Alabama black woman, refused to give up her seat on a bus to a white man and was arrested. The black community decided to call a boycott of the buses as a protest against segregated seating on the city's public transportation. Car pools were organized among blacks. Under the skillful leadership of the Reverend Dr. Martin Luther King Jr., a Baptist minister, the bus boycott was extraordinarily successful. Enduring intense hostility from many whites of the city, the black community persevered in the boycott month after month. In November 1956, the Supreme Court declared segregated seating in local transportation unconstitutional. Soon thereafter the blacks of Montgomery began using the city buses once more—and sat where they pleased. The Montgomery bus boycott had become the first direct community action by blacks to achieve national prominence.

CONFRONTATION IN LITTLE ROCK

Implicit in the *Brown v. Board of Education of Topeka* decision was the Supreme Court's understanding that enforcement of desegregation would require careful planning over a considerable period of time. The Eisenhower administration encouraged the states to work out their own plans. At hundreds of schools in the South integration was accomplished peacefully. But there were scattered incidents of violent opposition, the most prominent occurring in Little Rock, Arkansas.

In September 1957, that city's board of education was prepared to admit nine carefully selected black students to a white high school. Governor Orval Faubus of Arkansas, insisting that violence would break out if the students were admitted to classes, used the Arkansas national guard to bar them from the school building. President Eisenhower declared that Faubus's action violated national law. Obeying a federal court injunction, Faubus withdrew the national guard. But when a taunting mob prevented the black students from going into the high school, Eisenhower responded by ordering federal troops to Little Rock. During the entire academic year of 1957–58 the soldiers protected the eight remaining (one had withdrawn) black students.

THE CIVIL RIGHTS ACT OF 1957

Influenced by both the ruling of the Supreme Court for school desegregation and by the increasing activism of blacks to improve their condition, Congress passed a civil rights act—the first since the Reconstruction period. After long and hard debate, during which many conservative white southern legislators voiced strenuous objections to a civil rights measure, Congress passed the Civil Rights Act of 1957, which created a six-member commission to investigate the denial of voting rights and the violation of the equal protection of the laws. It was also to make recommendations for new legislation as it saw the need. The attorney general was authorized to obtain court orders to secure the right to vote anywhere in the nation.

THE CIVIL RIGHTS ACT OF 1960

The commission appointed by President Eisenhower under the Civil Rights Act of 1957 declared that the act was in itself ineffectual in protecting the voting rights of blacks. Congress then passed the Civil Rights Act of 1960, which empowered federal judges to appoint referees to assist blacks in registering and voting. Further, in order to halt a spate of recent bombings of churches and schools used by blacks, the act made it a federal crime to transport explosives across a state line in order to bomb a building or to cross a state line in order to escape prosecution for having bombed a building.

New States

The admission of Alaska and Hawaii to the Union put an end to the issue of whether the United States must be composed of contiguous land on the North American continent.

ALASKA

In January 1959, after Congress had approved the necessary enabling legislation, President Eisenhower issued a proclamation declaring Alaska the forty-ninth state of the Union. The new state ranked first in area and last in population. Alaska's importance to the rest of the nation was considered to be its vast natural resources, particularly its mineral wealth.

HAWAII

Bringing Alaska into the Union gave impetus to a half-century-old movement for granting statehood to Hawaii. In August 1959, after Congress had passed the required bill, President Eisenhower proclaimed Hawaii the fiftieth state of the Union. Reflecting the ethnic diversity of Hawaiian society, the first elected congressional delegation was composed of one senator of white mainland ancestry, one of Chinese ancestry, and a representative of Japanese ancestry. With Hawaii came the naval base at Pearl Harbor, the most important American naval station in the Pacific.

THE COLD WAR

One year after the end of World War II, relations began to deteriorate between the Western allies, under the general leadership of the United States, and the communist bloc, which was strictly led by the Soviet Union. According to the phrase used by Winston Churchill in 1946, an "iron curtain" had been dropped across Europe from north to south, establishing a barrier between Soviet-controlled Eastern Europe on one side and Western Europe plus the Western Hemisphere on the other. The persistent hostility between the Western and communist nations was soon called the Cold War.

Checking Communism in Europe

Underlying the struggle for power between the Western allies and the communist bloc was the knowledge that if the Cold War were to become "hot" over an issue on the European continent, it could possibly turn into an atomic war—and bring doom to humankind.

THE TRUMAN DOCTRINE

Early in 1947 Greece experienced attacks by native communist guerrilla bands that were receiving aid from communist nations to the north. In the same year the Soviet Union demanded that Turkey grant it military bases as well as concessions in the Dardanelles, the strait connecting the Black Sea and the Mediterranean. Truman reacted to the situation by delivering an address to Congress in March 1947, requesting an appropriation of $400 million for economic and military aid to bolster the governments of Greece and Turkey. Congress complied, and the assistance proved effective.

Truman's message was, however, more far-reaching than a request for aid to Greece and Turkey. The president called for the containment of Soviet expansion and pledged the use of American economic and military resources to help the "free peoples" of Europe resist communist aggression, whether by direct attack or subversion. This policy became known as the Truman Doctrine. In providing grounds for the principle of containment, the Truman Doctrine can be regarded as the basis for the American position in the Cold War.

THE MARSHALL PLAN

After Congress had provided assistance to Greece and Turkey, Secretary of State George C. Marshall recognized the need for the United States to support the economic and social recovery of Europe and thus preserve governments struggling with the effects of World War II. In June 1947, in an address at Harvard University, Marshall pointed out that the United States was anxious to cooperate with Europe if the nations of the continent were ready to formulate a program for mutual reconstruction. By declaring that

American policy would be directed "not against any country or doctrine but against hunger, poverty, desperation, and chaos," Marshall made it clear that the communist nations were welcome to participate in the program.

This offer was accepted by sixteen Western and Western-oriented nations, including Great Britain, France, Italy, Greece, and Turkey. In July 1947, the participatory nations sent representatives to a conference in Paris, where details were worked out for international cooperation along economic lines. The Soviet Union and its allies refused to send representatives, charging that the entire program was an American imperialist plot for the economic enslavement of Europe. In December 1947, Truman submitted to Congress the European Recovery Program, which incorporated much from the report of the Paris conference. A few months later, and after much discussion, Congress approved a modified version of the Truman administration's program.

Popularly called the Marshall Plan, the program was in existence from 1948 to 1951. Under the Marshall Plan the American government provided Europe with aid totaling approximately $15 billion, most of which was spent in the United States for foodstuffs, raw materials, and machinery. The impact of the Marshall Plan on the European nations was soon noticeable. It (1) promoted strong economic recovery, permitting many nations to surpass prewar levels of production; (2) spurred cooperative economic enterprises among Western European nations, such as the customs union established by Belgium, the Netherlands, and Luxembourg; (3) promoted political stability; and (4) stiffened the resistance of European nations against communist expansionism.

THE BERLIN AIRLIFT

In 1948 the Soviet Union refused to consider a Western proposal on the status of Berlin and also insisted that Soviet currency be the sole medium of exchange not only in the Soviet occupation zone of the city but also in the American, British, and French zones. The increasing tension precipitated strong Soviet action. In June 1948, the Soviet Union imposed a blockade on all surface traffic (road, rail, and canal) moving from the three western occupation zones of Germany through the Soviet occupation zone to the three western sectors of Berlin, which lay within the Soviet zone.

The Western powers, led by the United States, responded by establishing an air corridor between their zones in western Germany and their respective sectors of Berlin, along which they could fly supplies into the city. For more than ten months about a thousand planes a day flew cargoes of food, fuel, and other basic necessities to the more than 2 million people in Berlin's western zones. The massive airlift strikingly demonstrated the determination of the Western allies not to be forced into a policy of appeasing the Soviet Union.

The only option available to the Soviet Union to thwart the airlift was to attack the planes, but such action could very well have precipitated war. Finally, in May 1949, the Soviet Union announced that it would terminate the blockade if the three Western allies would lift the counterblockade that they had set up and if the foreign ministers of the four occupying powers would meet soon to enter into discussions on the future of Germany in general and of Berlin in particular.

THE NORTH ATLANTIC TREATY ORGANIZATION (NATO)

A number of Western observers felt that the Soviet announcement of a willingness to negotiate on the status of Germany had been induced in part by the success of the Western nations in achieving a treaty among themselves. In April 1949, twelve nations on both sides of the North Atlantic—the United States, Canada, Great Britain, France, Italy, Belgium, the Netherlands, Luxembourg, Portugal, Denmark, Norway, and Iceland—signed the North Atlantic Treaty, by which they would consider an attack upon any one of them as an attack upon all. The signatories pledged that they would go to the defense of an attacked member of the pact, if necessary with armed force. The membership of the alliance was increased to fifteen when it admitted Greece and Turkey in 1952, followed by West Germany in 1955. For the United States, becoming a party to the North Atlantic Treaty was a momentous decision, marking the nation's first peacetime military alliance with European nations.

To implement the defensive pact, the original signatories formed in 1950 the North Atlantic Treaty Organization (NATO), which integrated the military forces of member nations for optimum defense. NATO differed from previous alliances in that it provided not only for joint action in wartime but also for joint military and economic action in peacetime. The headquarters of NATO were established in Paris, and various regional military commands were set up. The command headquarters in Europe, named Supreme Headquarters, Allied Powers in Europe (SHAPE), was led by the supreme allied commander in Europe. The first to occupy the post was General Dwight D. Eisenhower. As a counterforce to NATO, the communist nations adopted the Warsaw Pact, a military alliance of seven Eastern European communist countries (East Germany was admitted in 1955), led by the Soviet Union.

After NATO was established there were a number of disputes among the member nations. Many difficulties were precipitated by France. In 1966 French president Charles de Gaulle, an ardent nationalist and archcritic of American influence in NATO, withdrew French military forces from NATO. He demanded that NATO troops in France be put under that country's control or be removed. He pledged, however, that France would still honor its commitments as a signatory to the original North Atlantic Treaty of 1949.

The following year the other nations withdrew their NATO troops from France and transferred NATO and SHAPE headquarters from Paris to Brussels, Belgium.

THE GENEVA SUMMIT CONFERENCE

In an attempt to ease Western-Soviet tensions the heads of the American, British, French, and Soviet governments met in July 1955 at Geneva, Switzerland, for the first summit conference (a meeting attended by two or more heads of state, usually representing both Western and communist nations; the term was originated by Winston Churchill in his post–World War II appeal for an international meeting "at the summit"). The United States was represented by President Eisenhower, Great Britain by Prime Minister Anthony Eden, France by Premier Edgar Fauré, and the Soviet Union by Premier Nikolai A. Bulganin and the first secretary of the Soviet Communist party, Nikita S. Khrushchev. (Bulganin headed the Soviet government in name only; Khrushchev held the real power.) The participants rejected war as an instrument of national policy. They agreed to increase economic and cultural contacts between the Western allies and the Soviet Union. They discussed the issues of political unification of Germany and disarmament by the leading powers but failed to reach an agreement on either matter. The discussion on disarmament prompted the participating nations to hold subsequent meetings on that issue; these also brought no conclusion. Although the conferees at Geneva settled only some of the important issues, they did conduct themselves in a strikingly affable manner, which generated for a brief time a spirit of goodwill between the Western allies and the Soviet Union.

THE HUNGARIAN REVOLT

In the post–World War II period the Soviet Union's allies—Poland, Czechoslovakia, Hungary, Romania, Bulgaria, and Albania—came under the control of Moscow. Yugoslavia also had a communist regime, but under Premier Josip Tito it frequently followed an independent line and consequently secured economic aid from the Western powers. In October 1956, a revolt against Soviet domination took place in Hungary. Hungarian premier Imre Nagy, a nationalistic communist and follower of Tito, demanded the immediate removal of Soviet troops from Hungary. He also announced his nation's withdrawal from the Warsaw Pact, the alliance of communist countries. The Soviet Union stated that it would make concessions. President Eisenhower publicly described these developments as the beginning of a wonderful new era for Eastern Europe.

However, Secretary of State John Foster Dulles had let it be understood regarding an earlier uprising against Soviet domination in Poland that the United States would not give military assistance to the insurgents. In November Soviet troops entered Hungary and crushed the revolt. A puppet government was set up under Janos Kadar, secretary of the Hungarian

Communist party. Soon after this successful Soviet retaliation, Eisenhower felt compelled to declare that American policy did not advocate uprisings within the nations allied with the Soviet Union. The final action taken by the United States concerning the short-lived revolt was to give asylum to thousands of Hungarians who had fled their homeland.

THE U-2 INCIDENT

In September 1959, Nikita S. Khrushchev, who was then premier of the Soviet Union as well as first secretary of the Soviet Communist party, made a tour of the United States upon President Eisenhower's invitation. The two leaders used the occasion to engage in some face-to-face negotiations and to lay plans for a new summit conference, the first since the 1955 Geneva meeting, to be held the following spring in Europe. On May 1, 1960, two weeks before the summit conference was to take place in Paris, an unarmed American U-2 reconnaissance plane was shot down deep within Soviet territory. On May 7 Khrushchev announced that the pilot, Francis Gary Powers, was alive and had confessed to high-altitude photographing of Soviet military installations. (Powers was subsequently tried in the Soviet Union for espionage, found guilty, and sentenced to ten years in prison, of which he served a year and a half before being exchanged for a Soviet agent.)

After Powers's admission Eisenhower stated that he himself had authorized the U-2 flights, which he defended as the only means of gathering certain information vital to the security of the United States. Nevertheless, he ordered future U-2 flights canceled. Such an admission of espionage activity by a head of government was unprecedented. By May 16 Eisenhower and Khrushchev, along with Prime Minister Harold Macmillan of Great Britain and President Charles de Gaulle of France, had assembled in Paris to begin the summit conference. But Khrushchev vilified Eisenhower and declared that he would not participate in the summit conference unless the president apologized for the U-2 flights. Eisenhower refused to do so, and Khrushchev went home in anger. The summit conference never took place.

The Korean War

An unprovoked assault upon South Korea by North Korean forces was regarded by many in the United States and in Western Europe as a signal that the Cold War was moving into the stage of widespread military hostilities.

THE DIVISION OF KOREA

At the end of World War II Japan was divested of Korea, which had long been its protectorate. Korea was divided at 38° north latitude into two zones of occupation; the northern part of the peninsula was commanded by Soviet troops and the southern part by American troops.

THE REPUBLIC OF KOREA

The United States and the Soviet Union failed to agree on the unification of Korea. After having trained and equipped a strong native army, the Soviet Union established a communist government in North Korea in 1948. Soviet troops then left. In the same year South Korean elections, under the supervision of the United Nations, resulted in the establishment of the Republic of Korea, with Dr. Syngman Rhee as head of an anticommunist government. President Rhee was an ardent nationalist who hoped eventually to incorporate North Korea into the Republic of Korea. In 1949 the last American occupying forces were withdrawn.

NORTH KOREAN AGGRESSION

In June 1950, without warning, North Korean troops, led by Soviet-trained officers and supplied with Soviet equipment, crossed the 38th parallel and invaded South Korea.

UNITED NATIONS ACTION

The United Nations Security Council, with the Soviet delegate absent, declared North Korea an aggressor and recommended that member nations of the world organization render military aid under its auspices to South Korea. The United Nations forces consisted of units from seventeen Western and Western-oriented nations, with the bulk of combat personnel furnished by the United States and South Korea. The United Nations forces in Korea were commanded by General Douglas MacArthur.

In the course of their military drive the North Korean forces had enjoyed tremendous success, occupying within three months all of South Korea except for a small enclave in the southeast. The United Nations forces under MacArthur then launched a counterattack that drove the enemy back across the 38th parallel and deep into North Korea, close to the border of the Chinese region of Manchuria. By November 1950, three-fourths of North Korea was occupied by United Nations troops.

CHINESE INTERVENTION

In November 1950, the new communist regime in neighboring China sent its troops across the Manchurian border into North Korea, apparently with the determination to defeat the United Nations forces and drive them from the entire Korean peninsula. The United Nations General Assembly voted, with opposition only from the Soviet Union and its allies, to declare China guilty of aggression.

DISMISSAL OF MacARTHUR

General MacArthur wanted to launch an all-out counteroffensive against the Chinese, even to the point of carrying the war into Communist China itself by attacking in Manchuria. Committed to conducting a limited war in

Asia, President Truman felt certain that an invasion of Manchuria would precipitate war with the Soviet Union and Communist China. Frequent disagreements between Truman and MacArthur over the way in which the Korean war should be conducted caused an open rupture between the two.

In April 1951, President Truman relieved the general of his command for disobeying an order to refrain from making foreign policy statements that were counter to the government's official position. MacArthur was replaced in Korea by General Matthew B. Ridgway. On returning to the United States, MacArthur was hailed by some as a hero. But many agreed with the president that the real issue in the Truman-MacArthur dispute was the subordination of the military to civil authority and that drastic action was needed in order to prevent the fighting in Korea from developing into a third world war.

THE ARMISTICE

In June 1951, after the North Korean and Communist Chinese troops had been checked by the United Nations forces just north of the 38th parallel, the Soviet Union suggested that discussions between the antagonists in Korea could lead to a cease-fire. Negotiations between the North Korean and Communist Chinese team on the one hand and the United Nations team on the other began promptly but dragged on for month after month, with each side trying to check the other's diplomatic moves. The truce talks took place mainly at Panmunjom, at the 38th parallel.

The issue on which the negotiations were deadlocked was that of repatriation of prisoners of war. The United Nations team insisted that each prisoner should be free to choose whether or not he wished to return to the nation for which he had been fighting, while the communist team demanded the compulsory repatriation of all. In December 1952, Eisenhower as president-elect put into effect a campaign promise he had made to visit the Korean front. Although not directly related to the truce negotiations at Panmunjom, his military inspection signified the great desire of Americans to end the war. An armistice was finally signed in July 1953, fixing the line of demarcation between North Korea and South Korea and providing for repatriation of prisoners of war on a voluntary basis.

AMERICAN WAR COSTS

In Korea about 55,000 American men died and some 104,000 were wounded in combat. The United States spent an estimated $18 billion on the war.

Combating Communist Expansion

While the leading nations of the Western allies continued to give full support to the United Nations, they formed new alliances in attempts to limit indirect as well as direct communist expansion.

THE CIVIL WAR IN CHINA

In the post–World War II period the Nationalist Chinese government under Generalissimo Chiang Kai-shek lost the people's support. The regime was widely criticized as being inefficient, corrupt, and unconcerned about much-needed economic and social reforms for both rural peasants and urban workers. The Chinese communists, led by Mao Tse-tung (later spelled Zedong), exploited the deep anti-Nationalist feelings throughout the nation. Supplied with equipment from the Soviet Union, they concentrated in the northern part of the nation and engaged in military action, achieving victory after victory over the Nationalist troops and, in the process, broadening their territorial base.

While in no way sympathetic toward the communists, the United States was reluctant to become enmeshed in what appeared to be a long civil war on the side of the Nationalist Chinese government, a World War II ally now held in disrepute. At the end of 1945 General George C. Marshall, who had recently retired as army chief of staff, was sent to China by President Truman to attempt to bring about a settlement between the communist and Nationalist factions. Marshall tried unsuccessfully to convince Chiang Kai-shek to introduce reforms, not only because they were needed but also because they would counteract communist propaganda. After six months of frustrating activity, Marshall managed to arrange a truce between the communists and Nationalists, but it was broken as soon as he returned to the United States.

When Marshall became secretary of state early in 1947 he argued successfully for the withdrawal of all American military forces from China, maintaining that support of Chiang Kai-shek's regime would require more men and matériel than the American government could, in practical terms, supply. American economic aid to the Nationalist forces, however, never stopped. During the next three years the communist troops continued to make steady and striking territorial gains. Ultimately, in December 1949, Chiang Kai-shek and his followers fled the Chinese mainland and set up the Nationalist government on the offshore island of Formosa (so named by early Portuguese explorers; it is called Taiwan by the Chinese). The communists immediately proclaimed the establishment of the People's Republic of China with Mao Zedong as chairman and Chou En-lai as premier.

Although many nations, including a number from the Western bloc, recognized the communist rule, the United States promptly accepted the regime on Taiwan as the true government of China. The United States viewed Taiwan, with its 10 million original inhabitants and the 2 million Nationalist (military and civilian) refugees from the mainland, as an important American military base in the Pacific, and the Nationalist army as a dependable military force to be used in case of need. Consequently, the United States extended economic and military aid to Taiwan and pledged to defend it against aggression. As for the People's Republic of China, with its population of 800 million, over the next two decades the United States consistently refused it recognition, prevented its admission to the United Nations, and maintained an embargo on trade with it.

THE POINT FOUR PROGRAM

In his 1949 inaugural address, President Truman advocated four major courses of action for the nation in its quest for international peace. The fourth point called for technical assistance to underdeveloped nations to raise their living standards. Congress responded to this recommendation by authorizing the Technical Assistance Program, known as the Point Four Program. Large sums of money were subsequently appropriated to meet the needs of the people of Asia, Africa, and Latin America. In so doing, the United States hoped to make the economic and social principles of communism less attractive to those people.

THE ANZUS PACT

In 1951 Australia, New Zealand, and the United States signed a mutual defense treaty. Called the ANZUS Pact from the first letters of the member nations' names, it declared that an attack upon any one of the signatories constituted a danger to all. Each nation pledged to act within its constitutional processes to meet the common danger.

SEATO

In 1954 eight nations—the United States, Great Britain, France, Australia, New Zealand, the Philippines, Thailand, and Pakistan—signed a collective defense treaty, forming what came to be called the Southeast Asia Treaty Organization (SEATO). The member nations pledged to act jointly against aggression toward any one of them. The United States became a signatory on condition that the aggression in question be considered to mean only that from the communist bloc of nations.

THE TREATY WITH NATIONALIST CHINA

In 1954 the United States signed a treaty with Nationalist China providing for mutual aid in the defense of Taiwan and the Pescadores, a group of islands belonging to Taiwan and lying in the strait between it and communist-held mainland China. Four years later Quemoy and Matsu, two offshore island groups that were occupied by the Nationalist government, were shelled from the mainland. The 1954 mutual defense treaty did not cover islands just off mainland China, such as Quemoy and Matsu. However, the United States chose to become involved in the shelling incident. It dispatched warships to escort—through nearby international waters—the Nationalist vessels carrying supplies to Quemoy.

The Middle East

After World War II both Great Britain and France, weakened by the effects of the recent armed conflict, steadily lost their influence in the Middle East. As a consequence, the United States found itself with increasing responsibilities in the area. The Arab nations, which had been so long under Western European domination, quickly learned how to play the United States against the Soviet Union and thus gain concessions from both powers.

THE SUEZ CANAL CRISIS

In 1955 Egypt began receiving military and technical aid from the Soviet Union and its allies. In attempting to forestall Soviet influence in the region, Secretary of State Dulles promised Egypt financial assistance to build a dam on the Nile River at Aswan. But with Egyptian president Gamal Abdel Nasser exhibiting increasing friendship for the communist bloc of nations and hostility toward the Western bloc, the Eisenhower administration, upon Dulles's strong recommendation, abruptly withdrew its offer of aid in 1956. Thereupon Nasser announced that the Suez Canal, operated by a company of mostly British and French stockholders, would be nationalized, making it clear that the tolls collected from operation of the waterway would be used for the construction of the Aswan dam.

In October 1956, Egypt was invaded by Great Britain and France in an effort to reestablish their control of the Suez Canal. Israel also invaded, in an attempt to stop periodic Egyptian guerrilla attacks upon its borders. The Soviet Union threatened to supply military aid to Egypt. President Eisenhower declared that although Nasser's actions had been provocative, the invasion was wrong, a position that angered Great Britain, France, and Israel as longtime allies of the United States. When action on the crisis by the United Nations Security Council was blocked by Great Britain and France in their capacity as permanent members of that body, the General Assembly—with the United States and the Soviet Union playing key roles— moved promptly, securing the withdrawal of the invading troops and the stationing of a United Nations emergency force in Egypt to patrol the area.

THE EISENHOWER DOCTRINE

As a result of the Suez Canal crisis, Soviet influence in the Middle East was enhanced. Aware that the region's political and economic instability made it vulnerable to the spread of communism, Eisenhower acted quickly. In January 1957, he asked Congress both to appropriate funds for economic and military assistance to Middle Eastern nations to help them preserve their independence and to permit the use of American armed forces if necessary to resist open communist aggression. Two months later Congress approved this policy, which came to be called the Eisenhower Doctrine. Although some nations, including Egypt and Syria, denounced the Eisenhower Doctrine as an attempt by the United States to dominate the region, many welcomed it. It remained an integral part of American foreign policy.

LEBANON AND JORDAN

In 1958 the regimes of both Lebanon and Jordan were threatened by internal subversion from dedicated followers of the staunchly pro-Soviet Nasser. Upon the request of President Camille Chamoun of Lebanon for American military assistance, the United States sent troops. At the same time Great Britain dispatched forces to Jordan upon the request of its King Hussein. The American and British moves were condemned as aggression by both the Soviet Union and Egypt. The United States and Great Britain insisted that the United Nations Security Council deal with the crisis. When a Soviet veto prevented action by that body, the General Assembly was called into special session. In an address to the General Assembly in August 1958, Eisenhower presented a basic plan for the political and economic stabilization of the Middle East under the supervision of the United Nations. A compromise resolution sponsored by the Arab nations was finally passed. American and British troops were withdrawn from the region after calm had been restored.

THE AFFLUENT SOCIETY

In the decade and a half after World War II the United States achieved a height of prosperity unmatched by that of any other nation in history. Both the war itself and the subsequent Cold War forced American industry to operate at its greatest levels, providing the most advanced standard of living experienced at any time.

The affluence of the period was all the more comforting to the American people since they had just undergone the worst depression in their history. The extensive business failures and massive unemployment of the 1930s were like a bad dream. The nation seemed to be arriving at the point where the desire for all sections of society to get a share of an economic "pie" was to be fulfilled. In addition to the satisfying availability of consumer goods, the swelling affluence was accompanied by the improved status of blacks, the increased employment of women, a strengthening of organized labor, the movement to the suburbs, an increased governmental commitment to education, and great advances in technology and medicine.

The post–World War II period was one of affluence, like that of the decade after World War I. But there the similarity—as important as it is—ends. For during the 1920s Americans looked upon the serious contemporary issues with complacency while engaging in unbridled pleasure-seeking. In the latter half of the 1940s and in the 1950s the knowledge that the many international crises resulting from the Cold War might turn into a nuclear conflict made people sober and anxious.

The Effects of Affluence

Unlike the prosperity that characterized the 1920s, the prosperity from 1940 to 1960 proved securely founded, considering the vast sums spent on defense during the Cold War and the ever-increasing purchasing of consumer goods.

STATISTICS

The extent of America's affluence can be seen in the statistics on the gross national product: It increased from about $205 billion in 1940 to about $500 billion in 1960 (a rise of almost 150 percent). It was estimated that within a decade and a half after World War II the 150 largest corporations owned approximately 50 percent of the nation's industrial wealth, which in turn equaled approximately 25 percent of that of the whole world.

In the decade and a half after World War II the unemployment rate was minimal, fluctuating between 3 and 5 percent. With virtually everyone in the available labor force employed, many with well-paying jobs, business firms strove to supply the American people with both essential and nonessential, albeit appealing, consumer goods.

THE RELENTLESSNESS OF POVERTY

Yet amid the affluence of the postwar period there were those who lived in want: whites in areas along the Appalachian mountain range, blacks in urban ghettos throughout the North, Indians on reservations that dotted the far West, Mexican-Americans in both rural and urban areas of the Southwest, and Puerto Ricans in New York City. In 1960, according to federal government findings, of the total American population of approximately 180 million, perhaps as many as 20 million (about 11 percent) lived at the poverty level.

Suburban Growth and Urban Transformation

A significant social change stemming from postwar affluence was the growth of the suburbs and the concomitant transformation of the urban centers. The movement to the suburbs had an extensive impact on the thoughts and actions of vast numbers of the American people.

STATISTICS

At the end of World War II the United States was predominantly urban. During the next fifteen years the population of the suburbs went from approximately 36 million to approximately 68 million (an increase of close to 100 percent); the population of the central cities went from approximately 52 million to approximately 58 million (an increase of about 12 percent). In the rural areas, the population actually declined, going from about 59 million to about 54 million. But what is just as important regarding the move to the suburbs is that it was made overwhelmingly by whites, drastically changing the racial composition of American cities. At the same time that whites, mostly affluent, were fleeing to the suburbs, poor blacks and Hispanic-Americans thronged into the inner cities. By 1960 blacks, who formed about 12 percent of the national population, accounted for approximately 20 percent of the population in over two hundred metropolitan areas. By the end of the next decade black Americans constituted about 70 percent of the population of Washington, D.C.; about 55 percent in Newark, New Jersey; and about 50 percent in Atlanta, Georgia. In more than half a dozen major cities, including Detroit and New Orleans, the black population was over 40 percent.

LIFE IN THE SUBURBS

To have one's own home with a bit of lawn on a tree-lined street was a traditional American dream. It was realized by many during the postwar years as a result of such things as the accessibility of inexpensive dwellings (standardized units were made possible by advances in mass-production and prefabrication methods), the availability through federal legislation of mortgage loans on quite favorable terms to World War II veterans, and the creation of a vast network of highways. The boom in housing construction was such that by 1960 approximately 25 percent of all the nation's dwelling units had been built during the preceding decade. Retail establishments came together in shopping malls conveniently located for their affluent suburban customers. The most serious charge leveled at the suburbs was their accentuation of racial separation.

Education

The vast economic and social changes that occurred during the period impelled many Americans to reexamine the goals of education, causing school administrators and teachers to redesign both curriculums and instruction methods.

ELEMENTARY EDUCATION

With the return to normal family life after the end of World War II, the birthrate began a long and marked rise, presenting challenges to the field of elementary education. The postwar "baby boom" required a massive effort to prepare additional teachers and to construct more classroom buildings. During the 1940s and 1950s elementary education increasingly came under attack as having become inadequate to its task. Most of the critics declared the cause to be what they considered the pernicious influence of John Dewey's philosophy. The critics favored a quick and full return to the arduous learning of the traditional academic disciplines.

SECONDARY EDUCATION

In 1960 approximately 85 percent of the nation's adolescents were in high school, a remarkable figure compared with that of approximately 10 percent in high school at the turn of the century.

HIGHER EDUCATION

After World War II the colleges and universities were deluged with former servicemen eager to make up for lost time. They were assisted in this aim with extensive financing provided by the federal "GI Bill." The veterans were sensitive to the value of higher education and conscientious in the pursuit of their studies.

Religion

Perhaps it was the concomitant anxieties of World War II and the Cold War that influenced many Americans to recommit themselves to organized religion. From 1940 to 1960, membership in churches and synagogues increased substantially. One manifestation of the surge in religious awakening was a tide of revivalism.

PROTESTANTISM

Two significant Protestant developments were the merging of bodies within a denomination and coalition among the various denominations, reversing the trend of extreme denominationalism, which had long dominated that wing of American Christianity. The National Council of the Churches of Christ in the United States, comprising twenty-six Protestant denominations plus four Eastern Orthodox bodies, was founded in 1950. The most famous Protestant revivalist was the Reverend William F. (Billy) Graham.

ROMAN CATHOLICISM

In relative membership growth, Roman Catholicism surpassed Protestantism. The most prominent expounder of Roman Catholic views on the moral and social issues then facing the American people was Bishop Fulton J. Sheen. Through a weekly television program, *Life Is Worth Living*, he gained an enormous following.

JUDAISM

In their desire to become thoroughly Americanized, many of the children of the Jewish immigrants of the late nineteenth and early twentieth centuries had become less than dedicated to the religious practices of their forebears, although they had retained the moral principles of their religion. The next generation, however, in part because of reaction to the Holocaust—the extermination of approximately 6 million Jews by the Nazi regime—and in part because of dissatisfaction with a blandly homogeneous American society, sought identity in a recommitment to the rituals and traditions of their ancestral faith.

Technology

The needs of World War II not only led to the development of the atomic bomb but also spurred rapid advances in electronics, which became the most important technological development of the 1940s and 1950s. By 1960 electronics was the nation's fourth-largest—and fastest-growing—industry, with sales totaling close to $13 billion. Automobile production also soared after the war.

THE COMPUTER

In 1944 Harvard University engineering professor Howard Acken developed the first digital computer, the operation of which was controlled by mechanical and electrical apparatus ("digital" refers to treating information in the form of words or solving problems expressed in words by converting the material into numbers and then calculating those numbers). Two years later research engineers at the University of Pennsylvania made the first totally electronic digital computer, whose circuits were controlled by vacuum tubes. In 1950 computers were introduced for business use. The machines manufactured during the rest of the decade, still controlled by vacuum tubes, were tremendous contraptions able to perform thousands of calculations a second. They were superseded early in the 1960s by computers controlled by transistors and able to perform approximately 1 million calculations a second. In 1955 the number of computers in use in the United States was about 300; by 1970 the number had increased to about 100,000. And as the years passed, virtually every sector of life found a use for computers.

THE TRANSISTOR

In 1947 three physicists at the Bell Telephone Laboratories—John Bardeen, Walter H. Brattain, and William Schockley—invented the transistor. Since the transistor presented much less bulk and much less weight than did a vacuum tube, a radio could now be carried in a pocket and a television set moved easily from one room to another.

THE AUTOMOBILE

During World War II the manufacture of automobiles was suspended, as the automakers turned to war production. After the war automobile production spurted to fulfill the public's desire, unsatisfied for four years, for new cars. In vastly increasing numbers, purchasers selected vehicles with such technical refinements as automatic transmission, power steering, and power brakes.

Medicine

A natural result of the postwar affluence was the ease with which Americans could pay for recently developed medical preparations and techniques. This made for a notable gain in health, perhaps the best index of which was a rise in life expectancy, from 62.9 years in 1940 to 69.7 in 1960.

ANTIBIOTICS

A component of the great strides in medicine was the use of a group of "wonder drugs" called antibiotics. Penicillin was discovered by British bacteriologist Alexander Fleming in 1928. It was more than a decade later, however, before the drug was proven useful in the treatment of a host of diseases, most effectively in combating scarlet fever, syphilis and gonorrhea, and most types of pneumonia. In the 1940s several different antibiotics were discovered, including streptomycin, which is particularly useful in controlling whooping cough and stomach infections.

DDT

The insecticide DDT (which is the popular abbreviation of its scientific name) was used by United States military forces during World War II in an attempt to eliminate typhus and malaria. However, some years later Rachel Carson, in her widely read book *Silent Spring* (1962), and others made it increasingly clear that the indiscriminate use of DDT and other insecticides had a seriously adverse effect upon the balance of nature by destroying large numbers of insects that constitute much of the food supply of several higher forms of animal life.

POLIO VACCINE

In 1953 Jonas Salk announced his development of a vaccine against poliomyelitis, and a vast immunization program throughout the nation was undertaken.

A FLOURISHING OF CULTURE

The affluence of the postwar period significantly aided the flourishing of art, literature, and music. With the advent of television, a revolution occurred in the fields of both entertainment and communication. A notable development in professional team sports was the breaking of the color barrier.

Art

The most significant new developments in American art were the emergence of the first major movement in painting that consciously rejected the imitation of a European style and the rise of modern sculpture.

PAINTING

During the mid-1940s and the 1950s many American painters turned from social criticism to a new movement called abstract expressionism. The traditional subject matter of painting, such as the human body, still life, or a rural scene, was of little or no concern. Within a basic structure of non-representational intent, the focus was upon such things as the utilization of space, of dimension (a huge canvas was often preferred), of surface texture (such as the distinctiveness of the brushstrokes), and of the interrelationship of colors. Abstract expressionism was the first major movement in American painting whose practitioners emphatically declined to imitate a European style. Indeed, the abstract expressionists affected the trend of painting outside the United States, exerting such influence that the painting center of the world shifted from Paris to New York City.

The members of the abstract expressionist school exhibited a broad diversity of styles. Jackson Pollock is acknowledged as the theoretician of the movement, and his work is considered to be its epitome. He created the "drip" technique, in which liquid paint is dribbled onto a large canvas placed on the floor or occasionally viscous paint is applied directly from the tube. Using this method, Pollock produced works consisting of whirling and crisscrossing lines of pigment that form a complicated and turbulent network. A typical painting is *Autumn Rhythm* (1950). Other leaders of the movement were the Dutch-born Willem de Kooning, and Mark Rothko.

Realism was by no means completely gone from American painting. The most acclaimed exponent of this genre was Andrew Wyeth.

Interestingly, the height of the abstract expressionist movement coincided with the enormous popularity of Anna Mary Robertson "Grandma" Moses and Norman Rockwell. The octogenarian Grandma Moses was the most famous American practitioner of the centuries-old tradition of primitive art (a genre in which works characterized by simple directness, two-dimensional flatness, and homeliness are executed by self-taught painters). Rockwell was the most successful illustrator of his time.

SCULPTURE

In sculpture the decades-old commitment to realism was challenged by Alexander Calder, who achieved fame with the creation of two types of abstract metal construction: the mobile, which hangs from the ceiling; and the stabile, which stands on the floor.

ARCHITECTURE

Some architects of the period repudiated the shunning of ornamentation associated with the International Style. Their resistance was based on the conviction that recent commercial buildings, with their starkly austere rectangular shapes, presented an unappealing sameness. The Finnish-born Eero

Saarinen and Edward Durrell Stone were among the leading architects who asserted this view.

Literature

During the 1940s and 1950s American novelists, poets, and playwrights continued to use established forms and techniques, but the playwrights seemed to do so with more notable creativity than did the novelists and poets.

THE NOVEL

The post–World War II generation of novelists leaned toward realism and naturalism in the honed form achieved during the two preceding decades. But in the view of many literary critics, the newcomers' clarity of goal and skill of style did not come up to those of the eminent novelists of the 1920s and 1930s.

Among the most acclaimed postwar writers were Norman Mailer, J. D. (Jerome David) Salinger, and Truman Capote. There was a spate of novels about World War II, perhaps the finest of which was Mailer's *The Naked and the Dead* (1948). Salinger made his mark with *The Catcher in the Rye* (1951), in which is depicted the frustrating attempts of an adolescent boy to defy the hypocrisy that pervades a society controlled by adults. Capote did not show an affinity for realism and naturalism. His works, such as *Other Voices, Other Rooms* (1948), focus on a world filled with fantasy and inhabited largely by grotesque persons.

POETRY

Three major poets of the 1940s and 1950s were William Carlos Williams, W. H. (Wystan Hugh) Auden, and Marianne Moore. Williams's most celebrated work is *Paterson* (1946–58), a five-volume poem that treats the ordinary daily activities and the historical events in that New Jersey city as a way to "explain" twentieth-century society. The British-born Auden's verse shows extraordinary technical proficiency. Moore's poetry earned distinction for its wit and keen images.

DRAMA

The great Eugene O'Neill had spent the 1930s concentrating on a cycle of plays, many of them autobiographical, most of which were not staged until the 1950s. *The Iceman Cometh* (1946), widely regarded as his finest work, deals with an annual visitor to a saloon who is convinced that by killing his wife he has released her from her illusions and burdens. Thus propelled, he engages in destructive and ultimately unsuccessful efforts to persuade the saloon's drunken patrons to give up their own illusions and return to the outside world. *Long Day's Journey into Night* (1956) is a treatment of the intense love-hate relationships among four family members (patterned after O'Neill's parents, older brother, and himself).

Thomas Lanier "Tennessee" Williams and Arthur Miller emerged to form, along with O'Neill, a triumvirate of the nation's finest playwrights. The prolific Williams was noted for an extensive use of deep symbolism and for a keen, poetic dialogue. A native of the South, he set many of his plays in that region, frequently depicting highly sensitive individuals (usually women) who retreated into self-delusion and memories in order to avoid what seemed certain doom from their current condition. His most successful plays were *The Glass Menagerie* (1945) and *A Streetcar Named Desire* (1947). Miller's style was clear-cut; it avoided symbolism, portrayed "ordinary" individuals, produced simple and direct dialogue, and placed the story in an average American middle-class home. *Death of a Salesman* (1949) is his masterpiece.

MAGAZINES

A striking move in periodical publishing was the reversal of the 1930s trend toward producing general-interest magazines, somewhat to the detriment of those that served a special-interest readership. Undoubtedly the most successful special-interest magazine was *TV Guide*, which appeared as a weekly in 1953. Another successful special-interest magazine was the monthly *Playboy*, founded in 1953 by Hugh Hefner. It contained such popular features as the centerfold of beautiful and provocative nude females and ultra-frank interviews with celebrities. The monthly *Sports Illustrated* appeared in 1954 as one more in an impressive collection of influential magazines published by the organization established by Henry R. Luce and his associates.

THE PAPERBACK REVOLUTION

Undoubtedly the major development in the field of publishing in the twentieth century was the successful marketing of softcover books. In 1939 Robert D. de Graff and three associates in conjunction with the Simon and Schuster publishing firm offered pocket-size paperbound reprints of the hardcover editions of ten best-selling books, with a price of twenty-five cents each. Within three months about 500,000 copies were sold. By the end of the 1950s approximately 350 million paperbacks were being purchased annually.

Music

The quality of orchestral music and opera during the postwar period equaled or surpassed that of the immediately preceding decades. The musical theater was revolutionized through a new conception of coordinating all the elements of a production. Country and western music gained steadily in popularity.

ORCHESTRAL COMPOSERS AND CONDUCTORS

The foremost composers of orchestral music were Aaron Copland, Walter Piston, and Roger Sessions. Copland's compositions frequently incorporated American folk tunes, as in the ballets *Billy the Kid* (1938) and *Appalachian Spring* (1944). Piston fused dissonant harmonies and jazz rhythms with the traditional classical musical forms. Sessions's music is vastly more complex than that of Copland or Piston. He virtually shunned melody in favor of intricate harmonic and rhythmic patterns.

The permanent conductor of the New York Philharmonic Symphony Orchestra during the late 1940s was the German-born Bruno Walter. In 1958 Leonard Bernstein was chosen the New York Philharmonic's first music director; for eleven years he held the post with distinction, conducting with an inimitable verve. Bernstein also turned his impressive musical talent to composing, producing well-received classical orchestral works, such as the *Jeremiah Symphony* (1942) and the orchestral ballet suite *Fancy Free* (1944), as well as musicals, including the long-standing favorite *West Side Story* (1957). The Boston Symphony Orchestra was led during the 1950s by the Frenchman Charles Munch. In 1938 the Philadelphia Orchestra selected as its principal conductor the Hungarian-born Eugene Ormandy. During a tenure of more than forty years he became well known for creating a uniquely sumptuous orchestral sound. Two other distinguished companies, the Chicago Symphony Orchestra and the Cleveland Orchestra, were led by Hungarian-born gifted precisionists, the former company by Fritz Reiner and the latter by George Szell.

CONCERT VIRTUOSOS

During the 1940s and 1950s there were four virtuosos who dominated concert playing: the Russian-born pianist Vladimir Horowitz; the Polish-born pianist Arthur Rubinstein; the Russian-born violinist Jascha Heifetz, who is considered by most critics to be the greatest twentieth-century player of the instrument; and the violinist Yehudi Menuhin.

OPERA

The most important twentieth-century composer of American operas was the Italian-born Gian-Carlo Menotti. Among his highly successful works were *The Medium* (1946) and *Amahl and the Night Visitors* (1951), the first opera composed for television.

In 1950 the Austrian-born Rudolf Bing became general manager of the Metropolitan Opera House. During a twenty-two-year tenure, he raised to even greater heights the company's high artistic standards. He engaged the company's first black singer, contralto Marian Anderson. Outstanding Metropolitan Opera tenors during the 1950s were Jan Peerce and Richard Tucker. Two much-acclaimed European sopranos were the Italian Renata Tebaldi and the Swede Birgit Nillson.

MUSICAL THEATER

In the 1940s a revolution in American musical theater was effected by the team of composer Richard Rodgers and lyricist Oscar Hammerstein II. Shortly before the death of Lorenz Hart, his lyricist for twenty-five years, Rodgers began his collaboration with Hammerstein. In contrast with Hart's somewhat sardonic lyrics, Hammerstein's were romantic and optimistic. Rodgers and Hammerstein endowed musical theater with a new stature through their harmonious coordination of dialogue, music, lyrics, and dance in the treatment of serious plots. All this was evidenced in their first show together: the towering *Oklahoma!* (1943), which is acknowledged as *the* American musical. *Oklahoma!*, which starred Alfred Drake, features the unforgettable songs "Oh, What a Beautiful Mornin'," "The Surrey with the Fringe on Top," and "People Will Say We're in Love." In her contribution to *Oklahoma!* ballet choreographer Agnes de Mille not only revolutionized the style of dance in musicals but also, in using dance to advance the plot, played a significant role in bringing about a basic change in musical theater itself. Other monumental hits by Rodgers and Hammerstein include *South Pacific* (1949), starring Mary Martin and Ezio Pinza, with "Some Enchanted Evening"; *The King and I* (1951), starring Gertrude Lawrence and Yul Brynner, with "Getting to Know You"; and *The Sound of Music* (1959), starring Mary Martin, with "Do Re Mi."

A new team of composer Frederick Loewe and lyricist Alan Jay Lerner produced two great works, *My Fair Lady* (1956) and *Camelot* (1960).

COUNTRY AND WESTERN MUSIC

The origin of country music is in the Southeast and that of western music is in the Southwest and West. The styles are very similar, each depending on the guitar, banjo, and fiddle for its distinctive sound. The lyrics focused largely on tribulations, such as unrequited love and the economic hardships of poor whites. During the 1920s the two styles were increasingly mingled. In the 1940s the music began to attract nationwide attention. The growing popularity was due in large part to the talent of singer Jimmie Rodgers.

LONG-PLAYING (LP) DISKS

One of the most important developments in twentieth-century music was the introduction, in 1948, of the long-playing phonograph record, invented by a team of research engineers headed by Peter Carl Goldmark. Recording on a single LP disk a body of music that had heretofore required five disks meant that within two decades virtually the entire repertory of both classical and light music appeared in compact form.

Motion Pictures

Early in the 1950s, because of intense competition from the new television industry, attendance in movie theaters began a steep decline, from which it was never able to rebound. Despite this decline, however, there was a select group of creative directors; there was a small group of stars whose popularity remained constant; and there was a large number of motion pictures still being produced.

DIRECTORS

Of the many fine directors of the period, two achieved particular eminence: the technician Alfred Hitchcock and the experimentalist Orson Welles. The British-born Hitchcock's forte was the thriller. He made more than two dozen, achieving the utmost in suspense with remarkable technical skill. Among his most popular works were *Rebecca* (1940), *Strangers on a Train* (1951), *North by Northwest* (1959), and *Psycho* (1960). Welles's first work was *Citizen Kane* (1941), which is considered by virtually all critics one of the very greatest motion pictures ever made. Welles was also its star. The film was loosely based on the life of newspaper publisher William Randolph Hearst. Stylistically, *Citizen Kane* was an exemplary work, encompassing devices—including close-ups, novel camera angles, striking group arrangements of performers, and overlapping conversations—that were brilliantly executed in a virtuosolike manner. Welles directed a few other highly regarded films, including *The Magnificent Ambersons* (1942) and *Touch of Evil* (1958). Besides directing, Welles performed to critical acclaim in several motion pictures directed by others.

STARS

There were a few stars who had started in films in the late 1920s or the 1930s, reached the heights of their popularity during the 1940s and 1950s, and retained beyond that period, indeed to the ends of their careers, the enduring loyalty of the movie-going public.

Clark Gable was the handsome and brash he-man. Humphrey Bogart was hard and cynical in almost every role. Spencer Tracy often depicted gruff characters. Gary Cooper and John Wayne played to perfection soft-spoken but courageous heroes. James Cagney was a feisty "little" guy. Henry Fonda evoked the decent and idealistic American. James Stewart endeared himself with his drawl and modest bearing. Cary Grant was elegant and urbane.

Among the female stars, four had exceptionally durable box-office attraction. Joan Crawford portrayed the strong-willed, intelligent type. Bette Davis with her expressive eyes filled the screen with a particular radiance. Marlene Dietrich was often cast as a seductive and mysterious woman. Katharine Hepburn achieved fame with her patrician appearance.

Three of the biggest new stars to emerge in the 1950s were Marilyn Monroe, Elizabeth Taylor, and Marlon Brando. Monroe was one of the top sex symbols in motion-picture history. Taylor was a woman of unsurpassed beauty who frequently chose roles that would display her ability to portray a fiery temperament. With a mumbling way of speaking and a "natural" manner, Brando was regarded by many as the best American film actor of his time.

MUSICALS

Hollywood retained its reputation for making the world's best motion picture musicals. Some of the most tastefully crafted among this type were *Meet Me in St. Louis* (1944), *An American in Paris* (1951), and *Singin' in the Rain* (1952).

WAR FILMS

The motion-picture industry responded to World War II by bringing forth a number of patriotic war films. Among the productions were four that became classics of the genre: *Casablanca* (1942), *Mrs. Miniver* (1942), *The Best Years of Our Lives* (1946), and *The Bridge on the River Kwai* (1957).

"MESSAGE" FILMS

The motion-picture industry continued the forthright treatment of various social injustices, a theme that had been handled with such commitment in the 1930s. *Gentleman's Agreement* (1947) examined the invidious effects of anti-Semitism in society. *On the Waterfront* (1954) explored the corruption in the New York City local of the longshoremen's union. But the 1940s and 1950s also saw added to this genre something new: films that dealt with human illness, both physical and mental. *The Lost Weekend* (1945) scrutinized an alcoholic's impairment, while *The Snake Pit* (1948) examined the appalling conditions in some mental institutions.

WIDE-SCREEN AND THREE-DIMENSIONAL INNOVATIONS

As a way of countering the threat of television, the film industry introduced new technology to heighten viewing enjoyment. Among the numerous innovations were two wide-screen systems—Cinerama, introduced in 1952, and Cinemascope, introduced in 1953—and a three-dimensional (3-D) process, introduced in 1952. Eventually deemed by both film critics and fans to be no substitute for a regular, well-directed and well-acted motion picture, none of these technical innovations continued to be used for more than a few years.

Television

A revolution in the presentation of entertainment and the transmittal of information was wrought by television—a revolution even more profound than that brought about earlier by motion pictures and radio.

BEGINNINGS

In 1930 the American Philo T. Farnsworth invented an electronic scanning system. That same year the National Broadcasting Company began operating an experimental television station in New York City. Franklin D. Roosevelt became the first president to appear on television when he opened the New York World's Fair in 1939. During World War II commercial television production was halted as part of the effort to manufacture war items. Within a year after the war, the medium swept the country with phenomenal force.

WIDE APPEAL

The number of families that owned television sets increased from approximately 15,000 in 1946 to close to 46 million in 1960. By the middle of the 1950s about 65 percent of the nation's homes contained sets, and by the decade's end about 90 percent did. In 1960, in those homes having at least one set, viewing was done an average of approximately five hours a day.

VARIETY SHOWS

With guest stars who could now be seen as well as heard, sight gags, attractive dancers in chorus lines, and lavish costumes and sets, the variety show was a "natural" for the new medium. The first big hit of television was in this genre: *Texaco Star Theater*, with comedian Milton Berle. Vastly more sophisticated was *Your Show of Shows*, starring Sid Caesar. The *Ed Sullivan Show* was a top favorite with television viewers for almost a quarter of a century.

SITUATION COMEDIES

Of the hundreds of situation comedies on television since its beginning, one of the most popular was *I Love Lucy*, with the inspired clown Lucille Ball. Another longtime favorite was *The Honeymooners*, starring the talented pair of Jackie Gleason and Art Carney.

ADVENTURE SERIALS

Evening telecasting included a multitude of adventure serials, mostly westerns and police dramas. To a much greater extent than were motion-picture westerns, television westerns were designed for an adult audience. So popular did the westerns become that by 1960 an average of four per evening appeared on the television screen, each very much like the other in characters and plots. The two biggest favorites were *Gunsmoke* and *Bonanza*. The indisputable top police drama was *Dragnet*, with Jack Webb as star, director, and sometimes scriptwriter. Winning fame for its realism, the serial portrayed the grueling work of police detectives in a large city.

SOAP OPERAS

A large portion of morning and early-afternoon telecasting was given over to daily half-hour segments of soap operas. Like those of radio, the television soap operas were aimed at housewives and focused on life's problems. *As the World Turns*, *Love of Life*, and *Search for Tomorrow* were especially popular.

CHILDREN'S SHOWS

From the outset television producers realized that the segment of the population most eager for their offerings in the morning, afternoon, and early evening would be children. The first successful children's program was the *Howdy Doody Show*, with Bob "Buffalo Bob" Smith, his freckle-cheeked puppet, Howdy Doody, and the mute clown, Clarabell. *Kukla, Fran and Ollie* featured a woman, Fran Allison, and two puppets, the clown, Kukla, and the dragon, Ollie (both were supplied movement and voice by Burr Tillstrom). Of a more educational nature was *Captain Kangaroo*, with the soft-spoken whimsical patter of Bob Keeshan.

TALK SHOWS

In the mid-1950s about 80 percent of those who owned television sets regularly stayed up until past midnight watching them. The most popular type of program presented late at night was the talk show. Of this genre the most successful by far was *The Tonight Show*, which went through a number of changes of host, regular cast, and format. The first host was Steve Allen; a few months after Allen left the show, Jack Paar became host.

QUIZ SHOWS

Enjoying constant and widespread appeal among television audiences were the quiz shows. Steadfastly popular was *What's My Line?* In *You Bet Your Life*, quizmaster Groucho Marx would elicit howls of delight from the audience with his mildly insulting side remarks during his interviews with contestants before the quiz. In 1955 *The $64,000 Question* premiered. The first of the "big-money" quiz shows, it was an immediate hit. But in 1958 the "big-money" quiz-show craze came to a sudden end in scandal. A former contestant on one of the programs publicly declared that they were rigged, correct answers by being "fed" beforehand to the more engaging contestants.

LIVE DRAMA

By the early 1950s many more live dramas were being presented each year on the television screen than on the stages of New York City theaters. Among the best of the dramatic series were *Kraft Television Theatre*, *Playhouse 90*, and *Studio One*. Some of the acclaimed original television dramas were Paddy Chayefsky's *Marty*, which is about a desolate butcher from the Bronx who finds solace in the companionship of a plain and shy woman as lonely as he; Rod Serling's *Requiem for a Heavyweight*; and Reginald Rose's *Twelve Angry Men*.

NEWS AND PUBLIC AFFAIRS

Leaders in the television industry soon began to tap the potential of their medium in news and public-affairs coverage. The institution of the American presidency, for example, was widely covered, and viewers were treated to inaugural ceremonies, national political conventions, presidential press conferences, and, in 1960, campaign debates. (In 1963 the networks stopped all regularly scheduled programming for three days to telecast only material associated with President John F. Kennedy's assassination and funeral.) The live televising of the 1951 hearings conducted by a Senate subcommittee on the investigation of crime in the nation and of the 1954 Army-McCarthy hearings drew millions of viewers.

Two highly regarded weekly public-affairs programs were *Face the Nation* and *Meet the Press*, on both of which a panel of print and television reporters questioned leading public figures. Both continued to be telecast into the 1990s. Among the most respected of the news analysts and nightly news-program anchors were Walter Cronkite, the team of Chester R. (Chet) Huntley and David Brinkley, and Edward R. Murrow.

SPORTS EVENTS

The large numbers of spectators who flocked to stadiums to see college and professional sports events in the 1940s and 1950s were "joined" by even larger numbers of spectators who watched the contests on television screens. The first televised World Series was that of 1947. The first televised heavyweight championship boxing match was held in 1946 between titleholder Joe Louis and contender Billy Conn. Professional football became a major televised sports.

FILMS

The early reaction of the motion-picture industry to television was utter indifference. By the end of the 1950s, however, the American motion-picture industry had completely reversed its attitude, welcoming the opportunity to realize a profit by selling its productions to the television networks.

Sports

One of the most significant developments in athletics during the 1940s and 1950s was the breaking down of the long-standing bar against hiring blacks, a situation prompted by the civil rights movement.

BASEBALL

A changing racial attitude was most notable in baseball, the professional sport in which the racial restriction had been strongest. The barrier was broken in the major leagues in 1947, when Jackie Robinson was hired by the Brooklyn Dodgers, through the efforts of general manager Branch Rickey. The following year half a dozen black players were on major-league teams. Two of the greatest hitters during the 1940s and 1950s—indeed, of all time—were Stanley (Stan) Musial and Theodore (Ted) Williams. Willie Howard Mays Jr. was another early black star. Charles Dillon "Casey" Stengel was not only one of America's greatest baseball managers but also perhaps the sport's most colorful personality, known particularly for his interviews, replete with his outrageously funny tortured syntax.

BOXING

After the great Joe Louis retired undefeated in 1949, the heavyweight crown passed to half a dozen others over the next decade. The most outstanding of Louis's successors were Rocky Marciano and Floyd Patterson.

TENNIS

In the 1940s and 1950s the game had its first Hispanic-American star, Richard Alonzo "Pancho" Gonzales. In 1957 Althea Gibson became the first black to capture the United States women's singles championship, also winning the British championship that same year. In 1958 she again took both titles.

GOLF

The player who most dominated professional golf during the 1940s and 1950s was William Benjamin (Ben) Hogan. The powerful-driving Samuel (Sam) Snead was another outstanding professional golfer. Mildred "Babe" Didrikson Zaharias is considered not only the best woman golfer of all time but also America's greatest all-around woman athlete.

Selected Readings

GENERAL WORKS:

Agar, Herbert. *The Price of Power: America Since 1945* (1957)
Baker, Donald G., and Charles H. Sheldon. *Postwar America: The Search for Identity* (1969)
Goldman, Eric F. *The Crucial Decade—and After: America, 1945–1960* (1961)
Jezer, Martin. *The Dark Ages: Life in the United States, 1945–1960* (1982)
Lewis, Peter. *The Fifties* (1977)
Miller, Douglas, and Marion Nowak. *The Fifties: The Way We Really Were* (1977)
Oakley, Ronald. *God's Country: America in the 1950s* (1986)

SPECIAL STUDIES:

Acheson, Dean. *Present at the Creation: My Years in the State Department* (1969)
Ambrose, Stephen E. *Eisenhower the President* (1984)
Barnouw, Erik. *Tube of Plenty: The Evolution of American Television* (1975)
Bloom, Jack. *Class, Race, and the Civil Rights Movement* (1987)
Brendon, Piers. *Ike* (1986)
Cummings, Bruce. *The Origins of the Korean War* (1980)
Dalfiume, Richard. *Desegregation of the U.S. Armed Forces* (1969)
Divine, Robert. *Eisenhower and the Cold War* (1981)
Downer, Alan S. *Fifty Years of American Drama, 1900–1950* (1951)
Eisenhower, Dwight D. *The White House Years* (2 vols., 1963–65)
Ewen, David. *Composers for the American Musical Theater* (1968)
Ferrell, Robert H. *Harry S. Truman and the Modern American Presidency* (1983)
Gaddis, John L. *The United States and the Origins of the Cold War* (1971)

Gottfried, Martin. *Broadway Musicals* (1979)

Greenstein, Fred. *The Hidden Hand Presidency: Eisenhower as Leader* (1982)

Harbutt, Fraser J. *The Iron Curtain: Churchill, America, and the Origins of the Cold War* (1986)

Hartmann, Susan M. *Truman and the 80th Congress* (1971)

Hess, Gary. *The United States' Emergence as a Southeast Asian Power, 1940–1950* (1987)

Hogan, Michael. *The Marshall Plan: America, Britain, and the Reconstruction of Western Europe, 1947–1952* (1987)

Iriye, Akira. *The Cold War in Asia* (1974)

Jackson, Kenneth T. *Crabgrass Frontier: The Suburbanization of the United States* (1985)

Kaplan, Laurence. *The United States and NATO* (1984)

Kaufman, Burton. *The Korean War* (1986)

Knight, Edgar W. *Fifty Years of American Education* (1951)

Konvitz, Milton R. *Expanding Liberties: Freedom's Gains in Postwar America* (1966)

LaFeber, Walter. *America, Russia, and the Cold War, 1945–1984* (1985)

Malone, Bill C. *Country Music U.S.A.: A Fifty Year History* (1969)

McCoy, Donald. *The Presidency of Harry S. Truman* (1984)

McCoy, Donald, and Richard Ruetter. *Quest and Response: Minority Rights and the Truman Administration* (1973)

Miller, Richard. *Truman: The Rise to Power* (1986)

Oliver, John W. *History of American Technology* (1956)

Oshinsky, Michael. *A Conspiracy So Immense: The World of Joe McCarthy* (1983)

Pollard, Robert. *Economic Security and the Origins of the Cold War* (1985)

Rae, John B. *The Road and the Car in American Life* (1971)

Rayback, Joseph G. *A History of American Labor* (1966)

Richardson, Elmo. *The Presidency of Dwight D. Eisenhower* (1979)

Rose, Barbara. *American Art Since 1900: A Critical History* (1967)

Ross, Irwin. *The Loneliest Campaign: The Truman Victory of 1948* (1968)

Rovere, Richard. *Senator Joe McCarthy* (1959)

Schickel, Richard. *Movies: The History of an Art and an Institution* (1965)

Schwartz, Bernard. *Inside the Warren Court* (1983)

Sitkoff, Harvard. *The Struggle for Black Equality, 1954–1980* (1981)

Sklar, Robert. *Movie-Made America: A Cultural History of American Movies* (1975)

Spanier, John W. *The Truman-MacArthur Controversy and the Korean War* (1959)

Taft, Philip. *Organized Labor in American History* (1964)

Theoharis, Athan G. *The Yalta Myths: An Issue in U.S. Politics, 1945–1955* (1970)

Truman, Harry S. *Memoirs* (2 vols., 1955–56)

Tsou, Tang. *America's Failure in China, 1941–1950* (1963)

Wilcox, Francis O., and H. Field Haviland Jr. *The United States and the United Nations* (1961)

Wood, Robert C. *Suburbia: Its People and Their Politics* (1959)

12

The New Frontier and the Great Society

1956 "Heartbreak Hotel" recorded by Presley

1957 Southern Christian Leadership Conference (SCLC) founded

Kerouac, *On the Road*

1959 Students for a Democratic Society (SDS) founded

1960 Sit-ins

Student Non-Violent Coordinating Committee (SNCC) founded

Kennedy elected president

1961 Executive order creates Peace Corps

Twenty-third Amendment ratified

Bay of Pigs invasion

Freedom Rides

Kennedy gives military aid to South Vietnam

Berlin Wall built

1962 University of Mississippi desegregated

Cuban Missile crisis

Friedan, *Feminine Mystique*

Warhol, *100 Cans*

Albee, *Who's Afraid of Virginia Woolf?*

Dylan, "Blowin' in the Wind"

1963 University of Alabama desegregated

Nuclear Test Ban Treaty signed

March on Washington

Kennedy assassinated; Johnson becomes president

1964   Twenty-fourth Amendment ratified

Civil Rights Act

Gulf of Tonkin Resolution

Economic Opportunity Act

Johnson elected president

1965   Civil rights march from Selma to Montgomery

Elementary and Secondary School Education Act

Medicare Act

Voting Rights Act

Housing and Urban Development Department created

1966   Transportation Department created

Masters and Johnson, *Human Sexual Response*

Black Panthers Party for Self-Defense founded

National Organization for Women (NOW) founded

1967   Twenty-fifth Amendment ratified

Six-Day War

Race riots in various cities, including Newark, Detroit, and Los Angeles

Balanchine, *Jewels*

1968   Tet Offensive

King assassinated

Militant students force Columbia University to cancel rest of semester

Vietnam peace negotiations begin in Paris

Kubrick, *2001: A Space Odyssey*

1969   Woodstock festival

1970   Gay Liberation Front founded

Sondheim, *Company*

1972   "Equal Rights" Amendment passed by Congress

In 1961 the elderly and staid Republican, Dwight D. Eisenhower, vacated the White House for the young and vigorous Democrat, John F. Kennedy. From the very beginning, the Kennedy administration captivated the American people with its distinctive verve. In accepting the presidential nomination Kennedy stated that Americans faced many domestic and foreign challenges constituting what he referred to as a New Frontier. As the geographic frontier of the past had afforded Americans many opportunities, this spiritual New Frontier offered them opportunities to effect economic and social reforms at home and to exercise moral and humane leadership abroad.

After Kennedy was assassinated, Lyndon B. Johnson assumed the presidential office and began firmly guiding the nation. In seeking to become president in his own right, Johnson spoke with emotion of achieving what he referred to as the Great Society. He promised a renewed attack by all the forces of government against poverty, disease, ignorance, and racial discrimination. When Kennedy assumed the presidency the civil rights movement had not long before entered a new stage, which came to be called the Black Revolution. During the Johnson administration the Black Revolution reached its startling climax.

In the field of foreign affairs, both Kennedy and Johnson were forced to contend with the constant perplexities of the Cold War. During the Kennedy administration the United States and the Soviet Union were brought to the brink of armed conflict. During the Johnson administration the United States became deeply immersed in a morass of fighting in Vietnam.

KENNEDY AND THE NEW FRONTIER

Following his inauguration, Kennedy attempted to persuade Congress to implement the domestic goals of the New Frontier. But the conservative coalition of Republican and southern Democratic legislators was able to thwart the full expectations of the executive branch. In dealing with the economy, the efforts of the administration were directed toward halting a spiraling inflation. As for civil rights, Kennedy, who had previously shown little interest in the trying status of the blacks, became more and more committed to their struggle for equality.

Election of 1960   The election was fiercely contested and turned out to be the closest in over seventy-five years.

DEMOCRATS

There were two aspirants to the presidential nomination who were notably able and aggressive: Senator John F. Kennedy of Massachusetts and Senate Majority Leader Lyndon B. Johnson of Texas. The delegates chose Kennedy to run for president and Johnson for vice-president. In so doing they presented the voters with a geographically balanced ticket.

REPUBLICANS

By the time the Republican national convention had begun its proceedings, Vice-President Nixon's nomination as standard-bearer appeared inevitable. As expected, he captured the prize on the first ballot. Henry Cabot Lodge, Jr., of Massachusetts, a former Republican senator and the current ambassador to the United Nations, was chosen as his running mate.

THE CAMPAIGN

An innovative feature of the campaign was a series of four one-hour televised debates, in which Kennedy and Nixon answered questions put to them by panels of news reporters. An estimated 75 million Americans watched. In the opinion of most political commentators, Kennedy probably won the debates by a slight margin. What was certain was that the senator, much less known than the vice-president, received valuable exposure to a national audience. Throughout the campaign Kennedy made two basic charges regarding the state of the nation as a result of the preceding seven and a half years of Republican rule: First, the United States was experiencing economic stagnation (he appealed for measures to "get the country moving again"); second, the United States was witnessing a decline in its power and prestige abroad. Nixon made vigorous efforts to refute both points.

KENNEDY'S NARROW VICTORY

Kennedy won 303 electoral votes; Nixon carried 219. Of a total of 68,337,642 popular votes, Kennedy received a plurality of only 118,550 over Nixon. This represented less than two-tenths of 1 percent of the ballots cast—the smallest percentage difference between the popular votes of two major presidential candidates since the election of 1884.

The Kennedy Administration

Kennedy was determined to be a dynamic president. He cherished the idea that it was the obligation of his office to help both the people of the United States and the people of the rest of the world.

THE PRESIDENT

Kennedy was a handsome, intelligent, and charming man. Having chosen politics as his profession, he practiced it with deep purpose and extraordinary daring. He made certain that nothing—including the heavy duties of the presidency—would curtail his intellectual and cultural growth.

INAUGURAL ADDRESS

Kennedy delivered a widely acclaimed inaugural address that focused on the sacrifices needed to ensure individual freedom and world peace. To the people of the United States he entreated: "Ask not what your country can do for you—ask what you can do for your country." To the people of the rest of the world he pledged that Americans would "pay any price, bear any burden, meet any hardship, support any friend, oppose any foe to assure the survival and the success of liberty."

THE CABINET

During his campaign Kennedy promised the voters that if elected he would name to his cabinet a "ministry of talent." His appointees were, on the whole, strong-willed men with administrative experience. Two of the leading posts were given to Republican businessmen: C. Douglas Dillon, a New York banker who had been ambassador to France during the Eisenhower administration, was named secretary of the treasury; Robert S. McNamara, president of the Ford Motor Company, became secretary of defense. Dean Rusk, president of the Rockefeller Foundation, an organization that aids projects to advance welfare and culture, was chosen secretary of state. Robert F. Kennedy, younger brother of the president, was appointed attorney general and soon became the leading figure in the cabinet.

New Frontier Legislation

Congress rejected Kennedy's most progressive legislative recommendations. It did, however, pass bills on housing, minimum wages, and the extension of social security. The Peace Corps, which was established by executive order, soon received support from Congress.

THE HOUSING ACT OF 1961

This act provided approximately $5 billion for slum clearance and housing projects.

THE MINIMUM WAGE ACT OF 1961

This measure increased the existing minimum wage to $1.25 an hour for close to 25 million workers. By the end of four years more than 3 million new workers would be included under the provisions of the law.

SOCIAL SECURITY AMENDMENTS OF 1961

Congress amended the Social Security Act to provide such benefits as aid to the children of unemployed workers and retirement funds, although in reduced amounts, to workers who chose to leave their jobs at the age of sixty-two rather than at sixty-five.

THE PEACE CORPS

Early in 1961 Kennedy issued an executive order creating the Peace Corps. This was an organization of persons who volunteered to serve as teachers and technicians to help raise the standard of living in under-developed countries of Africa, Asia, and Latin America. Six months later Congress appropriated funds to put the Peace Corps on a permanent basis. R. Sargent Shriver, Jr., the administrator of a Chicago commercial center and a brother-in-law of the president, was appointed to direct the program. Peace

Corps volunteers lived among the people of the countries they were serving and received modest financial allowances for their work.

Kennedy's Unachieved Goals

Kennedy failed to persuade Congress to accept the entire domestic program that he regarded as essential for improving the general condition of the American people. His proposals for aid to education, Medicare, and a department of urban affairs were all defeated by the coalition of Republicans and southern Democrats that had existed in Congress since the late 1930s. The coalition received help from various special-interest groups.

FEDERAL AID TO EDUCATION

Kennedy proposed a federal aid program for education that would help construct school buildings, increase teachers' salaries, and grant student scholarships. The proposal failed in Congress, largely because the Kennedy administration was unable to come to terms with the demand by Roman Catholic church leaders that parochial schools as well as public schools be given aid.

MEDICAL CARE FOR THE AGED

The Kennedy administration presented to Congress a plan known as Medicare to provide hospital and nursing care for the aged. Congress twice rejected the proposal. An important factor in the measure's defeat was the antipathy of the nation's largest organization of physicians, the American Medical Association, which repeatedly and vigorously characterized the plan as a step toward "socialized medicine."

DEPARTMENT OF URBAN AFFAIRS

Kennedy submitted a plan for the creation of a department of urban affairs. The proposal was defeated in Congress by the conservative coalition.

The Economy

From the beginning the Kennedy administration faced the problem of a stagnant economy. In order to stimulate economic growth it strove to foster stable prices for products sold at home as well as an increase in the volume of goods sold abroad.

CONFRONTATION WITH STEEL MANAGEMENT

The price of such a widely used commodity as steel has always had a significant effect upon numerous industrial costs. To help curb inflation, in the fall of 1961 Kennedy extracted from the steel managers a tacit agreement not to increase prices. Then in April 1962, the United States Steel Corporation suddenly announced an increase in the price of steel. Five other steel firms promptly did the same. An enraged Kennedy intervened immediately to divert government contracts for the purchase of steel to firms that had not raised their prices. This step compelled the "offending" companies to cancel the increase. The Kennedy administration was careful to explain that its action did not arise from any hostility toward business enterprise but was an attempt to halt inflation.

THE TRADE EXPANSION ACT

This law, passed in 1962, gave the president a great deal of flexibility in negotiating with the newly established European Economic Community (known as the Common Market), an economic union of six (later increased to nine) Western European nations formed to stimulate within each of them both industrial enterprise and employment. The Trade Expansion Act permitted the United States to compete for trade in a freer market than had previously existed by empowering the president to lower tariff duties by as much as 50 percent over a five-year period and to abolish tariff duties on a number of products exported by both the United States and the member nations of the Common Market.

The Black Revolution

Although measurable progress had been made in the 1950s toward school integration and safeguarding the right to vote, blacks became more and more forceful in their efforts to put an end to their "second-class citizenship." Early in 1960 a new direction in the civil rights movement began.

SIT-INS

Throughout the South black college students began to defy local laws and customs of racial segregation. The form of that protest was based on the principle of nonviolent resistance that the Reverend Martin Luther King had expounded during the highly successful Montgomery bus boycott of 1955–56. On February 1, 1960, four black students from the Agricultural and Technical College of North Carolina in Greensboro sat at a nearby Woolworth's "whites only" lunch counter, requested service, and refused to leave when they were denied it. The use of the sit-in was taken over by many college students, both black and white, and spread quickly throughout the South. The young people received a great deal of moral and financial support from such civil rights organizations as the National Association for the Advancement of Colored People (NAACP), directed by Roy Wilkins; the Southern Christian Leadership Conference (SCLC), under King; and the Congress of Racial Equality (CORE), led by James Farmer. In April 1960, at Shaw University in North Carolina, the Student Non-Violent Coordinating Committee (SNCC) was formed to bring into concerted action the efforts of the sit-in demonstrators. During 1960–61 eating facilities were desegregated in scores of southern towns and cities. By the end of 1961 approximately 75,000 students, both black and white, had made use of the sit-in. The sit-ins prompted kneel-ins at churches, read-ins at libraries, and wade-ins at beaches. Segregation as a way of life in the South was slowly disappearing.

FREEDOM RIDES

In May 1961, CORE began a campaign against the "whites only" facilities of bus terminals in the South. An integrated group known as the Freedom Riders set out by bus from Washington to New Orleans to put to the test the observance of the existing federal integration orders. The Freedom Riders were attacked by hostile mobs at several stops, with a number of serious incidents occurring in Alabama. Since the bus-company drivers would not subject themselves to further danger, the Freedom Riders were compelled to complete their trip by airplane. Soon more Freedom Riders took to buses throughout the South. In September 1961, the Interstate Commerce Commission, in response to a request by the Justice Department, issued an order prohibiting segregation on buses and in terminals used in interstate commerce. Not long afterward railroads and airlines voluntarily desegregated all their facilities.

DESEGREGATION OF UNIVERSITIES

Beginning in the 1950s a small number of black students were admitted to some white colleges and universities in the South. But black Americans were dissatisfied with the slow pace of this desegregation. In September 1962, James Meredith, a black air force veteran, obtained a federal court order that he be admitted to the University of Mississippi. But when he attempted to enroll, he repeatedly found his way barred, on two occasions by Governor Ross Barnett himself. Finally Meredith was accompanied to the campus by several hundred armed federal marshals. President Kennedy, in a television address, implored all those affected by the situation to comply with the law.

But to no avail. Rioting by students and local citizens erupted on the campus. Two persons were killed and scores were injured. Kennedy then ordered federal troops into the area, and calm was restored. The troops protected Meredith first as he enrolled and then as he pursued his studies until his graduation at the end of the academic year.

A repetition of the Mississippi incident threatened to occur at the University of Alabama. In June 1963, Governor George C. Wallace of Alabama personally barred the way of two black students when they tried to enroll for the summer session. But the governor immediately backed down when President Kennedy federalized units of the Alabama national guard and dispatched them to the campus.

MASS DEMONSTRATIONS

Blacks increased their demands for equal treatment in the spring of 1963, when they held mass demonstrations throughout the South. City after city felt the call for a complete end to segregation in all public facilities, including schools, libraries, stores, and restaurants. Many black leaders, following the philosophy of Dr. King, advocated that their followers use persistent pressure through nonviolent methods, such as petitions, boycotts, sit-ins, and orderly street demonstrations.

However, nonviolent protests, in the North as well as in the South, degenerated into violent clashes pitting blacks and their white sympathizers against police authorities who claimed they were complying with local laws. The attention of the nation was drawn to Birmingham, Alabama, where King himself was leading mass demonstrations to effect desegregation in the city. In May 1963, there was violence in Birmingham, as the police resorted to the use of high-pressure fire hoses, electric cattle prods, and dogs against the demonstrators. Leaders of the black and white communities soon reached agreement on a plan to desegregate the city. But in September violence erupted once more in Birmingham, when a bomb was thrown into a black church, killing four girls who were attending a Sunday-school class.

THE MARCH ON WASHINGTON

Believing that black protests could be better served if they were moved off the streets and into the courts, President Kennedy submitted a civil rights bill to Congress in June 1963. The proposed legislation prohibited a number of common discriminatory practices and granted the civil rights division of the Department of Justice increased authority to deal with instances of discrimination. Conservative white southern members of Congress quickly moved to block the measure.

That August, while legislators were debating the bill, black civil rights leaders organized the "March on Washington for Jobs and Freedom" to dramatize the need for such a measure. The civil rights groups received notable support from numerous service, religious, and labor organizations. More than 200,000 people (about 60,000 of whom were white) took part in what was the largest demonstration ever to take place in the nation's capital. The participants proceeded in orderly fashion from the Washington Monument to the Lincoln Memorial, where they listened to speeches by such prominent black leaders as the longtime civil rights activist and head of the Brotherhood of Sleeping Car Porters A. Philip Randolph, executive secretary of the NAACP Roy Wilkins, and Dr. King. Among the whites who spoke was the head of the United Auto Workers of America, Walter Reuther. In a memorable address King described his "dream" that his children might one day live in a nation where they would be judged not "by the color of their skin but by the content of their character."

The Assassination of Kennedy

The young and vigorous Kennedy became the fourth president to be killed by an assassin's bullet.

TRAGEDY IN DALLAS

Kennedy traveled to Texas in November 1963, to help reconcile the sharp differences between the conservative and liberal wings of the state's Democratic party before the 1964 election, in which he was planning to seek a second term as president. On November 22, while riding alongside his wife in a motorcade in Dallas, Kennedy was shot in the head and neck by a sniper. He died shortly afterward, without regaining consciousness. Less than two hours later Vice-President Lyndon B. Johnson, who had accompanied Kennedy on the political mission, took the presidential oath of office. Lee Harvey Oswald, a former marine who had established a reputation for participation in various communist causes, was charged with the murder. Two days after the assassination, as Oswald was about to be moved from one jail to another, and before a national television audience, Oswald was shot to death by Jack Ruby, a Dallas nightclub owner who had been a voluble admirer of the stricken president.

THE WARREN COMMISSION

Four days after Kennedy's funeral, President Johnson appointed a seven-member commission to conduct a thorough investigation of the assassination. Known as the Warren Commission after its chairman, Chief Justice Earl Warren, the commission received testimony from more than 500 people that filled twenty-six volumes. In an 888-page report issued in September 1964, the Warren Commission concluded that Oswald had killed President Kennedy and that Oswald and Ruby had each acted solely on his own.

In the following years many called for a new inquiry, contending that the commission had not delved enough into the possibility of a conspiracy. Thus the House of Representatives Select Committee on Assassination was established in 1973 to engage in another investigation. In January 1979, the committee issued its report, which concluded that there was indeed the possibility of conspiratorial action in the assassination of President Kennedy.

JOHNSON AND THE GREAT SOCIETY

In a number of addresses beginning in mid-1964 and culminating in his State of the Union message to Congress in January 1965, President Lyndon B. Johnson outlined the goals he cherished for the nation—goals that would bring about what he referred to as the Great Society. Johnson asserted that the federal government should assume a more commanding role than it had ever before played in improving the quality of life in the United States. In the Great Society no one would suffer from poverty, controllable diseases, lack of education, or racial injustice. The president's ability to transform his hopes into reality depended upon congressional approval of a program capable of being implemented in a practical way.

The Johnson Administration

Johnson assumed the duties of the presidency with a striking determination and intensity. His ability to get a job done, which he had exhibited brilliantly as the majority leader of the Senate, served him to good advantage in his new role.

THE PRESIDENT

Johnson's shrewdness and spirit of compromise made him one of the most successful politicians of his time. With those who worked under him he could be savagely demanding. He was a southwesterner through and through, with a drawl he seemed to take delight in.

THE CABINET

Wanting to indicate that he was anxious to continue the policies of the previous administration, Johnson asked the members of the Kennedy cabinet to remain in office. But within a year Attorney General Robert F. Kennedy, who had personal differences with the new president, resigned to run for the Senate. By the end of the following year Secretary of the Treasury C. Douglas Dillon had also relinquished his post.

Election of 1964

Contemporary political analysts agreed upon the meaning of the election: Since the beginning of the New Deal the voters, when given a clear-cut choice between a liberal and a conservative course for the nation, would make an overwhelming commitment to the former.

DEMOCRATS

The Democratic national convention acceded to virtually every wish of President Johnson. His nomination as the party's standard-bearer was inevitable. The liberal senator Hubert H. Humphrey of Minnesota was chosen as his running mate.

REPUBLICANS

The delegates to the Republican national convention nominated Senator Barry Goldwater of Arizona for president and Representative William Miller of New York for vice-president. Both were ultraconservative. The choice of Goldwater was a hard-fought and quite satisfying victory for the right wing over the usually strong internationalist left wing of the party.

THE CAMPAIGN

Goldwater maintained that his candidacy meant that for the first time since the 1932 Hoover-Roosevelt campaign the Republican party was offering the voters "a choice, not an echo [of the Democratic candidate]." On the domestic level, Goldwater recommended a rapid decrease in federal economic and social programs and a relaxation of government activity in the civil rights area. As for foreign affairs, he called for an extreme "get tough" policy toward the communist bloc. Johnson extolled the benefits that would accrue to all from the implementation of the Great Society, without ever describing precisely the various components of the program. He assumed a moderate position on relations with the communist nations.

JOHNSON'S LANDSLIDE VICTORY

Johnson received 43,167,000 popular votes to Goldwater's 27,146,000. The Democratic candidate was chosen president by the largest popular vote in the history of the nation. His 61.2 percent of the total vote topped Franklin D. Roosevelt's 60.8 percent in 1936 and Warren G. Harding's 60.4 percent in 1920. In the electoral college Johnson carried 486 votes to Goldwater's 52. Of the fifty states and the District of Columbia, Goldwater carried only five states in the South plus his home state of Arizona. (As a result of the Twenty-third Amendment to the Constitution, passed by Congress in 1960 and ratified in 1961, the eligible residents of the District could now vote in presidential elections.)

Social Legislation

For a time after he entered the White House, Johnson had little difficulty in securing from Congress the legislation he requested. Bill after bill was passed almost in the precise form that the president's advisors had suggested. But the spirit of cooperation began to wear thin in 1965, and Congress paid less attention to legislative proposals from the White House.

THE ECONOMIC OPPORTUNITY ACT

This measure, passed in 1964, provided close to $1 billion to undertake a "war on poverty." It established, among other things, a number of community-action projects to improve health and housing conditions and a Job Corps to train persons between the ages of sixteen and twenty-one in a variety of occupations. The Office of Economic Opportunity was created under the act to supervise the antipoverty program. Peace Corps director R. Sargent Shriver Jr. was chosen to head the new agency.

THE APPALACHIAN REGIONAL DEVELOPMENT ACT

This act, passed in 1965, authorized the expenditure of approximately $1 billion to provide relief to the people in the distressed areas along the Appalachian mountain range, which covers eleven states east of the Mississippi River from Pennsylvania to Alabama.

THE ELEMENTARY AND SECONDARY SCHOOL EDUCATION ACT

As a result of the provisions of this act, passed in 1965, students in elementary and secondary schools, including parochial and other private facilities, received governmental assistance indirectly through loans and grants to their schools. The act settled the controversy that had existed during the Kennedy administration over whether the federal government should grant such financial assistance to parochial educational institutions.

THE MEDICARE ACT

Despite widespread debate on the role of the federal government in providing medical care and the outspoken opposition of many of the nation's physicians, Congress finally, in 1965, enacted the plan called Medicare to provide hospital and nursing care for those sixty-five and over, to be financed from payments made to Social Security. Medicare became operative on July 1, 1965.

Government Reorganization and Reform

The need for the government to reorganize and reform itself was a continuing one. The Johnson administration directed some of its energy toward that end.

DEPARTMENT OF HOUSING AND URBAN DEVELOPMENT

In 1965 Congress created the Department of Housing and Urban Development. The new department was authorized to administer programs for the improvement of housing and community life in cities and their adjacent areas. Robert C. Weaver, who had held a variety of administrative posts in federal and state government, was appointed by Johnson as the first secretary of housing and urban development. Weaver became the first black cabinet member in the nation's history.

DEPARTMENT OF TRANSPORTATION

In 1966 Congress established the Department of Transportation to develop the policies and to supervise the programs of the federal government in the field of transportation. Johnson appointed Alan S. Boyd, who had served with distinction on the Florida Railroad and Utilities Commission, as the first secretary of transportation.

THE TWENTY-FIFTH AMENDMENT

President Eisenhower's three serious illnesses and President Kennedy's assassination made the American people keenly aware that the Constitution provided no procedure for replacing a disabled president. Passed by Congress in 1965 and ratified in 1967, the Twenty-fifth Amendment to the Constitution provided for the vice-president to assume the office of acting president in case the president should become incapacitated. The procedure was specified whereby the president would resume his office if he recovered. It also authorized the president, whenever the office of vice-president should become vacant, to appoint a new vice-president who would take office when confirmed by a majority of both houses of Congress. Thus a constitutional gap, which had troubled the nation for almost two hundred years, was filled.

The Climax of the Black Revolution

The Black Revolution, begun early in 1960, reached its climax during the Johnson administration, which was sympathetic to all but the violent aspects of the new activism.

THE TWENTY-FOURTH AMENDMENT

Since the end of the nineteenth century many of the southern states had adopted the poll tax as one method of keeping blacks from voting. By 1960 five southern states still retained it. Passed by Congress in 1962 and ratified in 1964, the Twenty-fourth Amendment to the Constitution prohibited the use of the poll tax as a requirement for voting in federal elections.

THE CIVIL RIGHTS ACT OF 1964

Largely as a result of pressure from President Johnson, a filibuster (the concerted use of dilatory tactics in a legislature to delay or prevent action) by conservative white southerners in the Senate was finally overcome. In July 1964, Congress passed a new civil rights act. The measure (1) strengthened voting rights protection; (2) prohibited discrimination in places of "public accommodation," such as stores, restaurants, hotels, and theaters; (3) required the federal government to withdraw financial assistance from any state or local program permitting discrimination in its operation; (4) authorized the attorney general to institute suits to desegregate schools; and (5) established the Equal Employment Opportunity Commission to foster compliance with the law forbidding discriminatory practices by employers and labor unions.

CONFRONTATION IN SELMA

It was soon evident that the Civil Rights Act of 1964 would be effective only if the American people decided to carry out its provisions in good faith. Crucial in the minds of many blacks was the issue concerning registration of voters. The act specifically forbade election officials to apply standards to black voting applicants that differed from those applied to white applicants. In 1965 Selma, Alabama, a community where black voters were few (approximately 350) in proportion to blacks who were of voting age (about 15,000), was chosen as a place to test the willingness of state and local officials to abide by the federal law.

Black voter registration was ferociously opposed by many whites, led by the county sheriff, who readily ordered the use of whips and clubs against demonstrators for black rights. What happened was a travesty, arousing Americans to the brutal ways in which the right to assemble, the right to petition, and the right to register were being denied to white citizens as well as black. The killing first of a black civil rights worker and then of a white one, a young minister from the North, attracted the attention of the nation.

THE VOTING RIGHTS ACT OF 1965

The events at Selma spurred President Johnson to address the Congress in March 1965, as he submitted legislation that he believed would give the federal government power to ensure nondiscriminatory procedures in all elections—federal, state, and local. The measure was necessary, the president insisted, in order to enforce the Fifteenth Amendment to the Constitution, which ninety-five years before had conferred on blacks the right to vote.

Congress responded positively. A new civil rights act was signed into law in August 1965. It contained the following provisions: (1) Literacy tests were to be suspended in any county where less than 50 percent of the voting-age population was registered or had cast ballots in 1964 (five southern states and portions of two others were affected by this); (2) federal examiners would be dispatched to register prospective voters in any county practicing voting discrimination; and (3) the attorney general was empowered to institute suits against the use of poll taxes (four southern states were affected by this).

MODERATE ORGANIZATIONS AND LEADERS

There was disagreement among the major black organizations and their leaders, especially after 1965, concerning the best strategy to use in the battle for equal treatment for blacks in a predominantly white society. The NAACP consistently rejected the use of violence. Roy Wilkins, executive secretary of the organization, ably presented the views of the moderates. The National Urban League had A. Whitney Young as its executive director. Young was an articulate spokesman for vigorous but nonviolent black community action. Established in 1957, the SCLC sought to end segregation in the use of public facilities and to end discrimination in employment and in voting. The founding president of the SCLC, the Reverend Martin Luther King, had difficulty reconciling his nonviolent methods with the demands of those blacks who advocated force as the way to get results. In April 1968, King was assassinated in Memphis, Tennessee. His death deepened the sense of bitterness and hostility among blacks, both moderate and militant.

MILITANT ORGANIZATIONS AND LEADERS

The Black Muslims, whose organization, the Nation of Islam, was founded in 1930, continued into the 1960s as a religious body that proclaimed the inherent superiority of the black over the white race and advocated the complete separation of the two. Although Elijah Muhammad was the revered spiritual leader of the Black Muslims, his most prominent follower, the ardent Malcolm X, was the body's leading spokesperson. In the mid-1960s both CORE and SNCC became radicalized. Founded in 1942 by James

Farmer, CORE, which had always encouraged the membership of whites, sought through nonviolent means to do away with racial discrimination. In 1966 Farmer resigned as head of CORE. Under such leaders as Roy Innes the organization became increasingly separatist in its philosophy. By 1967 SNCC had renounced its original commitment to nonviolent methods and began to force white members out of the organization. The fiery Stokely Carmichael, the new chairman of SNCC, popularized the slogan "Black Power," which the moderate NAACP, National Urban League, and SCLC rejected as being hate-fomenting. The Black Panther Party for Self-Defense was founded in California in 1966 by Huey Newton and Bobby Seale. Its most articulate spokesperson was Eldridge Cleaver. The Black Panthers advocated that blacks arm themselves in preparation for the direct violent confrontation with whites that they believed was certain to occur in the struggle for black liberation. As the years went by there were numerous violent encounters between the Black Panthers and the police. Emerging during the mid-1960s as a forceful intellectual leader in the black nationalist movement was the author LeRoi Jones, who assumed the African name Imamu Amiri Baraka.

URBAN GHETTOS

Germane to the black fight for an improved status was the fact that most black Americans had moved into the cities. By the mid-1960s close to 70 percent were living in metropolitan areas. Although they shared on a small scale in the national prosperity, their income level steadily fell behind that of white city dwellers. Because of their separation from whites through neighborhood housing patterns, schools that black children attended were segregated, not by law but in reality. A powerful theme running through all black objectives in the 1960s was the desire to break out of the ghetto's restrictions. Each summer from 1964 to 1967, riots erupted in the black sections of many northern cities. At times looting and gun battles between blacks and the police were rampant in the streets. Of the approximately fifty affected cities, those that suffered the most severe violence were Newark, Detroit, and Los Angeles. When the destruction finally came to an end, hundreds of people had been injured and scores had been killed.

A DIVIDED NATION HAS HOPE

President Johnson appointed a biracial and bipartisan eleven-member Advisory Commission on Civil Disorders, headed by former governor Otto Kerner of Illinois. The commission's unanimous report, issued in 1968, declared that the primary cause of the riots was the intolerable economic, social, and psychological conditions of urban blacks resulting from widespread and long-standing white racism. The report went on to state that some of the disturbances had been accentuated by the inefficiency of local police and national guard units called in to help restore order. "Our nation is moving toward two societies, one black and one white—separate and unequal," the commission concluded. Most Americans seemed to accept the fact that the problem existed. But there was hope. During the 1960s blacks had made considerable gains in achieving status—politically, economically, and socially. Symbolic of their new racial pride was the fact that in schools and colleges across the nation black students emphasized the importance of their own heritage by insisting on courses in black history and culture. And as never before, black Americans fought for and won acceptance by white Americans.

The Continuing Plight of the Indians

With the arrival of the whites from the European continent centuries before, the American Indians began suffering tragic unhappiness at their hands. For the past several decades their particular problems were poverty, inadequate education, and unemployment. In the 1960s the Indians exhibited a resurgence of militancy that fit into the pattern of the period.

TRENDS IN GOVERNMENT POLICY

The philosophy underlying both the Dawes Act of 1882 and the Burke Act of 1906—that Indians should adapt themselves completely to American society—was reversed in 1933 when Indian commissioner John Collier began to stress government interest in a revival of tribal arts and crafts. In 1934 Congress passed the Wheeler-Howard Act, fostering the efforts of tribes to govern themselves and to preserve their customs and traditions. Individuals could still seek a place outside the reservation, but tribal Indians were encouraged to cherish the heritage of their people.

INDIAN SELF-RELIANCE

In 1966 the Bureau of Indian Affairs of the Department of the Interior began to allow tribal councils greater independence and authority and also began implementing plans to improve the education of Indian youth. Many Indian tribes showed a militancy that rivaled that of many blacks. By the late 1960s most Indian leaders were determined that the affairs of the tribal Indians should be controlled not by the government but by the Indians themselves. Furthermore, throughout the nation tribes began developing many highly successful business enterprises on their reservations, engaging in such ventures as coal and oil production, small-articles manufacturing, and tourism. In 1970 about 67 percent of the more than 1 million Indians lived on one of the nation's 260 reservations. For most of them the primary decision was an individual choice between life on the reservation and entrance into the larger society dominated by whites.

The Cause of Hispanic-Americans

The long and hard struggle by blacks for equality of public treatment had a deep influence upon another group that was the victim of prejudice: Hispanic-Americans.

MEXICAN-AMERICANS

By far the largest group of Hispanic-Americans comprised those of Mexican background; by 1970 there were approximately 7.7 million, the vast majority of whom lived in the Southwest. In Los Angeles, the largest city in California and the second-largest city in the nation, Mexican-Americans constituted about 23.5 percent of the population by 1970. Until the mid-1960s, Mexican-Americans in the Southwest were the last to be employed in good times and the first to be dismissed in bad times. And when they worked, their pay was generally lower than that of others who performed the same jobs. Mexican-Americans were also subjected to discrimination in housing.

In the mid-1960s Mexican-Americans, who as a group had tended to refrain from drawing attention to their economic and social condition, began to organize. They strove to acquire all those elements—good education, well-paying jobs, decent housing—that constitute having "arrived" in American society. Important to the movement was the emphasis on the worth and beauty of Mexican-American culture. Militant members of the movement called themselves Chicanos (probably derived from *Mejicano*, the Spanish word for "Mexican"). The best-known Chicano was Cesar Chavez, who left social work to become a labor organizer in the Southwest among farm workers, many of whom were Mexican-Americans.

PUERTO RICANS

In the 1950s the government of Puerto Rico made a concerted effort, with aid from the United States, to develop production of agricultural commodities other than its principal crop, sugar, and to promote the growth of industry. It was hoped that such a policy would provide economic support for social and cultural opportunities, including a better school system, for the island's people.

As a result of the new economic program the Puerto Ricans' income rose significantly in the 1950s. Nevertheless, their standard of living was far below that of Americans in the continental United States. Consequently Puerto Ricans, as was their right as American citizens, began to move freely to the mainland, settling for the most part in and near New York City. By 1970 approximately 1.1 million Puerto Ricans lived in New York City itself, constituting approximately 16 percent of the population. As with every migrating group that had preceded them, they experienced culture shock and were subjected to various forms of discrimination. And as with every other migrating group, the Puerto Ricans took the initiative in order to achieve full equality. By establishing such self-help organizations as Aspira (meaning, in Spanish, "aspire") they sought to acquire, among other things, better employment and good housing. They were particularly concerned with the establishment of bilingual and bicultural educational programs for Puerto Rican and other Hispanic-American students.

CUBANS

During the 1960s hundreds of thousands of Cubans emigrated to the United States, most to flee the totalitarian regime of Premier Fidel Castro. By 1970 approximately 575,000 Cubans, the majority of whom were refugees, lived in the United States and were concentrated largely in Florida. About 225,000 Cubans were settled in the Miami metropolitan area, constituting about 67 percent of the population. Cherishing and retaining their Hispanic traditions and language while cautious about assimilating into the "anglo" way of life, the Cubans transformed Miami into a thriving bilingual and bicultural urban center.

Women's Liberation

The term "women's liberation" (familiarly shortened to "women's lib") was applied to a surge of activity during the 1960s in the women's rights movement, which had started in the nineteenth century and achieved a major goal with the granting of the suffrage to women in 1920.

OBJECTIVES

The basic objectives of the new feminists were full legal equality with men and the removal of economic and social discrimination between the sexes. Given high priority among their specific aims were an abortion without charge for any woman who requested it and the establishment of government-supported child-care centers.

NATIONAL ORGANIZATION FOR WOMEN

Particularly active leaders of the women's liberation movement were writers Betty Friedan and Gloria Steinem, and Bella Abzug and Shirley Chisholm, both New York City Democratic congressional representatives. To a large degree the movement was decentralized, with little conventional organizational makeup. Nevertheless, there were some organizations specifically created for the women's liberation cause. The largest and most influential was the National Organization for Women (NOW), formed in 1966 largely through the efforts of Friedan, whose widely read book *The Feminine Mystique* (1962) analyzed how society had assigned women the role of unthinking followers of men. NOW concentrated on legal and political action to achieve its goals.

THE EQUAL RIGHTS AMENDMENT

In 1972 the women's liberation movement finally persuaded Congress to pass the proposed Equal Rights Amendment to the Constitution, which declared that "equality of rights under the law shall not be denied or abridged on account of sex." But ratification was not achieved. By the end of the ten-year deadline the proposed amendment had won the approval of only thirty-five state legislatures, three short of the number required for it to be incorporated into the Constitution.

CONTINUANCE OF THE COLD WAR

The foreign policy of the Kennedy and Johnson administrations was controlled by the same factor that had regulated the diplomacy of the Truman and Eisenhower administrations—the Cold War. The conflict between the Western and communist nations forced Kennedy and Johnson to couple hardheadedness with the moral idealism that they said they would bring to American foreign policy. American-Soviet tensions were high. Kennedy expended massive energy to prevent Soviet challenges to the United States, both in Latin America and Europe, from erupting into armed conflict. On the other hand, Johnson led the nation deeper and deeper into the fighting in Vietnam.

Latin America

From the beginning of the Cold War the diplomacy of the United States was focused upon Europe and Asia. But the Kennedy administration did turn its attention to Latin America as a result of its interest in helping neighboring nations and its concern about the unrestrained activities of the Fidel Castro regime in Cuba.

THE ALLIANCE FOR PROGRESS

In March 1961, Kennedy proposed the creation of the Alliance for Progress to improve the quality of economic and social life in Latin America. Five months later, at a conference in Punta del Este, Uruguay, the charter of the new organization was adopted by the United States and all the Latin American nations except Cuba. The United States agreed to supply most of the funds for the projects under consideration for raising living standards in the area. But the Alliance for Progress eventually foundered, partly because private investors in the program became uneasy over the political instability of several of the republics that were to be assisted.

THE BAY OF PIGS

After Fidel Castro had seized power in Cuba in 1959 and established himself as premier, he used repressive measures against his countrymen, grew more and more virulently anti-American, and turned to the communist nations for economic and military support. Relations between Cuba and the United States deteriorated. Castro exacerbated the situation by demanding that the United States reduce the size of its embassy staff in Havana. In 1960 the Eisenhower administration responded by severing diplomatic relations.

With full authorization from Eisenhower and the somewhat reluctant approval of his successor, Kennedy, the Central Intelligence Agency secretly trained and equipped a group of Cuban refugees for an anti-Castro military operation. In April 1961, about 1,400 CIA-prepared Cuban refugees launched an invasion of their homeland at Bahía de Cochinos (Bay of Pigs) on the southern coast. The operation ended in utter failure, primarily because promised air support was withheld by the Kennedy administration. Many nations, including several in Latin America, condemned the role of the United States in the Bay of Pigs affair. President Kennedy publicly assumed responsibility for the debacle and resolved that in the future he would be much more careful in the execution of foreign policy.

Europe

As had presidents Truman and Eisenhower before them, Kennedy and Johnson recognized the salient fact that after World War II the Soviet Union had emerged as the most powerful nation in Europe.

THE BERLIN WALL

In June 1961, Soviet premier Nikita S. Khrushchev asserted that before the year's end his nation would sign a separate peace treaty with communist East Germany and make a demilitarized "free city" of West Berlin, which although lying within East Germany was still divided into American, British, and French occupation zones. The primary reason for the Soviet Union's desire to force the Western powers out of West Berlin and then to absorb it into East Germany was that West Berlin had been serving as a haven for many dissatisfied people fleeing from East Germany and other Eastern European communist countries.

Kennedy's response was prompt. In July he asserted that the Western powers had a right to remain in West Berlin and began to increase the American armed forces in Europe. The next month, in reply to Kennedy's action, the government of East Germany—supported by the Soviet Union—built a wall of concrete blocks and barbed wire between East Berlin and West Berlin, a construction that came to be called the Berlin Wall. Tension eventually eased, since the Soviet Union made no move to force the Western powers out of West Berlin and Khrushchev declared in October 1961 that he had decided not to sign a separate treaty with East Germany that year.

THE CUBAN MISSILE CRISIS

In the summer of 1962 Cuba began receiving from the Soviet Union large supplies of arms that both Castro and Khrushchev maintained were defensive in nature. However, American aerial photographs over Cuba indicated the existence of offensive missile bases being constructed by experts from the Soviet Union. In a television address on October 22 Kennedy announced that

he was ordering a naval "quarantine" (forced stoppage) of all offensive military equipment on its way to Cuba; he also demanded the prompt removal of the Soviet-installed missile bases. Some Soviet ships heading for Cuba altered their courses. Two Soviet ships bound for Cuba were stopped by American warships, searched for offensive military equipment, and then allowed to continue on their way after none was found.

After several days of suspense, Khrushchev began to yield. The premier ultimately offered to dismantle the missile bases and remove the offensive weapons if the United States would pledge not to invade Cuba. On October 26 Kennedy accepted the proposal. The American-Soviet crisis was at an end. The two nations had come perilously close to war. In the entire history of post–World War II Western-Soviet confrontations, none was more serious.

THE NUCLEAR TEST BAN TREATY

Soon after the Cuban missile crisis, relations between the United States and the Soviet Union began to improve. The Soviet leaders started to see new worth in a policy of peaceful coexistence with the Western nations. For one thing, the Soviet Union wanted a respite from the difficulties with the Western group in order to give attention to a serious rift between itself and the other power in the communist bloc, the People's Republic of China. Through the initiative of President Kennedy, representatives of the United States, Great Britain, and the Soviet Union met in Moscow during July–August 1963 to discuss the control of nuclear-weapons testing. A treaty was signed by which the three nations pledged not to conduct nuclear tests in the atmosphere and underwater. More than a hundred nations eventually signed the nuclear test ban treaty. Two recent nuclear powers, France and China, refused to become signatories.

The Middle East

The day after Israel declared its independence in 1948, all four bordering Arab states—Egypt, Lebanon, Syria, and Jordan—invaded the new nation intent on, but not succeeding in, destroying the Jewish state within their midst. The persistent hostility between Israel and the Arab nations was a constant threat to world peace, with serious consequences for the United States.

SIX-DAY WAR

After months of accusations and recriminations between the governments of Israel and Egypt, an Arab-Israeli war broke out in June 1967. Israel's victory within six days over Egypt and its allies, Syria and Jordan, resulted in the conquest of the Sinai Peninsula and the Gaza Strip from Egypt, the Golan Heights from Syria, and the West Bank of the Jordan River (called Judea and Samaria by Israel) including East Jerusalem, from Jordan. This led to a bitter quarrel over the new boundaries and an accelerated arms race between the Arab nations and Israel.

A CHANGE IN AMERICAN-SOVIET RELATIONS

The Arab-Israeli war could have been a prelude to a new world war, but the United States and the Soviet Union quickly indicated that they would not intervene in the conflict. Both powers had supplied arms and war matériel—the Soviet Union to the Arab nations and the United States to Israel—and neither could hold its allies in the Middle East to a peaceful course. Israel's swift victory over Egypt, Syria, and Jordan gave an important diplomatic advantage to the United States.

The Vietnam War

Native communist parties became more active in almost every Asian country after the victory of the communists in China in 1949. By 1960 communist pressure in Southeast Asia had made Indochina a danger spot, and ensuing warfare there continued through the next twelve years.

THE DIVISION OF VIETNAM

In the mid-nineteenth century France took over Vietnam, Laos, and Cambodia in Southeast Asia, combining them to form the colony of French Indochina. During World War II Japan conquered the region. Of the many native groups that conducted guerrilla warfare against the Japanese occupation, the most effective was the military arm of the communist-supported independence movement called the Viet Minh, which was led by Ho Chi Minh. At the end of World War II, Ho, as spokesperson for the Viet Minh, declared Vietnam an independent republic, soon affiliating it with the French Union, the association of France and its various overseas territories. In 1946, however, war erupted between the returning French and the Viet Minh. Most of the people of Vietnam who were noncommunist declined to aid the French, being even more antagonistic toward them than toward the Viet Minh. The fighting lasted until May 1954, when the French forces suffered a serious defeat at Dien Bien Phu.

The following month the foreign ministers of nineteen nations, including the United States, held a conference in Geneva to consider the situation in Indochina. The conference agreed to divide Vietnam into two parts and settled upon 17° north latitude as the line between the communist-based Republic of North Vietnam, under the presidency of Ho, and the Western-oriented Republic of South Vietnam. The agreement at Geneva also included a provision for the holding of elections two years later for the purpose of reuniting the two Vietnams. South Vietnam, however, supported by the United States, subsequently refused to conduct elections, in its concern that the immense popularity of Ho would result in the reunification of the two Vietnams under communist control.

AID UNDER KENNEDY

In South Vietnam, communist guerrillas, who were called the Viet Cong, strongly backed by communist North Vietnam, infiltrated the jungles, determined to overthrow the anticommunist government in the capital, Saigon. When South Vietnamese president Ngo Dinh Diem asked President Kennedy for assistance in 1961, an American advisory mission was sent to South Vietnam to bolster the government and strengthen the military forces fighting against the guerrilla tactics of the Viet Cong. Although American aid at first was limited to military equipment and supplies plus civilian and military advisors, the United States under Kennedy steadily became more deeply involved as North Vietnam, China, and the Soviet Union supplied more and more arms and ammunition to the guerrilla forces.

GULF OF TONKIN RESOLUTION

In early August 1964, in retaliation for the American navy's aid to South Vietnamese ships in their raids along the coast of North Vietnam, North Vietnamese patrol boats attacked an American destroyer in the Gulf of Tonkin. Two days later a disputable hostile action took place against the same American destroyer and another destroyer, an episode alleged by some United States officials to have occurred during a pitch-dark night under blindingly foul weather conditions and with faultily operated or poorly functioning radar and sonar equipment on the two American vessels. Nevertheless, upon President Johnson's urgent request, Congress passed on August 7, 1964, the Gulf of Tonkin Resolution by a 98 to 2 vote in the Senate and a unanimous vote in the House of Representatives. The resolution gave the president extraordinary authority in the use of military force in Southeast Asia.

AMERICAN MILITARY ESCALATION

In 1965 President Johnson approved the first air raids by American planes on strategic bases in North Vietnam, usually in support of the South Vietnamese air force. American policy was twofold: first, to destroy the sources of Soviet and Chinese aid to the Viet Cong that were located in the northern reaches of South Vietnam and the neighboring nations of Cambodia and Laos; second, to help change the corrupt and dictatorial government of South Vietnam into one that was popularly based. In order to carry out his policy, Johnson felt compelled to escalate steadily the level of United States military involvement in Vietnam. By 1966 there were 180,000 troops in the region; by 1967 there were 390,000; by 1968 there were 460,000; by 1969 there were 540,000, the largest number of troops that would be committed to the region.

THE TET OFFENSIVE

At the end of January 1968, in violation of a truce they had agreed to observe during Tet (the Vietnamese lunar New Year), North Vietnam and the Viet Cong began a surprise month-long massive attack, which soon came to be called the Tet Offensive, against more than a hundred cities and towns of South Vietnam. In Saigon they even entered the American embassy compound. The North Vietnamese and Viet Cong troops were ultimately beaten decisively, suffering appallingly heavy casualties.

Although North Vietnam and the Viet Cong experienced a military defeat, they won an unexpected political victory. Ever-growing numbers of Americans were becoming convinced, as they watched the Tet Offensive unfold on television, that despite what their political leaders were saying regarding United States involvement in Vietnam, there simply was no "light at the end of the tunnel." Thus in the United States there was rising opposition to American participation in the Vietnamese war.

PEACE NEGOTIATIONS BEGIN

In March 1968, President Johnson directed the cessation of American and South Vietnamese bombing of approximately 90 percent of North Vietnamese territory. In May the North Vietnamese government responded by sending representatives to a conference in Paris to discuss with American delegates the possibilities of a peaceful settlement of the conflict. Not until President Johnson ordered the cessation of all American bombing of North Vietnamese territory in October 1968 did the North Vietnamese delegates seriously begin to discuss proposals for peace. By that time there were delegates at the conference representing the United States, South Vietnam, North Vietnam, and the Viet Cong.

The United Nations

The Western bloc and the communist bloc were drawn into the difficult struggle for power in the Congo in late 1960, after the ninety-year Belgian colonial rule came to an end. This had repercussions at the United Nations.

CHOOSING A SECRETARY GENERAL

The efforts of the United Nations, led by Secretary General Dag Hammarskjöld, to establish order in the Congo were thwarted by commitments that the communist bloc had made to some African leaders. In the chaotic situation the United States strongly supported the approaches of the United Nations. Hammarskjöld gave his life trying to bring peace to the newly established Republic of the Congo; he was killed in an airplane crash on a mission to Africa in 1961. The Soviet Union refused to accept a new secretary general, demanding in place of the office a committee of three, one named by the Western nations, one by the communist nations, and one by the neutral nations. The matter was settled in 1962, when U Thant of Burma, acceptable to both the Western and communist blocs, was named to the post.

FINANCIAL DIFFICULTIES

At the same time that the Soviet Union was making objections to the appointment of a new secretary general, it was declining to pay its share of the expenses incurred by United Nations peace-keeping forces in the Congo. Since the United States insisted that no nation in financial arrears should be permitted to vote, the activities of the United Nations almost came to a stop. In 1965 a special committee of the General Assembly began work on a new plan for the financial support of United Nations activities. The plan was put into effect in 1966, when it received the support of both the United States and the Soviet Union.

THE TURBULENT ERA

The 1960s wrought a revolution in the life of the American people in many respects as profound as the American Revolution and the Civil War had. It was a turbulent era. The attitude of Americans during this period tended to be fearfully apprehensive. They were subject to the disillusioning Vietnam war and they agonized over its wrenchingly divisive nature. And yet the turmoil that diminished the nation and caused pessimism among its people had ultimately a beneficial sobering—indeed, maturing—effect. Through all the disturbance there were positive social strides. Blacks, Hispanic-Americans, and women, among other groups, achieved astounding gains in status. And there were other elements in the period's social ferment that had far-reaching and long-lasting effects on the nation. For example, young people rejected established principles of social conduct, and the sexual behavior of large numbers of people underwent a revolution. Educational institutions and religious bodies were not only influenced by the social movements of the period but became themselves very much a part of those changes.

Youth and the Counterculture

Concomitant with, and influenced by, the various political and social movements of the 1960s—opposition to the Vietnam war, the black struggle for equality of public treatment, women's liberation—was a youth movement that came to be known as the counterculture.

HIPPIES

Throughout the nation hundreds of thousands of young people, most from a white middle-class background, showed their disdain for such tenets of established American society as the respect for parental, religious, and governmental authority; the value of education; the importance of striving for economic security; and the worth of continent sexual behavior. Young men and women left school or quit their jobs; adopted unkempt clothing; wore long ungroomed hair; used drugs; became immersed in rock music; flocked to live together in a totally unstructured fashion in certain sections of some cities, such as the East Village of New York City and the Haight-Ashbury area of San Francisco, or in communes in the mountainous regions of the Northwest or the deserts of the Southwest. These youth were known as hippies (a term derived from the phrase "to be hip" in jazz vocabulary, meaning to be knowledgeable about current situations).

DRUG ABUSE

Although drug abuse was not confined to young people, very many of them committed to the counterculture relied on drugs on a fairly regular basis. The most widely used was marijuana, familiarly called "pot" or "grass." Of the pills that were "popped" (swallowed), the "uppers" (amphetamines) were taken to stimulate and the "downers" (barbiturates and tranquilizers) to sedate. Some young people addicted to heroin "mainlined" (injected it into a vein). Many who ingested LSD (lysergic acid diethylamide) did bodily injury to themselves while on a "trip" (a psychedelic drug experience).

THE WOODSTOCK FESTIVAL

In August 1969, near Woodstock, New York, almost 400,000 young men and women attended a weekend rock musical festival. The event became a vivid symbol of youth and the counterculture. Drug use, displays of nudity, uninhibited sexual encounters, and anti–Vietnam War sentiments were much in evidence.

STUDENT ACTIVISM

Many young people who felt their alienation from the so-called Establishment still remained at institutions of higher education and became dedicated activists. The Students for a Democratic society (SDS), founded in 1959 by Al Haber and Tom Hayden, had its first major base at the University of Michigan. Within three years chapters of the organization began protesting on a number of campuses against research being conducted by faculty and staff for the Vietnam war effort under the sponsorship of the Department of Defense; against the chemical firm that manufactured napalm (a component of the incendiary bombs and flamethrowers used by American troops in Vietnam), paying particular attention to its recruiting efforts among graduating students; and against the Reserve Officers' Training Corps (ROTC), an on-campus organization that prepared students to become military officers. In 1964 at the University of California at Berkeley the members of the Free Speech Movement on two occasions took over an administration building, refusing to leave until their demand for the right to voice their opinions on current issues was respected. In 1968 at Columbia University a number of militant student factions took over five buildings; occupied the office of the president; seized three administrators, whom they held as hostages for a day; and finally pressured the institution into suspending classes for the rest of the semester. By 1970 hundreds of thousands of students were among the millions of Americans who had participated in many rallies against the continuation of the war in Vietnam. Some student protesters publicly burned draft cards and raided draft-board offices, where they destroyed records.

A New Sexual Morality

The 1960s saw a revolution in the sexual beliefs and practices of Americans.

RESEARCH

Giving impetus to this basic change were published findings of researchers into human sexual behavior. Indiana University professor Alfred C. Kinsey and his associates, after a comprehensive investigation into sexual conduct, wrote *Sexual Behavior in the Human Male* (1948) and *Sexual Behavior in the Human Female* (1953), both of which provided factual support for the existence of widespread premarital and extramarital intercourse and of sexual acts that had long been considered by the vast majority of society to be "unnatural" and perhaps even sinful. The books by the sex-research team of William H. Masters and Virginia E. Johnson—*Human Sexual Response* (1966) and *Human Sexual Inadequacy* (1970), both focusing on the physiology of sexual behavior—challenged long-held beliefs.

PERSONAL CONDUCT

Women's use of the newly developed birth-control pill contributed to greater participation in premarital and extramarital intercourse. Many unwed mothers made no effort to conceal their status from the community. Young couples tried "living together" before deciding whether or not to get married. Numbers of married couples engaged in what soon came to be called "swinging": the exchange of sexual partners among two or more married couples. Responding to the freer attitudes regarding sexual conduct, tens of thousands of male and female homosexuals who had heretofore kept secret their sexual orientation, often out of a real concern for job security, openly declared themselves to be "gay," a word that was coming into increasing use to designate a homosexual individual or condition. In 1970 in New York City, homosexuals formed the Gay Liberation Front to contend militantly for the removal of the many and varied kinds of discrimination to which they had been for so long subjected.

EFFECTS ON CULTURE

Of course, the new sexual morality was reflected in literature, which began to incorporate the candid description of sexual acts and the use of explicit language. The theater, motion pictures, and television presented, in addition to explicit language, nudity and even sexual physical contact (the extent of these portrayals varied according to the accessibility of the medium to youngsters). Those who desired stronger fare were able to avail themselves of the offerings of the pornographic bookstores and movie houses.

Education

In the United States education had always been influenced by the social setting of the period, but during the 1960s this was particularly true.

ELEMENTARY EDUCATION

The movement of the 1940s and 1950s for a return to the traditional academic disciplines continued unabated. The cause was served by recently developed educational technology. For example, a number of schools tried instructing by closed-circuit television, in which a "master" teacher communicated with pupils in different classrooms in one or more buildings in a school system or even in more than one system.

SECONDARY EDUCATION

As in elementary education, technology was employed as a means of teaching the traditional disciplines. But a situation that hindered the movement prevailed in the high schools. The foment that had occurred on college and university campuses reached the high schools. And because the high-school students, not as sophisticated as the college and university students, responded in a less mature manner to the social tumult, the disquiet at the secondary level was even more distressing. In schools across the nation, students made increasing demands for greater latitude in the pursuit of their studies and for fewer personal restrictions, such as in language and attire. It was not long before this restiveness turned into a nightmarish scene in inner-city schools. The smoldering hostility between blacks on the one hand and Hispanic-Americans or whites on the other led to frequent physical confrontations.

HIGHER EDUCATION

The confrontational activities and violence on American campuses during the 1960s had significant consequences. There were deep negative ramifications. Perhaps most important, academic standards were impaired. In an effort to return the campuses to peace and stability, administrators and professors catered to students' demands, to the degree that they found themselves becoming untrue to what they had always believed were the methods and goals of higher education. For example, course requirements were made less rigorous; grades were inflated; and courses were added to the curriculum that were deemed "relevant" for modern society but lacked the traditional body of knowledge to be studied. And yet from the campus unrest there was a positive legacy too. As a result of their demands, students were now given an opportunity to influence such vital aspects as the appointment, promotion, and retention or dismissal of administrators and faculty members and the development of curriculum. Also, primarily as a result of student demands, courses on the history and culture of blacks and other minority groups and on women were developed. Furthermore, blacks and other minorities and women were admitted in ever-larger numbers to colleges and universities. The implementation of affirmative-action programs greatly increased the proportion of blacks and other minorities and women in college and university administrations and on faculties.

Religion

During the 1960s there was a halt in the tremendous increase in church and synagogue membership that had taken place during the 1940s and 1950s, although approximately 65 percent of the American people were still affiliated with organized religious bodies. Vast changes—some of them revolutionary—occurred within Protestantism, Roman Catholicism particularly, and Judaism.

PARTICIPATION BY RELIGIOUS LEADERS IN SOCIAL CAUSES

Organized religious bodies were very much affected by the social ferment of the period. Feeling a deep moral obligation, large numbers of ministers, priests, nuns, and rabbis played a leading role in such causes of the period as the struggle by blacks and other minority groups against discrimination; the women's liberation movement; the battle against poverty; the environmental crusade; and the opposition to the Vietnam war.

PROTESTANTISM

As a direct response to the women's liberation movement a few denominations—notably the Episcopal church—took the bold action of admitting women to the ministry. Protestantism continued to merge bodies within a denomination and to unify among the various denominations during the 1960s. But what was even more heartening to liberally inclined religious Americans was the fast-developing ecumenical spirit between Protestantism and Roman Catholicism. The long-standing hostility between the two wings of Christianity in the United States was largely dissipated as a result of continual dialogue that focused on the many similarities of dogma.

ROMAN CATHOLICISM

During 1962–65 the Second Vatican Council was held in Rome. The conference's liberal promulgations had an immediate and deep impact upon Catholicism in the United States. It modernized the life-styles of priests and nuns; increased the participation of the laity in religious services (the vernacular, or native language of a region, was now to be used in place of Latin) and other affairs of the church; advocated the coming together of Roman Catholic, Protestant, and Eastern Orthodox bodies for the unity of Christianity; and expressed respect for non-Christian religions and condemned any kind of discrimination, particularly anti-Semitism.

JUDAISM

Of the three bodies of the faith, the basic attitudes of the Orthodox branch underwent no significant changes, but those of the Conservative and Reform branches underwent substantial changes. Orthodox Judaism, however, largely through attracting many young adherents, experienced a resurgence of power and influence within Jewry. Perhaps the most notable development in Conservative Judaism was the new role of women. Increasingly, Conservative congregations permitted women to participate in the conduct of services and to hold lay offices, including the position of president. In the Reform branch, the change in status of women was quite similar to that in the Conservative. Furthermore, in some Reform congregations women even served as ordained rabbis. But another notable development in Reform Judaism was the reinstitution of the observance of many rituals and traditions that had long been abandoned.

ASIAN FAITHS

As part of their repudiation of the various elements of established American society, many young people turned away from the Christianity and Judaism of the Western world and affiliated themselves with Asian faiths. Of those, the most visible was the Hare Krishna sect, in which shaven-headed, saffron-robed adherents danced and chanted in the streets as part of their homage to Krishna, a Hindu god.

A DISTURBANCE-TINGED CULTURE

In all American history no better period than the 1960s can be offered to serve as an example of a time when a close link existed between social change and cultural development. To one degree or another, each facet of the advance of art, literature, and music reflected some aspect of the social climate of the period. An influential school of painters seemed to indict a society that had become consumer oriented and assembly-line dominated; architects created buildings that were abundantly diverse in conception and execution, a diversity that reflected the increasing differences of life-style among the nation's various economic and social groups. In a reciprocal manner, alienation from long-established principles of social conduct was the guiding force of an important stratum of literature, and that stratum made stronger the alienation of some groups, particularly the young. Newspaper publishing was a classic example of the fortunes of a business being thoroughly affected by changing economic and social patterns. In the field of music two genres enjoyed huge success. One was a very old and once the most exclusive aspect of the performing arts: ballet. The other was a new form appealing to the young in particular: rock 'n' roll.

Art

In painting a movement emerged that repudiated the nonrepresentational mode of the preceding period and was boldly representational. In sculpture the construction of massive pieces became predominant. In the field of architecture there evolved a tendency toward stylistic diversity.

PAINTING

In the late 1950s there was a growing disdain among some painters for abstract expressionism because of what they considered its overly austere quality and a kind of elitist commitment to that quality by its exponents. The demonstration of this feeling rapidly grew into a full-scale movement called pop art ("pop" was short for "popular"). The exponents of this movement attempted to produce works of art that would be both appealing and understandable to the masses. The new school realistically depicted ordinary objects, particularly consumer-oriented ones, from everyday American life. They appeared to be making a gently humorous indictment of the pervasive influence upon American society of a rampant consumerism fostered by the mass media.

Important in the pop-art movement were Andy Warhol and Roy Lichtenstein. The distinguishing feature of Warhol's work is the presentation of an image repeated to a point approaching monotony, a device interpreted by art critics as a wry commentary on the bombardment of the senses by standardized assembly-line products. Two of Warhol's most representative works are *100 Cans* (1962), which shows row upon row of soup cans on the shelves of a supermarket, and *Marilyn Six-Pack* (1962), a painting of three rows of two identical portraits of the film star Marilyn Monroe. Lichtenstein won recognition for his large-scale paintings of well-known comic strips, sometimes executed in their regular panel form.

SCULPTURE

The dominant movement in American sculpture was the use of welded metal to create abstract forms. David Smith was one of the first practitioners of this style. Members of this school turned frequently to creating massive pieces made of metal, many of which were on such an immense scale that they could not fit into a building but had to be placed outdoors in open spaces.

ARCHITECTURE

The trend in American architecture was an almost total abandonment of the International Style in favor of a diversity of styles—a movement that came to be called Postmodernism. The only rule seemed to be that there should be no rules. A prominent development was the return to the old, often with a recommitment to decoration. Outstanding examples of these structures were the compelling works of Philip Johnson, who had been an apostle of the International Style, and of the Chinese-American I. M. (Ieoh Ming) Pei.

Literature

The writings of most of the established novelists and poets were very little, if at all, influenced by the period's literary movement called the beat generation, which did, however, have a significant effect upon society itself. As was the case early in the twentieth century, an important segment of American drama came under the influence of European playwrights, persons this time who forswore the traditional elements of plays. Newspaper publishing, for a host of economic and social reasons, faced the most difficult set of circumstances with which it had been confronted in this century.

THE NOVEL

Among the best writers of the period were Saul Bellow, John Updike, and Philip Roth. Bellow, in such novels as *Herzog* (1964) and *Mr. Sammler's Planet* (1970), focused on the human being's attempts to discover a justification for existence. Updike achieved fame with *Rabbit, Run* (1960). In this novel a young man is unable to cope as a member of society. Roth, with a biting humor, depicted the fixed customs along with the thoughts and feelings of middle-class American Jews. His best-known novel is *Portnoy's Complaint* (1969).

The writings of the beat-generation movement, which began in the mid-1950s and lasted throughout the 1960s, enjoyed a wide popularity and had a notable impact upon a number of groups, especially the hippies. Beat writers were a small group of novelists and poets who in their works renounced the long-held attitudes of conventional American society, especially that which esteemed the acquisition of material wealth. They extolled the deep pleasure to be derived from a variety of experiences, including drug use; many and varied forms of sexual encounters; and the acceptance of an Asian religion, particularly Zen Buddhism, which would lead to a condition of complete bliss, or beatitude (hence the origin of the phrase "beat generation"). In literary style, they disdained the traditional forms and techniques and employed almost exclusively the patterns of vernacular American speech, including vulgarisms. They also relied heavily on the vocabulary of jazz. Jack Kerouac's *On the Road* (1957) is considered the epitome of the movement's thought and style. The novel portrays the sheer exhilaration of hitchhiking throughout the country and, in the process, being exposed to such things as drugs, unfettered sex, and Zen Buddhism.

POETRY

Widely acknowledged as the most influential American poet of his period, Robert Lowell wrote verse that came to be called "confessional poetry," in which he expresses human apprehensions and perplexities and the therapeutic value of relating them. The most representative poet of the beat generation was Allen Ginsberg, whose most famous work, *Howl* (1956), is a blistering censure of American social attitudes.

DRAMA

The most significant influence in American drama was theater of the absurd, which was developed largely from the works of the Romanian-born Frenchman Eugene Ionesco and the Irish-born Frenchman Samuel Beckett. This movement renounced such conventional elements of drama as readily perceivable plot, characters, and dialogue in order to convey a human existence so desperately bewildering that it becomes meaningless, even unreal. Edward Albee was not only the leading American advocate of theater of the absurd but also the most creative of the nation's contemporary playwrights. Crafted in a more conventional form than many of his other works is his best-known play, *Who's Afraid of Virginia Woolf?* (1962). It deals with a middle-aged college professor and his wife who mercilessly torment each other, revealing a marriage permeated with seething malice but a relationship they both desperately need.

During this period Neil Simon emerged as the most successful writer of comedy in the history of the American theater. His hallmark was the rapid offering of humorous one-liners. Among his more than a dozen hits were *The Odd Couple* (1965) and *The Sunshine Boys* (1972).

NEWSPAPERS

Beginning early in the 1960s a number of the nation's metropolitan newspapers were forced either to merge with other papers or to cease publication. The reasons included the increasing movement of middle-class people out of the cities; strong competition from television news and public-affairs coverage and from suburban newspapers; sharply rising expenses of production; and the costly effects of strikes, mostly for higher wages, particularly by the printers' union. The trend grew with such swiftness that by the mid-1960s only in New York City, Boston, and Washington, D.C., were there still three or more separately operated and competing dailies with large circulations.

Music

The 1960s saw the start of what was perhaps the zenith of musical activity in twentieth-century America. Symphony orchestras were ably led and the Metropolitan Opera House, along with opera companies throughout the nation, attracted ever-larger audiences. Ballet enjoyed for the first time a high level of popular esteem. And in the field of popular music, rock 'n' roll quickly captured the loyalty of the young.

ORCHESTRAL COMPOSERS AND CONDUCTORS

The works of the traditionalist Samuel Barber and the experimentalist John Cage represented the best of the opposite ends of the broad spectrum of orchestral musical composition in the 1960s. Barber's music, except for some dissonance and complex rhythmic patterns in his later compositions, was smoothly melodic. Cage was the supreme avant-gardist of the period. He often composed music devoid of harmonic and rhythmic patterns. He sometimes composed music by "chance"—determining, for example, such basic elements as the pitch and duration of notes by drawing a playing card or throwing dice. He even composed music that left to the performers the order of executing sections of a work or the deletion of sections.

In the 1970s the Bombay-born Zubin Mehta was music director of the New York Philharmonic Symphony Orchestra. During that period the Boston Symphony Orchestra had the Japanese Seiji Ozawa as its music director. The permanent conductor of the Chicago Symphony Orchestra in the late 1960s was the Hungarian-born Georg Solti. For fifty years, ending with his death in 1979, Arthur Fiedler conducted the Boston Pops Orchestra (the Boston Symphony minus its principal players). With a showmanlike manner, he brought "serious" music to millions of Americans, presenting programs that were a potpourri of "heavy" classics, "light" classics, and popular tunes mainly from the musical theater.

CONCERT VIRTUOSOS

Two of the most widely admired concert virtuosos were the violinist Isaac Stern and the Austrian-American pianist Rudolf Serkin.

OPERA

During the 1960s the Metropolitan Opera House attracted virtually all the world's finest singers. Soprano Maria Callas made her debut there in 1956. The two greatest stars of the Metropolitan were the Australian soprano Joan Sutherland and the Italian tenor Luciano Pavarotti. Another much-admired tenor was the Spanish-born Placido Domingo. An outstanding American singer was the black soprano Leontyne Price.

Widely acknowledged as the nation's most distinguished operatic company after the Metropolitan was the San Francisco Opera Company, founded in 1923. The company's reputation was regarded as a testament to the perfectionism of its Austrian-born general director, Kurt Herbert Adler.

Another leading opera house was the New York City Opera Company, established in 1944. The star of the house during the 1960s was the soprano Beverly Sills. Toward the end of her career she sang at the Metropolitan and subsequently became director of the New York City Opera Company.

BALLET

For the first four decades of the twentieth century there was practically no ballet in the United States; as in the preceding century, what little existed was imported from Europe. Great Russian ballet dancers such as Anna Pavlova and Vaslav Nijinsky toured the United States. In 1948 the New York City Ballet was established. It eventually became not only the premier ballet company in the United States but also ranked with the leading companies of the world. During the 1960s ballet became the most rapidly developing performing art in the nation. And New York City became the ballet center of the world.

The Russian-born and Russian-trained choreographer George Balanchine was associated with the New York City Ballet. He is acknowledged as the undisputed master of American ballet choreography. He created close to a hundred ballets, most with little or no plot and with greatly simplified costuming and staging, focusing on the execution of the dance itself. He was largely responsible for transforming the conventional role of the male dancer, who instead of merely supporting the female dancer was now given the opportunity to exhibit a graceful physical prowess, much of it in solo segments. Two of Balanchine's most popular works were *Entente Cordiale* (1958–77) and *Jewels* (1967). One of Balanchine's most gifted colleagues at the New York City Ballet was choreographer Jerome Robbins. Among the acclaimed principal dancers with the New York City Ballet were Maria Tallchief, Patricia McBride, Edward Villela, and Peter Martins.

The second leading ballet company in the nation was the American Ballet Theatre, founded in 1939.

Three of the world's finest dancers, Rudolph Nureyev, Natalia Makarova, and Mikhail Baryshnikov, all members of the famous Kirov Ballet of Leningrad, defected from the Soviet Union while on tour and settled in the United States to pursue their careers.

MUSICAL THEATER

Stephen Sondheim was a composer and lyricist of musicals who singlehandedly during the 1960s creatively effected a basic change in the integration of music and lyrics in the field. Of his most original works, the biggest success was *Company* (1970). Other top hits of the period were *Hello, Dolly!* (1964) and *Fiddler on the Roof* (1964).

ROCK 'N' ROLL

In the mid-1950s a new type of music appeared that was called rock 'n' roll. It was primarily a blending of black blues and white country and western. Instrumentally, there was a heavy reliance on the guitar and drums. The music quickly won an intense allegiance among the nation's youth. The lyrics usually dealt with the concerns of young men and women, such as the agonies of first love. The exaggerated beat, excessive volume, and energetic body movements of the performers made rock 'n' roll a musical symbol in the early 1960s of the antipathy of youth toward the quiet and orderly aspects of established American society. A top performer was Elvis Presley. Two of his most popular songs were "Heartbreak Hotel" and "Hound Dog."

In the mid-1960s the nature of rock 'n' roll was altered and the form became increasingly referred to simply as rock. The new direction stemmed from the influence of a number of British performing groups, particularly the Beatles and the Rolling Stones. The Beatles were John Lennon, Paul McCartney, George Harrison, and Ringo Starr. The Rolling Stones featured Mick Jagger as the lead vocalist. Under the pervasive influence of British rock groups, there was a deepening commitment to the black blues aspect of rock and a lessening attachment to the white country and western element. The playing (on instruments whose sounds were electronically amplified) and the singing became even louder and the body movements even more frenetic.

Soon afterward there occurred an equally significant modification of the style through its melding with folk music, resulting in what was called folk rock. Primarily responsible for this new development was Bob Dylan. After composing and singing in folk-music style his own songs of social protest, including "Blowin' in the Wind" (1962), Dylan began to absorb the elements of rock, writing and performing new songs with lyrics that angrily expressed the disaffection of the nation's young people.

It was not long before many rock groups were giving performances that were to one degree or another drug oriented: in the kinds of sounds, which conveyed a sense of drug-induced experiences; in the substance of the lyrics; and in the manner of the staging, particularly the lighting.

Selected Readings

GENERAL WORKS:

Burner, David, Robert D. Marcus, and Thomas R. West. *A Giant's Strength: America in the 1960s* (1971)

Gitlin, Todd. *The Sixties* (1987)

Matusow, Allen. *The Unraveling of America: A History of Liberalism in the 1960s (1984)*

O'Neill, William L. *Coming Apart: An Informal History of America in the 1960s* (1971)

Wright, Lawrence. *The New World: Growing Up in America, 1960–1984* (1988)

SPECIAL STUDIES:

Acuña, Rodolfo. *Occupied America: A History of Chicanos* (1980)

Allison, Graham T. *Essence of Decision: Explaining the Cuban Missile Crisis* (1971)

Barwick, Judith. *In Transition: How Feminism, Sexual Liberation, and the Search for Self-Fulfillment Have Altered America* (1979)

Bloom, Jack. *Class, Race, and the Civil Rights Movement* (1987)

Camarillo, Albert. *Hispanics in a Changing Society* (1979)

Caro, Robert. *Means of Ascent: The Years of Lyndon Johnson* (1990)

———. *The Path to Power: The Years of Lyndon Johnson* (1982)

Castro, Tony. *Chicano Power* (1974)

Chafe, William. *Women and Equality: Changing Patterns in American Culture* (1977)

Coles, Robert, and Geoffrey Stokes. *Sex and the American Teenager* (1985)

D'Emilio, John, and Estelle Freedman. *Intimate Matters: A History of Sexuality in America* (1988)

Dinnerstein, Leonard, and Frederick Cople Jaher, eds. *The Aliens: A History of Ethnic Minorities in America* (1970)

Duberman, Martin Bauml, Martha Vicinus, and George Chauncey Jr. *Hidden from History: Reclaiming the Gay and Lesbian Past* (1989)

FitzGerald, Frances. *Fire in the Lake: The Vietnamese and the Americans in Vietnam* (1972)

Freeman, Jo. *The Politics of Women's Liberation* (1975)

Geyelin, Philip. *Lyndon B. Johnson and the World* (1966)

Goldman, Eric F. *The Tragedy of Lyndon Johnson* (1968)

Halberstam, David. *The Best and the Brightest* (1972)

Heath, Jim F. *John F. Kennedy and the Business Community* (1969)

Herring, George. *America's Longest War* (1986)

Hilsman, Roger. *To Move a Nation: The Politics of Foreign Policy in the Administration of John F. Kennedy* (1967)

Hopkins, Jerry. *The Rock Story* (1970)

Hudson, Winthrop S. *Religion in America* (1973)

Johnson, Lady Bird. *A White House Diary* (1970)

Johnson, Lyndon Baines. *The Vantage Point: Perspectives of the Presidency, 1963–1969* (1971)

Josephy, Alvin M. Jr. *Red Power: The American Indians' Fight for Freedom* (1971)

Kahin, George. *Intervention: How America Became Involved in Vietnam* (1986)

Karnow, Stanley. *Vietnam* (1983)

Kearns, Doris. *Lyndon Johnson and the American Dream* (1976)

Kennedy, Robert F. *Thirteen Days: A Memoir of the Cuban Missile Crisis* (1969)

Kolodin, Irving. *The Story of the Metropolitan Opera: A Candid History* (1966)

LaFeber, Walter. *America, Russia, and the Cold War, 1945–1984* (1985)

Manchester, William. *The Death of a President* (1967)

Moore, Joan, and Harry Pachon. *Hispanics in the United States* (1985)

Oates, Stephen. *Let the Trumpet Sound: The Life and Times of Martin Luther King, Jr.* (1982)

O'Donnell, Kenneth P., and David F. Powers. *Johnny, We Hardly Knew Ye: Memoirs of John Fitzgerald Kennedy* (1972)

Olsen, James S., and Raymond Wilson. *Native Americans in the Twentieth Century* (1984)

Parmet, Herbert. *JFK—The Presidency of John F. Kennedy* (1983)

Powers, Thomas. *Vietnam: The War at Home* (1973)

Rose, Barbara. *American Art Since 1900: A Critical History* (1967)

Roszak, Theodore. *The Making of a Counter Culture* (1969)

Rupp, Leila J., and Verta Taylor. *Survival in the Doldrums: The American Women's Rights Movement, 1945 to the 1960s* (1987)

Schandler, Herbert. *The Unmaking of a President: Lyndon Johnson and Vietnam* (1977)

Schlesinger, Arthur M., Jr. *A Thousand Days: John F. Kennedy in the White House* (1965)

Sidey, Hugh. *A Very Personal Presidency: Lyndon Johnson in the White House* (1968)

Silberman, Charles E. *Crisis in Black and White* (1964)

———. *Crisis in the Classroom: The Remaking of American Education* (1970)

Sitkoff, Harvard. *The Struggle for Black Equality, 1954–1980* (1981)

Smith, Bradley. *The American Way of Sex* (1978)

Sorenson, Theodore C. *Kennedy* (1965)

Spector, Ronald. *The United States Army in Vietnam* (1983)

Summers, Harry, Jr. *On Strategy: A Critical Analysis of the Vietnam War* (1981)

White, Theodore H. *The Making of the President, 1960* (1961)

The Making of the President, 1964 (1965)

Wicker, Tom. *JFK and LBJ: The Influence of Personality upon Politics* (1968)

Wright, Nathan, Jr. *Black Power and Urban Unrest* (1967)

Zaroulis, Nancy, and Gerald Sullivan. *Who Spoke Up? American Protest Against War in Vietnam* (1984)

13

The Presidency in Disgrace and in Restoration

1968 Robert F. Kennedy assassinated

Nixon elected president

1969 American astronauts land on the moon

1970 United States invades Cambodia

Four students killed at Kent State University demonstration

1971 Twenty-sixth Amendment ratified

1972 Nixon and Mao hold meeting in China

Nixon and Brezhnev hold meeting in Soviet Union

SALT I treaty signed

Watergate break-in

Nixon reelected president

Coppola, *The Godfather*

1973 Vietnam cease-fire agreement signed

Senate Select Committee conducts televised hearings on Watergate

Yom Kippur War

Agnew resigns from vice-presidency; Ford appointed to replace him

"Saturday Night Massacre"

1974 Supreme Court orders Nixon to release Watergate conversations tapes

House Judiciary Committee recommends impeachment of Nixon

Nixon resigns; Ford becomes president

1975 North Vietnam absorbs South Vietnam

1976 Carter elected president

1977   Carter initiates "moral equivalent of war" on energy problem

Energy Department created

United States and Panama sign treaty turning over Canal to Panama

1978   Camp David accords

1979   United States and People's Republic of China establish diplomatic relations

Israel and Egypt sign peace treaty

United States and Soviet Union sign SALT II treaty

Iranian militants take American hostages

Soviet Union invades Afghanistan

1980   Carter withdraws SALT II treaty from Senate consideration to protest Soviet invasion of Afghanistan

United States boycotts Summer Olympic games in Moscow to protest Soviet invasion of Afghanistan

Health and Human Services Department created

Education Department created

Unlike the Kennedy and Johnson administrations, the Nixon administration shied away from a profound commitment to social programs and the civil rights movement. Despite his lack of success in solving domestic—particularly economic—problems, Nixon was easily reelected as president, primarily because he had a Democratic opponent who was unable to inspire widespread confidence in his judgment. Nixon achieved notable successes in the field of foreign affairs. He brought the Vietnam war to a close and initiated an era of détente (an easing or relaxation of strained relations and political tensions between nations) with the Soviet Union and the People's Republic of China. But the administration came to a crashing end before its time in the greatest political scandal in the nation's history.

Appointed rather than elected vice-president and then elevated to the highest office in the land by the unique resignation of the president, Gerald R. Ford attempted to wipe out the stain of the Nixon years. He inherited terrible economic problems.

The election of the Democrat Jimmy Carter to the presidency indicated an abrupt change in American politics. The hold of Nixon on the nation was now completely severed. Although Ford's character and style were far different from Nixon's, he had retained many of his immediate predecessor's staff members and had continued practically all of his policies. Carter appeared to Americans as a person filled with the conviction that the strength of the nation stemmed from its commitment to achieving justice for all and to improving the quality of life. But because of his management style and his strained relationship with Congress, he was never able to achieve the goals he had set for the American people.

NIXON AND THE DOMESTIC SCENE

Nixon turned back the trend of many of the policies on social matters supported by his two immediate predecessors. He vetoed a number of bills related to health and education. He impounded funds already appropriated by Congress for economic and social programs of which he himself disapproved. He disappointed those who desired more progress in the enforcement of civil rights legislation, particularly in school desegregation. A severe setback in the economy consistently bedeviled the Nixon administration. Soon after Nixon began his second term, his reputation plunged as the Watergate affair unfolded, revealing unprecedented corruption at the highest level of the executive branch.

Election of 1968

On two counts the election of 1968 was significant. It was a natural microcosm of the political and social turmoil of the decade, stemming primarily from the Vietnam war and the crusade for equality of treatment by blacks and other minority groups. Also it marked, through Nixon's victory, the start of a distinct era of narrow domestic politics and a turnabout in foreign policy.

DEMOCRATS

In March 1968, at the close of a television address on the war in Vietnam, President Johnson surprised the nation by saying: "I shall not seek and I will not accept the nomination of my party for another term as your president." Many political commentators felt certain that the decision resulted from his feeling that the voters were dissatisfied with his foreign policies, especially those regarding Vietnam, and with his failure to end racial unrest in the larger cities. Before his withdrawal as a candidate for reelection, Johnson had been severely challenged in the Democratic primaries, first by the ultraliberal and vocal anti–Vietnam War senator Eugene McCarthy of Minnesota and soon thereafter by an increasingly antiwar Senator Robert F. Kennedy of New York. After Kennedy had won the primary elections in several states, he was assassinated in June 1968, by an Arab-American who had apparently been infuriated by the senator's strong pro-Israel position. His death opened the way for Vice-President Hubert H. Humphrey, who had entered the presidential race when Johnson withdrew, as a defender of the administration's policies in Vietnam. After a bitter fight between the prowar and antiwar factions at the Democratic national convention in Chicago, the delegates nominated Humphrey for president and Senator Edmund S. Muskie of Maine for vice-president. While the proceedings were taking place, bloody clashes erupted on the streets of Chicago between antiwar and civil rights demonstrators—the vast majority of whom were young people—and the police.

REPUBLICANS

In a well-managed national convention the Republicans quickly nominated Richard M. Nixon for president and Governor Spiro T. Agnew of Maryland for vice-president. Agnew was a border-state politician who had publicly assailed militant black activism; his selection thus strengthened the ticket among white southern conservatives.

AMERICAN INDEPENDENTS

Former Democratic governor George C. Wallace of Alabama was nominated for president by the newly organized ultraconservative American Independent party. Wallace personally selected General Curtis E. LeMay, who had recently retired as chief of staff of the air force, as the vice-presidential nominee of the American Independents.

THE CAMPAIGN

The major issues of the campaign were the Vietnam war and urban unrest. The relatively moderate positions of the two major candidates on these matters were similar. Wallace, however, argued that the only satisfactory solution to the war in Southeast Asia was total American military victory. As for the riots in the cities, he guaranteed that if elected he would end them—with bayonets, if necessary. Further, Wallace called for a reversal of the federal government's commitment to desegregation, particularly in the areas of education and housing. Profiting from his experience in the exceedingly close presidential contest of 1960 against John F. Kennedy, Nixon gave skillful direction to the Republican campaign.

NIXON'S VICTORY

In popular votes, Nixon received 31,785,000; Humphrey, 31,275,000; Wallace, 9,906,000. Although the margin of victory in the popular vote between the two major contenders was indeed slim, Nixon received 302 electoral votes to 191 for Humphrey; Wallace carried 45. (When the electoral college balloted, one member who was pledged to Nixon switched to Wallace, finally giving him 46 votes. This action strengthened the demand that the procedure for choosing a president through an electoral college be reconsidered.) Although the Republicans increased their membership in both the Senate and House of Representatives, the Democrats still retained control of both houses.

The Nixon Administration

Nixon was one of the hardest-working occupants of the White House. He believed deeply in the need for a "strong" president, one who could fathom the desires of the broad base of the American people and bring their will to fruition.

THE PRESIDENT

Nixon was a "loner." Possessed of an inner conviction of the correctness of his own views and wary of the counsel of others, he shut himself off from the wide range of advisors a president usually has, even to the point of avoiding members of the cabinet. Try as he might to appear a "regular guy," his body seemed rigid, his smile forced, and his gestures mechanical.

THE CABINET

Initially Nixon sought for his cabinet individuals of well-established independence of thought and action, a practice he soon discontinued as he attempted to gain a tighter rein on the federal bureaucratic system. The original membership of the cabinet left some diverse constituencies unrepresented; it contained not one black, not one Jew, not one woman. The official family was decidedly conservative. Most of the members were from the business community. William P. Rogers, a New York lawyer and one of the president's closest friends, was named secretary of state. (In 1973 he was succeeded by Henry Kissinger, a former Harvard University professor who was an advisor to the Nixon administration on matters of foreign policy and security.) Republican representative Melvin P. Laird of Wisconsin was named head of the Department of Defense. John N. Mitchell, a New York lawyer who had been a partner of Nixon's, became attorney general. Of those serving in the cabinet, he became Nixon's most intimate advisor.

ASSISTANTS TO THE PRESIDENT

In time, the influence of cabinet officials declined and that of the head assistants to the president grew. White House chief of staff H. R. "Bob" Haldeman was an extraordinarily energetic, no-nonsense, power-wielding, devoted aide to the president. Domestic advisor John Erlichman was every bit as diligent and as dedicated to Nixon.

Appealing to the "Silent Majority"

Nixon sought the base of his support from what he called the "silent majority"—middle-class Americans who had grown weary of "big" government. To those people Nixon represented a rejection of governmental activism, particularly in the areas of civil rights and social welfare.

CIVIL RIGHTS

In his attempt to effect the switching of the conservative Democratic white voters of the solid South to the Republican party, Nixon embraced what soon came to be called the southern strategy. This pursuit prompted him to lessen the concern of the executive branch for diligent implementation of civil rights measures. Further, the Nixon administration recommended to Congress the passage of legislation prohibiting the busing of students solely for the purpose of achieving racial integration in the schools.

THE WELFARE PROGRAM

Nixon recommended drastic changes in the welfare system. In addition to supporting a guaranteed minimum income for every family, he advocated a tightening of the system. For example, every recipient of welfare assistance who was physically able would be required either to accept appropriate employment or to participate in a job-training program. The president's proposals were not approved by Congress.

LAW AND ORDER

Addressing himself to the often disruptive student demonstrations against the Vietnam war and the spate of black riots in a number of cities, plus the rapid increase of violent crime throughout the nation, Nixon made a strong appeal for the government to focus on law and order.

SUPREME COURT APPOINTMENTS

Nixon's first nomination to the Supreme Court—that of Warren E. Burger, a conservative judge of the United States Court of Appeals of the District of Columbia, to succeed Earl Warren as chief justice—was soon confirmed by the Senate. The president's next two nominees to the Court—conservative federal judges Clement Haynsworth Jr. of South Carolina and G. Harrold Carswell of Florida—were bitterly opposed by civil rights groups and organized labor. The Senate refused to confirm Haynsworth because he had heard a case in which he had a conflict of interest. It then rejected Carswell for his undistinguished reputation as a jurist and his record of racist views and actions. Nixon accused liberal Democratic senators of being biased against the seating of a southerner on the Supreme Court. Ultimately, Nixon did succeed in appointing three more conservative members to the Court, including a southerner. Becoming less liberal, the Court turned away from a broad interpretation of the Constitution and liberal activism toward a strict interpretation of the Constitution and the exercise of judicial restraint, particularly in the areas of civil rights and law and order.

The Economy

In order to deal with both a spiraling inflation and a deepening recession, the Nixon administration imposed a system of wage and price controls.

A PROGRAM FOR ECONOMIC RECOVERY

The Nixon administration initially attempted to stem increasing inflation by employing the usual approaches: (1) cutting back on government spending; (2) having the federal reserve banks charge high interest rates to commercial banks, so that the commercial banks in turn would charge high interest rates to the people and thereby discourage them from borrowing; and (3) using influence with businesses to have them curb large price increases and with labor unions to have them refrain from demanding large wage increases. But economic conditions became worse.

In addition to inflation, there was recession. The economy was stagnant, with an unemployment rate of almost 6 percent. In August 1971, Nixon implemented a new economic program with the following provisions: (1) a total restriction for ninety days on wage and price increases; (2) a reduction in personal income taxes and a repeal of the excise tax on automobiles, both achieved through congressional legislation, in order to spur the purchase of consumer goods and thus revive the economy; and (3) the appointment of a Cost of Living Council to supervise the freeze on wages and prices and to draft proposals for stability in the future. Labor leaders, led by President George Meany of the AFL-CIO, complained that while wages were frozen, businesses, despite frozen prices, were actually receiving higher profits through the new tax benefits.

PHASE TWO

In October 1971, just before the ninety-day freeze was to end, Nixon instituted what was soon called phase two of the administration's program to halt inflation. This phase included the establishment of a Pay Board, which limited wage increases to 5.5 percent, and the establishment of a Price Commission, which limited price increases to 2.5 percent. Within months labor leaders—particularly Meany once again—complained that although both wages and prices were restricted, business profits were not prohibited from increasing.

Government Reorganization and Reform

The Nixon administration, like many administrations before it, gave some attention to the matter of government reorganization and reform.

RESTRUCTURING THE POSTAL SYSTEM

In 1971 Congress disbanded the cabinet-level Post Office Department, headed by the postmaster general. Established in its place was the United States Postal Service, an independent agency within the executive branch of the government, headed by a postmaster general who was not a member of the cabinet. Rather than relying greatly on financial assistance from the government, as had the Post Office Department, the United States Postal Service was virtually to sustain itself from revenues collected for its services.

THE TWENTY-SIXTH AMENDMENT

During the Vietnam war the minimum age for military service was eighteen. All but a few of the states had long had a minimum voting age of twenty-one. To consider men old enough to go to war, risking death for their nation, yet too young to vote struck most of the American people as untenable. They decided through their legislators on both the federal and state levels that a change was in order. The Twenty-sixth Amendment to the Constitution, granting the suffrage to citizens who were eighteen years of age or older, was passed by Congress in March 1971 and ratified three months later. That November approximately 11 million Americans between the ages of eighteen and twenty-one were eligible to vote for the first time.

Election of 1972

Through a combination of bold moves in foreign policy and what was for him a fortunate choice of Democratic presidential and vice-presidential candidates and the subsequent conduct of the Democratic campaign, Nixon won a second term by an overwhelming popular-vote majority.

DEMOCRATS

The contest in the Democratic primaries aroused much interest among the American people. Senator George McGovern of South Dakota, promising major reforms both in his party and in the nation, won surprising victories in the primaries over other leading contenders: Senator Hubert H. Humphrey of Minnesota, Senator Edmund S. Muskie of Maine, Senator Henry M. Jackson of Washington, and Governor George C. Wallace of Alabama. (Wallace was paralyzed after being shot at a primary campaign rally and withdrew from the competition.) McGovern's supporters, among them many students and blacks and other minority groups, secured a majority of the delegates to the Democratic national convention, and he was easily nominated for president. Senator Thomas Eagleton of Missouri was selected as his running mate. Soon after the convention had adjourned, party leaders were stunned by the news that Eagleton had been hospitalized for mental depression three times during the 1960s. McGovern reluctantly decided to ask Eagleton to resign and to seek another running mate. The Democratic National Committee chose R. Sargent Shriver, Jr., former head of the Peace Corps.

REPUBLICANS

Early in 1972 minor challenges within the Republican party to the renomination of President Nixon and Vice-President Agnew were easily turned aside. The delegates to the national convention chose the same ticket that they had four years earlier.

THE CAMPAIGN

McGovern's campaign quickly lost the enthusiasm and momentum that had marked his efforts to win the Democratic nomination. In trying to gain the support of veteran party leaders, most of whom had opposed his nomination, McGovern forfeited some of his influence with the young reformers who had hoped that he would rebuild the Democratic party along ultraliberal lines. In his handling of such issues as unemployment, tax reform, amnesty for draft evaders in the Vietnam war, abortion, drug abuse, and crime, he gave many voters the impression of either wild radicalism or indecisiveness. Citing the heavy pressure of his presidential duties, Nixon spent little time campaigning. He tried to blunt the charges of the Democrats that his administration showed favoritism to special interests, had brought on inflation, was responsible for the high rate of unemployment, and was involved in a break-in of the Democratic national headquarters in the Watergate complex. In turn he argued that McGovern, if elected, would embark on unsound economic programs, so cut defense spending that the United States would be reduced to a second-rate power, and end the war in Vietnam so precipitately that American prisoners would be left in North Vietnam and the government of South Vietnam would collapse. For many voters the war issue seemed to be resolved in October 1972, when the governments in Hanoi, Saigon, and Washington announced simultaneously that they were ready to sign a cease-fire agreement as a prelude to a permanent peace settlement.

NIXON'S LANDSLIDE VICTORY

Nixon received 47,169,000 popular votes to McGovern's 29,170,000. He lost only one state, Massachusetts, and the District of Columbia. Nixon's 60.8 percent of the total vote narrowly missed equaling Lyndon B. Johnson's 61.2 percent of eight years earlier. In the electoral college Nixon had 520 votes and McGovern 17. But far from losing all its strength on the federal level, the Democratic party gained two more seats in the Senate, and although relinquishing thirteen seats in the House of Representatives, it retained a fifty-one-vote majority in that body. Only a little over half (55.4 percent) of the eligible voters bothered to cast ballots—a testimony, according to political analysts, to the disenchantment of the electorate with the candidates of both major parties.

A Controversial Vice-President

Spiro T. Agnew was probably the most controversial figure ever to occupy the second-highest office in the nation.

CONDUCT

The vice-president attracted attention as a defender of the conservative cause. While Nixon assumed the role of the sedate leader of the nation, he apparently gave Agnew the part of political counterattacker. Agnew played the part with stinging phraseology. He charged opponents of the Vietnam war with disloyalty, declaring that protests against the conflict were "encouraged by an effete corps of impudent snobs who characterize themselves as intellectuals." He found fault with intellectuals for being skeptical about the traditional values of American society, and he accused the major television networks of distorting the news. Although some right-wing members of the Republican party were pleased with Agnew's vituperation, many moderates seriously questioned whether their party would be helped by it.

RESIGNATION

Agnew's vice-presidency came to a sudden end after an investigation by the Justice Department produced evidence that as Baltimore county executive and as governor of Maryland he had accepted kickbacks from engineering and other firms doing business with the state. It was further alleged that he continued to receive bribes even while serving as vice-president. In October 1973, he resigned from the government, pleading "no contest" to the charge that he had evaded federal income tax when he was active in Maryland politics. He was sentenced to a three-year probation and fined $10,000. The light sentence was defended on the grounds of national interest. Nixon thereupon appointed Gerald R. Ford, minority leader of the House of Representatives, to be vice-president, according to the procedures set forth in the recently ratified Twenty-fifth Amendment.

The Watergate Scandal

The greatest political scandal in the nation's history was the Watergate affair. It destroyed the Nixon administration.

THE BREAK-IN

In June 1972, five men were arrested inside Democratic national headquarters in the Watergate, a complex of offices, hotels, and apartments in Washington, D.C. The five—and two others who were later apprehended for participating in the planning of the break-in—were in the employ of the Committee for the Re-election of the President (CREEP), an organization that had been set up under the indirect control of Nixon's leading White House advisors. In January 1973, the seven men were found guilty of conspiracy, burglary, and electronic eavesdropping. Two months later James McCord, one of the convicted burglars, wrote a letter to federal judge John J. Sirica, who had sat during the trial, charging that there had been a cover-up of the burglary by persons at the highest levels of the executive branch. President Nixon declared—and in the months ahead continued to do so—that he had possessed no prior knowledge of the break-in, nor of attempts to cover up the relationship between the men apprehended in the Watergate and CREEP.

THE SENATE SELECT COMMITTEE HEARINGS

Determined investigative reporting, notably by the team of Bob Woodward and Carl Bernstein of the *Washington Post*, helped bring about a Senate investigation. During May–August 1973, the Senate Select Committee on Presidential Campaign Activities, chaired by Democratic senator Sam J. Ervin Jr. of North Carolina, in the course of its investigation of corrupt campaign practices, conducted televised hearings on the Watergate affair. Among the most important witnesses who appeared before the committee were White House chief of staff H. R. Haldeman, White House domestic advisor John Erlichman, special counsel to the president John Dean III, and former attorney general John N. Mitchell. Dean testified that Mitchell, with the awareness of Haldeman and Erlichman, had consented to the burglary and that Nixon had approved the cover-up. Haldeman, Erlichman, and Mitchell each testified that the president had had no foreknowledge of the break-in or of the attempts to cover it up.

During the course of his testimony Mitchell described the campaign practices used under the auspices of CREEP as "White House horrors." In addition to burglarizing and wiretapping Democratic party offices, these "dirty tricks" on Democratic candidates included such tactics as harassing speakers and issuing fraudulent letters and leaflets.

THE DISMISSAL OF THE WATERGATE SPECIAL PROSECUTOR

In May 1973, Attorney General Elliot Richardson appointed Harvard University Law School professor Archibald Cox as special prosecutor to investigate the Watergate affair and allied acts of political corruption. Cox found much evidence of campaign espionage by CREEP, the use of illegal wiretapping by the Nixon administration, and large contributions by corporations to the Republican party for efforts expended on their behalf.

Meanwhile, during the course of the Senate Select Committee hearings, it was disclosed that beginning in 1971 President Nixon's conversations in the White House had been tape-recorded. Cox made vigorous efforts to obtain the tapes of conversations regarding the Watergate affair from Nixon, who in October 1973 refused to comply. Nixon ordered Cox dismissed. Attorney General Richardson and the next-highest Justice Department official resigned in protest. The dismissal and the resignations, all announced by the White House on the same evening, were collectively dubbed the "Saturday Night Massacre." Nixon's firing of Cox produced outrage across the nation and led the House of Representatives to empower its Judiciary Committee to begin the consideration of impeachment.

THE PRESIDENTIAL TAPES

Reacting to widespread anger and resentment, Nixon appointed Leon Jaworski, a well-respected Texas lawyer, as a new special prosecutor and made available to Judge Sirica tapes that had been sought by Cox. (Two of the nine subpoenaed tapes were claimed not to have existed, and one had an eighteen-and-a-half-minute gap.) Under continuing pressure from the public, in April 1974 Nixon submitted to the House Judiciary Committee edited typewritten transcripts of his taped conversations on the Watergate affair. Two months later the Supreme Court ordered the president to deliver to Jaworski other, previously subpoenaed, tapes on the cover-up in particular. Nixon's turning over the tapes did not stem the loss of confidence in him. By the summer of 1974 most Americans, according to the polls, were convinced that he had been involved at least in the cover-up of Watergate. There were demands for the president's resignation. But he announced time and again that he was determined to finish his term of office.

THE HOUSE JUDICIARY COMMITTEE HEARINGS

After completing its investigation, the House Judiciary Committee, headed by Democrat Peter W. Rodino Jr. of New Jersey, in July 1974 adopted by bipartisan votes three articles of impeachment against President Nixon. The first article, passed by a 27 to 11 vote, charged him with engaging in a "course of conduct" designed to obstruct justice in the Watergate case. The second, passed 28 to 10, charged him with abuse of power. The third, passed 21 to 17, charged him with unconstitutionally defying the subpoenas of the House Judiciary Committee.

The next step would have been for the House of Representatives as a whole to consider accepting or rejecting the impeachment articles adopted by its Judiciary Committee. If it approved the charges, it would recommend to the Senate that the president be brought to trial. If found guilty by a two-thirds vote of the Senate, which sits as a court in cases of impeachment, he would have been removed from office.

NIXON'S RESIGNATION

On August 5, 1974, Nixon admitted that he had been aware from the beginning of the attempts to cover up the Watergate break-in and that he had endeavored to prevent the Federal Bureau of Investigation from conducting an inquiry into the burglary. Recommendation by the House that Nixon be tried and his conviction by the Senate were now certainties. On August 9 Nixon resigned. In the history of the nation he was the first president to do so.

Vice-President Ford assumed the presidency. He soon issued a pardon to Nixon for any crime that he might have committed while occupying the presidential office. In January 1975, Nixon's leading associates—Haldeman, Erlichman, and Mitchell—were convicted for their participation in the Watergate affair. They joined fourteen former aides to Nixon or employees of CREEP who had already been found guilty of or had pleaded guilty to charges in the Watergate break-in and its cover-up. The Watergate scandal led to agitation within the federal government and the near paralysis of the

Nixon administration as it approached its end. More serious was that it caused among the American people a significant loss of confidence in government and a marked lack of respect for public officials.

FORD AND A POST-WATERGATE NATION

Gerald R. Ford viewed himself initially as an accidental and an interim president—and he was almost apologetic about performing his duties. But he soon gained confidence. The major domestic issue faced by the Ford administration was the economy, which was wracked by both the worst inflation in peacetime and the worst recession with its accompanying unemployment since the Great Depression of the 1930s.

The Ford Administration

Ford stripped the presidency of much of its excessive outward display. Eager for an exchange of ideas with both supporters and critics, he made himself available to people of substance in and out of government.

THE PRESIDENT

Ford had a friendly manner and kind disposition. He was not an innovator. But his candor, diligence, and modesty earned him a measure of respect from his associates. No dazzler, he was—in a word—uncomplicated.

THE CABINET

The new president immediately dispensed with his predecessor's exceedingly tight control of the executive branch in favor of the more usual approach of diffused authority. Members of the cabinet were free to act fully in those areas of concern for which they were responsible. Within six months after assuming office, Ford had largely reorganized the cabinet by changing four of its eleven members. The official family was given a diversity it had recently lacked, with the appointment of Edward H. Levi, a Jew and a Democrat who was president of the University of Chicago, as attorney general; John T. Dunlop, a Harvard University economics professor who had links with organized labor, as secretary of labor; Carla A. Hills, a woman who led the civil rights division of the Justice Department, as secretary of housing and urban development; and William T. Coleman, a black lawyer who had served as counsel to or as member of several federal government commissions, as secretary of transportation.

Domestic Issues

Ford's first—and surely most important—task was to restore the high repute of the presidency. After that, undoubtedly the most serious domestic concern during the Ford administration was the economy. The president also had to contend with the energy crisis.

LEADING A POST-WATERGATE NATION

As the first chief executive after the Watergate scandal, Ford cleansed the air of scheming actions. He sought the advice of people of divergent views from many sectors of society. He established frequent consultation with members of Congress. He instituted press conferences on a regular basis. All these were practices that had been allowed to lapse by his predecessor. Ford quickly put an end to the pervading nationwide bitterness and to the governmental impotence that had characterized the last stages of the Nixon administration. He took the people into his confidence. He faltered once in this regard—and badly—when he unexpectedly and precipitately granted Nixon a full pardon without obtaining either an admission of guilt or a revelation of all the facts regarding the former president's actions in the Watergate affair.

THE ECONOMY

The nation was suffering from both inflation and recession at the same time. The Ford administration seemed unsure as to which needed to be cured first. The president decided it was inflation. In order to combat inflation Ford advocated such measures as a sharp reduction in government spending, an increase in taxes, and the levying of higher duties on imported petroleum. But at the same time that he opposed as inflationary a plan of government spending to create employment for needy Americans, he approved programs that either directly or indirectly raised prices. For example, his energy-conservation plan was based on imposing higher costs for petroleum products. The government-authorized sale of huge amounts of wheat to the Soviet Union removed much of the crop from domestic consumption and thus increased the cost for the remaining portion.

Inflation remained high. At the beginning of 1975 the rate was 9 percent. The devastating effect on people's income of having to pay so much more for the necessities of life produced the worst economic slump since the Great Depression of the 1930s.

As for the effects of the recession, the unemployment rate was more than 8 percent throughout 1975, thus making it the most serious recession in three decades. Some government assistance was given to people hit hardest by the recession: Those in the lowest income brackets received tax reductions and there were extensions of the unemployment insurance periods. Ford was soon compelled to do an about-face. He concluded that the recession was just as bad for the nation as inflation. Thus early in 1975 he recommended an anti-recession program that included both a tax cut amounting to $16 billion for people with an annual income of less than $40,000 and a plan for public-service employment. But both inflation and recession continued unabated. At the end of 1976 the inflation rate was still 9 percent and the unemployment rate, due to the recession, was still more than 8 percent.

THE ENERGY CRISIS

The American people were troubled by the skyrocketing cost of gasoline and fuel oil as a result of the price levels established by the Organization of Petroleum Exporting Countries (OPEC), composed chiefly of Arab nations. President Ford proposed raising the price of domestic oil and natural gas in order to permit a rise in the cost of both, thereby reducing their consumption and helping alleviate the energy crisis.

CARTER AND A POLITICAL INTERLUDE

In the election of 1976 Jimmy Carter won the presidency from Gerald R. Ford, thus signaling the conclusion of the Nixon era in American politics. If the executive and legislative branches of the federal government, both now controlled by the same party for the first time in eight years, had worked together effectively, a period of significant social progress could have resulted. But this was not to be the case. Carter was never able to establish a sound working relationship with Congress. He acquired a reputation for being inconstant, if not in establishing domestic and foreign policies at least in choosing the methods for implementing them. The domestic issues on which the Carter administration expended the most effort were an economy significantly affected by inflation and a severe energy crisis.

Election of 1976

The Republican candidate, Gerald R. Ford, came nearer to being rejected by his party for the nomination than any incumbent president since Chester A. Arthur in 1884. After gaining the nomination, he rallied his forces to such a degree that he slashed his opponent's staggering lead in the polls to nearly nothing. Finally, however, he became the first occupant of the White House to lose an election since Herbert Hoover in 1932. The Democratic candidate, Jimmy Carter, rose from relative obscurity as a single-term governor to become the first president from the deep South since Zachary Taylor in 1848.

DEMOCRATS

Fifteen persons ran in the Democratic primaries. In a methodically planned and relentlessly pursued effort, former governor of Georgia Jimmy Carter won victory after victory in the primaries over more prominent contenders like Senator Henry M. Jackson of Washington and Governor George C. Wallace of Alabama. By the time of the Democratic national convention, Carter was virtually assured of becoming his party's standard-bearer. As expected, he was nominated for president on the first ballot. A prolonged search by Carter for a running mate ended in his selection of liberal senator Walter F. "Fritz" Mondale of Minnesota, a move that helped to reconcile liberals within the Democratic party who considered Carter to be somewhat conservative.

REPUBLICANS

For months before the Republican national convention, President Ford had to cope with an intense challenge for the presidential nomination from former governor of California Ronald Reagan, an exceedingly captivating personality who represented the right wing of the party. Before the opening of the convention, Reagan, in a bold gamble, declared that if nominated he wanted as his running mate Senator Richard Schweiker of Pennsylvania, regarded as the most liberal Republican in the Senate. Reagan's move so distressed his conservative supporters that he was immediately compelled to concentrate on retaining what delegate support he already held rather than on increasing it. In a discordant convention the delegates narrowly chose Ford over Reagan, thus defeating the strongest challenge to an incumbent president within his own party in close to a century. Upon Ford's request, the delegates named conservative Senator Robert J. Dole of Kansas as a candidate for vice-president, which appeased the right wing of the party.

THE CAMPAIGN

There were pronounced differences on a host of issues between the conservatively inclined Ford and the liberally inclined Carter. However, with the Watergate scandal unforgotten, both men tended to avoid dealing with the issues and instead strove to concentrate on portraying themselves as men deserving of trust. Ford declared that his candidacy represented continued quiet at home and peace abroad and continued reduction of the federal government's involvement in the affairs of local communities. Carter promised the American people full employment, national health care, welfare reform, tax reform, aid to the cities, a new energy policy, government reorganization and reform, and more "openness" in government.

During the campaign Ford and Carter engaged in three televised debates, the first to involve an incumbent president. Political commentators generally agreed that the debates were a draw. Dole and Mondale also participated in a televised debate (there was, at moments, considerable acrimony on Dole's part), the first ever between vice-presidential candidates.

According to polls at the outset of the campaign, Carter would achieve a landslide victory. But his lead soon began to narrow. Toward the end of the campaign it seemed as if Ford had gained enough strength to achieve an upset victory. But his cause lost precious momentum when he made a clumsy mistake in asserting that Eastern Europe, particularly Poland, was not under Soviet domination. Much time and energy were spent soothing the feelings of outraged Americans of Eastern European background. On the day before the election, the polls indicated that Carter's previous overwhelming lead had dwindled to practically nothing. The contest had become a toss-up.

CARTER'S VICTORY

In popular votes, Carter received 40,180,000 to Ford's 38,435,000. In the electoral college Carter carried 297 votes to Ford's 241, making it the closest electoral vote contest in sixty years. The support to the candidates broke along sectional lines. Carter captured all of the former Confederate states except Virginia, all of the border states except Oklahoma, and most of the large industrial states of the Northeast, including New York, Pennsylvania, and Massachusetts. Ford swept most of the Midwest and the entire far West. Carter achieved his victory by holding together the elements of the Democratic coalition of the New Deal period: organized labor, blacks and other minority groups, Roman Catholics, and the solid South. The Democratic party continued to enjoy its large majorities in Congress. In the Senate the membership consisted of 62 Democrats and 38 Republicans, exactly what it had been before the election. In the House of Representatives the Democrats controlled 293 seats and the Republicans 142, an addition of three seats to the already substantial margin held by the former. Voter participation sustained its downward trend. Of those eligible to vote, only 53.3 percent did so.

The Carter Administration

Carter continued with even greater resolve than Ford the effort to eliminate the "imperial" presidency that had reached its peak during the Nixon tenure. The first indication of this endeavor was the tone of Carter's inauguration, which was informal and modest. Also, Carter was determined to conduct an administration that was "open" and to prevent himself from being made inaccessible to the American people by a highly organized White House staff.

THE PRESIDENT

The constant toothy smile and the soft drawl of his native South belied the toughness and stubbornness of Jimmy Carter (his legal name was James Earl Carter Jr., but he had discontinued its use long ago). He was diligently methodical in all he undertook. He found deep satisfaction in familiarizing himself with all facets of a governmental issue. However, he so resisted delegating authority that critics accused him of overtaxing his much-admired mental and physical energies.

THE CABINET

Carter wished to give to cabinet members both an important role in policy-making and direct access to the president. Cyrus R. Vance, a New York lawyer who had been deputy secretary of defense in the Johnson administration, was named secretary of state. Harold Brown, who had been President Johnson's air force secretary and was president of the California Institute of Technology, was made secretary of defense. With the naming of Juanita M. Kreps, an economist and administrative vice-president of Duke University, as secretary of commerce and Patricia Roberts Harris, a black Washington lawyer and former ambassador to Luxembourg, as secretary of housing and urban development, the Carter cabinet became the first in the nation's history to have more than one woman.

Government Reorganization and Reform

Recognizing the value of the government's efforts to reorganize and reform its policies and procedures, the Carter administration played a major role in that regard.

DEPARTMENT OF ENERGY

Responding to President Carter's efforts to combat a serious energy crisis, in which the American people were increasingly troubled by the spiraling cost of gasoline, fuel oil, and natural gas, Congress established the Department of Energy in 1977. The department was authorized to develop the policies and to supervise the programs of the federal government in the field of energy. Carter appointed James F. Schlesinger, who had been the secretary of defense for both Nixon and Ford, as the nation's first secretary of energy.

DEPARTMENT OF HEALTH AND HUMAN SERVICES

Upon the recommendation of Carter, in 1980 Congress created from the Department of Health, Education, and Welfare two separate departments: the Department of Health and Human Services and the Department of Education. The newly established Department of Health and Human Services was to oversee all government agencies that had to do with the health and social and economic welfare of the American people. Patricia Roberts Harris, who had been a member of Carter's cabinet first as secretary of housing and urban development and then as secretary of health, education, and welfare, was appointed the first secretary of health and human services.

DEPARTMENT OF EDUCATION

The newly created Department of Education was authorized to administer all programs for the improvement of education. Carter appointed Shirley M. Hufstedler, who had served with distinction as a federal judge, as the first secretary of education.

Domestic Issues   As had been the case with the Nixon and Ford administrations, the most serious domestic matter confronting the Carter administration was the economy, with the energy crisis a further nagging concern.

THE ECONOMY

When Carter assumed office the inflation rate was 6 percent and the unemployment rate was 8 percent. Deciding that the latter condition needed attention first, the president with congressional cooperation implemented a sharp increase in government spending on public programs to provide jobs for those in need. Within two years the unemployment rate fell back to 6 percent.

On the other hand, the rate of inflation remained high. From the beginning of 1977 the 6 percent rate rose steadily until by the end of 1980 it had reached 12 percent, which was the highest inflation rate in over sixty years. Keenly troubled by the destructive impact upon American life of such accelerating inflation, the Carter administration turned to the same basic methods that his two immediate predecessors had used. The core of the plan was that the federal reserve banks would charge high interest rates to the commercial banks, which in turn would charge high interest rates to the people in order to discourage them from borrowing. But the interest rates kept spiraling, to the point where they reached into the unprecedented 20 percent range. The method was ineffective in lowering the inflation rate.

The economy even worsened. By 1980 the nation had entered a recession. The inflation rate rose to 13 points and the unemployment rate returned to 8 percent. By the time of Carter's reelection campaign the economy was stagnant—and much more so than it had ever been during the Nixon and Ford administrations.

THE ENERGY CRISIS

Like the Ford administration, the Carter administration was immediately forced to contend with a severe energy crisis resulting from the steadily rising price levels established by OPEC. Despite signs of an impending crisis, Americans had continued to use ever-larger amounts of petroleum products, with almost 50 percent coming from foreign sources. Although the rising cost of oil caused economic hardship, most people needed to drive automobiles and virtually all people needed to heat their homes.

In April 1977, Carter declared that combating the energy problem was "the moral equivalent of war" and that if the nation did not learn to prudently manage its shrinking energy supplies it was courting disaster. He proposed a plan that included the strict conservation of existing quantities of fuels; the implementation of higher prices for gasoline, fuel oil, and natural gas to reduce consumption; and the imposition of heavy penalties on organizations and individuals found guilty of the wasteful use of energy in all its forms. Congress, however, failed to pass legislation based on Carter's plan.

Two years later, within a period of but a few months, OPEC once again raised the average price of a barrel of oil by approximately 50 percent, immediately resulting in the spiraling cost of both gasoline and fuel oil for American consumers. In response, Carter offered a plan that included conservation of existing fuel supplies; the development of new sources of energy, such as nuclear power; and a long-range decrease in the importation of foreign oil. Further, as the central feature of the plan, he proposed the deregulation of the price of domestic oil in order to stimulate production by American oil companies. However, such deregulation resulted in American firms significantly raising the price of their gasoline to consumers. Between the higher price levels set by OPEC and the domestic-oil price deregulation arrangement, the average price of a gallon of regular gasoline nearly doubled, from seventy cents in 1977 to $1.30 in 1980. During those same years fuel oil increased from forty cents to about $1.00 a gallon.

A "CRISIS OF CONFIDENCE"

In a television address in July 1979, in which Carter outlined his program for resolving the energy problem, he declared that Americans were facing a "crisis of confidence." The president maintained that, as a result of having been subjected in successive order to such traumas as the Vietnam war, the Watergate scandal, the excessive demands of oil-exporting nations, and soaring inflation, people had begun to lose faith in their potential. He appealed to them to do everything possible to retrieve the old American tradition of self-reliance, lest the nation be at risk. Large numbers of Americans, however, and most Republican leaders, maintained that any "crisis of confidence" was in fact a crisis in presidential leadership.

A POLICY OF DÉTENTE

President Nixon's major concern in foreign affairs was the Vietnam war. After implementing a phased removal of American military forces from South Vietnam, he negotiated a cease-fire agreement with the government of North Vietnam. As for other aspects of foreign relations, the Nixon administration engaged in a historic policy of détente with the two leading communist nations, the Soviet Union and the People's Republic of China, and mediated, after a brief Arab-Israeli war, the creation of United Nations–sponsored buffer zones in the region.

President Ford continued the same basic foreign policy as his predecessor, including the pursuit of détente and the use of United States mediation to help bring permanent peace to the Middle East. Having little experience in international affairs, Ford permitted Secretary of State Henry Kissinger to take the lead in this aspect of his administration.

Carter declared at the very beginning of his presidency that he would conduct a foreign policy based on the moral and idealistic imperative to further the spread of human rights. But this goal soon proved to be too formidable a challenge to meet at all times. Eventually Carter, like Ford before him, maintained the foreign policy of steely realism established by Nixon, including the effort to ease strained relations and political tensions with the Soviet Union and communist China. In the Middle East Carter experienced both his most exhilarating diplomatic triumph and his most humiliating diplomatic defeat. He achieved his personal victory by skillfully mediating the difficult negotiations between Israel and Egypt that resulted in a peace treaty between the two longtime bitter enemies. But the United States suffered frustrating grief when, as part of a revolution in Iran, its embassy was taken over and fifty-two of its citizens were held as hostages for 444 days.

The End of the Vietnam War

The announced policy of the Nixon administration regarding the Vietnam war was to "wind down" the American involvement. The war was brought to a halt and a formal cease-fire agreement was signed, but fighting soon erupted again, leading to the collapse of South Vietnam.

PEACE NEGOTIATIONS CONTINUE

In 1969 President Nixon named Henry Cabot Lodge Jr., who had served as ambassador both to the United Nations and to South Vietnam, to head the American delegation to the peace talks in Paris, replacing veteran diplomat W. Averell Harriman, who had acted for the Johnson administration. In 1970 foreign-service official David K. Bruce was appointed to succeed Lodge.

ANTIWAR PROTESTS

While the peace negotiations dragged on, the first American troops were deliberately withdrawn from South Vietnam. The thrust soon thereafter by American forces into communist sanctuaries in neighboring Cambodia, ordered by Nixon in May 1970, aroused widespread opposition in the United States. By this time millions of Americans, including hundreds of thousands of students, had participated in rallies against the war. Some radical protesters publicly burned draft cards and raided draft-board offices, where they destroyed conscription records. Throughout the nation there were demonstrations.

Among the demonstrations against the government's military policy were many on college and university campuses. In one demonstration, at Kent State University in Ohio in May 1970, students were fired upon by members of the Ohio national guard and four were killed. The nation was shocked. Hundreds of other campuses experienced uprisings; there were demonstrations, confrontations between students and administrators, and building takeovers at such institutions as Harvard, Yale, and Cornell. And yet at the approximately 2,500 other colleges and universities throughout the nation, although students made demands, relative peace and stability prevailed.

VIETNAMIZATION POLICY

While carefully supervising a program of Vietnamization (training the forces of South Vietnam to assume full responsibility for military actions), the Nixon administration steadily withdrew American troops, until there were fewer than 25,000 in South Vietnam by the beginning of 1973.

CEASE-FIRE AGREEMENT

Although the peace talks in Paris were stalemated, the public discussions had been supplemented by private meetings between Henry Kissinger, then presidential advisor for foreign policy and security, and Le Duc Tho, North Vietnam's chief representative in Paris. In October 1972, a cease-fire agreement drafted by these two negotiators seemed to have been accepted by all sides. President Nixon, however, insisted that the terms of the settlement be clarified, and no truce was immediately reached.

In December 1972, the heavy American bombing campaign against the North Vietnamese capital of Hanoi and its harbor at Haiphong was resumed and the government of North Vietnam finally agreed to continue negotiations. In January 1973, a cease-fire in all of Vietnam went into effect. The document that was signed on January 27 provided that (1) all Americans involved in military combat would be withdrawn from Vietnam in sixty days; (2) the United States would remove or deactivate mines it had laid off the coast of Vietnam; (3) American prisoners of war held by North Vietnam would be turned over to American authorities within sixty days; (4) the

United States and North Vietnam would respect the right of the people of South Vietnam to self-determination; (5) the administration of South Vietnamese president Nguyen Van Thieu would continue, pending an election to be supervised by a council including representatives of the South Vietnamese government, the Viet Cong, and neutral factions; and (6) all aspects of the agreement would be supervised by an international commission with a 1,160-person force, consisting of troops from Canada, Poland, and Indonesia.

THE COLLAPSE OF SOUTH VIETNAM

Many issues were settled by the cease-fire accord, but tensions between North Vietnam and South Vietnam continued unabated. Fighting between South Vietnamese government troops and the communist guerrillas within South Vietnam began again. By the beginning of 1974 the fighting was constant and widespread. But it all ended suddenly. In March 1975, a partial retreat of South Vietnamese troops ordered by President Thieu turned into a rout. On April 30 North Vietnamese troops and communist guerrillas took over the South Vietnamese capital of Saigon. The government of South Vietnam promptly surrendered. Without delay Saigon was renamed Ho Chi Minh City in honor of the dead leader of North Vietnam. More than a century of Western domination, first by the French and then by the Americans, was over.

AMERICAN WAR COSTS

In the Vietnam war approximately 58,000 Americans died and about 154,000 were wounded in combat. As for financial expenditures, the United States spent approximately $141 billion.

Détente with the Communist Nations

President Nixon chose the election year of 1972 to begin a policy of détente with the communist nations. The new approach of the Nixon administration proved to be highly successful, prompting the Ford and Carter administrations to continue it enthusiastically.

NIXON AND THE SOVIET UNION

Although hostilities continued in Vietnam, with North Vietnam being supplied with Soviet arms, Nixon was welcomed in Moscow in May 1972. After discussions between the American president and the Soviet Communist party general secretary, Leonid I. Brezhnev, the two nations agreed to lower trade barriers, to cooperate on health and environmental projects, and to collaborate in space exploration. More significant was the signing of two treaties providing for the limitation of nuclear arsenals. The two accords were the result of the strategic arms limitation talks, popularly called SALT, which consisted of scores of meetings (beginning in 1970 in Helsinki, Finland) regarding the limitation by the two nations of their nuclear missile systems.

The first treaty put a limit on each nation of two sites for their antiballistic missile (ABM) defense systems. The second stabilized for five years the current level of each nation's offensive nuclear missile systems, both land-launched and submarine-launched. Finally, in Moscow Nixon and Brezhnev pledged themselves to work for an era of peaceful coexistence that might eventually lead to total disarmament.

NIXON AND CHINA

In February 1972, a few months before his trip to Moscow, Nixon went to Beijing (then called Peking) to confer with the chairman of the Chinese Communist party Mao Zedong and Premier Chou En-lai. After a week of private talks they agreed to work to "normalize" relations. This was the first contact between the two countries since a quarter-century earlier, when the communist Chinese had proclaimed the establishment of the People's Republic of China. (In 1971, several months before the meetings, the People's Republic of China had been admitted to the United Nations and Nationalist China on Taiwan had been expelled.) Sino-American trade and cultural and scientific exchanges were planned. In Beijing Nixon and Chou agreed that their two nations would remain in contact and arrange further joint efforts.

FORD AND A CONTINUANCE OF DÉTENTE

Despite some opposition from the conservative wing of his party, Ford carried on Nixon's policy of détente with the Soviet Union and communist China. Ford, however, was criticized for perhaps yielding too much, for not fully realizing that détente required some give and some take from each side. Within the framework of détente, Ford vigorously pursued the continuation of the strategic arms limitation talks.

CARTER AND THE SOVIET UNION

Upon taking office Carter eagerly adopted the policy of détente with the Soviet Union. In Vienna in June 1979, Carter and Soviet leader Brezhnev signed SALT II, providing for a further reduction of nuclear arsenals. According to the treaty, each nation was limited to 2,250 missile launchers, with no more than 1,320 of them to be equipped with missiles with multiple warheads (MIRVs, or Multiple Independently targeted Reentry Vehicle). The accord also limited the number of bombers that could carry long-range cruise missiles. In response to some conservatives' criticism that the terms were too favorable to the Soviet Union, Carter pointed out that the accord permitted the United States to continue developing a new type of intercontinental ballistic missile (ICBM) that was experimentally mobile and familiarly referred to as the MX.

Later that year the policy of détente foundered when the Soviet Union invaded Afghanistan to bolster the stability there of a Marxist regime that was under attack from Muslim rebels. Characterizing the Soviet military action as a menace to peace throughout the entire region, Carter put an embargo on grain that was to have been shipped to the Soviet Union. He called off all further American-Soviet cultural exchanges and considered the possibility of temporarily halting the sale of technological goods, such as computer systems. Further, and of greater consequence, Carter withdrew SALT II from the Senate while members of that body were considering ratification of the treaty.

Finally—in a dramatic act of supreme moral conduct in the pursuit of international relations—Carter announced that the United States would not participate in the Summer Olympic games to be held in 1980 in Moscow. Fifty other nations were convinced by the Carter administration to join in the boycott. Four years later, in retaliation for the 1980 boycott, the Soviet Union and a few other nations from the communist bloc refused to send their athletes to the Summer Olympic games held in 1984 in Los Angeles. Thus Carter, who upon taking office had eagerly embraced the policy of détente with the Soviet Union, put an end to that policy, bringing a return of the Cold War.

CARTER AND CHINA

Relations between the United States and the People's Republic of China were significantly improved through the efforts of the Carter administration. Carter completed the process of normalization of relations Nixon had initiated with his breakthrough visit to China in 1972. In January 1979, the two nations signed a treaty establishing full diplomatic relations, thirty years after the communists had established the People's Republic of China. (Before signing the treaty the United States severed diplomatic relations with the Nationalist Chinese government of Taiwan and abrogated its twenty-five-year-old mutual defense treaty with that government. Later, however, the United States set up unofficial diplomatic contacts with Taiwan and pledged limited aid for its defense.) Some months later in Washington, D.C., President Carter and Vice-Premier Deng Xiaoping of China, who was on a visit to the United States, formally agreed to implement large-scale cultural and technological exchanges between their nations. The two leaders also discussed extending Sino-American trade.

The Middle East

The long-standing tension between Israel and the Arab nations continued threatening to erupt into a war in which the United States could become a participant. It was also in this region that a new situation arose, an Islamic revolution in Iran, that led to a major foreign policy defeat for the United States.

THE YOM KIPPUR WAR

In October 1973, Egypt and Syria, with aid from Jordan, launched a sudden attack on Israel, which was caught by surprise since its people were at the time observing Yom Kippur (the Jewish high holy Day of Atonement). Egyptian forces crossed the Suez Canal to the east bank, into the Israeli-occupied Sinai peninsula. But by the time the fighting ceased two weeks later, Israeli troops had stopped the Egyptian advance and crossed the Suez Canal to the west bank. In addition, Israeli troops repulsed the Syrian forces on the Golan Heights between Israel and Syria.

MEDIATION BY KISSINGER

Under the auspices of the United Nations, in December 1973, representatives of Israel, Egypt, Syria, Jordan, the United States, and the Soviet Union met in Geneva to discuss a permanent peace settlement for the region. The following month, with Secretary of State Henry Kissinger as mediator, Israel and Egypt agreed to disengage their troops and to permit the creation of a United Nations–sponsored buffer zone in the Sinai, with Egyptian forces on the east bank of the Suez Canal and Israeli forces deeper into the Sinai. In May 1974, again through the mediation efforts of Kissinger, Israel and Syria decided on a disengagement of troops and the establishment on the Golan Heights of a buffer zone under the sponsorship of the United Nations.

FORD AND THE ARAB-ISRAELI CONFLICT

Moderating the pro-Israeli position he had held as a representative, Ford maintained that he would be "even-handed" toward Israel and the Arab nations in order to support Kissinger's efforts to achieve a permanent peace in the Middle East. In September 1975, Israel and Egypt signed an accord by which Israel made a further withdrawal from occupied territory in the Sinai in return for some political concessions by Egypt. The United States agreed to send 200 civilian technicians to a buffer zone between Israel and Egypt where they would operate early warning systems designed to detect any movement in the area by armed forces. The pact was a notable achievement for the Ford administration, which had expended tremendous energy toward its realization.

In January 1976 in the United Nations Security Council the United States vetoed a resolution affirming the right of the Palestinians to "establish an independent state in Palestine" and calling for a complete Israeli withdrawal from all Arab territories occupied as a result of the 1967 Middle East war. The United States argued that if the resolution had passed it would have created unbalanced conditions for negotiating a permanent peace between Israel and the Arab nations. In the spring of 1976 the American and Israeli governments found themselves in conflict. The United States wanted additional diplomatic movement in the Middle East and Israel hoped to defer it.

The American position was based on its belief that continued diplomatic activity would provide security against renewed fighting in the region.

THE CAMP DAVID ACCORDS

In 1977 President Anwar el-Sadat of Egypt astounded the world by making a momentous visit to Israel and delivering an unprecedented address to the Knesset, that nation's parliament. During his stay Sadat and his host, Prime Minister Menachem Begin of Israel, pledged that their nations would never again go to war against each other. Carter then invited the two Middle East leaders to meet at the presidential retreat at Camp David, Maryland, which they did in October 1978, to try to achieve an agreement. Sometimes reasoning with, sometimes cajoling the two strong-willed adversaries, Carter helped them forge two documents that came to be known as the Camp David accords.

One called for further negotiations to determine the future disposition of the West Bank and the Gaza Strip, Jordanian and Egyptian territory respectively, captured by Israel in the Six Day War of 1967 and occupied since then. The other provided for the gradual complete withdrawal of Israeli military forces from the Sinai peninsula and the establishment of normal diplomatic relations between Egypt and Israel. The Camp David accords would serve as the basis for the creation over the next few months of a comprehensive peace treaty. At a White House ceremony in March 1979, Begin and Sadat signed a peace treaty to which Carter affixed his signature as a witness. Thus for the first time since it had become a nation more than thirty years before, Israel was formally at peace with an Arab nation. Without Carter's diplomacy, it appeared certain, peace would not have been achieved.

THE IRANIAN HOSTAGE CRISIS

In the Persian Gulf region Iran was an important ally of the United States. The two nations had common interests relating to the oil industry and security matters evolving from Soviet expansionism in the area. However, the regime of the shah of Iran, Mohammed Reza Pahlevi, was repressive and corrupt. Large numbers of fervent Shiite Muslims were vigorously opposed to the Western-oriented rule of the shah and were determined to remove him from the throne and establish a fundamentalist Islamic republic.

Early in 1979 a bloody revolution quickly and overwhelmingly succeeded. The shah fled. The spiritual leader of the insurgents, the Ayatollah Ruholla Khomeini, an elderly and frail, fervently pious Islamic cleric, returned to Iran from a fifteen-year exile. He set up and zealously led an ultra-authoritarian Islamic republic that expunged virtually every aspect of modern Western-oriented culture. American interests in the Persian Gulf region were clearly threatened. In February 1979, the United States embassy in Teheran was attacked by an armed band that wounded two marines on duty and trapped the ambassador and his staff for about two hours inside the structure.

On November 4, 1979, a mob of approximately 500 students seized the embassy and took ninety hostages. The presence of the shah in the United States for cancer treatment had touched off the action. About two weeks later the militants released some of their captives, mainly women and blacks, and announced that they intended to try some of the remaining hostages for espionage. The students demanded the return of the deposed shah to Iran for trial before they would consider releasing any of the remaining hostages. The number of Americans in captivity would ultimately remain at fifty-two. The students' actions throughout had the full support of the Khomeini government.

In attempting to resolve the conflict an anguished Carter engaged in a number of actions, including freezing all Iranian assets in the United States and sending a naval task force to be within striking distance of Iranian territory. In April 1980, a United States military operation to rescue the hostages was aborted; equipment failed at a staging area in the Iranian desert about 200 miles southeast of Teheran. During the subsequent withdrawal from the area and while still on the ground a helicopter collided with a transport plane, killing eight servicemen. Secretary of State Cyrus R. Vance had argued against the rescue expedition, believing that the likelihood of success appeared too low and the risk of extensive loss of life of both the hostages and servicemen appeared too high. Vance resigned in the aftermath.

Three months after the failed rescue attempt the shah died. The Iranian leaders announced that his death did not mean the release of the fifty-two hostages.

Months later, on January 19, 1981, with the mediation of the Algerian government, the United States and Iran signed an accord on the release of the hostages. But Carter's expectation that the hostages would leave Iran by plane on that date—the last full day of his presidency—was not to be realized. The release was held up one more day. The airplane with the hostages on board left the ground moments after Reagan took the oath of office as president. There was a widespread belief that the timing was not by coincidence but by design on the part of Iran.

Central America

Carter's determination that the basis of his foreign policy would be the spread of human rights achieved fruition most successfully in Central America.

NICARAGUA

In 1978 Carter terminated economic and military aid to the repressive rightist regime of Anastasio Somoza Debayle in Nicaragua, basing the action on the long and extensive record of human rights violations in that nation. The following year Somoza resigned from office, having been under heavy diplomatic pressure from the United States and exposed to widespread armed attack from a leftist rebel group known as the Sandinista National Liberation Front, popularly referred to as the Sandinistas.

After Somoza's downfall a revolutionary junta controlled by the Sandinistas took political power. Despite its pronounced communist leanings, the new government quickly received ample financial support from the Carter administration as part of its effort to retain ties with Nicaragua and to prevent it from aligning itself with the Soviet Union and Cuba for military and financial assistance.

EL SALVADOR

In 1979 a coup led by military officers removed Carlos Humberto Romero from the presidency and set up a rightist junta made up of both military and civilian figures to govern a nation long wracked by violence between rightist and leftist forces. In 1980, during the savage armed conflict between the junta and communist guerrillas, who were aided by the Nicaraguan Sandinistas, three American nuns and a lay missionary were murdered. Although it was initially uncertain whether the junta or the antigovernment group was responsible for the killings (the government troops were subsequently proved to have committed the act), the Carter administration promptly cut off the financial aid it had been giving to the junta.

PANAMA

Over the years Panamanians had come to resent United States control of the ten-mile-wide canal zone and all that the established presence of a powerful foreign nation in their midst came to represent. In 1964 the United States and Panama began negotiating for the eventual transfer of the canal to Panama. In 1977 President Carter and President Omar Torrijos Herrera of Panama signed two accords. They constituted a treaty that revoked the Hay-Bunau-Varilla Treaty of 1903, which had granted the United States perpetual control of the canal zone, and would turn over the canal to Panama at the end of 1999. The following year, after acrimonious debate in the Senate, in which conservative members of that body argued against surrendering United States sovereignty, the treaty received one vote more than the two-thirds majority necessary under the Constitution for ratification. However, according to the pact the United States would still have the right to intervene to preserve the neutrality of the waterway.

PERSISTENCE OF SOCIAL FERMENT

The tumultuous social ferment of the 1960s persisted into the 1970s, though with diminished force. Americans experienced a disheartening loss of confidence in their government and lost respect for public officials as they witnessed the unfolding of a political scandal that resulted in the near paralysis and then the total destruction of a presidential administration. In their dependence upon petroleum, they became seemingly helpless captives of an association of oil-exporting nations patently unrestrained in their quest for wealth and power. They suffered cruelly from the devastating effect upon their lives of soaring inflation. The period witnessed a significant reversal of decades-old national migration patterns. The labor movement had to contend with considerable challenges. In technology, the penetration into space by the United States was a triumph second to none in the history of science—and adventure.

The Growth of Rural Areas and Small Towns

During the 1970s there was a marked reversal of long-continued migration patterns within the United States. For the first time in more than a century and a half, rural areas and small towns grew faster than did cities.

STATISTICS

During the 1960s, with people in large numbers still moving away from the nation's rural areas and small towns, the population of the nonmetropolitan areas increased by about 4.4 percent, whereas that of the metropolitan areas increased by about 17 percent. During the 1970s, however, the population of the rural areas and small towns increased by about 15.4 percent (from approximately 54.4 million to approximately 62.8 million), whereas that of the metropolitan areas increased by about only 9.1 percent (from approximately 148.8 million to approximately 162.4 million). But the people who left the urban areas did not generally move to farms. The trend of a steady percentage decline in the number of farm workers, begun in the last quarter of the nineteenth century, continued; by 1980 farm workers constituted 2.7 percent of the population. The greatest rise in population in both rural and urban areas during the decade occurred in the South, with an increase of 18.6 percent, and in the far West, with a spectacular increase of 26.5 percent.

CAUSES

The migration of large numbers of people to rural areas and small towns resulted from, among other things, the convenience of commuting over long distances by private automobile or public transportation, the relocation of business firms and industrial plants, and the development of retirement communities.

The Labor Movement

During the first six decades or so of the twentieth century, organized labor achieved many gains through carefully developed and vigorously implemented programs. But during the 1970s, although labor continued to win increased benefits, it faced serious challenges.

IMPROVED WORKING CONDITIONS

Throughout the twentieth century American laborers by effective organization improved their lot in many ways, including, for example, the shortening of their work hours. In 1900 a ten-hour workday and a six-day workweek were the norm; in 1940 it was an eight-hour workday and a six-day work week; in 1980 it was an eight-hour workday and five-day workweek. But more was achieved than that. By 1980 most workers were being given ten paid holidays a year, whereas in 1940 most had received five and in 1900 none. By 1980 most workers were also being given a two-week paid vacation each year, whereas in 1940 most had received one week without pay and in 1900 no vacation time.

MEMBERSHIP GAINS

In terms of membership there were some important gains during the 1970s. The recently organized United Farm Workers, after much bitter confrontation with large agricultural producers, finally achieved for its members far more satisfactory working conditions. White-collar employees, who had always been disinclined to join unions, regarding such an affiliation as a mark of lesser social status, were prompted to reconsider their attitudes in view of the increasing automation of office work. By 1980 close to 15 percent of the nation's white-collar workers had become union members. But the most telling gain in unionization was among government employees. During the 1960s the federal government took a position in favor of its employees unionizing. By the mid-1970s practically all state and local governments permitted their employees to organize and bargain collectively. For example, by 1980 about 570,000 public-school teachers belonged to the American Federation of Teachers, an affiliate of the AFL-CIO, and about 1.7 million belonged to the National Education Association, which, although it considered itself a professional group, conducted itself very much like a union, with, for example, its chapters resorting to strikes.

RECRUITING UNAFFILIATED WORKERS

As the 1970s drew to a close the AFL-CIO had to come to grips with the challenge of recruiting still unaffiliated workers. Between 1955, when the AFL-CIO was formed, and 1980 the nation's total labor force increased from about 68 million to about 104 million, but the portion in unions decreased from 34 percent to 22 percent. As for the AFL-CIO itself, in 1955 the organization had about 16 million members (21 percent of the labor force), whereas in 1980 it had about 13.6 million members (13 percent of the labor force).

Technology: Space Exploration

Spurred by competition between the United States and the Soviet Union, the exploration of space proceeded at a rapid rate. Each nation sent a number of spacecraft around the earth, around the sun, to the moon, and to the other planets.

ORBITING THE EARTH

In 1957 the Soviet Union launched the first unmanned spacecraft, *Sputnik* (Russian for "traveling companion"), that escaped the gravity of the earth. In 1958 the United States followed suit. Three years later humans themselves began to travel in space. The first to do so was Soviet cosmonaut Yuri A. Gagarin, who on April 12, 1961 made a single orbit around the earth. The following month American astronaut Alan B. Shepard Jr. rocketed 115 miles into space. In 1962 John H. Glenn Jr. became the first American to orbit the earth, doing so three times. In 1965 Virgil I. "Gus" Grissom and John Watts Young circled the earth three times in a two-person space capsule. By 1970 the two nations had sent approximately 25,000 unmanned satellites into orbit, of which almost 500 were still circling the earth a decade later.

LANDING ON THE MOON

The American project to land a person on the moon was called Project Apollo. In January 1967, a fire aboard the *Apollo I* spacecraft on its launching pad at Cape Kennedy, Florida, took the lives of Grissom, Edward H. White, and Roger Chaffee. There was intense national grief, and plans for the lunar project were delayed. But in December 1968, the *Apollo VIII* carried three men—Frank Borman, James A. Lovell, Jr., and William Anders—on a fantastic journey. During a 147-hour flight their spacecraft traveled approximately 240,000 miles from the earth to the moon, orbited the moon ten times, and returned to the earth, dropping into the Pacific Ocean.

On July 20, 1969, the ultimate goal of Project Apollo was achieved. Watched on television by hundreds of millions of people all over the earth, astronaut Neil A. Armstrong stepped onto the moon. "That's one small step for man, one giant leap for mankind," he said. Armstrong and his two fellow astronauts, Edwin E. "Buzz" Aldrin Jr. and Michael Collins, brought back from the moon's surface data of immense scientific value. Between July 1969 and December 1972 there were five landings on the moon. The last Apollo flight was made by Eugene Cernan, Harrison Schmitt, and Ron Evans. Cernan and Schmitt roamed the lunar surface for miles in a specially constructed jeeplike vehicle.

INTERNATIONAL COOPERATION

In July 1975, American astronauts and Soviet cosmonauts united their two spacecraft; then two of the Americans entered the Soviet spaceship and met its occupants face to face.

REACHING OTHER PLANETS

In October 1975, two unmanned Soviet craft landed on Venus (the second body in space to be "visited" by humans) and relayed photographs back to earth.

On July 20, 1976, seven years to the day after a person first walked on the moon, the unmanned American craft *Viking I* landed on Mars. This was the culmination of an eleven-month voyage to a planet approximately 230 million miles from the earth. *Viking I* and the identical *Viking II*, which landed six weeks later, conducted a number of scientific experiments, including scooping up Martian soil and pouring it into their miniature biological laboratories to analyze it for evidence of life.

In March 1979, the American spacecraft *Voyager I*, and in July 1979, the identical *Voyager II*, both of which had been launched in 1977, passed within about 400,000 miles of the solar system's largest planet, Jupiter, transmitting an enormous amount of data and stunning photographs of the planet and its five largest moons. After passing Jupiter, *Voyager I* went on to explore the second-largest planet, Saturn, and its environs in November 1980; *Voyager II* did the same in August 1981. *Voyager II* reached Uranus, approximately 1.8 billion miles from earth, in 1986, and Neptune, approximately 2.8 billion miles from earth, in 1989. Thus by 1990 only one planet of the solar system—distant Pluto—had yet to be reconnoitered by spacecraft from earth.

SHUTTLING

In April 1981, two American astronauts cruised for three days in the reusable winged and wheeled shuttle spacecraft *Columbia* and then returned to earth in a "soft" landing, a feat that augured the making of routine commuter trips into space.

A MORE TRADITIONAL CULTURE

As the 1960s melded into the 1970s, the intimate relationship between social change and cultural development continued. Social turbulence did lessen during the period, and cultural activity reflected that. A quieter, more traditional—albeit vigorous—cultural scene thus emerged. That phenomenon could be readily observed in motion-picture production and in sports. The motion-picture industry operated in a much altered way. As for sports, no other area of American cultural development manifested such significant gains in status by blacks.

Motion Pictures

In order to continue as a viable part of the field of popular entertainment, the motion-picture industry felt compelled to accommodate itself to changing economic and social conditions. It did so. And despite difficult circumstances, great films with great performances were still made.

NEW TRENDS

Three factors in particular were most responsible for significant new trends in filmmaking: the steeply climbing costs of production, particularly during the inflationary economy of the 1970s; the developing public taste for realism over romanticism, with a readier acceptance of—even a desire for—the depiction of violence and explicit sexual activity; and finally, the constant competition of television. The solution arrived at by the heads of the film industry was to make fewer but better movies.

By the 1970s the motion-picture and television industries had come to terms with each other. At first the studios sold to the television networks individual films that had already been shown in movie houses. Later they sold large portions of their entire stock of already screened films in package deals. Further, the studios began to make films specifically for television viewing. Ironically, by 1980 Americans were seeing more movies than ever in the past, but they were seeing them at home on television.

DIRECTORS

In the 1970s two young directors, Francis Ford Coppola and Peter Bogdanovich, gained prominence. Coppola's *The Godfather* (1972) and *The Godfather, Part II* (1974), which were done on a grand scale, soon achieved legendary status in motion-picture history. Bogdanovich's *The Last Picture Show* (1971) offered a haunting image of a Texas hamlet during the 1950s, while *Paper Moon* (1973) presented a slick Bible salesman and a nimble-witted little girl who became his associate as they "worked" the Midwest during the 1930s.

STARS

During the 1960s and 1970s film stars were of a different kind from those of the preceding decades. On the whole, they disdained a life of glamour off the screen. They tried a wide variety of roles instead of being a "type" that a studio head and his publicity department had created. Such were top stars Paul Newman, Robert Redford, Jane Fonda, and Robert DeNiro.

MUSICALS

Hollywood made fewer musicals that were conceived and executed for the screen and turned more to the musical theater for material. By the end of the 1970s almost all the top hit musicals of Broadway had been adapted to the screen, including *Hello, Dolly!* (1969) and *Fiddler on the Roof* (1971). Many film critics believed that although the motion-picture industry gained a measure of security by screening an already established hit, it lost something in integral spontaneity.

COMEDIES

After about two decades of a relatively small output of comedies, most of them unremarkable, the genre burst forth with a new vigor in the 1970s. Hardly any topic was now considered too delicate for a blatantly comedic treatment. All this was due in large part to the talent of two filmmakers who wrote or co-wrote the screenplays for, directed and acted in, their productions: Mel Brooks and Woody Allen. *Blazing Saddles* (1974) by Brooks and *Annie Hall* (1977) by Allen were especially well-received efforts.

GANGSTER FILMS

The enthusiasm of the public for gangster films during the 1930s was spent soon after that decade. It was not until the late 1960s and the 1970s that the enthusiasm was revived by the appearance of three extraordinarily fine productions with new perceptions of the genre, particularly in presenting characters in well-rounded completeness and showing violence realistically: *Bonnie and Clyde* (1967), *The Godfather* (1972), and *The Godfather, Part II* (1974).

HORROR FILMS

Creatures of horror in both human and nonhuman form in *Rosemary's Baby* (1968) and *The Exorcist* (1973) were top box-office draws.

WESTERNS

Westerns began to appear that, except for the setting and the background of the characters, were so different from past westerns that the public had some difficulty recognizing them as being in the same category. No longer was it a simple matter of "good guys" against "bad guys"; it was a probing of individuals' motives. An excellent example of this development was *Butch Cassidy and the Sundance Kid* (1969), starring Paul Newman and Robert Redford, which was a breezy account of two appealingly personable outlaws.

WAR FILMS

Whereas the vast majority of war movies used to treat the United States as totally good and its enemies as totally bad, while romanticizing actual combat, the films of the 1970s were more balanced, most of them tending to condemn war itself and to present battle scenes in a gruesomely realistic manner. *Patton* (1970) was about World War II. *M∗A∗S∗H* (1970) depicted the conduct of an army field hospital staff that treated soldiers wounded in the Korean war. *The Deer Hunter* (1979) portrayed three young friends whose lives, as well as the lives of those they left behind, were affected by their military experience in the Vietnam war.

SCIENCE-FICTION FILMS

The exploration of space was a natural impetus to the making of a spate of science-fiction movies, and advanced technology enabled special-effects experts to make scenes that were wondrous to behold. The great science-fiction films of the period were striking testimony to the remarkably creative talent of their directors: *2001: A Space Odyssey* (1968), directed by Stanley Kubrick; *Star Wars* (1977), directed by George Lucas; and *Close Encounters of the Third Kind* (1977), directed by Steven Spielberg.

Sports

Beginning in the 1960s and throughout the 1970s two notable developments occurred in sports. First, after the long-standing policy of refusing to hire blacks was abandoned in the 1940s and 1950s, teams, particularly in football and basketball, were more and more dominated both in numbers and skills by black players. Second, women finally came into their own in professional athletics, especially in tennis.

BASEBALL

Despite the increasingly strong popularity of the other spectator sports, baseball retained its image as the national game. Two of the greatest batters in the history of the sport were Mickey Mantle and Louis (Hank) Aaron. In 1974 Aaron broke Babe Ruth's almost forty-year-old record of 714 home runs in regular-season major-league play. In 1975 Frank Robinson became the first black manager in major league baseball.

BOXING

If one person were to be chosen as the preeminent athlete of the period, it would certainly be the magnetic black boxer Muhammad Ali. (He was originally named Cassius Marcellus Clay Jr. but adopted a new name after becoming a Black Muslim.) Ali was the first person to win the heavyweight championship for a third time, doing so in 1978.

FOOTBALL

During the 1960s and 1970s professional football captured fans in a manner reminiscent of the sport's popularity in the 1920s. This was due in large part to the achievements of a number of extraordinarily able and charismatic coaches and players. The outstanding coach of the late 1960s was Vincent (Vince) Lombardi. He was the personification of tough-mindedness: "Winning isn't everything, it's the only thing!" was his announced philosophy. Among the most accomplished players of the period were John (Johnny) Unitas and Joseph (Joe) Namath.

BASKETBALL

Professional basketball reached the height of its popularity, with teams now increasingly dominated by black players who had earlier enjoyed highly successful college basketball careers. Oscar Robertson (called the "Big O") exerted a profound influence upon professional basketball with his brilliant technique. The seven-foot-one-inch-tall Wilton (Wilt) Chamberlain is regarded as the best offensive player of all time in professional basketball. About a half-inch taller than Chamberlain was Kareem Abdul-Jabbar (originally named Lew Alcindor, he assumed a new name after becoming a Black Muslim), who was consistently one of the leading scorers every season during the 1970s.

TENNIS

Held in high regard by tennis fans was James (Jimmy) Connors. In 1979, 1980, and 1981 John McEnroe won the United States men's singles championship, making him the first player since the extraordinary Bill Tilden of the 1920s to capture a national title three consecutive times. McEnroe's displays of hot temper during matches, usually in reaction to officials' decisions, earned him a reputation as the "bad boy" of tennis.

If there was one sport in which women came into their own it was professional tennis, with fans following the careers of female players as eagerly as they did those of male players. The two top women stars of the game were Billie Jean King and Chris Evert Lloyd.

GOLF

Foremost in professional golf were Arnold Palmer and Jack Nicklaus. Nicklaus is perhaps the greatest player in the history of professional golf. Between 1962 and 1980 he won the following titles: the Masters five times (thus becoming the first person ever to win it that many times), the United States Open four times, and the British Open three times.

Selected Readings

GENERAL WORKS:

Barnet, Richard. *The Lean Years* (1980)

Carroll, Peter. *It Seemed Like Nothing Happened: The Tragedy and Promise of America in the 1970s* (1982)

Dolan, Paul J., and Edward G. Quinn, eds. *The Sense of the 70s: A Rhetorical Reader* (1978)

Freedman, Leonard, ed. *Issues of the Seventies* (1970)

Hougan, Jim. *Decadence: Radical Nostalgia, Narcissism, and Decline in the 1970s* (1975)

SPECIAL STUDIES:

Bernstein, Carl, and Bob Woodward. *All the President's Men* (1974)

Bono, Philip, and Kenneth Gotland. *Frontiers of Space* (1976)

Brodie, Fawn. *Richard Nixon* (1981)

Calleo, Peter. *The Imperious Economy* (1982)

Carter, Jimmy. *Keeping the Faith* (1982)

————. *Why Not the Best?* (1975)

Dean, John. *Blind Ambition* (1976)

Deibel, Terry. *Presidents, Public Opinion, and Power: The Nixon, Carter, and Reagan Years* (1987)

Ford, Gerald. *A Time to Heal* (1979)

Goldfield, Michael. *The Decline of Organized Labor in the United States,* (1987)

Kalb, Marvin and Bernard. *Kissinger* (1974)

Kissinger, Henry. *The White House Years* (1979)

————. *Years of Upheaval* (1982)

Lukas, J. Anthony. *Nightmare: The Underside of the Nixon Years* (1976)

McCarthy, Mary. *The Mask of State: Watergate Portraits* (1974)

Mankiewicz, Frank. *Perfectly Clear: Nixon from Whittier to Watergate* (1973)

————. *U. S. v. Richard Nixon, The Final Crisis* (1975)

Mazlish, Bruce. *In Search of Nixon: A Psychohistorical Inquiry* (1972)

Michener, James A. *Sports in America* (1976)

Nixon, Richard. *RN: The Memoirs of Richard Nixon* (1978)

Panetta, Leon E., and Peter Gall. *Bring Us Together: The Nixon Team and the Civil Rights Retreat* (1971)

Pipes, Richard. *U.S.-Soviet Relations in the Era of Détente* (1981)

Porter, Gareth. *A Peace Denied: The United States, Vietnam, and the Paris Agreement* (1976)

Quandt, William. *Camp David* (1986)

Ramazani, R. K. *The U.S. and Iran* (1982)

Rather, Dan, and Gary Gates. *The Palace Guard* (1974)

Reeves, Richard. *A Ford, Not a Lincoln* (1975)

Reichley, A. James. *Conservatives in an Age of Change: The Nixon and Ford Administrations* (1981)

Safire, William. *Before the Fall* (1975)

Schlesinger, Arthur M., Jr. *The Imperial Presidency* (1973)

Schrags, Peter. *Test of Loyalty: Daniel Ellsberg and the Rituals of Secret Government* (1974)

Sklar, Robert. *Movie-Made America: A Cultural History of American Movies* (1975)

terHorst, J. F. *Gerald Ford and the Future of the Presidency* (1974)

Tillman, Seth. *The United States in the Middle East* (1982)

Warner, Sam Bass, Jr. *The Urban Wilderness: A History of the American City* (1972)

White, Theodore H. *Breach of Faith* (1975)

————. *The Making of the President, 1968* (1969)

————. *The Making of the President, 1972* (1973)

Wills, Garry. *Nixon Agonistes* (1971)

14

The Triumph of Conservatism

1978 Congress passes legislation making the legal mandatory retirement age seventy

VCR introduced

1980 Reagan elected president

1981 Reagan fires striking air-traffic controllers

1983 241 marines in Lebanon killed in terrorist attack

United States invades Grenada

1984 Reagan reelected president

1985 Gramm-Rudman-Hollings Act

1986 United States bombs Libya

Iran-Contra scandal revealed

1987 Combined Congressional Committees conducts televised hearings on Iran-Contra scandal

Stock market plunge

Senate rejects Bork nomination to Supreme Court

United States and Soviet Union sign I.N.F. treaty

1988 Bush elected president

1989 United States invades Panama

1990 Senate confirms Souter appointment to Supreme Court

Burns, *The Civil War*

1991 Persian Gulf War

Throughout his campaign in the election of 1980 the unabashedly conservative Republican presidential candidate Ronald Reagan assailed the belief that had remained virtually an article of faith since Franklin D. Roosevelt's New Deal: that the federal government was responsible for the social welfare of its citizens. The election of Reagan to the presidency marked the beginning of a new direction in America. Reagan wanted—and was able to some degree—to turn the nation away from "big" government to one embracing the previous laissez-faire system. The major domestic issue faced by the Reagan administration was the economy, which was wracked simultaneously by both inflation and recession. During the last two years of Reagan's second term the nation was gripped by the Iran-Contra affair, the worst political scandal since Watergate. As a result, the president's leadership ability and his popularity were quickly diminished.

Unlike his immediate predecessor in the White House, whom he had served as vice-president with scrupulous loyalty, George Bush was no ideologue. Although embracing a set of basically conservative principles, Bush was a political, economic, and social moderate, who established a reputation as a president with a temperate approach to most issues, both domestic and foreign. As with the Reagan administration, the most serious domestic matter that the Bush administration had to contend with was the economy. However, with the Bush administration, focus was on a determined attempt, in cooperation with a Democratic-controlled Congress, to reduce the huge budget deficit by a prudent combination of increased taxation and decreased spending.

In foreign affairs the Reagan administration, while not completely abandoning the position of the three preceding administrations of pursuing détente with the Soviet Union, showed an inclination to take a harder line in its dealings with that nation. Eventually Reagan restrained his militancy. The Bush administration was a beneficiary of both the Soviet Union's initiatives to end the Cold War and the subsequent disintegration of the Soviet-controlled communist bloc of nations. In other parts of the world, both the Reagan and Bush administrations had to contend with continuous turmoil in the Middle East, which ultimately turned into war in the Persian Gulf region, as well as dictatorial regimes and political coups in Central America and the Caribbean.

REAGAN AND A COUNTER-REVOLUTIONARY AGENDA

Reagan launched a frontal assault on federal laws implementing the many and expensive social welfare programs passed during the previous two decades, especially those of Johnson's Great Society. He sought to shift responsibility for overseeing the remaining social welfare programs from the federal government to the state and local governments. Further, he forcefully criticized the power and activities of the federal regulatory agencies. On important domestic issues, Reagan racked up a record of hard-line thinking and action on civil rights, organized labor, and a host of social issues, including abortion, consumerism, and environmentalism. As for the rampant inflation and recession, the president decided it was the former that needed to be cured first.

Election of 1980

In his attempt to win a second term Jimmy Carter was burdened with a record that could be easily assailed. On the domestic scene, the nation was experiencing an economy beset by high rates of inflation and unemployment and by a severe energy crisis. In foreign affairs the nation was continuing to grapple agonizingly with the long-standing Iranian hostage crisis. In addition, Carter was opposed by a Republican candidate of compelling attractiveness who conducted his campaign with notable finesse.

DEMOCRATS

Carter decided to seek election to a second term. His principal rival in the Democratic caucuses and primaries was liberal senator Edward M. "Ted" Kennedy of Massachusetts. Initially Kennedy did well. But his quest for the Democratic nomination for president faltered with the recalling of his involvement in an accident at Chappaquidick, Massachusetts, in 1969. A young woman passenger in an automobile driven by the senator drowned when it plunged off a bridge. The charge raised at the time of the accident that Kennedy possessed a flawed character, was revived with stunning effect.

Carter chose not to make personal appearances in the various primaries, asserting that he could not leave Washington, D.C., as he was needed there during the nagging Iranian hostage crisis. Nevertheless, he emerged victorious. At the convention Kennedy released his delegates before the balloting began. With virtually no opposition, Carter was easily renominated on the first ballot. So too was Vice-President Walter F. Mondale.

REPUBLICANS

An early strong contender in the Republican caucuses and primaries was the moderate George Herbert Walker Bush, who had served in the federal government in various capacities, including those of representative from Texas, ambassador to the United Nations, and director of the CIA. But after a faltering performance at the very beginning, former governor Ronald Wilson Reagan of California won repeated victories in his party's primary elections. As expected, at the Republican national convention he captured the presidential nomination on the first ballot. In a carefully crafted plan to gain support from moderate Republicans, who were unhappy about the choice of a standard-bearer who was the idol of the party's right wing, Reagan attempted to convince former president Ford to accept second place on the ticket. Ford showed interest. However, some of Reagan's closest advisors became uneasy, feeling that Ford had demanded too much power and authority in the decision making. Thus the deal fell through. Reagan then requested that the delegates at the convention choose Bush as his running mate, which they did promptly and enthusiastically.

INDEPENDENTS

Members of the newly formed National Unity party, popularly called Independents, nominated former Republican representative John M. Anderson of Illinois for president. He selected as his running mate former Democratic governor Patrick J. Lucey of Wisconsin. The platform adopted was generally conservative on fiscal matters, calling for a modest reduction in taxation and spending, and somewhat liberal on social issues and foreign policy, advocating further attempts at achieving détente with the communist nations.

THE CAMPAIGN

The Democrats attempted to make Reagan the central issue in the campaign. They depicted the Republican candidate as woefully unknowledgeable on a host of issues, due largely, it was implied, to the effects of advanced age. Further, they characterized Reagan as insensitive to the cause of civil rights and as irresponsibly advocating a reversal of the policy of détente with the Soviet Union.

But Reagan and his surrogates succeeded in making Carter's presidential record the focus of the campaign. Reagan charged that his opponent had pursued a domestic policy that resulted in high inflation and a high unemployment rate and conducted a foreign policy that made the United States appear weak and vacillating, most prominently in the Iranian hostage crisis.

Anderson had a modest organization and limited campaign funds. But the intellectually nimble and highly articulate third-party candidate hoped to attract to his cause both Democrats and Republicans who were disaffected with the political philosophy and past performance of the major parties' standard-bearers. However, he made little headway during the campaign.

In the single televised debate between the two leading candidates, Reagan successfully deflected Carter's attack on his ultraconservative political philosophy and past record. The Republican candidate was most effective with the viewers when he faced the camera directly and asked the estimated 95 million viewers, "Are you better off than you were four years ago?" Most political commentators concluded that Reagan won the debate handily.

REAGAN'S LANDSLIDE VICTORY

In popular votes, Reagan received 43,899,000; Carter, 35,481,000; Anderson, 5,719,000. Reagan carried 489 electoral votes to Carter's 49, while Anderson got none. Carter won only six regionally scattered states, including his home state of Georgia, and the District of Columbia. Reagan swept to victory by demolishing the Democratic coalition of the New Deal period that Carter had previously been able to hold together. Almost half of organized labor, approximately one-third of Hispanic Americans, a significant minority of Jews, a vast majority of Roman Catholics, and virtually all of the solid South voted for Reagan. Blacks alone from that coalition held firm for the Democratic candidate.

The magnitude of Reagan's victory carried over to the congressional vote. The Republicans won command of the Senate for the first time in more than a quarter century, gaining twelve seats and achieving a fifty-three-vote majority in that body. They also gained thirty-three seats in the still Democratically controlled House of Representatives.

The Reagan Administration

Unlike many of his predecessors, who tried to realize a large number of objectives, Reagan managed his administration so as to achieve just a few things with bulldog tenacity, such as lowering taxes and raising the defense budget. A carefully chosen White House staff skillfully arranged his workday to glean the most from positive media coverage, particularly that of the television evening news programs, in order to issue a flow of positive symbols and images of his presidency. His assistants also saw to it that he was able to distance himself from the sorts of crises that would normally touch a nation's chief executive, earning him the nickname of the Teflon president. (Teflon is the trademark name of a chemical coating used on cooking utensils to prevent sticking.)

THE PRESIDENT

At age sixty-nine Reagan was the oldest person ever elected to the nation's highest office. He was amiable and usually showed notable self-confidence. He was viewed as a hands-off administrator, one who chose capable associates and gave them wide latitude to do a job without his frequent checking up. He was the opposite of a workaholic, regularly leaving his desk in the Oval Office early enough to spend the evening in rest and recreation. Another nickname given him was the Great Communicator, derived from a skill that was honed from long years as a motion-picture actor and television personality.

THE CABINET

The Reagan cabinet, in keeping with the president's governmental and political philosophy, was a model of conservatism. Former economics professor and corporate executive George P. Shultz became the secretary of state (following Alexander M. Haig Jr.'s brief stint in that post). Heading the Department of Defense was another corporate executive, the hard-driving Caspar W. Weinberger. At the beginning of Reagan's second term the capable, energetic, and frequently abrasive secretary of the treasury Donald T. Regan and the equally capable, energetic, and usually affable White House chief of staff James A. Baker III together simply informed the president that they had decided to switch jobs. The president immediately acquiesced. Of all the members of the cabinet, Reagan's closest friend was Edwin Meese III, who served as the second attorney general. Meese received much criticism for his ultraconservative stance on many legal matters and for his less than firm control of his department. Reagan also appointed as his first secretary of the interior James Watt, who systematically saw to it that enforcement of existing regulations on environmental matters would be less than strictly enforced. Lauro F. Cavazos became the first Hispanic-American cabinet member in the nation's history when he was appointed during the last year of Reagan's tenure to be his secretary of education.

Battling "Big" Government

Reagan had a stated mission: to reverse what he conceived to be a process in existence since the New Deal, by which the federal government increasingly supervised and controlled every facet of life in the United States. At times the new president sounded as if he actually considered the very government he headed to be an enemy to be vanquished. In his inaugural address Reagan said that "government is not the solution to our problems; government is the problem." Soon after entering the White House he vowed to the American people that he would "get the government off our backs."

SHIFTING RESPONSIBILITY TO STATE AND LOCAL GOVERNMENTS

In order to realize his goal, Reagan advocated that except for such obviously federal governmental matters as foreign policy and national defense, the state and local governments should assume most of the authority and responsibility for matters heretofore handled by the federal government. Reagan's critics charged that his proposals would merely transfer the costly, but necessary, programs from one level of government to another, relieving the fiscal pressure upon the government over which he presided.

DEREGULATION

The Reagan administration asserted that the methods of the federal government regulating agencies were for the most part heavy-handed, wasteful of time and energy, and exceedingly costly. In addition, it maintained that the regulations imposed upon private businesses stifled initiative and consequently development. Reagan, with determination exhibited both in the signals to incumbent administrators and in his appointment of new administrators who shared his philosophy, saw to the reduction in the efficacy of regulation. The policy of deregulation could be observed in agencies such as the Consumer Product Safety Commission, the Environmental Protection Agency (EPA), and the Occupational Safety and Health Administration (OSHA), where high-level administrators and middle-level supervisors made certain that the rules were laxly enforced.

CUTTING SOCIAL PROGRAMS

Aided by a fairly large bloc of conservatives in Congress, particularly in the Senate, the Reagan administration embarked on a successful course of action to reduce federal support—moral and financial—to a host of social program: for example, people receiving hospital or nursing care under Medicare had to pay more for it, people getting unemployment compensation had to accept less, and people receiving food stamps had to live on decreased allotments.

Conservative Stance on Domestic Issues

Reagan was vigorously conservative in his views on the whole range of critical domestic issues that faced the nation during the 1980s. Large numbers of Americans held the same views as he did, with hopes that as president he could translate those views into results.

CIVIL RIGHTS

Black Americans and other minority groups complained that the Reagan administration's philosophy and action on civil rights were unsympathetic to such a degree that decades of progress in the struggle for equality of public treatment were being undone. Reagan maintained unequivocally that he was in no way biased against anyone because of race, religion, ethnic background, or national origin. And he was ready with a host of anecdotal incidents from his personal and professional life substantiating this. Americans were ready to accept this.

But the civil rights record of his presidency was clearly and constantly unhelpful. The president belatedly came to give lukewarm backing to an amendment to the Voting Rights Act of 1965 passed overwhelmingly by Congress. The amendment extended the highly successful use of federal governmental power to ensure nondiscriminatory procedures in all elections. Reagan supported the Justice Department in its efforts to undo several affirmative-action hiring programs that had given employment preference to individuals based on race, ethnicity, or gender. His effort was thwarted by a ruling of the Supreme Court in 1986 that upheld the practice of affirmative action to redress past discrimination against blacks and other minorities. In the area of education, the president was opposed to the busing of students to achieve racial balance. He instructed the Internal Revenue Service to discontinue the barring of tax exemptions for private schools that discriminated against black applicants for admission. The latter action was subsequently invalidated by a Supreme Court ruling. Finally, Reagan appointees to the Civil Rights Commission were individuals whose philosophy and record pertaining to the protection of civil rights were undistinguished.

LABOR

Soon after taking office Reagan showed his attitude toward organized labor. In mid-1981 members of the Professional Airline Traffic Controller Organization (PATCO), a union of federal government employees, struck for, among other things, higher wages and shorter hours, admittedly defying a government prohibition of the right to walk off the job. After a back-to-work order was issued by a federal judge three days after the job action started, Reagan's response was swift and, according to critics, brutal. He fired all air-traffic controllers still on strike, revoked the federal government's certification of the union, and directed the Department of Transportation to begin to hire and train air-traffic controller recruits to fill the approximately 12,000 positions now vacant.

ABORTION

Reagan was an outspoken opponent of abortion and gave generous and frequent encouragement to the membership of anti-abortion organizations. He stated his unequivocal hope that the Supreme Court would reverse itself and overturn the decision in the *Roe* v. *Wade* case of 1973, which permitted abortion on demand.

EDUCATION

Reagan thought that the federal government should decrease its role in education and let the state and local governments have greater autonomy than in the recent past. He declared his intention either to abolish the recently established Department of Education and allow some of its responsibilities to be absorbed by other federal agencies or to replace the department with an agency at less than cabinet level. Congress, however, was not convinced of the feasibility of this and did not pass the requisite legislation.

PRAYER IN THE PUBLIC SCHOOLS

Not only did Reagan extol the virtue of prayer in the public schools but he also announced his preference for the spoken rather than silent type. After Congress failed to pass legislation providing for either one, he made a plea for an amendment to the Constitution that would permit group prayer in the public elementary and secondary schools. The Moral Majority, an influential, politically oriented, ultraconservative religious organization founded in 1979 and headed by Baptist minister Jerry Falwell, received lavish presidential support in its crusade for public-school prayer, as well as in its opposition to abortion and pornography.

GUN CONTROL

On March 30, 1981, as he was leaving a hotel in Washington, D.C., where he had delivered an address, Reagan was shot in the side and severely wounded. Also shot in the attack were two security officers and the president's press secretary, James Brady, who received grave head wounds. Charged with the attacks was John W. Hinckley Jr., who was subsequently found not guilty by reason of insanity and was placed in an institution for the mentally ill. Although the deranged young man used a cheap handgun (commonly called a "Saturday night special") that he had bought without difficulty, the president was unalterably opposed to comprehensive legislation limiting the purchase and use of guns. However, Brady's wife, Sarah, and ultimately Brady himself, became leading advocates of gun-control legislation.

CONSUMERISM

Reagan was severely criticized by consumer groups for his lack of sympathy for their cause. According to consumerists, the president was hostile to the establishment of a federal consumer-protection agency and lax in overseeing the enforcement of already existing consumer-oriented laws.

ENVIRONMENTALISM

The environmentalists found even greater fault with Reagan than did the consumerists. Environmental groups pointed out that the president had assumed an anti-environmental position on the use of land for industrial purposes and on the production of nuclear energy. They also noted he had backed down on such specific issues as water pollution and auto-emission standards.

The Economy

Undoubtedly the most serious domestic concern that the Reagan administration had to contend with was the economy. The nation was suffering from a stagnant economy and continuing inflation.

SUPPLY-SIDE ECONOMICS

To revitalize the economy and to combat inflation the Reagan administration adopted a plan based on the theory of supply-side economics. This theory maintained that lowering taxes would help the growth of business and thus produce a greater and more varied amount of goods at competitive prices, prompting increased buying on the part of consumers and thereby stimulating the total economy. This approach to recovery was soon called Reaganomics.

INFLATION

At the beginning of 1981 the rate of inflation reached 13.2 percent. The devastating effect of such inflation produced the worst economic crisis since the Great Depression of the 1930s. Particularly hurt were the elderly trying to get along on small incomes, with increases in the cost of living far outstripping their means to pay. In order to combat inflation, President Reagan advocated such measures as a sharp reduction in government spending, except for defense expenditures, and a decrease in taxes. But at the same time that he assaulted as inflationary a plan of government spending to create jobs for many of the almost 8 million workers (more than 7 percent of the total labor force) who were unemployed, he approved certain programs that either directly or indirectly raised prices. For example, his energy conservation plan was based in part on the imposition of higher costs for petroleum products.

Early in 1981 the president recommended to Congress an anti-inflation program that included a sharp reduction in government spending, which affected many long-standing social programs, and a substantial lowering of the personal income tax. Initially, a majority of the members in both houses of Congress, including virtually all Republicans and a large number of conservative Democrats, supported his plan. By the fall of 1982 the inflation rate had decreased to 6.7 percent. But high unemployment continued; over 11 million people (more than 10 percent of the total labor force) were out of work, making for the highest rate of joblessness since the Great Depression.

TAX REDUCTIONS

In mid-1981 Reagan won a tremendous victory when Congress passed the tax-cut bill he had recommended. The legislation provided for a decrease in personal income taxes across the board for all income groups: a 5 percent reduction in 1981, an additional 10 percent in 1982, and another 10 percent in 1983. At first taxpayers were ecstatic, but it soon became apparent that the new rates greatly favored the high-income taxpayer.

In 1986 Congress passed the Tax Reform Act, providing for the first substantial revamping of the federal income tax system in more than forty years. The act replaced the tax-rate schedule with just three separate and distinct rates on individuals (and in so doing, decreased the financial load for most payers), exempted from any tax payments millions of families with low incomes, reduced the top tax rate for corporations by thirteen percentage points, and eliminated for both individuals and businesses a wide range of tax deductions.

THE GRAMM-RUDMAN-HOLLINGS ACT

At the same time that the deep reductions in taxes were being implemented, there was a monumental rise in military expenditures, totalling approximately $1.5 trillion during the first term. The Reagan administration vigorously advocated a considerable increase in defense spending in order to strengthen the nation's security in an unsettled world. With a lack of sufficient revenue (resulting from the tax reductions) to fully pay for the spiraling costs of military personnel and equipment, the national debt rose in runaway fashion. Between 1981 and 1986 the debt had doubled, from $1 trillion to $2 trillion. In order to avert an eventual fiscal catastrophe the federal government deemed it essential to stop spending more money than it took in. In 1985 Congress passed an act sponsored by Republican representative Phil Gramm of Texas, Republican senator Warren B. Rudman of New Hampshire, and Democratic senator Ernest F. Hollings of North Carolina. The Gramm-Rudman-Hollings Act (in referring to the law the third legislator's name was often omitted) provided for the revision of procedures to be used in the federal budget system; prescribed trimming many government programs, wherever it was deemed necessary, in order to gradually get rid of the huge national debt; and ordered reduction of the budget deficit to zero by 1991.

The Energy Crisis

As had been the case with the Ford and Carter administrations, the Reagan administration had to deal with a serious energy crisis.

DEREGULATION

Believing that the federal government should decrease its participation in the field of energy and allow the American petroleum and natural-gas companies to have greater latitude, President Reagan announced his desire to dismantle the Department of Energy. Its functions would be performed by other agencies of the federal government. To help alleviate the energy crisis, in 1981 the president by executive decree removed government regulations on the price of domestic oil and natural gas, thus permitting a rise in the cost of both. His purpose was twofold: first, to reduce the consumption of those two high-demand commodities; second, to stimulate a search for additional energy sources by the American oil and natural-gas firms. Opposed to the president's plan, yet unable to agree among themselves, the Democratic leaders in Congress, the lower house of which their party controlled, failed to formulate an acceptable counterproposal.

CONSERVATION AND ALTERNATIVE SOURCES

There was much discussion about but little meaningful effort made toward becoming less dependent on petroleum through conservation and the use of alternative energy sources: electric batteries for running automobiles; the "old standby" of coal (there was a three-hundred-year supply), with the problem of pollutants released into the atmosphere; wind power; solar power; and nuclear power, with the dangers of harmful substances escaping from nuclear plants, explosions of nuclear reactors, and the safe disposal of radioactive waste.

Election of 1984

Having become the most popular president since Franklin D. Roosevelt, Reagan sought reelection and appeared certain of success.

DEMOCRATS

The leading contenders for the Democratic presidential nomination were former vice-president Walter F. Mondale; Senator Gary Hart of Colorado; and the Reverend Jesse L. Jackson, a Chicago-based civil rights activist. Jackson's quest for the presidency brought a new and exciting element to national politics. He was the first black American to make a full-scale bid for the presidential nomination of a major political party. With spellbinding oratory he presented his ultraliberal domestic and foreign policy views. He worked energetically to rally what he termed the "rainbow coalition" of the various racial and ethnic groups, many members of which were economically and socially disadvantaged. Despite his limited appeal to most traditional Democrats, Jackson won almost 20 percent of the primary votes cast. Mondale, having secured the commitment of an overwhelming majority of the delegates to the Democratic national convention by the time it began its proceedings, easily won the nomination.

The Democratic party produced another historic advance in American politics. Upon Mondale's request, the delegates to the convention selected Representative Geraldine Ferraro of New York for second place on the ticket, marking the first time that a major political party chose a woman as its candidate for vice-president. Ferraro's selection was viewed by many political analysts as a bold gamble to attract enough women voters to thwart the reelection plans of an immensely popular president.

REPUBLICANS

Proceedings took place as expected at the Republican national convention. President Reagan and Vice-President Bush were renominated virtually without opposition.

THE CAMPAIGN

Mondale assaulted Reagan's economic policy as one that benefited the wealthy and harmed both the middle class and the poor. As for Reagan's record on foreign affairs, Mondale charged that it showed neither advances in extending détente with the communist nations nor significant developments in achieving political stability in the Middle East and Central America.

Reagan's response was that the people were better off economically than when he assumed the presidency four years earlier and that the nation was not involved in armed conflict anywhere in the world. Besides, the vast majority of the American people were simply "taken" with their president, who exuded geniality and good humor and could soothe away anxiety with mellifluously uttered phrases about the newfound opportunities he foresaw for the nation in the future. Probably the single most emotional issue of the campaign was taxation. The differing positions of the candidates were clear-cut. Mondale acknowledged that if elected he would feel compelled to recommend an increase in taxes to reduce the huge budget deficit. Reagan said there would be a tax increase only "over [his] dead body." Of the two televised debates held between the presidential candidates, political analysts generally concluded that Mondale won the first and Reagan the second.

REAGAN'S LANDSLIDE VICTORY

The balloting resulted in a second victory for Reagan; his success was even greater than that of four years earlier. He received 54,451,000 popular votes to Mondale's 37,565,000. Reagan was reelected by the fifth largest popular vote in the history of the nation, receiving 58.9 percent of the total vote cast. He carried every state except his opponent's home state of Minnesota and he lost the District of Columbia, thus capturing 525 out of 538 electoral votes, making it the greatest triumph in the electoral college since Franklin D. Roosevelt achieved his stunning victory in 1936. As he had in his landslide victory of four years earlier, Reagan attained success by adding to the traditional Republican backing a large percentage of most of the elements of the decades-old Democratic coalition. But the size of Reagan's victory was not reflected in the congressional vote. In fact the Republican party lost two seats in the Senate, although it retained a slim majority in that body. As for the House of Representatives, although the Republican party increased its membership by fourteen seats it remained very much in the minority.

The Iran-Contra Scandal

The worst crisis of the Reagan presidency began about halfway through the second term. It was disclosed that the administration had secretly sold arms to Iran in violation of both United States law and stated government policy. It had diverted a portion of the money received to aid rebels called Contras in their opposition to the leftist regime in Nicaragua, illegally circumventing legislation prohibiting American assistance to the Nicaraguan insurgents.

THE REVELATIONS

In November 1986, a Lebanese journal reported that six months earlier former national security advisor Robert C. McFarlane had gone on a secret diplomatic mission to Iran, accompanying a shipment of military equipment to the virulently anti-American government of that nation. After denying the report, Reagan finally conceded that for the past year and a half the United States had been shipping arms in order to cultivate relationship with moderate elements in Iran that could eventually lead to a bettering of relations. Soon it became clear that another reason was to gain the government's assistance in securing the release of seven Americans being held hostage by Iranian-backed Shiite militants in Lebanon. Reagan announced that the arms shipment would stop in order to dispel the "widespread but mistaken" view that his administration had been exchanging arms for hostages.

The most startling revelation of the affair then erupted. Marine Corps lieutenant colonel Oliver L. North, a member of the staff of the National Security Council who was part of that organization's team charged with developing and executing the Iranian arms deal, had been diverting millions of dollars toward payment for equipment for the Nicaraguan Contras, despite congressional legislation prohibiting such assistance from the United States. President Reagan quickly dismissed North and his superior, the national security advisor, Vice-Admiral John M. Poindexter. President Reagan would continue to defend his administration's secret dealings with Iran, yet maintained he had no knowledge of the diversion of money from the arms sales to help the Contras.

THE TOWER COMMISSION

In December 1986, in an effort to deflect criticism, Reagan appointed a three-person commission to investigate the activities of the National Security Council staff. Known as the Tower Commission after its chairperson, former Republican senator John G. Tower of Texas, the panel issued a report three months later that characterized the president as a casual administrator who was not fully attentive to his duties and who had failed, in particular, to sufficiently supervise members of his staff, many of whom engaged in a course of conduct that ill-served the president and the nation itself. As for the policies pursued by the administration relating to Iran and the Contras, the Tower Commission described them as being underpinned by deception and disregard for the laws of the nation.

THE COMBINED CONGRESSIONAL
SELECT INVESTIGATING COMMITTEES HEARINGS

In December 1986, both the Senate and the House of Representatives appointed select committees to investigate the Iran-Contra affair. During May–August 1987, the combined committees, chaired by Democratic senator Daniel K. Inouye of Hawaii, conducted televised hearings. Among the witnesses who appeared were McFarlane, North, and Poindexter. McFarlane testified that Reagan had frequently been apprised of the arms sales progress and had approved measures suggested for freeing the hostages in

Lebanon. As for the Contras, McFarlane asserted that after Congress had ended financial assistance to the Contras, Reagan had instructed certain staff members of the National Security Council to do anything that was within their power to ensure that the Contras remained a viable insurgent group.

North testified that he had never informed the president about any specific aspects of the dealings with Iran and had never informed him of sending military equipment to the Contras. But North said that he had always assumed that the president was aware of what he was doing and gave his approval of such activities. As for funding the Contras, North declared that he had sent by way of Poindexter five memorandums to Reagan requesting permission to divert profits from the arms sales to the Nicaraguan rebels. North hinted that William J. Casey, the recently deceased former director of the CIA, had supplied the creative inspiration and direction for the project of funding the Contras with some of the profits from the Iranian arms sales.

Poindexter testified that he had kept the president uninformed about precise elements of the Iranian negotiations and that it was he himself who had authorized the diversion of money, never getting Reagan's approval nor briefing him about it. North and Poindexter declared further that they were convinced that they had pursued courses of action that were in keeping with the president's desires and that would ultimately benefit the United States and its allies but that they had purposely misled members of Congress about their deeds.

In November 1987, the combined congressional select committees issued a 690-page report. It was skeptical of the plausibility of the testimonies of both North and Poindexter. The committee unsparingly took Reagan to task. It concluded that Reagan had failed to implement faithfully the congressional legislation pertaining to dealings with Iran and the Contras and that he had not properly supervised his staff. Thus Reagan was to be held fully responsible for the questionable, even illegal acts committed by those who served him. In short, the report stated that if the president of the United States had not known what was going on while he was in charge, he should have.

THE INDEPENDENT COUNSEL

Upon Reagan's request, a federal court in December 1986 appointed former federal judge Lawrence E. Walsh as an independent counsel (special prosecutor) to look into charges that members of the president's staff had knowingly broken the law in implementing American foreign policy on Iran and the Contras. In turn, a federal grand jury, in March 1988, indicted four key individuals, including North and Poindexter. In 1989 North was found guilty of three counts: obstructing a congressional investigation, falsifying and destroying National Security Council documents, and illegally accepting a gift. He was sentenced to two years' probation and 1,200 hours of community service and fined $150,000. He appealed his conviction, and a year later a higher court reversed it in part and ordered a review of his entire case. Poindexter was found guilty and sentenced to six months in prison but appealed the decision of the court.

Supreme Court Appointments

Reagan's most enduring legacy may well be to the federal judiciary. By the time he left office, he had appointed more than half of the 761 members of the federal courts. Most were white males with a conservative judicial philosophy, large numbers of whom were quite young and thus expected to have many years of service ahead of them.

INITIAL SELECTIONS

Reagan's first appointment to the Supreme Court in 1981 was an Arizona state judge, Sandra Day O'Connor. Although she was a conservative, the president received praise from many segments of society, even liberal Americans, because O'Connor became the first woman in the nation's history to serve on the Supreme Court. In 1986, Reagan named Associate Justice William H. Rehnquist, the most conservative member of the Court, to succeed the retiring Warren E. Burger as chief justice. The elevation of Rehnquist left a vacancy that the president immediately filled with a brilliant conservative federal judge, Antonin Scalia, who became the first person of Italian background to serve on the highest court.

THE BORK NOMINATION AND AFTERMATH

The president's next nomination to the Court, in 1986, was Robert H. Bork, an ultraconservative former professor of law and federal judge. The nomination was vociferously opposed by liberal and moderate groups that characterized Bork not as merely a conservative but as a frighteningly right-wing extremist. The Senate, by a vote of fifty-eight to forty-two, refused to confirm him. Another conservative federal judge, Douglas H. Ginzburg, was then nominated, but days after admitting that he had used marijuana not only as a college student but also as a law professor, he requested that his name be withdrawn. Reagan then nominated conservative federal judge Anthony Kennedy of California, who was confirmed by a unanimous vote of the Senate in 1988. The Supreme Court, which had begun to lose its liberal stamp with the Nixon appointments, achieved with the Reagan appointments a solid conservative majority of 5 to 4.

The Stock-Market Plunge

In 1987 the stock market plunged. But unlike the stock-market crash of 1929, it took place within an economy that was performing briskly and thus did not become the first step toward depression.

FRENZIED ACTIVITY

For a number of weeks beginning in late August 1987, the prices of securities on the New York stock market gradually declined. Then on October 19 the stock market plummeted a startling 508 points. On that day approximately 600 million shares were traded and more than $500 billion in the market value of listed stocks were wiped out. The debacle set a record as the worst day by far in the history of the New York Stock Exchange.

BASIC CAUSE

Financial experts generally agreed that the collapse was due largely to program trading, in which major traders on the New York Stock Exchange bought and sold huge blocks of securities in a matter of seconds, based on computer analysis of even the smallest differences between current and projected future prices of securities.

BUSH AND A MODERATE APPROACH

As vice-president to Ronald Reagan for eight years, George Bush exhibited an impeccable loyalty to the chief executive. When he was elected president, Bush pursued his own management methodology and political philosophy. Bush would be a "hands-on" administrator. Despite repeated affirmations of allegiance to the nation's conservative agenda, Bush was in reality a political, economic, and social moderate. From the very beginning his presidency would be known for its temperate approach. In addition, he was a pragmatist. Unwilling ever to become a captive to a particular ideology in the conduct of either domestic matters or foreign affairs, he made it quite clear to allies and adversaries alike that he was ready to accommodate himself to the situation at hand whenever he felt it was necessary to do so.

Election of 1988

George Bush became the first incumbent vice-president to be elected to the nation's highest office since Martin Van Buren in 1836. His achievement was due in large part to waging one of the most negative campaigns in the history of American national politics.

DEMOCRATS

A particularly spirited, at times quite heated, competition prevailed in the Democratic caucuses and primaries. The leading aspirants to the presidential nomination were former senator Gary Hart of Colorado; senators Joseph R. Biden Jr. of Delaware, Albert Gore Jr. of Tennessee, and Paul

Simon of Illinois; Representative Richard A. Gephardt of Missouri; Governor Michael S. Dukakis of Massachusetts; former governor Bruce E. Babbitt of Arizona; and the Reverend Jesse Jackson. In the early stages Hart showed the greatest momentum, but his candidacy was ended by extensive media coverage of his extramarital relationship with a young woman. Other candidates were eliminated with low percentages of primary election votes, leaving the field to Dukakis and Jackson. Despite the ultraliberal Jackson's formidable presence, Dukakis finally emerged the victor in the primaries and was nominated for president on the first ballot by the Democratic national convention. The matter of second place on the ticket proved to be more difficult. Jackson stated unequivocally that he wanted to become the vice-presidential candidate of his party. But there was concern that, as a black American with ultraliberal views, he would cause conservative members of the party to desert the Democratic ticket. Thus the delegates, acting upon Dukakis's cautious recommendation, chose conservative senator Lloyd Bentsen of Texas for vice-president.

REPUBLICANS

The Republican party caucuses and primaries were wide open. Candidates included Vice-President George Bush; Senator Robert J. Dole of Kansas; Representative Jack F. Kemp of New York; former governor Pierre S. "Pete" du Pont IV of Delaware; former secretary of state Alexander M. Haig Jr.; and the television evangelist Reverend Marion "Pat" Robertson. Bush eventually pulled ahead of the others and received enough delegate commitments to be assured of the nomination at the Republican national convention. For vice-president, Bush tapped the ultraconservative Senator J. Danforth "Dan" Quayle of Indiana. Many criticized Bush for passing over several prominent, harder-working "heavyweights" among the Republicans in the Senate. Furthermore, it was made known that during the Vietnam war Quayle had joined the national guard in order to avoid being drafted.

THE CAMPAIGN

Polls conducted at the beginning of the campaign showed that the voters preferred Dukakis to Bush by about a 20-percent margin. Dukakis was viewed as a serious-minded and highly competent governor under whose leadership his state had gained a new economic vigor. Bush was considered by many to be a lackluster and somewhat ineffectual public official who owed his rise to national prominence to a series of appointments by various Republican administrations. But Dukakis's lead quickly and steadily dissolved. The reason, political commentators universally agreed, was the overwhelming influence of negative campaigning. Rather than focus on significant domestic and foreign policy issues facing the American people, the race deteriorated into an extensive use of negative campaigning, in which each candidate attacked his opponent's record, freely using exaggerations, half-truths, innuendos, and omissions. The Republican candidate's campaign managers and television consultants vastly outmaneuvered and outperformed their Democratic counterparts. The Republicans succeeded in characterizing Dukakis as a coddler of criminals, too dangerously liberal for the nation's good, and unpatriotic. Many Democratic voters concluded that Dukakis and his advisors bungled by not responding promptly to the distortions of their candidate's ideology, positions on the issues, and public record. In the two televised debates Dukakis was judged to have been so "wooden" that it worked to his great disadvantage with the voters. During the last few weeks before the election the main feature in Bush's stump speeches was his promise of "no new taxes!" with the admonition to doubters: "Read my lips." As the campaign drew to a close, the polls showed that Bush would be a certain and easy winner.

BUSH'S VICTORY

Bush polled 47,946,000 popular votes to Dukakis's 41,016,000 and received 426 electoral votes to Dukakis's 112. Bush captured all of New England except for his opponent's home state of Massachusetts, all of the large industrial states of the Northeast except New York, all of the border states except West Virginia, the entire South, and most of the Midwest and far West, totaling forty states in all. Added to Dukakis's ten states was the District of Columbia. Despite Bush's victory, the Democrats maintained their control both of the Senate, with a 55 to 45 majority, and of the House of Representatives, with a 260 to 175 majority.

The Bush Administration

From the beginning the guiding principles of the Bush administration were made clear. Bush relied on a decision-making procedure in which he would hear the widest possible range of options from as many advisors as possible and then select a course that, more often than not, was in the center of a continuum of alternatives. Bush was eager to have a cooperative rather than a confrontational relationship with Congress.

THE PRESIDENT

Bush was a tall, lanky public servant of patrician origins who tried to project an image of having sprung from "just folks." He took delight in the traditional American virtues. He was, in a word, "cautious." Avoiding blunders appeared to be his priority objective. Only rarely did he take a bold gamble in handling a problem that demanded his attention. However, he did seem to genuinely enjoy surprising the nation every now and then, particularly in making appointments.

THE CABINET

Although the new president turned to conservative white males like himself in background and temperament for the three senior posts in the cabinet—secretary of state, secretary of the treasury, and attorney general—he did give the cabinet a diversity that the American people had come to expect. James A. Baker III, who had been Reagan's chief of staff and secretary of the treasury as well as Bush's extraordinarily skilled campaign manager, was named secretary of state. Baker was also the president's most trusted advisor; his counsel was not limited to foreign affairs. After the Senate rejected former Republican senator John G. Tower of Texas, Bush chose hard-working Republican representative Dick Cheney of Wyoming as secretary of defense. The cabinet also included Elizabeth Dole, who had been secretary of transportation in the Reagan administration, as secretary of labor; Louis W. Sullivan, a black physician who was dean of a medical school, as secretary of health and human services; and Jack Kemp, who had been a conservative Republican representative of New York, as secretary of housing and urban development.

Domestic Issues

The domestic problems facing Bush were basically those that had been troubling the nation since the 1970s. The most serious domestic matter was surely the economy, particularly the huge budget deficit. Difficult social issues like abortion, drug abuse, and education also demanded attention.

REDUCING THE BUDGET DEFICIT

In July 1990, Bush retracted his paramount pledge of "Read my lips: no new taxes!" Confronted with a huge federal budget deficit that had to be lowered as required by the Gramm-Rudman-Hollings Act, the president agreed in writing that it was "clear" to *him* that there was a need for increased "tax revenues." The national debt stood at $3 trillion, and Bush aimed at beginning to decrease it by reducing the 1991 deficit by $40 billion and cutting $500 billion from the deficit over the next five years. To accomplish this goal a deal was struck between the Bush administration and congressional Democratic leaders. The president agreed to raise taxes and to cut military appropriations; the Democrats agreed to cut spending for such entitlement programs as Social Security and Medicare. Republican candidates in the 1990 congressional elections were unhappy about having to abandon their long-standing charge that their Democratic opponents were imbued with a "tax and spend" philosophy.

THE S&L SCANDAL

Soon after taking office Bush had to contend with a crucial state of affairs in the savings and loan (S&L) field. It was a matter that would result in extraordinary costs to the government and that could be politically explosive for the administration. Under Reagan's policy of diminished regulation of the S&L industry, hundreds of institutions were not even examined because the Reagan administration had refused to increase the number of personnel engaged in that work. In turn, a large number of firms granted imprudently large loans and made flagrantly ill-advised investments based on poorly managed investigations. S&L officers took funds in order to enrich themselves, amassing huge sums of money for personal use.

Most members of Congress, both Democrats and Republicans, played a part in bringing about the debacle. Most accepted substantial contributions to their election campaigns from S&Ls. In 1982 Congress passed legislation allowing the S&Ls, which had heretofore been limited to granting home mortgages, to invest in virtually any kind of business enterprise. Because of uncurbed mismanagement and wanton dishonesty, about 15 percent of the more than 3,000 S&Ls were close to or actually insolvent. And of the hundreds of institutions taken over by the federal government, over 60 percent were discovered to be riddled with rampant fraud. By law the federal government guaranteed deposits up to $100,000 in the event of the failure of an S&L institution. In 1989 Congress appropriated $166 billion to rescue the foundering industry. However, within a year most economists estimated that the ultimate cost could be as much as $500 billion, or about $2,000 for each and every inhabitant of the United States. That sum would have to be taken from the nation's taxpayers.

THE SUPREME COURT AND ABORTION

Over the years Bush had come to adopt Reagan's opposition to abortion for any reason. In 1989 the Supreme Court, with its new conservative majority, voted 5 to 4 to uphold a Missouri law that restricted a woman's access to an abortion. Furthermore, the Court agreed to consider three more cases, the decisions of which could reverse its earlier position in *Roe v. Wade* (1973) that, according to the Constitution, a woman has the fundamental right to an abortion. In 1990 William J. Brennan Jr., the leader of the Court's liberal bloc, retired. Three days after Brennan resigned, the president nominated David H. Souter, a conscientious, competent, and conservative former New Hampshire state judge and newly appointed federal judge. He was confirmed by the Senate with limited opposition.

THE WAR ON DRUGS

To deal with the problem of drug abuse Congress created the office of director of national drug control policy to coordinate the activities of the various federal government agencies playing a role in the war on drugs: the Drug Enforcement Administration, the Federal Bureau of Investigation, and the United States Custom Service. Bush appointed William J. Bennett, who had been secretary of education in the Reagan cabinet, as the first director (or so-called drug czar).

EDUCATION

Despite a 1988 campaign pledge that he would become the "education president," Bush's performance on education by the end of 1990 was poor—long on rhetoric and short on initiative. Leadership at the highest level of the Department of Education offered no creative or provocative ideas to educators. Furthermore, the Bush administration was reluctant to spend even the amount that it had estimated was necessary for the betterment of education. In the first budget he submitted to Congress, Bush requested about $3 billion less for educational purposes than Reagan had asked for in his last budget.

ENVIRONMENTALISM

The Bush administration made a break with the Reagan administration on many environmental issues. In 1989 Bush recommended to Congress that it strengthen the Clean Air Act of 1970 to combat more stringently toxic air pollution and acid rain. Congress responded quickly with the requisite legislation.

END OF THE COLD WAR

The United States pursuit of détente with the communist nations begun in the early 1970s remained a cornerstone of American foreign policy throughout the 1980s. Toward the end of that decade there was a sudden dramatic move on the part of the Soviet Union to bring détente to its logical end. On December 7, 1988, in an address to the United Nations, Mikhail Gorbachev, general secretary of the Communist party of the Soviet Union, unilaterally proclaimed that the Cold War was over. Gorbachev declared his intention to establish an entirely new and genuinely cooperative relationship between the United States and the Soviet Union. The Soviet Union would embark on a determined course of permitting freedom of expression for its citizens, implementing some capitalistic practices, and significantly reducing both its nuclear and conventional armaments. According to Gorbachev, the embodying principles of the new era in the Soviet Union would be *glasnost* (Russian for "openness") and *perestroika* (Russian for "restructuring").

The end of the Cold War was good news for the United States, but there still existed trouble spots in the world: the Middle East with its constant unrest and Central America and the Caribbean with various rightist and leftist regimes attempting to grasp power. The unsettled conditions in the Middle East finally erupted into the Persian Gulf war.

Détente with the Communist Nations

Reagan did not entirely abandon détente with the Soviet Union and the People's Republic of China, but he exhibited a combative manner in dealing with the former. However, during his second term, he tempered his militant stance. Bush encountered an entirely new set of circumstances in dealing with communist nations. While he was president-elect, the Soviet Union had announced that the Cold War was an unhappy situation of the past.

REAGAN AND THE SOVIET UNION

Halfway through his first term Reagan publicly denounced Soviet communism as "the focus of evil in the modern world" and depicted the Soviet Union itself as "an evil empire." The administration refused to revive the SALT II accord providing for the further reduction of American and Soviet nuclear arsenals. Instead, Reagan proposed the Strategic Defense Initiative (SDI), popularly called Star Wars. The system would use advanced technology to construct a shield to be positioned in space to seek out and strike down Soviet missiles before they could reach American targets. SDI was criticized on many grounds: that it was probably not technologically workable; that it would be monumentally expensive to research and build; and that it violated the antiballistic missile (ABM) defense system provisions of the SALT treaty of 1972. Despite these criticisms, the Reagan administration declared its resolve to make Star Wars a reality.

After his reelection, Reagan moderated his aggressive posture in dealing with the Soviet Union, mainly in response to overtures from that nation's new leadership. In early 1985 Mikhail Gorbachev became the general secretary of the Soviet Communist party. The new leader committed himself to the policy of détente between the United States and the Soviet Union, appealed for extensive reductions in the nuclear arsenals of both nations, and suggested that he and Reagan meet as soon as possible to attempt to resolve the differences existing between the two nations.

A series of summit conferences took place. In November 1985, at Geneva, Switzerland, Reagan and Gorbachev met for the first time. They discussed a wide range of issues, including the control of nuclear weapons and human rights. Gorbachev vigorously insisted that Reagan relinquish his cherished SDI project and Reagan just as vigorously declined to do so. The differences were wide and the exchanges were sometimes harsh. No formal comprehensive agreements were achieved.

In October 1986, Reagan and Gorbachev met in Reykjavik, Iceland, where the Soviet leader offered to reduce his nation's stockpile of both medium- and long-range nuclear missiles if Reagan would agree to a ten-year moratorium on certain key aspects of the SDI program. The president unequivocally refused to abandon any aspect of the project. The summit was concluded precipitately and unceremoniously.

Success came the following year. In December 1987, in Washington, D.C., Reagan and Gorbachev signed the Intermediate Nuclear Forces (INF) treaty, the first accord providing for comprehensive nuclear arms control. According to the treaty, the United States would destroy 358 of its inter-mediate-range ballistic and cruise missiles and the Soviet Union would destroy 573 of theirs. Since one type of Soviet missile slated for destruction carried three warheads apiece, the total number of nuclear warheads that the Soviet Union had agreed to destroy was about four times that of the United States. To ensure compliance, there was to be a carefully developed system of verification procedures.

In the spring of 1988 Reagan visited the Soviet Union, where he was warmly received by the people. However, the first formal meeting of Reagan and Gorbachev was discordant, due in large part to Reagan's bringing up what he characterized as a sorrowful record of human rights in the Soviet Union. Yet Reagan appeared as if he no longer perceived the Soviet Union to be an "evil empire."

REAGAN AND CHINA

In April 1984, Reagan was welcomed in Beijing, where he engaged in cordial discussions with leaders of the People's Republic of China. The two nations signed a series of agreements relating to cultural, technological, and commercial concerns. Thus Reagan extended the policy of détente with the People's Republic of China that had been initiated by Nixon and continued by Carter.

BUSH AND THE SOVIET UNION

Bush's most important challenges—and opportunities—in foreign affairs came in his response to the Soviet overture regarding a new phase in United States–Soviet relations. But the ending of the Cold War was only one of the factors to affect the relationship between the two nations. In the spring of 1988 there began—astonishingly—within the communist bloc a revolt against communism. In the Soviet Union, the People's Republic of China, and throughout Soviet-controlled Eastern Europe— East Germany, Hungary, Poland, Czechoslovakia, Bulgaria, Romania— uprisings occurred. In November 1989, citizens of both West Berlin and East Berlin demolished the Berlin Wall, which had separated them for almost three decades. Hundreds of thousands of East Berliners poured into West Berlin. More astounding was that the Soviet Union allowed (whether willingly or not) each of those nations of Eastern Europe to go its separate way, free from political, economic, social—and military—domination by the Kremlin in Moscow.

Further, in the spring of 1990 there were increasing demands for secession within the Soviet Union from some of the fifteen republics having large numbers of nationalistic ethnic groups. The drive for political independence was particularly strong in the Baltic republics of Estonia, Latvia, and Lithuania, as well as Georgia and Azerbaijan. It even appeared as if the Soviet Union might disintegrate as a political entity.

On September 12, 1990, the four main allied nations that had defeated Nazi Germany in 1945—the United States, Great Britain, France, and the Soviet Union—signed a treaty with the two Germanys to reunify them on October 3, 1990, thus formally establishing a single German republic. Reunified Germany would be a member of NATO, just as West Germany had been since 1955.

All the while, Gorbachev had to contend with a faltering economy and with serious challenges to his leadership from both the left and right of the political spectrum within the Communist party, and to the policies he set for the nation.

Amid all of these developments, the United States was an idle and not unhappy spectator. President Bush had to formulate and conduct policy regarding the Soviet Union at a time of awesome changes.

In December 1989, Bush and Gorbachev met in Malta. They pledged to sign treaties during the following year regulating the stockpiling and deployment of both conventional and long-range nuclear weapons. During late May and early June 1990, the two leaders met in Washington, D.C. With a measure of joyous solemnity, they declared that the decade-old Cold War between the Western and Communist nations was over. They left for future discussions the structure of Europe in a post–Cold War era.

In September 1990 in Helsinki, Finland, Bush and Gorbachev held their third summit, convened in response to Iraq's recent invasion of Kuwait. The meeting between the leaders of the United States and the Soviet Union was the first one to be convened as a result of an international crisis since the Cold War had ended. The joint communiqué issued at the conclusion provided striking evidence of the vastly improved relations between the two superpowers and their willingness to act in concert if at all possible. Bush and Gorbachev pledged jointly to pursue a course that would compel Iraq to withdraw completely from Kuwait, even to the point of their resorting to nonpeaceful means to accomplish the objective.

BUSH AND CHINA

In the spring of 1989 the policy of détente with the People's Republic of China experienced a setback. Thousands of students congregated in Tiananmen Square in the center of Beijing and demonstrated for political reform that would guarantee freedom of expression and other civil rights. The unarmed demonstrators were brutally attacked by government troops;

perhaps as many as 2,000 people were killed in the assault. The Bush administration issued a formal protest against the use of force, stopped arms sales and financial aid to the government and called upon other nations to do the same, and ordered a halt to high-level diplomatic dealings. (However, the president twice sent two of his high-level aides to Beijing on secret visits.) Although he was pressured by many who represented a wide spectrum of political views to sever diplomatic relations with China, Bush refused to do so, attesting that formal contact was necessary in order for the United States to convince China to adopt democratic changes.

Turmoil in the Middle East

The unending turmoil, with frequent eruptions of violence, in the Middle East was a continuing source of concern for both the Reagan and Bush administrations. The United States was in a unique position to play the role of broker in peace negotiations between Israel and the moderate Arab nations.

REAGAN AND LEBANON

In June 1982, Israel made a military incursion into Lebanon. Its goal was to drive out units of the Palestine Liberation Organization (PLO), a group dedicated to the establishment of a Palestinian state and the destruction of Israel, which had been conducting guerrilla attacks upon Israel's northern border. Within two months Israel forced the expulsion of PLO members, including its chairman, Yasir Arafat, who were taken in by other Arab nations. During the Israeli incursion the government of Lebanon—which had already been experiencing civil war—disintegrated. Social and economic chaos ensued amid constant and fierce violence among the various antagonistic Christian and Muslim sects.

To help bring order, the Reagan administration sent marines to Lebanon to join a multinational military force that included French and Italian units. Israel soon withdrew its troops to southern Lebanon, where it set up a security zone to protect northern Israel against guerrilla raids from Lebanese territory. After the Israeli pullout, the multinational peacekeeping force came under frequent attack from several of the Lebanese armed groups.

Over the next two years the United States sustained major terrorist strikes. In April 1983, sixty-three people died and many more were wounded when the United States embassy in Beirut was demolished by a terrorist bombing. The Islamic Jihad (Arabic for "Holy War"), a terrorist group with close ties to Iran, claimed responsibility for the act. That October a Muslim terrorist drove a truck with 2,500 pounds of TNT into the United States marines' headquarters. The structure was completely destroyed. In the rubble were the bodies of 241 marines. The organization believed to be responsible was a Muslim terrorist group with links to either Iran or Syria. Two minutes after the attack, another truck filled with explosives blew up a barracks occupied by a French peacekeeping unit, killing fifty-eight and wounding many others.

In the aftermath, the Reagan administration was criticized for having troops in a nation so beset with political instability and continuous armed hostility. A special commission concluded there had been inadequate security at the marine headquarters. In February 1984, Reagan ordered all marine units to withdraw completely from Lebanon. The following September a bombing at the new United States embassy in Beirut killed forty and wounded many others. The Islamic Jihad again claimed responsibility for the terrorist act.

Throughout the 1980s in Lebanon, Westerners, mostly Americans, were kidnapped by militant Shiite Muslim groups. Some in captivity were put to death or died from lack of proper medical care; others were released only after many months and even years. By 1990 seven Americans and fourteen citizens of other Western nations were still being held.

REAGAN AND TERRORISM

The mid-1980s was a period of widespread terrorism, emanating predominantly from the Middle East. Thousands of people were bombed, shot, hijacked, and kidnapped as part of a method of action for achieving political goals. Among the innocent victims were Americans, causing the Reagan administration to increase the effectiveness of its security measures. In June 1985, armed members of the Hezbollah (Arabic for "Party of God"), an organization of militant Shiite Muslims, supplied and financed by Iran, hijacked a jet with 104 American travelers shortly after takeoff from Athens, Greece. A United States navy diver was brutally killed by the terrorists. After seventeen days the hijackers freed the remaining thirty-nine hostages, convinced that Israel had agreed in behind-the-scenes negotiations to their demand that more than 700 mostly Shiite Lebanese and Palestinians held in prison would be released. Israel soon did so.

The following October armed members of the PLO seized the Italian cruise ship *Achille Lauro*. A wheelchair-bound American Jewish passenger was shot dead; his body was then thrown overboard. The terrorists surrendered after the Egyptian government agreed to fly them to safety in Tunisia. But United States navy jets forced the airplane to land in Sicily. The Italian government imprisoned the terrorists but allowed their leader to escape.

In April 1986, a West Berlin discothèque frequented by American service personnel was bombed, resulting in the deaths of two and the wounding of more than 200. The West German government concluded that a Libyan-sponsored terrorist group committed the act. In retaliation, American airplanes conducted a surprise raid on the Tripoli base of Libyan leader Colonel Muammar el-Qaddafi, killing more than a dozen persons, including his baby daughter.

REAGAN AND THE ISRAELI-PALESTINIAN CONFLICT

In December 1987 in the Israeli-occupied West Bank and Gaza Strip there began the *intifada* (Arabic for "uprising"), in which bands of Palestinians, mostly boys and young men, on an almost daily basis threw rocks and stones at Israeli soldiers of occupation, who resorted to firing upon the demonstrators. Within a year more than 300 Palestinians and about a dozen Israelis were killed in the clashes.

The Reagan administration, which was supportive of Israel, did not engage in the efforts necessary to further the peace process between Israel and the Arab nations, as had been done with a notable amount of success by the three preceding administrations. While opposing the establishment of a Palestinian state in the West Bank and Gaza, the Reagan administration was against the annexation of the West Bank and Gaza by Israel. Instead, it supported the granting of self-determination to the Palestinians in a confederation with Jordan, the very position held by liberal elements of Israeli society.

In mid-1988 King Hussein of Jordan disavowed all obligations pertaining to the West Bank. Israel and the United States were thus left to deal either with the Palestinians themselves or with the PLO. In late 1988 the PLO proclaimed the creation of the independent state of Palestine. Shortly thereafter PLO chairman Yasir Arafat publicly announced that he recognized Israel's right to exist, renounced the use of terrorism, and accepted two long-standing United Nations Security Council resolutions, 232 and 338, that had been passed as the basis for a comprehensive peace settlement in the Middle East. By accepting those three conditions, Arafat met requirements that made it possible for the United States to end a thirteen-year-old ban it had imposed on contacts with the PLO. In December 1988, the Reagan administration began limited formal discussions with the PLO in Tunisia. Israel was horrified and tried unsuccessfully to convince Reagan that Arafat could not be trusted.

BUSH AND THE ISRAELI-PALESTINIAN CONFLICT

As the *intifada* accelerated, with a rising death toll among both the Palestinians and the Israelis, the United States realized that it had to seize whatever opportunities presented themselves for a negotiated settlement before widespread armed conflict engulfed the volatile region. The Bush administration was fully aware that only the United States would be accepted by most as a credible mediator between the Arabs and the Israelis. Only the United States would be accepted as an effective guarantor of a settlement. Compared with all preceding administrations, the Bush administration perhaps showed the least sympathy toward Israel. Nevertheless, it exhibited a greater readiness to engage in the process of resolving the Israeli-Palestinian conflict. The administration implied that the conservative government of Prime Minister Yitzhak Shamir of Israel was not sincere in wanting an agreement with the Palestinians. It continued the direct talks with the PLO.

However, in May 1990, guerrillas of the Palestine Liberation Front, a faction within the PLO, raided Israel. All the terrorists were either captured or killed before they could carry out their mission. Those apprehended stated that their assignment had been to kill Israeli civilians. The Bush administration informed PLO leaders that unless they unequivocally condemned the raid and expelled the member group that acknowledged responsibility for it, the United States would find it no longer possible to maintain the formal contact. The PLO withheld specific denunciation of the attack. Accordingly, Bush suspended the dialogue with the PLO, despite appeals from Arab nations to reconsider.

The Persian Gulf War

Iraq invaded and occupied Kuwait and posed a military threat to Saudi Arabia, producing a crisis in the Persian Gulf region that eventually led to war between the United States and its allies and Iraq.

IRAQI INVASION OF KUWAIT

On August 2, 1990 Iraq invaded neighboring Kuwait. Iraqi forces induced Kuwait's government leaders to flee, occupied the nation's capital, and took possession of extensive petroleum reserves. Within a few weeks Iraqi secret police and soldiers began to loot, torture, and murder Kuwaitis. President Saddam Hussein of Iraq, a particularly cunning and ruthless dictator, asserted that the invasion was the only course of action remaining to him in his dispute with that nation. Kuwait had lent Hussein billions of dollars to help finance his eight-year war with Iran. Iraq maintained that its efforts to repay the loan were hindered by Kuwait's increased petroleum output, which had driven down the price of oil on the world market, seriously hurting Iraq's economy since petroleum constituted 90 percent of its exports.

RESPONDING WITH ECONOMIC SANCTIONS AND A MILITARY BUILDUP

A critical aspect of the industrialized nations' response to Iraq's aggression was the control of oil reserves. Iraq itself possessed about 10 percent of the world's supply of petroleum, Kuwait about 10 percent, and Saudi Arabia about 25 percent. National leaders everywhere were keenly aware of the implications to the world economy of a totally uninhibited despot controlling half of the world's oil.

The United Nations Security Council condemned the invasion and called for the immediate withdrawal of all Iraqi forces from Kuwait. Instead, the following day Iraq positioned troops close to the border of Saudi Arabia. The Security Council next invoked comprehensive economic sanctions against

Iraq. It later adopted a resolution granting nations the right to enforce the blockade by having their ships stop vessels that appeared to be bound from or to Iraq and board them for inspection. Iraq very soon directed its vessels to offer no resistance to the stop-and-search measure.

As for the United States response to the conflict, President Bush characterized the conduct of Iraq as "naked aggression" and stated that the only acceptable outcome was the complete withdrawal of the Iraqis from Kuwait. Reflecting the views of virtually the entire membership of Congress and the vast majority of the American people, the president declared that Iraq presented a threat to Saudi Arabia and pledged to help Saudi forces defend that nation's independence.

Within six days after the invasion the president began sending troops and massive amounts of military arms and equipment to Saudi Arabia and the neighboring waterways. The Bush administration called the military deployment Operation Desert Shield. By mid-January 1991 the United States—in what was the largest military buildup since the Vietnam war—had deployed to the region approximately 540,000 servicemen and -women, more than 1,350 aircraft, and about 100 ships. The United States ordered some of its navy vessels to the region to enforce a blockade of all exports from Iraq and all goods imported to Iraq (with the exception of certain foodstuffs and medical supplies). By a vote of the Arab League, with the opposition of only Libya and the PLO, Egyptian, Syrian, and Moroccan troops were also sent to Saudi territory to join Saudi and escaped Kuwaiti troops in the defense. Twenty-seven nations joined the United States in the area by providing troops, such as Great Britain and France, or by contributing naval forces, such as the Soviet Union, Canada, and Italy.

HOSTAGE-HOLDING

Two and a half weeks into the conflict Hussein announced that the approximately 17,000 foreigners who had been working in or visiting Iraq or Kuwait when the invasion took place were now being held as hostages. They would be permitted to leave when the United States withdrew its military forces from Saudi Arabia. Upon Bush's rejection of the offer, Hussein moved about 700 American, British, French, German, and Japanese male detainees to various industrial centers and military installations to serve as human shields to deter air attacks. Hussein finally relented by allowing all of the hostages to depart.

IRAQI ANNEXATION OF KUWAIT

Iraq declared the annexation of Kuwait as a province and consequently ordered all nations having embassies in Kuwait to close them. But in order to defy Iraq's attempts simply to eliminate a sovereign nation, many countries, including the United States, for a period of time kept reduced staffs in their embassies as a sign that—although without sufficient food and water—they were technically still open.

RESORTING TO MILITARY FORCE

On November 29, 1990, the Security Council approved a resolution authorizing the use of force against Iraq if it did not withdraw from Kuwait by January 15, 1991. On January 9, 1991, Secretary of State Baker and Iraqi foreign minister Tariq Aziz met in Geneva to resolve the crisis by diplomacy but they failed to reach an agreement. On January 12, after a debate marked by strikingly thoughtful eloquence, Congress, with a close vote in the Senate, authorized the president to wage war. Those who had opposed authorization in favor of continuing the economic sanctions against Iraq, once the vote was taken, immediately gave their full support to the prosecution of the war. As for the American people, the vast majority supported the president in his belief that if Iraq did not withdraw peacefully from Kuwait then armed force would have to be used to dislodge it. The Bush administration decided to name the anticipated military assault Operation Desert Storm.

Seven hours after the Security Council's January 15 deadline for the Iraqi withdrawal from Kuwait, the United States and coalition partners Great Britain, Italy, Saudi Arabia, and Kuwait launched an air offensive against Iraq and Iraqi troops in Kuwait. After a few days of engaging in thousands of bombing missions, the United States and its allies achieved air supremacy in the region. A six-week-long massive air assault of more than 100,000 sorties devastated Iraq's infrastructure. The precision bombing in the Iraqi capital of Baghdad and elsewhere effectively destroyed virtually all military installations while keeping civilian casualties to a minimum.

Hussein attempted to alienate Arab nations from the coalition with efforts to provoke noncombatant Israel into entering the war. Iraq fired a series of its Soviet-made Scud missiles on Israel, but American Patriot anti-missile missiles shipped to Israel and operated by American and Israeli crews intercepted them, permitting only minor harm to life and property. (Saudi Arabia was also attacked by Scud missiles.) Upon the earnest appeals of the United States, Israel, with much anguish, restrained itself from retaliating.

President Bush declared that if Iraq did not withdraw from Kuwait by February 23, the coalition partners would institute a ground war. A few days before the deadline, the Soviet Union, which had been for many years the chief supplier of arms and military advisors to Iraq, its longtime chief client in the region, offered a peace proposal. Hussein showed interest in the bid but failed to accept it immediately. On February 23, the United States and its allies began a large-scale land attack across the entire front into Kuwait, and American, British, and French troops struck deep into southeastern Iraqi territory, outflanking and encircling Hussein's forces. The coalition forces won a stunning victory in a one-hundred-hour ground war. Kuwait, which had been ravaged by the Iraqis, was liberated. Iraq's threatened use of chemical weapons never occurred. The Iraqi retreat turned into a rout. An estimated 100,000 Iraqi soldiers were killed in the onslaught. Approximately 80,000 demoralized Iraqi troops surrendered.

AFTERMATH

On March 2, in a desert area of occupied southeastern Iraq, at a meeting between allied and Iraqi military leaders the Iraqi delegation accepted all the demands that were presented to it for turning the provisional truce into a permanent cease-fire formally ending the Persian Gulf War, including rescinding the annexation of Kuwait, accepting liability for war damages, restoring all seized Kuwaiti assets, and promptly returning all prisoners of War and Kuwaiti civilian detainees. In agreeing to the allied terms the government of Iraq had, in essence, surrendered.

At war's end virtually every American had nothing but the utmost praise for President Bush for showing such good judgment throughout the entire conflict in the Persian Gulf region and felt deep gratitude to both Bush and the armed services, which had been brilliantly led by General H. Norman Schwarzkopf, commander of the United States forces in the Persian Gulf war, for achieving a military victory so quickly and with so few allied casualties.

AMERICAN WAR COSTS

In the Persian Gulf war, 125 American service personnel were killed in battle and 83 died of other causes, including 29 (three of whom were women) in an Iraqi Scud missile attack on a barracks in Saudi Arabia miles behind the front. Another 213 were wounded in combat. The United States spent approximately $45 billion on the war.

Central America and the Caribbean

Both the Reagan and Bush administrations pursued a foreign policy in Central America and the Caribbean that was committed to stemming radical national movements. But their endeavors were ineffective due largely to congressional opposition to United States intervention in the internal affairs of nations in the region. However, each president had one notable success: Reagan in Grenada and Bush in Panama.

REAGAN AND NICARAGUA

Reagan was absolutely convinced that the repressive Marxist Sandinista junta, headed by Daniel Ortega Saavedra, was fast transforming Nicaragua into a close client of the Soviet Union, thus posing a threat to the political stability and security of other nations in the region. A more specific and immediate concern was that the Sandinista government was giving substantial military and financial assistance to the leftist insurgents fighting against the United States–backed government in neighboring El Salvador. Many members of Congress, both Democrats and Republicans, reacted negatively to the Reagan administration's view, maintaining that the president was overstating the threat to Central America from the Soviet Union and relying too much on American military forces to resolve the political problems that existed in the area. Consequently, in 1982, Congress passed the Boland Amendment. Named after its sponsor, Democratic representative Edward Boland of Massachusetts, it prohibited the Department of Defense and the CIA from training or giving military supplies to any person attempting to overthrow the government of Nicaragua.

The Reagan administration resorted to covert measures. The CIA secretly provided extensive training to an existing military group of anti-Sandinista Nicaraguans known as the Contras. In early 1983 the Contras began engaging in bold guerrilla maneuvers. But when it became known that CIA-sponsored agents had laid mines in three harbors of Nicaragua, damaging commercial vessels, Congress immediately canceled all American assistance to the Contras. Despite the Reagan administration's hopes, the Contras were not able to overpower the entrenched Sandinistas.

BUSH AND NICARAGUA

Reagan's policy toward Nicaragua was rejected by Bush, who fully realized the pitfalls were he to continue his immediate predecessor's course of action. Conceding that the policy of military aid for the Contras had failed, the Bush administration in 1989 assented to financial assistance for humanitarian—not military—purposes to help the rebel group switch from being insurgents to becoming part of the nation's legitimate political system. This plan meshed with a similar one advanced two years earlier by the heads of five Latin American governments.

REAGAN AND EL SALVADOR

Armed conflict of many years' duration between the rightist government and the communist guerillas was still raging in El Salvador when in December 1980 José Napoleon Duarte, a moderate conservative whose candidacy had been sponsored by the ruling junta, was elected president. He was the first civilian to attain that office in almost fifty years. Soon after Reagan became president he sent American military advisors to assist the government of El Salvador and reinstated the financial aid that Carter had discontinued following the murder of three American nuns and a lay missionary by the former government's troops.

In the 1984 Salvadoran presidential election Duarte won reelection. He then implemented a number of social and economic reforms. He was not successful, however, against either the right-wing guerrillas and their notorious "death squads" or the left-wing guerrillas, both of which groups had killed thousands. The ferocious civil war continued unabated.

THE INVASION OF GRENADA

In October 1983, ultraleftist political and military figures on the Caribbean island nation of Grenada staged a coup against the incumbent leftist government of Prime Minister Maurice Bishop and set up a regime with even closer links to both the Soviet Union and Cuba than had been maintained by the Bishop government. The Reagan administration was particularly worried about the construction of an airport, with financial and technological assistance from Cuba, whose facilities could accommodate Soviet and Cuban fighter aircraft. Six days after the coup United States forces invaded the nation and ousted the Marxist regime.

President Reagan offered a number of reasons for having taken military action, such as ensuring the safety of about a thousand Americans living in Grenada and complying with an appeal from the six-member Organization of Eastern Caribbean States to drive out ultraleftist revolutionary elements from the region. Under American patronage and guidance, Grenada established a politically moderate, provisional democratic government, which promptly received helpful financial aid from the United States.

Despite condemnation of the invasion by the United Nations, several Latin American countries, and many Democratic members of Congress, the vast majority of American citizens supported their president for what they considered a bold and morally correct course of action.

THE INVASION OF PANAMA

During the late 1980s relations between the United States and Panama grew steadily worse. Manuel Antonio Noriega, the Panamanian president, was a crafty, brutal autocrat who became increasingly more provocative in his anti-American conduct. Both the Reagan and Bush administrations tried a variety of approaches—unsuccessfully—to bring an end to the Noriega regime, including the imposition of economic sanctions, the use of massive amounts of propaganda, and the encouragement of a coup. Noriega became more repressive toward the Panamanian people and more erratic and reckless in his dealings with the United States. In December 1989, the Panamanian legislature, which Noriega controlled, named him "Maximum Leader" and declared that as a result of provocative American acts a state of war existed between the United States and Panama.

Three days after the Panamanian legislature's action, maintaining that the safety of Americans living and working in Panama was at risk, Bush secretly authorized the immediate invasion of Panama. The goals were to capture Noriega and take him to the United States for trial on charges of smuggling drugs into the United States and to help set up a democratic government led by Guillermo Endora, the candidate who had appeared to win the most recent presidential election. The American troops swiftly defeated the Panamanian military forces and seized control of most of the nation. At about the time the invasion began, at a United States military base in Panama, Endora took the oath of office as president of a new government.

Noriega escaped and was given refuge in the Vatican embassy in Panama City. However, after eleven days he gave himself up to American authorities and was flown to the United States to stand trial on drug charges. All the while, Noriega accused the United States of being totally cynical. For years he had been supplying valuable information to the CIA, and the leadership of that organization, including at one time Bush, was fully aware that while doing so he had been involved in drug trafficking.

At home most members of Congress, both Democrats and Republicans, reflecting the thinking of the American people, applauded the president for his success in what was considered a proper effort. The Panamanians themselves expressed gratitude to the United States for ejecting a despotic leader. Latin American nations formally condemned the intervention but subsequently conveyed to the United States in a variety of ways their satisfaction with the ultimate political result.

The United Nations

Within forty-five years of its founding in 1945 as a deliberative association of fifty-one members, most of which were Western democratic nations, the United Nations became by 1990 an often unwieldy association of 160 members.

THE UNITED STATES OUTVOTED

More than two-thirds of the members were Third World nations. Well before the 1990s the United States was being continually outvoted in the United Nations General Assembly. The votes of the less-developed countries, acting in solidarity, could carry any proposition. Time and again the Western democracies, particularly the United States, were subjected to public denunciation by the Third World delegates, who in private maintained that this should in no way adversely affect the continuation of long-standing economic assistance to their regions from the Western governments.

THE DEFENSE OF THE ORGANIZATION

Defenders of the United Nations cautioned against excessive disillusionment with the world organization, maintaining that current world problems were too large and complex to be treated by any one nation or small group of nations.

THE RETURN TO SOCIAL CALM

With the coming of the 1980s there was a return to social calm in the United States. Of course, Americans confronted such serious social problems as drug abuse and AIDS. But the social turmoil of the 1960s that persisted in diminished form into the 1970s was over. Nevertheless, significant changes took place in society. For example, the structure and values of the family experienced profound changes, and the elderly effectively banded together to obtain accommodations for their special needs.

The Population

In 1980 the population of the United States was approximately 226.5 million—an increase from that at the beginning of the century of about 200 percent.

RACIAL BACKGROUNDS

Of the total number, 173.7 million (76.7 percent) were non-Hispanic whites; 26.5 million (11.7 percent) were blacks; 14.6 million (6.4 percent) were Hispanic-Americans; 1.1 million were American Indians; and 3.5 million were Asians, mostly Chinese and Japanese, but including a substantially larger number of Vietnamese and Koreans than in previous counts.

FASTEST-GROWING MINORITY

Hispanic-Americans formed the nation's fastest-growing minority group during the 1970s at 2.2 percent annually, compared, for example, with 1.3 percent for blacks.

The Family

The "typical" American family of the first half of the twentieth century—with the father as undisputed head and sole economic support, the mother as housekeeper and child nurturer, and the several offspring as dutiful respecters of their parents—was no more.

CHANGING ATTITUDES

By 1980 only 7 percent of the nation's families fit the long-standing "typical" family pattern. Largely as a result of the women's rights movement of the 1960s a new relationship between men and women developed, effecting profound changes in the structure and values of the family itself. Of the married women who worked, most did so to add to their spouses' incomes to be better able to meet family expenses. But there were now other compelling reasons for a woman to seek employment, including a fervent disinclination to be "tied down" to household chores, a desire for the social and intellectual stimulation of pursuing a career, and a realization of the worth of establishing herself in a particular line of work before her children grew up and left home. As a result of changing social attitudes, divorce laws were liberalized in state after state.

TRENDS WITHIN THE FAMILY STRUCTURE

By the 1980s certain basic trends within the family structure were clearly in evidence: The average number of children in a family had decreased from three or four to one or two; the portion of employed married women with children in school had reached approximately 55 percent; the divorce rate had increased by more than 100 percent, with 38 percent of all first marriages being dissolved; the proportion of children who lived in a home with only one parent had reached approximately 35 percent; the percentage of households in which a woman was the head had risen by about 35 percent.

Senior Citizens

The steady increase in life expectancy that had been continuing since the beginning of the twentieth century had a considerable effect upon many facets of society during the 1980s.

EFFECTS OF ACTIVISM

By 1980 approximately 25 million Americans were sixty-five years of age or older. Referred to as senior citizens, they successfully used their strength as a special-interest group, relying on their cause's strong appeal to the collective conscience of younger people and on their power as a voting bloc. For example, the age at which the vast majority of Americans had traditionally retired was sixty-five. In 1978 Congress made the legal mandatory retirement age seventy. Understandably, many younger Americans were vexed by the possibility that the older people who chose to remain employed would prevent many younger people either from being hired or from being promoted. On the local and state levels, the elderly were allowed reductions on such things as the price of admission to motion-picture theaters and museums, the fares on public transportation, and the rate of taxation on their homes. Home-construction firms played an important role in serving the elderly by developing, mostly in mild-weather regions such as Florida and the Southwest, retirement villages that served the needs of older people, with comfortable housing, shopping facilities, leisure activities, and medical care.

CRISIS IN SOCIAL SECURITY

By the 1980s a crisis arose regarding the solvency of the Social Security system, since for many years larger sums had been paid to its beneficiaries than had been put in by wage earners enrolled in the system who were not yet drawing benefits. Thus in order to prevent Social Security from running out of funds, methods were adopted to get the system back on a stable financial course.

Technology: Land and Air Transportation

Because of the difficult economic conditions and the changing social circumstances of the late 1970s and the 1980s, the automobile, airline, and railroad industries all suffered traumatic experiences, with many enterprises even facing the stark issue of survival.

THE AUTOMOBILE

By 1980 over 125 million cars were on the roads—something like one vehicle for every two persons in the nation. Astoundingly, one out of every six employed Americans earned a living directly or indirectly because of automobiles.

The American automobile industry faced two major crises. There was a reaction against what seemed to many the automobile industry's emphasis on selling superpowerful vehicles with little apparent concern for safety features. An early and leading exponent of this position was consumer advocate Ralph Nader, who condemned the automakers for paying little attention to safety standards and proposed a more carefully conceived and executed automobile design. As a result of disclosures by Nader and others, Congress passed legislation requiring a comprehensive group of strict safety standards to be imposed on all vehicles.

The other crisis faced by the American automobile industry was stiff competition from European and Japanese car manufacturers. The situation stemmed from the energy pinch. Compared with the automobiles produced in the United States, those produced in other nations were smaller and their engines were more fuel efficient and therefore a great deal more economical to run. Thus foreign car manufacturers produced vehicles in the 1980s that very many American consumers purchased.

The changing pattern of the percentage shares of car sales in the United States by domestic and foreign automakers was striking. In 1975 the percentage shares were: domestic producers, 81.8; foreign manufacturers, 18.2. In 1980 the percentage shares were: domestic producers, 73.5; foreign manufacturers, 26.5. Of the purchase of imported vehicles in the United States, the Japanese makes constituted approximately 80 percent. In 1980 the domestic automobile industry had its worst sales year since 1961. Early in the 1980s the American automobile manufacturers, in response to the public's demand for small, fuel-efficient cars, began in earnest to turn them out in large numbers, setting themselves the formidable task of first catching up with and then surpassing their foreign competition.

THE AIRPLANE

In 1970 the commercial airlines flew about 170 million passengers about 132 billion miles. In 1980 they flew about 297 million passengers about 254 billion miles. Until 1958 the planes used by the American airlines were of the piston-engine and propeller type, but in that year jet-engine aircraft were introduced. Early in the 1960s the largest jets could carry about 150 passengers; in the late 1970s the largest could hold about 500. By the 1980s, as a result of advances in aeronautical engineering, jets sped along at approximately six hundred miles an hour at a height of about 30,000 feet.

During the early 1980s the airlines faced a crisis—a severe drop in income—as a result of being compelled to pay amounts for fuel because of the demands of OPEC.

THE RAILROADS

For decades the level of freight handling by the railroads remained relatively constant. But this was not the case with passenger travel. In 1940 the nation's airlines annually carried fewer than 5 percent of the number of passengers domestically that the railroads did; in 1990 the railroads carried fewer than 5 percent of the number of passengers domestically that the airlines did.

In 1970 Congress established the National Railway Passenger Corporation, called Amtrak, the unified national railroad system. In order to revitalize and repopularize rail transportation the federal government committed itself to improving the efficiency and comfort of passenger trains. However, with the difficult economic conditions of the early 1980s, the executive branch decided to greatly reduce federal government subsidies to Amtrak, a decrease that resulted in the discontinuance of most passenger travel service.

Medicine

Significant developments in medicine included improvements in cancer therapy, the transplanting of vital organs, and the use of new methods in the treatment of heart disease. Two grave medical problems of the period were drug abuse and AIDS.

CANCER THERAPY

During the 1980s about a million new cases of cancer among the American people were diagnosed annually and about 400,000 died of the disease, which, after heart disease, was the principal cause of death in the nation. In 1940 about 20 percent of those having cancer could be expected to live for five years; in 1980 about 40 percent were expected to do so, and the survival rate was improving rapidly. The gains in a patient's chances of surviving reflected improvements in the use of traditional methods of treatment—surgery, radiation, and chemotherapy—as well as new methods.

ORGAN TRANSPLANTS

An astonishing advance in medicine was the transplanting of vital organs from one person to another. Kidney-, liver-, and heart-transplant operations were successfully performed. Kidney transplants in particular became routine in the United States during the 1980s.

TREATMENT OF HEART DISEASE

By 1980 the annual number of heart transplants declined because of the shortage of donors and because of the destruction of the transplanted organs by the patients' natural immune defenses. The transplant operation was largely superseded by either the performance of coronary bypass surgery—by 1980 about 100,000 such operations were being performed annually—or the placing within the body of a pacemaker—by 1980 about 600,000 people kept their hearts beating in a steady rhythm with the help of such devices.

DRUG ABUSE

In the 1980s the drug of greatest consequence to the nation was cocaine. The middle- and upper-class Americans who were "on" (using) cocaine, which was usually "snorted" (inhaled in powdered form through the nostrils), had to spend an average of $10,000 a year to assure a steady supply for a "fix." Their number was estimated in 1980 to be 2 million but had dropped significantly by 1990. However, the use of crack, a derivative of cocaine, soared rapidly by 1990 among blacks and other minorities living in inner-city ghettos, largely because of a sharp decrease in the price for the substance as the supply greatly increased.

Amid the illegal use of drugs was the legal consumption of alcoholic beverages. In 1990 about 12 million adults were alcoholics or frequently drank to excess.

AIDS

The new sexual morality of Americans in the 1960s and 1970s was checked in the 1980s and 1990s by the spread of sexually transmitted diseases. The most devastating of these was AIDS (acquired immune deficiency syndrome). In 1981 the first documented case of the disease was reported. The two highest-risk groups in society were intravenous drug users who shared hypodermic needles, and homosexuals. By 1990 approximately 95,000 people had died of AIDS. And according to various studies, as many as one million Americans could become infected within five years. Research to develop a vaccine against the AIDS virus was intensive but unsuccessful as the 1990s began.

DEVELOPMENT OF HEALTH CONSCIOUSNESS

During the 1980s there was a tremendous increase in the number of Americans who became avidly committed to sustaining good health through a regimen of prudent physical conduct. In order to achieve better health, people altered their life-styles in four basic ways: they stopped overeating, stopped heavy drinking of alcoholic beverages, stopped smoking, and engaged in regular exercise. Physical-fitness establishments, often called health spas, sprouted up throughout the nation. By the mid-1980s approximately 47 percent of the population exercised regularly. In 1990 the most favored forms of exercise were tennis, bicycling, and jogging.

THE TELEVISION CULTURE

Put simply, television was the most powerful tool of communication in the history of humankind. Toward the end of the twentieth century television became unequivocally the all-pervading and most influential art form and the all-pervading information transmitter. Television and its complements—the videocassette recorder, the videodisk player, and the camcorder—with the tremendous advantage of entertaining and informing within the comfort and convenience of the home, were a supreme technological accomplishment of which the American people were enormously proud and grateful.

Television

In 1990 virtually 100 percent of America's households contained television sets. There were about 160 million sets in use in the nation. Viewing was done an average of approximately six hours a day.

SITUATION COMEDIES

The nature of situation comedies of the 1980s was determined by the appearance in 1971 of one series: *All in the Family.* Unlike its predecessors in the genre, this show did not rely on constrainedly "tame" subject matter but focused openly on controversial topics, such as racial, religious, and ethnic prejudice and sexual conduct. The program starred Carroll O'Connor as the supreme bigot Archie Bunker and Jean Stapleton as his obtuse wife, Edith. Consistently popular also was *The Mary Tyler Moore Show.* Into the 1990s both of these classic situation comedies, as reruns, were still loved by television audiences.

TALK SHOWS

Retaining its long-standing record as the most-watched offering in this genre was *The Tonight Show.* Johnny Carson, who became the host of the program in 1962, remained so into the 1990s.

NEWS AND PUBLIC AFFAIRS

In 1980 about 35 million households regularly viewed the nightly news programs on the three major commercial networks (the American Broadcasting Company, the Columbia Broadcasting System, and the National Broadcasting Company).

The most popular program in the field of news and public affairs in the 1980s was *60 Minutes*. A single installment of this documentary series almost always covered three news stories, each quite different from the others in content and treatment, resulting in an appealingly diversified package. Among the news correspondents narrating the stories were Mike Wallace, Harry Reasoner, and Morley Safer.

In 1979, after more than three decades of consideration by its members, the House of Representatives began telecasting its routine proceedings on public television and on a few cable television systems. Although the Senate for many years had permitted the telecasting of its committee hearings, it was not until 1986 that it started telecasting its routine proceedings. The telecasting of proceedings of the United States Supreme Court, strongly opposed by a majority of its members, was at the beginning of the 1990s still not realized.

PUBLIC TELEVISION

By 1980 members of more than 45 million households viewed public television with some regularity. The close to 300 stations in the nationwide noncommercial system telecast both American and foreign programs, concentrating on dramas, classical music, and documentaries, many of which dealt with art, literature, and music as well as with the natural sciences.

The most successful by far of public television's offerings was a series titled *Masterpiece Theater*, comprising a number of British dramatic productions, which premiered in 1970 and continued running into the 1990s. It was elegantly hosted by the British-born social commentator Alistair Cooke. In 1990 the zenith in the history of television documentaries was reached with the presentation on public television of the twelve-hour series *The Civil War*, produced and directed by Ken Burns. The production was the most-watched series ever to be presented on public television. As critics of the cultural scene almost unanimously agreed, this was television at its best—entertaining and informative and yet not pandering.

COLOR

In 1956 WNBQ-TV (later renamed WMAQ-TV) in Chicago became the first station in the United States to telecast all its local programs in color. By the late 1960s the three major commercial networks were telecasting all their programs in color. In 1965 about 3 million households had color television sets; in 1970 about 24 million households did; in 1980 about 76 million households (virtually all that owned television sets) did.

CABLE

In the 1950s cable television was introduced on a small scale. By 1990 about 58 percent of American homes that had television subscribed to the service of one of the approximately 9,000 cable television companies.

Initially, cable television was installed in areas where the images and sound on sets hooked up to rooftop antennas to pull television signals from the atmosphere were of poor quality because of the physical remoteness of the regions or because of interference from land formations. By the late 1970s, however, most families subscribing to cable television did so more for the greater variety of program offerings. A significant achievement in cable television in the 1980s was the creation of the Cable News Network (CNN) by media entrepreneur Ted Turner.

HIGH-DEFINITION TELEVISION (HDTV)

In the 1990s television viewers experienced a development as profound as that of the introduction in the 1950s of color and cable: the availability of high-definition television (HDTV). The HDTV images were as sharp and bright as those in a motion picture projected on a theater screen. This was achieved by increasing the number of horizontal scanning bars covering the television screen.

Complements to Television

The most important development in the television industry during the 1980s was the increasing popularity of three complementary devices: the videocassette recorder, the videodisk player, and the camcorder.

VIDEOCASSETTE RECORDER (VCR)

In 1978 the videocassette recorder (VCR) was introduced. By 1990 approximately 78 percent of American homes that had television sets had VCRs. The stock of commercially produced videocassettes continually expanded to encompass many offerings within a wide variety of categories.

VIDEODISK PLAYER

Introduced in 1979, the videodisk player was another device that made it possible for one to determine exactly what to view on the television set and when to view it. By 1990 commercially produced videodisk sales reached an annual total of approximately 16 million annually. The advantage of the videodisk-player system over the videocassette-recorder system was that it provided both images and sounds of far superior quality; its disadvantage was that it could play only commercially produced disks and could not record programs from the television set as could the videocassette-recorder system.

THE CAMCORDER

In the late 1980s the camcorder (camera and recorder) became one of the hottest items in the consumer electronics field, quickly and almost completely superseding the home-movie camera. Two hours' worth of videotape costing $5 could be exposed by the camcorder and then be immediately played back on the VCR connected to the television set, whereas an equivalent amount of silent home-movie film would cost more than $500 to purchase and then have commercially developed.

INFLUENCE

By the 1990s the VCR, videodisk player, and camcorder significantly bolstered television in its capability to let Americans entertain and inform themselves.

Selected Readings

GENERAL WORKS:

Boag, David, ed. *Assessing the Reagan Years* (1988)

Johnson, Haynes. *Sleepwalking Through History: America in the Reagan Years* (1991)

Wills, Gary. *Reagan's America: Innocents at Home* (1987)

SPECIAL STUDIES:

Ackerman, Frank. *Reaganomics* (1982)

Altman, Dennis. *AIDS in the Mind of America* (1986)

Barrett, Lawrence I. *Gambling with History: Ronald Reagan in the White House* (1984)

Dallek, Robert. *Ronald Reagan: The Politics of Symbolism* (1984)

Deaver, Michael. *Behind the Scenes: In Which the Author Talks about Ronald and Nancy Reagan ... and Himself* (1987)

Dugger, Ronnie. *On Reagan: The Man & His Presidency* (1983)

Hagstrom, Jerry. *Beyond Reagan: The New Landscape of American Politics* (1988)

Haig, Alexander M., Jr. *Caveat: Realism, Reagan, and Foreign Policy* (1984)

Krieger, Joel. *Reagan, Thatcher, and the Politics of Decline* (1986)

Lash, Jonathan. *A Season of Spoils: The Story of the Reagan Administration's Attack on the Environment* (1984)

Mandelbaum, Michael. *Reagan and Gorbachev* (1987)

Mayer, Jane. *Landslide: The Unmaking of the President, 1984–1988* (1988)

Miller, Judith, and Laurie Mylroie. *Saddam Hussein and the Crisis in the Gulf* (1990)

Noonan, Peggy. *What I Saw at the Revolution: A Political Life in the Reagan Era* (1990)

Reagan, Ronald. *An American Life* (1990)

Regan, Donald T. *For the Record: From Wall Street to Washington* (1988)

Stockman, David. *The Triumph of Politics: The Inside Story of the Reagan Revolution* (1986)

Talbott, Strobe. *Deadly Gambits: The Reagan Administration and the Stalemate in Nuclear Arms Control* (1984)

———. *The Russians and Reagan* (1984)

Winship, Michael. *Television* (1988)

Appendices

Appendix A

PRESIDENTS AND SECRETARIES OF STATE

President		Secretary of State	
1. George Washington	1789–1797	Thomas Jefferson	1789
		Edmund Randolph	1794
		Timothy Pickering	1795
2. John Adams	1797–1801	Timothy Pickering	
		John Marshall	1800
3. Thomas Jefferson	1801–1809	James Madison	1801
4. James Madison	1809–1817	Robert Smith	1809
		James Monroe	1811
5. James Monroe	1817–1825	John Quincy Adams	1817
6. John Quincy Adams	1825–1829	Henry Clay	1825
7. Andrew Jackson	1829–1837	Martin Van Buren	1829
		Edward Livingston	1831
		Louis McLane	1833
		John Forsyth	1834
8. Martin Van Buren	1837–1841	John Forsyth	
9. William Henry Harrison	1841	Daniel Webster	1841
10. John Tyler	1841–1845	Daniel Webster	
		Hugh S. Legaré	1843
		Abel P. Upshur	1843
		John C. Calhoun	1844
11. James Knox Polk	1845–1849	James Buchanan	1845
12. Zachary Taylor	1849–1850	John M. Clayton	1849
13. Millard Fillmore	1850–1853	Daniel Webster	1850
		Edward Everett	1852
14. Franklin Pierce	1853–1857	William L. Marcy	1853
15. James Buchanan	1857–1861	Lewis Cass	1857
		Jeremiah S. Black	1860
16. Abraham Lincoln	1861–1865	William H. Seward	1861
17. Andrew Johnson	1865–1869	William H. Seward	
18. Ulysses S. Grant	1869–1877	Elihu B. Washburne	1869
		Hamilton Fish	1869
19. Rutherford B. Hayes	1877–1881	William M. Evarts	1877
20. James A. Garfield	1881	James G. Blaine	1881

President		Secretary of State	
21. Chester A. Arthur	1881–1885	James G. Blaine	
		F. T. Frelinghuysen	1881
22. Grover Cleveland	1885–1889	Thomas F. Bayard	1885
23. Benjamin Harrison	1889–1893	James G. Blaine	1889
		John W. Foster	1892
24. Grover Cleveland	1893–1897	Walter Q. Gresham	1893
		Richard Olney	1895
25. William McKinley	1897–1901	John Sherman	1897
		William R. Day	1898
		John Hay	1898
26. Theodore Roosevelt	1901–1909	John Hay	
		Elihu Root	1905
		Robert Bacon	1909
27. William H. Taft	1909–1913	Philander C. Knox	1909
28. Woodrow Wilson	1913–1921	William J. Bryan	1913
		Robert Lansing	1915
		Bainbridge Colby	1920
29. Warren G. Harding	1921–1923	Charles E. Hughes	1921
30. Calvin Coolidge	1923–1929	Charles E. Hughes	
31. Herbert C. Hoover	1929–1933	Frank B. Kellogg	1925
		Henry L. Stimson	1929
32. Franklin D. Roosevelt	1933–1945	Cordell Hull	1933
		Edward R. Stettinius	1945
33. Harry S. Truman	1945–1953	Edward R. Stettinius	
		James F. Byrnes	1945
		George C. Marshall	1947
		Dean Acheson	1949
34. Dwight D. Eisenhower	1953–1961	John Foster Dulles	1953
		Christian Herter	1959
35. John F. Kennedy	1961–1963	Dean Rusk	1961
36. Lyndon B. Johnson	1963–1969	Dean Rusk	
37. Richard M. Nixon	1969–1974	William P. Rogers	1969
		Henry Kissinger	1973
38. Gerald R. Ford	1974–1977	Henry Kissinger	
39. Jimmy Carter	1977–1981	Cyrus R. Vance	1977
		Edmund Muskie	1980
40. Ronald W. Reagan	1981–1989	Alexander M. Haig Jr.	1981
		George P. Shultz	1982
41. George H. Bush	1989–	James A. Baker III	1989

Appendix B

ADMISSION OF STATES INTO THE UNION

State	Year of Admission
1. Delaware	1787
2. Pennsylvania	1787
3. New Jersey	1787
4. Georgia	1788
5. Connecticut	1788
6. Massachusetts	1788
7. Maryland	1788
8. South Carolina	1788
9. New Hampshire	1788
10. Virginia	1788
11. New York	1788
12. North Carolina	1789
13. Rhode Island	1790
14. Vermont	1791
15. Kentucky	1792
16. Tennessee	1796
17. Ohio	1803
18. Louisiana	1812
19. Indiana	1816
20. Mississippi	1817
21. Illinois	1818
22. Alabama	1819
23. Maine	1820
24. Missouri	1821
25. Arkansas	1836
26. Michigan	1837
27. Florida	1845
28. Texas	1845
29. Iowa	1846
30. Wisconsin	1848
31. California	1850
32. Minnesota	1858
33. Oregon	1859

State	Year of Admission
34. Kansas	1861
35. West Virginia	1863
36. Nevada	1864
37. Nebraska	1867
38. Colorado	1876
39. North Dakota	1889
40. South Dakota	1889
41. Montana	1889
42. Washington	1889
43. Idaho	1890
44. Wyoming	1890
45. Utah	1896
46. Oklahoma	1907
47. New Mexico	1912
48. Arizona	1912
49. Alaska	1959
50. Hawaii	1959

Appendix C

TERRITORIAL EXPANSION OF THE UNITED STATES

Territory	Year	Method of Acquisition
Original states and territories	1783	Treaty with Great Britain
Louisiana Purchase	1803	Purchase from France
Florida	1819	Treaty with Spain
Texas	1845	Anexation of independent nation
Oregon	1846	Treaty with Great Britain
Mexican Cession	1848	Conquest from Mexico
Gadsden Purchase	1853	Purchase from Mexico
Alaska	1867	Purchase from Russia
Hawaii	1898	Annexation of independent nation
Puerto Rico	1899	Conquest from Spain
Guam	1899	Conquest from Spain
The Philippines	1899	Conquest from Spain (granted independence in 1946)
American Samoa	1900	Treaty with Great Britain and Germany
Panama Canal Zone	1904	Treaty with Panama (returned to Panama by treaty in 1978)
Corn Islands	1916	Treaty with Nicaragua (returned to Nicaragua by treaty in 1971)
Virgin Islands	1917	Purchase from Denmark
Pacific Islands Trust	1947	Trusteeship under United Nations (some granted independence)

Others (Midway, Wake, and other islands)

Appendix D

POPULATION OF THE UNITED STATES

Census	Population
1790	3,929,214
1800	5,308,483
1810	7,239,881
1820	9,638,453
1830	12,866,020
1840	17,069,453
1850	23,191,876
1860	31,443,321
1870	38,558,371
1880	50,155,783
1890	62,947,714
1900	75,994,575
1910	91,972,266
1920	105,710,620
1930	122,775,046
1940	131,669,275
1950	150,697,361
1960	179,323,175
1970	203,302,031
1980	226,504,825
1990	248,723,165

Index